Life of

Napoleon Bonaparte

By Sir Walter Scott

Volume II

Sir Walter Scott

Life of
Napoleon Bonaparte
Volume II
1827

Published by
Omnia Veritas Ltd

Omnia Veritas

www.omnia-veritas.com

Vincennes

CHAPTER I **21**

Corsica—Family of Buonaparte—Napoleon born 15th August, 1769—His early habits—Sent to the Royal Military School at Brienne—His great Progress in Mathematical Science—Deficiency in Classical Literature—Anecdotes—Removed to the General School of Paris—When in his Seventeenth Year, appointed Second Lieutenant of Artillery—His early Politics—Promoted to a Captaincy—Pascal Paoli—Napoleon sides with the French Government against Paoli—And is banished from Corsica—Visits Marseilles, and publishes the Souper de Beaucaire. 21

CORSICA 22
BRIENNE 26
VALENCE—AUXONNE 31
PAOLI—CORSICA 34

CHAPTER II **39**

Siege of Toulon—Recapitulation—Buonaparte appointed to the Command of the Artillery at Toulon—Finds every thing in disorder—His plan for obtaining the Surrender of the Place—Adopted—Anecdotes during the Siege—Allied troops resolve to evacuate Toulon—Dreadful Particulars of the Evacuation—England censured on this occasion—Lord Lynedoch—Fame of Buonaparte increases, and he is appointed Chief of Battalion in the Army of Italy—Joins Headquarters at Nice—On the Fall of Robespierre, Buonaparte superseded in command—Arrives in Paris in May, 1795, to solicit employment—He is unsuccessful—Retrospect of the Proceedings of the National Assembly—Difficulties in forming a new Constitution—Appointment of the Directory—of the Two Councils of Elders and of Five Hundred—Nation at large, and Paris in particular, disgusted with their pretensions—Paris assembles in Sections—General Danican appointed their Commander-in-Chief—Menou appointed by the Directory to disarm the National Guards—but suspended for incapacity—Buonaparte appointed in his room—The Day of the Sections—Conflict betwixt the Troops of the Convention under Buonaparte, and those of the Sections of Paris under Danican—The latter defeated with much slaughter—Buonaparte appointed Second in Command of the Army of the Interior—then General-in-Chief—Marries Madame Beauharnais—Her Character—Buonaparte immediately afterwards joins the Army of Italy. 39

SIEGE OF TOULON 40

EVACUATION OF TOULON 48
SAORGIO 52
RETROSPECT 56
NEW CONSTITUTION 62
THE SECTIONS 67

THE DIRECTORY. 74
JOSEPHINE BEAUHARNAIS. 75

CHAPTER III 79

The Alps—Feelings and Views of Buonaparte on being appointed to the Command of the Army of Italy—General Account of his new Principles of Warfare—Mountainous Countries peculiarly favourable to them—Retrospect of Military Proceedings since October 1795—Hostility of the French Government to the Pope—Massacre of the French Envoy Basseville, at Rome—Austrian Army under Beaulieu—Napoleon's Plan for entering Italy—Battle of Montenotte, and Buonaparte's first Victory—Again defeats the Austrians at Millesimo—and again under Colli—Takes possession of Cherasco—King of Sardinia requests an Armistice, which leads to a Peace, concluded on very severe Terms—Close of the Piedmontese Campaign—Napoleon's Character at this period......................... 79

COMMANDER-IN-CHIEF..80
SYSTEM OF TACTICS..84
THE POPE 86
BATTLE OF MONTENOTTE 90
BATTLE OF MILLESIMO 92
ACTION OF DEGO...93
ARMISTICE OF CHERASCO..97

CHAPTER IV 101

Farther progress of the French Army under Buonaparte—He crosses the Po, at Placenza, on 7th May—Battle of Lodi takes place on the 10th, in which the French are victorious—Remarks on Napoleon's Tactics in this celebrated Action—French take possession of Cremona and Pizzighitone—Milan deserted by the Archduke Ferdinand and his Duchess—Buonaparte enters Milan on the 15th May—General situation of the Italian States at this period—Napoleon inflicts Fines upon the neutral and unoffending States of Parma and Modena, and extorts the surrender of some of their finest Pictures—Remarks upon this novel procedure... 101

PROGRESS OF THE FRENCH ARMY..101
TORTONA...104
PASSAGE OF THE PO 104
BATTLE OF LODI 107
PIZZIGHITONE 113
SITUATION OF THE ITALIAN STATES 116
SEIZURE OF WORKS OF ART...118
WORKS OF ART 120

CHAPTER V **129**

Directory proposes to divide the Army of Italy betwixt Buonaparte and Kellermann—Buonaparte resigns, and the Directory give up the point—Insurrection against the French at Pavia—crushed—and the Leaders shot—Also at the Imperial Fiefs, and Lugo, quelled and punished in the same way—Reflections—Austrians defeated at Borghetto, and retreat behind the Adige—Buonaparte narrowly escapes being made Prisoner at Valeggio—Mantua blockaded—Verona occupied by the French—King of Naples secedes from Austria—Armistice purchased by the Pope—The Neutrality of Tuscany violated, and Leghorn occupied by the French Troops—Views of Buonaparte respecting the Revolutionizing of Italy—He temporizes—Conduct of the Austrian Government at this Crisis—Beaulieu displaced, and succeeded by Wurmser—Buonaparte sits down before Mantua. 129

REVOLT OF PAVIA *131*
BATTLE OF BORGHETTO *134*
FORTRESS OF MANTUA *136*
VERONA—LOUIS XVIII *138*
LEGHORN VIOLATED *141*
VIEWS AGAINST ITALY *145*
BEAULIEU DISPLACED *147*

CHAPTER VI **151**

Campaign on the Rhine—General Plan—Wartensleben and the Archduke Charles retire before Jourdan and Moreau—The Archduke forms a junction with Wartensleben, and defeats Jourdan, who retires—Moreau, also, makes his celebrated Retreat through the Black Forest—Buonaparte raises the Siege of Mantua, and defeats the Austrians at Salo and Lonato—Misbehaviour of the French General Valette, at Castiglione—Lonato taken, with the French Artillery, on 3d August—Retaken by Massena and Augereau—Singular escape of Buonaparte from being captured at Lonato—Wurmser defeated between Lonato and Castiglione, and retreats on Trent and Roveredo—Buonaparte resumes his position before Mantua—Effects of the French Victories on the different Italian States—Inflexibility of Austria—Wurmser recruited—Battle of Roveredo—French victorious, and Massena occupies Trent—Buonaparte defeats Wurmser at Primolano—and at Bassano, 8th September—Wurmser flies to Vicenza—Battle of Saint-George—Wurmser finally shut up within the walls of Mantua. 151

CAMPAIGN ON THE RHINE.. 151

ADVANCE OF WURMSER *153*
BATTLE OF LONATO *156*
ESCAPE AT LONATO *159*

INFLEXIBILITY OF AUSTRIA 161
THE TYROL 164
BATTLE OF BASSANO 167
ACTION OF CEREA...170

CHAPTER VII 173

Corsica reunited with France—Critical situation of Buonaparte in Italy at this period—The Austrian General Alvinzi placed at the head of a new Army—Various Contests, attended with no decisive result—Want of Concert among the Austrian Generals—French Army begin to murmur—First Battle of Arcola—Napoleon in personal danger—No decisive result—Second Battle of Arcola—The French victorious—Fresh want of concert among the Austrian Generals—General Views of Military and Political Affairs, after the conclusion of the fourth Italian Campaign—Austria commences a fifth Campaign—but has not profited by experience—Battle of Rivoli, and Victory of the French—Further successful at La Favorita—French regain their lost ground in Italy—Surrender of Mantua—Instances of Napoleon's Generosity. 173

CORSICA REUNITED WITH FRANCE..*173*
ALVINZI *174*
MURMURS OF THE TROOPS *178*
FIRST BATTLE OF ARCOLA *181*
SECOND BATTLE OF ARCOLA *184*
FRENCH AND AUSTRIAN ARMIES...*187*
AUSTRIAN PLAN OF OPERATIONS..*188*
BATTLE OF RIVOLI *191*
BATTLE OF LA FAVORITA *194*
SURRENDER OF MANTUA *196*

CHAPTER VIII 201

Situation and Views of Buonaparte at this period—His politic Conduct towards the Italians—Popularity—Severe terms of Peace proposed to the Pope—rejected—Napoleon differs from the Directory, and Negotiations are renewed—but again rejected—The Pope raises his army to 40,000 Men—Napoleon invades the Papal Territories—The Papal Troops defeated near Imola—and at Ancona—which is captured—Loretto taken—Clemency of Buonaparte to the French recusant Clergy—Peace of Tolentino—Napoleon's Letter to the Pope—San Marino—View of the Situation of the different Italian States—Rome—Naples—Tuscany—Venice.. 201

PRE-EMINENCE OF NAPOLEON *201*
CONDUCT TO THE ITALIANS *204*
POLITIC CONDUCT *207*

NEGOTIATIONS WITH THE POPE 210
INVASION OF THE PAPAL TERRITORIES 213
CAPTURE OF LORETTO 215
TREATY OF TOLENTINA 218
REPUBLIC OF SAN MARINO... 220

CHAPTER IX 225

Archduke Charles—Compared with Napoleon—Fettered by the Aulic Council—Napoleon, by a stratagem, passes the Tagliamento, and compels the Archduke to retreat—Gradisca carried by storm—Chusa-Veneta taken—Trieste and Fiume occupied—Venice breaks the Neutrality—Terrified on learning that an Armistice had taken place betwixt France and Austria—The Archduke retreats by hasty marches on Vienna—The Government irresolute—and the Treaty of Leoben signed—Venice makes humiliating submissions—Napoleon's Speech to her Envoys—He declares War against Venice, and evades obeying the orders of the Directory to spare it—The Great Council, on 31st May, concede everything to Buonaparte—Terms granted. 225

ARCHDUKE CHARLES.. 225
FRENCH PLAN OF THE CAMPAIGN... 227
TRIESTE AND FIUME 231
OVERTURES OF PEACE 234
THE ARCHDUKE'S RETREAT... 236
PEACE OF LEOBEN 239
TREATY OF LEOBEN.. 241
VENICE 243

CHAPTER X 251

Napoleon's Amatory Correspondence with Josephine—His Court at Montebello—Negotiations and Pleasure mingled there—Genoa—Revolutionary spirit of the Genoese—They rise in insurrection, but are quelled by the Government, and the French plundered and imprisoned—Buonaparte interferes, and appoints the Outlines of a new Government—Sardinia—Naples—The Cispadane, Transpadane, and Emilian Republics, united under the name of the Cisalpine Republic—The Valteline—The Grisons—The Valteline united to Lombardy—Great improvement of Italy, and the Italian Character, from these changes—Difficulties in the way of Pacification betwixt France and Austria—The Directory and Napoleon take different Views—Treaty of Campo Formio—Buonaparte takes leave of the Army of Italy, to act as French Plenipotentiary at Rastadt.. 251

COURT AT MONTEBELLO 252
GENOA 254

CISALPINE REPUBLIC *258*
TREATY OF CAMPO-FORMIO *259*
CONGRESS OF RASTADT *265*

CHAPTER XI **267**

Retrospect—The Directory—they become unpopular—Causes of their unpopularity—Also at enmity among themselves—State of public feeling in France—In point of numbers, favourable to the Bourbons; but the Army and monied Interest against them—Pichegru, head of the Royalists, appointed President of the Council of Five Hundred—Barbé Marbois, another Royalist, President of the Council of Ancients—Directory throw themselves upon the succour of Hoche and Buonaparte—Buonaparte's personal Politics discussed—Pichegru's Correspondence with the Bourbons—known to Buonaparte—He despatches Augereau to Paris—Directory arrest their principal Opponents in the Councils on the 18th Fructidor, and Banish them to Guiana—Narrow and Impolitic Conduct of the Directory to Buonaparte—Projected Invasion of England. 267

RETROSPECT *267*
THE DIRECTORY *268*
PICHEGRU *273*
INTRIGUES OF PICHEGRU *277*
AUGEREAU DESPATCHED TO PARIS *279*
THE EIGHTEENTH FRUCTIDOR *281*
THE DIRECTORY *283*

CHAPTER XII **287**

View of the respective Situations of Great Britain and France, at the Period of Napoleon's return from Italy—Negotiations at Lisle—Broken off—Army of England decreed, and Buonaparte named to the Command—He takes up his Residence in Paris—Public Honours—The real Views of the Directory discovered to be the Expedition to Egypt—Armies of Italy and the Rhine, compared and contrasted—Napoleon's Objects and Motives in heading the Egyptian Expedition—those of the Directory regarding it—Its actual Impolicy—Curious Statement by Miot—The Armament sails from Toulon, on 19th May 1798—Napoleon arrives before Malta on 10th June—Proceeds on his course, and, escaping the British Squadron, lands at Alexandria on the 1st July—Description of the various Classes who inhabit Egypt:—1. The Fellahs and Bedouins—2. The Cophts—3. The Mamelukes—Napoleon issues a Proclamation against the Mamelukes—Marches against them on the 7th July—Discontent of the French Troops—Battle of the Pyramids on 21st of July—Cairo surrenders................... 287

NEGOTIATIONS AT LISLE *288*

PARIS—MADAME DE STAËL	289
PARIS—PUBLIC HONOURS	292
EXPEDITION TO EGYPT	296
ARMIES OF ITALY AND THE RHINE	298
EXPEDITION TO EGYPT	300
SAILS FROM TOULON	307
VOYAGE TO EGYPT	308
MAMELUKES	311
MARCH TO CAIRO	313
BATTLE OF THE PYRAMIDS	315

CHAPTER XIII 319

French Fleet—Conflicting Statements of Buonaparte and Admiral Gantheaume—Battle of Aboukir on 1st August, 1798—The French Admiral, Brueyes, killed, and his Ship, L'Orient, blown up—The Victory complete—Effects of this disaster—Means by which Napoleon proposed to establish himself in Egypt—His Administration, in many respects, praiseworthy—in others, his Conduct absurd—He aspires to be regarded an Envoy of the Deity—His endeavours to propitiate the Porte—The Fort of El Arish falls into his hands—Massacre of Jaffa—Admitted by Buonaparte himself—His Arguments in its defence—Replies to them—General Conclusions—Plague in the French Army—Napoleon's Humanity and Courage upon this occasion—Proceeds against Acre to attack Djezzar Pacha—Sir Sidney Smith—His Character—Captures a French Convoy, and throws himself into Acre—French arrive before Acre on 17th March, 1799, and effect a breach on the 28th, but are driven back—Assaulted by an Army of Moslems assembled without the Walls of Acre, whom they defeat and disperse—Personal Misunderstanding and Hostility betwixt Napoleon and Sir Sidney Smith—Explained—Buonaparte is finally compelled to raise the Siege. 319

FRENCH FLEET	319
BATTLE OF ABOUKIR	321
ADMINISTRATION IN EGYPT	324
INSURRECTION IN CAIRO	328
OTTOMAN PORTE	330
MASSACRE OF JAFFA	332
SAINT JEAN D'ACRE	336
SIEGE OF ACRE	338
THE SIEGE OF ACRE RAISED	343

CHAPTER XIV 345

Discussion concerning the alleged Poisoning of the Sick in the Hospitals at Jaffa—Napoleon acquitted of the charge—French Army re-enter Cairo on the 14th June—Retrospect of what had taken place in Upper and Lower Egypt during

Napoleon's Absence—Incursion of Murad Bey—18,000 Turks occupy Aboukir—Attacked and defeated—This Victory terminates Napoleon's Career in Egypt—Admiral Gantheaume receives Orders to make ready for Sea—On the 22d August Napoleon embarks for France—Arrives in Ajaccio on the 30th September—and lands at Frejus on the 9th October. 345

POISONING OF THE SICK AT JAFFA *345*
THE TURKISH ARMY AT ABOUKIR *350*
TURKS DEFEATED AT ABOUKIR *351*
SITUATION AND PROSPECTS *352*
AJACCIO *357*

CHAPTER XV 359

Retrospect of Public Events since the Departure of Napoleon for Egypt—Invasion and Conquest of Switzerland—Seizure of Turin—Expulsion of the Pope—The Neapolitans declare War against France—The French enter Naples—Disgraceful Avarice exhibited by the Directory—Particularly in their Negotiations with the United States of America—Russia comes forward in the general Cause—Her Strength and Resources—Reverses of the French in Italy, and on the Rhine—Insurrections in Belgium and Holland against the French—Anglo-Russian Expedition sent to Holland—The Chouans again in the Field—Great and Universal Unpopularity of the Directory—State of Parties in France—Law of Hostages—Abbé Siêyes becomes one of the Directory—His Character and Genius—Description of the Constitution proposed by him for the Year Three—Ducos, Gohier, and Moulins, also introduced into the Directory—Family of Napoleon strive to keep him in the Recollection of the People—Favourable Change in the French Affairs—Holland Evacuated by the Anglo-Russian Army—Korsakow defeated by Massena—and Suwarrow retreats before Lecourbe. ... 359

EXPULSION OF THE POPE *361*
NEGOTIATIONS WITH AMERICA *363*
SUWARROW *365*
"THE MODÉRÉS" *368*
CONSTITUTION FOR THE YEAR THREE *371*
DUCOS—GOHIER—MOULINS *374*
JOURDAN *377*

CHAPTER XVI 379

General rejoicing on the return of Buonaparte—Advances made to him on all sides—Napoleon coalesces with Siêyes—Revolution of the 18th Brumaire (Nov. 9)—Clashing Views of the Councils of Ancients, and the Five Hundred—Barras and his Colleagues resign—Proceedings of the Councils on the 18th—and 19th—Sittings removed from Paris to St. Cloud—Commotion in the Council of Five

Hundred—Napoleon menaced and assaulted, and finally, extricated by his Grenadiers—Lucien Buonaparte, the President, retires from the Hall—Declares the Council dissolved—Provisional Consular Government of Buonaparte, Siêyes, and Ducos. 379

PARIS.. 379
STATE OF PARTIES... 382
THE EIGHTEENTH BRUMAIRE 386
ARENA.. 398

CHAPTER XVII..**401**

Clemency of the New Consulate—Beneficial change in the Finances—Law of Hostages repealed—Religious liberty allowed—Improvements in the War Department—Pacification of La Vendée—Ascendancy of Napoleon—Disappointment of Siêyes—Committee formed to consider Siêyes' Plan of a Constitution—Rejected as to essentials—A new one adopted, monarchical in every thing but form—Siêyes retires from public life—General view of the new Government—Despotic Power of the First Consul. 401

THE PROVISIONAL GOVERNMENT 401
IMPROVEMENT IN WAR DEPARTMENT 404
DISAPPOINTMENT OF SIÊYES.. 407
DISCUSSION ON THE CONSTITUTION... 409
CONSULAR GOVERNMENT 412
THE CONSULATE 418

CHAPTER XVIII...**423**

Proceedings of Buonaparte in order to consolidate his power—His great success—Causes that led to it—Cambacérès and Le Brun chosen Second and Third Consuls—Talleyrand appointed Minister for Foreign Affairs, and Fouché Minister of Police—Their Characters—Other Ministers nominated—Various Changes made, in order to mark the Commencement of a new Era—Napoleon addresses a Letter personally to the King of England—Answered by Lord Grenville—Negotiation for Peace that followed, speedily broken off—Campaigns in Italy, and on the Rhine—Successes of Moreau—Censured by Napoleon for Over-caution—The Charge considered—The Chief Consul resolves to bring back, in Person, Victory to the French Standards in Italy—His Measures for that purpose... 423

CAMBACÉRÈS—LEBRUN—TALLEYRAND... 427
VARIOUS CHANGES.. 430
LETTER TO THE KING OF ENGLAND 432
EXTERNAL SITUATION OF FRANCE... 434

SUCCESSES OF MOREAU 437
PLAN OF THE CAMPAIGN 439

CHAPTER XIX **441**

    The Chief Consul leaves Paris on 6th May, 1800—Has an Interview with Necker at Geneva on 8th—Arrives at Lausanne on the 13th—Various Corps put in motion to cross the Alps—Napoleon, at the head of the Main Army, marches on the 15th, and ascends Mont St. Bernard—On the 16th, the Vanguard takes possession of Aosta—Fortress and Town of Bard threaten to baffle the whole plan—The Town is captured—and Napoleon contrives to send his Artillery through it, under the fire of the Fort, his Infantry and Cavalry passing over the Albaredo—Lannes carries Ivrea—Recapitulation—Operations of the Austrian General Melas—At the commencement of the Campaign, Melas advances towards Genoa—Actions betwixt him and Massena—In March, Lord Keith blockades Genoa—Melas compelled to retreat—Enters Nice—Recalled from thence by the news of Napoleon's having crossed Mont St. Bernard—Genoa surrenders—Buonaparte enters Milan—Battle of Montebello—The Chief Consul is joined by Desaix—Battle of Marengo on the 14th—Death of Desaix—Capitulation on the 15th, by which Genoa, &c., are yielded—Napoleon returns to Paris on the 2d July. 441

    PASSAGE OF THE GREAT ST. BERNARD 443
    BARD 445
    OPERATIONS OF MELAS 448
    MASSENA SURRENDERS GENOA 451
    SITUATION OF MELAS 454
    DESAIX—MARENGO 456
    MARENGO 457
    PARIS 464

CHAPTER XX **467**

    Napoleon offers, and the Austrian Envoy accepts, a new Treaty—The Emperor refuses it, unless England is included—Negotiations with England—fail—Renewal of the War—Armistice—Resumption of Hostilities—Battle of Hohenlinden—Other Battles—The Austrians agree to a separate Peace—Treaty of Luneville—Convention between France and the United States—The Queen of Naples repairs to Petersburgh—Paul receives her with cordiality, and applies in her behalf to Buonaparte—His Envoy received at Paris with the utmost distinction, and the Royal Family of Naples saved for the present—Rome restored to the authority of the Pope—Napoleon demands of the King of Spain to declare War against Portugal—Olivenza and Almeida taken—Malta, after a Blockade of Two Years, obliged to submit to the English. 467

    NEGOTIATIONS WITH ENGLAND 468

ARMISTICE	471
NAPLES	473
SUWARROW	476
NAPLES	479
ROME—PEACE WITH PORTUGAL	481

CHAPTER XXI **485**

Internal Government of France—General Attachment to the Chief Consul—Plot to remove him by Assassination—Defeated—Vain hopes of the Royalists, that Napoleon would restore the Bourbons—Infernal Machine—It fails—Suspicion first falls on the Republicans—The actual Conspirators executed—Use made by Buonaparte of the Conspiracy to consolidate Despotism—System of Police—Fouché—His Skill, Influence, and Power—Apprehension entertained by the Chief Consul of the effects of Literature—Persecution of Madame de Staël—The Concordat—Plan for a general System of Jurisprudence—Amnesty granted to the Emigrants—Plans of Public Education—Hopes of a General Peace.................... 485

INTERNAL GOVERNMENT OF FRANCE	485
PLOT TO ASSASSINATE THE FIRST CONSUL	486
THE ROYALISTS	488
THE INFERNAL MACHINE	491
SPECIAL CRIMINAL TRIBUNAL	495
THE HAUTE POLICE	498
THE POLICE	501
THE CONCORDAT	503
PUBLIC EDUCATION	509

CHAPTER XXII **513**

Return to the external Relations of France—Her universal Ascendency—Napoleon's advances to the Emperor Paul—Plan of destroying the British Power in India—Right of Search at Sea—Death of Paul—Its effects on Buonaparte—Affairs of Egypt—Assassination of Kleber—Menou appointed to succeed him—British Army lands in Egypt—Battle and Victory of Alexandria—Death of Sir Ralph Abercromby—General Hutchinson succeeds him—The French General Belliard capitulates—as does Menou—War in Egypt brought to a victorious Conclusion. 513

THE EMPEROR PAUL	513
DEATH OF THE EMPEROR PAUL	516
ASSASSINATION OF KLEBER	519
BRITISH EXPEDITION TO EGYPT	521

CHAPTER XXIII **525**

Preparations for the Invasion of Britain—Nelson put in command of the Sea—Attack of the Boulogne Flotilla—Pitt leaves the Ministry—succeeded by Mr. Addington—Negotiations for Peace—Just punishment of England, in regard to the conquered Settlements of the enemy—Forced to restore them all, save Ceylon and Trinidad—Malta is placed under the guarantee of a Neutral Power—Preliminaries of Peace signed—Joy of the English Populace, and doubts of the better classes—Treaty of Amiens signed—The ambitious projects of Napoleon, nevertheless, proceed without interruption—Extension of his power in Italy—He is appointed Consul for life, with the power of naming his Successor—His Situation at this period. 525

PITT LEAVES THE MINISTRY *526*
TREATY OF AMIENS *527*
PROJECTS OF AMBITION—CONSUL FOR LIFE *531*
CONSUL FOR LIFE *532*

CHAPTER XXIV **537**

Different Views entertained by the English Ministers and the Chief Consul of the effects of the Treaty of Amiens—Napoleon, misled by the Shouts of a London Mob, misunderstands the Feelings of the People of Great Britain—His continued encroachments on the Independence of Europe—His conduct to Switzerland—Interferes in their Politics, and sets himself up, uninvited, as Mediator in their concerns—Ney enters Switzerland at the head of 40,000 men—The patriot, Reding, disbands his Forces, and is imprisoned—Switzerland is compelled to furnish France with a Subsidiary Army of 16,000 Troops—The Chief Consul adopts the title of Grand Mediator of the Helvetic Republic............................. 537

TREATY OF AMIENS *538*
SWITZERLAND *542*
HELVETIC REPUBLIC *547*

APPENDIX **549**

No. I. Buonaparte's letter to General Paoli. 549
No. II. Letter of Napoleon Buonaparte to M. Matteo Buttafuoco, deputy from Corsica to the National Assembly. 552
No. III. The Supper of Beaucaire. *July 29, 1793.* 565
No. IV. Letters of Napoleon to Josephine. 575

(1.) Napoleon to Josephine *575*
(2.) *577*

- (3.) 577
- (4.) 577
- (5.) 578
- (6.) 581

No. V. Descent of the french in south wales, under general tate 583
No. VI. Buonaparte's camp library 586
No. VII. Buonaparte, member of the national institute, commander-in-chief, to the people of Egypt 589
No. VIII. Historical notes on the eighteenth brumaire. 591

Chapter I

Corsica—Family of Buonaparte—Napoleon born 15th August, 1769—His early habits—Sent to the Royal Military School at Brienne—His great Progress in Mathematical Science—Deficiency in Classical Literature—Anecdotes—Removed to the General School of Paris—When in his Seventeenth Year, appointed Second Lieutenant of Artillery—His early Politics—Promoted to a Captaincy—Pascal Paoli—Napoleon sides with the French Government against Paoli—And is banished from Corsica—Visits Marseilles, and publishes the Souper de Beaucaire.

The island of Corsica was, in ancient times, remarkable as the scene of Seneca's exile, and in the last century was distinguished by the memorable stand which the natives made in defence of their liberties against the Genoese and French, during a war which tended to show the high and indomitable spirit of the islanders, united as it is with the fiery and vindictive feelings proper to their country and climate.

In this island, which was destined to derive its future importance chiefly from the circumstance, Napoleon Buonaparte, or Bonaparte,[1] had his origin. His family was noble, though not of

---

[1] There was an absurd debate about the spelling of the name, which became, as trifles often do, a sort of party question. Buonaparte had disused the superfluous *u*, which his father retained in the name, and adopted a more modern spelling. This was represented on one side as an attempt to bring his name more nearly to the French idiom; and, as if it had been a matter of the last moment, the vowel was obstinately replaced in the name, by a class of writers who deemed it politic not to permit the successful general to relinquish the slightest mark of his Italian extraction, which was in every respect impossible for him either to conceal or to deny, even if he had nourished such an idea. In his baptismal register, his name is spelled Napoleone Bonaparte, though the father subscribes, Carlo Buonaparte. The spelling seems to have been quite indifferent.—S.—"During Napoleon's first campaign in Italy, he dropped the *u*. In this change he had no other motive than to assimilate the orthography to the pronunciation, and to abbreviate his signature."—Bourrienne, tom. i., p. 3.

much distinction, and rather reduced in fortune. Flattery afterwards endeavoured to trace the name which he had made famous, into remote ages, and researches were made through ancient records, to discover that there was one Buonaparte who had written a book,[2] another who had signed a treaty—a female of the name who had given birth to a pope,[3] with other minute claims of distinction, which Napoleon justly considered as trivial, and unworthy of notice. He answered the Emperor of Austria, who had a fancy of tracing his son-in-law's descent from one of the petty sovereigns of Treviso, that he was the Rodolph of Hapsbourg of his family; and to a genealogist, who made a merit of deducing his descent from some ancient line of Gothic princes, he caused reply to be made, that he dated his patent of nobility from the battle of Montenotte, that is, from his first victory.[4]

CORSICA

All that is known with certainty of Napoleon's family may be told in few words. The Buonapartes were a family of some distinction in the middle ages;[5] their names are inscribed in the Golden Book at Treviso, and their armorial bearings are to be seen on several houses in Florence. But attached, during the civil war, to the party of the Ghibellines, they of course were persecuted by the Guelphs; and being exiled from Tuscany, one of the family took refuge in Corsica, and there established himself and his successors, who were regularly enrolled among the noble natives of the island, and enjoyed all the privileges of gentle blood.

---

[2] The book alluded to is entitled "Ragguaglio Storico di tutto l'occorso, giorno per giorno, nel Sacco de Roma dell anno 1527, scritto da Jacopo Buonaparte, gentiluomo Samminiatese, chi vi si trovò presente." In 1568, a Giuseppe Buonaparte published a comedy, entitled "La Vedova." Copies of both these works are in the British Museum.
[3] Paul the Fifth.
[4] "I sent Clarke to Florence as ambassador, where he employed himself in nothing but turning over the old musty records of the place, in search of proofs of the nobility of my family. He so plagued me with letters upon the subject, that I was forced to bid him cease from troubling either his head or mine with this nonsense about nobility,—that I was the *first* of my family."—Napoleon, *Voice*, &c., vol. i., p. 401.
[5] "They were of Tuscan origin. In the middle ages they figured as senators of the republics of Florence, San Miniato, Bologna, Sarzana, and Treviso, and as prelates attached to the Court of Rome."—Napoleon, *Memoirs*, vol. iii., y. 7.

The father of Napoleon, Charles Buonaparte, was the principal descendant of this exiled family. He was regularly educated at Pisa, to the study of the law, and is stated to have possessed a very handsome person, a talent for eloquence, and a vivacity of intellect, which he transmitted to his son. He was a patriot also and a soldier, and assisted at the gallant stand made by Paoli against the French. It is said he would have emigrated along with Paoli, who was his friend, but was withheld by the influence of his father's brother, Lucien Buonaparte, who was Archdeacon of the Cathedral of Ajaccio, and the wealthiest person of the family.

It was in the middle of civil discord, fights, and skirmishes, that Charles Buonaparte married Lætitia Ramolini, one of the most beautiful young women of the island, and possessed of a great deal of firmness of character. She partook the dangers of her husband during the years of civil war, and is said to have accompanied him on horseback in some military expeditions, or perhaps hasty flights, shortly before her being delivered of the future emperor.[6] Though left a widow in the prime of life, she had already born her husband thirteen children, of whom five sons and three daughters survived him. I. Joseph, the eldest, who, though placed by his brother in an obnoxious situation, as intrusive King of Spain, held the reputation of a good and moderate man. II. Napoleon himself. III. Lucien, scarce inferior to his brother in ambition and talent. IV. Louis, the merit of whose character consists in its unpretending worth, and who renounced a crown rather than consent to the oppression of his subjects. V. Jerome, whose disposition is said to have been chiefly marked by a tendency to dissipation. The females were, I. Maria Anne, afterwards Grand Duchess of Tuscany, by the name of Eliza.[7] II. Maria Annonciada, who became Maria Pauline, Princess of Borghese.[8] III. Carlotta, or Caroline, wife of Murat, and Queen of Naples.

---

[6] Las Cases, vol. i., p. 108.
[7] Died at Trieste, 9th August, 1820. "On accidentally reading, at St. Helena, the account of her death, Napoleon exclaimed, 'Eliza has just shown us the way; death, which seemed to have overlooked our family, now begins to strike it. I shall be the next to follow her to the grave.'"—Antommarchi, vol. i., p. 384.
[8] She died at the Borghese Palace, near Florence, 9th June, 1825.

The family of Buonaparte being reconciled to the French government after the emigration of Paoli, enjoyed the protection of the Count de Marbœuf, the French Governor of Corsica, by whose interest Charles was included in a deputation of the nobles of the island, sent to Louis XVI. in 1779. As a consequence of this mission, he was appointed to a judicial situation—that of assessor of the Tribunal of Ajaccio—the income of which aided him to maintain his increasing family, which the smallness of his patrimony, and some habits of expense, would otherwise have rendered difficult. Charles Buonaparte, the father of Napoleon, died at the age of about forty years, of an ulcer in the stomach, on the 24th February 1785.[9] His celebrated son fell a victim to the same disease. During Napoleon's grandeur, the community of Montpellier expressed a desire to erect a monument to the memory of Charles Buonaparte. His answer was both sensible and in good taste. "Had I lost my father yesterday," he said, "it would be natural to pay his memory some mark of respect consistent with my present situation. But it is twenty years since the event, and it is one in which the public can take no concern. Let us leave the dead in peace."

The subject of our narrative was born upon the 15th day of August 1769, at his father's house in Ajaccio, forming one side of a court which leads out of the Rue Charles.[10] We read with interest, that his mother's good constitution, and bold character of mind, having induced her to attend mass upon the day of his birth, (being the Festival of the Assumption,) she was obliged to return home immediately, and as there was no time to prepare a bed or bedroom, she was delivered of the future victor upon a temporary couch prepared for her accommodation, and covered with an ancient piece of tapestry, representing the heroes of the Iliad. The infant was christened by the name of Napoleon, an obscure saint, who had dropped to leeward, and fallen altogether out of the calendar, so that his namesake never knew which day he was to celebrate as the

---

[9] "I was quietly pursuing my studies whilst my father was struggling against the violence of a painful agony. He died, and I had not the consolation to close his eyes: that sad duty was reserved for Joseph, who acquitted himself of it with all the zeal of an affectionate son."—Napoleon, Antommarchi, vol. i., p. 240.

[10] "The patrimonial house of Napoleon, at present in the possession of M. Ramolini, member of the Chamber of Deputies for the department of Corsica, continues an object of great veneration with travellers and military men."—Benson's *Corsica*, p. 4.

festival of his patron. When questioned on this subject by the bishop who confirmed him, he answered smartly, that there were a great many saints, and only three hundred and sixty-five days to divide amongst them. The politeness of the Pope promoted the patron in order to compliment the god-child, and Saint Napoleon des Ursins was accommodated with a festival. To render this compliment, which no one but a Pope could have paid, still more flattering, the feast of Saint Napoleon was fixed for the 15th August, the birthday of the Emperor, and the day on which he signed the Concordat.[11] So that Napoleon had the rare honour of promoting his patron saint.

The young Napoleon had, of course, the simple and hardy education proper to the natives of the mountainous island of his birth, and in his infancy was not remarkable for more than that animation of temper, and wilfulness and impatience of inactivity, by which children of quick parts and lively sensibility are usually distinguished.[12] The winter of the year was generally passed by the family of his father at Ajaccio, where they still preserve and exhibit, as the ominous plaything of Napoleon's boyhood, the model of a brass cannon, weighing about thirty pounds.[13] We leave it to philosophers to inquire, whether the future love of war was suggested by the accidental possession of such a toy; or whether the tendency of the mind dictated the selection of it; or, lastly, whether the nature of the pastime, corresponding with the taste which chose it, may not have had each their action and reaction, and contributed between them to the formation of a character so warlike.

The same traveller who furnishes the above anecdote, gives an interesting account of the country retreat of the family of Buonaparte, during the summer.

Going along the sea-shore from Ajaccio towards the Isle Sanguinière, about a mile from the town, occur two stone pillars, the remains of a door-way, leading up to a dilapidated villa, once the

---

[11] Las Cases, vol. i., p. 120.
[12] "In my infancy I was noisy and quarrelsome, and feared nobody. I beat one, scratched another, and made myself formidable to all."—Napoleon, Antommarchi, vol. i., p. 327.
[13] Benson's Sketches of Corsica, p. 4.—S.

residence of Madame Buonaparte's half-brother on the mother's side, whom Napoleon created Cardinal Fesch.[14] The house is approached by an avenue, surrounded and overhung by the cactus and other shrubs, which luxuriate in a warm climate. It has a garden and a lawn, showing amidst neglect, vestiges of their former beauty, and the house is surrounded by shrubberies, permitted to run to wilderness. This was the summer residence of Madame Buonaparte and her family. Almost enclosed by the wild olive, the cactus, the clematis, and the almond-tree, is a very singular and isolated granite rock, called Napoleon's grotto, which seems to have resisted the decomposition which has taken place around. The remains of a small summer-house are visible beneath the rock, the entrance to which is nearly closed by a luxuriant fig-tree. This was Buonaparte's frequent retreat, when the vacations of the school at which he studied permitted him to visit home.—How the imagination labours to form an idea of the visions, which, in this sequestered and romantic spot, must have arisen before the eyes of the future hero of a hundred battles!

BRIENNE

The Count de Marbœuf, already mentioned as Governor of Corsica, interested himself in the young Napoleon, so much as to obtain him an appointment [April, 1779] to the Royal Military School at Brienne, which was maintained at the royal expense, in order to bring up youths for the engineer and artillery service. The malignity of contemporary historians has ascribed a motive of gallantry towards Madame Buonaparte as the foundation of this kindness; but Count Marbœuf had arrived at a period of life when such connexions are not to be presumed, nor did the scandal receive any currency from the natives of Ajaccio.

Nothing could be more suitable to the nature of young Buonaparte's genius, than the line of study which thus fortunately was opened before him. His ardour for the abstract sciences amounted to a passion, and was combined with a singular aptitude

---

[14] The mother of Letitia Ramolini, wife of Carlo Buonaparte, married a Swiss officer in the French service, named Fesch, after the death of Letitia's father.—S.

for applying them to the purposes of war, while his attention to pursuits so interesting and exhaustless in themselves, was stimulated by his natural ambition and desire of distinction. Almost all the scientific teachers at Brienne, being accustomed to study the character of their pupils, and obliged by their duty to make memoranda and occasional reports on the subject, spoke of the talents of Buonaparte, and the progress of his studies, with admiration. Circumstances of various kinds, exaggerated or invented, have been circulated concerning the youth of a person so remarkable. The following are given upon good authority.[15]

The conduct of Napoleon among his companions, was that of a studious and reserved youth, addicting himself deeply to the means of improvement, and rather avoiding than seeking the usual temptations to dissipation of time. He had few friends, and no intimates; yet at different times when he chose to exert it, he exhibited considerable influence over his fellow-students, and when there was any joint plan to be carried into effect, he was frequently chosen dictator of the little republic.

In the time of winter, Buonaparte upon one occasion engaged his companions in constructing a fortress out of the snow, regularly defended by ditches and bastions, according to the rules of fortification. It was considered as displaying the great powers of the juvenile engineer in the way of his profession, and was attacked and defended by the students, who divided into parties for the purpose, until the battle became so keen that their superiors thought it proper to proclaim a truce.

The young Buonaparte gave another instance of address and enterprise upon the following occasion. There was a fair held annually in the neighbourhood of Brienne, where the pupils of the Military School used to find a day's amusement; but on account of a quarrel betwixt them and the country people upon a former occasion, or for some such cause, the masters of the institution had

---

[15] They were, many years since, communicated to the author by Messrs. Joseph and Louis Law, brothers of General Lauriston, Buonaparte's favourite aide-de-camp. These gentlemen, or at least Joseph, were educated at Brienne, but at a later period than Napoleon. Their distinguished brother was his contemporary.—S.

directed that the students should not, on the fair day, be permitted to go beyond their own precincts, which were surrounded with a wall. Under the direction of the young Corsican, however, the scholars had already laid a plot for securing their usual day's diversion. They had undermined the wall which encompassed their exercising ground, with so much skill and secrecy, that their operations remained entirely unknown till the morning of the fair, when a part of the boundary unexpectedly fell, and gave a free passage to the imprisoned students, of which they immediately took the advantage, by hurrying to the prohibited scene of amusement.

But although on these, and perhaps other occasions, Buonaparte displayed some of the frolic temper of youth, mixed with the inventive genius and the talent for commanding others by which he was distinguished in after time, his life at school was in general that of a recluse and severe student, acquiring by his judgment, and treasuring in his memory, that wonderful process of almost unlimited combination, by means of which he was afterwards able to simplify the most difficult and complicated undertakings. His mathematical teacher was proud of the young islander, as the boast of his school, and his other scientific instructors had the same reason to be satisfied.

In languages Buonaparte was less a proficient, and never acquired the art of writing or spelling French, far less foreign languages, with accuracy or correctness; nor had the monks of Brienne any reason to pride themselves on the classical proficiency of their scholar. The full energies of his mind being devoted to the scientific pursuits of his profession, left little time or inclination for other studies.

Though of Italian origin, Buonaparte had not a decided taste for the fine arts, and his taste in composition seems to have leaned towards the grotesque and the bombastic. He used always the most exaggerated phrases; and it is seldom, if ever, that his bulletins present those touches of sublimity which are founded on dignity and simplicity of expression.

Notwithstanding the external calmness and reserve of his deportment, he who was destined for such great things, had, while yet a student at Brienne, a full share of that ambition for distinction and dread of disgrace, that restless and irritating love of fame, which is the spur to extraordinary attempts. Sparkles of this keen temper sometimes showed themselves. On one occasion, a harsh superintendent imposed on the future Emperor, for some trifling fault, the disgrace of wearing a penitential dress, and being excluded from the table of the students, and obliged to eat his meal apart. His pride felt the indignity so severely, that it brought on a severe nervous attack; to which, though otherwise of good constitution, he was subject upon occasions of extraordinary irritation. Father Petrault,[16] the professor of mathematics, hastened to deliver his favourite pupil from the punishment by which he was so much affected.

It is also said that an early disposition to the popular side distinguished Buonaparte even when at Brienne. Pichegru, afterwards so celebrated, who acted as his monitor in the military school, (a singular circumstance,) bore witness to his early principles, and to the peculiar energy and tenacity of his temper. He was long afterwards consulted whether means might not be found to engage the commander of the Italian armies in the royal interest. "It will be but lost time to attempt it," said Pichegru. "I knew him in his youth—his character is inflexible—he has taken his side, and he will not change it."[17]

In October, 1784, Napoleon Buonaparte, then only fifteen years old, was, though under the usual age, selected by M. de Keralio,[18] the inspector of the twelve military schools, to be sent to

---

[16] Father Petrault was subsequently secularized, and joined the army of Italy, where he served his pupil in the capacity of secretary. On Buonaparte's return from Egypt, he found him a corpulent financier; but commencing usurer, he was soon reduced to beggary. Napoleon granted him a pension sufficient for his subsistence.—Las Cases, vol. i., p. 119.
[17] Las Cases, vol. i., p. 120.
[18] The following is a copy of Keralio's report:—"M. de Buonaparte, (Napoleon,) born 15th August, 1769, height four feet, ten inches, ten lines, has finished his fourth course; of good constitution, excellent health, of submissive character, upright, grateful, and regular in conduct; has always been distinguished for application to the mathematics. He is tolerably well acquainted with history and geography; he is deficient in the ornamental branches, and in Latin, in which he has only completed his fourth course. He will make an excellent

have his education completed in the general school of Paris. It was a compliment paid to the precocity of his extraordinary mathematical talent, and the steadiness of his application. While at Paris he attracted the same notice as at Brienne; and among other society, frequented that of the celebrated Abbé Raynal, and was admitted to his literary parties. His taste did not become correct, but his appetite for study in all departments was greatly enlarged; and notwithstanding the quantity which he daily read, his memory was strong enough to retain, and his judgment sufficiently ripe to arrange and digest, the knowledge which he then acquired; so that he had it at his command during all the rest of his busy life. Plutarch was his favourite author; upon the study of whom he had so modelled his opinions and habits of thought, that Paoli afterwards pronounced him a young man of an antique caste, and resembling one of the classical heroes.[19]

Some of his biographers have, about this time, ascribed to him the anecdote of a certain youthful pupil of the military school, who desired to ascend in the car of a balloon with the æronaut Blanchard, and was so mortified at being refused, that he made an attempt to cut the balloon with his sword.[20] The story has but a flimsy support, and indeed does not accord well with the character of the hero, which was deep and reflective, as well as bold and determined, and not likely to suffer its energies to escape in idle and useless adventure.

A better authenticated anecdote states, that at this time he expressed himself disrespectfully towards the king in one of his letters to his family. According to the practice of the school, he was obliged to submit the letter to the censorship of M. Domairon, the professor of belles lettres, who, taking notice of the offensive passage, insisted upon the letter being burnt, and added a severe rebuke. Long afterwards, in 1802, M. Domairon appeared at Napoleon's levee; when the first consul reminded his old tutor

---

sailor: he deserves to pass to the military school at Paris."—M. de Keralio, a highly accomplished man, who had been tutor in the royal family of Bavaria, died in 1793.
[19] "Paoli often patted me on the head, saying, 'You are one of Plutarch's men.' He divined that I should be something extraordinary."—Napoleon, *Voice*, &c., vol. i., p. 251.
[20] "This story, though incorrect as to Napoleon, was true as to one of his comrades, Dupont de Chambon."—Arnoult, *Vie de Napoleon*, p. 3.

good-humouredly, that times had changed considerably since the burning of the letter.

VALENCE—AUXONNE

Napoleon Buonaparte, in his seventeenth year, [September, 1785,] received his first commission as second lieutenant in the regiment of La Fère, or first artillery, then quartered at Valence. He mingled with society when he joined his regiment, more than he had hitherto been accustomed to do; mixed in public amusements, and exhibited the powers of pleasing which he possessed in an uncommon degree, when he chose to exert them. His handsome and intelligent features, with his active and neat, though slight figure, gave him additional advantages. His manners could scarcely be called elegant, but made up in vivacity and variety of expression, and often in great spirit and energy, for what they wanted in grace and polish.

In 1786, he became an adventurer for the honours of literature also, and was anonymously a competitor for the prize offered by the Academy of Lyons on Raynal's question, "What are the principles and institutions, by application of which mankind can be raised to the highest pitch of happiness?" The prize was adjudged to the young soldier. It is impossible to avoid feeling curiosity to know the character of the juvenile theories respecting government, advocated by one who at length attained the power of practically making what experiments he pleased. Probably his early ideas did not exactly coincide with his more mature practice; for when Talleyrand, many years afterwards, got the Essay out of the records of the Academy, and returned it to the author, Buonaparte destroyed it, after he had read a few pages.[21] He also laboured under the temptation of writing a journey from Valence to Mount Cenis, after the manner of Sterne, which he was fortunate enough finally to resist.[22] The affectation which pervades Sterne's peculiar style of

---

[21] Las Cases, vol. i., p. 129. A copy of the Essay had, however, been taken by his brother Louis. It was published in 1826 by Gourgaud.
[22] Las Cases, vol. i., p. 135.

composition, was not likely to be simplified under the pen of Buonaparte.

In 1789, Buonaparte, then quartered at Auxonne, had composed a work, which might form two volumes, on the political, civil, and military history of Corsica. He addressed a letter to General Paoli, then residing in London, on the subject of the proposed work, and the actual condition of his countrymen.[23] He also submitted it to the Abbé Raynal, who recommended the publication of it.[24] With this view, Buonaparte invited M. Joly, a bookseller of Dole, to visit him at Auxonne. He came, he says, and found the future Emperor in a naked barrack room, the sole furniture of which consisted of a wretched bed without curtains, a table placed in the embrasure of a window, loaded with books and papers, and two chairs. His brother Louis, whom he was teaching mathematics, lay on a wretched mattress, in an adjoining closet. M. Joly and the author agreed on the price of the impression of the book, but Napoleon was at the time in uncertainty whether he was to remain at Auxonne or not. The work was never printed, nor has a trace of it been discovered.[25]

In 1790, Buonaparte, still at Auxonne, composed a political tract in the form of a letter to M. de Buttafuoco, major-general, and deputy of the Corsican noblesse in the National Assembly. A hundred copies were printed and sent to Corsica; where it was adopted and republished by the patriotic society of Ajaccio,[26] who passed a resolution, attaching the epithet *infamous*, to the name of their noble deputy.[27]

---

[23] A copy of this letter is given in the Appendix, No. I. A few months after it was written, Paoli, in consequence of Mirabeau's motion for the recall of the Corsican exiles, left England for Corsica.
[24] Las Cases, vol. ii., p. 345.
[25] "This passage is not correct. I recollect very well, that, on my account, a larger and more commodious apartment was assigned to my brother than to the other officers of the same rank. I had a good chamber and an excellent bed. My brother directed my studies, but I had proper masters, even in literature."—Louis Buonaparte, p. 26.
[26] Norvins, tom. i., p. 19.
[27] The letter to Buttafuoco is a diatribe against that Corsican nobleman, who had been, during the wars with France, a strong opponent of the liberties of his country. He had been, of course, the enemy of the family of Paoli, to which Napoleon at this time was warmly attached. We have preserved the composition entire, because, though the matter be

Sterner times were fast approaching, and the nation was now fully divided by those factions which produced the Revolution. The officers of Buonaparte's regiment were also divided into Royalists and Patriots; and it is easily to be imagined, that the young and the friendless stranger and adventurer should adopt that side to which he had already shown some inclination, and which promised to open the most free career to those who had only their merit to rely upon. "Were I a general officer," he is alleged to have said, "I would have adhered to the King; being a subaltern, I join the Patriots."

There was a story current, that in a debate with some brother officers on the politics of the time, Buonaparte expressed himself so outrageously, that they were provoked to throw him into the Saone, where he had nearly perished. But this is an inaccurate account of the accident which actually befell him. He was seized with the cramp when bathing in the river. His comrades saved him with difficulty; but his danger was matter of pure chance.

Napoleon has himself recorded that he was a warm patriot during the whole sitting of the National Assembly; but that, on the appointment of the Legislative Assembly, he became shaken in his opinions. If so, his original sentiments regained force; for we shortly afterwards find him entertaining such as went to the extreme heights of the Revolution.

Early in the year 1792, Buonaparte became a captain in the artillery by seniority; and in the same year, being at Paris, he witnessed the two insurrections of the 20th June and 10th August. He was accustomed to speak of the insurgents as the most despicable banditti, and to express with what ease a determined officer could have checked these apparently formidable, but dastardly and unwieldy masses.[28] But, with what a different feeling of interest would Napoleon have looked on that infuriated populace, those still resisting though overpowered Swiss, and that burning palace, had any seer whispered to him, "Emperor that shall be, all

---

uninteresting, the rough and vivid style of invective is singularly characteristic of the fiery youth, whose bosom one of his teachers compared to a volcano surcharged with molten granite, which it poured forth in torrents, whenever his passions were excited.—See Appendix, No. II.

[28] See *ante*, vol. i. Las Cases, vol. iii., p. 143; and Bourrienne, tom. i., p. 48.

this blood and massacre is but to secure your future empire!" Little anticipating the potent effect which the passing events were to bear on his own fortune, Buonaparte, anxious for the safety of his mother and family, was now desirous to exchange France for Corsica, where the same things were acting on a less distinguished stage.

PAOLI—CORSICA

It was a singular feature in the French Revolution, that it brought out from his retirement the celebrated Pascal Paoli, who, long banished from Corsica, the freedom and independence of which he had so valiantly defended, returned from exile with the flattering hope of still witnessing the progress of liberty in his native land. On visiting Paris, he was received there with enthusiastic veneration, and the National Assembly and Royal Family contended which should show him most distinction. He was created president of the department, and commander of the national guard of his native island, and used the powers intrusted to him with great wisdom and patriotism.

But Paoli's views of liberty were different from those which unhappily began to be popular in France. He was desirous of establishing that freedom, which is the protector, not the destroyer of property, and which confers practical happiness, instead of aiming at theoretical perfection. In a word, he endeavoured to keep Corsica free from the prevailing infection of Jacobinism; and in reward, he was denounced in the Assembly. Paoli, summoned to attend for the purpose of standing on his defence, declined the journey on account of his age, but offered to withdraw from the island.

A large proportion of the inhabitants took part with the aged champion of their freedom, while the Convention sent an expedition, at the head of which were La Combe Saint Michel,[29] and

---

[29] La Combe Saint Michel was afterwards employed by Napoleon in Italy, Spain, and Germany. He died in 1812.

Salicetti,[30] one of the Corsican deputies to the Convention, with the usual instructions for bloodshed and pillage issued to their commissaries.[31]

Buonaparte was in Corsica, upon leave of absence from his regiment, when these events were taking place; and although he himself, and Paoli, had hitherto been on friendly terms, the young artillery officer did not hesitate which side to choose. He embraced that of the Convention with heart and hand; and his first military exploit was in the civil war of his native island. In the year 1793, he was despatched from Bastia, in possession of the French party, to surprise his native town Ajaccio, then occupied by Paoli or his adherents. Buonaparte was acting provisionally, as commanding a battalion of national guards. He landed in the gulf of Ajaccio with about fifty men, to take possession of a tower called the Torre di Capitello, on the opposite side of the gulf, and almost facing the city. He succeeded in taking the place; but as there arose a gale of wind which prevented his communicating with the frigate which had put him ashore, he was besieged in his new conquest by the opposite faction, and reduced to such distress, that he and his little garrison were obliged to feed on horse-flesh. After five days he was relieved by the frigate, and evacuated the tower, having first in vain attempted to blow it up. The Torre di Capitello still shows marks of the damage it then sustained, and its remains may be looked on as a curiosity, as the first scene of *his* combats, before whom

"Temple and tower Went to the ground."[32]

---

[30] During the reign of Joseph, he was appointed minister of police at Naples, where he died in 1809.
[31] Napoleon, Memoirs, vol. iv., p. 51.
[32] Such is the report of the Corsicans concerning the alleged first exploit of their celebrated countryman. See Benson's *Sketches*, p. 4. But there is room to believe that Buonaparte had been in action so early as February, 1793. Admiral Truguet, with a strong fleet, and having on board a large body of troops, had been at anchor for several weeks in the Corsican harbours, announcing a descent upon Sardinia. At length, having received on board an additional number of forces, he set sail on his expedition. Buonaparte is supposed to have accompanied the admiral, of whose talent and judgment he is made in the Saint Helena MSS., to speak with great contempt. Buonaparte succeeded in taking some batteries in the straits of Saint Bonifacio; but the expedition proving unsuccessful, they were speedily abandoned.—S.—For an account of the expedition to Sardinia, see *Napoleon's Memoirs*, vol. i., p. 5.

The strength of Paoli increasing, and the English preparing to assist him, Corsica became no longer a safe or convenient residence for the Buonaparte family. Indeed, both Napoleon and his brother Joseph, who had distinguished themselves as partisans of the French, were subjected to a decree of banishment from their native island; and Madame Buonaparte, with two of her daughters, set sail under their protection, and settled for a time, first at Nice, and afterwards at Marseilles, where the family remained in obscurity, until the dawning prospects of Napoleon afforded him the means of assisting them.

One small fountain at Ajaccio is pointed out as the only ornament which, in after days, his bounty bestowed on his birth-place.[33] He might perhaps think it impolitic to do any thing which might remind the country he ruled that he was not a child of her soil, nay, was in fact very near having been born an alien, for Corsica was not united to, or made an integral part of France, until June 1769, a few weeks only before Napoleon's birth. This stigma was repeatedly cast upon him by his opponents, some of whom reproached the French with having adopted a master, from a country from which the ancient Romans were unwilling even to choose a slave; and Napoleon may have been so far sensible to it, as to avoid showing any predilection to the place of his birth, which might bring the circumstance strongly under observation of the great nation, with which he and his family seemed to be indissolubly united. But as a traveller already quoted, and who had the best opportunities to become acquainted with the feelings of the proud islanders, has expressed it,—"The Corsicans are still highly patriotic, and possess strong local attachment—in their opinion, contempt for the country of one's birth is never to be redeemed by any other qualities. Napoleon, therefore, certainly was not popular in Corsica, nor is his memory cherished there."[34]

The feelings of the parties were not unnatural on either side. Napoleon, little interested in the land of his birth, and having such

---

[33] "As you quit the town, the first object that presents itself is a little fountain on the left, which, except the pavement of the quay, is the only public work of Buonaparte, for the place of his birth."—Benson.
[34] Benson's Sketches of Corsica, p. 121.—S.

an immense stake in that of his adoption, in which he had every thing to keep and lose,[35] observed a policy towards Corsica which his position rendered advisable; and who can blame the high-spirited islanders, who, seeing one of their countrymen raised to such exalted eminence, and disposed to forget his connexion with them, returned with slight and indifference the disregard with which he treated them?

On his return from Corsica, Buonaparte had arrived at Nice, and was preparing to join his regiment, when General Degear, who commanded the artillery of "the army of Italy," then encamped round the city, required his services, and employed him in several delicate operations. Shortly after, the insurrection of Marseilles broke out—a movement consequent upon the arrest of the leaders of the Girondist party in the Convention, on the first Prairial (31st May;) and which extended with violence into the departments. The insurgents of Marseilles organized a force of six thousand men, with which they took possession of Avignon, and thereby intercepted the communications of the army of Italy. The general-in-chief being much embarrassed by this circumstance, sent Buonaparte to the insurgents, to try to induce them to let the convoys pass. In July he went to Marseilles and Avignon, had interviews with the leaders, convinced them that it was their own interest not to excite the resentment of the army of Italy, and in fine secured the transit of the convoys.

During his residence at Marseilles, when sent to the insurgents, having, he says, an opportunity of observing all the weakness and incoherence of their means of resistance, he drew up a little pamphlet, which he called "*Le Souper de Beaucaire*," and which he published in that city. "He endeavoured," he says, "to open the eyes of these frantic people, and predicted that the only result of their revolt would be to furnish a pretext to the men of blood of the day, for sending the principal persons amongst them to the scaffold." "It produced," he adds, "a very powerful effect, and

---

[35] Not literally, however; for it is worth mentioning, that when he was in full-blown possession of his power, an inheritance fell to the family, situated near Ajaccio, and was divided amongst them. The First Consul, or Emperor, received an olive garden as his share.—*Sketches of Corsica.*—S.

contributed to calm the agitation which prevailed."[36] During these proceedings Toulon had surrendered to the English. Buonaparte was ordered on service to the siege of that town, and joined the army on the 12th of September.

---

[36] Montholon, tom. iii., p. 14.—Nothing can be more inaccurate than to term the *Souper de Beaucaire* a Jacobin pamphlet, although it is unquestionably written to urge the Federalists to submit to their inevitable fate, and avert extremity by doing so in time. The work is nearly free from the cant language of the day. There is no mention of liberty, equality, fraternity, or the rights of man, &c.—no abstract discussion of political principles. The whole merits of the dispute betwixt Paris and the departments are hurried over with little or no argument. Buonaparte urges the Marseillois to submission, not because the principles which dictated their insurrection were erroneous, but because they had not means to maintain successful resistance; not because they had been confuted by the Jacobins in argument, but because they were unequal to the task of contending with them by force. In after time, however, he called in and destroyed every copy of the *Souper de Beaucaire* which could be found, so that only one remained, from which the recent reprint of Monsieur Pancoucke has been executed.—S.—As remarkable specimens of Napoleon's easy style and habits of thinking, the opening and closing parts of this pamphlet are given, translated into English, in No. III. of the Appendix to this volume.

Chapter II

Siege of Toulon—Recapitulation—Buonaparte appointed to the Command of the Artillery at Toulon—Finds every thing in disorder—His plan for obtaining the Surrender of the Place—Adopted—Anecdotes during the Siege—Allied troops resolve to evacuate Toulon—Dreadful Particulars of the Evacuation—England censured on this occasion—Lord Lynedoch—Fame of Buonaparte increases, and he is appointed Chief of Battalion in the Army of Italy—Joins Headquarters at Nice—On the Fall of Robespierre, Buonaparte superseded in command—Arrives in Paris in May, 1795, to solicit employment—He is unsuccessful—Retrospect of the Proceedings of the National Assembly—Difficulties in forming a new Constitution—Appointment of the Directory—of the Two Councils of Elders and of Five Hundred—Nation at large, and Paris in particular, disgusted with their pretensions—Paris assembles in Sections—General Danican appointed their Commander-in-Chief—Menou appointed by the Directory to disarm the National Guards—but suspended for incapacity—Buonaparte appointed in his room—The Day of the Sections—Conflict betwixt the Troops of the Convention under Buonaparte, and those of the Sections of Paris under Danican—The latter defeated with much slaughter—Buonaparte appointed Second in Command of the Army of the Interior—then General-in-Chief—Marries Madame Beauharnais—Her Character—Buonaparte immediately afterwards joins the Army of Italy.

SIEGE OF TOULON

The siege of Toulon was the first incident of importance, which enabled Buonaparte to distinguish himself in the eyes of the French Government, and of the world at large.

Buonaparte's professional qualifications were still better vouched than the soundness of his political principles, though these were sufficiently decided. The notes which the inspectors of the Military School always preserve concerning their scholars, described his genius as being of the first order; and to these he owed his promotion to the rank of a lieutenant-colonel of artillery, with the command of the artillery during this siege.

We have already mentioned that a general diffidence, and dread of the proceedings of the Jacobins, joined to the intrigues of the Girondists, had, after the fall of the latter party, induced several of the principal towns in France to take arms against the Convention, or rather against the Jacobin party, who had attained the complete mastery in that body. We have also said that Toulon, taking a more decided step than either Marseilles or Lyons, had declared for the King and the Constitution of 1791, and invited the support of the English and Spanish squadrons, who were cruising upon the coast. A disembarkation was made, and a miscellaneous force, hastily collected, of Spaniards, Sardinians, Neapolitans, and English, was thrown into the place.

This was one of the critical periods when vigorous measures, on the part of the allies, might have produced marked effects on the result of the war. Toulon is the arsenal of France, and contained at that time immense naval stores, besides a fleet of seventeen sail of the line ready for sea, and thirteen or fourteen more, which stood in need of refitting. The possession of it was of the last importance, and with a sufficiently large garrison, or rather an army strong enough to cover the more exposed points without the town, the English might have maintained their footing at Toulon, as they did at a later period both at Lisbon and Cadiz. The sea would, by maintaining the defensive lines necessary to protect the roadstead, have been entirely at the command of the besieged; and they could have been supplied with provisions in any quantity from Sicily, or the Barbary States, while the besiegers would have experienced great difficulty, such was the dearth in Provence at the time, in supporting their own army. But to have played this bold game, the presence of an army, instead of a few battalions, would have been requisite; and a general of consummate ability must have held the chief command. This was the more especially necessary, as Toulon, from the nature of the place, must have been defended by a war of posts, requiring peculiar alertness, sagacity, and vigilance. On the other hand, there were circumstances very favourable for the defence, had it been conducted with talent and vigour. In order to invest Toulon on the right and left side at once, it was necessary there should be two distinct blockading armies; and these could scarce communicate with each other, as a steep ridge of mountains, called Pharon, must interpose betwixt them. This gave opportunity to the besieged to combine their force, and choose the object of attack when they sallied; while, on the other hand, the two bodies of besiegers could not easily connect their operations, either for attack or defence.

Lord Mulgrave,[37] who commanded personally in the place, notwithstanding the motley character of the garrison, and other discouraging circumstances, began the defence with spirit. Sir George Keith Elphinstone[38] also defeated the Republicans at the mountain pass, called Ollioules. The English for some time retained possession of this important gorge, but were finally driven out from it. Cartaux, a republican general whom we have already mentioned,[39] now advanced on the west of Toulon, at the head of a very considerable army, while General Lapoype blockaded the city on the east, with a part of the army of Italy. It was the object of the French to approach Toulon on both sides of the mountainous ridge, called Pharon. But on the east the town was covered by the strong and regular fort of La Malgue, and on the west side of the road by a less formidable work, called Malbosquet. To support Malbosquet, and to protect the entrance to the roadstead and harbour, the English engineers fortified with great skill an eminence, called Hauteur de

---

[37] His lordship died the 7th of April, 1831.
[38] In 1797 created Baron Keith. He died in 1823.
[39] See *ante*, vol. i.

Grasse. The height bent into a sort of bay, the two promontories of which were secured by redoubts, named L'Eguillette and Balagnier, which communicated with and supported the new fortification, which the English had termed Fort Mulgrave.

Several sallies and skirmishes took place, in most of which the Republicans were worsted. Lieutenant-General O'Hara arrived from Gibraltar with reinforcements, and assumed the chief command.

Little could be said for the union of the commanders within Toulon; yet their enterprises were so far successful, that the French began to be alarmed at the slow progress of the siege. The dearth of provisions was daily increasing, the discontent of the people of Provence was augmented; the Catholics were numerous in the neighbouring districts of Vivarais and Lower Languedoc; and Barras and Fréron wrote from Marseilles [Dec. 1] to the Convention, suggesting that the siege of Toulon should be raised, and the besieging army withdrawn beyond the Durance.[40] But while weaker minds were despairing, talents of the first order were preparing to achieve the conquest of Toulon.

When Napoleon arrived at the scene of action, and had visited the posts of the besieging army, he found so many marks of incapacity, that he could not conceal his astonishment. Batteries had been erected for destroying the English shipping, but they were three gun-shots' distance from the point which they were designed to command; red-hot balls were preparing, but they were not heated in furnaces beside the guns, but in the country-houses in the neighbourhood at the most ridiculous distance, as if they had been articles of easy and ordinary transportation. Buonaparte with difficulty obtained General Cartaux's permission to make a shot or two by way of experiment; and when they fell more than half-way short of the mark, the general had no excuse but to rail against the

---

[40] This letter appeared in the *Moniteur*, 10th December, 1793. But as the town of Toulon was taken a few days afterwards, the Convention voted the letter a fabrication.—S.—"This was unfair; for it was genuine, and gave a just idea of the opinion that prevailed when it was written, respecting the issue of the siege, and of the difficulties that prevailed in Provence."—Napoleon, *Memoirs*, vol. i., p. 22.

aristocrats, who had, he said, spoiled the quality of the powder with which he was supplied.[41]

The young officer of artillery, with prudence, and at the same time with spirit, made his remonstrances to the member of Convention, Gasparin,[42] who witnessed the experiment, and explained the necessity of proceeding more systematically, if any successful result was expected.

At a council of war, where Gasparin presided, the instructions of the Committee of Public Safety were read, directing that the siege of Toulon should be commenced according to the usual forms, by investing the body of the place, in other words, the city itself. The orders of the Committee of Public Safety were no safe subject of discussion or criticism for those who were to act under them; yet Buonaparte ventured to recommend their being departed from on this important occasion. His comprehensive genius had at once discovered a less direct, yet more certain manner, of obtaining the surrender of the place. He advised, that, neglecting the body of the town, the attention of the besiegers should be turned to attain possession of the promontory called Hauteur de Grasse, by driving the besiegers from the strong work of fort Mulgrave, and the two redoubts of L'Eguillette and Balagnier, by means of which the English had established the line of defence necessary to protect the fleet and harbour. The fortress of Malbosquet, on the same point, he also recommended as a principal object of attack. He argued, that if the besiegers succeeded in possessing themselves of these fortifications, they must obtain a complete command of the roads where the English fleet lay, and oblige them to put to sea. They would, in the same manner, effectually command the entrance of the bay, and prevent supplies or provisions from being thrown into the city. If the garrison were thus in danger of being totally cut off from supplies by their vessels being driven from their anchorage, it was natural to suppose that the English troops would rather

---

[41] Las Cases, vol. i., p. 140.
[42] It was to Gasparin that Napoleon was indebted for the triumph of his plan over the objections of the committees of the Convention. He preserved a grateful recollection of this circumstance, as appears by his will. It was Gasparin, he used to say, who had first opened his career.—Las Cases, vol. i., p. 144.

evacuate Toulon, than remain within the place, blockaded on all sides, until they might be compelled to surrender by famine.

The plan was adopted by the council of war after much hesitation, and the young officer by whom it was projected received full powers to carry it on. He rallied round him a number of excellent artillery officers and soldiers; assembled against Toulon more than two hundred pieces of cannon, well served; and stationed them so advantageously, that he annoyed considerably the English vessels in the roads, even before he had constructed those batteries on which he depended for reducing forts Mulgrave and Malbosquet, by which they were in a great measure protected.

In the meanwhile, General Doppet, formerly a physician, had superseded Cartaux, whose incapacity could no longer be concealed by his rhodomontading language; and, wonderful to tell, it had nearly been the fate of the ex-doctor to take Toulon, at a time when such an event seemed least within his calculation. A tumultuary attack of some of the young French Carmagnoles on a body of Spanish troops which garrisoned fort Mulgrave, had very nearly been successful. Buonaparte galloped to the spot, hurrying his reluctant commander along with him, and succours were ordered to advance to support the attack, when an aide-de-camp was shot by Doppet's side; on which the medical general, considering this as a bad symptom, pronounced the case desperate, and, to Buonaparte's great indignation, ordered a retreat to be commenced. Doppet being found as incapable as Cartaux, was in his turn superseded by Dugommier, a veteran who had served for fifty years, was covered with scars, and as fearless as the weapon he wore.

From this time the commandant of artillery, having the complete concurrence of his general, had no doubt of success. To ensure it, however, he used the utmost vigilance and exertion, and exposed his person to every risk.

One of the dangers which he incurred was of a singular character. An artilleryman being shot at the gun which he was serving, while Napoleon was visiting a battery, he took up the dead man's rammer, and, to give encouragement to the soldiers, charged the gun repeatedly with his own hands. In consequence of using this implement he caught an infectious cutaneous complaint, which, being injudiciously treated and thrown inward, was of great prejudice to his health until after his Italian campaigns, when he was completely cured by Dr. Corvissart; after which, for the first time, he showed that tendency to *embonpoint* which marked the latter part of his life.[43]

Upon another occasion, while Napoleon was overlooking the construction of a battery, which the enemy endeavoured to interrupt by their fire, he called for some person who could write, that he might dictate an order. A young soldier stepped out of the ranks, and resting the paper on the breast-work, began to write accordingly. A shot from the enemy's battery covered the letter with earth the instant it was finished. "Thank you—we shall have no occasion for sand this bout," said the military secretary. The gaiety and courage of the remark drew Buonaparte's attention on the young man, who was the celebrated General Junot, afterwards created Duke D'Abrantes.[44] During this siege, also, he discovered the talents of Duroc, afterwards one of his most faithful adherents. In these and many other instances, Buonaparte showed his extensive knowledge of mankind, by the deep sagacity which enabled him to discover and attach to him those whose talents were most capable of rendering him service.

Notwithstanding the influence which the commandant of artillery had acquired, he found himself occasionally thwarted by the members of the Convention upon mission to the siege of Toulon, who latterly were Fréron, Ricord, Salicetti, and the younger Robespierre. These representatives of the people, knowing that their commission gave them supreme power over generals and armies, never seem to have paused to consider whether nature or education had qualified them to exercise it, with advantage to the public and credit to themselves. They criticized Buonaparte's plan of attack, finding it impossible to conceive how his operations, being directed against detached fortifications at a distance from Toulon, could be eventually the means of placing the town itself with facility in their

---

[43] Las Cases, vol. i., p. 147.
[44] Las Cases, vol. i., p. 154.

hands. But Napoleon was patient and temporizing; and having the good opinion of Salicetti, and some intimacy with young Robespierre, he contrived to have the works conducted according to his own plan.

The presumption of these dignitaries became the means of precipitating his operations. It was his intention to complete his proposed works against fort Mulgrave before opening a large and powerful battery, which he had constructed with great silence and secrecy against Malbosquet, so that the whole of his meditated assault might confound the enemy by commencing at the same time. The operations being shrouded by an olive plantation, had been completed without being observed by the English, whom Buonaparte proposed to attack on the whole line of defence simultaneously. Messrs. Fréron and Robespierre, however, in visiting the military posts, stumbled upon this masked battery; and having no notion why four mortars and eight twenty-four pounders should remain inactive, they commanded the fire to be opened on Malbosquet without any farther delay.

General O'Hara, confounded at finding this important post exposed to a fire so formidable and unexpected, determined by a strong effort to carry the French battery at once. Three thousand men[45] were employed in this sally; and the general himself, rather contrary to what is considered the duty of the governor of a place of importance, resolved to put himself at their head. The sally was at first completely successful; but while the English pursued the enemy too far, in all the confidence of what they considered as assured victory, Buonaparte availed himself of some broken ground and a covered way, to rally a strong body of troops, bring up reserves, and attack the scattered English both in flank and rear. There was a warm skirmish, in which Napoleon himself received a bayonet wound in the thigh, by which, though a serious injury, he was not, however, disabled. The English were thrown into irretrievable confusion, and retreated, leaving their general wounded, and a prisoner in the hands of the enemy. It is singular, that during his long warfare, Buonaparte was never personally engaged with the British, except in his first, and at Waterloo, his last and fatal battle.

---

[45] Napoleon says six thousand.—Gourgaud, tom. i., p. 17.

The attack upon Acre can scarce be termed an exception, as far as his own person was concerned.

The loss of their commandant, added to the discouragement which began to prevail among the defenders of Toulon, together with the vivacity of the attack which ensued, seem finally to have disheartened the garrison. Five batteries were opened on fort Mulgrave, the possession of which Buonaparte considered as ensuring success. After a fire of twenty-four hours, Dugommier and Napoleon resolved to try the fate of a general attack, for which the representatives of the people showed no particular zeal. The attacking columns advanced before day, during a heavy shower of rain. They were at first driven back on every point by the most determined opposition; and Dugommier, as he saw the troops fly in confusion, exclaimed, well knowing the consequences of bad success to a general of the Republic, "I am a lost man!"[46] Renewed efforts, however, at last prevailed; the Spanish artillerymen giving way on one point, the fort fell [Dec. 18] into the possession of the French, who showed no mercy to its defenders.[47]

Three hours, according to Buonaparte, after the fort was taken, the representatives of the people appeared in the trenches, with drawn swords, to congratulate the soldiers on their successful valour, and hear from their commandant of artillery, the reiterated assurance, that, this distant fort being gained, Toulon was now their own. In their letter to the Convention, the deputies gave a more favourable account of their own exploits, and failed not to represent Ducos, Salicetti, and young Robespierre, as leading the attack with sabre in hand, and, to use their own phrase, showing the troops the road to victory.[48] On the other hand, they ungraciously forgot, in their despatches, to mention so much as the name of Buonaparte, to whom the victory was entirely to be ascribed.[49]

---

[46] Gourgaud, tom. i., p. 24.
[47] Jomini, tom. iv., p. 223; Toulongeon, tom. iv., p. 88; Napoleon's Memoirs, vol. i., p. 25; Rivington's Annual Register, 1793, p. 415.
[48] Moniteur, 28th December.
[49] "Amongst those who chiefly distinguished themselves are the citizens Buonaparte, commandant of the artillery, Arena, and Gervoni."—Dugommier *to the Minister of War.*

EVACUATION OF TOULON

In the meantime, Napoleon's sagacity was not deceived in the event. The officers of the allied troops, after a hurried council of war, resolved to evacuate Toulon, since the posts gained by the French must drive the English ships from their anchorage, and deprive them of a future opportunity of retreating, if they neglected the passing moment. Lord Hood alone urged a bolder resolution, and recommended the making a desperate effort to regain fort Mulgrave, and the heights which it commanded. But his spirited counsel was rejected, and the evacuation resolved on;[50] which the panic of the foreign troops, especially the Neapolitans, would have rendered still more horrible than it proved, but for the steadiness of the British seamen.

The safety of the unfortunate citizens, who had invoked their protection, was not neglected even amid the confusion of the retreat. The numerous merchant vessels and other craft, offered means of transportation to all, who, having to fear the resentment of the Republicans, might be desirous of quitting Toulon. Such was the dread of the victors' cruelty, that upwards of fourteen thousand persons accepted this melancholy refuge.[51] Meantime there was other work to do.

It had been resolved, that the arsenal and naval stores, with such of the French ships as were not ready for sea, should be destroyed; and they were set on fire accordingly. This task was in a great measure intrusted to the dauntless intrepidity of Sir Sydney Smith, who carried it through with a degree of order, which, everything considered, was almost marvellous. The assistance of the Spaniards was offered and accepted; and they undertook the duty of scuttling and sinking two vessels used as powder magazines, and destroying some part of the disabled shipping. The rising conflagration growing redder and redder, seemed at length a great volcano, amid which were long distinctly seen the masts and yards

---

[50] Rivington's Annual Register, 1793, p. 415.
[51] James's Naval History, vol. i., p. 115; Thiers, tom. vi., p. 59.—"The total number borne away amounted to 14,877."—*Mémoires de Joubert*, p. 75.

of the burning vessels, and which rendered obscurely visible the advancing bodies of Republican troops, who attempted on different points to push their way into the place. The Jacobins began to rise in the town upon the flying Royalists;—horrid screams and yells of vengeance, and revolutionary chorusses, were heard to mingle with the cries and plaintive entreaties of the remaining fugitives, who had not yet found means of embarkation. The guns from Malbosquet, now possessed by the French, and turned on the bulwarks of the town, increased the uproar. At once a shock, like that of an earthquake, occasioned by the explosion of many hundred barrels of gunpowder, silenced all noise save its own, and threw high into the midnight heaven a thousand blazing fragments, which descended, threatening ruin wherever they fell. A second explosion took place, as the other magazine blew up, with the same dreadful effects.

This tremendous addition to the terrors of the scene, so dreadful in itself, was owing to the Spaniards setting fire to those vessels used as magazines, instead of sinking them, according to the plan which had been agreed upon. Either from ill-will, carelessness, or timidity, they were equally awkward in their attempts to destroy the dismantled ships intrusted to their charge, which fell into the hands of the French but little damaged. The British fleet, with the flotilla crowded with fugitives which it escorted, left Toulon without loss, notwithstanding an ill-directed fire maintained on them from the batteries which the French had taken.

It was upon this night of terror, conflagration, tears, and blood, that the star of Napoleon first ascended the horizon; and though it gleamed over many a scene of horror ere it set, it may be doubtful whether its light was ever blended with those of one more dreadful.

The capture of Toulon crushed all the hopes of resistance to the Jacobins, which had been cherished in the south of France. There was a strong distrust excited against England, who was judged only desirous to avail herself of the insurrection of these unhappy citizens to cripple and destroy the naval power of France, without the wish of effectually assisting the Royalists. This was an unjust belief, but it cannot be denied that there were specious grounds for the accusation. The undertaking the protection of a city in such a situation as that of Toulon, if the measure was embraced at all, should have been supported by efforts worthy of the country whose assistance was implored and granted. Such efforts were not made, and the assistance actually afforded was not directed by talent, and was squandered by disunion. The troops showed gallantry; but the leaders, excepting the naval officers, evinced little military skill, or united purpose of defence. One gentleman, then in private life, chancing to be in Toulon at the time, distinguished himself as a volunteer,[52] and has since achieved a proud career in the British army. Had he, or such as he, been at the head of the garrison, the walls of Toulon might have seen a battle like that of Barossa, and a very different result of the siege might probably have ensued.

So many of the citizens of Toulon concerned in the late resistance had escaped, by the means provided by the English, that Republican vengeance could not collect its victims in the usual numbers.[53] Many were shot, however, and it has been said that Buonaparte commanded the artillery, by which, as at Lyons, they were exterminated; and also that he wrote a letter to Fréron and the younger Robespierre, congratulating them and himself on the execution of these aristocrats, and signed Brutus Buonaparte, Sans-Culotte. If he actually commanded at this execution, he had the poor apology, that he must do so or himself perish; but, had the fact and the letter been genuine, there has been enough of time since his downfall to prove the truth of the accusation, and certainly enough of writers disposed to give these proofs publicity. He himself positively denied the charge; and alleged that the victims were shot by a detachment of what was called the Revolutionary Army, and not by troops of the line.[54] This we think highly probable. Buonaparte has besides affirmed, that far from desiring to sharpen the vengeance of the Jacobins, or act as their agent, he hazarded the displeasure of those whose frown was death, by interposing his protection to save the unfortunate family of Chabrillan, emigrants

---

[52] Mr. Graham of Balgowan, now Lord Lynedoch. He marched out on one of the sorties, and when the affair became hot, seized the musket and cartouch-box of a fallen soldier, and afforded such an example to the troops, as contributed greatly to their gaining the object desired.—S.

[53] Jomini, tom. iv., p. 226; Lacretelle, tom. xi., p. 189.

[54] Montholon, tom. iii., p. 13; Jomini, tom. iv., p. 226; Las Cases, vol. i., p. 153.

and aristocrats, who, being thrown by a storm on the coast of France, shortly after the siege of Toulon, became liable to punishment by the guillotine, but whom he saved by procuring them the means of escape by sea.[55]

In the meanwhile, the young general of artillery was rapidly rising in reputation. The praises which were suppressed by the representatives of the people, were willingly conferred and promulgated by the frank old veteran, Dugommier. Buonaparte's name was placed on the list of those whom he recommended for promotion, with the pointed addition, that if neglected, he would be sure to force his own way.[56] He was accordingly confirmed in his provisional situation of chief of battalion, and appointed [March] to hold that rank in the army of Italy. Before joining that army, the genius of Napoleon was employed by the Convention in surveying and fortifying the sea-coast of the Mediterranean; a very troublesome task, as it involved many disputes with the local authorities of small towns and villages, and even hamlets, all of whom wished to have batteries erected for their own special protection, without regard to the general safety. It involved him, moreover, as we shall presently see, in some risk with the Convention at home.

The chief of battalion discharged his task scientifically. He divided the necessary fortifications into three classes, distinguishing those designed to protect harbours and roadsteads, from such as were intended to defend anchorages of less consequence, and both from the third class, which were to be placed on proper situations, to prevent insults and partial descents on the coast by an enemy superior at sea. Napoleon dictated to General Gourgaud[57] hints on

---

[55] Las Cases, vol. i., p. 152.
[56] "Dugommier wrote to the Committee of Public Safety, soliciting the rank of brigadier-general for him, and concluded with these words, 'Reward this young man, and promote him, for should he be ungratefully treated, he will promote himself.'"—Napoleon, *Montholon*, tom. iii., p. 15.
Dugommier was killed on the following November, by the bursting of a field-piece. Napoleon bequeathed to his descendant 100,000 francs, "as a testimonial of gratitude for the esteem, affection, and friendship of that brave and intrepid general."
[57] Gourgaud, tom. i., p. 30.

this subject, which must be of consequence to the sea-coasts which need such military defences.[58]

Having made his report to the Convention, Buonaparte proceeded to join the headquarters of the French army, then lying at Nice, straitened considerably and hemmed in by the Sardinians and Austrians, who, after some vain attempts of General Brunet[59] to dislodge them, had remained masters of the Col de Tende, and lower passes of the Alps, together with the road leading from Turin to Nice by Saorgio.

SAORGIO

Buonaparte had influence enough to recommend with success to the general, Dumerbion,[60] and the representatives of the people, Ricord and Robespierre, a plan for driving the enemy out of this position, forcing them to retreat beyond the higher Alps, and taking Saorgio; all which measures succeeded as he had predicted.[61] Saorgio surrendered, [April 29,] with much stores and baggage, and the French army obtained possession of the chain of the higher Alps, which, being tenable by defending few and difficult passes, placed a great part of the army of Italy, (as it was already termed, though only upon the frontier,) at disposal for actual service.[62]

---

[58] An Englishman will probably remember the sublime passage in "The Mariners of England:"—
"Britannia needs no bulwark, No towers along the steep; Her march is on the mountain-wave, Her home is on the deep."
[59] "Brunet being unjustly accused of favouring the insurrection at Marseilles, was delivered up to the Revolutionary Tribunal at Paris, and perished on the scaffold."—Napoleon, *Montholon*, tom. iii., p. 21.
[60] "An old and brave officer. His military knowledge was considerable, but he was confined to his bed by the gout half his time."—Napoleon, *Gourgaud*, tom. i., p. 42.
"Happily, he allowed himself to be directed entirely by the young Buonaparte."—Thiers, tom. vi., p. 288.
[61] Gourgaud, tom. i., p. 42.
[62] Jomini, tom. v., p. 204; Thiers, tom. vi., p. 283; Montholon, tom. iii., p. 30; Botta, tom. i., p. 190. General Dumerbion, in his despatch to the government, describing his successes, says, "It is to the talent of General Buonaparte that I am indebted for the skilful plans which have assured our victory."

While directing the means of attaining these successes, Buonaparte, at the same time, acquired a complete acquaintance with that Alpine country, in which he was shortly to obtain victories in his own name, not in that of others, who obtained reputation by acting on his suggestions. But, while he was thus employed, he was involved in an accusation before the Convention, which, had his reputation been less for approved patriotism, might have cost him dear.

In his plans for the defence of the Mediterranean, Napoleon had proposed repairing an old state prison at Marseilles, called fort Saint Nicholas, that it might serve as a powder Magazine. This plan his successor on the station proceeded to execute, and by doing so, gave umbrage to the patriots, who charged the commandant of artillery then at Marseilles, and superintending the work, with an intention to rebuild this fort, to serve as a Bastile for controlling the good citizens. The officer being summoned to the bar of the Convention, proved that the plan was not his own, but drawn out by Buonaparte. The representatives of the army in Italy, however, not being able to dispense with his services, wrote to the Convention in his behalf, and gave such an account of the origin and purpose of the undertaking, as divested it of all shade of suspicion even in the suspicious eye of the Committee of Public Safety.[63]

In the remainder of the year 1794, there was little service of consequence in the army of Italy, and the 9th and 10th Thermidor (27th and 28th July) of that year, brought the downfall of Robespierre, and threatened unfavourable consequences to Buonaparte, who had been in close communication with the tyrant's brother, and was understood to have participated in the tone of exaggerated patriotism affected by his party. He endeavoured to shelter himself under his ignorance of the real tendency of the proceedings of those who had fallen,—an apology which resolves itself into the ordinary excuse, that he found his late friends had not been the persons he took them for. According to this line of defence, he made all haste to disclaim accession to the political schemes of which they were accused. "I am somewhat affected," he

---

[63] Gourgaud, tom. i., p. 48.

wrote to a correspondent,[64] "at the fate of the younger Robespierre; but, had he been my brother, I would have poniarded him with my own hand, had I been aware that he was forming schemes of tyranny."

Buonaparte's disclamations do not seem at first to have been favourably received. His situation was now precarious; and when those members were restored to the Convention, who had been expelled and proscribed by the Jacobins, it became still more so. The reaction of the moderate party, accompanied by horrible recollections of the past, and fears for the future, began now to be more strongly felt, as their numbers in the Convention acquired strength. Those officers who had attached themselves to the Jacobin party, were the objects of their animosity; and, besides, they were desirous to purify the armies, as far as possible, of those whom they considered as their own enemies, and those of good order; the rather, that the Jacobinical principles still continued to be more favoured in the armies than in the interior. To the causes of this we have before alluded; but it may not be unnecessary to repeat, that the soldiers had experienced all the advantages of the fierce energies of a government which sent them out to conquest, and offered them the means of achieving it; and they had not been witnesses to the atrocities of their tyranny in the interior.

Before the downfall of Robespierre took place, Buonaparte had received regular but secret instructions to examine the fortifications of Genoa. M. Ricord, by whom these instructions had been signed, having now been superseded, and the younger Robespierre guillotined, Albitte, Salicetti, and Laporte, the new superintendents of the army of Italy, were pleased to suspect that Buonaparte had engaged in some plot of betraying Genoa to the enemy: he was arrested accordingly early in August; but his papers effectually established his innocence, and after the lapse of a fortnight he was released.[65]

---

[64] General Tilly. See *Nouvelle Biog. de Bruxelles*, 1822.
[65] "In the despatch of Salicetti and Albitte to the Government, dated 24th August, they declare, that there existed no foundation for the charges made against him."—Jomini, tom. vi., p. 114; *Bourrienne et ses Erreurs*, tom. i., p. 27.

In March 1795, he was sent to Toulon to take the command of the artillery in an expedition destined against Rome; but this scheme was not persevered in. During his visit to Toulon, however, he had the opportunity of saving from the violence of the populace, a party of unfortunate emigrants, including the noble family of Chabrillant, who had been landed from a Spanish prize. His influence with some cannoneers who had served under him during the siege, enabled him to rescue these individuals; and he unhesitatingly did so, though at considerable risk to himself. On his rejoining the troops in the Maritime Alps, near the end of March, he found the army about to be altered in some parts of its organization, and placed under the command of General Kellermann. A recent arrangement had recalled to the service many officers of high rank who had of late been unemployed; and he, as the youngest on the list of generals, could not only not be allowed to retain his command of the artillery in the army of Kellermann, but was removed to the infantry. He repaired therefore to Paris, with the view of soliciting professional employment elsewhere, and especially of remonstrating against his permanent removal from the branch of the service in which he had spent so many years. On his way to the capital he visited his mother at Marseilles, and found his brother Joseph respectably married in that city.

On reaching Paris in May, he found his pretensions thwarted by Aubry, the President of the Military Committee, who was disposed to treat with little attention his statement respecting the siege of Toulon, and his two years of successful service in the army of Italy. When, in the heat of discussion, Aubry objected his youth, Buonaparte replied, that presence in the field of battle ought to anticipate the claim of years. The president, who had not been much in action, considered his reply as a personal insult; and Napoleon, disdaining farther answer, tendered his resignation.[66] It was not, however, accepted; and he still remained in the rank of expectants, but among those whose hopes were entirely dependent upon their merits.[67]

---

[66] Montholon, tom. iii., p. 50; Las Cases, vol. i., p. 155; Louis Buonaparte, p. 14.
[67] Buonaparte is represented by some writers as having at this period found his situation extremely embarrassing, even as regarded pecuniary means, in the capital of which he was

It may be observed that, at a subsequent period, Aubry, being among those belonging to Pichegru's party who were banished to Cayenne, was excepted from the decree which permitted the return of those unfortunate exiles, and died at Demerara.

Meantime, his situation becoming daily more unpleasant, Buonaparte solicited Barras and Fréron, who, as Thermidoriens, had preserved their credit, for occupation in almost any line of his profession, and even negotiated for permission to go into the Turkish service, to train the Mussulmans to the use of artillery. A fanciful imagination may pursue him to the rank of pacha, or higher; for, go where he would, he could not have remained in mediocrity. His own ideas had a similar tendency. "How strange," he said, "it would be, if a little Corsican officer of artillery were to become King of Jerusalem!" He was offered a command in La Vendée, which he declined to accept, and was finally named to command a brigade of artillery in Holland. But it was in a land where there still existed so many separate and conflicting factions, as in France, that he was doomed to be raised, amid the struggles of his contending countrymen, and upon their shoulders and over their heads, to the very highest eminence to which fortune can exalt an individual. The times required such talents as his, and the opportunity for exercising them soon arose.

RETROSPECT

The French nation were in general tired of the National Convention, which successive proscriptions had drained of all the talent, eloquence, and energy it had once possessed; and that Assembly had become hateful and contemptible to all men, by suffering itself to be the passive tool of the Terrorists for two years, when, if they had shown proper firmness, the revolution of the 9th Thermidor might as well have been achieved at the beginning of that frightful anarchy, as after that long period of unheard-of

---

at no distant period to be the ruler. Among others who are said to have assisted him was the celebrated actor Talma; and such may have been the case; but the story of Talma's having been acquainted with Napoleon at the Academy of Brienne, and at that early period predicting the greatness of "*le petit Buonaparte*," has been expressly contradicted by Louis, the ex-King of Holland, who was at this epoch in Paris along with his brother.

suffering. The Convention was not greatly improved in point of talent, even by the return of their banished brethren; and, in a word, they had lost the confidence of the public entirely. They therefore prepared to gratify the general wish by dissolving themselves.

But before they resigned their ostensible authority, it was necessary to prepare some mode of carrying on the government in future.

The Jacobin constitution of 1793 still existed on paper; but although there was an unrepealed law, menacing with death any one who should propose to alter that form of government, no one appeared disposed to consider it as actually in exercise; and, notwithstanding the solemnity with which it had been received and ratified by the sanction of the national voice, it was actually passed over and abrogated as a matter of course, by a tacit but unanimous consent. Neither was there any disposition to adopt the Girondist constitution of 1791, or to revert to the democratic monarchy of 1792, the only one of these models which could be said to have had even the dubious endurance of a few months. As at the general change of the world, all former things were to be done away—all was to be made anew.

Each of these forms of government had been solemnized by the national oaths and processions customary on such occasions; but the opinion was now universally entertained, that not one of them was founded on just principles, or contained the power of defending itself against aggression, and protecting the lives and rights of the subject. On the other hand, every one not deeply interested in the late anarchy, and implicated in the horrid course of bloodshed and tyranny which was its very essence, was frightened at the idea of reviving a government which was a professed continuation of the despotism ever attendant upon a revolution, and which, in all civilized countries, ought to terminate with the extraordinary circumstances by which revolution has been rendered necessary. To have continued the revolutionary government, indeed, longer than this, would have been to have imitated the conduct of an ignorant empiric, who should persist in subjecting a convalescent patient to the same course of exhausting and dangerous medicines, which a regular physician would discontinue as soon as the disease had been brought to a favourable crisis.

It seems to have been in general felt and admitted, that the blending of the executive and legislative power together, as both had been exercised by the existing Convention, opened the road to the most afflicting tyranny; and that to constitute a stable government, the power of executing the laws, and administering the ministerial functions, must be vested in some separate individuals, or number of individuals, who should, indeed, be responsible to the national legislature for the exercise of this power, but neither subject to their direct control, nor enjoying it as emanating immediately from their body. With these reflections arose others, on the utility of dividing the legislative body itself into two assemblies, one of which might form a check on the other, tending, by some exercise of an intermediate authority, to qualify the rash rapidity of a single chamber, and obstruct the progress of any individual, who might, like Robespierre, obtain a dictatorship in such a body, and become, in doing so, an arbitrary tyrant over the whole authorities of the state. Thus, loth and late, the French began to cast an eye on the British constitution, and the system of checks and balances upon which it is founded, as the best means of uniting the protection of liberty with the preservation of order. Thinking men had come gradually to be aware, that in hopes of getting something better than a system which had been sanctioned by the experience of ages, they had only produced a set of models, which were successively wondered at, applauded, neglected, and broken to pieces, instead of a simple machine, capable, in mechanical phrase, of working well.

Had such a feeling prevailed during the commencement of the Revolution, as was advocated by Mounier and others,[68] France and Europe might have been spared the bloodshed and distress which afflicted them during a period of more than twenty years of war, with all the various evils which accompanied that great convulsion. France had then a king; nobles, out of whom a senate might have been selected; and abundance of able men to have formed a lower house, or house of commons. But the golden opportunity was passed over; and when the architects might, perhaps, have been

---

[68] See *ante*, vol. i.

disposed to execute the new fabric which they meditated, on the plan of a limited monarchy, the materials for the structure were no longer to be found.

The legitimate King of France no doubt existed, but he was an exile in a foreign country; and the race of gentry, from whom a house of peers, or hereditary senate, might have been chiefly selected, were to be found only in foreign service, too much exasperated by their sufferings to admit a rational hope that they would ever make any compromise with those who had forced them from their native land, and confiscated their family property. Saving for these circumstances, and the combinations which arose out of them, it seems very likely, that at the period at which we have now arrived, the tide, which began to set strongly against the Jacobins, might have been adroitly turned in favour of the Bourbons. But, though there was a general feeling of melancholy regret, which naturally arose from comparing the peaceful days of the monarchy with those of the Reign of Terror,—the rule of Louis the XVI. with that of Robespierre,—the memory of former quiet and security with the more recent recollections of blood and plunder,—still it seems to have existed rather in the state of a predisposition to form a royal party, than as the principle of one already existing. Fuel was lying ready to catch the flame of loyalty, but the match had not yet been applied; and to counteract this general tendency, there existed the most formidable obstacles.

In the first place, we have shown already the circumstances by which the French armies were strongly attached to the name of the Republic, in whose cause all their wars had been waged, and all their glory won; by whose expeditious and energetic administration the military profession was benefited, while they neither saw nor felt the misery entailed on the nation at large. But the French soldier had not only fought in favour of democracy, but actively and directly against royalty. As *Vive la République* was his war-cry, he was in La Vendée, on the Rhine, and elsewhere, met, encountered, and sometimes defeated and driven back, by those who used the opposite signal-word, *Vive le Roi*. The Royalists were, indeed, the most formidable opponents of the military part of the French nation; and such was the animosity of the latter at this period to the idea of returning to the ancient system, that if a general could have been found capable of playing the part of Monk, he would probably have experienced the fate of La Fayette and Dumouriez.

A second and almost insuperable objection to the restoration of the Bourbons, occurred in the extensive change of property that had taken place. If the exiled family had been recalled, they could not, at this very recent period, but have made stipulations for their devoted followers, and insisted that the estates forfeited in their cause, should have been compensated or restored; and such a resumption would have inferred ruin to all the purchasers of national demesnes, and, in consequence, a general shock to the security of property through the kingdom.

The same argument applied to the Church lands. The Most Christian King could not resume his throne, without restoring the ecclesiastical establishment in part, if not in whole. It was impossible to calculate the mass of persons of property and wealth, with their various connexions, who, as possessors of national demesnes, that is, of the property of the Church, or of the emigrants, were bound by their own interest to oppose the restoration of the Bourbon family. The revolutionary government had followed the coarse, but striking and deeply politic, admonition of the Scottish Reformer—"Pull down the nests," said Knox, when he urged the multitude to destroy churches and abbeys, "and the rooks will fly off." The French government, by dilapidating and disposing of the property of the emigrants and clergy, had established an almost insurmountable barrier against the return of the original owners. The cavaliers in the great Civil War of England had been indeed fined, sequestrated, impoverished; but their estates were still, generally speaking, in their possession; and they retained, though under oppression and poverty, the influence of a national aristocracy, diminished, but not annihilated. In France, that influence of resident proprietors had all been transferred to other hands, tenacious in holding what property they had acquired, and determined to make good the defence of it against those who claimed a prior right.

Lastly, the fears and conscious recollections of those who held the chief power in France for the time, induced them to view their own safety as deeply compromised by any proposition of restoring the exiled royal family. This present sitting and ruling Convention had put to death Louis XVI.,—with what hope of safety could they install his brother on the throne? They had formally, and in full conclave, renounced belief in the existence of a Deity—with what consistence could they be accessory to restore a national church? Some remained Republicans from their heart and upon conviction; and a great many more of the deputies could not abjure democracy, without confessing at the same time, that all the violent measures which they had carried through for the support of that system, were so many great and treasonable crimes.

These fears of a retributive reaction were very generally felt in the Convention. The Thermidoriens, in particular, who had killed Robespierre, and now reigned in his stead, had more substantial grounds of apprehension from any counter-revolutionary movement, than even the body of the representatives at large, many of whom had been merely passive in scenes where Barras and Tallien had been active agents. The timid party of The Plain might be overawed by the returning prince; and the members of the Girondists, who could indeed scarce be said to exist as a party, might be safely despised. But the Thermidoriens themselves stood in a different predicament. They were of importance enough to attract both detestation and jealousy; they held power, which must be an object of distrust to the restored monarch; and they stood on precarious ground, betwixt the hatred of the moderate party, who remembered them as colleagues of Robespierre and Danton, and that of the Jacobins, who saw in Tallien and Barras deserters of that party, and the destroyers of the power of the Sans-Culottes. They had, therefore, just reason to fear, that, stripped of the power which they at present possessed, they might become the unpitied and unaided scapegoats, to expiate all the offences of the Revolution.

Thus each favourable sentiment towards the cause of the Bourbons was opposed; I. By their unpopularity with the armies; II. By the apprehensions of the confusion and distress which must arise from a general change of property; and III. By the conscious fears of those influential persons, who conceived their own safety concerned in sustaining the republican model.

Still, the idea of monarchy was so generally received as the simplest and best mode of once more re-establishing good order and a fixed government, that some statesmen proposed to resume the form, but change the dynasty. With this view, divers persons were suggested by those, who supposed that by passing over the legitimate heir to the crown, the dangers annexed to his rights and claims might be avoided, and the apprehended measures of resumption and reaction might be guarded against. The son of the Duke of Orleans was named, but the infamy of his father clung to him. In another wild hypothesis the Duke of York, or the Duke of Brunswick, were suggested as fit to be named constitutional Kings of France. The Abbé Sièyes is said to have expressed himself in favour of the prince last named.[69]

But without regarding the wishes or opinions of the people without doors, the Convention resolved to establish such a model of government as should be most likely to infuse into a republic something of the stability of a monarchical establishment; and thus repair at once former errors, and preserve an appearance of consistency in the eyes of Europe.

NEW CONSTITUTION

For this purpose eleven commissioners, chiefly selected amongst the former Girondists, were appointed [April] to draw up a new Constitution upon a new principle, which was again to receive the universal adhesion of the French by acclamation and oath, and to fall, in a short time, under the same neglect which had attended every preceding model. This, it was understood, was to be so constructed, as to unite the consistency of a monarchical government with the name and forms of a democracy.

---

[69] The Memoirs published under the name of Fouché make this assertion. But although that work shows great intimacy with the secret history of the times, it is not to be implicitly relied upon.—S.

That the system now adopted by the French commissioners might bear a form corresponding to the destinies of the nation, and flattering to its vanity, it was borrowed from that of the Roman republic, an attempt to imitate which had already introduced many of the blunders and many of the crimes of the Revolution. The executive power was lodged in a council of five persons, termed Directors, to whom were to be consigned the conduct of peace and war, the execution of the laws, and the general administration of the government. They were permitted no share of the legislative authority.

This arrangement was adopted to comply with the jealousy of those, who, in the individual person of a single Director, holding a situation similar to that of the Stadtholder in Holland, or the President of the United States, saw something too closely approaching to a monarchical government. Indeed, it is said, Louvet warned them against establishing such an office, by assuring them, that when they referred the choice of the individual who was to hold it, to the nation at large, they would see the Bourbon heir elected.[70] But the inconvenience of this pentarchy could not be disguised; and it seemed to follow as a necessary consequence of such a numerous executive council, either that there would be a schism, and a minority and majority established in that pre-eminent body of the state, where unity and vigour were chiefly requisite, or else that some one or two of the ablest and most crafty among the Directors would establish a supremacy over the others, and use them less as their colleagues than their dependents. The legislators, however, though they knew that the whole Roman empire was found insufficient to satiate the ambition of three men, yet appeared to hope that the concord and unanimity of their five directors might continue unbroken, though they had but one nation to govern; and they decided accordingly.

The executive power being thus provided for, the legislative body was to consist of two councils; one of Elders, as it was called, serving as a House of Lords; another of Youngers, which they termed, from its number, the Council of Five Hundred. Both were elective, and the difference of age was the only circumstance which

---

[70] "Peut-être un jour, on vous nommerait un Bourbon."—Thiers, tom. viii., p. 10.

placed a distinction betwixt the two bodies. The members of the Council of Five Hundred were to be at least twenty-five years old, a qualification which, after the seventh year of the Republic, was to rise to thirty years complete. In this assembly laws were to be first proposed; and, having received its approbation, they were to be referred to the Council of Ancients. The requisites to sit in the latter senate, were the age of forty years complete, and the being a married man or a widower. Bachelors, though above that age, were deemed unfit for legislation, perhaps from want of domestic experience.

The Council of Ancients had the power of rejecting the propositions laid before them by the Council of Five Hundred, or, by adopting and approving them, that of passing them into laws. These regulations certainly gained one great point, in submitting each proposed legislative enactment to two separate bodies, and of course, to mature and deliberate consideration. It is true, that neither of the councils had any especial character, or separate interest which could enable or induce the Ancients, as a body, to suggest to the Five Hundred a different principle of considering any proposed measure, from that which was likely to occur to them in their own previous deliberation. No such varied views, therefore, were to be expected, as must arise between assemblies composed of persons who differ in rank or fortune, and consequently view the same question in various and opposite lights. Still, delay and reconsideration were attained, before the irrevocable fiat was imposed upon any measure of consequence; and so far much was gained. An orator was supposed to answer all objections to the system of the two councils thus constituted, when he described that of the Juniors as being the imagination, that of the Ancients as being the judgment of the nation; the one designed to invent and suggest national measures, the other to deliberate and decide upon them. This was, though liable to many objections, an ingenious illustration indeed; but an illustration is not an argument, though often passing current as such.

On the whole, the form of the Constitution[71] of the year Three, *i. e.* 1795, showed a greater degree of practical efficacy, sense, and consistency, than any of those previously suggested; and in the introduction, though there was the usual proclamation of the rights of man, his duties to the laws and to the social system were for the first time enumerated in manly and forcible language, intimating the desire of the framers of these institutions to put a stop to the continuation of revolutionary violence in future.

But the constitution, now promulgated, had a blemish common to all its predecessors; it was totally new, and unsanctioned by the experience either of France or any other country; a mere experiment in politics, the result of which could not be known until it had been put in exercise, and which, for many years at least, must be necessarily less the object of respect than of criticism. Wise legislators, even when lapse of time, alteration of manners, or increased liberality of sentiment, require corresponding alterations in the institutions of their fathers, are careful, as far as possible, to preserve the ancient form and character of those laws, into which they are endeavouring to infuse principles and a spirit accommodated to the altered exigencies and temper of the age. There is an enthusiasm in patriotism as well as in religion. We value institutions, not only because they are ours, but because they have been those of our fathers; and if a new constitution were to be presented to us, although perhaps theoretically showing more symmetry than that by which the nation had been long governed, it would be as difficult to transfer to it the allegiance of the people, as it would be to substitute the worship of a Madonna, the work of modern art, for the devotion paid by the natives of Saragossa to their ancient Palladium, Our Lady of the Pillar.

But the constitution of the year Three, with all its defects, would have been willingly received by the nation in general, as affording some security from the revolutionary storm, had it not been for a selfish and usurping device of the Thermidoriens to mutilate and render it nugatory at the very outset, by engrafting

---

[71] "Its authors were Lesage, Daunou, Boissy d'Anglas, Creuzée-Latouche, Berlier, Louvet, Lareveillère-Lepaux, Languinais, Durand-Maillanne, Baudin des Ardennes, and Thibaudeau."—Thiers, tom. viii., p. 9.

upon it the means of continuing the exercise of their own arbitrary authority. It must never be forgotten, that these conquerors of Robespierre had shared all the excesses of his party before they became his personal enemies; and that when deprived of their official situations and influence, which they were likely to be by a representative body freely and fairly elected, they were certain to be exposed to great individual danger.

Determined, therefore, to retain the power in their own hands, the Thermidoriens suffered, with an indifference amounting almost to contempt, the constitution to pass through, and be approved of by, the Convention. But, under pretence that it would be highly impolitic to deprive the nation of the services of men accustomed to public business, they procured [Aug. 22] two decrees to be passed; the first ordaining the electoral bodies of France to choose, as representatives to the two councils under the new constitution, at least two-thirds of the members presently sitting in Convention; and the second declaring, that in default of a return of two-thirds of the present deputies, as prescribed, the Convention themselves should fill up the vacancies out of their own body; in other words, should name a large proportion of themselves their own successors in legislative power.[72]

These decrees were sent down to the Primary Assemblies of the people, and every art was used to render them acceptable.

But the nation, and particularly the city of Paris, generally revolted at this stretch of arbitrary authority. They recollected, that all the members who had sat in the first National Assembly, so remarkable for talent, had been declared ineligible, on that single account, for the second legislative body; and now, men so infinitely the inferiors of those who were the colleagues of Mirabeau, Mounier, and other great names, presumed not only to declare themselves eligible by re-election, but dared to establish two-thirds of their number as indispensable ingredients of the legislative assemblies, which, according to the words alike and spirit of the constitution, ought to be chosen by the free voice of the people. The electors, and particularly those of the sections of Paris, angrily

---

[72] Thiers, tom. viii., p. 13.

demanded to know, upon what public services the deputies of the Convention founded their title to a privilege so unjust and anomalous. Among the more active part of them, to whom the measure was chiefly to be ascribed, they saw but a few reformed Terrorists, who wished to retain the power of tyranny, though disposed to exercise it with some degree of moderation, and the loss of whose places might be possibly followed by that of their heads; in the others, they only beheld a flock of timid and discountenanced Helots, willing to purchase personal security at the sacrifice of personal honour and duty to the public; while in the Convention as a body, who pronounced so large a proportion of their number as indispensable to the service of the state, judging from their conduct hitherto, they could but discover an image composed partly of iron, partly of clay, deluged with the blood of many thousand victims—a pageant without a will of its own, and which had been capable of giving its countenance to the worst of actions, at the instigation of the worst of men—a sort of Moloch, whose name had been used by its priests to compel the most barbarous sacrifices. To sum up the whole, these experienced men of public business, without whose intermediation it was pretended the national affairs could not be carried on, could only shelter themselves from the charge of unbounded wickedness, by pleading their unlimited cowardice, and by poorly alleging that for two years they had sat, voted, and deliberated under a system of compulsion and terror. So much meanness rendered those who were degraded by it unfit, not merely to rule, but to live; and yet two-thirds of their number were, according to their own decrees, to be intruded on the nation as an indispensable portion of its representatives.

THE SECTIONS

Such was the language held in the assemblies of the sections of Paris, who were the more irritated against the domineering and engrossing spirit exhibited in these usurping enactments, because it was impossible to forget that it was their interference, and the protection afforded by their national guard, which had saved the Convention from massacre on more occasions than one.

In the meanwhile, reports continued to be made from the Primary Assemblies, of their adhesion to the constitution, in which they were almost unanimous, and of their sentiments concerning the two decrees, authorizing and commanding the re-election of two-thirds of the Convention, on which there existed a strong difference of opinion. The Convention, determined, at all rates, to carry through with a high hand the iniquitous and arbitrary measure which they proposed, failed not to make these reports such as they desired them to be, and announced that the two decrees had been accepted by a majority of the Primary Assemblies. The citizens of Paris challenged the accuracy of the returns—alleged that the reports were falsified—demanded a scrutiny, and openly bid defiance to the Convention. Their power of meeting together in their sections, on account of the appeal to the people, gave them an opportunity of feeling their own strength, and encouraging each other by speeches and applauses. They were further emboldened and animated by men of literary talent, whose power was restored with the liberty of the press.[73] Finally, they declared their sittings permanent, and that they had the right to protect the liberties of France. The greater part of the national guards were united on this occasion against the existing government; and nothing less was talked of, than that they should avail themselves of their arms and numbers, march down to the Tuileries, and dictate law to the Convention with their muskets, as the revolutionary mob of the suburbs used to do with their pikes.

The Convention, unpopular themselves, and embarked in an unpopular cause, began to look anxiously around for assistance. They chiefly relied on the aid of about five thousand regular troops, who were assembled in and around Paris. These declared for government with the greater readiness, that the insurrection was of a character decidedly aristocratical, and that the French armies, as already repeatedly noticed, were attached to the Republic. But besides, these professional troops entertained the usual degree of contempt for the national guards, and on this account alone were quite ready to correct the insolence of the *pekins*,[74] or *muscadins*,[75]

---

[73] "La Harpe, Lacretelle, jun., Suard, Morellet, Vaublanc, Pastoret, Dupont de Nemours, Quatremère de Quincy, Delalot, Marchenna, and General Miranda, all either published pamphlets or made speeches in the sections."—Thiers, tom. viii., p. 15.

[74] *Pekins*, a word of contempt, by which the soldiers distinguished those who did not belong to their profession.—S.

who usurped the dress and character of soldiers. The Convention had also the assistance of several hundred artillerymen, who, since the taking of the Bastile, had been always zealous democrats. Still apprehensive of the result, they added to this force another of a more ominous description. It was a body of volunteers, consisting of about fifteen hundred men, whom they chose to denominate the Sacred Band, or the Patriots of 1789. They were gleaned out of the suburbs, and from the jails, the remnants of the insurrectional battalions which had formed the body-guard of Hébert and Robespierre, and had been the instruments by which they executed their atrocities. The Convention proclaimed them men of the 10th of August—undoubtedly, they were also men of the massacres of September. It was conceived that the beholding such a pack of blood-hounds, ready to be let loose, might inspire horror into the citizens of Paris, to whom their very aspect brought so many fearful recollections. It did so, but it also inspired hatred; and the number and zeal of the citizens, compensating for the fury of the Terrorists, and for the superior discipline of the regular troops to be employed against them, promised an arduous and doubtful conflict.

Much, it was obvious, must depend on the courage and conduct of the leaders.

The sections employed, as their commander-in-chief, General Danican, an old officer of no high reputation for military skill, but otherwise a worthy and sincere man. The Convention at first made choice of Menou, and directed him, supported by a strong military force, to march into the section Le Pelletier, and disarm the national guards of that district. This section is one of the most wealthy, and of course most aristocratic, in Paris, being inhabited by bankers, merchants, the wealthiest class of tradesmen, and the better orders in general. Its inhabitants had formerly composed the battalion of national guards des Filles Saint Thomas, the only one which, taking part in the defence of the Tuileries, shared the fate of the Swiss Guards upon the memorable 10th of August. The section continued to entertain sentiments of the same character, and when Menou appeared at the head of his forces, accompanied by La Porte, a member of the Convention, he found the citizens under arms, and

---

[75] *Muscadins*, fops—a phrase applied to the better class of *Sans-Culottes*.—S.

exhibiting such a show of resistance, as induced him, after a parley, to retreat without venturing an attack upon them.

Menou's indecision showed that he was not a man suited to the times, and he was suspended from his command by the Convention, and placed under arrest. The general management of affairs and the direction of the Conventional forces, was then committed to Barras; but the utmost anxiety prevailed among the members of the committees by whom government was administered, to find a general of nerve and decision enough to act under Barras, in the actual command of the military force, in a service so delicate, and times so menacing. It was then that a few words from Barras, addressed to his colleagues, Carnot and Tallien, decided the fate of Europe for wellnigh twenty years, "I have the man," he said, "whom you want, a little Corsican officer, who will not stand upon ceremony."[76]

The acquaintance of Barras and Buonaparte had been, as we have already said, formed at the siege of Toulon, and the former had not forgotten the inventive and decisive genius of the young officer to whom the conquest of that city was to be ascribed. On the recommendation of Barras, Buonaparte was sent for. He had witnessed the retreat of Menou, and explained with much simplicity the causes of that check, and the modes of resistance which ought to be adopted in case of the apprehended attack. His explanations gave satisfaction. Buonaparte was placed at the head of the Conventional forces, and took all the necessary precautions to defend the same palace which he had seen attacked and carried by a body of insurgents on the 10th of August. But he possessed far more formidable means of defence than were in the power of the unfortunate Louis. He had two hundred pieces of cannon, which his high military skill enabled him to distribute to the utmost advantage. He had more than five thousand regular forces, and about fifteen hundred volunteers. He was thus enabled to defend the whole circuit of the Tuileries; to establish posts in all the avenues by which it could be approached; to possess himself of the bridges, so as to

---

[76] "For several months, Napoleon, not being actively employed, laboured in the military committee, and was well acquainted with Carnot and Tallien, whom he saw daily. How, then, could Barras make them the proposal attributed to him?"—Louis Buonaparte, p. 17.

prevent co-operation between the sections which lay on the opposite banks of the river; and finally, to establish a strong reserve in the Place Louis Quinze, or, as it was then called, Place de la Révolution. Buonaparte had only a few hours to make all these arrangements, for he was named in place of Menou late on the night before the conflict.

A merely civic army, having no cannon, (for the field-pieces, of which each section possessed two, had been almost all given up to the Convention after the disarming the suburb of Saint Antoine,) ought to have respected so strong a position as the Tuileries, when so formidably defended. Their policy should have been, as in the days of Henry II., to have barricaded the streets at every point, and cooped up the Conventional troops within the defensive position they had assumed, till want of provisions obliged them to sally at disadvantage, or to surrender. But a popular force is generally impatient of delay. The retreat of Menou had given them spirit, and they apprehended, with some show of reason, that the sections, if they did not unite their forces, might be attacked and disarmed separately. They therefore resolved to invest the Convention in a hostile manner, require of the members to recall the obnoxious decrees, and allow the nation to make a free and undictated election of its representatives.

On the thirteenth Vendemaire, corresponding to the 4th October, the civil affray, commonly called the Day of the Sections, took place. The national guards assembled, to the number of thirty thousand men and upwards, but having no artillery. They advanced by different avenues, in close columns, but everywhere found the most formidable resistance. One large force occupied the quays on the left bank of the Seine, threatening the palace from that side of the river. Another strong division advanced on the Tuileries, through the Rue St. Honoré, designing to debouche on the palace, where the Convention was sitting, by the Rue de Echelle. They did so, without duly reflecting that they were flanked on most points by strong posts in the lanes and crossings, defended by artillery.

The contest began in the Rue St. Honoré. Buonaparte had established a strong post with two guns at the cul-de-sac Dauphine, opposite to the church of St. Roche. He permitted the imprudent Parisians to involve their long and dense columns in the narrow street without interruption, until they established a body of grenadiers in the front of the church, and opposite to the position at the cul-de-sac. Each party, as usual, throws on the other the blame of commencing the civil contest for which both were prepared. But all agree the firing commenced with musketry. It was instantly followed by discharges of grape-shot and cannister, which, pointed as the guns were, upon thick columns of the national guards, arranged on the quays and in the narrow streets, made an astounding carnage. The national guards offered a brave resistance, and even attempted to rush on the artillery, and carry the guns by main force. But a measure which is desperate enough in the open field, becomes impossible when the road to assault lies through narrow streets, which are swept by the cannon at every discharge. The citizens were compelled to give way. By a more judicious arrangement of their respective forces, different results might have been hoped; but how could Danican, in any circumstances have competed with Buonaparte? The affair, in which several hundred men were killed and wounded, was terminated as a general action in about an hour; and the victorious troops of the Convention, marching into the different sections, completed the dispersion and disarming of their opponents, an operation which lasted till late at night.

The Convention used this victory with the moderation which recollection of the Reign of Terror had inspired. Only two persons suffered death for the Day of the Sections. One of them, La Fond, had been a garde de corps, was distinguished for his intrepidity, and repeatedly rallied the national guard under the storm of grape shot. Several other persons having fled, were in their absence capitally condemned, but were not strictly looked after; and deportation was the punishment inflicted upon others. The accused were indebted for this clemency chiefly to the interference of those members of the Convention, who, themselves exiled on the 31st of May, had suffered persecution and learned mercy.

The Convention showed themselves at the same time liberal to their protectors. General Berruyer,[77] who commanded the volunteers of 1789, and other general officers employed on the Day of the Sections, were loaded with praises and preferment. But a separate triumph was destined to Buonaparte, as the hero of the day. Five days after the battle, Barras solicited the attention of the Convention to the young officer, by whose prompt and skilful dispositions the Tuileries had been protected on the 13th Vendemaire, and proposed that they should approve of General Buonaparte's appointment as second in command of the army of the interior, Barras himself still remaining commander-in-chief. The proposal was adopted by acclamation. The Convention retained their resentment against Menou, whom they suspected of treachery; but Buonaparte interfering as a mediator, they were content to look over his offence.

After this decided triumph over their opponents, the Convention ostensibly laid down their authority, and retiring from the scene in their present character, appeared upon it anew in that of a Primary Assembly, in order to make choice of such of their members as, by virtue of the decrees of two-thirds, as they were called, were to remain on the stage, as members of the Legislative Councils of Elders and Five Hundred.

After this change of names and dresses, resembling the shifts of a strolling company of players, the two-thirds of the old Convention, with one-third of members newly elected, took upon them the administration of the new constitution. The two re-elected thirds formed a large proportion of the councils, and were, in some respects, much like those unfortunate women, who, gathered from jails and from the streets of the metropolis, have been sometimes sent out to foreign settlements; and, however profligate their former lives may have been, often regain character, and become tolerable members of society, in a change of scene and situation.

---

[77] In 1796, the Directory appointed Berruyer commander of the Hôpital des Invalides, which situation he held till his death, in 1804.

THE DIRECTORY

The Directory consisted of Barras, Siêyes, Reubel, Latourneur de la Manche, and Reveillière-Lepaux, to the exclusion of Tallien, who was deeply offended. Four of these directors were reformed Jacobins, or Thermidoriens; the fifth, Reveillière-Lepaux, was esteemed a Girondist. Siêyes, whose taste was rather for speculating in politics than acting in them, declined what he considered a hazardous office, and was replaced by Carnot.

The nature of the insurrection of the Sections was not ostensibly royalist, but several of its leaders were of that party in secret, and, if successful, it would most certainly have assumed that complexion. Thus, the first step of Napoleon's rise commenced by the destruction of the hopes of the House of Bourbon, under the reviving influence of which, twenty years afterwards, he himself was obliged to succumb. But the long path which closed so darkly, was now opening upon him in light and joy. Buonaparte's high services, and the rank which he had obtained, rendered him now a young man of the first hope and expectation, mingling on terms of consideration among the rulers of the state, instead of being regarded as a neglected stranger, supporting himself with difficulty, and haunting public offices and bureaux in vain, to obtain some chance of preferment, or even employment.

From second in command, the new general soon became general-in-chief of the army of the interior, Barras having found his duties as a director incompatible with those of military command. He employed his genius, equally prompt and profound, in improving the state of the military forces; and, in order to prevent the recurrence of such insurrections as that of the 13th Vendemaire, or Day of the Sections, and as the many others by which it was preceded, he appointed and organized a guard for the protection of the representative body.

As the dearth of bread, and other causes of disaffection, continued to produce commotions in Paris, the general of the interior was sometimes obliged to oppose them with a military force. On one occasion, it is said, that when Buonaparte was anxiously admonishing the multitude to disperse, a very bulky woman exhorted them to keep their ground. "Never mind these coxcombs with the epaulets," she said; "they do not care if we are all starved, so they themselves feed and get fat."—"Look at me, good woman," said Buonaparte, who was then as thin as a shadow, "and tell me which is the fatter of us two." This turned the laugh against the Amazon, and the rabble dispersed in good-humour.[78] If not among the most distinguished of Napoleon's victories, this is certainly worthy of record, as achieved at the least cost.

Meantime, circumstances, which we will relate, according to his own statement, introduced Buonaparte to an acquaintance, which was destined to have much influence on his future fate. A fine boy of ten or twelve years old, presented himself at the levee of the general of the interior, with a request of a nature unusually interesting. He stated his name to be Eugene Beauharnais, son of the ci-devant Vicomte de Beauharnais, who, adhering to the revolutionary party, had been a general in the Republican service upon the Rhine, and falling under the causeless suspicion of the Committee of Public Safety, was delivered to the Revolutionary Tribunal, and fell by its sentence just four days before the overthrow of Robespierre. Eugene was come to request of Buonaparte, as general of the interior, that his father's sword might be restored to him. The prayer of the young supplicant was as interesting as his manners were engaging, and Napoleon felt so much interest in him, that he was induced to cultivate the acquaintance of Eugene's mother, afterwards the Empress Josephine.[79]

JOSEPHINE BEAUHARNAIS

This lady was a Creolian, the daughter of a planter in St. Domingo. Her name at full length was Marie-Joseph Rose Detacher de la Pagérie. She had suffered her share of revolutionary miseries. After her husband, General Beauharnais, had been deprived of his command, she was arrested as a suspected person, and detained in prison till the general liberation, which succeeded the revolution of

---
[78] Las Cases, tom. i., p. 161.
[79] Montholon, tom. iii., p. 82.

9th Thermidor. While in confinement, Madame Beauharnais had formed an intimacy with a companion in distress, Madame Fontenai, now Madame Tallien,[80] from which she derived great advantages after her friend's marriage. With a remarkably graceful person, amiable manners, and an inexhaustible fund of good humour, Madame Beauharnais was formed to be an ornament to society. Barras, the Thermidorien hero, himself an ex-noble, was fond of society, desirous of enjoying it on an agreeable scale, and of washing away the dregs which Jacobinism had mingled with all the dearest interests of life. He loved show, too, and pleasure, and might now indulge both without the risk of falling under the suspicion of incivism, which, in the Reign of Terror, would have been incurred by any attempt to intermingle elegance with the enjoyments of social intercourse. At the apartments which he occupied as one of the directory, in the Luxemburg palace, he gave its free course to his natural taste, and assembled an agreeable society of both sexes. Madame Tallien and her friend formed the soul of these assemblies, and it was supposed that Barras was not insensible to the charms of Madame Beauharnais,—a rumour which was likely to arise, whether with or without foundation.

When Madame Beauharnais and General Buonaparte became intimate, the latter assures us, and we see no reason to doubt him, that although the lady was two or three years older than himself,[81] yet being still in the full bloom of beauty, and extremely agreeable in her manners, he was induced, solely by her personal charms, to make her an offer of his hand, heart, and fortunes,—little supposing, of course, to what a pitch the latter were to arise.

Although he himself is said to have been a fatalist, believing in destiny and in the influence of his star, he knew nothing, probably, of the prediction of a negro sorceress, who, while Marie-Joseph was but a child, prophesied she should rise to a dignity greater than that of a queen, yet fall from it before her death.[82] This was one of those

---

[80] See vol. i.
[81] Buonaparte was then in his twenty-sixth year. Josephine gave herself in the marriage contract for twenty-eight.—S.
[82] A lady of high rank, who happened to live for some time in the same convent at Paris, where Josephine was also a pensioner or boarder, heard her mention the prophecy, and told it herself to the author, just about the time of the Italian expedition, when Buonaparte

vague auguries, delivered at random by fools or imposters, which the caprice of Fortune sometimes matches with a corresponding and conforming event. But without trusting to the African sibyl's prediction, Buonaparte may have formed his match under the auspices of ambition as well as love. The marrying Madame Beauharnais was a mean of uniting his fortune with those of Barras and Tallien, the first of whom governed France as one of the directors; and the last, from talents and political connexions, had scarcely inferior influence. He had already deserved well of them for his conduct on the Day of the Sections, but he required their countenance to rise still higher; and without derogating from the bride's merits, we may suppose her influence in their society corresponded with the views of her lover. It is, however, certain, that he always regarded her with peculiar affection; that he relied on her fate, which he considered as linked with and strengthening his own; and reposed, besides, considerable confidence in Josephine's tact and address in political business. She had at all times the art of mitigating his temper, and turning aside the hasty determinations of his angry moments, not by directly opposing, but by gradually parrying and disarming them. It must be added, to her great praise, that she was always a willing, and often a successful advocate, in the cause of humanity.

They were married 9th March 1796; and the dowery of the bride was the chief command of the Italian armies, a scene which opened a full career to the ambition of the youthful general. Buonaparte remained with his wife only three days after his marriage, hastened to see his family, who were still at Marseilles, and having enjoyed the pleasure of exhibiting himself as a favourite of Fortune in the city which he had lately left in a very subordinate capacity, proceeded rapidly to commence the career to which Fate called him, by placing himself at the head of the Italian army.[83]

---

was beginning to attract notice. Another clause is usually added to the prediction—that the party whom it concerned should die in an hospital, which was afterwards explained as referring to Malmaison. This the author did not hear from the same authority. The lady mentioned used to speak in the highest terms of the simple manners and great kindness of Madame Beauharnais.—S.

[83] "It was I who proposed Buonaparte for the command of the army of Italy, not Barras."—Carnot, *Réponse à Bailleul.*

"Napoleon owed the appointment to the command of the army of Italy to his signal services under Dumerbion."—Jomini, tom. viii., p. 49.

Chapter III

The Alps—Feelings and Views of Buonaparte on being appointed to the Command of the Army of Italy—General Account of his new Principles of Warfare—Mountainous Countries peculiarly favourable to them—Retrospect of Military Proceedings since October 1795—Hostility of the French Government to the Pope—Massacre of the French Envoy Basseville, at Rome—Austrian Army under Beaulieu—Napoleon's Plan for entering Italy—Battle of Montenotte, and Buonaparte's first Victory—Again defeats the Austrians at Millesimo—and again under Colli—Takes possession of Cherasco—King of Sardinia requests an Armistice, which leads to a Peace, concluded on very severe Terms—Close of the Piedmontese Campaign—Napoleon's Character at this period.

Napoleon has himself observed, that no country in the world is more distinctly marked out by its natural boundaries than Italy.[84] The Alps seem a barrier erected by Nature herself, on which she has inscribed in gigantic characters, "Here let ambition be staid." Yet this tremendous circumvallation of mountains, as it could not prevent the ancient Romans from breaking out to desolate the world, so it has been in like manner found, ever since the days of Hannibal, unequal to protect Italy herself from invasion. The French nation, in the times of which we treat, spoke indeed of the Alps as a natural boundary, so far as to authorise them to claim all which lay on the western side of these mountains, as naturally pertaining to their dominions; but they never deigned to respect them as such, when the question respected their invading, on their own part, the territories of other states, which lay on or beyond the formidable frontier. They assumed the law of natural limits as an

---

[84] Napoleon, Memoirs, tom. iii., p. 91.

unchallengeable rule when it made in favour of France, but never allowed it to be quoted against her interest.

COMMANDER-IN-CHIEF

During the Revolutionary War, the general fortune of battle had varied from time to time in the neighbourhood of these mighty boundaries. The King of Sardinia[85] possessed almost all the fortresses which command the passes on these mountains, and had therefore been said to wear the keys of the Alps at his girdle. He had indeed lost his Dukedom of Savoy, and the County of Nice, in the late campaigns; but he still maintained a very considerable army, and was supported by his powerful ally the Emperor of Austria, always vigilant regarding that rich and beautiful portion of his dominions which lies in the north of Italy. The frontiers of Piedmont were therefore covered by a strong Austro-Sardinian army, opposed to the French, of which Napoleon had been just named commander-in-chief. A strong Neapolitan force[86] was also to be added, so that in general numbers their opponents were much superior to the French; but a great part of this force was cooped up in garrisons which could not be abandoned.

It may be imagined with what delight the general, scarce aged twenty-six, advanced to an independent field of glory and conquest, confident in his own powers, and in the perfect knowledge of the country, which he had acquired when by his scientific plans of the campaign, he had enabled General Dumerbion to drive the Austrians back, and obtain possession of the Col di Tende, Saorgio, and the gorges of the higher Alps.[87] Buonaparte's achievements had hitherto been under the auspices of others. He made the dispositions before Toulon, but it was Dugommier who had the credit of taking the place. Dumerbion, as we have just said, obtained the merit of the advantages in Piedmont. Even in the civil turmoil of the 13th Vendemaire, his actual services had been overshadowed by

---

[85] Victor Amadeus III. He was born in 1726, and died in 1796.
[86] "The Neapolitan army was 60,000 strong; the cavalry was excellent."—Napoleon, *Memoirs*, tom. iii., p. 134.
[87] Viz. in April, 1794.—See Napoleon, Memoirs, tom. iii., p. 28.

the official dignity of Barras as commander-in-chief. But if he reaped honour in Italy, the success would be exclusively his own; and that proud heart must have throbbed to meet danger upon such terms; that keen spirit have toiled to discover the means of success.

For victory he relied chiefly upon a system of tactics hitherto unpractised in war, or at least upon any considerable or uniform scale. It may not be unnecessary to pause, to take a general view of the principles which he now called into action.

Nations in the savage state, being constantly engaged in war, always form for themselves some peculiar mode of fighting, suited to the country they inhabit, and to the mode in which they are armed. The North-American Indian becomes formidable as a rifleman or sharpshooter, lays ambuscades in his pathless forests, and practises all the arts of irregular war. The Arab, or Scythian, manœuvres his clouds of cavalry, so as to envelope and destroy his enemy in his deserts by sudden onsets, rapid retreats, and unexpected rallies; desolating the country around, cutting off his antagonist's supplies, and practising, in short, the species of war proper to a people superior in light cavalry.

The first stage of civilisation is less favourable to success in war. As a nation advances in the peaceful arts, and the character of the soldier begins to be less familiarly united with that of the citizen, this system of natural tactics falls out of practice; and when foreign invasion, or civil broils, call the inhabitants to arms, they have no idea save that of finding out the enemy, rushing upon him, and committing the event to superior strength, bravery, or numbers. An example may be seen in the great Civil War of England, where men fought on both sides, in almost every county of the kingdom, without any combination, or exact idea of uniting in mutual support, or manœuvring so as to form their insulated bands into an army of preponderating force. At least, what was attempted for that purpose must have been on the rudest plan possible, where, even in actual fight, that part of an army which obtained any advantage, pursued it as far as they could, instead of using their success for the support of their companions; so that the main body was often defeated when a victorious wing was in pursuit of those whom their first onset had broken.

But—as war becomes a profession, and a subject of deep study—it is gradually discovered, that the principles of tactics depend upon mathematical and arithmetical science; and that the commander will be victorious who can assemble the greatest number of forces upon the same point at the same moment, notwithstanding an inferiority of numbers to the enemy when the general force is computed on both sides. No man ever possessed in a greater degree than Buonaparte, the power of calculation and combination necessary for directing such decisive manœuvres. It constituted, indeed, his *secret*—as it was for some time called—and that secret consisted in an imagination fertile in expedients which would never have occurred to others; clearness and precision in forming his plans; a mode of directing with certainty the separate moving columns which were to execute them, by arranging so, that each division should arrive on the destined position at the exact time when their service was necessary; and above all, in the knowledge which enabled such a master-spirit to choose the most fitting subordinate implements, to attach them to his person, and, by explaining to them so much of his plan as it was necessary each should execute, to secure the exertion of their utmost ability in carrying it into effect.

Thus, not only were his manœuvres, however daring, executed with a precision which warlike operations had not attained before his time; but they were also performed with a celerity which gave them almost always the effect of surprise. Napoleon was like lightning in the eyes of his enemies; and when repeated experience had taught them to expect this portentous rapidity of movement, it sometimes induced his opponents to wait, in a dubious and hesitating posture, for attacks, which, with less apprehension of their antagonist, they would have thought it more prudent to frustrate and to anticipate.

Great sacrifices were necessary to enable the French troops to move with that degree of celerity which Buonaparte's combinations required. He made no allowance for impediments or unexpected obstacles; the time which he had calculated for execution of manœuvres prescribed, was on no account to be exceeded—every sacrifice was to be made of baggage, stragglers, even artillery, rather than the column should arrive too late at the point of its destination. Hence, all that had hitherto been considered as essential not only to the health, but to the very existence of an army, was in a great measure dispensed with in the French service; and, for the first time, troops were seen to take the field without tents, without camp-equipage, without magazines of provisions, without military hospitals;—the soldiers eating as they could, sleeping where they could, dying where they could; but still advancing, still combating, and still victorious.

It is true that the abandonment of every object, save success in the field, augmented frightfully all the usual horrors of war. The soldier, with arms in his hands, and wanting bread, became a marauder in self-defence; and, in supplying his wants by rapine, did mischief to the inhabitants, in a degree infinitely beyond the benefit he himself received; for it may be said of military requisition, as truly as of despotism, that it resembles the proceedings of a savage, who cuts down a tree to come at the fruit. Still, though purchased at a high rate, that advantage was gained by this rapid system of tactics, which in a slower progress, during which the soldier was regularly maintained, and kept under the restraint of discipline, might have been rendered doubtful. It wasted the army through disease, fatigue, and all the consequences of want and toil; but still the victory was attained, and that was enough to make the survivors forget their hardships, and to draw forth new recruits to replace the fallen. Patient of labours, light of heart and temper, and elated by success beyond all painful recollections, the French soldiers were the very men calculated to execute this desperate species of service under a chief, who, their sagacity soon discovered, was sure to lead to victory all those who could sustain the hardships by which it was to be won.

SYSTEM OF TACTICS

The character of the mountainous countries, among which he was, for the first time, to exercise his system, was highly favourable to Buonaparte's views. Presenting many lines and defensible positions, it induced the Austrian generals to become stationary, and occupy a considerable extent of ground, according to their old system of tactics. But though abounding in such positions as might at first sight seem absolutely impregnable, and were too often trusted to as such, the mountains also exhibited to the sagacious eye of a great captain, gorges, defiles, and difficult and unsuspected points of access, by which he could turn the positions that appeared in front so formidable; and, by threatening them on the flank and on the rear, compel the enemy to a battle at disadvantage, or to a retreat with loss.

The forces which Buonaparte had under his command were between fifty and sixty thousand good troops, having, many of them, been brought from the Spanish campaign, in consequence of the peace with that country; but very indifferently provided with clothing, and suffering from the hardships they had endured in those mountainous, barren, and cold regions.[88] The cavalry, in particular, were in very poor order; but the nature of their new field of action not admitting of their being much employed, rendered this of less consequence. The misery of the French army, until these Alpine campaigns were victoriously closed by the armistice of Cherasco, could, according to Buonaparte's authority,[89] scarce bear description. The officers for several years had received no more than eight livres a-month (twenty pence sterling a-week) in name of pay, and staff-officers had not amongst them a single horse. Berthier preserved, as a curiosity, an order of the day, dated Albenga, directing an advance of four Louis d'or to every general of division, to enable them to enter on the campaign.[90] Among the generals to

---

[88] Napoleon states his fighting force, fit for duty, at about 30,000 men.—Montholon, tom. iii., p. 140; Jomini, tom. viii., p. 59, at 42,400.
[89] Las Cases, tom. i., p. 162.
[90] This reminds us of the liberality of the Kings of Brentford to their Knightsbridge forces—
First King. Here, take five guineas to these warlike men.

whom this paltry supply was rendered acceptable by their wants, were, or might have been, many whose names became afterwards the praise and dread of war.[91] Augereau, Massena,[92] Serrurier, Joubert, Lasnes, and Murat, all generals of the first consideration, served under Buonaparte in his first Italian campaign.

The position of the French army had repeatedly varied since October 1795, after the skirmish at Cairo. At that time the extreme left of the line, which extended from south to north, rested upon the Col d'Argentine, and communicated with the higher Alps—the centre was on the Col di Tende and Mount Bertrand—the left occupied the heights of Saint Bertrand, Saint Jacques, and other ridges running in the same direction, which terminated on the Mediterranean shore, near Finale.

The Austrians, strongly reinforced, attacked this line, and carried the heights of Mont Saint Jacques; and Kellermann, after a vain attempt to regain that point of his position, retreated to the line of defence more westward, which rests on Borghetto. Kellermann, an active and good brigade officer, but without sufficient talent to act as commander-in-chief, was superseded, and Scherer was placed in command of the army of Italy. He risked a battle with the Austrians near Loana, in which the talents of Massena and Augereau were conspicuous; and by the victory which ensued, the French regained the line of Saint Jacques and Finale, which Kellermann had been forced to abandon; so that in a general point of view, the relative position of the two opposed armies was not very different from that in which they had been left by Buonaparte.[93]

Second King. And here, five more, which makes the sum just ten.
Herald. We have not seen so much the Lord knows when!—S.
[91] "The state of the finances was such, that the government, with all its efforts, could only furnish the chest of the army, at the opening of the campaign, with 2000 louis in specie, and a million in drafts, part of which were protested."—Napoleon, *Montholon*, tom. iii., p. 140; Thiers, tom. viii., p. 174.
[92] "An idea of the penury of the army may be collected from the correspondence of the commander-in-chief, who appears to have once sent Massena a supply of twenty-four francs to provide for his official expenses."—Jomini, tom. viii., p. 96.
[93] Napoleon, Memoirs, tom. iii., p. 54.

THE POPE

But though Scherer had been thus far victorious, he was not the person to whom the Directory desired to intrust the daring plan of assuming the offensive on a grand scale upon the Alpine frontier, and, by carrying their arms into Italy, compelling the Austrians to defend themselves in that quarter, and to diminish the gigantic efforts which that power had hitherto continued with varied success, but unabated vigour, upon the Rhine. The rulers of France had a farther object in this bold scheme. They desired to intimidate, or annihilate and dethrone the Pope. He was odious to them as head of the Church, because the attachment of the French clergy to the Roman See, and the points of conscience which rested upon that dependence, had occasioned the recusancy of the priests, especially of those who were most esteemed by the people, to take the constitutional oath. To the Pope, and his claims of supremacy, were therefore laid the charge of the great civil war in La Vendée, and the general disaffection of the Catholics in the south of France.

But this was not the only cause of the animosity entertained by the Directory against the head of the Catholic Church. They had, three years before, sustained an actual injury from the See of Rome, which was yet unavenged. The people of Rome were extremely provoked that the French residing there, and particularly the young artists, had displayed the three-coloured cockade, and were proposing to exhibit the scutcheon containing the emblems of the Republic, over the door of the French consul. The Pope, through his minister, had intimated his desire that this should not be attempted, as he had not acknowledged the Republic as a legitimate government. The French, however, pursued their purpose; and the consequence was, that a popular commotion arose, which the papal troops did not greatly exert themselves to suppress. The carriage of the French envoy, or chargé des affaires, named Basseville, was attacked in the streets, and chased home; his house was broken into by the mob, and he himself, unarmed and unresisting, was cruelly assassinated. The French Government considered this very naturally as a gross insult, and were the more desirous of avenging it, that by doing so they would approach nearer to the dignified conduct of the Roman Republic, which, in good or evil, seems always to have been their model. The affair happened in 1793, but was not forgotten in 1796.[94]

The original idea entertained by the French Government for prosecuting their resentment, had been by a proposed landing at Civita Vecchia with an army of ten thousand men, marching to Rome, and exacting from the pontiff complete atonement for the murder of Basseville. But as the English fleet rode unopposed in the Mediterranean, it became a matter of very doubtful success to transport such a body of troops to Civita Vecchia by sea, not to mention the chance that, even if safely landed, they would have found themselves in the centre of Italy, cut off from supplies and succours, assaulted on all hands, and most probably blockaded by the British fleet. Buonaparte, who was consulted, recommended that the north of Italy should be first conquered, in order that Rome might be with safety approached and chastised; and this scheme, though in appearance scarce a less bold measure, was a much safer one than the Directory had at first inclined to, since Buonaparte would only approach Rome in the event of his being able to preserve his communications with Lombardy and Tuscany, which he must conquer in the first place.[95]

The plan of crossing the Alps and marching into Italy, suited in every respect the ambitious and self-confident character of the general to whom it was now intrusted. It gave him a separate and independent authority, and the power of acting on his own judgment and responsibility; for his countryman Salicetti, the deputy who accompanied him as a commissioner of the Government, was not probably much disposed to intrude his opinions. He had been Buonaparte's patron, and was still his friend.[96] The young general's mind was made up to the alternative of conquest or ruin, as may be judged from his words to a friend at taking leave of him. "In three

---

[94] "He received a thrust of a bayonet in the abdomen: he was dragged into the streets, holding his bowels in his hands, and at length left on a field-bed in a guard-house, where he expired."—Montholon, tom. iii., p. 41; Botta, Storia d'Italia, tom. i., p. 271. Basseville, in 1789, was editor of the *Mercure National*. He published *Elémens de Mythologie*, &c.
[95] Montholon, tom. iii., p. 43; Thibaudeau, Hist. Gen. de Napoleon, tom. i., p. 139; Jomini, tom. viii., p. 49.
[96] "Salicetti was never the personal friend of Napoleon, but of his brother Joseph; with whom, in 1792 and 1793, he had been member for the department of Corsica."—Joseph Buonaparte, *Notes sur les Mémoires de Bourrienne*, tom. i., p. 238.

months," he said, "I will be either at Milan or at Paris;" intimating at once his desperate resolution to succeed, and his sense that the disappointment of all his prospects must be the consequence of a failure.

On the 27th of March Buonaparte reached Nice. The picture of the army which General Scherer[97] laid before him, was even worse than he had formed any idea of. The supply of bread was very uncertain; distributions of meat had long ceased; and for means of conveyance there were only mules, and not above five hundred of these could be reckoned upon.

The headquarters had never been removed from Nice, since the commencement of the war: they were instantly ordered to be transferred to Albenga. On the march thither, along the rugged and precipitous shore of the Mediterranean, the staff, broken with the rear and baggage of the army, were exposed to the cannonade of Nelson's squadron; but the young commander-in-chief would not allow the columns to halt, for the purpose either of avoiding or of returning it.[98] On the 3rd of April, the army reached port Maunie, near Oneglia, and on the 4th arrived at Albenga; where, with the view of animating his followers to ambitious hopes, he addressed the army of Italy to the following purpose:—"Soldiers, you are hungry and naked.—The Republic owes you much, but she has not the means to acquit herself of her debts. The patience with which you support your hardships among these barren rocks is admirable, but it cannot procure you glory. I am come to lead you into the most fertile plains that the sun beholds—Rich provinces, opulent towns, all shall be at your disposal—Soldiers, with such a prospect before you, can you fail in courage and constancy?" This was showing the deer to the hound when the leash is about to be slipped.

---

[97] "I am particularly gratified with my reception by General Scherer; who, by his honourable deportment and readiness to supply me with all useful information, has acquired a right to my gratitude. To great facility in expressing himself, he unites an extent of general and military knowledge, which may probably induce you to deem his services useful in some important station."—Napoleon *to the Directory, March 30.*

[98] Jomini, tom. viii., p. 62; Thiers, tom. viii., p. 329.

The Austro-Sardinian army, to which Buonaparte was opposed, was commanded by Beaulieu, an Austrian general of great experience and some talent, but no less than seventy-five years old; accustomed all his life to the ancient rules of tactics, and unlikely to suspect, anticipate, or frustrate, those plans, formed by a genius so fertile as that of Napoleon.

Buonaparte's plan for entering Italy differed from that of former conquerors and invaders, who had approached that fine country by penetrating or surmounting at some point or other her Alpine barriers. This inventive warrior resolved to attain the same object, by turning round the southern extremity of the Alpine range, keeping as close as possible to the shores of the Mediterranean, and passing through the Genoese territory by the narrow pass called the Boccheta leading around the extremity of the mountains, and betwixt these and the sea. Thus he proposed to penetrate into Italy, by the lowest level which the surface of the country presented, which must be of course where the range of the Alps unites with that of the Apennines. The point of junction where these two immense ranges of mountains touch upon each other, is at the heights of Mount Saint Jacques, above Genoa, where the Alps, running north-westward, ascend to Mont Blanc, their highest peak, and the Apennines, running to the south-east, gradually elevate themselves to Monte Velino, the tallest mountain of the range.

To attain his object of turning the Alps in the manner proposed, it was necessary that Buonaparte should totally change the situation of his army; those occupying a defensive line, running north and south, being to assume an offensive position, extending east and west. Speaking of an army as of a battalion, he was to form into column upon the right of the line which he had hitherto occupied. This was an extremely delicate operation, to be undertaken in presence of an active enemy, his superior in numbers; nor was he permitted to execute it uninterrupted.

No sooner did Beaulieu learn that the French general was concentrating his forces, and about to change his position, than he hastened to preserve Genoa, without possession of which, or at least of the adjacent territory, Buonaparte's scheme of advance could scarce have been accomplished. The Austrian divided his army into three bodies. Colli, at the head of a Sardinian division, he stationed on the extreme right at Ceva; his centre division, under D'Argenteau, having its head at Sasiello, had directions to march on a mountain called Montenotte, with two villages of the same name, near to which was a strong position at a place called Montelegino, which the French had occupied in order to cover their flank during their march towards the east. At the head of his left wing, Beaulieu himself moved from Novi upon Voltri, a small town within ten miles of Genoa, for the protection of that ancient city, whose independence and neutrality were like to be held in little reverence. Thus it appears, that while the French were endeavouring to penetrate into Italy by an advance from Sardinia by the way of Genoa, their line of march was threatened by three armies of Austro-Sardinians, descending from the skirts of the Alps, and menacing to attack their flank. But though a skilful disposition, Beaulieu's had, from the very mountainous character of the country, the great disadvantage of wanting connexion between the three separate divisions; neither, if needful, could they be easily united on any point desired, while the lower line, on which the French moved, permitted constant communication and co-operation.

BATTLE OF MONTENOTTE

On the 10th of April, D'Argenteau, with the central division of the Austro-Sardinian army, marched on Montenotte, while Beaulieu on the left attacked the van of the French army, which had come as far as Voltri. General Cervoni, commanding the French division which sustained the attack of Beaulieu, was compelled to fall back on the main body of his countrymen; and had the assault of D'Argenteau been equally animated, or equally successful, the fame of Buonaparte might have been stifled in the birth. But Colonel Rampon, a French officer, who commanded the redoubts near Montelegino, stopped the progress of D'Argenteau by the most determined resistance. At the head of not more than fifteen hundred men, whom he inspired with his own courage, and caused to swear either to maintain their post or die there,[99] he continued to defend

---

[99] Thiers, tom. viii., p. 178; Lacretelle, tom. xiii., p. 153.

the redoubts, during the whole of the 11th, until D'Argenteau, whose conduct was afterwards greatly blamed for not making more determined efforts to carry them, drew off his forces for the evening, intending to renew the attack next morning.

But, on the morning of the 12th, the Austrian general found himself surrounded with enemies. Cervoni, who retreated before Beaulieu, had united himself with La Harpe, and both advancing northward during the night of the 11th, established themselves in the rear of the redoubts of Montelegino, which Rampon had so gallantly defended. This was not all. The divisions of Augereau and Massena had marched, by different routes, on the flank and on the rear of D'Argenteau's column; so that next morning, instead of renewing his attack on the redoubts, the Austrian general was obliged to extricate himself by a disastrous retreat, leaving behind him colours and cannon, a thousand slain, and two thousand prisoners.[100]

Such was the battle of Montenotte, the first of Buonaparte's victories; eminently displaying that truth and mathematical certainty of combination,[101] which enabled him on many more memorable occasions, even when his forces were inferior in numbers, and apparently disunited in position, suddenly to concentrate them and defeat his enemy, by overpowering him on the very point where he thought himself strongest. He had accumulated a superior force on the Austrian centre, and destroyed it, while Colli, on the right, and Beaulieu himself, on the left, each at the head of numerous forces, did not even hear of the action till it was fought and won.[102]

In consequence of the success at Montenotte, and the close pursuit of the defeated Austrians, the French obtained possession of Cairo, which placed them on that side of the Alps which slopes towards Lombardy, and where the streams from these mountains run to join the Po.

---

[100] Napoleon, Memoirs, tom. iii., p. 145; Jomini, tom. viii., p. 70; Las Cases, tom. ii., p. 187.
[101] "Napoleon placed himself on a ridge in the centre of his divisions, the better to judge of the turn of affairs, and to prescribe the manœuvres which might become necessary."— Jomini, tom. viii., p. 72.
[102] Montholon, tom. iii., p. 145; Las Cases, tom. ii., p. 190; Thiers, tom. viii., p. 178.

Beaulieu had advanced to Voltri, while the French withdrew to unite themselves in the attack upon D'Argenteau. He had now to retreat northward with all haste to Dego, in the valley of the river Bormida, in order to resume communication with the right wing of his army, consisting chiefly of Sardinians, from which he was now nearly separated by the defeat of the centre. General Colli, by a corresponding movement on the right, occupied Millesimo, a small town about nine miles from Dego, with which he resumed and maintained communication by a brigade stationed on the heights of Biastro. From the strength of this position, though his forces were scarce sufficiently concentrated, Beaulieu hoped to maintain his ground till he should receive supplies from Lombardy, and recover the consequences of the defeat at Montenotte. But the antagonist whom he had in front had no purpose of permitting him such respite.

BATTLE OF MILLESIMO

Determined upon a general attack on all points of the Austrian position, the French army advanced in three bodies upon a space of four leagues in extent. Augereau, at the head of the division which had not fought at Montenotte, advanced on the left against Millesimo; the centre, under Massena, directed themselves upon Dego, by the vale of the Bormida; the right wing, commanded by La Harpe, proceeded by the heights of Cairo, for the purpose of turning Beaulieu's left flank. Augereau, whose division had not engaged at the battle of Montenotte, was the first who came in contact with the enemy. He attacked General Colli on the 13th April. His troops, emulous of the honour acquired by their companions, behaved with great bravery, rushed upon the outposts of the Sardinian army at Millesimo, forced, and retained possession of the gorge by which it was defended, and thus separated from the Sardinian army a body of about two thousand men, under the Austrian General Provera, who occupied a detached eminence called Cossaria, which covered the extreme left of General Colli's position. But the Austrian showed the most obstinate courage. Although surrounded by the enemy, he threw himself into the ruinous castle of Cossaria, which crowned the eminence, and showed a disposition to maintain the place to the last; the rather that, as he could see from the turrets of his stronghold the Sardinian troops, from whom he had been separated, preparing to fight on the ensuing day, he might reasonably hope to be disengaged.[103]

Buonaparte in person came up; and seeing the necessity of dislodging the enemy from this strong post, ordered three successive attacks to be made on the castle. Joubert, at the head of one of the attacking columns, had actually, with six or seven others, made his way into the outworks, when he was struck down by a wound in the head. General Banel, and Adjutant-general Quénin fell, each at the head of the column which he commanded; and Buonaparte was compelled to leave the obstinate Provera in possession of the castle for the night. The morning of the 14th brought a different scene. Contenting himself with blockading the castle of Cossaria, Buonaparte now gave battle to General Colli, who made every effort to relieve it. These attempts were all in vain. He was defeated and cut off from Beaulieu; he retired as well as he could upon Ceva, leaving to his fate the brave General Provera, who was compelled to surrender at discretion.

ACTION OF DEGO

On the same day, Massena, with the centre, attacked the heights of Biastro, being the point of communication betwixt Beaulieu and Colli, while La Harpe, having crossed the Bormida, where the stream came up to the soldiers' middle, attacked in front and in flank the village of Dego, where the Austrian commander-in-chief was stationed. The first attack was completely successful,—the heights of Biastro were carried, and the Piedmontese routed. The assault of Dego was not less so, although after a harder struggle. Beaulieu was compelled to retreat, and was entirely separated from the Sardinians, who had hitherto acted in combination with him. The defenders of Italy now retreated in different directions, Colli

---

[103] Montholon, tom. iii., p. 146; Las Cases, tom. ii., p. 192; Jomini, tom. viii., p. 76.

moving westward towards Ceva, while Beaulieu, closely pursued through a difficult country, retired upon D'Aqui.[104]

Even the morning after the victory, it was nearly wrested out of the hands of the conquerors. A fresh division of Austrians, who had evacuated Voltri later than the others, and were approaching to form a junction with their general, found the enemy in possession of Beaulieu's position. They arrived at Dego like men who had been led astray, and were no doubt surprised at finding it in the hands of the French. Yet they did not hesitate to assume the offensive, and by a brisk attack drove out the enemy, and replaced the Austrian eagles in the village. Great alarm was occasioned by this sudden apparition; for no one among the French could conceive the meaning of an alarm beginning on the opposite quarter to that on which the enemy had retreated, and without its being announced from the outposts towards D'Aqui.

Buonaparte hastily marched on the village. The Austrians repelled two attacks; at the third, General Lanusse, afterwards killed in Egypt, put his hat upon the point of his sword, and advancing to the charge, penetrated into the place. Lannes also, afterwards Duke of Montebello, distinguished himself on the same occasion by courage and military skill, and was recommended by Buonaparte to the Directory for promotion. In this battle of Dego, more commonly called of Millesimo, the Austro-Sardinian army lost five or six thousand men, thirty pieces of cannon, with a great quantity of baggage. Besides, the Austrians were divided from the Sardinians; and the two generals began to show, not only that their forces were disunited, but that they themselves were acting upon separate motives; the Sardinians desiring to protect Turin, whereas the movements of Beaulieu seemed still directed to prevent the French from entering the Milanese territory.[105]

Leaving a sufficient force on the Bormida to keep in check Beaulieu, Buonaparte now turned his strength against Colli, who, overpowered, and without hopes of succour, abandoned his line of defence near Ceva, and retreated to the line of the Tanaro.

---

[104] Las Cases, tom. ii., p. 193; Montholon, tom. iii., p. 148; Thiers, tom. viii., p. 181.
[105] Montholon, tom. iii., p. 148; Las Cases, tom. ii., p. 193; Lacretelle, tom. xiii., p. 59.

Napoleon, in the meantime, fixed his head-quarters at Ceva, and enjoyed from the heights of Montezemoto, the splendid view of the fertile fields of Piedmont stretching in boundless perspective beneath his feet, watered by the Po, the Tanaro, and a thousand other streams which descend from the Alps. Before the eyes of the delighted army of victors lay this rich expanse like a promised land; behind them was the wilderness they had passed;—not indeed, a desert of barren sand, similar to that in which the Israelites wandered, but a huge tract of rocks and inaccessible mountains, crested with ice and snow, seeming by nature designed as the barrier and rampart of the blessed regions which stretched eastward beneath them. We can sympathize with the self-congratulation of the general who had surmounted such tremendous obstacles in a way so unusual. He said to the officers around him, as they gazed upon this magnificent scene, "Hannibal took the Alps by storm. We have succeeded as well by taming their flank."[106]

The dispirited army of Colli was attacked at Mondovi during his retreat, by two corps of Buonaparte's army, from two different points, commanded by Massena and Serrurier. The last general, the Sardinian repulsed with loss; but when he found Massena, in the meantime, was turning the left of his line, and that he was thus pressed on both flanks, his situation became almost desperate.[107] The cavalry of the Piedmontese made an effort to renew the combat. For a time they overpowered and drove back those of the French; and General Stengel, who commanded the latter, was slain in attempting to get them into order.[108] But the desperate valour of Murat, unrivalled perhaps in the heady charge of cavalry combat, renewed the fortune of the field; and the horse, as well as the infantry of Colli's army, were compelled to a disastrous retreat. The defeat was decisive; and the Sardinians, after the loss of the best of

---

[106] "Annabal a forcé les Alpes; nous nous les avons tournées!"—Napoleon, *Montholon*, tom. iii., p. 151.
[107] "The rapidity of Massena's movements was a subject of astonishment and terror with the Piedmontese, who regarded him as a rebel. He was born at Nice, but attached himself early in his youth to the French service. The Revolution found him a sergeant in the Royal Italian regiment."—Lacretelle, tom. xiii., p. 161.
[108] "General Stengel, a native of Alsace, was an excellent hussar officer; he had served under Dumouriez, and in the other campaigns of the North; he was adroit, intelligent, and active, combining the qualities of youth with those of maturity, he was the true general for advanced posts."—Napoleon, *Montholon*, tom. iii., p. 152.

their troops, their cannon, baggage, and appointments, and being now totally divided from their Austrian allies, and liable to be overpowered by the united forces of the French army, had no longer hopes of effectually covering Turin. Buonaparte, pursuing his victory, took possession of Cherasco, within ten leagues of the Piedmontese capital.[109]

Thus Fortune, in the course of a campaign of scarce a month, placed her favourite in full possession of the desired road to Italy by command of the mountain-passes, which had been invaded and conquered with so much military skill. He had gained three battles over forces far superior to his own; inflicted on the enemy a loss of twenty-five thousand men in killed, wounded, and prisoners; taken eighty pieces of cannon, and twenty-one stand of colours;[110] reduced to inaction the Austrian army; almost annihilated that of Sardinia; and stood in full communication with France upon the eastern side of the Alps, with Italy lying open before him, as if to invite his invasion. But it was not even with such laurels, and with facilities which now presented themselves for the accomplishment of new and more important victories upon a larger scale, and with more magnificent results, that the career of Buonaparte's earliest campaign was to be closed. The head of the royal house of Savoy, if not one of the most powerful, still one of the most distinguished in Europe, was to have the melancholy experience, that he had encountered with the Man of Destiny, as he was afterwards proudly called, who, for a time, had power, in the emphatic phrase of Scripture, "to bind kings with chains, and nobles with fetters of iron."

The shattered relics of the Sardinian army had fallen back, or rather fled, to within two leagues of Turin, without hope of being again able to make an effectual stand. The Sovereign of Sardinia, Savoy, and Piedmont, had no means of preserving his capital, nay, his existence on the continent, excepting by an almost total submission to the will of the victor. Let it be remembered, that Victor Amadeus the Third was the descendant of a race of heroes,

---

[109] Montholon, tom. iii., p. 151; Jomini, tom. viii., p. 93.
[110] Murat was despatched to Paris with them, and the treaty for the armistice of Cherasco. His arrival, by way of Mount Cenis, with so many trophies, and the King of Sardinia's submission, caused great joy in the capital. Junot, who had been despatched after the battle of Millesimo by the Nice road, arrived later than Murat.

who, from the peculiar situation of their territories, as constituting a neutral ground of great strength betwixt France and the Italian possessions of Austria, had often been called on to play a part in the general affairs of Europe, of importance far superior to that which their condition as a second-rate power could otherwise have demanded. In general, they had compensated their inferiority of force by an ability and gallantry which did them the highest credit, both as generals and as politicians; and now Piedmont was at the feet, in her turn, of an enemy weaker in numbers than her own. Besides the reflections on the past fame of his country, the present humiliating situation of the King was rendered more mortifying by the state of his family connexions. Victor Amadeus was the father-in-law of Monsieur (Louis XVIII.,) and of the Comte d'Artois, (afterwards Charles X.) He had received his sons-in-law at his court at Turin, had afforded them an opportunity of assembling around them their forces, consisting of the emigrant noblesse, and had strained all the power he possessed, and in many instances successfully, to withstand both the artifices and the arms of the French Republicans. And now, so born, so connected, and with such principles, he was condemned to sue for peace, on any terms which might be dictated, from a General of France, aged twenty-six years, who, a few months before, was desirous of an appointment in the artillery service of the Grand Signior.

ARMISTICE OF CHERASCO

Under these afflicting circumstances, a suspension of hostilities was requested by the King of Sardinia; and, on the 24th April, conferences were held at Carru, the headquarters of the French, but an armistice could only be purchased by placing two of the King's strongest fortresses—Coni and Tortona, in the hands of the French, and thus acknowledging that he surrendered at discretion. The armistice was agreed on [April 28] at Cherasco, but commissioners were sent by the King to Paris, to arrange with the Directory the final terms of peace. These were such as victors give to the vanquished.

Besides the fortresses already surrendered, the King of Sardinia was to place in the hands of the French five others of the first importance. The road from France to Italy was to be at all times open to the French armies; and indeed the King, by surrender of the places mentioned, had lost the power of interrupting their progress. He was to break off every species of alliance and connexion with the combined powers at war with France, and become bound not to entertain at his court, or in his service, any French emigrants whatever, or any of their connexions; nor was an exception even made in favour of his own two daughters. In short, the surrender was absolute.[111] Victor Amadeus exhibited the utmost reluctance to subscribe this treaty, and did not long survive it.[112] His son succeeded in name to the kingdom of Piedmont; but the fortresses and passes, which had rendered him a prince of some importance, were, excepting Turin, and one or two of minor consequence, all surrendered into the hands of the French.

Viewing this treaty with Sardinia as the close of the Piedmontese campaign, we pause to consider the character which Buonaparte displayed at that period. The talents as a general which he had exhibited were of the very first order. There was no disconnexion in his objects; they were all attained by the very means he proposed, and the success was improved to the utmost. A different conduct usually characterises those who stumble unexpectedly on victory, either by good fortune or by the valour of their troops. When the favourable opportunity occurs to such leaders, they are nearly as much embarrassed by it as by a defeat. But Buonaparte, who had foreseen the result of each operation by his sagacity, stood also prepared to make the most of the advantages which might be derived from it.

His style in addressing the Convention was, at this period, more modest and simple, and therefore more impressive, than the figurative and bombastic style which he afterwards used in his bulletins. His self-opinion, perhaps, was not risen so high as to

---

[111] The treaty was concluded at Paris, on the 15th May. For a copy of it, see *Annual Register*, vol. xxxviii., p. 262.
[112] Victor Amadeus died of apoplexy, in the following October, and was succeeded by his son, Charles Emanuel.

permit him to use the sesquipedalian words and violent metaphors, to which he afterwards seems to have given a preference. We may remark also, that the young victor was honourably anxious to secure for such officers as distinguished themselves, the preferment which their services entitled them to.[113] He urges the promotion of his brethren in arms in almost every one of his despatches,—a conduct not only just and generous, but also highly politic. Were his recommendations successful, their general had the gratitude due for the benefit; were they overlooked, thanks equally belonged to him for his good wishes, and the resentment for the slight attached itself to the government, who did not give effect to them.

If Buonaparte spoke simply and modestly on his own achievements, the bombast which he spared was liberally dealt out to the Convention by an orator named Daubermesnil, who invokes all bards, from Tyrtæus and Ossian down to the author of the Marseillois Hymn—all painters, from Apelles to David—all musicians, from Orpheus to the author of the *Chant du départ*, to sing, paint, and compose music, upon the achievements of the General and Army of Italy.[114]

With better taste, a medal of Buonaparte was struck in the character of the Conqueror of the battle of Montenotte. The face is extremely thin, with lank hair, a striking contrast to the fleshy square countenance exhibited on his later coins. On the reverse, Victory, bearing a palm branch, a wreath of laurel, and a naked sword, is seen flying over the Alps. This medal we notice as the first of the splendid series which records the victories and honours of Napoleon, and which was designed by Denon as a tribute to the genius of his patron.

---

[113] See Correspondence Inédite, tom. i., p. 85.
[114] See the speech in the *Moniteur*, No. 233, 12th May.

Chapter IV

Farther progress of the French Army under Buonaparte—He crosses the Po, at Placenza, on 7th May—Battle of Lodi takes place on the 10th, in which the French are victorious—Remarks on Napoleon's Tactics in this celebrated Action—French take possession of Cremona and Pizzighitone—Milan deserted by the Archduke Ferdinand and his Duchess—Buonaparte enters Milan on the 15th May—General situation of the Italian States at this period—Napoleon inflicts Fines upon the neutral and unoffending States of Parma and Modena, and extorts the surrender of some of their finest Pictures—Remarks upon this novel procedure.

PROGRESS OF THE FRENCH ARMY

The ardent disposition of Buonaparte did not long permit him to rest after the advantages which he had secured. He had gazed on Italy with an eagle's eye; but it was only for a moment, ere stooping on her with the wing, and pouncing on her with the talons, of the king of birds.

A general with less extraordinary talent would perhaps have thought it sufficient to have obtained possession of Piedmont, revolutionizing its government as the French had done that of Holland, and would have awaited fresh supplies and reinforcements from France before advancing to farther and more distant conquests, and leaving the Alps under the dominion of a hostile, though for the present a subdued and disarmed monarchy. But Buonaparte had studied the campaign of Villars in these regions, and was of opinion that it was by that general's hesitation to advance boldly into Italy, after the victories which the Marshal de Coigni had obtained at Parma and Guastalla, that the enemy had been enabled to assemble an accumulating force, before which the French were compelled to retreat.[115] He determined, therefore, to give the Republic of Venice, the Grand Duke of Tuscany, and other states in Italy, no time to muster forces, and take a decided part, as they were likely to do, to oppose a French invasion. Their terror and surprise could not fail to be increased by a sudden irruption; while months, weeks, even days of consideration, might afford those states, attached as the rulers must be to their ancient oligarchical forms of government, time and composure to assume arms to maintain them. A speedy resolution was the more necessary, as Austria, alarmed for her Italian possessions, was about to make every effort for their defence. Orders had already been sent by the Aulic Council of War to detach an army of thirty thousand men, under Wurmser, from the Army of the Rhine to the frontiers of Italy. These were to be strengthened by other reinforcements from the interior, and by such forces as could be raised in the mountainous district of the Tyrol, which furnishes perhaps the most experienced and most formidable sharpshooters in the world. The whole was to be united to the fragments of Beaulieu's defeated troops. If suffered to form a junction, and arrange their plans for attack or defence, an army, of force so superior to the French in numbers, veterans in discipline, and commanded by a general like Wurmser, was likely to prevent all the advantages which the French might gain by a sudden irruption, ere an opposition so formidable was collected and organized. But the daring scheme which Napoleon contemplated, corresponding to the genius of him who had formed it, required to be executed with caution, united with secrecy and celerity. These were the more necessary, as, although the thanks of the French Government had been voted to the army of Italy five times in the course of a month, yet the Directory, alarmed at the more doubtful state of hostilities upon the Rhine, had turned their exertions chiefly in that direction; and, trusting to the skill of their general, and the courage of his troops, had not transmitted recruits and supplies upon the scale necessary for the great undertakings which he meditated. But *Italiam—Italiam!*[116]—the idea

---

[115] Montholon, tom. iii., p. 162.
[116] "—procul obscuros colles humilemque videmus Italiam. Italiam! primus conclamat Achates; Italiam! læto socii clamore salutant."
Virg. *Æneid*, Book III.—S.

of penetrating into a country so guarded and defended by nature, as well as by military skill, the consciousness of having surmounted obstacles of a nature so extraordinary, and the hope that they were approaching the reward of so many labours—above all, their full confidence in a leader, who seemed to have bound Victory to his standard—made the soldiers follow their general, without counting their own deficiencies, or the enemy's numbers.[117]

To encourage this ardour, Buonaparte circulated an address,[118] in which, complimenting the army on the victories they had gained, he desired them at the same time "to consider nothing as won so long as the Austrians held Milan, and while the ashes of those who had conquered the Tarquins were soiled by the presence of the assassins of Basseville." It would appear that classical allusions are either familiar to the French soldiers, or that, without being more learned than others of their rank, they are pleased with being supposed to understand them. They probably considered the oratory of their great leader as soldier-like words, and words of exceeding good command. The English soldier, addressed in such flights of eloquence, would either have laughed at them, or supposed that he had got a crazed play-actor put over him, instead of a general. But there is this peculiar trait in the French character, that they are willing to take every thing of a complimentary kind in the manner in which it seems to be meant. They appear to have made that bargain with themselves on many points, which the audience usually do in a theatre,—to accept of the appearance of things for the reality. They never inquire whether a triumphal arch is of stone or of wood; whether a scutcheon is of solid metal, or only gilt; or whether a speech, of which the tendency is flattering to their

---

"Now every star before Aurora flies, Whose glowing blushes streak the purple skies; When the dim hills of Italy we view'd, That peep'd by turns, and dived beneath the flood, Lo! Italy appears, Achates cries, And, Italy! with shouts the crowd replies."
Dryden.

[117] "The army, on reaching the Adige, will command all the states of the House of Austria in Italy, and all those of the Pope on this side of the Apennines; it will be in a situation to proclaim the principles of liberty, and to excite Italian patriotism against the sway of foreigners. The word *Italiam. Italiam!* proclaimed at Milan, Bologna, and Verona, will produce a magical effect."—Napoleon, *Montholon*, tom. iii., p. 165.

[118] It was dated Cherasco, April the 26th, and sufficiently proves, that notwithstanding all their victories, many of the soldiery, nay, even of the superior officers, were still alarmed at the magnitude of the enterprise on which Napoleon was entering with apparently very inadequate resources.

national vanity, contains genuine eloquence, or only tumid extravagance.

TORTONA

All thoughts were therefore turned to Italy. The fortress of Tortona was surrendered to the French by the King of Sardinia; Buonaparte's headquarters were fixed there, [May 4.] Massena concentrated another part of the army at Alexandria, menacing Milan, and threatening, by the passage of the Po, to invade the territories belonging to Austria on the northern bank of that stream. As Buonaparte himself observed, the passage of a great river is one of the most critical operations in modern war; and Beaulieu had collected his forces to cover Milan, and prevent the French, if possible, from crossing the Po. But, in order to avert the dangerous consequences of attempting to force his passage on the river, defended by a formidable enemy in front, Buonaparte's subtle genius had already prepared the means for deceiving the old Austrian respecting his intended operations.

PASSAGE OF THE PO

Valenza appeared to be the point of passage proposed by the French; it is one of those fortresses which cover the eastern frontier of Piedmont, and is situated upon the Po. During the conferences previous to the armistice of Cherasco, Buonaparte had thrown out hints as if he were particularly desirous to be possessed of this place, and it was actually stipulated in the terms of the treaty, that the French should occupy it for the purpose of effecting their passage over the river. Beaulieu did not fail to learn what had passed, which coinciding with his own ideas of the route by which Buonaparte meant to advance upon Milan, he hastened to concentrate his army on the opposite bank, at a place called Valeggio, about eighteen miles from Valenza, the point near which he expected the attempt to be made, and from which he could move easily in any direction towards the river, before the French could send over any considerable force. Massena also countenanced this report, and riveted the attention of the Austrians on Valenza, by pushing strong reconnoitring parties from Alexandria in the direction of that fortress. Besides, Beaulieu had himself crossed the Po at this place, and, like all men of routine—(for such he was though a brave and approved soldier)—he was always apt to suppose that the same reasons which directed himself, must needs seem equally convincing to others. In almost all delicate affairs, persons of ordinary talents are misled by their incapacity to comprehend, that men of another disposition will be likely to view circumstances, and act upon principles, with an eye and opinion very different from their own.

But the reports which induced the Austrian general to take the position at Valeggio, arose out of a stratagem of war. It was never Buonaparte's intention to cross the Po at Valenza. The proposal was a feint to draw Beaulieu's attention to that point, while the French accomplished the desired passage at Placenza, nearly fifty miles lower down the river than Valeggio, where their subtle general had induced the Austrians to take up their line of defence. Marching for this purpose with incredible celerity, Buonaparte, on the 7th of May, assembled his forces at Placenza, when their presence was least expected, and where there were none to defend the opposite bank, except two or three squadrons of Austrians, stationed there merely for the purpose of reconnoitring. General Andréossi (for names distinguished during those dreadful wars begin to rise on the narrative, as the stars glimmer out on the horizon) commanded an advanced guard of five hundred men. They had to pass in the common ferry-boats, and the crossing required nearly half an hour; so that the difficulty, or rather impossibility, of achieving the operation, had they been seriously opposed, appears to demonstration. Colonel Lannes threw himself ashore first with a body of grenadiers, and speedily dispersed the Austrian hussars, who attempted to resist their landing. The vanguard having thus opened the passage, the other divisions of the army were enabled to cross in succession, and in the course of two days the whole were in the Milanese territory, and on the left bank of the Po. The military manœuvres, by means of which Buonaparte achieved, without the loss of a man, an operation of so much consequence, and which, without such address as he displayed, must have been attended with great loss, and risk of failure, have often been considered as among his most masterly movements.

Beaulieu, informed too late of the real plans of the French general, moved his advanced guard, composed of the division of General Liptay, from Valeggio towards the Po, in the direction of Placenza. But here also the alert general of the French had been too rapid in his movements for the aged German. Buonaparte had no intention to wait an attack from the enemy with such a river as the Po in his rear, which he had no means of recrossing if the day should go against him; so that a defeat, or even a material check, would have endangered the total loss of his army. He was, therefore, pushing forward in order to gain ground on which to manœuvre, and the advanced divisions of the two armies met at a village called Fombio, not far from Casal, on the 8th of May. The Austrians threw themselves into the place, fortified and manned the steeples, and whatever posts else could be made effectual for defence, and reckoned upon defending themselves there until the main body of Beaulieu's army should come up to support them. But they were unable to sustain the vivacity of the French onset, to which so many successive victories had now given a double impulse. The village was carried at the bayonet's point; the Austrians lost their cannon, and left behind one-third of their men, in slain, wounded, and prisoners. The wreck of Liptay's division saved themselves by crossing the Adda at Pizzighitone, while they protected their retreat by a hasty defence of that fortress.[119]

Another body of Austrians having advanced from Casal, to support, it may be supposed, the division of Liptay, occasioned a great loss to the French army in the person of a very promising officer. This was General La Harpe, highly respected and trusted by Buonaparte, and repeatedly mentioned in the campaigns of Piedmont. Hearing the alarm given by the out-posts, when the Austrian patrols came in contact with them, La Harpe rode out to satisfy himself concerning the nature and strength of the attacking party. On his return to his own troops, they mistook him and his attendants for the enemy, fired upon, and killed him. He was a Swiss by birth, and had been compelled to leave his country on account of

---

[119] Montholon, tom. iii., p. 169; Thibaudeau, tom. i., p 206; Jomini, tom. viii., p. 117.

his democratical opinions; a grenadier, says Buonaparte, in stature and in courage, but of a restless disposition. The soldiers with the superstition belonging to their profession, remarked, that during the battle of Fombio, on the day before, he was less animated than usual, as if an obscure sense of his approaching fate already overwhelmed him.[120]

The Austrian regiment of cavalry which occasioned this loss, after some skirmishing, was content to escape to Lodi, a point upon which Beaulieu was again collecting his scattered forces, for the purpose of covering Milan, by protecting the line of the Adda.

BATTLE OF LODI

"The passage of the Po," said Buonaparte, in his report to the Directory, "had been expected to prove the boldest and most difficult manœuvre of the campaign, nor did we expect to have an action of more vivacity than that of Dego. But we have now to recount the battle of Lodi."[121] As the conqueror deservedly congratulated himself on this hard-won victory, and as it has become in a manner especially connected with his name and military character, we must, according to our plan, be somewhat minute in our details respecting it.

The Adda, a large and deep river, though fordable at some places and in some seasons, crosses the valley of the Milanese, rising in the Tyrolese Alps, and joining the Po at Pizzighitone; so that, if the few points at which it can be crossed are fortified or defended, it forms a line covering all the Milanese territory to the eastward, from any force approaching from the direction of Piedmont. This line Beaulieu proposed to make good against the victor before whom he had so often retreated, and he conjectured (on this occasion rightly) that, to prosecute his victory by marching upon Milan, Buonaparte would first desire to dislodge the covering army from the line of the Adda, as he could not safely advance to the capital of Lombardy,

---

[120] Montholon, tom. iii., p. 172.
[121] Moniteur, No. 241, May 20.

leaving the enemy in possession of such a defensive line upon their flank. He also conjectured that this attempt would be made at Lodi.

This is a large town, containing twelve thousand inhabitants. It has old Gothic walls, but its chief defence consists in the river Adda, which flows through it, and is crossed by a wooden bridge about five hundred feet in length. When Beaulieu, after the affair of Fombio, evacuated Casal, he retreated to this place with about ten thousand men. The rest of his army was directed upon Milan and Cassano, a town situated, like Lodi, upon the Adda.

Buonaparte calculated that, if he could accomplish the passage of the Adda at Lodi, he might overtake and disperse the remainder of Beaulieu's army, without allowing the veteran time to concentrate them for farther resistance in Milan, or even for rallying under the walls of the strong fortress of Mantua. The judgment of the French general was in war not more remarkable for seizing the most advantageous moment of attack, than for availing himself to the very uttermost of success when obtained. The quick-sighted faculty and power of instant decision with which nature had endowed him, had, it may be supposed, provided beforehand for the consequences of the victory ere it was yet won, and left no room for doubt or hesitation when his hopes had become certainties. We have already remarked, that there have been many commanders, who, after an accidental victory, are so much at a loss what is next to be done, that while they are hesitating, the golden moments pass away unimproved; but Buonaparte knew as well how to use advantages, as to obtain them.

Upon the 10th day of May, attended by his best generals, and heading the choicest of his troops, Napoleon pressed forward towards Lodi. About a league from Casal, he encountered the Austrian rear-guard, who had been left, it would appear, at too great a distance from the main body. The French had no difficulty in driving these troops before them into the town of Lodi, which was but slightly defended by the few soldiers whom Beaulieu had left on the western or right side of the Adda. He had also neglected to destroy the bridge, although he ought rather to have supported a defence on the right bank of the river, (for which the town afforded many facilities,) till the purpose of destruction was completed, than have allowed it to exist. If his rear-guard had been actually stationed in Lodi, instead of being so far in the rear of the main body, they might, by a protracted resistance from the old walls and houses, have given time for this necessary act of demolition.

But though the bridge was left standing, it was swept by twenty or thirty Austrian pieces of artillery, whose thunders menaced death to any who should attempt that pass of peril. The French, with great alertness, got as many guns in position on the left bank, and answered this tremendous fire with equal spirit. During this cannonade, Buonaparte threw himself personally amongst the fire, in order to station two guns loaded with grape-shot in such a position, as rendered it impossible for any one to approach for the purpose of undermining or destroying the bridge; and then calmly proceeded to make arrangements for a desperate attempt.

His cavalry was directed to cross, if possible, at a place where the Adda was said to be fordable,—a task which they accomplished with difficulty. Meantime, Napoleon observed that the Austrian line of infantry was thrown considerably behind the batteries of artillery which they supported, in order that they might have the advantage of a bending slope of ground, which afforded them shelter from the French fire. He therefore drew up a close column of three thousand grenadiers, protected from the artillery of the Austrians by the walls and houses of the town, and yet considerably nearer to the enemy's line of guns on the opposite side of the Adda than were their own infantry, which ought to have protected them. The column of grenadiers, thus secured, waited in comparative safety, until the appearance of the French cavalry, who had crossed the ford, began to disquiet the flank of the Austrians. This was the critical moment which Buonaparte expected. A single word of command wheeled the head of the column of grenadiers to the left, and placed it on the perilous bridge. The word was given to advance, and they rushed on with loud shouts of *Vive la République!* But their appearance upon the bridge was the signal for a redoubled shower of grape-shot, while from the windows of the houses on the left side of the river, the soldiers who occupied them poured volley after volley of musketry on the thick column as it endeavoured to force its way over the long bridge. At one time the French grenadiers, unable to sustain this dreadful storm, appeared for an instant to hesitate. But Berthier, the chief of Buonaparte's staff, with Massena, L'Allemagne, and Corvini, hurried to the head of the column, and by their presence and gallantry renewed the resolution of the soldiers, who now poured across the bridge. The Austrians had but one resource left; to rush on the French with the bayonet, and kill, or drive back into the Adda, those who had forced their passage, before they could deploy into line, or receive support from their comrades, who were still filing along the bridge. But the opportunity was neglected, either because the troops, who should have executed the manœuvre, had been, as we have already noticed, withdrawn too far from the river; or because the soldiery, as happens when they repose too much confidence in a strong position, became panic-struck when they saw it unexpectedly carried. Or it may be, that General Beaulieu, so old and so unfortunate, had somewhat lost that energy and presence of mind which the critical moment demanded. Whatever was the cause, the French rushed on the artillerymen, from whose fire they had lately suffered so tremendously, and, unsupported as they were, had little difficulty in bayoneting them.

The Austrian army now completely gave way, and lost in their retreat, annoyed as it was by the French cavalry, upwards of twenty guns, a thousand prisoners, and perhaps two thousand more wounded and slain.[122]

Such was the famous passage of the Bridge of Lodi; achieved with such skill and gallantry, as gave the victor the same character for fearless intrepidity, and practical talent in actual battle, which the former part of the campaign had gained him as a most able tactician.

Yet this action, though successful, has been severely criticized by those who desire to derogate from Buonaparte's military talents. It has been said, that he might have passed over a body of infantry at the same ford where the cavalry had crossed; and that thus, by manœuvring on both sides of the river, he might have compelled the Austrians to evacuate their position on the left bank of the Adda,

---

[122] Montholon, tom. iii., p. 173; Jomini, tom. viii., p. 126; Thibaudeau, tom. i., p. 218.

without hazarding an attack upon their front, which could not but cost the assailants very dearly.

Buonaparte had perhaps this objection in his recollection when he states, that the column of grenadiers was so judiciously sheltered from the fire until the moment when their wheel to the left brought them on the bridge, that they only lost two hundred men[123] during the storm of the passage. We cannot but suppose, that this is a very mitigated account of the actual loss of the French army. So slight a loss is not to be easily reconciled with the horrors of the battle, as he himself detailed them in his despatches; nor with the conclusion, in which he mentions, that of the sharp contests which the army of Italy had to sustain during the campaign, none was to be compared with that "terrible passage of the bridge of Lodi."[124]

In fact, as we may take occasion to prove hereafter, the Memoranda of the great general, dictated to his officers at Saint Helena, have a little too much the character of his original bulletins; and, while they show a considerable disposition to exaggerate the difficulties to be overcome, the fury of the conflict, and the exertions of courage by which the victory was attained, show a natural inconsistency, from the obvious wish to diminish the loss which was its unavoidable price.

But, admitting that the loss of the French had been greater on this occasion than their general cared to recollect or acknowledge, his military conduct seems not the less justifiable.

Buonaparte appears to have had two objects in view in this daring exploit. The first was, to improve and increase the terror into which his previous successes had thrown the Austrians, and to impress on them the conviction, that no position, however strong, was able to protect them against the audacity and talent of the French. This discouraging feeling, exemplified by so many defeats, and now by one in circumstances where the Austrians appeared to have every advantage, it was natural to suppose, would hurry Beaulieu's retreat, induce him to renounce all subsequent attempts

---

[123] "The loss of the French was only four hundred men."—Thibaudeau, tom. i., p. 218.
[124] Moniteur, No. 241, May 20.

to cover Milan, and rather to reunite the fragments of his army, particularly that part of Liptay's division, which, after being defeated at Fombio, had thrown themselves into Pizzighitone. To have manœuvred slowly and cautiously, would not have struck that terror and confusion which was inspired by the desperate attack on the position at Lodi. Supposing these to have been his views, the victor perfectly succeeded; for Beaulieu, after his misadventure, drew off without any farther attempt to protect the ancient capital of Lombardy, and threw himself upon Mantua, with the intention of covering that strong fortress, and at the same time of sheltering under it the remains of his army, until he could form a junction with the forces which Wurmser was bringing to his assistance from the Rhine.

Buonaparte himself has pointed out a second object, in which he was less successful. He had hoped the rapid surprise of the bridge of Lodi might enable him to overtake or intercept the rest of Beaulieu's army, which, as we have said, had retreated by Cassano. He failed, indeed, in this object; for these forces also made their way into the Mantuan territory, and joined Beaulieu, who, by crossing the classical Mincio, placed another strong line of military defence betwixt him and his victor. But the prospect of intercepting and destroying so large a force, was worth the risk he encountered at Lodi,[125] especially taking into view the spirit which his army had acquired from a long train of victory, together with the discouragement which had crept into the Austrian ranks from a uniform series of defeats.

It should also be remembered, in considering the necessity of forcing the bridge of Lodi, that the ford over the Adda was crossed with difficulty even by the cavalry, and that when once separated by the river, the communication between the main army and the detachment of infantry, (which his censors say Napoleon should have sent across in the same manner,) being in a great degree interrupted, the latter might have been exposed to losses, from

---

[125] "Vandémiaire and Montenotte," said the Emperor, "never induced me to look upon myself as a man of a superior class: it was not till after Lodi that I was struck with the possibility of my becoming a decisive actor on the scene of political events. It was then that the first spark of my ambition was kindled."—Las Cases, tom. i., p. 150.

which Buonaparte, situated as he was on the right bank, could have had no means of protecting them.

PIZZIGHITONE

Leaving the discussion of what might have been, to trace that which actually took place, the French cavalry pursued the retreating Austrians as far as Cremona, of which they took possession. Pizzighitone was obliged to capitulate, the garrison being cut off from all possibility of succour. About five hundred prisoners surrendered in that fortress; the rest of Liptay's division, and other Austrian corps, could no otherwise escape, than by throwing themselves into the Venetian territory.

It was at this time that Buonaparte had some conversation with an old Hungarian officer made prisoner in one of the actions, whom he met with at a bivouac by chance, and who did not know him. The veteran's language was a curious commentary on the whole campaign; nay, upon Buonaparte's general system of warfare, which appeared so extraordinary to those who had long practised the art on more formal principles. "Things are going on as ill and as irregularly as possible," said the old martinet. "The French have got a young general, who knows nothing of the regular rules of war; he is sometimes on our front, sometimes on the flank, sometimes on the rear. There is no supporting such a gross violation of rules."[126] This somewhat resembles the charge which foreign tacticians have brought against the English, that they gained victories by continuing, with their insular ignorance and obstinacy, to fight on, long after the period when, if they had known the rules of war, they ought to have considered themselves as completely defeated.

A peculiar circumstance is worth mentioning. The French soldiers had a mode at that time of amusing themselves, by conferring an imaginary rank upon their generals, when they had done some remarkable exploit. They showed their sense of the bravery displayed by Buonaparte at the Battle of Lodi, by creating

---

[126] Montholon, tom. iii., p, 178.

him a Corporal; and by this phrase, of the *Little Corporal*, he was distinguished in the intrigues formed against him, as well as those which were carried on in his favour; in the language of Georges Cadoudal, who laid a scheme for assassinating him, and in the secret consultation of the old soldiers and others, who arranged his return from Elba.[127]

We are now to turn for a time from war to its consequences, which possess an interest of a nature different from the military events we have been detailing.

The movements which had taken place since the King of Sardinia's defeat, had struck terror into the Government of Milan, and the Archduke Ferdinand, by whom Austrian Lombardy was governed. But while Beaulieu did his best to cover the capital by force of arms, the measures resorted to by the Government were rather of a devotional than warlike character. Processions were made, relics exposed, and rites resorted to, which the Catholic religion prescribes as an appeal to Heaven in great national calamities. But the saints they invoked were deaf or impotent; for the passage of the bridge of Lodi, and Beaulieu's subsequent retreat to Mantua, left no possibility of defending Milan. The archduke and his duchess immediately left Milan, followed by a small retinue, and leaving only a moderate force in the citadel, which was not in a very defensible condition. Their carriages passed through a large crowd which filled the streets. As they moved slowly along, the royal pair were observed to shed natural tears, at leaving the capital of these princely possessions of their house. The people observed a profound silence, only broken by low whispers. They showed neither joy nor sorrow at the event which was passing—all thoughts were bent in anxious anticipation upon what was to happen next.[128]

When the archduke had departed, the restraint which his presence had imposed from habit and sentiment, as much as from

---

[127] "How subtle is the chain which unites the most trivial circumstances to the most important events! Perhaps this very nickname contributed to the Emperor's miraculous success on his return from Elba in 1815. While he was haranguing the first battalion he met, which he found it necessary to parley with, a voice from the ranks exclaimed, 'Vive notre petit Caporal!—We will never fight against him.'"—Las Cases, tom. i., p. 170.

[128] Thiers, tom. viii., p. 207.

fear of his authority, was of course removed, and many of the Milanese citizens began, with real or affected zeal for republicanism, to prepare themselves for the reception of the French. The three-coloured cockade was at first timidly assumed; but the example being shown, it seemed as if these emblems had fallen like snow into the caps and hats of the multitude. The imperial arms were removed from the public buildings, and a placard was put on the palace of the government with an inscription—"This house is to be let—apply for the keys to the French Commissioner Salicetti." The nobles hastened to lay aside their armorial bearings, their servants' liveries, and other badges of aristocracy. Meantime the magistrates caused order to be maintained in the town, by regular patrols of the burgher guard. A deputation of the principal inhabitants of Milan, with Melzi[129] at its head, was sent to the victorious general with offers of full submission, since there was no longer room for resistance, or for standing upon terms.

On the 15th of May, Buonaparte made his public entry into Milan, under a triumphal arch prepared for the occasion, which he traversed, surrounded by his guards, and took up his residence in the archiepiscopal palace. The same evening a splendid entertainment was given, and the Tree of Liberty, (of which the aristocrats observed, that it was a bare pole without either leaves or fruit, roots or branches,) was erected with great form in the principal square. All this affectation of popular joy did not disarm the purpose of the French general, to make Milan contribute to the relief of his army. He imposed upon the place a requisition of twenty millions of livres, but offered to accept of goods of any sort in kind, and at a rateable valuation; for it may be easily supposed that specie, the representative of value, must be scarce in a city circumstanced as Milan was.[130] The public funds of every description, even those dedicated to the support of hospitals, went into the French military chest; the church-plate was seized as a part of the requisition; and, when all this was done, the citizens were burdened with the charge of finding rations for fifteen thousand

---

[129] "It was in memory of this mission, that Napoleon, when King of Italy, created the duchy of Lodi, in favour of Melzi."—Montholon, tom. iii., p. 179.
[130] Botta, tom. i., p. 431; Jomini, tom. viii., p. 179; Thibaudeau, tom. i., p. 234; Thiers, tom. viii., p. 208.

men daily, by which force the citadel, with its Austrian garrison, was instantly to be blockaded.[131]

SITUATION OF THE ITALIAN STATES

While Lombardy suffered much, the neighbouring countries were not spared. The reader must be aware, that for more than a century Italy had been silently declining into that state of inactivity which succeeds great exertion, as a rapid and furious blaze sinks down into exhaustion and ashes. The keen judgment of Napoleon had seen, that the geographical shape of Italy, though presenting in many respects advantages for a great and commercial nation, offered

---

[131] On the 20th, Buonaparte addressed the following remarkable order of the day to the army:—

"Soldiers! you have rushed like a torrent from the top of the Apennines: you have overthrown, dispersed, all that opposed your march. Piedmont, delivered from Austrian tyranny, indulges her natural sentiments of peace and friendship towards France. Milan is yours; and the republican flag waves throughout Lombardy. The Dukes of Parma and Modena are indebted for their political existence only to your generosity. The army which so proudly threatened you, can now find no barrier to protect it against your courage: neither the Po, the Ticino, nor the Adda, could stop you a single day: those vaunted bulwarks of Italy opposed you in vain; you passed them as rapidly as the Apennines. These great successes have filled the heart of your country with joy; your representatives have ordered a festival to commemorate your victories, which has been held in every commune of the republic. There your fathers, your mothers, your wives, sisters, and mistresses, rejoiced in your victories, and proudly boasted of belonging to you. Yes, soldiers! you have done much.—But remains there nothing more to perform? Shall it be said of us, that we know how to conquer, but not how to make use of victory? Shall posterity reproach us with having found our Capua in Lombardy?—But I see you already hasten to arms; an effeminate repose is tedious to you; the days which are lost to glory, are lost to your happiness. Well, then! let us set forth; we have still forced marches to make, enemies to subdue, laurels to gather, injuries to avenge! Let those who have sharpened the daggers of civil war in France, who have basely murdered our ministers, and burnt our ships at Toulon, tremble! The hour of vengeance has struck. But let the people of all countries be free from apprehension; we are the friends of the people everywhere, and more particularly of the descendants of Brutus and Scipio, and the great men whom we have taken for our models. To restore the capitol, to replace there the statues of the heroes who rendered it illustrious, with suitable honours, to awaken the Roman people, stupified by several ages of slavery—such is the fruit of our victories. They will form an historical era for posterity: yours will be the immortal glory of having changed the face of the finest part of Europe. The French people, free, respected by the whole world, will give to Europe a glorious peace, which will indemnify her for the sacrifices of every kind, which, for the last six years, she has been making. You will then return to your homes; and your countrymen will say, as they point you out—'*He belonged to the army of Italy.*'"—*Moniteur*, No. 254, June 2.

On reading over this proclamation one day at St. Helena, the Emperor exclaimed—"And yet they have the folly to say I could not write!"—Las Cases, tom. iii., p. 86.

this main impediment to its separate existence as one independent state, that its length being too great in proportion to its breadth, there was no point sufficiently central to preserve the due influence of a metropolis in relation to its extreme northern and southern provinces; and that the inhabitants of Naples and Lombardy being locally so far divided, and differing in climate, habits, and the variety of temper which climate and habits produce, could hardly be united under the same government. From these causes Italy was, after the demolition of the great Roman Empire, early broken up into different subdivisions, which, more civilized than the rest of Europe at the time, attracted in various degrees the attention of mankind; and at length, from the sacerdotal power of Rome, the wealth and extensive commerce of Venice and Genoa, the taste and splendour of Florence, and the ancient fame of the metropolis of the world, became of importance much over-proportioned to their actual extent of territory. But this time had passed away, and the Italian states, rich in remembrances, were now comparatively poor in point of immediate consequence in the scale of nations. They retained their oligarchical or monarchical forms and constitutions, as in the more vigorous state of their existence, but appeared to have lost their energies both for good and evil. The proud and jealous love which each Italian used to bear towards his own province was much abated; the hostility of the factions which divided most of their states, and induced the citizens to hazard their own death or exile in the most trifling party quarrel, had subsided into that calm, selfish indifference, which disregards public interests of all kinds. They were ill governed, in so far as their rulers neglected all means of benefiting the subjects or improving the country; and they were thus far well-governed, that, softened by the civilisation of the times, and perhaps by a tacit sense of their own weakness, their rulers had ceased, in a great measure, to exercise with severity the despotic powers with which they were in many cases invested, though they continued to be the cause of petty vexations, to which the natives had become callous. The Vatican slept like a volcano, which had exhausted its thunders; and Venice, the most jealous and cruel of oligarchies, was now shutting her wearied eyes, and closing her ears, against informers and spies of state. The Italian states stood, therefore, like a brotherhood of old trees, decayed at heart and root, but still making some show of branches and leaves; until the French invasion rushed down, like the whirlwind which lays them prostrate.

In the relations between France and Italy, it must be observed, that two of the most considerable of these states, Tuscany and Venice, were actually in league with the former country, having acknowledged the republic, and done nothing to deserve the chastisement of her armies. Others might be termed neutral, not having perhaps deemed themselves of consequence sufficient to take part in the quarrel of the coalesced powers against France. The Pope had given offence by the affair of Basseville, and the encouragement which his countenance afforded to the non-conforming clergy of France. But, excepting Naples and Austrian Lombardy, no state in Italy could be exactly said to be at open war with the new republic. Buonaparte was determined, however, that this should make no difference in his mode of treating them.

SEIZURE OF WORKS OF ART

The first of these slumbering potentates with whom he came in contact, was the Duke of Parma.[132] This petty sovereign, even before Buonaparte entered Milan, had deprecated the victor's wrath; and although neither an adherent of the coalition, nor at war with France, he found himself obliged to purchase an armistice by heavy sacrifices. He paid a tribute of two millions of livres, besides furnishing horses and provisions to a large amount, and agreeing to deliver up twenty of the finest paintings in his cabinet, to be chosen by the French general.[133]

The next of these sufferers was the Duke of Modena.[134] This prince was a man of moderate abilities; his business was hoarding money, and his pleasure consisted in nailing up, with his own princely hands, the tapestry which ornamented churches on days of high holiday; from which he acquired the nickname of "the royal upholsterer." But his birth was illustrious as the descendant of that celebrated hero of Este, the patron of Tasso and of Ariosto; and his alliance was no less splendid, having married the sister of the

---

[132] Frederic, Duke of Parma, grandson of Philip V. of Spain, was born in 1751. On his death, in 1802, the duchy was united to France, in virtue of the convention of 1801.
[133] Montholon, tom. iii., p. 173; Lacretelle, tom. xiii., p. 172; Thibaudeau, tom. i., p. 211. See the Treaty, Annual Register, vol. xxxviii., p. 233.
[134] Hercules III., Renaud d'Este, last Duke of Modena, was born in 1727 and died in 1797.

unfortunate Marie Antoinette, and of Joseph the Second: then his daughter was married to the Archduke Ferdinand, the Governor of Milan. Notwithstanding his double connexion with the Imperial family, the principality of Modena was so small that he might have been passed over as scarce worthy of notice, but for the temptation of his treasures, in the works of art, as well as in specie. On the approach of a column of the French army to Modena, the duke fled from his capital, but sent his brother, the Chevalier d'Este, to capitulate with Napoleon, [May 20.][135]

It might have been urged in his favour, that he was no avowed partner in the coalition; but Buonaparte took for granted his good-will towards his brother-in-law the Emperor of Austria, and esteemed it a crime deserving atonement.[136] Indeed it was one which had not been proved by any open action, but neither could it admit of being disproved. The duke was therefore obliged to purchase the privilege of neutrality, and to expiate his supposed good inclination for the house of Austria. Five millions and a half of French livres, with large contributions in provisions and accoutrements, perhaps cost the Duke of Modena more anxious thoughts than he had bestowed on the misfortunes of his imperial relatives.

To levy on obnoxious states or princes the means of paying or accommodating troops, would have been only what has been practised by victors in all ages. But an exaction of a new kind was now for the first time imposed on these Italian Princes. The Duke of Modena, like the Duke of Parma, was compelled to surrender twenty of his choicest pictures, to be selected at the choice of the French general, and the persons of taste with whom he might advise. This was the first time that a demand of this nature had been made in modern times in a public and avowed manner,[137] and we

---

[135] Lacretelle, tom. xiii., p. 187; Montholon, tom. iii., p. 187.
[136] "The duke is avaricious. His only daughter and heiress is married to the Archduke of Milan. The more you squeeze from him, the more you take from the House of Austria."—Lallemant to Buonaparte, 14th May; *Correspondence Inédite*, tom. i., p. 169.
[137] Montholon, tom. iii., p. 174.

must pause to consider the motives and justice of such a requisition.[138]

WORKS OF ART

Hitherto, works of art had been considered as sacred, even during the utmost extremities of war. They were judged to be the property, not so much of the nation or individuals who happened to possess them, as of the world in general, who were supposed to have a common interest in these productions, which, if exposed to become the ordinary spoils of war, could hardly escape damage or destruction. To take a strong example of forbearance, Frederick of Prussia was a passionate admirer of the fine arts, and no scrupulous investigator of the rights conferred by conquest, but rather disposed to stretch them to the uttermost. Yet, when he obtained possession of Dresden under circumstances of high irritation, Frederick respected the valuable gallery, cabinets, and museums of the capital of Saxony, and preserved their contents inviolate, as a species of property which could not, and ought not, to fall within the rights of a conqueror. He considered the elector as only the keeper of the gallery; and regarded the articles which it contained as belonging to the civilized world at large.

There are persons who demand the cause of this distinction, and require to know why works of art, the value of which is created solely by the opinion of those who pretend to understand them, and is therefore to be regarded as merely imaginary, or, as it is called by lawyers, a mere *pretium affectionis*, should be exempted from that martial law which disposes at pleasure of the real property of the vanquished.

It might easily be shown in reply, that the respect due to genius of the highest order, attaches with a sort of religious zeal to

---

[138] "The republic had already received, by the same title, and placed in its Museum, the *chefs-d'œuvre* of the Dutch and Flemish schools. The Romans carried away from conquered Greece the statues which adorn the capitol. Every capital of Europe contained the spoils of antiquity, and no one had ever thought of imputing it to them as a crime."—Thibaudeau, tom. i., p. 214.

the objects of our admiration in the fine arts, and renders it a species of sacrilege to subject them to the chances of war. It has besides already been hinted, that these chefs-d'œuvre being readily liable to damage, scarcely admitting of being repaired, and absolutely incapable of being replaced, their existence is hazarded by rendering them the objects of removal, according to the fluctuation of victory.

But it is surely sufficient to say, that wherever the progress of civilisation has introduced rules to qualify and soften the extremities of war, these should be strictly adhered to. In the rudest ages of society, man avails himself of the right of the strongest in the fullest extent. The victor of the Sandwich islands devours his enemy—the North American Indian tortures him to death—almost all savage tribes render their prisoners slaves, and sell them as such. As society advances, these inhumanities fall out of practice; and it is unnecessary to add, that, as the victorious general deserves honourable mention in history, who, by his clemency, relaxes in any respect the rigorous laws of conquest, so he must be censured in proportion whose conduct tends to retrograde towards the brutal violence of primitive hostility.

Buonaparte cannot be exempted from this censure. He, as the willing agent of the Directory under whose commands he acted, had resolved to disregard the neutrality which had hitherto been considered as attaching to the productions of the fine arts, and, for the first time, had determined to view them as the spoils of conquest. The motive is more easily discovered than justified.

In the Reign of Terror and Equality, the fine arts, with every thing connected with cultivated feelings, had been regarded as inconsistent with the simplicity of the Republican character; and, like the successful fanatics of England, and the first enthusiastic votaries of the Koran, the true Sans-Culottes were disposed to esteem a taste which could not generally exist without a previous superior education, as something aristocratic, and alien from the imaginary standard of equality, to which it was their purpose to lower all the exertions of intellect, as well as the possession of property. Palaces were therefore destroyed, and monuments broken to pieces.

But this brutal prejudice, with the other attempts of these frantic democrats to bring back the world to a state of barbarism, equally in moral and in general feeling, was discarded at the fall of the Jacobin authority. Those who succeeded to the government, exerted themselves laudably in endeavouring rather to excite men's minds to a love of those studies and tastes, which are ever found to humanize and soften the general tone of society, and which teach hostile nations that they have points of friendly union, even because they unite in admiring the same masterpieces of art. A museum was formed at Paris, for the purpose of collecting and exhibiting to public admiration paintings and statues, and whatever was excellent in art, for the amusement of the citizens, whose chief scene of pleasure hitherto had been a wild and ill-regulated civic festival, to vary the usual exhibition of the procession of a train of victims moving towards the guillotine. The substitution of such a better object of popular attention was honourable, virtuous, and politic in itself, and speedily led the French people, partly from taste, partly from national vanity, to attach consequence to the fine arts and their productions.

Unfortunately there were no ordinary measures by which the French, as purchasers, could greatly augment the contents of their Museum; and more unfortunately for other nations, and ultimately for themselves, they had the power and the will to increase their possessions of this kind, without research or expense, by means of the irresistible progress of their arms. We have no right to say that this peculiar species of spoliation originated with Buonaparte personally. He probably obeyed the orders of the Directory; and, besides, instances might no doubt be found in the history of all nations, of interesting articles of this nature having been transferred by the chance of war from one country to another, as in cases of plunder of an ordinary description, which, though seldom avowed or defended, are not the less occasionally practised. But Napoleon was unquestionably the first and most active agent, who made such exactions a matter of course, and enforced them upon principle; and that he was heartily engaged in this scheme of general plunder, is sufficiently proved from his expressions to the Directory, upon transmitting those paintings which the Duke of Modena, the first sufferer on this system, was compelled to surrender, and which were transferred to Paris as the legitimate spoils of war.

But before copying the terms in which Napoleon announces the transmission of masterpieces of art to the National Museum, it ought to be remarked, that the celebrated Saint Jerome, by Correggio, which he mentions with a sort of insulting triumph, was accounted so valuable, that the Duke of Modena offered two millions of livres as the ransom of that picture alone. This large sum the French general, acting on the principle which many in his situation were tempted to recognise, might have safely converted to his own use, under the certainty that the appropriation, indispensable as his services were to the government, would neither have been inquired into nor censured. But avarice cannot be the companion, far less the controller, of ambition. The feelings of the young victor were of a character too elevated to stoop to the acquisition of wealth; nor was his career, at that or any other period, sullied by this particular and most degrading species of selfishness. When his officers would have persuaded him to accept the money, as more useful for the army, he replied, that the two millions of livres would soon be spent, but the Correggio[139] would remain an ornament of the city of Paris for ages, and inspire the production of future masterpieces.[140]

In his despatch to the Directory, of 17th Floreal (8th of May,) Napoleon desires to have some artists sent to him, who might collect the monuments of art; which shows that the purpose of seizing upon them had been already formed.[141] In the letter which accompanied the transmission of the pictures, he has these

---

[139] Montholon, tom. iii., p. 174.

[140] "Is it, then, so difficult for Sir Walter to justify the motive which induced Napoleon to prefer works of art? It was a motive too great and too praiseworthy to need justification."—Louis Buonaparte, p. 21.

[141] On the 7th of May, Carnot had written to Buonaparte—"The executive Directory is convinced, citizen-general, that you consider the glory of the fine arts connected with that of the army under your command. Italy is, in great part, indebted to them for her riches and renown; but the time is arrived when their reign must pass into France to strengthen and embellish that of liberty. The National Museum must contain the most distinguished monuments of all the arts, and you will neglect no opportunity of enriching it with such as it expects from the present conquests of the army of Italy, and those which may follow," &c.—*Correspondence Inédite*, tom. i., p. 155.

remarkable expressions:—"You will receive the articles of the suspension of arms which I have granted to the Duke of Parma. I will send you as soon as possible the finest pictures of Correggio, amongst others a Saint Jerome, which is said to be his masterpiece. I must own that the saint takes an unlucky time to visit Paris, but I hope you will grant him the honours of the Museum."[142]

The same system was followed at Milan, where several of the most valuable articles were taken from the Ambrosian collection. The articles were received in the spirit with which they were transmitted. The most able critics were despatched to assist the general in the selection of the monuments of the fine arts to be transferred to Paris, and the Secretary-general of the Lyceum, confounding the possession of the production of genius with the genius itself which created them, congratulated his countrymen on the noble dispositions which the victors had evinced. "It is no longer blood," said the orator, "which the French soldier thirsts for. He desires to lead no slaves in triumph behind his chariot—it is the glorious spoils of the arts and of industry with which he longs to decorate his victories—he cherishes that devouring passion of great souls, the love of glory, and the enthusiasm for high talents, to which the Greeks owed their astonishing successes. It was the defence of their temples, their monuments, their statues, their great artists, that stimulated their valour. It was from such motives they conquered at Salamis and at Marathon. It is thus that our armies advance, escorted by the love of arts, and followed by sweet peace, from Coni to Milan, and soon to proceed from thence to the proud basilic of St. Peter's." The reasoning of the Secretary of the Lyceum is lost amidst his eloquence; but the speech, if it means any thing, signifies, that the seizing on those admired productions placed the nation which acquired the forcible possession of them, in the same condition as if she had produced the great men by whom they were achieved;—just as the ancient Scythians believed they became inspired with the talents and virtues of those whom they murdered. Or, according to another interpretation, it may mean that the French, who fought to deprive other nations of their property, had as praiseworthy motives of action as the Greeks, who made war in defence of that which was their own. But however their conduct

---

[142] Moniteur, 25th Floreal, 16th May.

might be regarded by themselves, it is very certain that they did by no means resemble those whose genius set the example of such splendid success in the fine arts. On the contrary, the classical prototype of Buonaparte in this transaction, was the Roman Consul Mummius, who violently plundered Greece of those treasures of art, of which he himself and his countrymen were insensible to the real and proper value.

It is indeed little to the purpose, in a moral point of view, whether the motive for this species of rapine were or were not genuine love of the art. The fingering connoisseur who secretes a gem, cannot plead in mitigation, that he stole it, not on account of the value of the stone, but for the excellence of the engraving; any more than the devotee who stole a Bible could shelter herself under a religious motive. But, in truth, we do not believe that the French or their general were actuated on this occasion by the genuine love of art. This taste leads men to entertain respect for the objects which it admires; and feeling its genuine influence, a conqueror would decline to give an example of a species of rapine, which, depriving those objects of admiration of the protection with which the general sentiment of civilized nations had hitherto invested them, must hold them up, like other ordinary property, as a prey to the strongest soldier. Again, we cannot but be of opinion, that a genuine lover of the arts would have hesitated to tear those paintings from the churches or palaces, for the decoration of which they had been expressly painted, and where they must always have been seen to the best effect, whether from the physical advantages of the light, size of apartment, and other suitable localities connected with their original situation, or from the moral feelings which connect the works themselves with the place for which they were primarily designed, and which they had occupied for ages. The destruction of these mental connexions, which give so much additional effect to painting and statuary, merely to gratify the selfish love of appropriation, is like taking a gem out of the setting, which in many cases may considerably diminish its value.

We cannot, therefore, believe, that this system of spoliation was dictated by any sincere and manly love of the arts, though this was so much talked of in France at the time. It must, on the contrary, be ascribed to the art and ambition of the Directory who ordered, and the general who obeyed; both of whom, being sensible that the national vanity would be flattered by this species of tribute, hastened to secure it an ample gratification. Buonaparte, in particular, was at least sufficiently aware, that, with however little purity of taste the Parisians might look upon these exquisite productions, they would be sufficiently alive to the recollection, that, being deemed by all civilized people the most admirable specimens in the world, the valour of the French armies, and the skill of their unrivalled general, had sent them to adorn the metropolis of France; and might hope, that once brought to the prime city of the Great Nation, such chefs-d'œuvre could not again be subject to danger by transportation, but must remain there, fixed as household gods, for the admiration of posterity. So hoped, as we have seen, the victor himself; and doubtless with the proud anticipation, that in future ages the recollection of himself, and of his deeds, must be inseparably connected with the admiration which the Museum, ordained and enriched by him, was calculated to produce.

But art and ambition are apt to estimate the advantages of a favourite measure somewhat too hastily. By this breach of the law of nations, as hitherto acknowledged and acted upon, the French degraded their own character, and excited the strongest prejudice against their rapacity among the Italians, whose sense of injury was in proportion to the value which they set upon those splendid works, and to the dishonour which they felt at being forcibly deprived of them. Their lamentations were almost like those of Micah the Ephraimite, when robbed of "the graven image, and the Teraphim, and the Ephod, and the molten image," by the armed and overbearing Danites—"Ye have taken away my gods that I have made, and what have I more?"

Again, by this unjust proceeding, Buonaparte prepared for France and her capital the severe moral lesson inflicted upon her by the allies in 1815. Victory has wings as well as Riches; and the abuse of conquest, as of wealth, becomes frequently the source of bitter retribution. Had the paintings of Correggio, and other great masters, been left undisturbed in the custody of their true owners, there could not have been room, at an after period, when looking around the Louvre, for the reflection, "Here once were disposed the treasures of art, which, won by violence, were lost by defeat."[143]

---

[143] See also Lacretelle's "Digression sur l'enlèvement de statues, tableaux, &c."—*Hist.*, tom. xiii., p. 172.

Chapter V

Directory proposes to divide the Army of Italy betwixt Buonaparte and Kellermann—Buonaparte resigns, and the Directory give up the point—Insurrection against the French at Pavia—crushed—and the Leaders shot—Also at the Imperial Fiefs, and Lugo, quelled and punished in the same way—Reflections—Austrians defeated at Borghetto, and retreat behind the Adige—Buonaparte narrowly escapes being made Prisoner at Valeggio—Mantua blockaded—Verona occupied by the French—King of Naples secedes from Austria—Armistice purchased by the Pope—The Neutrality of Tuscany violated, and Leghorn occupied by the French Troops—Views of Buonaparte respecting the Revolutionizing of Italy—He temporizes—Conduct of the Austrian Government at this Crisis—Beaulieu displaced, and succeeded by Wurmser—Buonaparte sits down before Mantua.

Occupying Milan, and conqueror in so many battles, Buonaparte might be justly considered as in absolute possession of Lombardy, while the broken forces of Beaulieu had been compelled to retreat under that sole remaining bulwark of the Austrian power, the strong fortress of Mantua, where they might await such support as should be detached to them through the Tyrol, but could undertake no offensive operations. To secure his position, the Austrian general had occupied the line formed by the Mincio, his left flank resting upon Mantua, his right upon Peschiera, a Venetian city and fortress, but of which he had taken possession, against the reclamation of the Venetian government, who were desirous of observing a neutrality between such powerful belligerents, not perhaps altogether aware how far the victor, in so dreadful a strife, might be disposed to neglect the general law of nations. The Austrian defence on the right was prolonged by the lago di Guarda, a large lake out of which the

Mincio flows, and which, running thirty-five miles northward into the mountains of the Tyrol, maintained uninterrupted Beaulieu's communication with Germany.

Buonaparte, in the meantime, permitted his forces only the repose of four or five days, ere he again summoned them to active exertion. He called on them to visit the Capitol, there to re-establish (he ought to have said to *carry away*) the statues of the great men of antiquity, and to change, or rather renovate, the destinies of the finest district of Europe. But while thus engaged, he received orders from Paris respecting his farther proceedings, which must have served to convince him that *all* his personal enemies, all who doubted and feared him, were not to be found in the Austrian ranks.

The Directory themselves had begun to suspect the prudence of suffering the whole harvest of success which Italy afforded, to be reaped by the adventurous and haughty character who had first thrust in the sickle. They perhaps felt already an instinctive distrust of the waxing influence, which was destined one day to overpower their own. Under some such impression, they resolved [May 7] to divide the army of Italy betwixt Buonaparte and Kellermann, directing the former general to pass the Po, and advance southward on Rome and Naples, with twenty thousand men, while Kellermann, with the other moiety of the Italian army, should press the siege of Mantua, and make head against the Austrians.[144]

This was taking Buonaparte's victory out of his grasp; and he resented the proposal accordingly, by transmitting his resignation [May 14,] and declining to have any concern in the loss of his army, and the fruits of his conquests. He affirmed, that Kellermann, with an army reduced to twenty thousand men, could not face Beaulieu, but would be speedily driven out of Lombardy; and that, in consequence, the army which advanced southward would be overwhelmed and destroyed. One bad general, he said, was better than two good ones.[145] The Directory must have perceived from

---

[144] See Letter of the Directory to Buonaparte, May 7; Correspondence Inédite, tom. i., p. 145; and Montholon, tom. iv., p. 447.

[145] "Je crois qu'il faut plutôt un mauvais général que deux bons. La guerre est comme le gouvernement—*c'est une affaire de tact.*"—*Correspondence Inédite*, tom. i., p. 160.

such a reply, the firm and inflexible nature of the man they had made the leader of their armies, but they dared not, such was his reputation, proceed in the plan they had formed for the diminution of his power; and, perhaps for the first time since the Revolution, the executive government of France was compelled to give way to a successful general, and adopt his views instead of their own. The campaign was left to his sole management;[146] he obtained an ascendancy which he took admirable care not to relinquish, and it became the only task of the Directory, so far as Italy was concerned, to study phrases for intimating their approbation of the young general's measures.

Whatever were the ultimate designs of Buonaparte against Rome, he thought it prudent to suspend them until he should be free from all danger of the Austrians, by the final defeat of Beaulieu. For this object, he directed the divisions of his army towards the right bank of the Mincio, with a view of once more forcing Beaulieu's position, after having taken precautions for blockading the citadel of Milan, where the Austrians still held out, and for guarding Pavia and other points, which appeared necessary to secure his conquests.

REVOLT OF PAVIA

Napoleon himself fixed his headquarters at Lodi, upon the 24th of May. But he was scarcely arrived there, when he received the alarming intelligence, that the city of Pavia, with all the surrounding districts, were in arms in his rear; that the tocsin was ringing in every village, and that news were circulated, that the Prince of Condé's army, united with a strong Austrian force, had descended from the Tyrol into Italy. Some commotions had shown themselves in Milan, and the Austrian garrison there made demonstrations towards favouring the insurrection in Pavia, where the insurgents were

---

[146] "You appear desirous, citizen-general, to continue to conduct the whole series of the military operations of the present campaign in Italy. The Directory have maturely reflected on this proposition, and the confidence they have in your talents and Republican zeal, has decided this question in the affirmative."—Carnot to Buonaparte, 21st May; *Correspondence Inédite*, tom. i., p. 202.

completely successful, and had made prisoners a French corps of three hundred men.

Buonaparte represents these disturbances as effected by Austrian agents;[147] but he had formerly assured us, that the Italians took little interest in the fate of their German masters. The truth is, that, having entered Italy with the most flattering assurances of observing respect for public and private property, the French had alienated the inhabitants, by exacting the contributions which they had imposed on the country with great severity. As Catholics, the Italians were also disgusted with the open indignities thrown on the places and objects of public worship, as well as on the persons and character of their priests.[148]

The nobles and the clergy naturally saw their ruin in the success of the French; and the lower classes joined them for the time, from dislike to foreigners, love of national independence, resentment of the exactions made, and the acts of sacrilege committed by the ultramontane invaders. About thirty thousand insurgents were in arms; but having no regular forces on which to rest as a rallying point, they were ill calculated to endure the rapid assault of the disciplined French.

Buonaparte, anxious to extinguish a flame so formidable, instantly returned from Lodi to Milan, at the head of a strong division, took order for the safety of the capital of Lombardy, and moved next morning towards Pavia, the centre of the insurrection. The village of Benasco, which was defended against Lannes, was taken by storm, the inhabitants put to the sword, and the place plundered and burnt. Napoleon himself arrived before Pavia, blew the gates open with his cannon, dispersed with ease the half-armed insurgents, and caused the leaders of the insurrection to be put to death, for having attempted to defend the independence of their country. He then seized on the persons of many inhabitants, and

---

[147] Montholon, tom. iii., p. 196.
[148] It has been alleged, that in a farce exhibited on the public stage by authority of Buonaparte, the Pope was introduced in his pontifical dress. This, which could not be looked on as less than sacrilege by a Catholic population, does not accord with the general conduct of Buonaparte. See, however, *"Tableau des Premières Guerres de Buonaparte,"* Paris, 1815, par Le Chevalier Mechaud de Villelle, p. 41.—S.

sent them to Paris as hostages for the subjection of their fellow-citizens.[149]

The French general published a proclamation in the Republican style, in which he reproaches the insurgents for presuming to use arms in defence of their country, and menaces with fire and sword whatever individuals should in future prosecute the same daring course. He made his threat good some weeks afterwards, when a similar insurrection took place in those districts called the Imperial Fiefs,[150] and still later, when an effort at resistance was attempted in the town of Lugo. On both occasions, the leaders of the armed inhabitants were tried by a military commission, condemned, and shot. On the last, indeed, to revenge the defeat sustained by a squadron of French dragoons, Lugo was taken by storm, pillaged, burnt, and the men put to the sword; while some credit seems to be taken by Buonaparte in his despatches, for the clemency of the French, which spared the women and children.[151]

It is impossible to read the account of these barbarities, without contrasting them with the opinions professed on other occasions, both by the republican and imperial governments of France. The first of these exclaimed as at an unheard of cruelty, when the Duke of Brunswick, in his celebrated proclamation, threatened to treat as a brigand every Frenchman, not being a soldier, whom he should find under arms, and to destroy such villages as should offer resistance to the invading army. The French at that time considered with justice, that, if there is one duty more holy than another, it is that which calls on men to defend their

---

[149] "The pillage lasted several hours; but occasioned more fear than damage; it was confined to some goldsmiths' shops. The selection of the hostages fell on the principal families. It was conceived to be advantageous that some of the persons of most influence should visit France. In fact, they returned a few months after, several of them having travelled in all our provinces, where they had adopted French manners."—Napoleon, *Montholon*, tom. iii., p. 200.
"Pavia," said the Emperor, "is the only place I ever gave up to pillage. I had promised it to the soldiers for twenty-four hours; but after three hours I could bear it no longer, and put an end to it. Policy and morality are equally opposed to the system. Nothing is so certain to disorganize and completely ruin an army."—Las Cases, tom. iv., p. 326. See also Botta, tom. v., p. 465; Jomini, tom. viii., p. 137; and Lacretelle, tom. xiii., p. 199.
[150] Montholon, tom. iii., p. 227.
[151] Montholon, tom. iii., p. 227.

native country against invasion. Napoleon, being emperor, was of the same opinion in the years 1813 and 1814, when the allies entered the French territories, and when, in various proclamations, he called on the inhabitants to rise against the invaders with the implements of their ordinary labour when they had no better arms, and "to shoot a foreigner as they would a wolf." It would be difficult to reconcile these invitations with the cruel vengeance taken on the town of Lugo,[152] for observing a line of conduct which, in similar circumstances, Buonaparte so keenly and earnestly recommended to those whom fortune had made his own subjects.

The brief insurrection of Pavia suppressed by these severities, Buonaparte once more turned his thoughts to the strong position of the Austrians, with the purpose of reducing Beaulieu to a more decided state of disability, before he executed the threatened vengeance of the Republic on the Sovereign Pontiff. For this purpose he advanced to Brescia, and manœuvred in such a manner as induced Beaulieu, whom repeated surprises of the same kind had not put upon his guard, to believe, that either the French general intended to attempt the passage of the Mincio at the small but strong town of Peschiera, where that river issues from the lago di Guarda, or else that, marching northward along the eastern bank, he designed to come round the head of the lake, and thus turn the right of the Austrian position. While Beaulieu disposed his forces as expecting an attack on the right of his line, Buonaparte, with his usual celerity, proposed to attack him on the centre, at Borghetto, a town situated on the Mincio, and commanding a bridge over it, above ten miles lower than Peschiera.

BATTLE OF BORGHETTO

On the 30th May, the French general attacked with superior force, and repulsed across the Mincio, an Austrian corps who endeavoured to cover the town. The fugitives attempted to demolish the bridge, and did break down one of its arches. But the French, rushing forward with impetuosity, under cover of a heavy

---

[152] "The examples of the Imperial Fiefs and Lugo, though extremely severe, were indispensable, and authorised by the usage of war."—Jomini, tom. viii., p. 156.

fire, upon the retreating Austrians, repaired the broken arch so as to effect a passage, and the Mincio, passed as the Po and the Adda had been before, ceased in its turn to be a protection to the army drawn up behind it.

Beaulieu, who had his headquarters at Valeggio, a village nearly opposite to Borghetto, hastened to retreat, and evacuating Peschiera, marched his dismayed forces behind the Adige, leaving five hundred prisoners, with other trophies of victory, in the hands of the French. Buonaparte had designed that this day of success should have been still more decisive; for he meditated an attack upon Peschiera at the moment when the passage at Borghetto was accomplished; but ere Augereau, to whom this manœuvre was committed, had time to approach Peschiera, it was evacuated by the Austrians, who were in full retreat by Castel Nuovo, protected by their cavalry.[153]

The left of the Austrian line, cut off from the centre by the passage of the French, had been stationed at Puzzuolo, lower on the Mincio. When Sebottendorf, who commanded the Imperial troops stationed on the left bank, heard the cannonade, he immediately ascended the river, to assist his commander-in-chief to repel the French, or to take them in flank if it was already crossed. The retreat of Beaulieu made both purposes impossible; and yet this march of Sebottendorf had almost produced a result of greater consequence than would have been the most complete victory.

The French division which first crossed the Mincio, had passed through Valeggio without halting, in pursuit of Beaulieu, by whom the village had been just before abandoned. Buonaparte with a small retinue remained in the place, and Massena's division were still on the right bank of the Mincio, preparing their dinner. At this moment the advanced guard of Sebottendorf, consisting of hulans and hussars, pushed into the village of Valeggio. There was but barely time to cry to arms, and, shutting the gates of the inn, to employ the general's small escort in its defence, while Buonaparte, escaping by the garden, mounted his horse and galloped towards Massena's division. The soldiers threw aside their cookery, and

---

[153] Montholon, tom. iii., p. 204; Jomini, tom. viii., p. 140.

marched instantly against Sebottendorf, who, with much difficulty, and not without loss, effected a retreat in the same direction as his commander-in-chief Beaulieu. This personal risk induced Buonaparte to form what he called the corps of guides, veterans of ten years' service at least, who were perpetually near his person, and, like the *Triarii* of the Romans, were employed only when the most desperate efforts of courage were necessary. Bessières, afterwards Duke of Istria, and Marshal of France, was placed at the head of this chosen body, which gave rise to the formation of the celebrated Imperial Guards of Napoleon.[154]

FORTRESS OF MANTUA

The passage of the Mincio obliged the Austrians to retire within the frontier of the Tyrol; and they might have been considered as completely expelled from Italy, had not Mantua and the citadel of Milan still continued to display the Imperial banners. The castle of Milan was a place of no extraordinary strength, the surrender of which might be calculated on so soon as the general fate of war had declared itself against the present possessors. But Mantua was by nature one of those almost impregnable fortresses, which may long, relying on its own resources, defy any compulsion but that of famine.

The town and fortress of Mantua are situated on a species of island, five or six leagues square, called the seraglio, formed by three lakes, which communicate with, or rather are formed by, the Mincio. This island has access to the land by five causeways, the most important of which was in 1796 defended by a regular citadel, called, from the vicinity of a ducal palace, La Favorità. Another was defended by an intrenched camp, extending between the fortress and the lake. The third was protected by a horn-work. The remaining two causeways were only defended by gates and draw-bridges. Mantua, low in situation, and surrounded by water, in a warm climate, is naturally unhealthy; but the air was likely to be still more destructive to a besieging army, (which necessarily lay in many respects more exposed to the elements, and were besides in greater

---

[154] Montholon, tom. iii., p. 206.

numbers, and less habituated to the air of the place,) than to a garrison who had been seasoned to it, and were well accommodated within the fortress.

To surprise a place so strong by a coup-de-main was impossible, though Buonaparte represents his soldiers as murmuring that such a desperate feat was not attempted. But he blockaded Mantua [June 4] with a large force, and proceeded to take such other measures to improve his success, as might pave the way to future victories. The garrison was numerous, amounting to from twelve to fourteen thousand men; and the deficiencies of the fortifications, which the Austrians had neglected in over security, were made up for by the natural strength of the place. Yet of the five causeways, Buonaparte made himself master of four; and thus the enemy lost possession of all beyond the walls of the town and citadel, and had only the means of attaining the mainland through the citadel of La Favorità. Lines of circumvallation were formed, and Serrurier was left in blockade of the fortress, which the possession of four of the accesses enabled him to accomplish with a body of men inferior to the garrison.[155]

To complete the blockade, it was necessary to come to some arrangement with the ancient republic of Venice. With this venerable government Napoleon had the power of working his own pleasure; for although the state might have raised a considerable army to assist the Austrians, to whom its senate, or aristocratic government, certainly bore good will, yet, having been in amity with the French Republic, they deemed the step too hazardous, and vainly trusting that their neutrality would be respected, they saw the Austrian power completely broken for the time, before they took any active measures either to stand in their defence, or to deprecate the wrath of the victor. But when the line of the Mincio was forced, and Buonaparte occupied the Venetian territory on the left bank, it was time to seek by concessions that deference to the rights of an independent country which the once haughty aristocracy of Venice had lost a favourable opportunity of supporting by force.

---

[155] Napoleon, Memoirs, tom. iii., p. 209.

VERONA—LOUIS XVIII

There was one circumstance which rendered their cause unfavourable. Louis XVIII., under the title of a private person, the Comte de Lille, had received the hospitality of the republic, and was permitted to remain at Verona, living in strict seclusion. The permission to entertain this distinguished exile, the Venetian government had almost mendicated from the French revolutionary rulers, in a manner which we would term mean, were it not for the goodness of the intention, which leads us to regard the conduct of the ancient mistress of the Adriatic with pity rather than contempt. But when the screen of the Austrian force no longer existed between the invading armies of France and the Venetian territories—when the final subjugation of the north of Italy was resolved on—the Directory peremptorily demanded, and the senate of Venice were obliged to grant, an order, removing the Comte de Lille from the boundaries of the republic.

The illustrious exile protested against this breach of hospitality, and demanded, before parting, that his name, which had been placed on the golden book of the republic, should be erased, and that the armour presented by Henry IV. to Venice, should be restored to his descendant.[156] Both demands were evaded, as might have been expected in the circumstances, and the future monarch of France left Verona on the 21st of April, 1796, for the army of the Prince of Condé, in whose ranks he proposed to place himself, without the purpose of assuming any command, but only that of fighting as a volunteer in the character of the first gentleman in France. Other less distinguished emigrants, to the number of several hundreds, who had found an asylum in Italy, were, by the successes at Lodi and Borghetto, compelled to fly to other countries.

Buonaparte, immediately after the battle of Borghetto, and the passage of the Mincio, occupied the town of Verona [June 3,] and did not fail to intimate to its magistrates, that if the *Pretender*, as he termed him, to the throne of France, had not left Verona before his arrival, he would have burnt to the ground a town which,

---

[156] Daru, Hist. de Venise; tom. v., p. 436; Thibaudeau, tom. i., p. 257.

acknowledging him as King of France, assumed, in doing so, the air of being itself the capital of that republic.[157] This might, no doubt, sound gallant in Paris; but Buonaparte knew well that Louis of France was not received in the Venetian territory as the successor to his brother's throne, but only with the hospitality due to an unfortunate prince, who, suiting his claim and title to his situation, was content to shelter his head, as a private man might have done, from the evils which seemed to pursue him.

The neutrality of Venice was, however, for the time admitted, though not entirely from respect for the law of nations; for Buonaparte is at some pains to justify himself for not having seized without ceremony on the territories and resources of that republic, although a neutral power as far as her utmost exertions could preserve neutrality. He contented himself for the time with occupying Verona, and other dependencies of Venice upon the line of the Adige. "You are too weak," he said to the Proveditore Foscarelli, "to pretend to enforce neutrality, with a few hundred Sclavonians, on two such nations as France and Austria. The Austrians have not respected your territory where it suited their purpose, and I must, in requital, occupy such part as falls within the line of the Adige."[158]

But he considered that the Venetian territories to the westward should in policy be allowed to retain the character of neutral ground, which The Government, as that of Venice was emphatically called, would not, for their own sakes, permit them to lose; while otherwise, if occupied by the French as conquerors, these timid neutrals might, upon any reverse, have resumed the character of fierce opponents. And, at all events, in order to secure a territory as a conquest, which, if respected as neutral, would secure itself, there would have been a necessity for dividing the French forces, which it was Buonaparte's wish to concentrate. From interested motives, therefore, if not from respect to justice, Buonaparte deferred seizing the territory of Venice when within his grasp, conscious that the total defeat of the Austrians in Italy would, when accomplished, leave the prey as attainable, and more defenceless

---

[157] Moniteur, No. 267, June 17; Montholon, tom. iv., p. 121.
[158] Thiers, tom. viii., p. 225.

than ever. Having disposed his army in its position, and prepared some of its divisions for the service which they were to perform as moveable columns, he returned to Milan to reap the harvest of his successes.

The first of these consisted in the defection of the King of Naples from the cause of Austria, to which, from family connexion, he had yet remained attached, though of late with less deep devotion. His cavalry had behaved better during the engagements on the Mincio, than has been of late the custom with Neapolitan troops, and had suffered accordingly. The King, discouraged with the loss, solicited an armistice, which he easily obtained [June 5]; for his dominions being situated at the lower extremity of Italy, and his force extending to sixty thousand men at least, it was of importance to secure the neutrality of a power who might be dangerous, and who was not, as matters stood, under the immediate control of the French. A Neapolitan ambassador was sent to Paris to conclude a final peace; in the meanwhile, the soldiers of the King of the Two Sicilies were withdrawn from the army of Beaulieu, and returned to their own country. The dispositions of the Court of Naples continued, nevertheless, to vacillate, as opportunity of advantage, joined with the hatred of the Queen, (sister of Marie Antoinette,) or the fear of the French military superiority, seemed to predominate.[159]

The storm now thickened round the devoted head of the Pope. Ferrara and Bologna, the territories of which belonged to the Holy See, were occupied by the French troops. In the latter place, four hundred of the Papal troops were made prisoners, with a cardinal who acted as their officer. The latter was dismissed on his parole. But when summoned to return to the French headquarters, his eminence declined to obey, and amused the republican officers a good deal, by alleging, that the Pope had dispensed with his engagement. Afterwards, however, there were officers of no mean rank in the French service, who could contrive to extricate themselves from the engagement of a parole, without troubling the Pope for his interference on the occasion. Influenced by the approaching danger, the Court of Rome sent Azara, the Spanish

---

[159] Montholon, tom. iii., p. 213; Thibaudeau, tom. i., p. 275.

minister, with full powers to treat for an armistice. It was a remarkable part of Buonaparte's character, that he knew as well when to forbear as when to strike. Rome, it was true, was an enemy whom France, or at least its present rulers, both hated and despised; but the moment was then inopportune for the prosecution of their resentment. To have detached a sufficient force in that direction, would have weakened the French army in the north of Italy, where fresh bodies of German troops were already arriving, and might have been attended with great ultimate risk, since there was a possibility that the English might have transported to Italy the forces which they were about to withdraw from Corsica, amounting to six thousand men. But, though these considerations recommended to Napoleon a negotiation with the Pope, his holiness was compelled to purchase the armistice [June 23] at a severe rate. Twenty-one millions of francs, in actual specie, with large contributions in forage and military stores, the cession of Ancona, Bologna, and Ferrara, not forgetting one hundred of the finest pictures, statues, and similar objects of art, to be selected according to the choice of the committee of artists who attended the French army, were the price of a respite which was not of long duration. It was particularly stipulated, with republican ostentation, that the busts of the elder and younger Brutus were to be among the number of ceded articles, and it was in this manner that Buonaparte made good his vaunt, of establishing in the Roman capitol the statues of the illustrious and classical dead.[160]

LEGHORN VIOLATED

The Archduke of Tuscany was next to undergo the republican discipline. It is true, that prince had given no offence to the French Republic; on the contrary, he had claims of merit with them, from having been the very first power in Europe who acknowledged them as a legal government, and having ever since been in strict amity with them. It seemed also, that while justice required he should be spared, the interest of the French themselves did not oppose the conclusion. His country could have no influence on the fate of the impending war, being situated on the western side of the Apennines.

---

[160] Montholon, tom. iii., p. 221; Thiers, tom. viii., p. 236.

In these circumstances, to have seized on his museum, however tempting, or made requisitions on his territories, would have appeared unjust towards the earliest ally of the French Republic; so Buonaparte contented himself with seizing on the grand duke's seaport of Leghorn [June 27,] confiscating the English goods which his subjects had imported, and entirely ruining the once flourishing commerce of the dukedom. It was a principal object with the French to seize the British merchant vessels, who, confiding in the respect due to a neutral power, were lying in great numbers in the harbour; but the English merchantmen had such early intelligence as enabled them to set sail for Corsica, although a very great quantity of valuable goods fell into the possession of the French.

While the French general was thus violating the neutrality of the grand duke, occupying by surprise his valuable seaport, and destroying the commerce of his state, the unhappy prince was compelled to receive him at Florence,[161] with all the respect due to a valued friend, and profess the utmost obligation to him for his lenity, while Manfredini, the Tuscan minister, endeavoured to throw a veil of decency over the transactions at Leghorn, by allowing that the English were more masters in that port than was the grand duke himself. Buonaparte disdained to have recourse to any paltry apologies. "The French flag," he said, "has been insulted in Leghorn—You are not strong enough to cause it to be respected. The Directory has commanded me to occupy the place."[162] Shortly after, Buonaparte, during an entertainment given to him by the grand duke at Florence, received intelligence that the citadel of Milan had at length surrendered. He rubbed his hands with self-congratulation, and turning to the grand duke, observed, "that the Emperor, his brother, had now lost his last possession in Lombardy."

When we read of the exactions and indignities to which the strong reduce the weak, it is impossible not to remember the simile of Napoleon himself, who compared the alliance of France and an inferior state, to a giant embracing a dwarf. "The poor dwarf," he

---

[161] "Il parcourut avet le grand-duc la célèbre galerie et n'y remarqua que trop la Vénus de Medicis."—Lacretelle, tom. xiii., p. 190.
[162] Montholon, tom. iii., p. 226; Pommereuil, Campagnes de Buonaparte, p. 78.

added, "may probably be suffocated in the arms of his friend; but the giant does not mean it, and cannot help it."

While Buonaparte made truce with several of the old states in Italy, or rather adjourned their destruction in consideration of large contributions, he was far from losing sight of the main object of the French Directory, which was to cause the adjacent governments to be revolutionized and new-modelled on a republican form, corresponding to that of the Great Nation herself.

This scheme was, in every respect, an exceedingly artful one. In every state which the French might overrun or conquer, there must occur, as we have already repeatedly noticed, men fitted to form the members of revolutionary government, and who, from their previous situation and habits, must necessarily be found eager to do so. Such men are sure to be supported by the rabble of large towns, who are attracted by the prospect of plunder, and by the splendid promises of liberty, which they always understand as promising the equalization of property. Thus provided with materials for their edifice, the bayonets of the French army were of strength sufficient to prevent the task from being interrupted, and the French Republic had soon to greet sister states, under the government of men who held their offices by the pleasure of France, and who were obliged, therefore, to comply with all her requisitions, however unreasonable.

This arrangement afforded the French government an opportunity of deriving every advantage from the subordinate republics, which could possibly be drained out of them, without at the same time incurring the odium of making the exactions in their own name. It is a custom in some countries, when a cow who has lost her calf will not yield her milk freely, to place before the refractory animal the skin of her young one stuffed, so as to have some resemblance to life. The cow is deceived by this imposture, and yields to be milked upon seeing this representative of her offspring. In like manner, the show of independence assigned to the Batavian, and other associated republics, enabled France to drain these countries of supplies, which, while they had the appearance of being given to the governments of those who granted the supplies, passed, in fact, into the hands of their engrossing ally. Buonaparte was sufficiently aware that it was expected from him to extend the same system to Italy, and to accelerate, in the conquered countries of that fertile land, this species of political regeneration; but it would appear that, upon the whole, he thought the soil scarcely prepared for a republican harvest. He mentions, no doubt, that the natives of Bologna and Reggio, and other districts, were impatient to unite with the French as allies, and intimate friends; but even these expressions are so limited as to make it plain that the feelings of the Italians in general were not as yet favourable to that revolution which the Directory desired, and which he endeavoured to forward.

He had, indeed, in all his proclamations, declared to the inhabitants of the invaded countries, that his war was not waged with them but with their governments, and had published the strictest orders for the discipline to be observed by his followers. But though this saved the inhabitants from immediate violence at the hand of the French soldiery, it did not diminish the weight of the requisitions with which the country at large was burdened, and to which poor and rich had to contribute their share. They were pillaged with regularity, and by order, but they were not the less pillaged; and Buonaparte himself has informed us, that the necessity of maintaining the French army at their expense very much retarded the march of French principles in Italy. "You cannot," he says, with much truth, "at the same moment strip a people of their substance, and persuade them, while doing so, that you are their friend and benefactor."

He mentions also in the St. Helena manuscripts,[163] the regret expressed by the wise and philosophical part of the community, that the revolution of Rome, the source and director of superstitious opinions, had not been commenced; but frankly admits that the time was not come for going to such extremities, and that he was contented with plundering the Roman See of its money and valuables, waiting until the fit moment should arrive of totally destroying that ancient hierarchy.

---

[163] Montholon, tom. iii., p. 222.

VIEWS AGAINST ITALY

It was not without difficulty that Buonaparte could bring the Directory to understand and relish these temporizing measures. They had formed a false idea of the country, and of the state and temper of the people, and were desirous at once to revolutionize Rome, Naples, and Tuscany.

Napoleon, more prudently, left these extensive regions under the direction of their old and feeble governments, whom he compelled, in the interim, to supply him with money and contributions, in exchange for a protracted existence, which he intended to destroy so soon as the fit opportunity should offer itself. What may be thought of this policy in diplomacy, we pretend not to say; but in private life it would be justly branded as altogether infamous. In point of morality, it resembles the conduct of a robber, who, having exacted the surrender of the traveller's property, as a ransom for his life, concludes his violence by murder. It is alleged, and we have little doubt with truth, that the Pope was equally insincere, and struggled only, by immediate submission, to prepare for the hour when the Austrians should strengthen their power in Italy. But it is the duty of the historian loudly to proclaim, that the bad faith of one party in a treaty forms no excuse for that of the other; and that national contracts ought to be, especially on the stronger side, as pure in their intent, and executed as rigidly, as if those with whom they were contracted were held to be equally sincere in their propositions. If the more powerful party judge otherwise, the means are in their hand to continue the war; and they ought to encounter their more feeble enemy by detection, and punishment of his fraud, not by anticipating the same deceitful course which their opponent has resorted to in the consciousness of his weakness,—like a hare which doubles before the hounds when she has no other hope of escape. It will be well with the world, when falsehood and finesse are as thoroughly exploded in international communication, as they are among individuals in all civilized countries.

But though those states, whose sovereigns could afford to pay for forbearance, were suffered for a time to remain under their ancient governments, it might have been thought that Lombardy, from which the Austrians had been almost totally driven, and where, of course, there was no one to compound with on the part of the old government, would have been made an exception. Accordingly, the French faction in these districts, with all the numerous class who were awakened by the hope of national independence, expected impatiently the declaration of their freedom from the Austrian yoke, and their erection, under the protection of France, into a republic on the same model with that of the Great Nation. But although Buonaparte encouraged men who held these opinions, and writers who supported them, he had two weighty reasons for procrastinating on this point. First, if France manumitted Lombardy, and converted her from a conquered province into an ally, she must in consistency have abstained from demanding of the liberated country those supplies, by which Buonaparte's army was entirely paid and supported. Again, if this difficulty could be got over, there remained the secret purpose of the Directory to be considered. They had determined, when they should make peace with the Emperor of Austria, to exact the cession of Belgium and the territory of Luxembourg, as provinces lying convenient to France, and had resolved, that under certain circumstances, they would even give up Lombardy again to his dominion, rather than not obtain these more desirable objects. To erect a new republic in the country which they were prepared to restore to its former sovereign, would have been to throw a bar in the way of their own negotiation. Buonaparte had therefore the difficult task of at once encouraging, on the part of the republicans of Lombardy, the principles which induced them to demand a separate government, and of soothing them to expect with patience events, which he was secretly conscious might possibly never come to pass. The final issue shall be told elsewhere. It may be just necessary to observe, that the conduct of the French towards the republicans whom they had formed no predetermination to support, was as uncandid as towards the ancient governments whom they treated with. They sold to the latter false hopes of security, and encouraged the former to express sentiments and opinions, which must have exposed them to ruin, in case of the restoration of Lombardy to its old rulers, an event which the Directory all along contemplated in secret. Such is, in almost all cases, the risk incurred by a domestic faction, who trust to carry their peculiar objects in the bosom of their own country by means of a foreign nation. Their too powerful auxiliaries are ever ready to sacrifice them to their own views of emolument.

Having noticed the effect of Buonaparte's short but brilliant campaign on other states, we must observe the effects which his victories produced on Austria herself. These were entirely consistent with her national character. The same tardiness which has long made the government of Austria slow in availing themselves of advantageous circumstances, cautious in their plans, and unwilling to adopt, or indeed to study to comprehend, a new system of tactics, even after having repeatedly experienced its terrible efficacies, is combined with the better qualities of firm determination, resolute endurance, and unquenchable spirit. The Austrian slowness and obstinacy, which have sometimes threatened them with ruin, have, on the other hand, often been compensated by their firm perseverance and courage in adversity.

Upon the present occasion, Austria showed ample demonstration of the various qualities we have ascribed to her. The rapid and successive victories of Buonaparte, appeared to her only the rash flight of an eaglet, whose juvenile audacity had overestimated the strength of his pinion. The Imperial Council resolved to sustain their diminished force in Italy, with such reinforcements as might enable them to reassume the complete superiority over the French, though at the risk of weakening their armies on the Rhine. Fortune in that quarter, though of a various complexion, had been, on the whole, more advantageous to the Austrians than elsewhere, and seemed to authorise the detaching considerable reinforcements from the eastern frontier, on which they had been partially victorious, to Italy, where, since Buonaparte had descended from the Alps, they had been uniformly unfortunate.

BEAULIEU DISPLACED

Beaulieu, aged and unlucky, was no longer considered as a fit opponent to his inventive, young, and active adversary. He was as full of displeasure, it is said, against the Aulic Council, for the associates whom they had assigned him, as they could be with him for his bad success.[164] He was recalled, therefore, in that species of disgrace which misfortune never fails to infer, and the command of his remaining forces, now drawn back and secured within the passes of the Tyrol, was provisionally assigned to the veteran Melas.

Meanwhile Wurmser, accounted one of the best of the Austrian generals, was ordered to place himself at the head of thirty thousand men from the Imperial forces on the Rhine, and, traversing the Tyrol, and collecting what recruits he could in that warlike district, to assume the command of the Austrian army, which, expelled from Italy, now lay upon its frontiers, and might be supposed eager to resume their national supremacy in the fertile climate out of which they had been so lately driven.

Aware of the storm which was gathering, Buonaparte made every possible effort to carry Mantua before arrival of the formidable Austrian army, whose first operation would doubtless be to raise the siege of that important place. A scheme to take the city and castle by surprise, by a detachment which should pass to the Seraglio, or islet on which Mantua is situated, by night and in boats, having totally failed, Buonaparte was compelled to open trenches, and proceed as by regular siege. The Austrian general, Canto D'Irles, when summoned to surrender it, replied that his orders were to defend the place to extremity. Napoleon, on his side, assembled all the battering ordnance which could be collected from the walls of the neighbouring cities and fortresses, and the attack and defence commenced in the most vigorous manner on both sides; the French making every effort to reduce the city before Wurmser should open his campaign, the governor determined to protract his resistance, if

---

[164] The following letter appears in the journals as an intercepted despatch from Beaulieu to the Aulic Council of War. It seems worthy of preservation, as expressing the irritated feelings with which the veteran general was certainly affected, whether he wrote the letter in question or not. It will be recollected, that D'Argenteau, of whom he complains, was the cause of his original misfortunes at Montenotte. See *ante*, p. . "I asked you for a *general*, and you have sent me Argenteau—I am quite aware that he is a great lord, and that he is to be created Field-marshal of the Empire, to atone for my having placed him under arrest—I apprise you that I have no more than twenty thousand men remaining, and that the French are sixty thousand strong. I apprise you farther, that I will retreat to-morrow—next day—the day after that—and every day—even to Siberia itself, if they pursue me so far. My age gives me a right to speak out the truth. Hasten to make peace on any condition whatever."—*Moniteur*, 1796, No. 269.—S.

possible, until he was relieved by the advance of that general. But although red-hot balls were expended in profusion, and several desperate and bloody assaults and sallies took place, many more battles were to be fought, and much more blood expended, before Buonaparte was fated to succeed in this important object.[165]

---

[165] Montholon, tom. iii., p. 229; Jomini, tom. viii., p. 163.

Chapter VI

Campaign on the Rhine—General Plan—Wartensleben and the Archduke Charles retire before Jourdan and Moreau—The Archduke forms a junction with Wartensleben, and defeats Jourdan, who retires—Moreau, also, makes his celebrated Retreat through the Black Forest—Buonaparte raises the Siege of Mantua, and defeats the Austrians at Salo and Lonato—Misbehaviour of the French General Valette, at Castiglione—Lonato taken, with the French Artillery, on 3d August—Retaken by Massena and Augereau—Singular escape of Buonaparte from being captured at Lonato—Wurmser defeated between Lonato and Castiglione, and retreats on Trent and Roveredo—Buonaparte resumes his position before Mantua—Effects of the French Victories on the different Italian States—Inflexibility of Austria—Wurmser recruited—Battle of Roveredo—French victorious, and Massena occupies Trent—Buonaparte defeats Wurmser at Primolano—and at Bassano, 8th September—Wurmser flies to Vicenza—Battle of Saint-George—Wurmser finally shut up within the walls of Mantua.

CAMPAIGN ON THE RHINE

The reader must, of course, be aware, that Italy, through which we are following the victorious career of Napoleon, was not the only scene of war betwixt France and Austria, but that a field of equally strenuous and much more doubtful contest was opened upon the Rhine, where the high military talents of the Archduke Charles were opposed to those of Moreau and Jourdan.

The plan which the Directory had adopted for the campaign of 1796 was of a gigantic character, and menaced Austria, their most powerful enemy upon the continent, with nothing short of total destruction. It was worthy of the genius of Carnot, by whom it was formed, and of Napoleon and Moreau, by whom it had been revised and approved. Under sanction of this general plan, Buonaparte regulated the Italian campaign in which he had proved so successful; and it had been schemed, that to allow Austria no breathing space, Moreau, with the army of the Sambre and Meuse, should press forward on the eastern frontier of Germany, supported on the left by Jourdan, at the head of the army of the Rhine, and that both generals should continue to advance, until Moreau should be in a position to communicate with Buonaparte through the Tyrol. When this junction of the whole forces of France, in the centre of the Austrian dominions, was accomplished, it was Carnot's ultimate plan that they should advance upon Vienna, and dictate peace to the Emperor under the walls of his capital.[166]

Of this great project, the part intrusted to Buonaparte was completely executed, and for some time the fortune of war seemed equally auspicious to France upon the Rhine as in Italy. Moreau and Jourdan crossed that great national boundary at Neuwied and Kehl, and moved eastward through Germany, forming a connected front of more than sixty leagues in breadth, until Moreau had actually crossed the river Lech, and was almost touching with his right flank the passes of the Tyrol, through which he was, according to the plan of the campaign, to have communicated with Buonaparte.

During this advance of two hostile armies, amounting each to seventy-five thousand men, which filled all Germany with consternation, the Austrian leader Wartensleben was driven from position to position by Jourdan, while the Archduke Charles was equally unable to maintain his ground before Moreau. The imperial generals were reduced to this extremity by the loss of the army, consisting of from thirty to thirty-five thousand men, who had been detached under Wurmser to support the remains of Beaulieu's forces, and reinstate the Austrian affairs in Italy, and who were now

---

[166] See Correspondence Inédite, tom. i., p. 12; Montholon, tom. iv., p. 372; Jomini, tom. viii., p. 388.

on their march through the Tyrol for that purpose. But the archduke was an excellent and enterprising officer, and at this important period he saved the empire of Austria by a bold and decided manœuvre. Leaving a large part of his army to make head against Moreau, or at least to keep him in check, the archduke moved to the right with the rest, so as to form a junction with Wartensleben, and overwhelm Jourdan with a local superiority of numbers, being the very principle on which the French themselves achieved so many victories. Jourdan was totally defeated, and compelled to make a hasty and disorderly retreat, which was rendered disastrous by the insurrection of the German peasantry around his fugitive army. Moreau, also unable to maintain himself in the heart of Germany, when Jourdan, with the army which covered his left flank, was defeated, was likewise under the necessity of retiring, but conducted his retrograde movement with such dexterity, that his retreat through the Black Forest, where the Austrians hoped to cut him off, has been always judged worthy to be compared to a great victory.[167] Such were the proceedings on the Rhine, and in the interior of Germany, which must be kept in view as influencing at first by the expected success of Moreau and Jourdan, and afterwards by their actual failure, the movements of the Italian army.[168]

ADVANCE OF WURMSER

As the divisions of Wurmser's army began to arrive on the Tyrolese district of Trent, where the Austrian general had fixed his head-quarters, Buonaparte became urgent, either that reinforcements should be despatched to him from France, or that the armies of the Rhine should make such a movement in advance towards the point where they might co-operate with him, as had been agreed upon at arranging the original plan of the campaign.

---

[167] "That retreat was the greatest blunder that ever Moreau committed. If he had, instead of retreating, made a détour, and marched in the rear of Prince Charles, he would have destroyed or taken the Austrian army. The Directory, jealous of me, wanted to divide, if possible, the stock of military reputation; and as they could not give Moreau credit for a victory, they caused his retreat to be extolled in the highest terms: although even the Austrian generals condemned him for it."—Napoleon, *Voice*, &c., vol. ii., p. 40. See also Gourgaud, tom. i., p. 157.

[168] Montholon, tom. iii., pp. 292-307; Jomini, tom. viii., pp. 178-194.

But he obtained no succours; and though the campaign on the Rhine commenced, as we have seen, in the month of June, yet that period was too late to afford any diversion in favour of Napoleon, Wurmser and his whole reinforcements being already either by that time arrived, or on the point of arriving, at the place where they were to commence operations against the French army of Italy.[169]

The thunder-cloud which had been so long blackening on the mountains of the Tyrol, seemed now about to discharge its fury. Wurmser, having under his command perhaps eighty thousand men, was about to march from Trent against the French, whose forces, amounting to scarce half so many, were partly engaged in the siege of Mantua, and partly dispersed in the towns and villages on the Adige and Chiese, for covering the division of Serrurier, which carried on the siege. The Austrian veteran, confident in his numbers, was only anxious so to regulate his advance, as to derive the most conclusive consequences from the victory which he doubted not to obtain. With an imprudence which the misfortunes of Beaulieu ought to have warned him against, he endeavoured to occupy with the divisions of his army so large an extent of country, as rendered it very difficult for them to maintain their communications with each other. This was particularly the case with his right wing under Quasdonowich, the Prince of Reuss, and General Ocskay, who were detached down the valley of the river Chiese, with orders to direct their march on Brescia. This division was destined to occupy Brescia, and cut off the retreat of the French in the direction of Milan. The left wing of Wurmser's army, under Melas, was to descend the Adige by both banks at once, and manœuvre on Verona, while the centre, commanded by the Austrian field-marshal in person, was to march southward by the left bank of the lago di Guarda, take possession of Peschiera, which the French occupied, and, descending the Mincio, relieve the siege of Mantua. There was this radical error in the Austrian plan, that, by sending the right wing by the valley of Chiese, Wurmser placed the broad lake of Guarda, occupied by a French flotilla, between that division and the rest of his army, and of course made it impossible for the centre and left to

---

[169] Montholon, tom. iii., p. 234.

support Quasdonowich, or even to have intelligence of his motions or his fate.[170]

The active invention of Buonaparte, sure as he was to be seconded by the zeal and rapidity of the French army, speedily devised the means to draw advantage from this dislocation of the Austrian forces. He resolved not to await the arrival of Wurmser and Melas, but, concentrating his whole strength, to march into the valley of Chiese, and avail himself of the local superiority thus obtained, to attack and overpower the Austrian division left under Quasdonowich, who was advancing on Brescia, down the eastern side of the lake. For this purpose one great sacrifice was necessary. The plan inevitably involved the raising of the siege of Mantua. Napoleon did not hesitate to relinquish this great object, at whatever loss, as it was his uniform system to sacrifice all secondary views, and to incur all lesser hazards, to secure what he considered as the main object of the campaign. Serrurier, who commanded the blockading army, was hastily ordered to destroy as much as possible of the cannon and stores which had been collected with so much pains for the prosecution of the siege.[171] A hundred guns were abandoned in the trenches, and Wurmser, on arriving at Mantua, found that Buonaparte had retired with a precipitation resembling that of fear.[172]

On the night of the 31st July this operation took place, and, leaving the division of Augereau at Borghetto, and that of Massena at Peschiera, to protect, while it was possible, the line of the Mincio, Buonaparte rushed, at the head of an army which his combinations had rendered superior, upon the right wing of the Austrians, which had already directed its march to Lonato, near the bottom of the lago di Guarda, in order to approach the Mincio, and resume its communication with Wurmser. But Buonaparte, placed by the celerity of his movements between the two hostile armies, defeated

---

[170] Montholon, tom. iii., p. 235; Jomini, tom. viii., p. 302.
[171] Jomini, tom. viii., p. 314; Montholon, tom. iii., p. 239.
[172] "Napoleon despatched Louis in the greatest haste to Paris, with an account of what had taken place. Louis left his brother with regret on the eve of the battle, to become the bearer of bad news. 'It must be so,' said Napoleon, 'but before you return you will have to present to the Directory the colours which we shall take to-morrow.'"—Louis Buonaparte, tom. i., p 63.

one division of the Austrian right at Salo, upon the lake, and another at Lonato. At the same time, Augereau and Massena, leaving just enough of men at their posts of Borghetto and Peschiera to maintain a respectable defence against Wurmser, made a forced march to Brescia, which they supposed to be still occupied by a third division of the Austrian right wing. But that body, finding itself insulated, and conceiving that the whole French army was debouching on them from different points, was already in full retreat towards the Tyrol, from which it had advanced with the expectation of turning Buonaparte's flank, and destroying his retreat upon Milan. Some French troops were left to accelerate their flight, and prevent their again making head, while Massena and Augereau, rapidly countermarching, returned to the banks of the Mincio to support their respective rear-guards, which they had left at Borghetto and Peschiera, on the line of that river.

BATTLE OF LONATO

They received intelligence, however, which induced them to halt upon this counter-march. Both rear-guards had been compelled to retire from the line of the Mincio, of which river the Austrians had forced the passage. The rear-guard of Massena, under General Pigeon, had fallen back in good order, so as to occupy Lonato; that of Augereau fled with precipitation and confusion, and failed to make a stand at Castiglione, which was occupied by Austrians, who intrenched themselves there. Valette, the officer who commanded this body, was deprived of his commission in presence of his troops for misbehaviour,[173] an example which the gallantry of the French generals rendered extremely infrequent in their service.

Wurmser became now seriously anxious about the fate of his right wing, and determined to force a communication with Quasdonowich at all risks. But he could only attain the valley of the Chiese, and the right bank of the lago di Guarda, by breaking a passage through the divisions of Massena and Augereau. On the 3d of August, at break of day, two divisions of Austrians, who had

---

[173] Buonaparte to the Directory; Moniteur, No. 328; Jomini, tom. viii., p. 318; Botta, tom. ii., p. 64.

crossed the Mincio in pursuit of Pigeon and Valette, now directed themselves, with the most determined resolution, on the French troops, in order to clear the way between the commander-in-chief and his right wing.

The late rear-guard of Massena, which, by his counter-march, had now become his advanced-guard, was defeated, and Lonato, the place which they occupied, was taken by the Austrians, with the French artillery, and the general officer who commanded them. But the Austrian general, thus far successful, fell into the great error of extending his line too much towards the right, in order, doubtless, if possible, to turn the French position on their left flank, thereby the sooner to open a communication with his own troops on the right bank of the lago di Guarda, to force which had been his principal object in the attack. But, in thus manœuvring,[174] he weakened his centre, an error of which Massena instantly availed himself. He formed two strong columns under Augereau, with which he redeemed the victory, by breaking through and dividing the Austrian line, and retaking Lonato at the point of the bayonet. The manœuvre is indeed a simple one, and the same by which, ten years afterwards, Buonaparte gained the battle of Austerlitz; but it requires the utmost promptitude and presence of mind to seize the exact moment for executing such a daring measure to advantage. If it is but partially successful, and the enemy retains steadiness, it is very perilous; since the attacking column, instead of flanking the broken divisions of the opposite line, may be itself flanked by decided officers and determined troops, and thus experience the disaster which it was their object to occasion to the enemy. On the present occasion, the attack on the centre completely succeeded. The Austrians, finding their line cut asunder, and their flanks pressed by the victorious columns of the French, fell into total disorder. Some, who were farthest to the right, pushed forward, in hopes to unite themselves to Quasdonowich, and what they might find remaining of the original right wing; but these were attacked in front by General Soret, who had been active in defeating Quasdonowich upon the 30th July, and were at the same time pursued by another detachment of the French, which had broken through their centre.

---

[174] "Sa manœuvre me parut un sûr garant de la victoire."—Buonaparte to the Directory, 6th August.

Such was the fate of the Austrian right at the battle of Lonato, while that of the left was no less unfavourable. They were attacked by Augereau with the utmost bravery, and driven from Castiglione, of which they had become masters by the bad conduct of Valette. Augereau achieved this important result at the price of many brave men's lives;[175] but it was always remembered as an essential service by Buonaparte, who afterwards, when such dignities came in use, bestowed on Augereau the title of Duke of Castiglione.[176] After their defeat, there can be nothing imagined more confused or calamitous than the condition of the Austrian divisions, who, having attacked, without resting on each other, found themselves opposed and finally overwhelmed by an enemy who appeared to possess ubiquity, simply from his activity and power of combining his forces.

A remarkable instance of their lamentable state of disorder and confusion, resembling in its consequences more than one example of the same sort, occurred at Lonato. It might, with any briskness of intelligence, or firmness of resolution, have proved a decisive advantage to their arms; it was, in its result, a humiliating illustration, how completely the succession of bad fortune had broken the spirit of the Austrian soldiers. The reader can hardly have forgotten the incident at the battle of Millesimo, when an Austrian column which had been led astray, retook, as if it were by chance, the important village of Dego;[177] or the more recent instance, when a body of Beaulieu's advanced guard, alike unwittingly, had nearly made Buonaparte prisoner in his quarters.[178] The present danger arose from the same cause, the confusion and want of combination of the enemy; and now, as in the former perilous occurrences, the very same circumstances which brought on the danger, served to ward it off.

---

[175] Buonaparte, in his despatch to the Directory, states the loss of the Austrians at from two to three thousand killed, and four thousand prisoners; Jomini, tom. viii., p. 325, says, "three thousand killed, wounded, or prisoners."

[176] "That day was the most brilliant of Augereau's life, nor did Napoleon ever forget it."—Montholon, tom. iii., p. 255.

[177] See *ante*.

[178] See *ante*.

ESCAPE AT LONATO

A body of four or five thousand Austrians, partly composed of those who had been cut off at the battle of Lonato, partly of stragglers from Quasdonowich, received information from the peasantry, the French troops, having departed in every direction to improve their success, had only left a garrison of twelve hundred men in the town of Lonato. The commander of the division resolved instantly to take possession of the town, and thus to open his march to the Mincio, to join Wurmser. Now, it happened that Buonaparte himself, coming from Castiglione with only his staff for protection, had just entered Lonato. He was surprised when an Austrian officer was brought before him blindfolded, as is the custom on such occasions, who summoned the French commandant of Lonato to surrender to a superior force of Austrians, who, he stated, were already forming columns of attack to carry the place by irresistible force of numbers. Buonaparte, with admirable presence of mind, collected his numerous staff around him, caused the officer's eyes to be unbandaged, that he might see in whose presence he stood, and upbraided him with the insolence of which he had been guilty, in bringing a summons of surrender to the French commander-in-chief in the middle of his army.[179] The credulous officer, recognising the presence of Buonaparte, and believing it impossible that he could be there without at least a strong division of his army, stammered out an apology, and returned to persuade his dispirited commander to surrender himself, and the four thousand men and upwards whom he commanded, to the comparatively small force which occupied Lonato. They grounded their arms accordingly, to one-fourth of their number, and missed an inviting and easy opportunity of carrying Buonaparte prisoner to Wurmser's headquarters.

The Austrian general himself, whose splendid army was thus destroyed in detail, had been hitherto employed in revictualling Mantua, and throwing in supplies of every kind; besides which, a

---

[179] "Go and tell your general," said Napoleon, "that I give him eight minutes to lay down his arms; he is in the midst of the French army; after that time there are no hopes for him."—Montholon, tom. iii., p. 246; Jomini, tom. viii., p. 326. But see Botta, tom. i., p. 546.

large portion of his army had been detached in the vain pursuit of Serrurier, and the troops lately engaged in the siege, who had retreated towards Marcaria. When Wurmser learned the disasters of his right wing, and the destruction of the troops despatched to form a communication with it, he sent to recall the division which we have mentioned, and advanced against the French position between Lonato and Castiglione, with an army still numerous, notwithstanding the reverses which it had sustained. But Buonaparte had not left the interval unimproved. He had recalled Serrurier from Marcaria, to assail the left wing and the flank of the Austrian field-marshal. The opening of Serrurier's fire was a signal for a general attack on all points of Wurmser's line. He was defeated, and nearly made prisoner; and it was not till after suffering great losses in the retreat and pursuit, that he gained with difficulty Trent and Roveredo, the positions adjacent to the Tyrol, from which he had so lately sallied with such confidence of victory. He had lost perhaps one half of his fine army, and the only consolation which remained was, that he had thrown supplies into the fortress of Mantua. His troops also no longer had the masculine confidence which is necessary to success in war. They were no longer proud of themselves and of their commanders; and those, especially, who had sustained so many losses under Beaulieu, could hardly be brought to do their duty, in circumstances where it seemed that Destiny itself was fighting against them.

The Austrians are supposed to have lost nearly forty thousand men in these disastrous battles. The French must have at least suffered the loss of one-fourth of the number, though Buonaparte confesses only to seven thousand men;[180] and their army, desperately fatigued by so many marches, such constant fighting, and the hardships of a campaign, where even the general for seven days never laid aside his clothes, or took any regular repose, required some time to recover their physical strength.

---

[180] "In the different engagements between the 29th July and the 12th August, the French army took 15,000 prisoners, 70 pieces of cannon, and nine stand of colours, and killed or wounded 25,000 men; the loss of the French army was 7000 men."—Montholon, tom. iii., p. 251.

Meantime, Napoleon resumed his position before Mantua; but the want of battering cannon, and the commencement of the unhealthy heats of autumn, amid lakes and inundations, besides the great chance of a second attack on the part of Wurmser, induced him to limit his measures to a simple blockade, which, however, was so strict as to retain the garrison within the walls of the place, and cut them off even from the islet called the Seraglio.

The events of this hurried campaign threw light on the feelings of the different states of Italy. Lombardy in general remained quiet, and the citizens of Milan seemed so well affected to the French, that Buonaparte, after the victory of Castiglione, returned them his thanks in name of the Republic.[181] But at Pavia, and elsewhere, a very opposite disposition was evinced; and at Ferrara, the Cardinal Mattei, archbishop of that town, made some progress in exciting an insurrection. His apology, when introduced to Buonaparte's presence to answer for his conduct, consisted in uttering the single word *Peccavi!* and Napoleon, soothed by his submission, imposed no punishment on him for his offence,[182] but, on the contrary, used his mediation in some negotiations with the court of Rome. Yet though the Bishop of Ferrara, overawed and despised, was permitted to escape, the conduct of his superior, the Pope, who had shown vacillation in his purposes of submission, when he heard of the temporary raising of Mantua, was carefully noted and remembered for animadversion, when a suitable moment should occur.

INFLEXIBILITY OF AUSTRIA

Nothing is more remarkable, during these campaigns, than the inflexibility of Austria, which, reduced to the extremity of distress by

---

[181] "Your people render themselves daily more worthy of liberty, and they will, no doubt, one day appear with glory on the stage of the world."—*Moniteur*, No. 331, Aug. 9.

[182] "When brought before the Commander-in-chief, he answered only by the word *peccavi*, which disarmed the victor, who merely confined him three months in a religious house."—Montholon, tom. iii., p. 254.

Mattei was born at Rome in 1744. Compelled, in 1810, to repair to France with his colleagues, he was banished by Napoleon to Rhetel, for refusing to be present at his marriage with Maria Louisa. The cardinal died in 1820.

the advance of Moreau and Jourdan into her territories, stood nevertheless on the defensive at every point, and by extraordinary exertions again recruited Wurmser with fresh troops, to the amount of twenty thousand men; which reinforcement enabled that general, though under no more propitious star, again to resume the offensive, by advancing from the Tyrol. Wurmser, with less confidence than before, hoped now to relieve the siege of Mantua a second time, and at a less desperate cost, by moving from Trent towards Mantua, through the defiles formed by the river Brenta. This manœuvre he proposed to execute with thirty thousand men, while he left twenty thousand, under General Davidowich, in a strong position at or near Roveredo, for the purpose of covering the Tyrol; an invasion of which district, on the part of the French, must have added much to the general panic which already astounded Germany, from the apprehended advance of Moreau and Jourdan from the banks of the Rhine.

Buonaparte penetrated the design of the veteran general, and suffered him without disturbance to march towards Bassano upon the Brenta, in order to occupy the line of operations on which he intended to manœuvre, with the secret intention that he would himself assume the offensive, and overwhelm Davidowich as soon as the distance betwixt them precluded a communication betwixt that general and Wurmser. He left General Kilmaine, an officer of Irish extraction[183] in whom he reposed confidence, with about three thousand men, to cover the siege of Mantua, by posting himself under the walls of Verona, while, concentrating a strong body of forces, Napoleon marched upon the town of Roveredo, situated in the valley of the Adige, and having in its rear the strong position of Calliano. The town is situated on the high road to Trent, and Davidowich lay there with twenty-five thousand Austrians, intended to protect the Tyrol, while Wurmser moved down the Brenta, which runs in the same direction with the Adige, but at about thirty miles' distance, so that no communication for mutual support could take place betwixt Wurmser and his lieutenant-general. It was upon Davidowich that Buonaparte first meant to pour his thunder.

---

[183] Kilmaine was born at Dublin in 1754. He distinguished himself at Jemappes and in La Vendée, and was selected to command the "*Army of England*," but died at Paris in 1799.

Sept. 4.

The battle of Roveredo, fought upon the 4th of September, was one of that great general's splendid days. Before he could approach the town, one of his divisions had to force the strongly intrenched camp of Mori, where the enemy made a desperate defence. Another attacked the Austrians on the opposite bank of the Adige, (for the action took place on both sides of the river,) until the enemy at length retreated, still fighting desperately. Napoleon sent his orders to General Dubois, to charge with the first regiment of hussars:—he did so, and broke the enemy, but fell mortally wounded with three balls. "I die," he said, "for the Republic—bring me but tidings that the victory is certain."[184]

The retreating enemy were driven through the town of Roveredo, without having it in their power to make a stand. The extreme strength of the position of Calliano seemed to afford them rallying ground. The Adige is there bordered by precipitous mountains, approaching so near its course, as only to leave a pass of forty toises' breadth between the river and the precipice, which opening was defended by a village, a castle, and a strong defensive wall resting upon the rock, all well garnished with artillery. The French, in their enthusiasm of victory, could not be stopped even by these obstacles. Eight pieces of light artillery were brought forward, under cover of which the infantry charged and carried this strong position; so little do natural advantages avail when the minds of the assailants are influenced with an opinion that they are irresistible, and those of the defenders are depressed by a uniform and uninterrupted course of defeat. Six or seven thousand prisoners, and fifteen pieces of cannon captured, were the fruits of this splendid victory; and Massena the next morning took possession of Trent in the Tyrol, so long the stronghold where Wurmser had maintained his headquarters.[185]

The wrecks of Davidowich's army fled deeper into the Tyrol, and took up their position at Lavisa, a small village on a river of a similar name, about three leagues to the northward of Trent, and

---
[184] Buonaparte to the Directory, 6th September.
[185] Jomini, tom. ix., p. 107; Thibaudeau, tom. ii., p. 5; Montholon, tom. iii., p. 259.

situated in the principal road which communicates with Brixen and Inspruck. Buonaparte instantly pursued them with a division of his army, commanded by Vaubois, and passed the Lavisa with his cavalry, while the enemy were amused with an assault upon the bridge. Thus he drove them from their position, which, being the entrance of one of the chief defiles of the Tyrol, it was of importance to secure, and it was occupied accordingly by Vaubois with his victorious division.

THE TYROL

Buonaparte, in consequence of his present condition, became desirous to conciliate the martial inhabitants of the Tyrol, and published a proclamation, in which he exhorted them to lay down their arms, and return to their homes; assuring them of protection against military violence, and labouring to convince them, that they had themselves no interest in the war which he waged against the Emperor and his government, but not against his subjects.[186] That his conduct might appear to be of a piece with his reasoning, Napoleon issued an edict, disuniting the principality of Trent from the German empire, and annexing it in point of sovereignty to the French Republic, while he intrusted, or seemed to intrust, the inhabitants themselves with the power of administering their own laws and government.

Bounties which depended on the gift of an armed enemy, appeared very suspicious to the Tyrolese, who were aware that, in fact, the order of a French officer would be more effectual law, whenever that nation had the power, than that of any administrator of civil affairs whom they might themselves be permitted to choose. As for the proclamation, the French general might as well have wasted his eloquence on the rocks of the country. The Tyrol, one of the earliest possessions of the House of Austria, had been uniformly governed by those princes with strict respect to the privileges of the inhabitants, who were possessed already of complete personal freedom. Secured in all the immunities which were necessary for their comfort, these sagacious peasants saw nothing to expect from

---

[186] Montholon, tom. iii., p. 263.

the hand of a stranger general, excepting what Buonaparte himself has termed, those vexations necessarily annexed to a country which becomes the seat of war, and which, in more full detail, include whatever the avarice of the general, the necessities of the soldiers, not to mention the more violent outrage of marauders and plunderers, may choose to exact from the inhabitants. But, besides this prudent calculation of consequences, the Tyrolese felt the generous spirit of national independence, and resolved that their mountains should not be dishonoured by the march of an armed enemy, if the unerring rifle-guns of their children were able to protect their native soil from such indignity. Every mode of resistance was prepared; and it was then that those piles of rocks, stones, and trunks of trees, were collected on the verge of the precipices which line the valley of the Inn, and other passes of the Tyrol, but which remained in grim repose till rolled down, to the utter annihilation of the French and Bavarian invaders in 1809, under the direction of the valiant Hofer and his companions in arms.

More successful with the sword than the pen, Buonaparte had no sooner disposed of Davidowich and his army, than he began his operations against Wurmser himself, who had by this time learned the total defeat of his subordinate division, and that the French were possessed of Trent. The Austrian field-marshal immediately conceived that the French general, in consequence of his successes, would be disposed to leave Italy behind, and advance to Inspruck, in order to communicate with the armies of Moreau and Jourdan, which were now on the full advance into Germany. Instead, therefore, of renouncing his own scheme of relieving Mantua, Wurmser thought the time favourable for carrying it into execution; and in place of falling back with his army on Friuli, and thus keeping open his communication with Vienna, he committed the great error of involving himself still deeper in the Italian passes to the southward, by an attempt, with a diminished force, to execute a purpose, which he had been unable to accomplish when his army was double the strength of the French. With this ill-chosen plan, he detached Mezaros with a division of his forces, to manœuvre on Verona, where, as we have seen, Buonaparte had stationed Kilmaine to cover the siege, or rather the blockade, of Mantua. Mezaros departed accordingly, and leaving Wurmser at Bassano on the Brenta, marched south-westward towards the collateral valley of the Adige, and attacked Kilmaine, who, by drawing his men under cover of the fortifications of Verona, made a resolute defence. The Austrian general, finding it impossible to carry the place by a coup-de-main, was meditating to cross the Adige, when he was recalled by the most urgent commands to rejoin Wurmser with all possible despatch.

As soon as Buonaparte learned this new separation of Wurmser from a large division of his army, he anticipated the possibility of defeating the field-marshal himself, driving him from his position at Bassano, and of consequence, cutting off at his leisure the division of Mezaros, which had advanced so far to the southward as effectually to compromise its safety.

To execute this plan required the utmost rapidity of movement; for, should Wurmser learn that Buonaparte was advancing towards Bassano, in time to recall Mezaros, he might present a front too numerous to be attacked with hope of success. There are twenty leagues' distance betwixt Trent and Bassano, and that ground was to be traversed by means of very difficult roads, in the space of two days at farthest. But it was in such circumstances that the genius of Napoleon triumphed, through the enthusiastic power which he possessed over the soldiery, and by which he could urge them to the most incredible exertions. He left Trent on the 6th September, at break of day, and reached, in the course of the evening, Borgo di Val Lugano, a march of ten French leagues. A similar forced march of five leagues and upwards, brought him up with Wurmser's advanced-guard, which was strongly posted at Primolano.

The effect of the surprise, and the impetuosity of the French attack surmounted all the advantages of position. The Austrian double-lines were penetrated by a charge of three French columns—the cavalry occupied the high-road, and cut off the enemy's retreat on Bassano—in a word, Wurmser's vanguard was totally destroyed, and more than four thousand men laid down their arms.[187] From Primolano the French, dislodging whatever enemies they encountered, advanced to Cismone, a village, where a river of the same name unites with the Brenta. There they halted exhausted with fatigue; and on that evening no sentinel in the army endured more privations than Napoleon himself, who took up his quarters for the night without either staff-officers or baggage, and was glad to accept a share of a private soldier's ration of bread, of which the poor fellow lived to remind his general when he was become Emperor.[188]

BATTLE OF BASSANO

Cismone is only about four leagues from Bassano, and Wurmser heard with alarm, that the French leader, whom he conceived to be already deeply engaged in the Tyrolese passes, had destroyed his vanguard, and was menacing his own position. It was under this alarm that he despatched expresses, as already mentioned, to recall Mezaros and his division. But it was too late; for that general was under the walls of Verona, nigh fifteen leagues from Wurmser's position, on the night of the 7th September, when the French army was at Cismone, within a third part of that distance. The utmost exertions of Mezaros could only bring his division as far as Montebello, upon the 8th September, when the battle of Bassano seemed to decide the fate of his unfortunate commander-in-chief.

Sept. 8.

This victory was as decisive as any which Buonaparte had hitherto obtained. The village of Salagna was first carried by main force, and then the French army, continuing to descend the defiles of the Brenta, attacked Wurmser's main body, which still lay under his own command in the town of Bassano. Augereau penetrated into the town upon the right, Massena upon the left. They bore down all opposition, and seized the cannon by which the bridge was defended, in spite of the efforts of the Austrian grenadiers, charged

---

[187] Buonaparte to the Directory, 8th September; Montholon, tom. iii., p. 265. Jomini, tom. ix., p. 114, estimates the prisoners at fully from twelve to fifteen hundred.
[188] At the camp of Boulogne, in 1805.

with the duty of protecting Wurmser and his staff, who were now in absolute flight.

The field-marshal himself, with the military chest of his army, nearly fell into the hands of the French; and though he escaped for the time, it was after an almost general dispersion of his troops.[189] Six thousand Austrians surrendered to Buonaparte;[190] Quasdonowich, with three or four thousand men, effected a retreat to the north-east, and gained Friuli; while Wurmser himself, finding it impossible to escape otherwise, fled to Vicenza in the opposite direction, and there united the scattered forces which still followed him, with the division of Mezaros. When this junction was accomplished, the aged marshal had still the command of about sixteen thousand men, out of sixty thousand, with whom he had, scarce a week before, commenced the campaign. The material part of his army, guns, waggons, and baggage, was all lost—his retreat upon the hereditary states of Austria was entirely cut off—the flower of his army was destroyed—courage and confidence were gone—there seemed no remedy but that he should lay down his arms to the youthful conqueror by whose forces he was now surrounded on all sides, without, as it appeared, any possibility of extricating himself. But Fate itself seemed to take some tardy compassion on this venerable and gallant veteran, and not only adjourned his final fall, but even granted him leave to gather some

---

[189] Napoleon the same night visited the field of battle, and he told this anecdote of it at St. Helena—"In the deep silence of a beautiful moonlight night," said the Emperor, "a dog leaping suddenly from beneath the clothes of his dead master, rushed upon us, and then immediately returned to his hiding-place, howling piteously. He alternately licked his master's face, and again flew at us; thus at once soliciting aid and threatening revenge. Whether owing to my own particular mood of mind at the moment, the time, the place, or the action itself, I know not, but certainly no incident on any field of battle ever produced so deep an impression on me. I involuntarily stopped to contemplate the scene. This man, thought I, must have had among his comrades friends; and here he lies forsaken by all except his dog! What a strange being is man! and how mysterious are his impressions! I had, without emotion, ordered battles which were to decide the fate of the army; I had beheld with tearless eyes, the execution of those operations, in the course of which numbers of my countrymen were sacrificed; and here my feelings were roused by the mournful howling of a dog. Certainly at that moment I should have been easily moved by a suppliant enemy; I could very well imagine Achilles surrendering up the body of Hector at the sight of Priam's tears."—Las Cases, tom. ii., p. 403. See also Arnault, Hist. de Napoleon; and Thibaudeau, tom. ii., p. 11.

[190] Montholon, tom. iii., p. 266; Buonaparte, in his letter to the Directory, says 5000; Jomini, tom. ix., p. 116, reduces them to 2000.

brief-dated laurels, as the priests of old were wont to garland their victims before the final sacrifice.

Surrounded by dangers, and cut off from any other retreat, Wurmser formed the gallant determination to throw himself and his remaining forces into Mantua, and share the fate of the beleaguered fortress which he had vainly striven to relieve. But to execute this purpose it was necessary to cross the Adige, nor was it easy to say how this was to be accomplished. Verona, one point of passage, was defended by Kilmaine, who had already repulsed Mezaros. Legnago, where there was a bridge, was also garrisoned by the French; and Wurmser had lost his bridge of pontoons at the battle of Bassano. At the village of Albarado, however, there was an established ferry, totally insufficient for passing over so considerable a force with the necessary despatch, but which Wurmser used for the purpose of sending across two squadrons of cavalry, in order to reconnoitre the blockade of Mantua, and the facilities which might present themselves for accomplishing a retreat on that fortress. This precaution proved for the time the salvation of Wurmser, and what remained of his army.

Fortune, which has such influence in warlike affairs, had so ordered it, that Kilmaine, apprehending that Wurmser would attempt to force a passage at Verona, and desirous to improve his means of resistance against so great a force, had sent orders that the garrison of four hundred men who guarded the bridge at Legnago should join him at Verona, and that an equal number should be detached from the blockade of Mantua, to supply their place on the Lower Adige. The former part of his command had been obeyed, and the garrison of Legnago were on their march for Verona. But the relief which was designed to occupy their post, though on their way to Legnago, had not yet arrived. The Austrian cavalry, who had passed over at Albarado, encountering this body on its march from the vicinity of Mantua, attacked them with spirit, and sabred a good many. The commander of the French battalion, confounded at this appearance, concluded that the whole Austrian army had gained the right bank of the Adige, and that he should necessarily be cut off if he prosecuted his march to Legnago. Thus the passage at that place was left altogether undefended; and Wurmser, apprised of this unhoped-for chance of escape, occupied the village, and took possession of the bridge.[191]

Buonaparte, in the meantime, having moved from Bassano to Arcola in pursuit of the defeated enemy, learned, at the latter place, that Wurmser still lingered at Legnago, perhaps to grant his troops some indispensable repose, perhaps to watch whether it might be even yet possible to give the slip to the French divisions by which he was surrounded, and, by a rapid march back upon Padua, to regain his communication with the Austrian territories, instead of enclosing himself in Mantua. Buonaparte hastened to avail himself of these moments of indecision. Augereau was ordered to march upon Legnago by the road from Padua, so as to cut off any possibility of Wurmser's retreat in that direction; while Massena's division was thrown across the Adige by a ferry at Ronco, to strengthen General Kilmaine, who had already occupied the line of a small river called the Molinella, which intersects the country between Legnago and Mantua. If this position could be made good, it was concluded that the Austrian general, unable to reach Mantua, or to maintain himself at Legnago, must even yet surrender himself and his army.

ACTION OF CEREA

On the 12th September, Wurmser began his march. He was first opposed at Cerea, where Murat and Pigeon had united their forces. But Wurmser made his dispositions, and attacked with a fury which swept out of the way both the cavalry and infantry of the enemy, and obtained possession of the village. In the heat of the skirmish, and just when the French were giving way, Buonaparte himself entered Cerea, with the purpose of personally superintending the dispositions made for intercepting the retreat of Wurmser, when, but for the speed of his horse, he had nearly fallen as a prisoner into the hands of the general whose destruction he was labouring to ensure. Wurmser arrived on the spot a few minutes afterwards, and gave orders for a pursuit in every direction; commanding, however, that the French general should, if possible,

---

[191] Jomini, tom. ix., p. 116; Thibaudeau, tom. ii., p. 54; Montholon, tom. iii., p. 267.

be taken alive—a conjunction of circumstances worthy of remark, since it authorised the Austrian general for the moment to pronounce on the fate of him, who, before and after was the master of his destiny.

Having again missed this great prize, Wurmser continued his march all night, and turning aside from the great road, where the blockading army had taken measures to intercept him, he surprised a small bridge over the Molinella, at a village called Villa Impenta, by which he eluded encountering the forces of Kilmaine. A body of French horse, sent to impede his progress, was cut to pieces by the Austrian cavalry. On the 14th, Wurmser obtained a similar success at Duc Castelli, where his cuirassiers destroyed a body of French infantry; and having now forced himself into a communication with Mantua, he encamped between the suburb of Saint George and the citadel, and endeavoured to keep open the communication with the country, for the purpose of obtaining a supply of forage and provisions.

Sept. 19.

But it was not Buonaparte's intention to leave him undisturbed in so commodious a position. Having received the surrender of an Austrian corps which was left in Porto Legnago, and gleaned up such other remnants of Wurmser's army as could not accompany their general in his rapid march to Mantua, he resolved once more to force his way into the islet of the Seraglio, upon which Mantua is built, and confine the besieged within the walls of their garrison. On the 19th, after a very severe and bloody action, the French obtained possession of the suburb of Saint George, and the citadel termed La Favorita, and a long series of severe sallies and attacks took place, which, although gallantly fought by the Austrians, generally tended to their disadvantage, so that they were finally again blockaded within the walls of the city and castle.[192]

The woes of war now appeared among them in a different and even more hideous form than when inflicted with the sword alone. When Wurmser threw himself into Mantua, the garrison might

---

[192] Montholon, tom. iii., p. 271; Jomini, tom. ix., p. 126.

amount to twenty-six thousand men; yet, ere October was far advanced, there were little above the half of the number fit for service. There were nearly nine thousand sick in the hospitals,—infectious diseases, privations of every kind, and the unhealthy air of the lakes and marshes with which they were surrounded, had cut off the remainder. The French also had lost great numbers; but the conquerors could reckon up their victories, and forget the price at which they had been purchased.

It was a proud vaunt, and a cure in itself for many losses, that the minister of war had a right to make the following speech to the Directory, at the formal introduction of Marmont, then aide-de-camp of Buonaparte, and commissioned to present on his part the colours and standards taken from the enemy:—"In the course of a single campaign," he truly said, "Italy had been entirely conquered—three large armies had been entirely destroyed—more than fifty stand of colours had been taken by the victors—forty thousand Austrians had laid down their arms—and, what was not the least surprising part of the whole, these deeds had been accomplished by an army of only thirty thousand Frenchmen, commanded by a general scarce twenty-six years old."[193]

---

[193] Moniteur, No. 13, October 4.

CHAPTER VII

Corsica reunited with France—Critical situation of Buonaparte in Italy at this period—The Austrian General Alvinzi placed at the head of a new Army—Various Contests, attended with no decisive result—Want of Concert among the Austrian Generals—French Army begin to murmur—First Battle of Arcola—Napoleon in personal danger—No decisive result—Second Battle of Arcola—The French victorious—Fresh want of concert among the Austrian Generals—General Views of Military and Political Affairs, after the conclusion of the fourth Italian Campaign—Austria commences a fifth Campaign—but has not profited by experience—Battle of Rivoli, and Victory of the French—Further successful at La Favorita—French regain their lost ground in Italy—Surrender of Mantua—Instances of Napoleon's Generosity.

CORSICA REUNITED WITH FRANCE

About this period the reunion of Corsica with France took place. Buonaparte contributed to this change in the political relations of his native country indirectly, in part by the high pride which his countrymen must have originally taken in his splendid career; and he did so more immediately, by seizing the town and port of Leghorn, and assisting those Corsicans, who had been exiled by the English party, to return to their native island.[194] He intimated the event to the Directory, and stated that he had appointed Gentili, the principal partisan of the French, to govern the island provisionally; and that the Commissioner Salicetti was to

---

[194] Jomini, tom. ix., p. 153; Thibaudeau, tom. ii., p. 32; Montgaillard, tom. iv., p. 468.

set sail for the purpose of making other necessary arrangements.[195] The communication is coldly made, nor does Buonaparte's love of his birth-place induce him to expatiate upon its importance, although the Directory afterwards made the acquisition of that island a great theme of exultation. But his destinies had called him to too high an elevation to permit his distinguishing the obscure islet which he had arisen from originally. He was like the young lion, who, while he is scattering the herds and destroying the hunters, thinks little of the forest-cave in which he first saw the light.[196]

Indeed, Buonaparte's situation, however brilliant, was at the same time critical, and required his undivided thoughts. Mantua still held out, and was likely to do so. Wurmser had caused about three-fourths of the horses belonging to his cavalry to be killed and salted for the use of the garrison, and thus made a large addition, such as it was, to the provisions of the place. His character for courage and determination was completely established; and being now engaged in defending a fortress by ordinary rules of art, which he perfectly understood, he was in no danger of being over-reached and out-manœuvred by the new system of tactics, which occasioned his misfortunes in the open field.

ALVINZI

While, therefore, the last pledge of Austria's dominions in Italy was confided to such safe custody, the Emperor and his ministers were eagerly engaged in making a new effort to recover

---

[195] "Gentili and all the refugees landed in October, 1796, in spite of the English cruisers. The republicans took possession of Bastia and of all the fortresses. The English hastily embarked. The King of England wore the Corsican crown only two years. This whim cost the British treasury five millions sterling. John Bull's riches could not have been worse employed."—Napoleon, *Montholon*, tom. iii., p. 58.

[196] It is fair to add, however, that Buonaparte in his Memoirs, while at St. Helena, gives a sketch of the geographical description and history of Corsica, and suggests several plans for the civilisation of his countrymen,—one of which, the depriving them of the arms which they constantly wear, might be prudent were it practicable, but certainly would be highly unpalatable. There occurs an odd observation, "that the Crown of Corsica must, on the temporary annexation of the island to Great Britain, have been surprised at finding itself appertaining to the successor of Fingal." Not more, we should think, than the diadem of France, and the iron crown of Italy, may have marvelled at meeting on the brow of a Corsican soldier of fortune.—S.

their Italian territories. The defeat of Jourdan, and the retreat of Moreau before the Archduke Charles, had given the Imperialists some breathing time, and enabled them, by extensive levies in the warlike province of Illyria, as well as draughts from the army of the Rhine, to take the field with a new army, for the recovery of the Italian provinces, and the relief of Mantua. By orders of the Aulic Council, two armies were assembled on the Italian frontier; one at Friuli, which was partly composed of that portion of the army of Wurmser, which, cut off from their main body at the battle of Bassano, had effected, under Quasdonowich, a retreat in that direction; the other was to be formed on the Tyrol. They were to operate in conjunction, and both were placed under the command of Marshal Alvinzi,[197] an officer of high reputation, which was then thought merited.

Thus, for the fourth time, Buonaparte was to contest the same objects on the same ground, with new forces belonging to the same enemy. He had, indeed, himself, received from France, reinforcements to the number of twelve battalions, from those troops which had been formerly employed in La Vendée. The army, in general, since victory had placed the resources of the rich country which they occupied at the command of their leader, had been well supplied with clothes, food, and provisions, and were devotedly attached to the chief who had conducted them from starving on the barren Alps into this land of plenty, and had directed their military efforts with such skill, that they could scarce ever be said to have failed of success in whatever they undertook under his direction.

Napoleon had also on his side the good wishes, if not of the Italians in general, of a considerable party, especially in Lombardy, and friends and enemies were alike impressed with belief in his predestined success. During the former attempts of Wurmser, a contrary opinion had prevailed, and the news that the Austrians were in motion, had given birth to insurrections against the French in many places, and to the publication of sentiments unfavourable to them almost every where. But now, when all predicted the certain success of Napoleon, the friends of Austria remained quiet, and the numerous party who desire in such cases to keep on the winning

---

[197] Alvinzi was, at this time, seventy years of age. He died in 1810.

side, added weight to the actual friends of France, by expressing their opinions in her favour. It seems, however, that Victory, as if displeased that mortals should presume to calculate the motives of so fickle a deity, was, on this occasion, disposed to be more coy than formerly even to her greatest favourite, and to oblige him to toil harder than he had done even when the odds were more against him.[198]

Davidowich commanded the body of the Austrians which was in the Tyrol, and which included the fine militia of that martial province. There was little difficulty in prevailing on them to advance into Italy, convinced as they were that there was small security for their national independence while the French remained in possession of Lombardy. Buonaparte, on the other hand, had placed Vaubois in the passes upon the river Lavisa, above Trent, to cover that new possession of the French Republic, and check the advance of Davidowich. It was the plan of Alvinzi to descend from Friuli, and approach Vicenza, to which place he expected Davidowich might penetrate by a corresponding movement down the Adige. Having thus brought his united army into activity, his design was to advance on Mantua, the constant object of bloody contention. He commenced his march in the beginning of October, 1796.

As soon as Buonaparte heard that Alvinzi was in motion, he sent orders to Vaubois to attack Davidowich, and to Massena to advance to Bassano upon the Brenta, and make head against the Austrian commander-in-chief. Both measures failed in effect.

Nov. 5.

Vaubois indeed made his attack, but so unsuccessfully, that after two days' fighting he was compelled to retreat before the Austrians, to evacuate the city of Trent, and to retreat upon Calliano, already mentioned as a very strong position, in the previous account of the battle of Roveredo. A great part of his opponents being Tyrolese, and admirably calculated for mountain warfare, they forced Vaubois from a situation which was almost impregnable; and their army, descending the Adige upon the right

---

[198] Montholon, tom. iii., p. 345; Thibaudeau, tom. ii., p. 82.

bank, appeared to manœuvre with the purpose of marching on Montebaldo and Rivoli, and thus opening the communication with Alvinzi.

On the other hand, though Massena had sustained no loss, for he avoided an engagement, the approach of Alvinzi, with a superior army, compelled him to evacuate Bassano, and to leave the enemy in undisputed possession of the valley of the Brenta. Buonaparte, therefore, himself saw the necessity of advancing with Augereau's division, determined to give battle to Alvinzi, and force him back on the Piave before the arrival of Davidowich. But he experienced unusual resistance; and it is amid complaints of the weather, of misadventures and miscarriages of different sorts, that he faintly claims the name of a victory for his first encounter with Alvinzi. It is clear that he had made a desperate attempt to drive the Austrian general from Bassano—that he had not succeeded; but, on the contrary, was under the necessity of retreating to Vicenza. It is further manifest, that Buonaparte was sensible this retreat did not accord well with his claim of victory; and he says, with a consciousness which is amusing, that the inhabitants of Vicenza were surprised to see the French army retire through their town, as they had been witnesses of their victory on the preceding day.[199] No doubt there was room for astonishment if the Vicenzans had been as completely convinced of the fact as Buonaparte represents them. The truth was, Buonaparte was sensible that Vaubois, being in complete retreat, was exposed to be cut off unless he was supported, and he hasted to prevent so great a loss, by meeting and reinforcing him. His own retrograde movement, however, which extended as far as Verona, left the whole country betwixt the Brenta and Adige open to the Austrians; nor does there occur to those who read the account of the campaign, any good reason why Davidowich and Alvinzi, having no body of French to interrupt their communication, should not instantly have adjusted their operations on a common basis.[200] But it was the bane of the Austrian tactics, through the whole war, to neglect that connexion and co-operation betwixt their separate divisions, which is essential to secure the general result of a campaign. Above all, as Buonaparte himself

---

[199] Montholon, tom. iii., p. 345; Thibaudeau, tom. ii., p. 109.
[200] Jomini, tom. ix., p. 165.

remarked of them, their leaders were not sufficiently acquainted with the value of time in military movements.

Napoleon having retreated to Verona, where he could at pleasure assume the offensive by means of the bridge, or place the Adige between himself and the enemy, visited, in the first place, the positions of Rivoli and Corona, where were stationed the troops which had been defeated by Davidowich.

MURMURS OF THE TROOPS

They appeared before him with dejected countenances, and Napoleon upbraided them with their indifferent behaviour. "You have displeased me," he said;—"You have shown neither discipline, nor constancy, nor bravery. You have suffered yourselves to be driven from positions where a handful of brave men might have arrested the progress of a large army. You are no longer French soldiers.—Let it be written on their colours—'They are not of the Army of Italy.'" Tears, and groans of sorrow and shame, answered this harangue—the rules of discipline could not stifle their sense of mortification, and several of the grenadiers, who had deserved and wore marks of distinction, called out from the ranks—"General, we have been misrepresented—Place us in the advance, and you may then judge whether we do not belong to the army of Italy." Buonaparte having produced the necessary effect, spoke to them in a more conciliatory tone; and the regiments who had undergone so severe a rebuke, redeemed their character in the subsequent part of the campaign.[201]

While Napoleon was indefatigable in concentrating his troops on the right bank of the Adige, and inspiring them with his own spirit of enterprise, Alvinzi had taken his position on the left bank, nearly opposite to Verona. His army occupied a range of heights called Caldiero, on the left of which, and somewhat in the rear, is the little village of Arcola, situated among marshes, which extend around the foot of that eminence. Here the Austrian general had

---

[201] Montholon, tom. iii., p. 349.

stationed himself, with a view, it may be supposed, to wait until Davidowich and his division should descend the right bank of the Adige, disquiet the French leader's position on that river, and give Alvinzi himself the opportunity of forcing a passage.

Buonaparte, with his usual rapidity of resolution, resolved to drive the Austrian from his position on Caldiero, before the arrival of Davidowich. But neither on this occasion was fortune propitious to him.[202] A strong French division, under Massena, attacked the heights amid a storm of rain; but their most strenuous exertions proved completely unsuccessful, and left to the general only his usual mode of concealing a check, by railing at the elements.[203]

The situation of the French became critical, and, what was worse, the soldiers perceived it; and complained that they had to sustain the whole burden of the war, had to encounter army after army, and must succumb at last under the renewed and unwearied efforts of Austria. Buonaparte parried these natural feelings as well as he could,[204] promising that their conquest of Italy should be speedily sealed by the defeat of this Alvinzi; and he applied his whole genius to discover the means of bringing the war to an effective struggle, in which he confided that, in spite of numbers, his own talents, and the enterprising character of an army so often victorious, might assure him a favourable result. But it was no easy way to discover a mode of attacking, with even plausible hopes of success. If he advanced northward on the right bank to seek out and destroy Davidowich, he must weaken his line on the Adige, by the troops withdrawn to effect that purpose; and during his absence, Alvinzi would probably force the passage of the river at some point, and thus have it in his power to relieve Mantua. The heights of Caldiero, occupied by the Austrian main body, and lying in his front, had, by dire experiment, been proved impregnable.

---

[202] Jomini, tom. ix., p. 170; Thibaudeau, tom. ii., p. 112.
[203] "The rain fell in torrents; the ground was so completely soaked, that the French artillery could make no movement, whilst that of the Austrians, being in position, and advantageously placed, produced its full effect."—Montholon, tom. iii., p. 352.
[204] "We have but one more effort to make, and Italy is our own. The enemy is, no doubt, more numerous than we are, but half his troops are recruits; when he is beaten, Mantua must fall, and we shall remain masters of all. From the smiling flowery bivouacs of Italy, you cannot return to the Alpine snows. Succours are on the road; only beat Alvinzi, and I will answer for your future welfare."—Montholon, tom. iii., p. 355.

In these doubtful circumstances the bold scheme occurred to the French general, that the position of Caldiero, though it could not be stormed, might be turned, and that by possessing himself of the village of Arcola, which lies to the left, and in the rear of Caldiero, the Austrians might be compelled to fight to disadvantage. But the idea of attacking Arcola was one which would scarce have occurred to any general save Buonaparte.

Arcola is situated upon a small stream called the Alpon, which, as already hinted, finds its way into the Adige, through a wilderness of marshes, intersected with ditches, and traversed by dikes in various directions. In case of an unsuccessful attack, the assailants were like to be totally cut off in the swamps. Then to debouche from Verona, and move in the direction of Arcola, would have put Alvinzi and his whole army on their guard. Secrecy and celerity are the soul of enterprise. All these difficulties gave way before Napoleon's genius.

Verona, it must be remembered, is on the left bank of the Adige—on the same with the point which was the object of Buonaparte's attack. At nightfall, the whole forces at Verona were under arms; and leaving fifteen hundred men under Kilmaine to defend the place from any assault, with strict orders to secure the gates, and prevent all communication of his nocturnal expedition to the enemy, Buonaparte commenced his march at first to the rear, in the direction of Peschiera; which seemed to imply that his resolution was at length taken to resign the hopes of gaining Mantua, and perhaps to abandon Italy. The silence with which the march was conducted, the absence of all the usual rumours which used in the French army to precede a battle, and the discouraging situation of affairs, appeared to presage the same issue. But after the troops had marched a little way in this direction, the heads of columns were wheeled to the left, out of the line of retreat, and descended the Adige as far as Ronco, which they reached before day. Here a bridge had been prepared, by which they passed over the river, and were placed on the same bank with Arcola, the object of their attack, and lower than the heights of Caldiero.

FIRST BATTLE OF ARCOLA

Nov. 15.

There were three causeways by which the marsh of Arcola is traversed—each was occupied by a French column. The central column moved on the causeway which led to the village so named. The dikes and causeways were not defended, but Arcola and its bridge were protected by two battalions of Croats with two pieces of cannon, which were placed in a position to enfilade the causeway. These received the French column with so heavy a fire on its flank, that it fell back in disorder. Augereau rushed forward upon the bridge with his chosen grenadiers; but enveloped as they were in a destructive fire, they were driven back on the main body.

Alvinzi, who conceived it only an affair of light troops, sent, however, forces into the marsh by means of the dikes which traversed them, to drive out the French. These were checked by finding that they were to oppose strong columns of infantry, yet the battle continued with unabated vigour. It was essential to Buonaparte's plan that Arcola should be carried; but the fire continued tremendous. At length, to animate his soldiers to a final exertion, he caught a stand of colours, rushed on the bridge, and planted them there with his own hand. A fresh body of Austrians arrived at that moment, and the fire on flank blazed more destructively than ever. The rear of the French column fell back; the leading files, finding themselves unsupported, gave way; but, still careful of their general, bore him back in their arms through the dead and dying, the fire and the smoke. In the confusion he was at length pushed into the marsh. The Austrians were already betwixt him and his own troops, and he must have perished or been taken, had not the grenadiers perceived his danger. The cry instantly arose, "Forward—forward—save the general!" Their love to Buonaparte's person did more than even his commands and example had been able to accomplish.[205] They returned to the charge, and at length

---

[205] "This was the day of military devotedness. Lannes, who had been wounded at Governolo, had hastened from Milan; he was still suffering; he threw himself between the enemy and Napoleon, and received three wounds. Muiron, Napoleon's aide-de-camp, was

pushed the Austrians out of the village; but not till the appearance of a French corps under General Guieux had turned the position, and he had thrown himself in the rear of it. These succours had passed at the ferry of Alborado, and the French remained in possession of the long-contested village. It was at the moment a place of the greatest importance; for the possession of it would have enabled Buonaparte, had the Austrians remained in their position, to operate on their communications with the Brenta, interpose between Alvinzi and his reserves, and destroy his park of artillery. But the risk was avoided by the timely caution of the Austrian field-marshal.[206]

Alvinzi was no sooner aware that a great division of the French army was in his rear than, without allowing them time for farther operations, he instantly broke up his position on Caldiero, and evacuated these heights by a steady and orderly retreat. Buonaparte had the mortification to see the Austrians effect this manœuvre by crossing a bridge in their rear over the Alpon, and which could he have occupied, as was his purpose, he might have rendered their retreat impossible, or at least disastrous. As matters stood, however, the village of Arcola came to lose its consequence as a position, since, after Alvinzi's retreat, it was no longer in the rear, but in the front of the enemy.

Buonaparte remembered he had enemies on the right as well as the left of the Adige; and that Davidowich might be once more routing Vaubois, while he was too far advanced to afford him assistance. He therefore evacuated Arcola, and the village of Porcil, situated near it, and retreating to Ronco, recrossed the river, leaving only two demi-brigades in advance upon the left bank.

The first battle of Arcola, famous for the obstinacy with which it was disputed, and the number of brave officers and men who fell, was thus attended with no decisive result. But it had checked the inclination of Alvinzi to advance on Verona—it had delayed all communication betwixt his army and that of the Tyrol—

---

killed in covering his general with his own body. Heroic and affecting death!"—Napoleon, *Memoirs*, tom. iii., p. 362.
[206] Jomini, tom. ix., p. 180; Thibaudeau, tom. ii., p. 117.

above all, it had renewed the Austrians' apprehensions of the skill of Buonaparte and the bravery of his troops, and restored to the French soldiery the usual confidence of their national character.

Nov. 16.

Buonaparte remained stationary at Ronco until next morning at five o'clock, by which time he received intelligence that Davidowich had lain quiet in his former position; that he had no cause to be alarmed for Vaubois' safety, and might therefore operate in security against Alvinzi. This was rendered the more easy, (16th November,) as the Austrian general, not aware of Buonaparte's having halted his army at Ronco, imagined he was on his march to concentrate his forces nearer Mantua, and hastened therefore to overwhelm the rear-guard, whom he expected to find at the ferry. Buonaparte spared them the trouble of a close advance to the Adige. He again crossed to the left side, and again advanced his columns upon the dikes and causeways which traversed the marshes of Arcola. On such ground, where it was impossible to assign to the columns more breadth than the causeways could accommodate, the victorious soldiers of France had great advantage over the recent levies of Austria; for though the latter might be superior in number on the whole, success must in such a case depend on the personal superiority of the front or leading files only. The French, therefore, had the first advantage, and drove back the Austrians upon the village of Arcola; but here, as on the former day, Alvinzi constituted his principal point of defence, and maintained it with the utmost obstinacy.

After having repeatedly failed when attacking in front a post so difficult of approach, Napoleon endeavoured to turn the position by crossing the little river Alpon, near its union with the Adige. He attempted to effect a passage by means of fascines, but unsuccessfully; and the night approached without any thing effectual being decided. Both parties drew off, the French to Ronco, where they recrossed the Adige; the Austrians to a position behind the well-contested village of Arcola.

The battle of the 16th November was thus far favourable to the French, that they had driven back the Austrians, and made many prisoners in the commencement of the day; but they had also lost many men; and Napoleon, if he had gained ground in the day, was fain to return to his position at night, lest Davidowich, by the defeat of Vaubois, might either relieve Mantua, or move on Verona. The 17th was to be a day more decisive.

SECOND BATTLE OF ARCOLA

Nov. 17.

The field of battle, and the preliminary manœuvres, were much the same as on the preceding day; but those of the French were nearly disconcerted by the sinking of one of the boats which constituted their bridge over the Adige. The Austrians instantly advanced on the demi-brigade which had been stationed on the left bank to defend the bridge. But the French having repaired the damage, advanced in their turn, and compelled the Austrians to retreat upon the marsh. Massena directed his attack on Porcil—General Robert pressed forward on Arcola. But it was at the point where he wished to cross the Alpon that Buonaparte chiefly desired to attain a decided superiority; and in order to win it, he added stratagem to audacity. Observing one of his columns repulsed, and retreating along the causeway, he placed the 32d regiment in ambuscade in a thicket of willows which bordered the rivulet, and saluting the pursuing enemy with a close, heavy, and unexpected fire, instantly rushed to close with the bayonet, and attacking the flank of a column of nearly three thousand Croats, forced them into the marsh, where most of them perished.

It was now that, after a calculation of the losses sustained by the enemy, Napoleon conceived their numerical superiority so far diminished, and their spirit so much broken, that he need no longer confine his operations to the dikes, but meet his enemy on the firm plain which extended beyond the Alpon. He passed the brook by means of a temporary bridge which had been prepared during night, and the battle raged as fiercely on the dry level, as it had done on the dikes and amongst the marshes.

The Austrians fought with resolution, the rather that their left, though stationed on dry ground, was secured by a marsh which Buonaparte had no means of turning. But though this was the case, Napoleon contrived to gain his point by impressing on the enemy an idea that he had actually accomplished that which he had no means of doing. This he effected by sending a daring officer, with about thirty of the guides, (his own body-guards they may be called,) with four trumpets; and directing these determined cavaliers to charge, and the trumpets to sound, as if a large body of horse had crossed the marsh. Augereau attacked the Austrian left at the same moment; and a fresh body of troops advancing from Legnago, compelled them to retreat, but not to fly.

Alvinzi was now compelled to give way, and commence his retreat on Montebello. He disposed seven thousand men in echelon to cover this movement, which was accomplished without very much loss; but his ranks had been much thinned by the slaughter of the three battles of Arcola. Eight thousand men has been stated as the amount of his losses.[207] The French who made so many and so sanguinary assaults upon the villages, must also have suffered a great deal. Buonaparte acknowledges this in energetic terms. "Never," he writes to Carnot, "was field of battle so disputed. I have almost no generals remaining—I can assure you that the victory could not have been gained at a cheaper expense. The enemy were numerous, and desperately resolute."[208] The truth is, that Buonaparte's mode of striking terror by these bloody and desperate charges in front upon strong positions, was a blemish in his system. They cost many men, and were not uniformly successful. That of Arcola was found a vain waste of blood, till science was employed instead of main force, when the position was turned by Guieux on the first day; and on the third, by the troops who crossed the Alpon.

---

[207] Jomini, tom. ix., p. 101. Napoleon estimates the loss of Alvinzi, in the three days' engagements, at 18,000 men including 6000 prisoners. Montholon, tom. iii., p. 370.
[208] Letter to the Directory, 19th November.

The tardy conduct of Davidowich, during these three undecided days of slaughterous struggle, is worthy of notice and censure. It would appear that from the 10th November that general had it in his power to attack the division which he had hitherto driven before him, and that he had delayed doing so till the 16th; and on the 18th, just the day after Alvinzi had made his retreat, he approached Verona on the right bank. Had these movements taken place before Alvinzi's defeat, or even during any of the three days preceding, when the French were engaged before Arcola, the consequences must have been very serious. Finding, however, that Alvinzi had retreated, Davidowich followed the same course, and withdrew into the mountains, not much annoyed by the French, who respected the character of his army, which had been repeatedly victorious, and felt the weakness incident to their own late losses.[209]

Another incidental circumstance tends equally strongly to mark the want of concert and communication among the Austrian generals. Wurmser, who had remained quiet in Mantua during all the time when Alvinzi and Davidowich were in the neighbourhood, made a vigorous sally on the 23d November; when his doing so was of little consequence, since he could not be supported.

Thus ended the fourth campaign undertaken for the Austrian possessions in Italy. The consequences were not so decidedly in Buonaparte's favour as those of the three former. Mantua, it is true, had received no relief; and so far the principal object of the Austrians had miscarried. But Wurmser was of a temper to continue the defence till the last moment, and had already provided for a longer defence than the French counted upon, by curtailing the rations of the garrison. The armies of Friuli and the Tyrol had also, since the last campaign, retained possession of Bassano and Trent, and removed the French from the mountains through which access is gained to the Austrian hereditary dominions. Neither had Alvinzi suffered any such heavy defeat as his predecessors Beaulieu or Wurmser; while Davidowich, on the contrary, was uniformly

---

[209] "The French army re-entered Verona in triumph by the Venice gate, three days after having quitted that city almost clandestinely by the Milan gate. It would be difficult to conceive the astonishment and enthusiasm of the inhabitants."—Montholon, tom. iii., p. 370.

successful, had he known how to avail himself of his victories. Still the Austrians were not likely, till reinforced again, to interrupt Buonaparte's quiet possession of Lombardy.

During two months following the battle of Arcola and the retreat of the Austrians, the war which had been so vigorously maintained in Italy experienced a short suspension, and the attention of Buonaparte was turned towards civil matters—the arrangement of the French interests with the various powers of Italy, and with the congress of Lombardy, as well as the erection of the districts of Bologna, Ferrara, Reggio, and Modena, into what was called the Transpadane Republic. These we shall notice elsewhere, as it is not advisable to interrupt the course of our military annals, until we have recounted the last struggle of the Austrians for the relief of Mantua.

FRENCH AND AUSTRIAN ARMIES

It must be in the first place observed, that whether from jealousy or from want of means, supplies and recruits were very slowly transmitted from France to their Italian army. About seven thousand men, who were actually sent to join Buonaparte, scarcely repaired the losses which he had sustained in the late bloody campaigns.[210] At the same time the treaty with the Pope being broken off, the supreme pontiff threatened to march a considerable army towards Lombardy. Buonaparte endeavoured to supply the want of reinforcements by raising a defensive legion among the Lombards, to which he united many Poles. This body was not fit to be brought into line against the Austrians, but was more than sufficient to hold at bay the troops of the papal see, who have never enjoyed of late years a high degree of military reputation.

Meantime Austria, who seemed to cling to Italy with the tenacity of a dying grasp, again, and now for the fifth time, recruited her armies on the frontier, and placing Alvinzi once more at the

---

[210] "You announce the arrival of 10,000 men from the Army of the Ocean, and a like number from that of the Rhine; but they have not arrived, and should they not come speedily, you will sacrifice an army ardently devoted to the Constitution."—Buonaparte to the Directory, 28th December.

head of sixty thousand men, commanded him to resume the offensive against the French in Italy.[211] The spirit of the country had been roused instead of discouraged by the late defeats. The volunteer corps, consisting of persons of respectability and consideration, took the field, for the redemption, if their blood could purchase it, of the national honour. Vienna furnished four battalions, which were presented by the Empress with a banner, that she had wrought for them with her own hands. The Tyrolese also thronged once more to their sovereign's standard, undismayed by a proclamation made by Buonaparte after the retreat from Arcola, and which paid homage, though a painful one, to these brave marksmen. "Whatever Tyrolese," said this atrocious document, "is taken with arms in his hand, shall be put to instant death." Alvinzi sent abroad a counter proclamation, "that for every Tyrolese put to death as threatened, he would hang up a French officer." Buonaparte again replied, "that if the Austrian general should use the retaliation he threatened, he would execute in his turn officer for officer out of his prisoners, commencing with Alvinzi's own nephew, who was in his power." A little calmness on either side brought them to reflect on the cruelty of aggravating the laws of war, which are already too severe; so that the system of military execution was renounced on both sides.

AUSTRIAN PLAN OF OPERATIONS

But notwithstanding this display of zeal and loyalty on the part of the Austrian nation, its councils do not appear to have derived wisdom from experience. The losses sustained by Wurmser and by Alvinzi, proceeded in a great measure from the radical error of having divided their forces, and commenced the campaign on a double line of operation, which could not, or at least were not made to, correspond and communicate with each other. Yet they commenced this campaign on the same unhappy principles. One army descending from the Tyrol upon Montebaldo, the other was to

---

[211] "The Austrian army amounted to from 65,000 to 70,000 fighting men, and 6000 Tyrolese, besides 24,000 men of the garrison of Mantua."—Montholon, tom. iii., p. 404.
"After the battle of Arcola, the active French army amounted to 36,380 while 10,230 formed the blockade of Mantua."—Jomini, tom. ix., p. 262.

march down by the Brenta on the Paduan territory, and then to operate on the lower Adige, the line of which, of course, they were expected to force, for the purpose of relieving Mantua. The Aulic Council ordered that these two armies were to direct their course so as to meet, if possible, upon the beleaguered fortress. Should they succeed in raising the siege, there was little doubt that the French must be driven out of Italy; but even were the scheme only partially successful, still it might allow Wurmser with his cavalry to escape from that besieged city, and retreat into the Romagna, where it was designed that he should, with the assistance of his staff and officers, organize and assume the command of the papal army. In the meantime, an intelligent agent was sent to communicate, if possible, with Wurmser.[212]

This man fell into the hands of the besiegers. It was in vain that he swallowed his despatches, which were inclosed in a ball of wax; means were found to make the stomach render up its trust, and the document which the wax enclosed was found to be a letter, signed by the Emperor's own hand, directing Wurmser to enter into no capitulation, but to hold out as long as possible in expectation of relief, and if compelled to leave Mantua, to accept of no conditions, but to cut his way into the Romagna, and take upon himself the command of the papal army. Thus Buonaparte became acquainted with the storm which was approaching, and which was not long of breaking.[213]

Alvinzi, who commanded the principal army, advanced from Bassano to Roveredo upon the Adige. Provera, distinguished for his gallant defence of Cossaria, during the action of Millesimo,[214] commanded the divisions which were to act upon the lower Adige. He marched as far as Bevi l'Acqua, while his advanced guard, under Prince Hohenzollern, compelled a body of French to cross to the right bank of the Adige.

Jan. 12.

---

[212] Montholon, tom. iii., p. 405; Jomini, tom. ix., p. 263.
[213] Montholon, tom. iii., p. 406.
[214] See *ante*.

Buonaparte, uncertain which of these attacks he was to consider as the main one, concentrated his army at Verona, which had been so important a place during all these campaigns as a central point, from which he might at pleasure march either up the Adige against Alvinzi, or descend the river to resist the attempts of Provera. He trusted that Joubert, whom he had placed in defence of La Corona, a little town which had been strongly fortified for the purpose, might be able to make a good temporary defence. He despatched troops for Joubert's support to Castel Nuovo, but hesitated to direct his principal force in that direction until ten in the evening of 13th January, when he received information that Joubert had been attacked at La Corona by an immense body, which he had resisted with difficulty during the day, and was now about to retreat, in order to secure the important eminence at Rivoli, which was the key of his whole position.[215]

Judging from this account, that the principal danger occurred on the upper part of the Adige, Buonaparte left only Augereau's division to dispute with Provera the passage of that river on the lower part of its course. He was especially desirous to secure the elevated and commanding position of Rivoli, before the enemy had time to receive his cavalry and cannon, as he hoped to bring on an engagement ere he was united with those important parts of his army. By forced marches Napoleon arrived at Rivoli at two in the morning of the 14th, and from that elevated situation, by the assistance of a clear moonlight, he was able to discover, that the bivouac of the enemy was divided into five distinct and separate bodies, from which he inferred that their attack the next day would be made in the same number of columns.[216]

The distance at which the bivouacs were stationed from the position of Joubert, made it evident to Napoleon that they did not mean to make their attack before ten in the morning, meaning probably to wait for their infantry and artillery. Joubert was at this time in the act of evacuating the position which he only occupied by a rear-guard. Buonaparte commanded him instantly to counter-march and resume possession of the important eminence of Rivoli.

---

[215] Jomini, tom. ix., p. 268.
[216] Montholon, tom. iii., p. 410.

BATTLE OF RIVOLI

Jan. 14.

A few Croats had already advanced so near the French line as to discover that Joubert's light troops had abandoned the chapel of Saint Marc, of which they took possession. It was retaken by the French, and the struggle to recover and maintain it brought on a severe action, first with the regiment to which the detachment of Croats belonged, and afterwards with the whole Austrian column which lay nearest to that point, and which was commanded by Ocskay. The latter was repulsed, but the column of Kobler pressed forward to support them, and having gained the summit, attacked two regiments of the French who were stationed there, each protected by a battery of cannon. Notwithstanding this advantage, one of the regiments gave way, and Buonaparte himself galloped to bring up reinforcements. The nearest French were those of Massena's division, which, tired with the preceding night's march, had lain down to take some rest. They started up, however, at the command of Napoleon, and suddenly arriving on the field, in half an hour the column of Kobler was beaten and driven back. That of Liptay advanced in turn; and Quasdonowich, observing that Joubert, in prosecuting his success over the division of Ocskay, had pushed forward and abandoned the chapel of Saint Marc, detached three battalions to ascend the hill, and occupy that post. While the Austrians scaled, on one side, the hill on which the chapel is situated, three battalions of French infantry, who had been countermarched by Joubert to prevent Quasdonowich's purpose, struggled up the steep ascent on another point. The activity of the French brought them first to the summit, and having then the advantage of the ground, it was no difficult matter for them to force the advancing Austrians headlong down the hill which they were endeavouring to climb. Meantime, the French batteries thundered on the broken columns of the enemy—their cavalry made repeated charges, and the whole Austrians who had been engaged fell into inextricable disorder. The columns which had advanced were irretrievably defeated; those who remained were in such a condition, that to attack would have been madness.

Amid this confusion, the division of Lusignan, which was the most remote of the Austrian columns, being intrusted with the charge of the artillery and baggage of the army, had, after depositing these according to order, mounted the heights of Rivoli, and assumed a position in rear of the French. Had this column attained the same ground while the engagement continued in front, there can be no doubt that it would have been decisive against Napoleon. Even as it was, their appearance in the rear would have startled troops, however brave, who had less confidence in their general; but those of Buonaparte only exclaimed, "There arrive farther supplies to our market," in full reliance that their commander could not be out-manœuvred. The Austrian division, on the other hand, arriving after the battle was lost, being without artillery or cavalry, and having been obliged to leave a proportion of their numbers to keep a check upon a French brigade, felt that, instead of being in a position to cut off the French, by attacking their rear while their front was engaged, they themselves were cut off by the intervention of the victorious French betwixt them and their defeated army. Lusignan's division was placed under a heavy fire of the artillery in reserve, and was soon obliged to lay down its arms. So critical are the events of war, that a military movement, which, executed at one particular period of time, would have ensured victory, is not unlikely, from the loss of a brief interval, to occasion only more general calamity.[217] The Austrians, on this, as on some other occasions, verified too much Napoleon's allegation, that they did not sufficiently consider the value of time in military affairs.

The field of Rivoli was one of the most desperate that Buonaparte ever won, and was gained entirely by superior military skill, and not by the overbearing system of mere force of numbers, to which he has been accused of being partial.[218] He himself had his horses repeatedly wounded in the course of the action, and exerted

---

[217] It is represented in some military accounts, that the division which appeared in the rear of the French belonged to the army of Provera, and had been detached by him on crossing the Adige, as mentioned below. But Napoleon's Saint Helena manuscripts prove the contrary. Provera only crossed on the 14th January, and it was on the morning of the same day that Napoleon had seen the five divisions of Alvinzi, that of Lusignan which afterwards appeared in the rear of his army being one, lying around Joubert's position of Rivoli.—S.— See Montholon, tom. iii., p. 415, and Jomini, tom. ix., p. 284.
[218] Jomini, tom. ix., pp. 275, 287; Montholon, tom. iii., p. 408.

to the utmost his personal influence to bring up the troops into action where their presence was most required.[219]

Alvinzi's error, which was a very gross one, consisted in supposing that no more than Joubert's inconsiderable force was stationed at Rivoli, and in preparing, therefore, to destroy him at his leisure; when his acquaintance with the French celerity of movement[220] ought to have prepared him for the possibility of Buonaparte's night march, by which, bringing up the chosen strength of his army into the position where the enemy only expected to find a feeble force, he was enabled to resist and defeat a much superior army, brought to the field upon different points, without any just calculation on the means of resistance which were to be opposed; without the necessary assistance of cavalry and artillery; and, above all, without a preconcerted plan of co-operation and mutual support. The excellence of Napoleon's manœuvres was well supported by the devotion of his generals, and the courage of his soldiers. Massena, in particular, so well seconded his general, that afterwards, when Napoleon, as Emperor, conferred on him the title of Duke, he assigned him his designation from the battle of Rivoli.[221]

Almost before this important and decisive victory was absolutely gained, news arrived[222] which required the presence of Buonaparte elsewhere. On the very same day of the battle, Provera, whom we left manœuvring on the Lower Adige, threw a bridge of pontoons over that river, where the French were not prepared to oppose his passage, and pushed forward to Mantua, the relief of which fortress he had by stratagem nearly achieved. A regiment of his cavalry, wearing white cloaks, and resembling, in that particular, the first regiment of French hussars, presented themselves before the suburb of Saint George, then only covered by a mere line of

---

[219] "This day the general-in-chief was several times surrounded by the enemy; he had several horses killed."—Montholon, tom. iii., p. 415.
[220] "The Roman legions are reported to have marched twenty-four miles a-day; but our brigades, though fighting at intervals, march thirty."—Buonaparte to the Directory.
[221] "It was after the battle of Rivoli, that Massena received from Buonaparte and the army the title of 'enfant chéri de la victoire,'" &c.—Thibaudeau, tom. ii., p. 195.
[222] "At two o'clock in the afternoon, in the midst of the battle of Rivoli."—Montholon, tom. iii., p. 416.

circumvallation. The barricades were about to be opened without suspicion, when it occurred to a sagacious old French sergeant, who was beyond the walls gathering wood, that the dress of this regiment of white cloaks was fresher than that of the French corps, called Bertini's, for whom they were mistaken. He communicated his suspicions to a drummer who was near him; they gained the suburb, and cried to arms, and the guns of the defences were opened on the hostile cavalry, whom they were about to have admitted in the guise of friends.[223]

Jan. 16

About the time that this incident took place, Buonaparte himself arrived at Roverbella, within twelve miles of Mantua, to which he had marched with incredible despatch from the field of battle at Rivoli, leaving to Massena, Murat, and Joubert, the task of completing his victory, by the close pursuit of Alvinzi and his scattered forces.

BATTLE OF LA FAVORITA

In the meanwhile, Provera communicated with the garrison of Mantua across the lake, and concerted the measures for its relief with Wurmser. On the 16th of January, being the morning after the battle of Rivoli, and the unsuccessful attempt to surprise the suburb of Saint George, the garrison of Mantua sallied from the place in strength, and took post at the causeway of La Favorita, being the only one which is defended by an enclosed citadel or independent fortress. Napoleon, returning at the head of his victorious forces, surrounded and attacked with fury the troops of Provera, while the blockading army compelled the garrison, at the bayonet's point, to re-enter the besieged city of Mantua. Provera, who had in vain, though with much decision and gallantry, attempted the relief of Mantua, which his Imperial master had so much at heart, was compelled to lay down his arms with a division of about five thousand men, whom he had still united under his person. The

---

[223] Montholon, tom. iii., p. 416.

detached corps which he had left to protect his bridge, and other passes in his rear, sustained a similar fate. Thus one division of the army, which had commenced the campaign of January only on the 7th of that month, were the prisoners of the destined conqueror before ten days had elapsed. The larger army, commanded by Alvinzi, had no better fortune. They were closely pursued from the bloody field of Rivoli, and never were permitted to draw breath or to recover their disorder. Large bodies were intercepted and compelled to surrender, a practice now so frequent among the Austrian troops, that it ceased to be shameful.[224]

Nevertheless, one example is so peculiar as to deserve commemoration, as a striking instance of the utter consternation and dispersion of the Austrians after this dreadful defeat, and of the confident and audacious promptitude which the French officers derived from their unvaried success. René, a young officer, was in possession of the village called Garda, on the lake of the same name, and, in visiting his advanced posts, he perceived some Austrians approaching, whom he caused his escort to surround and make prisoners. Advancing to the front to reconnoitre, he found himself close to the head of an imperial column of eighteen hundred men, which a turning in the road had concealed till he was within twenty yards of them. "Down with your arms!" said the Austrian commandant; to which René answered with the most ready boldness,—"Do *you* lay down your arms! I have destroyed your advanced guard, as witness these prisoners—ground your arms or no quarter." And the French soldiers, catching the hint of their leader, joined in the cry of "Ground your arms." The Austrian officer hesitated, and proposed to enter into capitulation; the Frenchman would admit of no terms but instant and immediate surrender. The dispirited imperialist yielded up his sword, and commanded his soldiers to imitate his example. But the Austrian soldiers began to suspect the truth; they became refractory, and refused to obey their leader, whom René addressed with the utmost apparent composure. "You are an officer, sir, and a man of honour—you know the rules of war—you have surrendered—you are therefore my prisoner, but I rely on your parole. Here, I return your sword—compel your men to submission, otherwise I direct

---

[224] Montholon, tom. iii., p. 417; Jomini, tom. ix., p. 293.

against you the division of six thousand men who are under my command." The Austrian was utterly confounded, betwixt the appeal to his honour and the threat of a charge from six thousand men. He assured René he might rely on his punctilious compliance with the parole he had given him; and speaking in German to his soldiers, persuaded them to lay down their arms, a submission which he had soon afterwards the satisfaction to see had been made to one-twelfth part of their number.

Amid such extraordinary success, the ground which the French had lost in Italy was speedily resumed. Trent and Bassano were again occupied by the French. They regained all the positions and strongholds which they had possessed on the frontiers of Italy before Alvinzi's first descent, and might perhaps have penetrated deeper into the mountainous frontier of Germany but for the snow which choked up the passes.[225]

SURRENDER OF MANTUA

One crowning consequence of the victories of Rivoli and of La Favorita, was the surrender of Mantua itself, that prize which had cost so much blood, and had been defended with such obstinacy.

Feb. 2.

For several days after the decisive actions which left him without a shadow of hope of relief, Wurmser continued the defence of the place in a sullen yet honourable despair, natural to the feelings of a gallant veteran, who, to the last, hesitated between the desire to resist, and the sense that, his means of subsistence being almost totally expended, resistance was absolutely hopeless. At length he sent his aide-de-camp, Klenau, (afterwards a name of celebrity,) to the headquarters of Serrurier, who commanded the blockade, to treat of a surrender. Klenau used the customary language on such

---

[225] "The trophies acquired in the course of January were 25,000 prisoners, twenty-four colours and standards, and sixty pieces of cannon; on the whole, the enemy's loss was at least 35,000 men. Bessières carried the colours to Paris. The prisoners were so numerous that they created some difficulty."—Montholon, tom. iii., p. 419.

occasions. He expatiated on the means which he said Mantua still possessed of holding out, but said, that as Wurmser doubted whether the place could be relieved in time, he would regulate his conduct as to immediate submission, or farther defence, according to the conditions of surrender to which the French generals were willing to admit him.

A French officer of distinction was present, muffled in his cloak, and remaining apart from the two officers, but within hearing of what had passed. When their discussion was finished, this unknown person stepped forward, and taking a pen wrote down the conditions of surrender to which Wurmser was to be admitted—conditions more honourable and favourable by far than what his extremity could have exacted. "These," said the unknown officer to Klenau, "are the terms which Wurmser may accept at present, and which will be equally tendered to him at any period when he finds farther resistance impossible. We are aware he is too much a man of honour to give up the fortress and city, so long and honourably defended, while the means of resistance remain in his power. If he delays accepting the conditions for a week, for a month, for two months, they shall be equally his when he chooses to accept them. Tomorrow I pass the Po, and march upon Rome." Klenau, perceiving that he spoke to the French commander-in-chief, frankly admitted that the garrison could not longer delay surrender, having scarce three days' provisions unconsumed.[226]

This trait of generosity towards a gallant but unfortunate enemy, was highly favourable to Buonaparte. The taste which dictated the stage-effect of the cloak may indeed be questioned; but the real current of his feeling towards the venerable object of his respect, and at the same time compassion, is ascertained otherwise. He wrote to the Directory on the subject, that he had afforded to Wurmser such conditions of surrender as became the generosity of the French nation towards an enemy, who, having lost his army by misfortune, was so little desirous to secure his personal safety, that he threw himself into Mantua, cutting his way through the blockading army; thus voluntarily undertaking the privations of a

---

[226] Montholon, tom. iii., p. 420.

siege, which his gallantry protracted until almost the last morsel of provisions was exhausted.[227]

But the young victor paid still a more delicate and noble-minded compliment, in declining to be personally present when the veteran Wurmser had the mortification to surrender his sword, with his garrison of twenty thousand men, ten thousand of whom were fit for service. This self-denial did Napoleon as much credit nearly as his victory, and must not be omitted in a narrative, which, often called to stigmatize his ambition and its consequences, should not be the less ready to observe marks of dignified and honourable feeling. The history of this remarkable man more frequently reminds us of the romantic and improbable victories imputed to the heroes of the romantic ages, than of the spirit of chivalry attributed to them; but in this instance Napoleon's conduct towards Wurmser may be justly compared to that of the Black Prince to his royal prisoner, King John of France.

Serrurier, who had conducted the leaguer, had the honour to receive the surrender of Wurmser, after the siege of Mantua had continued for six months, during which the garrison is said by Napoleon to have lost twenty-seven thousand men by disease, and in the various numerous and bloody sallies which took place. This decisive event put an end to the war in Italy. The contest with Austria was hereafter to be waged on the hereditary dominions of that haughty power.

The French, possessed of this grand object of their wishes, were not long in displaying their national characteristics. Their military and prescient sagacity was evinced in employing one of the most celebrated of their engineers, to improve and bring nearly to perfection the defence of a city which may be termed the citadel of Italy. They set afoot, besides, civic feasts and ceremonies, and among others, one in honour of Virgil, who, being the panegyrist of an emperor, was indifferently selected as the presiding genius of an infant republic. Their cupidity was evinced by their artists' exercising their ingenuity in devising means to cut from the wall and carry off the fresco paintings, by Titian, of the wars between the Gods and

---

[227] Buonaparte to the Directory, 15 Pluviose, 3d February.

the Giants, at all risks of destroying what could never be replaced. Luckily, the attempt was found totally unadvisable.

Chapter VIII

Situation and Views of Buonaparte at this period—His politic Conduct towards the Italians—Popularity—Severe terms of Peace proposed to the Pope—rejected—Napoleon differs from the Directory, and Negotiations are renewed—but again rejected—The Pope raises his army to 40,000 Men—Napoleon invades the Papal Territories—The Papal Troops defeated near Imola—and at Ancona—which is captured—Loretto taken—Clemency of Buonaparte to the French recusant Clergy—Peace of Tolentino—Napoleon's Letter to the Pope—San Marino—View of the Situation of the different Italian States—Rome—Naples—Tuscany—Venice.

PRE-EMINENCE OF NAPOLEON

The eyes of all Europe were now riveted on Napoleon Buonaparte, whose rise had been so sudden, that he was become the terror of empires and the founder of states—the conqueror of the best generals and most disciplined troops in Europe; within a few months after he had been a mere soldier of fortune, rather seeking for subsistence than expecting honourable distinction. Such sudden elevations have occasionally happened amid semi-barbarous nations, where great popular insurrections, desolating and decisive revolutions, are common occurrences, but were hitherto unheard of in civilized Europe. The pre-eminence which he had suddenly obtained had, besides, been subjected to so many trials, as to afford every proof of its permanence. Napoleon stood aloft, like a cliff on which successive tempests had expended their rage in vain. The means which raised him were equally competent to make good his greatness. He had infused into the armies which he commanded the firmest reliance on his genius, and the greatest love for his person; so that he could always find agents ready to execute his most difficult commands. He had even inspired them with a portion of his own indefatigable exertion and his commanding intelligence. The maxim which he inculcated upon them when practising those long and severe marches which formed one essential part of his system, was, "I would rather gain victory at the expense of your legs than at the price of your blood."[228] The French, under his training, seemed to become the very men he wanted, and to forget in the excitation of war and the hope of victory, even the feelings of weariness and exhaustion. The following description of the French soldier by Napoleon himself, occurs in his despatches to the Directory during his first campaign in Italy:—

"Were I to name all those who have been distinguished by acts of personal bravery, I must send the muster-roll of all the grenadiers and carabineers of the advanced-guard. They jest with danger, and laugh at death; and if any thing can equal their intrepidity, it is the gaiety with which, singing alternately songs of love and patriotism, they accomplish the most severe forced marches. When they arrive at their bivouac, it is not to take their repose, as might be expected, but to tell each his story of the battle of the day, and produce his plan for that of to-morrow; and many of them think with great correctness on military subjects. The other day I was inspecting a demi-brigade, and as it filed past me, a common chasseur approached my horse, and said, 'General, you ought to do so and so.'—'Hold your peace, you rogue!' I replied. He disappeared immediately, nor have I since been able to find him out. But the manœuvre which he recommended was the very same which I had privately resolved to carry into execution."[229]

To command this active, intelligent, and intrepid soldiery, Buonaparte possessed officers entirely worthy of the charge; men young, or at least not advanced in years, to whose ambition the Revolution, and the wars which it had brought on, had opened an unlimited career, and whose genius was inspired by the plans of their leader, and the success which attended them. Buonaparte, who had his eye on every man, never neglected to distribute rewards and

---

[228] Louis Buonaparte, tom. ii., p. 60.
[229] Letter to the Directory, June 1; Moniteur, No. 264.

punishments, praise and censure with a liberal hand, or omitted to press for what latterly was rarely if ever denied to him—the promotion of such officers as particularly distinguished themselves. He willingly assumed the task of soothing the feelings of those whose relations had fallen under his banners. His letter of consolation to General Clarke upon the death of young Clarke, his nephew, who fell at Arcola, is affecting, as showing that amid all his victories he felt himself the object of reproach and criticism.[230] His keen sensitiveness to the attacks of the public press attended him through life, and, like the slave in the triumphal car, seemed to remind him, that he was still a mortal man.

It should farther be remarked, that Napoleon withstood, instantly and boldly, all the numerous attempts made by commissaries, and that description of persons, to encroach upon the fund destined for the use of the army. Much of his public, and more of his private correspondence, is filled with complaints against these agents, although he must have known that, in attacking them, he disobliged men of the highest influence, who had frequently some secret interest in their wealth. But his military fame made his services indispensable, and permitted him to set at defiance the enmity of such persons, who are generally as timid as they are sordid.

Towards the general officers there took place a gradual change of deportment, as the commander-in-chief began to feel gradually, more and more, the increasing sense of his own personal importance. We have been informed by an officer of the highest rank, that, during the earlier campaigns, Napoleon used to rejoice with, and embrace them as associates, nearly on the same footing,

---

[230] Letter from Napoleon to General Clarke, 25 Brumaire, 15th Nov. 1796.—"Your nephew has been slain on the field of battle at Arcola. The young man had been familiar with arms—had led on columns, and would have been one day an excellent officer. He has died with glory in the face of the enemy. He did not suffer for an instant. What man would not envy such a death? Who is he that would not accept as a favourable condition the choice of thus escaping from the vicissitudes of a contemptible world? Who is there among us who has not a hundred times regretted that he has not been thus withdrawn from the powerful effects of calumny, of envy, and of all the odious passions which seem the almost exclusive directors of the conduct of mankind?"—This letter, remarkable in many respects, will remind the English reader of Cato's exclamation over the body of his son—"Who would not be this youth!"—S.

engaged in the same tasks. After a period, his language and carriage became those of a frank soldier, who, sensible of the merit of his subordinate assistants, yet makes them sensible, by his manner, that he is their commander-in-chief. When his infant fortunes began to come of age, his deportment to his generals was tinctured with that lofty courtesy which princes use towards their subjects, and which plainly intimated, that he held them as subjects in the war, not as brethren.[231]

CONDUCT TO THE ITALIANS

Napoleon's conduct towards the Italians individually was, in most instances, in the highest degree prudent and political; while, at the same time, it coincided, as true policy usually does, with the rules of justice and moderation, and served, in a great measure, to counterbalance the odium which he incurred by despoiling Italy of the works of art, and even by his infringements on the religious system of the Catholics.

On the latter subject, the general became particularly cautious, and his dislike or contempt of the Church of Rome was no longer shown in that gross species of satire which he had at first given loose to. On the contrary, it was veiled under philosophical indifference; and, while relieving the clergy of their worldly possessions, Napoleon took care to avoid the error of the Jacobins; never proposing their tenets as an object of persecution, but protecting their persons, and declaring himself a decided friend to general toleration on all points of conscience.

---

[231] "Decrès has often told me, that he was at Toulon when he first heard of Napoleon's appointment to the command of the army of Italy. He had known him well at Paris, and thought himself on terms of perfect familiarity with him. 'Thus,' said he, 'when we learned that the new general was about to pass through the city, I hastened to him full of eagerness and joy; the door of the apartment was thrown open, and I was on the point of rushing towards him with my wonted familiarity, but his attitude, his look, the tone of his voice, suddenly deterred me. Not that there was any thing offensive either in his appearance or manner; but the impression he produced was sufficient to prevent me from ever again attempting to encroach upon the distance that separated us."—Las Cases, tom. i., p. 164.

In point of politics, as well as religion, the opinions of Buonaparte appear to have experienced a great change. It may be doubted, indeed, if he ever in his heart adopted those of the outrageous Jacobins.[232] At all events, his clear and sound good sense speedily made him aware, that such a violence on the established rules of reason and morality, as an attempt to make the brutal strength of the multitude the forcible controller of those possessed of the wisdom, property, and education of a country, is too unnatural to remain long, or to become the basis of a well-regulated state. Being at present a Republican of the Thermidorien party, Buonaparte, even though he made use of the established phrases, Liberty and Equality, acknowledged no dignity superior to citizen, and *thee'd* and *thou'd* whomsoever he addressed, was permitted to mix many grains of liberality with those democratic forms. Indeed, the republican creed of the day began to resemble the leathern apron of the brazier, who founded a dynasty in the East—his descendants continued to display it as their banner, but enriched it so much with gems and embroidery, that there was little of the original stuff to be discovered.

Jacobinism, for example, being founded on the principle of assimilating the national character to the gross ignorance of the lower classes, was the natural enemy of the fine arts and of literature, whose productions the Sans-Culottes could not comprehend, and which they destroyed for the same enlightened reasons that Jack Cade's followers hanged the clerk of Chatham, with his pen and inkhorn about his neck.[233] Buonaparte, on the contrary, saw that knowledge, of whatever kind, was power; and therefore he distinguished himself honourably amidst his victories, by seeking the conversation of men distinguished for literary attainments, and displaying an interest in the antiquities and curiosities of the towns which he visited, that could not but seem

---

[232] Even when before Toulon, he was not held by clear-sighted persons to be a very orthodox Jacobin. General Cartaux, the stupid Sans-Culotte under whom he first served, was talking of the young commandant of artillery with applause, when his wife, who was somewhat first in command at home, advised him not to reckon too much on that young man, "who had too much sense to be long a Sans-Culotte."—"Sense! Female-citizen Cartaux," said her offended husband, "do you take us for fools?"—"By no means," answered the lady; "but his sense is not of the same kind with yours."—S.—Las Cases, vol. i., p. 144.
[233] *Second Part of King Henry VI., Act 4., Scene 2.*

flattering to the inhabitants. In a letter addressed publicly to Oriani,[234] a celebrated astronomer, he assures him, that all men of genius, all who had distinguished themselves in the republic of letters, were to be accounted natives of France, whatever might be the actual place of their birth. "Hitherto," he said, "the learned in Italy did not enjoy the consideration to which they were entitled—they lived retired in their laboratories and libraries, too happy if they could escape the notice, and consequently the persecution, of kings and priests. It is now no longer thus—there is no longer religious inquisition, nor despotic power. Thought is free in Italy. I invite the literary and scientific persons to consult together, and propose to me their ideas on the subject of giving new vigour and life to the fine arts and sciences. All who desire to visit France will be received with distinction by the government. The people of France have more pride in enrolling among their citizens a skilful mathematician, a painter of reputation, a distinguished man in any class of literature, than in adding to their territories a large and wealthy city. I request, citizen, that you will make my sentiments known to the most distinguished literary persons in the state of Milan."[235] To the municipality of Pavia he wrote, desiring that the professors of their celebrated university should resume their course of instruction under the security of his protection, and inviting them to point out to him such measures as might occur, for giving a more brilliant existence to their ancient seminaries.

The interest which he thus took in the literature and literary institutions of Italy was shown by admitting men of science or letters freely to his person. Their communication was the more flattering, that being himself of Italian descent, and familiar with the beautiful language of the country from his infancy, his conversation with men of literary eminence was easily conducted. It may be mentioned episodically, that Napoleon found a remnant of his

---

[234] "At St. Helena Napoleon had preserved a distinct recollection of this celebrated man. He described his timidity and embarrassment at the sight of the stately retinue of the staff, which quite dazzled him: 'You are here with your friends; we honour learning, and only wish to show the respect we entertain for it!'—'Ah! general, excuse me, but this splendour quite overpowers me!' He, however, recovered his self-possession, and held with Napoleon a long conversation, which produced in his mind a feeling of surprise, such as he could not for a long time overcome. He was unable to conceive how it was possible to have acquired, at the age of twenty-six, so much glory and science."—Antommarchi, tom. i., p. 368.

[235] Antommarchi, tom. i., p. 367.

family in Italy, in the person of the Abbate Gregorio Buonaparte, the only remaining branch of that Florentine family, of whom the Corsican line were cadets. He resided at San Miniato, of which he was canon, and was an old man, and said to be wealthy. The relationship was eagerly acknowledged, and the general, with his whole staff, dined with the Canon Gregorio. The whole mind of the old priest was wrapt up in a project of obtaining the honours of regular canonization for one of the family called Bonaventura, who had been a Capuchin in the seventeenth century, and was said to have died in the odour of sanctity, though his right to divine honours had never been acknowledged.[236] It must have been ludicrous enough to have heard the old man insist upon a topic so uninteresting to Napoleon, and press the French republican general to use his interest with the Pope. There can be little doubt that the holy father, to have escaped other demands, would have canonized a whole French regiment of Carmagnoles, and ranked them with the old militia of the calendar, the Theban Legion. But Napoleon was sensible that any request on such a subject coming from him, would be only ludicrous.[237]

POLITIC CONDUCT

The progress which Buonaparte made personally in the favour of the Italians, was, doubtless, a great assistance to the propagation of the new doctrines which were connected with the French Revolution, and was much aided by the trust which he seemed desirous to repose in the natives of the country. He retained, no doubt, in his own hands, the ultimate decision of every thing of consequence; but in matters of ordinary importance, he permitted and encouraged the Italians to act for themselves, in a manner they had not been accustomed to under their German masters. The internal government of their towns was intrusted to provisional

---

[236] Antommarchi, tom. i., p. 135.
[237] Las Cases says, that afterwards the Pope himself touched on the same topic, and was disposed to see the immediate guidance and protection afforded by the consanguinean Saint Bonaventura in the great deeds wrought by his relation. It was said of the church-endowing saint, David King of Scotland, that he was a sore saint for the Crown; certainly, Saint Bonaventura must have been a sore saint for the Papal See. The old abbé left Napoleon his fortune, which he conferred on some public institution.—S.

governors, chosen without respect to rank, and the maintenance of police was committed to the armed burghers, or national guards. Conscious of the importance annexed to these privileges, they already became impatient for national liberty. Napoleon could hardly rein back the intense ardour of the large party among the Lombards who desired an immediate declaration of independence, and he had no other expedient left than to amuse them with procrastinating excuses, which enhanced their desire of such an event, while they delayed its gratification. Other towns of Italy,—for it was among the citizens of the towns that these sentiments were chiefly cultivated,—began to evince the same wish to new-model their governments on the revolutionary system; and this ardour was chiefly shown on the southern side of the Po.

It must be remembered, that Napoleon had engaged in treaty with the Duke of Modena, and had agreed to guarantee his principality, on payment of immense contributions in money and stores, besides the surrender of the most valuable treasures of his museum. In consequence, the Duke of Modena was permitted to govern his states by a regency, he himself fixing his residence in Venice. But his two principal towns, Reggio and Modena, especially the former, became desirous of shaking off his government. Anticipating in doing so the approbation of the French general and government, the citizens of Reggio rose in insurrection, expelled from their town a body of the ducal troops, and planted the tree of liberty, resolved, as they said, to constitute themselves a free state, under the protection of the French Republic. The ducal regency, with a view of protecting Modena from a similar attempt, mounted cannon on their ramparts, and took other defensive measures.

Buonaparte affected to consider these preparations as designed against the French; and marching a body of troops, took possession of the city without resistance, deprived the duke of all the advantages which he had purchased by the mediation of the celebrated Saint Jerome, and declared the town under protection of France. Bologna and Ferrara, legations appertaining to the Papal See, had been already occupied by French troops, and placed under the management of a committee of their citizens. They were now encouraged to coalesce with Reggio and Modena. A congress of a hundred delegates from the four districts was summoned, to effect the formation of a government which should extend over them all. The congress met accordingly, engaged their constituents in a perpetual union, under title of the Cispadane Republic, from their situation on the right of the river Po; thus assuming the character of independence, while in fact they remained under the authority of Buonaparte, like clay in the hands of the potter, who may ultimately model it into any shape he has a mind. In the meantime, he was careful to remind them, that the liberty which it was desirable to establish, ought to be consistent with due subjection to the laws. "Never forget," he said, in reply to their address announcing their new form of government, "that laws are mere nullities without the force necessary to support them. Attend to your military organization, which you have the means of placing on a respectable footing—you will be more fortunate than the people of France, for you will arrive at liberty without passing through the ordeal of revolution."[238]

This was not the language of a Jacobin; and it fortifies the belief, that even now, while adhering ostensibly to the republican system, Buonaparte anticipated considerable changes in that of France.

Meanwhile the Lombards betrayed much uneasiness at seeing their neighbours outstrip them in the path of revolution, and of nominal independence. The municipality of Milan proceeded to destroy all titles of honour, as a badge of feudal dependence, and became so impatient, that Buonaparte was obliged to pacify them by a solemn assurance that they should speedily enjoy the benefits of a Republican constitution; and, to tranquillize their irritation, placed them under the government of a provisional council, selected from all classes, labourers included.

Jan. 3.

This measure made it manifest, that the motives which had induced the delay of the French Government to recognise the independence (as they termed it) of Lombardy, were now of less

---

[238] Montholon, tom. iii., p. 382; tom. iv., p. 179.

force; and in a short time, the provisional council of Milan, after some modest doubts on their own powers, revolutionized their country, and assumed the title of the Transpadane Republic, which they afterwards laid aside, when, on their union with the Cispadane, both were united under the name of the Cisalpine Commonwealth. This decisive step was adopted 3d January, 1797. Decrees of a popular character had preceded the declaration of independence, but an air of moderation was observed in the revolution itself. The nobles, deprived of their feudal rights and titular dignities, were subjected to no incapacities; the reformation of the Church was touched upon gently, and without indicating any design of its destruction. In these particulars, the Italian commonwealth stopped short of their Gallic prototype.[239]

NEGOTIATIONS WITH THE POPE

If Buonaparte may be justly charged with want of faith, in destroying the authority of the Duke of Modena, after having accepted of a price for granting him peace and protection, we cannot object to him the same charge for acceding to the Transpadane Republic, in so far as it detached the legations of Ferrara and Bologna from the Roman See. These had been in a great measure reserved for the disposal of the French, as circumstances should dictate, when a final treaty should take place betwixt the Republic and the Sovereign Pontiff. But many circumstances had retarded this pacification, and seemed at length likely to break it off without hope of renewal.

If Buonaparte is correct in his statement, which we see no reason to doubt, the delay of a pacification with the Roman See was chiefly the fault of the Directory, whose avaricious and engrossing spirit was at this period its most distinguishing characteristic. An armistice, purchased by treasure, by contributions, by pictures and statues, and by the cession of the two legations of Bologna and Ferrara, having been mediated for his Holiness by the Spanish ambassador Azara, the Pope sent two plenipotentiaries to Paris to treat of a definitive peace. But the conditions proposed were so

---

[239] Montholon, tom. v., p. 179.

severe, that however desperate his condition, the Pope found them totally inadmissible. His Holiness was required to pay a large contribution in grain for ten years, a regular tribute of six millions of Roman crowns for six years, to cede to France in perpetuity the ports of Ancona and Civita Vecchia, and to declare the independence of Ferrara, Bologna, and Ravenna. To add insult to oppression, the total cession of the Clementine Museum was required, and it was stipulated that France should have under management of her minister at Rome, a separate tribunal for judging her subjects, and a separate theatre for their amusement. Lastly, the secular sovereignty of the dominions of the Church was to be executed by a senate and a popular body.[240]

These demands might have been complied with, although they went the length of entirely stripping his Holiness of the character of a secular prince. But there were others made on him, in his capacity of head of the Church, which he could not grant, if he meant in future to lay claim to any authority under that once venerable title. The Sovereign Pontiff was required to recall all the briefs which he had issued against France since 1789, to sanction the constitutional oath which released the French clergy from the dominion of the Holy See, and to ratify the confiscation of the church-lands. Treasures might be expended, secular dignities resigned, and provinces ceded; but it was clear that the Sovereign Pontiff could not do what was expressly contrary to the doctrines of the Church which he represented. There were but few clergymen in France who had hesitated to prove their devotion to the Church of Rome, by submitting to expulsion, rather than take the constitutional oath. It was now for the Head of the Church to show in his own person a similar disinterested devotion to her interests.

Accordingly, the College of Cardinals having rejected the proposals of France, as containing articles contrary to conscience, the Pope declared his determination to abide by the utmost extremity, rather than accede to conditions destructive, degrading, and, in his opinion, impious. The Directory instantly determined on the total ruin of the Pope, and of his power, both spiritual and temporal.

---

[240] Montholon, tom. iii., p. 384.

Napoleon dissented from the opinion of the Government. In point of moral effect, a reconciliation with the Pope would have been of great advantage to France, and have tended to reunite her with other Catholic nations, and diminish the horror with which she was regarded as sacrilegious and atheistical. Even the army of the Holy See was not altogether to be despised, in case of any reverse taking place in the war with the Austrians. Under these considerations, he prevailed on the Directory to renew the negotiations at Florence.[241] But the French commissioners, having presented as preliminaries sixty indispensable conditions, containing the same articles which had been already rejected, as contrary to the conscience of the Pontiff, the conferences broke up; and the Pope, in despair, resolved to make common cause with the House of Austria, and have recourse to the secular force, which the Roman See had disused for so many years.[242]

It was a case of dire necessity; but the arming of the Pope's government, whose military force had been long the subject of ridicule,[243] against the victorious conqueror of five Austrian armies, reminds us of Priam, when, in extremity of years and despair, he buckled on his rusty armour, to oppose age and decrepitude to the youthful strength of Pyrrhus.[244] Yet the measures of Sextus indicated considerable energy. He brought back to Rome an instalment of sixteen millions of stipulated tribute, which was on the road to Buonaparte's military chest—took every measure to increase his army, and by the voluntary exertions of the noble families of Rome, he actually raised it to forty thousand men, and placed at its head the same General Colli, who had commanded with credit the troops of Sardinia during the campaign on the Alps. The utmost pains were

---

[241] Montholon, tom. iii., p. 386.
[242] Thibaudeau, tom. ii., p. 55; Letter de Cacault à Buonaparte, Correspondence Inédite, tom. ii., pp. 114-125; Montholon, tom. iii., p. 387.
[243] Voltaire, in one of his romances, terms the Pope an old gentleman, having a guard of one hundred men, who mount guard with umbrellas, and who make war on nobody.—S.
[244] "Arma diu senior desueta trementibus ævo Circumdat nequicquam humeris, et inutile ferrum Cingitur"——
Æneid, Lib. II.
"He—when he saw his regal town on fire, His ruin'd palace, and his entering foes, On every side inevitable woes; In arms disused invests his limbs, decay'd, Like them, with age; a late and useless aid."
Dryden.

taken by the clergy, both regular and secular, to give the expected war the character of a crusade, and to excite the fierce spirit of those peasantry who inhabit the Apennines, and were doubly disposed to be hostile to the French, as foreigners and as heretics. The Pope endeavoured also to form a close alliance with the King of the Two Sicilies, who promised in secret to cover Rome with an army of thirty thousand men. Little reliance was indeed to be placed in the good faith of the Court of Naples; but the Pope was compared, by the French envoy, Cacault,[245] to a man who, in the act of falling, would grasp for support at a hook of red-hot iron.[246]

INVASION OF THE PAPAL TERRITORIES

While the Court of Rome showed this hostile disposition, Napoleon reproached the French Government for having broken off the negotiation, which they ought to have protracted till the event of Alvinzi's march into Italy was known; at all events, until their general had obtained possession of the sixteen millions, so much wanted to pay his forces. In reply to his remonstrances, he received permission to renew the negotiations upon modified terms. But the Pope had gone too far to recede. Even the French victory of Arcola, and the instant threats of Buonaparte to march against him at the head of a flying column, were unable to move his resolution. "Let the French general march upon Rome," said the Papal minister; "the Pope, if necessary, will quit his capital. The farther the French are drawn from the Adige, the nearer they are to their ultimate destruction."[247] Napoleon was sensible, on receiving a hostile answer, that the Pope still relied on the last preparations which were made for the relief of Mantua, and it was not safe to attempt his chastisement until Alvinzi and Provera should be disposed of. But the decisive battles of Rivoli and La Favorita having ruined these armies, Napoleon was at leisure to execute his purpose of crushing the power, such as it was, of the Holy See. For this purpose he

---

[245] Cacault was born at Nantes in 1742. During the Consulate, he was chosen a member of the Senate. He published a translation of Lessing's Historical Sketch of the Drama. He died in 1805.

[246] "La cour de Rome, au desespoir, saisirait un fer rouge: elle s'abandonne à l'impulsion bruyante des Napolitains."—*Correspondence Inédite*, tom. ii., p. 119.

[247] Montholon, tom. iii., p. 387.

despatched Victor with a French division of four thousand men, and an Italian army of nearly the same force, supplied by Lombardy and by the Transpadane republic, to invade the Territories of the Church on the eastern side of Italy, by the route of Imola.

Feb. 3.

Meantime, the utmost exertions had been made by the clergy of Romagna, to raise the peasants in a mass, and a great many obeyed the sound of the tocsin. But an insurrectionary force is more calculated to embarrass the movements of a regular army, by alarms on their flanks and rear, by cutting off their communications, and destroying their supplies, defending passes, and skirmishing in advantageous positions, than by opposing them in the open field. The Papal army, consisting of about seven or eight thousand men, were encamped on the river Senio, which runs on the southward of the town of Imola, to dispute the passage. The banks were defended with cannon; but the river being unusually low, the French crossed about a league and a half higher up than the position of the Roman army, which, taken in the rear, fled in every direction, after a short resistance. A few hundreds were killed, among whom were several monks, who, holding the crucifix in their hand, had placed themselves in the ranks to encourage the soldiers. Faenza stood out and was taken by storm; but the soldiers were withheld from pillage by the generosity or prudence of Napoleon,[248] and he dismissed the prisoners of war[249] to carry into the interior of the country the news of their own defeat, of the irresistible superiority of the French army, and of the clemency of their general.[250]

Feb. 4.

---

[248] "This is the same thing as happened at Pavia," said the soldiers, by way of demanding the pillage of the place. "No," answered Napoleon; "at Pavia they had revolted after taking an oath, and they wanted to massacre our soldiers who were their guests. These are only senseless people, who must be conquered by clemency."—Montholon, tom. iv., p. 18.

[249] Napoleon addressed them thus in Italian—"I am the friend of all the nations of Italy, and particularly of the people of Rome. You are free; return to your families, and tell them that the French are the friends of religion, order, and the poor."—Montholon, tom. iv., p. 19.

[250] Jomini, tom. ix., p. 307; Montholon, tom. iv., p. 7; Thibaudeau, tom. ii., p. 220.

Next day, three thousand of the Papal troops, occupying an advantageous position in front of Ancona, and commanded by Colli, were made prisoners without firing a shot; and Ancona was taken after slight resistance, though a place of some strength. A curious piece of priestcraft had been played off in this town, to encourage the people to resistance. A miraculous image was seen to shed tears, and the French artists could not discover the mode in which the trick was managed until the image was brought to headquarters, when a glass shrine, by which the illusion was managed, was removed. The Madonna was sent back to the church which owned her, but apparently had become reconciled to the foreign visitors, and dried her tears in consequence of her interview with Buonaparte.[251]

CAPTURE OF LORETTO

On the 10th of February, the French, moving with great celerity, entered Loretto, where the celebrated Santa Casa is the subject of the Catholic's devotional triumph, or secret scorn, according as his faith or his doubts predominate. The wealth which this celebrated shrine is once supposed to have possessed by gifts of the faithful, had been removed by Colli—if, indeed, it had not been transported to Rome long before the period of which we treat; yet, precious metal and gems to the amount of a million of livres, fell into the possession of the French, whose capture was also enriched by the holy image of our Lady of Loretto, with the sacred porringer, and a bedgown of dark-coloured camlet, warranted to have belonged to the Blessed Virgin.[252] This image, said to have been of celestial workmanship, was sent to Paris, but was restored to the Pope in 1802. We are not informed that any of the treasures were given back along with the Madonna, to whom they had been devoted.

---

[251] "Monge was sent to the spot. He reported that the Madonna actually wept. The chapter received orders to bring her to headquarters. It was an optical illusion, ingeniously managed by means of a glass."—Montholon, tom. iv., p. 12.
[252] "It is a wooden statue clumsily carved; a proof of its antiquity. It was to be seen for some years at the National Library."—Montholon, tom. iv., p. 13.

As the French army advanced upon the Roman territory, there was a menace of the interference of the King of Naples, worthy to be mentioned, both as expressing the character of that court, and showing Napoleon's readiness in anticipating and defeating the arts of indirect diplomacy.

The Prince of Belmonte-Pignatelli, who attended Buonaparte's headquarters, in the capacity, perhaps, of an observer, as much as of ambassador for Naples, came to the French general in secrecy, to show him, under strict confidence, a letter of the Queen of the Two Sicilies, proposing to march an army of thirty thousand men towards Rome. "Your confidence shall be repaid," said Buonaparte, who at once saw through the spirit of the communication—"You shall know what I have long since settled to do in case of such an event taking place." He called for the portfolio containing the papers respecting Naples, and presented to the disconcerted Prince the copy of a despatch written in November preceding, which contained this passage:—"the approach of Alvinzi would not prevent my sending six thousand men to chastise the court of Rome; but as the Neapolitan army might march to their assistance, I will postpone this movement till after the surrender of Mantua; in which case, if the King of Naples should interfere, I shall be able to spare twenty-five thousand men to march against his capital, and drive him over to Sicily." Prince Pignatelli was quite satisfied with the result of this mutual confidence, and there was no more said of Neapolitan armed interference.[253]

From Ancona, the division commanded by Victor turned westward to Foligno, to unite itself with another column of French which penetrated into the territories of the Church by Perugia, which they easily accomplished. Resistance seemed now unavailing. The Pope in vain solicited his subjects to rise against the second Alaric, who was approaching the Holy City. They remained deaf to his exhortations, though made in the names of the Blessed Virgin, and of the Apostles Peter and Paul, who had of old been the visible protectors of the metropolis of the Christian world in a similar emergency. All was dismay and confusion in the patrimony of Saint

---

[253] Jomini, tom. ix., p. 311; Thibaudeau, tom. iii., p. 228.

Peter's, which was now the sole territory remaining in possession of his representative.

But there was an unhappy class of persons, who had found shelter in Rome, rather than disown whose allegiance they had left their homes, and resigned their means of living. These were the recusant French clergy, who had refused to take the constitutional oath and who now, recollecting the scenes which they witnessed in France, expected little else, than that, on the approach of the Republican troops, they would, like the Israelitish captain, be slain between the horns of the very altar at which they had taken refuge. It is said that one of their number, frantic at the thoughts of the fate which he supposed awaited them, presented himself to Buonaparte, announced his name and condition, and prayed to be led to instant death. Napoleon took the opportunity to show once more that he was acting on principles different from the brutal and persecuting spirit of Jacobinism. He issued a proclamation, in which, premising that the recusant priests, though banished from the French territory, were not prohibited from residing in countries which might be conquered by the French arms, he declares himself satisfied with their conduct. The proclamation goes on to prohibit, under the most severe penalty, the French soldiery, and all other persons, from doing any injury to these unfortunate exiles. The convents are directed to afford them lodging, nourishment, and fifteen French livres (twelve shillings and sixpence British) monthly, to each individual, for which the priest was to compensate by saying masses *ad valorem*;—thus assigning the Italian convents payment for their hospitality, in the same coin with which they themselves requited the laity.

Perhaps this liberality might have some weight with the Pope in inducing him to throw himself upon the mercy of France, as had been recommended to him by Buonaparte in a confidential communication through the superior of the monastic order of Camalduli, and more openly in a letter addressed to Cardinal Mattei. The King of Naples made no movement to his assistance. In fine, after hesitating what course to take, and having had at one time his equipage ready harnessed to leave Rome and fly to Naples, the Pontiff judged resistance and flight alike unavailing, and chose the humiliating alternative of entire submission to the will of the conqueror.

It was the object of the Directory entirely to destroy the secular authority of the Pope, and to deprive him of all his temporalities. But Buonaparte foresaw, that whether the Roman territories were united with the new Cispadane republic, or formed into a separate state, it would alike bring on prematurely a renewal of the war with Naples, ere the north of Italy was yet sufficiently secure to admit the marching a French force into the southern extremities of the Italian peninsula, exposed to descents of the English, and insurrections in the rear. These Napoleon foresaw would be the more dangerous and difficult to subdue, that, though he might strip the Pope of his temporalities, he could not deprive him of the supremacy assigned him in spiritual matters by each Catholic; which, on the contrary, was, according to the progress of human feeling, likely to be the more widely felt and recognised in favour of a wanderer and a sufferer for what would be accounted conscience-sake, than of one who, submitting to circumstances, retained as much of the goods of this world as the clemency of his conqueror would permit.[254]

TREATY OF TOLENTINA

Influenced by these considerations, Buonaparte admitted the Pope to a treaty, which terminated in the peace of Tolentino, by which Sextus purchased such a political existence as was left to him, at the highest rate which he had the least chance of discharging. Napoleon mentions, as a curious instance of the crafty and unscrupulous character of the Neapolitans, that the same Pignatelli, whom we have already commemorated, attached himself closely to the plenipotentiaries during the whole treaty of Tolentino; and in his ardour to discover whether there existed any secret article betwixt the Pope and Buonaparte which might compromise the interests of

---

[254] Montholon, tom. iv., p. 16.

his master, was repeatedly discovered listening at the door of the apartment in which the discussions were carried on.[255]

Feb. 19.

The articles which the Pope was obliged to accept at Tolentino,[256] included the cession of Avignon and its territories, the appropriation of which by France, had never yet been recognised; the resigning the legations of Bologna, Ferrara, and Romagna; the occupation of Ancona, the only port excepting Venice, which Italy has in the Adriatic; the payment of thirty millions of livres, in specie or in valuable effects; the complete execution of the article in the armistice of Bologna respecting the delivery of paintings, manuscripts, and objects of art; and several other stipulations of similar severity.[257]

Buonaparte informs us, that it was a principal object in this treaty to compel the abolition of the Inquisition, from which he had only departed in consequence of receiving information, that it had ceased to be used as a religious tribunal, and subsisted only as a court of police. The conscience of the Pope seemed also so tenderly affected by the proposal, that he thought it safe to desist from it.

The same despatch, in which Buonaparte informs the Directory, that his committee of artist collectors "had made a good harvest of paintings in the Papal dominions, and which, with the objects of art ceded by the Pope, included almost all that was curious and valuable, excepting some few objects at Turin and Naples," conveyed to them a document of a very different kind. This was a respectful and almost reverential letter from Napoleon to the Pope,[258] recommending to his Holiness to distrust such persons

---

[255] Montholon, tom. iv., p. 25.
[256] For a copy of the Treaty of Tolentino, see Annual Register, vol. xxxix., p. 328, and Montholon, tom. iv., p. 18.
[257] "One of the negotiators of the Pope observed to Buonaparte that he was the only Frenchman who had marched against Rome since the Constable Bourbon; but what rendered this circumstance still more singular was, that the history of the first expedition, under the title of 'The Sacking of Rome' was written by Jacopo Buonaparte, an ancestor of him who executed the second."—Las Cases, tom. i., p. 98.
[258] "The Directory adopted the most insulting forms in communicating with the Pope; the general wrote to him with respect. The Directory endeavoured to overthrow the authority

as might excite him to doubt the good intentions of France, assuring him that he would always find the Republic most sincere and faithful, and expressing in his own name the perfect esteem and veneration which he entertained for the person of his Holiness, and the extreme desire which he had to afford him proofs to that effect.[259]

This letter furnished much amusement at the time, and seemed far less to intimate the sentiments of a sans-culotte general, than those of a civilized highwayman of the old school of Macheath, who never dismissed the travellers whom he had plundered, without his sincere good wishes for the happy prosecution of their journey.

REPUBLIC OF SAN MARINO

A more pleasing view of Buonaparte's character was exhibited about this time, in his conduct towards the little interesting republic of San Marino. That state, which only acknowledges the Pope as a protector, not as a sovereign, had maintained for very many years an independence, which conquerors had spared either in contempt or in respect. It consists of a single mountain and a single town, and boasts about seven thousand inhabitants, governed by their own laws. Citizen Monge, the chief of the committee of collecting artists, was sent deputy to San Marino to knit the bands of amity between the two republics,—which might well resemble a union between Lilliput and Brobdingnag. There were no pictures in the little republic, or they might have been a temptation to the citizen collector. The people of San Marino conducted themselves with much sagacity; and although more complimentary to Buonaparte than Diogenes to Alexander the Great, when he came to visit the philosopher in his tub, they showed the same judgment in eschewing too much courtesy.[260] They respectfully declined an accession of territory, which could but have involved them in subsequent quarrels with the sovereign from whom it was to be

---

of the Pope; Napoleon preserved it. The Directory banished and proscribed priests; Napoleon commanded his soldiers, wherever they might fall in with them, to remember that they were Frenchmen and their brothers."—Las Cases, tom. i., p. 170.
[259] Montholon, tom. iv., p. 25; Thibaudeau, tom. ii., p. 287.
[260] Botta, tom. ii., p. 199; Thibaudeau, tom. ii., p. 239.

wrested, and only accepted as an honorary gift the present of four field pieces, being a train of artillery upon the scale of their military force, and of which, it is to be hoped, the Captain Regents of the little contented state will never have any occasion to make use.[261]

Rome might, for the present at least, be considered as completely subjugated. Naples was at peace, if the signature of a treaty can create peace. At any rate, so distant from Rome, and so controlled by the defeat of the Papal arms—by the fear that the English fleet might be driven from the Mediterranean—and by their distance from the scene of action—the King of the Two Sicilies, or rather his wife, the high-spirited daughter of Maria Theresa, dared not offer the least interference with the purposes of the French general. Tuscany had apparently consented to owe her political existence to any degree of clemency or contempt which Buonaparte might extend to her; and, entertaining hopes of some convention betwixt the French and English, by which the grand duke's port of Leghorn might be restored to him, remained passive as the dead. The republic of Venice alone, feeling still the stimulus arising from her ancient importance, and yet painfully conscious of her present want of power, strained every exertion to place herself in a respectable attitude. That city of lofty remembrances, the Tyre of the middle ages, whose traders were princes, and her merchants the honourable of the earth, fallen as she was from her former greatness, still presented some appearance of vigour. Her oligarchical government, so long known and so dreaded, for jealous precautions, political sagacity, the impenetrability of their plans, and the inflexibility of their rigour, still preserved the attitude of independence, and endeavoured, by raising additional regiments of Sclavonians, disciplining their peasantry, who were of a very martial character, and forming military magazines of considerable extent, to maintain such an aspect as might make their friendship to be courted, and their enmity to be feared. It was already evident that the Austrians, notwithstanding all their recent defeats, were again about to make head on their Italo-German frontier; and France, in opposing them, could not be indifferent to the neutrality of Venice, upon whose territories, to all appearance, Buonaparte must have

---

[261] For an interesting sketch of the republic of San Marino, see Seward's *Anecdotes of Distinguished Persons*, vol. iii., p. 276.

rested the flank of his operations, in case of his advancing towards Friuli. So circumstanced, and when it was recollected that the mistress of the Adriatic had still fifty thousand men at her command, and those of a fierce and courageous description, chiefly consisting of Sclavonians, Venice, even yet, was an enemy not to be lightly provoked. But the inhabitants were not unanimous, especially those of the Terra Firma, or mainland, who, not being enrolled in the golden book of the insular nobility of Venice, were discontented, and availed themselves of the encouragement and assistance of the new-created republics on the Po to throw off their allegiance. Brescia and Bergamo, in particular, were clamorous for independence.

Napoleon saw, in this state of dissension, the means of playing an adroit game; and while, on the one hand, he endeavoured to restrain, till a more favourable opportunity, the ardour of the patriots, he attempted on the other, to convince the Senate, that they had no safe policy but in embracing at once the alliance of France, offensive and defensive, and joining their forces to those of the army with which he was about to move against the Austrians. He offered, on these conditions, to guarantee the possessions of the republic, even without exacting any modification of their oligarchical constitution. But Venice declared for an impartial neutrality.[262] It had been, they said, their ancient and sage policy, nor would they now depart from it. "Remain then neuter," said Napoleon; "I consent to it. I march upon Vienna, yet will leave enough of French troops in Italy to control your republic.—But dismiss these new levies; and remark, that if, while I am in Germany, my communications shall be interrupted, my detachments cut off, or my convoys intercepted in the Venetian territories, the date of your republic is terminated. She will have brought on herself annihilation."[263]

Lest these threats should be forgotten while he was at a distance, he took the best precautions in his power, by garrisoning advantageous points on the line of the Adige; and trusting partly to this defence, partly to the insurgents of Bergamo and Brescia, who,

---

[262] Botta, tom. ii., p. 252; Daru, Hist. de Venise, tom. v., p. 544.
[263] Montholon, tom. iv., p. 130.

for their own sakes, would oppose any invasion of the mainland by their Venetian masters, whose yoke they had cast aside, Napoleon again unfurled his banners, and marched to new triumphs over yet untried opponents.

Chapter IX

Archduke Charles—Compared with Napoleon—Fettered by the Aulic Council—Napoleon, by a stratagem, passes the Tagliamento, and compels the Archduke to retreat—Gradisca carried by storm—Chusa-Veneta taken—Trieste and Fiume occupied—Venice breaks the Neutrality—Terrified on learning that an Armistice had taken place betwixt France and Austria—The Archduke retreats by hasty marches on Vienna—The Government irresolute—and the Treaty of Leoben signed—Venice makes humiliating submissions—Napoleon's Speech to her Envoys—He declares War against Venice, and evades obeying the orders of the Directory to spare it—The Great Council, on 31st May, concede everything to Buonaparte—Terms granted.

ARCHDUKE CHARLES

The victories of the Archduke Charles on the Rhine, and his high credit with the soldiery, seemed to point him out as the commander falling most naturally to be employed against the young general of the French republic, who, like a gifted hero of romance, had borne down successively all opponents who had presented themselves in the field. The opinions of Europe were suspended concerning the probable issue of the contest. Both generals were young, ambitious, enthusiastic in the military profession, and warmly beloved by their soldiers. The exploits of both had filled the trumpet of Fame; and although Buonaparte's success had been less uninterrupted, yet it could not be denied, that if the Archduke's plans were not equally brilliant and original with those of his great adversary, they were just and sound, and had been attended repeatedly with great results, and by the defeat of such men as Moreau and Jourdan. But there were two particulars in which the Austrian prince fell far short of Napoleon,—first, in that ready, decided, and vigorous confidence, which seizes the favourable instant for the execution of plans resolved upon,—and, secondly, in having the disadvantage to be subjected, notwithstanding his high rank, to the interference of the Aulic Council; who, sitting at Vienna, and ignorant of the changes and vicissitudes of the campaign, were yet, by the ancient and jealous laws of the Austrian empire, entitled to control his opinion, and prescribe beforehand the motions of the armies, while the generals, intrusted with the execution of their schemes, had often no choice left but that of adherence to their instructions, however emerging circumstances might require a deviation.[264]

But although the encounter betwixt these two distinguished young generals be highly interesting, our space will not permit us to detail the campaigns of Austria at the same length as those of Italy. The latter formed the commencement of Buonaparte's military career, and at no subsequent period of his life did he achieve the same wondrous victories against such immense odds, or with such comparatively inadequate means. It was also necessary, in the outset of his military history, to show, in minute detail, the character of his tactics, and illustrate that spirit of energetic concentration, which, neglecting the extremities of an extended line of operations, combined his whole strength, like a bold and skilful fencer, for one thrust at a vital part, which, if successful, must needs be fatal. The astonishing rapidity of his movements, the audacious vivacity of his attack, having been so often described in individual cases, may now be passed over with general allusions; nor will we embarrass ourselves and our readers with minute details of positions, or encumber our pages with the names of obscure villages, unless when there is some battle calling for a particular narrative, either from its importance or its singularity.

By the direction of the Aulic Council, the Archduke Charles had taken up his position at Friuli, where it had been settled that the sixth Austrian army, designed to act against Buonaparte for the

---

[264] "The Aulic Council at Vienna, that pernicious tribunal which, in the Seven Years' War, called Laudon to account for taking Schweidnitz without orders, has destroyed the schemes of many an Austrian general, for though plans of offensive operations may succeed when concerted at home, it is impossible to frame orders for every possible contingency."—Gentz, *on the Fall of Prussia.*

defence of the Italo-German frontier, should be assembled. This position was strangely preferred to the Tyrol, where the Archduke could have formed a junction ten days sooner with an additional force of forty thousand men from the army of the Rhine, marching to reinforce his own troops,—men accustomed to fight and conquer under their leader's eye; whilst those with whom he occupied Friuli, and the line of the Piave, belonged to the hapless Imperial forces, which, under Beaulieu, Wurmser, and Alvinzi, had never encountered Buonaparte without incurring some notable defeat.

FRENCH PLAN OF THE CAMPAIGN

While the Archduke was yet expecting those reinforcements which were to form the strength of his army, his active adversary had been joined by more than twenty thousand men, sent from the French armies on the Rhine, and which gave him at the moment a numerical superiority over the Austrian general. Instead, therefore, of waiting, as on former occasions, until the Imperialists should commence the war by descending into Italy, Napoleon resolved to anticipate the march of the succours expected by the Archduke, drive him from his position on the Italian frontiers, and follow him into Germany, even up to the walls of Vienna. No scheme appeared too bold for the general's imagination to form, or his genius to render practicable; and his soldiers, with the view before them of plunging into the midst of an immense empire, and placing chains of mountains betwixt them and every possibility of reinforcement or communication, were so confident in the talents of their leader, as to follow him under the most undoubting expectation of victory. The Directory had induced Buonaparte to expect a co-operation by a similar advance on the part of the armies of the Rhine, as had been attempted in the former campaign.

Buonaparte took the field in the beginning of March, advancing from Bassano.[265] The Austrians had an army of

---

[265] At Bassano, on the 9th of March, Buonaparte thus addressed the troops—"Soldiers! the taking of Mantua has put an end to the war of Italy. You have been victorious in fourteen pitched battles and seventy actions; you have taken 100,000 prisoners, 500 field-pieces, 2000 heavy cannon, and four pontoon trains. The contributions laid on the countries you have conquered have fed, maintained, and paid the army; besides which you have sent

observation under Lusignan on the bank of the Piave, but their principal force was stationed upon the Tagliamento, a river whose course is nearly thirty miles more to the eastward, though collateral with the Piave. The plains on the Tagliamento afforded facilities to the Archduke to employ the noble cavalry who have always been the boast of the Austrian army; and to dislodge him from the strong country which he occupied, and which covered the road that penetrates between the mountains and the Adriatic, and forms the mode of communication in that quarter betwixt Vienna and Italy, through Carinthia, it was not only necessary that he should be pressed in front—a service which Buonaparte took upon himself—but also that a French division, occupying the mountains on the Prince's right, should precipitate his retreat, by maintaining the perpetual threat of turning him on that wing. With this view, Massena had Buonaparte's orders, which he executed with equal skill and gallantry. He crossed the Piave about the eleventh March, and ascending that river, directed his course into the mountains towards Belluno, driving before him Lusignan's little corps of observation, and finally compelling his rear-guard, to the number of five hundred men, to surrender.

The Archduke Charles, in the meantime, continued to maintain his position on the Tagliamento, and the French approached the right bank, with Napoleon at their head, determined apparently to force a passage. Artillery and sharpshooters were disposed in such a manner as to render this a very hazardous attempt, while two beautiful lines of cavalry were drawn up, prepared to charge any troops who might make their way to the left bank, while they were yet in the confusion of landing.

A very simple stratagem disconcerted this fair display of resistance. After a distant cannonade, and some skirmishing, the

---

thirty millions to the minister of finance for the use of the public treasury. You have enriched the Museum of Paris with 300 masterpieces of the arts of ancient and modern Italy, which it had required thirty centuries to produce. You have conquered for the Republic the finest countries in Europe. The Kings of Sardinia and Naples, the Pope, and the Duke of Parma, are separated from the coalition. You have expelled the English from Leghorn, Genoa, and Corsica. Yet higher destinies await you! You will prove yourselves worthy of them! Of all the foes who combined to stifle the Republic in its birth, the Emperor alone remains before you," &c.

French army drew off, as if despairing to force their passage, moved to the rear, and took up apparently their bivouac for the night. The Archduke was deceived. He imagined that the French, who had marched all the preceding night, were fatigued, and he also withdrew from the bank of the river to his camp. But two hours afterwards, when all seemed profoundly quiet, the French army suddenly got under arms, and, forming in two lines, marched rapidly to the side of the river, ere the astonished Austrians were able to make the same dispositions as formerly for defence. Arrived on the margin, the first line instantly broke up into columns, which, throwing themselves boldly into the stream, protected on the flanks by the cavalry, passed through and attained the opposite bank.[266] They were repeatedly charged by the Austrian cavalry, but it was too late—they had gotten their footing, and kept it. The Archduke attempted to turn their flank, but was prevented by the second line of the French, and by their reserve of cavalry. He was compelled to retreat, leaving prisoners and cannon in the hands of the enemy. Such was the first disastrous meeting between the Archduke Charles and his future relative.[267]

March 16.

The Austrian prince had the farther misfortune to learn, that Massena had, at the first sound of the cannonade, pushed across the Tagliamento, higher up than his line of defence, and destroying what troops he found before him, had occupied the passes of the Julian Alps at the sources of that river, and thus interposed himself between the imperial right wing and the nearest communication with Vienna. Sensible of the importance of this obstacle, the Archduke hastened, if possible, to remove it. He brought up a fine column of grenadiers from the Rhine, which had just arrived at Klagenfurt, in his rear, and joining them to other troops, attacked Massena with the utmost fury, venturing his own person like a private soldier, and once or twice narrowly escaping being made prisoner. It was in vain—all in vain. He charged successively and

---

[266] "The river is pretty deep, and a bridge would have been desirable; but the good-will of the soldiers supplied that deficiency. A drummer was the only person in danger, and he was saved by a woman who swam after him."—Montholon, tom. iv., p. 73.
[267] Montholon, tom. iv., p. 72; Jomini, tom. x., p. 33.

repeatedly, even with the reserve of the grenadiers, but no exertion could change the fortune of the day.[268]

March 19.

Still the Archduke hoped to derive assistance from the natural or artificial defences of the strong country through which he was thus retreating, and in doing so was involuntarily introducing Buonaparte, after he should have surmounted the border frontier into the most fertile provinces of his brother's empire. The Lisonzo, usually a deep and furious torrent, closed in by a chain of impassable mountains, seemed to oppose an insurmountable barrier to his daring pursuers. But nature, as well as events, fought against the Austrians. The stream, reduced by frost, was fordable in several places. The river thus passed, the town of Gradisca, which had been covered with field-works to protect the line of the Lisonzo, was surprised and carried by storm, and its garrison of two thousand five hundred men made prisoners, by the divisions of Bernadotte and Serrurier.

Pushed in every direction, the Austrians sustained every day additional and more severe losses. The strong fort of Chiusa-Veneta was occupied by Massena, who continued his active and indefatigable operations on the right of the retreating army. This success caused the envelopement, and dispersion or surrender, of a whole division of Austrians, five thousand of whom remained prisoners, while their baggage, cannon, colours, and all that constituted them an army, fell into the hands of the French. Four generals were made prisoners on this occasion; and many of the mountaineers of Carniola and Croatia, who had joined the Austrian army from their natural love of war, seeing that success appeared to have abandoned the imperial cause, became despondent, broke up their corps, and retired as stragglers to their villages.

---

[268] Jomini, tom. x., p, 38; Montholon, tom. iv., p. 77.

TRIESTE AND FIUME

Buonaparte availed himself of their loss of courage, and had recourse to proclamations, a species of arms which he valued himself as much upon using to advantage, as he did upon his military fame. He assured them that the French did not come into their country to innovate on their rights, religious customs, and manners. He exhorted them not to meddle in a war with which they had no concern, but encouraged them to afford assistance and furnish supplies to the French army, in payment of which he proposed to assign the public taxes which they had been in the habit of paying to the Emperor.[269] His proposal seems to have reconciled the Carinthians to the presence of the French, or, more properly speaking, they submitted to the military exactions which they had no means of resisting.[270] In the meanwhile, the French took possession of Trieste and Fiume, the only seaports belonging to Austria, where they seized much English merchandise, which was always a welcome prize, and of the quicksilver mines of Idria, where they found a valuable deposit of that mineral.

Napoleon repaired the fortifications of Klagenfurt, and converted it into a respectable place of arms, where he established his headquarters. In a space of scarce twenty days, he had defeated the Austrians in ten combats, in the course of which Prince Charles had lost at least one-fourth of his army. The French had surmounted the southern chain of the Julian Alps; the northern line could, it was supposed, offer no obstacle sufficient to stop their irresistible general; and the Archduke, the pride and hope of the Austrian armies, had retired behind the river Mehur, and seemed to be totally without the means of covering Vienna.

There were, however, circumstances less favourable to the French, which require to be stated. When the campaign commenced, the French general Joubert was posted with his

---

[269] Montholon, tom. iv., p. 81.
[270] "No extraordinary contribution was levied, and the inhabitants gave no occasion for complaint of any kind. The English merchandise at Trieste was confiscated. Quicksilver, to the value of several millions, from the mine of Idria, was found in the imperial warehouses."—Montholon, tom. iv., p. 82.

division in the gorge of the Tyrol above Trent, upon the same river Levisa, the line of which had been lost and won during the preceding winter. He was opposed by the Austrian generals Kerpen and Laudon, who, besides some regular regiments, had collected around them a number of the Tyrolese militia, who among their own mountains were at least equally formidable. They remained watching each other during the earlier part of the campaign; but the gaining of the battle of the Tagliamento was the signal for Joubert to commence the offensive. His directions were to push his way through the Tyrol to Brixen, at which place Napoleon expected he might hear news of the advance of the French armies from the Rhine, to co-operate in the march upon Vienna. But the Directory, fearing perhaps to trust nearly the whole force of the Republic in the hands of a general so successful and so ambitious as Napoleon, had not fulfilled their promises in this respect. The army of Moreau had not as yet crossed the Rhine.

Joubert, thus disappointed of his promised object, began to find himself in an embarrassing situation. The whole country was in insurrection around him, and a retreat in the line by which he had advanced, might have exposed him to great loss, if not to destruction. He determined, therefore, to elude the enemy, and by descending the river Drave, to achieve a junction with his commander-in-chief Napoleon. He accomplished his difficult march by breaking down the bridges behind him, and thus arresting the progress of the enemy; but it was with difficulty, and not without loss, that he effected his proposed union, and his retreat from the Tyrol gave infinite spirits not only to the martial Tyrolese, but to all the favourers of Austria in the North of Italy. The Austrian general Laudon sallied from the Tyrol at the head of a considerable force, and compelled the slender body of French under Balland, to shut themselves up in garrisons; and their opponents were for the moment again lords of a part of Lombardy. They also re-occupied Trieste and Fiume, which Buonaparte had not been able sufficiently to garrison; so that the rear of the French army seemed to be endangered.[271]

---

[271] Jomini, tom. x., p. 56; Montholon, tom. iv., p. 83.

The Venetians, at this crisis, fatally for their ancient republic, if indeed its doom had not, as is most likely, been long before sealed, received with eager ears the accounts, exaggerated as they were by rumour, that the French were driven from the Tyrol, and the Austrians about to descend the Adige, and resume their ancient empire in Italy. The Senate were aware that neither their government nor their persons were acceptable to the French general, and that they had offended him irreconcilably by declining the intimate alliance and contribution of troops which he had demanded. He had parted from them with such menaces as were not easily to be misunderstood. They believed, if his vengeance might not be instant, it was only the more sure; and conceiving him now deeply engaged in Germany, and surrounded by the Austrian levies en masse from the warlike countries of Hungary and Croatia, they imagined that throwing their own weight into the scale at so opportune a moment, must weigh it down for ever. To chastise their insurgent subjects of Bergamo and Brescia, was an additional temptation.

April 16.

Their mode of making war savoured of the ancient vindictive temper ascribed to their countrymen. An insurrection was secretly organized through all the territories which Venice still possessed on the mainland, and broke out, like the celebrated Sicilian vespers, in blood and massacre. In Verona they assassinated more than a hundred Frenchmen, many of them sick soldiers in the hospitals[272]—an abominable cruelty which could not fail to bring a curse on their undertaking. Fioravante, a Venetian general, marched at the head of a body of Sclavonians to besiege the forts of Verona, into which the remaining French had made their retreat, and where they defended themselves. Laudon made his appearance with his Austrians and Tyrolese, and it seemed as if the fortunes of Buonaparte had at length found a check.

---

[272] See the report of the agents of the Venetian government.—Daru, tom. v., p. 584. Napoleon says, "the fury of the people carried them so far as to murder *four hundred sick in the hospitals.*"—Montholon, tom. iv., p. 133.

OVERTURES OF PEACE

But the awakening from this pleasing dream was equally sudden and dreadful. News arrived that preliminaries of peace had been agreed upon, and an armistice signed between France and Austria. Laudon, therefore, and the auxiliaries on whom the Venetians had so much relied, retired from Verona. The Lombards sent an army to the assistance of the French. The Sclavonians, under Fioravante, after fighting vigorously, were compelled to surrender. The insurgent towns of Vicenza, Treviso, and Padua, were again occupied by the Republicans. Rumour proclaimed the terrible return of Napoleon and his army, and the ill-advised Senate of Venice were lost in stupor, and scarce had sense left to decide betwixt unreserved submission and hopeless defence.

It was one of the most artful rules in Buonaparte's policy, that when he had his enemy at decided advantage, by some point having been attained which seemed to give a complete turn to the campaign in his favour, he seldom failed to offer peace, and peace upon conditions much more favourable than perhaps the opposite party expected. By doing this, he secured such immediate and undisputed fruits of his victory, as the treaty of peace contained; and he was sure of means to prosecute farther advantages at some future opportunity. He obtained, moreover, the character of generosity; and, in the present instance, he avoided the great danger of urging to bay so formidable a power as Austria, whose despair might be capable of the most formidable efforts.

March 31.

With this purpose, and assuming for the first time that disregard for the usual ceremonial of courts, and etiquette of politics, which he afterwards seemed to have pleasure in displaying, he wrote a letter in person to the Archduke Charles on the subject of peace.

This composition affects that abrupt laconic severity of style, which cuts short argument, by laying down general maxims of philosophy of a trite character, and breaks through the usual laboured periphrastic introductions with which ordinary politicians preface their proposals, when desirous of entering upon a treaty. "It is the part of a brave soldier," he said, "to make war, but to wish for peace. The present strife has lasted six years. Have we not yet slain enough of men, and sufficiently outraged humanity? Peace is demanded on all sides. Europe at large has laid down the arms assumed against the French Republic. Your nation remains alone in hostility, and yet blood flows faster than ever. This sixth campaign has commenced under ominous circumstances.—End how it will, some thousands of men more will be slain on either side; and at length, after all, we must come to an agreement, for every thing must have an end at last, even the angry passions of men. The Executive Directory made known to the Emperor their desire to put a period to the war which desolates both countries, but the intervention of the Court of London opposed it. Is there then no means of coming to an understanding, and must we continue to cut each other's throats for the interests or passions of a nation, herself a stranger to the miseries of war? You, the general-in-chief, who approach by birth so near to the crown, and are above all those petty passions which agitate ministers, and the members of government, will you resolve to be the benefactor of mankind, and the true saviour of Germany? Do not suppose that I mean by that expression to intimate, that it is impossible for you to defend yourself by force of arms; but under the supposition, that fortune were to become favourable to you, Germany would be equally exposed to ravage. With respect to my own feelings, general, if this proposition should be the means of saving one single man's life, I should prefer a civic crown so merited, to the melancholy glory attending military success."

The whole tone of the letter is ingeniously calculated to give the proposition the character of moderation, and at the same time to avoid the appearance of too ready an advance towards his object. The Archduke, after a space of two days, returned this brief answer, in which he stripped Buonaparte's proposal of its gilding, and treated it upon the footing of an ordinary proposal for a treaty of peace, made by a party, who finds it convenient for his interest:— "Unquestionably, sir, in making war, and in following the road prescribed by honour and duty, I desire as much as you the attainment of peace for the happiness of the people, and of humanity. Considering, however, that in the situation which I hold, it is no part of my business to inquire into and determine the quarrel of the belligerent powers; and that I am not furnished on the part of the Emperor with any plenipotentiary powers for treating, you will excuse me, general, if I do not enter into negotiation with you touching a matter of the highest importance, but which does not lie within my department. Whatever shall happen, either respecting the future chances of the war, or the prospect of peace, I request you to be equally convinced of my distinguished esteem."[273]

The Archduke would willingly have made some advantage of this proposal by obtaining an armistice of five hours, sufficient to enable him to form a junction with the corps of Kerpen, which, having left the Tyrol to come to the assistance of the commander-in-chief, was now within a short distance. But Buonaparte took care not to permit himself to be hampered by any such ill-timed engagement, and, after some sharp fighting, in which the French, as usual, were successful, he was able to interpose such a force as to prevent the junction taking place.

Two encounters followed at Neumark and at Unzmark—both gave rise to fresh disasters, and the continued retreat of the Archduke Charles and the Imperial army. The French general then pressed forward on the road to Vienna, through mountain-passes and defiles, which could not have been opened otherwise than by turning them on the flank. But these natural fastnesses were no longer defences. Judenburg, the capital of Upper Styria, was abandoned to the French without a blow, and shortly after Buonaparte entered Gratz, the principal town of Lower Styria, with the same facility.

THE ARCHDUKE'S RETREAT

The Archduke now totally changed his plan of warfare. He no longer disputed the ground foot by foot, but began to retreat by

---

[273] Montholon, tom. iv., p. 91.

hasty marches towards Vienna, determined to collect the last and utmost strength which the extensive states of the Emperor could supply, and fight for the existence, it might be, of his brother's throne, under the walls of his capital. However perilous this resolution might appear, it was worthy of the high-spirited prince by whom it was adopted; and there were reasons, perhaps, besides those arising from soldierly pride and princely dignity, which seemed to recommend it.

The army with which the enterprising French general was now about to debouche from the mountains, and enter the very centre of Germany, had suffered considerably since the commencement of the campaign, not only by the sword, but by severity of weather, and the excessive fatigue which they endured in executing the rapid marches, by which their leader succeeded in securing victory; and the French armies on the Rhine had not, as the plan of the campaign dictated, made any movement in advance corresponding with the march of Buonaparte.

Nor, in the country which they were about to enter with diminished forces, could Buonaparte trust to the influence of the same moral feeling in the people invaded, which had paved the way to so many victories on the Rhine. The citizens of Austria, though living under a despotic government, are little sensible of its severities, and are sincerely attached to the Emperor, whose personal habits incline him to live with his people without much form, and mix in public amusements, or appear in the public walks, like a father in the midst of his family. The nobility were as ready as in former times to bring out their vassals, and a general knowledge of discipline is familiar to the German peasant as a part of his education. Hungary possessed still the high spirited race of barons and cavaliers, who, in their great convocation in 1740, rose at once, and drawing their sabres, joined in the celebrated exclamation, "*Moriamur pro rege nostro, Maria Teresa!*" The Tyrol was in possession of its own warlike inhabitants, all in arms, and so far successful, as to have driven Joubert out of their mountains. Trieste and Fiume were retaken in the rear of the French army. Buonaparte had no line of communication when separated from Italy, and no means of obtaining supplies, but from a country which would probably be soon in insurrection in his rear, as well as on his flanks. A battle lost, when there was neither support, reserve, nor place of arms nearer than Klagenfurt, would have been annihilation. To add to these considerations, it was now known that the Venetian republic had assumed a formidable and hostile aspect in Italy; by which, joined to a natural explosion of feeling, religious and national, the French cause was considerably endangered in that country. There were so many favourers of the old system, together with the general influence of the Catholic clergy, that it seemed not unlikely this insurrection might spread fast and far. Italy, in that case, would have been no effectual place of refuge to Buonaparte or his army. The Archduke enumerated all these advantages to the Cabinet of Vienna, and exhorted them to stand the last cast of the bloody die.

But the terror, grief, and confusion, natural in a great metropolis, whose peace for the first time for so many years was alarmed with the approach of the unconquered and apparently fated general, who having defeated and destroyed five of their choicest armies, was now driving under its walls the remnants of the last, though commanded by that prince whom they regarded as the hope and flower of Austrian warfare, opposed this daring resolution. The alarm was general, beginning with the court itself; and the most valuable property and treasure were packed up to be carried into Hungary, where the royal family determined to take refuge. It is worthy of mention, that among the fugitives of the Imperial House was the Archduchess Maria Louisa, then between five and six years old, whom our imagination may conceive agitated by every species of childish terror derived from the approach of the victorious general on whom she was, at a future and similar crisis, destined to bestow her hand.

The cries of the wealthy burghers were of course for peace. The enemy were within fourteen or fifteen days' march of their walls; nor had the city (perhaps fortunately) any fortifications, which in the modern state of war could have made it defensible even for a day. They were, moreover, seconded by a party in the Cabinet; and, in short, whether it chanced for good or for evil, the selfish principle of those who had much to lose, and were timid in proportion, predominated against that, which desired at all risks the continuance of a determined and obstinate defence. It required many lessons to convince both sovereign and people, that it is better to put all on the hazard—better even to lose all, than to sanction the being pillaged at different times, and by degrees, under pretence of friendship and amity. A bow which is forcibly strained back will regain its natural position; but if supple enough to yield of itself to the counter direction, it will never recover its elasticity.

PEACE OF LEOBEN

The affairs, however, of the Austrians were in such a condition, that it could hardly be said whether the party who declared for peace, to obtain some respite from the distresses of the country, or those who wished to continue war with the chances of success which we have indicated, advised the least embarrassing course. The Court of Vienna finally adopted the alternative of treaty, and that of Leoben was set on foot.

Generals Bellegarde and Merfield, on the part of the Emperor, presented themselves at the headquarters of Buonaparte, 13th April, 1797, and announced the desire of their sovereign for peace. Buonaparte granted a suspension of arms, to endure for five days only; which was afterwards extended, when the probability of the definitive treaty of peace was evident.

It is affirmed, that in the whole discussions respecting this most important armistice, Napoleon—as a conqueror, whose victories had been in a certain degree his own, whose army had been supported and paid from the resources of the country which he conquered, who had received reinforcements from France only late and reluctantly, and who had recruited his army by new levies among the republicanized Italians—maintained an appearance of independence of the Government of France. He had, even at this period, assumed a freedom of thought and action, the tenth part of the suspicion attached to which would have cost the most popular general his head in the times of Danton and Robespierre. But, though acquired slowly, and in counteraction to the once overpowering, and still powerful, democratic influence, the authority of Buonaparte was great; and, indeed, the power which a conquering general attains, by means of his successes, in the bosom of his soldiers, becomes soon formidable to any species of government, where the soldier is not intimately interested in the liberties of the subject.

Yet it must not be supposed that Napoleon exhibited publicly any of that spirit of independence which the Directory appear to have dreaded, and which, according to the opinion which he himself intimates, seems to have delayed the promised co-operation, which was to be afforded by the eastern armies on the banks of the Rhine. Far from testifying such a feeling, his assertion of the rights of the Republic was decidedly striking, of which the following is a remarkable instance. The Austrian commissioner, in hopes to gain some credit for the admission, had stated in the preliminary articles of the convention, as a concession of consequence, that his Imperial Majesty acknowledged the French Government in its present state. "Strike out that condition," said Buonaparte sternly, "the French Republic is like the sun in heaven. The misfortune lies with those who are so blind as to be ignorant of the existence of either."[274] It was gallantly spoken; but how strange to reflect, that the same individual, in three or four years afterwards, was able to place an extinguisher on one of those suns, without even an eclipse being the consequence.[275]

It is remarkable also, that while asserting to foreigners this supreme dignity of the French Republic, Buonaparte should have departed so far from the respect he owed its rulers. The preliminaries of peace were proposed for signature on the 18th April. But General Clarke, to whom the Directory had committed full powers to act in the matter, was still at Turin. He was understood to be the full confidant of his masters, and to have instructions to watch the motions of Buonaparte, nay, to place him under arrest, should he see cause to doubt his fealty to the French Government. Napoleon, nevertheless, did not hesitate to tender his

---

[274] Montholon, tom. iv., p. 101.
[275] Buonaparte first mentions this circumstance as having taken place at Leoben, afterwards at the definitive treaty of Campo Formio. The effect is the same, wherever the words were spoken.—S.

individual signature and warranty, and these were readily admitted by the Austrian plenipotentiaries;—an ominous sign of the declension of the powers of the Directory, considering that a military general, without the support even of the commissioners from the government, or proconsuls, as they were called, was regarded as sufficient to ratify a treaty of such consequence. No doubt seems to have been entertained that he had the power to perform what he had guaranteed; and the part which he acted was the more remarkable, considering the high commission of General Clarke.[276]

TREATY OF LEOBEN

The articles in the treaty of Leoben remained long secret; the cause of which appears to have been, that the high contracting parties were not willing comparisons should be made between the preliminaries as they were originally settled, and the strange and violent altercations which occurred in the definitive treaty of Campo Formio. These two treaties of pacification differed, the one from the other, in relation to the degree and manner how a meditated partition of the territory of Venice, of the Cisalpine republic, and other smaller powers was to be accomplished, for the mutual benefit of France and Austria. It is melancholy to observe, but it is nevertheless an important truth, that there is no moment during which independent states of the second class have more occasion to be alarmed for their security, than when more powerful nations in their vicinity are about to conclude peace. It is so easy to accommodate these differences of the strong at the expense of such weaker states, as, if they are injured, have neither the power of making their complaints heard, nor of defending themselves by force, that, in the iron age in which it has been our fate to live, the

---

[276] "On the 27th of April, the Marquis de Gallo presented the preliminaries, ratified by the Emperor, to Napoleon at Gratz. It was in one of these conferences, that one of the plenipotentiaries, authorised by an autograph letter of the Emperor, offered Napoleon to procure him, on the conclusion of a peace, a sovereignty of 250,000 souls in Germany, for himself and his family, in order to place him beyond the reach of republican ingratitude. The general smiled, he desired the plenipotentiary to thank the Emperor for this proof of the interest he took in his welfare, and said, that he wished for no greatness or riches, unless conferred on him by the French people."—Montholon, tom. iv., p. 103.

injustice of such an arrangement has never been considered as offering any counterpoise to its great convenience, whatever the law of nations might teach to the contrary.

It is unnecessary to enter upon the subject of the preliminaries of Leoben, until we notice the treaty of Campo Formio, under which they were finally modified, and by which they were adjusted and controlled. It may be, however, the moment to state, that Buonaparte was considerably blamed, by the Directory and others, for stopping short in the career of conquest, and allowing the House of Austria terms which left her still formidable to France, when, said the censors, it would have cost him but another victory to blot the most constant and powerful enemy of the French Republic out of the map of Europe; or, at least, to confine her to her hereditary states in Germany. To such criticism he replied, in a despatch to the Directory from Leoben, during the progress of the treaty: "If, at the commencement of these Italian campaigns, I had made a point of going to Turin, I should never have passed the Po—had I insisted prematurely on advancing to Rome, I could never have secured Milan—and now, had I made an indispensable object of reaching Vienna, I might have destroyed the Republic."[277]

Such was his able and judicious defence of a conduct, which, by stopping short of some ultimate and extreme point apparently within his grasp, extracted every advantage from fear, which despair perhaps might not have yielded him, if the enemy had been driven to extremity. And it is remarkable, that the catastrophe of Napoleon himself was a corollary of the doctrine which he now laid down; for, had he not insisted upon penetrating to Moscow, there is no judging how much longer he might have held the empire of France.

The contents of the treaty of Leoben, so far as they were announced to the representatives of the French nation by the Directory, only made known, as part of the preliminaries, that the cession of the Belgic provinces, and of such a boundary as France might choose to demand upon the Rhine, had been admitted by Austria; and that she had consented to recognise a single republic in

---

[277] Correspondence Inédite tom. ii., p. 564. See also Jomini, tom. ix., Pièces Justificatives, Nos. 1 and 2.

Italy, to be composed out of those which had been provisionally established. But shortly afterwards it transpired, that Mantua, the subject of so much and such bloody contest, and the very citadel of Italy, as had appeared from the events of these sanguinary campaigns, was to be resigned to Austria, from whose tenacious grasp it had been wrenched with so much difficulty. This measure was unpopular; and it will be found that Buonaparte had the ingenuity, in the definitive treaty of peace, to substitute an indemnification, which he ought not to have given, and which was certainly the last which the Austrians should have accepted.

VENICE

April 9

It was now the time for Venice to tremble. She had declared against the French in their absence; her vindictive population had murdered many of them; the resentment of the French soldiers was excited to the utmost, and the Venetians had no right to reckon upon the forbearance of their general. The treaty of Leoben left the Senate of that ancient state absolutely without support; nay, as they afterwards learned, Austria, after pleading their cause for a certain time, had ended by stipulating for a share of their spoils, which had been assigned to her by a secret article of the treaty. The doom of the oligarchy was pronounced ere Buonaparte had yet traversed the Noric and Julian Alps, for the purpose of enforcing it. By a letter to the doge, dated from the capital of Upper Styria, Napoleon, bitterly upbraiding the Senate for requiting his generosity with treachery and ingratitude, demanded that they should return by his aide-de-camp who bore the letter, their instant choice betwixt war and peace, and allowing them only four-and-twenty hours to disperse their insurgent peasantry, and submit to his clemency.[278]

Junot, introduced into the Senate, made the threats of his master ring in the astounded ears of the members, and by the blunt and rough manner of a soldier, who had risen from the ranks, added

---

[278] Daru, tom. v., p. 568; Montholon, tom. iv., p. 135.

to the dismay of the trembling nobles. The Senate returned a humble apology to Buonaparte, and despatched agents to deprecate his wrath. These envoys were doomed to experience one of those scenes of violence which were in some degree natural to this extraordinary man, but to which in certain cases he seems to have designedly given way, in order to strike consternation into those whom he addressed. "Are the prisoners at liberty?" he said, with a stern voice, and without replying to the humble greetings of the terrified envoys. They answered with hesitation that they had liberated the French, the Polish, and the Brescians, who had been made captive in the insurrectionary war. "I will have them all—all!" exclaimed Buonaparte—"all who are in prison on account of their political sentiments. I will go myself to destroy your dungeons on the Bridge of Tears—opinions shall be free—I will have no Inquisition. If all the prisoners are not set at instant liberty, the English envoy dismissed, the people disarmed, I declare instant war. I might have gone to Vienna if I had listed—I have concluded a peace with the Emperor—I have eighty thousand men, twenty gun-boats—I will hear of no Inquisition, and no Senate either—I will dictate the law to you—I will prove an Attila to Venice. If you cannot disarm your population, I will do it in your stead—your government is antiquated—it must crumble to pieces."[279]

While Buonaparte, in these disjointed yet significant threats, stood before the deputies like the Argantes of Italy's heroic poet, and gave them the choice of peace and war with the air of a superior being, capable at once to dictate their fate, he had not yet heard of the massacre of Verona, or of the batteries of a Venetian fort on the Lido having fired upon a French vessel, which had run into the port to escape the pursuit of two armed Austrian ships. The vessel was alleged to have been sunk, and the master and some of the crew to have been killed. The news of these fresh aggressions did not fail to aggravate his indignation to the highest pitch. The terrified deputies ventured to touch with delicacy on the subject of pecuniary atonement. Buonaparte's answer was worthy of a Roman. "If you could proffer me," he said, "the treasures of Peru—if you could

---

[279] See, in Daru, tom. v., p. 605, the report of the two envoys, Dona and Justiniani.

strew the whole district with gold, it could not atone for the French blood which has been treacherously spilt."[280]

May 3.

Accordingly, on the 3d of May, Buonaparte declared war against Venice, and ordered the French minister to leave the city; the French troops, and those of the new Italian republics, were at the same time commanded to advance, and to destroy in their progress, wherever they found it displayed, the winged Lion of Saint Mark, the ancient emblem of Venetian sovereignty. The declaration is dated at Palma Nova.[281]

It had been already acted upon by the French who were on the Venetian frontier, and by La Hotze, a remarkable character, who was then at the head of the army of the Italian republics of the new model, and the forces of the towns of Brescia and Bergamo, which aspired to the same independence. This commander was of Swiss extraction; an excellent young officer, and at that time enamoured of liberty on the French system, though he afterwards saw so much reason to change his opinions, that he lost his life, as we may have occasion to mention, fighting under the Austrian banners.

The terrified Senate of Venice proved unworthy descendants of the Zenos, Dandolos, and Morosinis, as the defenders of Christendom, and the proud opposers of Papal oppression. The best resource they could imagine to themselves, was to employ at Paris those golden means of intercession which Buonaparte had so sturdily rejected. Napoleon assures us, that they found favour by means of these weighty arguments. The Directory, moved, we are informed, by the motives of ten millions of French francs, transmitted from Venice in bills of exchange, sent to the general of Italy orders to spare the ancient senate and aristocracy. But the

---

[280] "Non, non, quand vous couvriez cette plage d'or, tous vos tresors, tout l'or du Pérou, ne peuvent payer le sang Français."—Daru, tom. v., p. 619.
[281] For a copy of this manifesto against Venice, see *Moniteur*, No. 239, May 16, and *Annual Register*, vol. xxxiv., p. 337. "As soon as it was made public, the whole Terra Firma revolted against the capital. Every town proclaimed its independence, and constituted a government for itself. Bergamo, Brescia, Padua, Vicenza, Bassano, and Udine, formed so many separate republics."—Montholon, tom. iv., p. 143.

account of the transaction, with the manner in which the remittances were distributed, fell into the hands of Napoleon, by despatches intercepted at Milan. The members of the French Government, whom these documents would have convicted of peculation and bribery, were compelled to be silent; and Buonaparte, availing himself of some chicanery as to certain legal solemnities, took it on him totally to disregard the orders he had received.

The Senate of Venice, rather stupified than stimulated by the excess of their danger, were holding on the 30th April, a sort of privy council in the apartments of the doge, when a letter from the commandant of their flotilla informed them, that the French were erecting fortifications on the low grounds contiguous to the lagoons or shallow channels which divide from the main-land and from each other the little isles on which the amphibious mistress of the Adriatic holds her foundation; and proposing, in the blunt style of a gallant sailor, to batter them to pieces about their ears before the works could be completed.[282] Indeed, nothing would have been more easy than to defend the lagoons against an enemy, who, notwithstanding Napoleon's bravado, had not even a single boat. But the proposal, had it been made to an abbess and a convent of nuns, could scarce have appeared more extraordinary than it did to these degenerate nobles. Yet the sense of shame prevailed; and though trembling for the consequences of the order which they issued, the Senate directed that the admiral should proceed to action.[283] Immediately after the order was received, their deliberations were interrupted by the thunder of the cannon on either side—the Venetian gun-boats pouring their fire on the van of the French army, which had begun to arrive at Fusini.

To interrupt these ominous sounds, two plenipotentiaries were despatched to make intercession with the French general; and, to prevent delay, the doge himself undertook to report the result.

The Grand Council was convoked on the 1st of May, when the doge, pale in countenance, and disconcerted in demeanour, proposed, as the only means of safety, the admission of some

---

[282] Daru, tom. vi., p. 9.
[283] Daru, tom. vi., p. 10.

democratic modifications into their forms, under the direction of General Buonaparte; or, in other words, to lay their institutions at the feet of the conqueror, to be remodelled at his pleasure. Of six hundred and nineteen patricians, only twenty-one dissented from a vote which inferred the absolute surrender of their constitution. The conditions to be agreed on were, indeed, declared subject to the revision of the Council; but this, in the circumstances, could only be considered as a clause intended to save appearances. The surrender must have been regarded as unconditional and total.[284]

Amidst the dejection and confusion which possessed the Government, some able intriguer (the secretary, it was said, of the French ambassador at Venice, whose principal had been recalled) contrived to induce the Venetian Government to commit an act of absolute suicide, so as to spare Buonaparte the trouble and small degree of scandal which might attach to totally destroying the existence of the republic.

On the 9th of May, as the committee of the Great Council were in close deliberation with the doge, two strangers intruded upon those councils, which heretofore—such was the jealous severity of the oligarchy—were like those of supernatural beings; those who looked on them died. But now, affliction, confusion, and fear, had withdrawn the guards from these secret and mysterious chambers and laid open to the intrusion of strangers those stern haunts of a suspicious oligarchy, where, in other days, an official or lictor of the Government might have been punished with death even for too loud a foot-fall, far more for the fatal crime of having heard more than was designed to come to his knowledge. All this was now ended; and without check or rebuke the two strangers were permitted to communicate with the Senate by writing. Their advice, which had the terms of a command, was, to anticipate the intended reforms of the French—to dissolve the present Government—throw open their prisons—disband their Sclavonian soldiers—plant the tree of liberty on the place of Saint Mark, and to take other popular measures of the same nature, the least of which, proposed

---

[284] Daru, tom. vi., p. 13.

but a few months before, would have been a signal of death to the individual who had dared to hint at it.[285]

An English satirist has told us a story of a man persuaded by an eloquent friend, to hang himself, in order to preserve his life. The story of the fall of Venice vindicates the boldness of the satire. It does not appear that Buonaparte could have gone farther; nay, it seems unlikely he would have gone so far, as was now recommended.

As the friendly advisers had hinted that the utmost speed was necessary, the committee scarce interposed an interval of three days, between receiving the advice and recommending it to the Great Council; and began in the meanwhile to anticipate the destruction of their government and surrender of their city, by dismantling their fleet and disbanding their soldiers.

At length, the Great Council assembled on the 12th of May. The doge had commenced a pathetic discourse on the extremities to which the country was reduced, when an irregular discharge of fire-arms took place under the very windows of the council-house. All started up in confusion. Some supposed the Sclavonians were plundering the citizens; some that the lower orders had risen on the nobility; others, that the French had entered Venice, and were proceeding to sack and pillage it. The terrified and timid counsellors did not wait to inquire what was the real cause of the disturbance, but hurried forward, like sheep, in the path which had been indicated to them. They hastened to despoil their ancient government of all authority, to sign in a manner its sentence of civil death—added every thing which could render the sacrifice more agreeable to Buonaparte—and separated in confusion, but under the impression that they had taken the best measure in their power for quelling the tumult, by meeting the wishes of the predominant party. But this was by no means the case. On the contrary, they had the misfortune to find that the insurrection, of which the firing was the signal, was directed not against the aristocrats, but against those who proposed the surrender of the national independence. Armed bands shouted, "Long live Saint Mark, and perish foreign domination!"

---

[285] Daru, tom. vi., p. 32.

Others indeed there were, who displayed in opposition three-coloured banners, with the war-cry of "Liberty for ever!" The disbanded and mutinous soldiers mixed among these hostile groups, and threatened the town with fire and pillage.[286]

Amid this horrible confusion, and while the parties were firing on each other, a provisional government was hastily named. Boats were despatched to bring three thousand French soldiers into the city. These took possession of the place of Saint Mark,[287] while some of the inhabitants shouted; but the greater part, who were probably not the less sensible of the execrable tyranny of the old aristocracy, saw it fall in mournful silence, because there fell along with the ancient institutions of their country, however little some of these were to be regretted, the honour and independence of the state itself.

The terms which the French granted, or rather imposed, appeared sufficiently moderate, so far as they were made public. They announced, that the foreign troops would remain so long, and no longer, than might be necessary to protect the peace of Venice[288]—they undertook to guarantee the public debt, and the payment of the pensions allowed to the impoverished gentry. They required, indeed, the continuance of the prosecution against the commander of that fort of Luco who had fired on the French vessel; but all other offenders were pardoned, and Buonaparte afterwards suffered even this affair to pass into oblivion; which excited doubt whether the transaction had ever been so serious as had been alleged.

Five secret and less palatable articles attended these avowed conditions. One provided for the various exchanges of territory which had been already settled at the Venetian expense betwixt Austria and France. The second and third stipulated the payment of

---

[286] Daru, tom. vi., p. 36.
[287] Daru, tom. vi., p. 40.
[288] "The French troops entered Venice on the 16th of May. The partisans of liberty immediately met in a popular assembly. The aristocracy was destroyed for ever; the democratic constitution of twelve hundred was proclaimed. Dandolo was placed at the head of all the city. The Lion of St. Mark and the Corinthian horses were carried to Paris."—Montholon, tom. iv., p. 142.

three millions of francs in specie, and as many in naval stores. Another prescribed the cession of three ships of war, and of two frigates, armed and equipped. A fifth ratified the exaction, in the usual style of French cupidity, of twenty pictures and five hundred manuscripts.[289]

It will be seen hereafter what advantages the Venetians purchased by all these unconscionable conditions. At the moment, they understood that the stipulations were to imply a guarantee of the independent existence of their country as a democratical state. In the meanwhile, the necessity for raising the supplies to gratify the rapacity of the French, obliged the provisional government to have recourse to forced loans; and in this manner they inhospitably plundered the Duke of Modena (who had fled to Venice for refuge when Buonaparte first entered Lombardy) of his remaining treasure, amounting to one hundred and ninety thousand sequins.

---

[289] "General Bernadotte carried the colours taken from the Venetian troops to Paris. These frequent presentations of colours were, at this period, very useful to the government; for the disaffected were silenced and overawed by this display of the spirit of the armies."— Montholon, tom. iv., p. 145.

Chapter X

Napoleon's Amatory Correspondence with Josephine—His Court at Montebello—Negotiations and Pleasure mingled there—Genoa—Revolutionary spirit of the Genoese—They rise in insurrection, but are quelled by the Government, and the French plundered and imprisoned—Buonaparte interferes, and appoints the Outlines of a new Government—Sardinia—Naples—The Cispadane, Transpadane, and Emilian Republics, united under the name of the Cisalpine Republic—The Valteline—The Grisons—The Valteline united to Lombardy—Great improvement of Italy, and the Italian Character, from these changes—Difficulties in the way of Pacification betwixt France and Austria—The Directory and Napoleon take different Views—Treaty of Campo Formio—Buonaparte takes leave of the Army of Italy, to act as French Plenipotentiary at Rastadt.

When peace returns, it brings back the domestic affections, and affords the means of indulging them. Buonaparte was yet a bridegroom, though he had now been two years married, and upwards. A part of his correspondence with his bride has been preserved, and gives a curious picture of a temperament as fiery in love as in war. The language of the conqueror, who was disposing of states at his pleasure, and defeating the most celebrated commanders of the time, is as enthusiastic as that of an Arcadian. We cannot suppress the truth, that (in passages which we certainly shall not quote) it carries a tone of indelicacy, which, notwithstanding the intimacy of the married state, an English husband would not use, nor an English wife consider as the becoming expression of connubial affection. There seems no doubt, however, that the attachment which these letters indicate was perfectly sincere, and on one occasion at least, it was chivalrously expressed;—"Wurmser shall buy dearly the tears which he makes you shed."[290]

It appears from this correspondence that Josephine had rejoined her husband, under the guardianship of Junot, when he returned from Paris, after having executed his mission of delivering to the Directory, and representatives of the French people, the banners and colours taken from Beaulieu. In December, 1796, Josephine was at Genoa, where she was received with studied magnificence, by those in that ancient state who adhered to the French interest, and where, to the scandal of the rigid Catholics, the company continued assembled, at a ball given by M. de Serva, till a late hour on Friday morning, despite the presence of a senator having in his pocket, but not venturing to enforce, a decree of the senate for the better observation of the fast day upon the occasion. These, however, were probably only occasional visits; but after the signature of the treaty of Leoben, and during the various negotiations which took place before it was finally adjusted, as ratified at Campo Formio, Josephine lived in domestic society with her husband, at the beautiful seat, or rather palace, of Montebello.

This villa, celebrated from the important negotiations of which it was the scene, is situated a few leagues from Milan, on a gently sloping hill, which commands an extensive prospect over the fertile plains of Lombardy. The ladies of the highest rank, as well as those celebrated for beauty and accomplishments,—all, in short, who could add charms to society,—were daily paying their homage to Josephine, who received them with a felicity of address which seemed as if she had been born for exercising the high courtesies that devolved upon the wife of so distinguished a person as Napoleon.

COURT AT MONTEBELLO

Negotiations proceeded amid gaiety and pleasure. The various ministers and envoys of Austria, of the Pope, of the Kings of

---

[290] For some curious extracts from this Correspondence, see Appendix, No. IV.

Naples and Sardinia, of the Duke of Parma, of the Swiss Cantons, of several of the Princes of Germany,—the throng of generals, of persons in authority, of deputies of towns,—with the daily arrival and despatch of numerous couriers, the bustle of important business, mingled with fêtes and entertainments, with balls and with hunting parties,—gave the picture of a splendid court, and the assemblage was called accordingly, by the Italians, the Court of Montebello. It was such in point of importance; for the deliberations agitated there were to regulate the political relations of Germany, and decide the fate of the King of Sardinia, of Switzerland, of Venice, of Genoa: all destined to hear from the voice of Napoleon, the terms on which their national existence was to be prolonged or terminated.

Montebello was not less the abode of pleasure. The sovereigns of this diplomatic and military court made excursions to the lago Maggiore, to lago di Como, to the Borromean islands, and occupied at pleasure the villas which surround those delicious regions. Every town, every village, desired to distinguish itself by some peculiar mark of homage and respect to him, whom they then named the Liberator of Italy.[291] These expressions are in a great measure those of Napoleon himself, who seems to have looked back on this period of his life with warmer recollections of pleasurable enjoyment than he had experienced on any other occasion.

It was probably the happiest time of his life. Honour, beyond that of a crowned head, was his own, and had the full relish of novelty to a mind which two or three years before was pining in obscurity. Power was his, and he had not experienced its cares and risks; high hopes were formed of him by all around, and he had not yet disappointed them. He was in the flower of youth, and married to the woman of his heart. Above all, he had the glow of Hope, which was marshalling him even to more exalted dominion; and he had not yet become aware that possession brings satiety, and that all earthly desires and wishes terminate, when fully attained, in vanity and vexation of spirit.

---

[291] Montholon, tom. iv., p. 147.

The various objects which occupied Buonaparte's mind during this busy yet pleasing interval, were the affairs of Genoa, of Sardinia, of Naples, of the Cisalpine republic, of the Grisons, and lastly, and by far the most important of them, the definitive treaty with Austria, which involved the annihilation of Venice as an independent state.

GENOA

Genoa, the proud rival of Venice, had never attained the same permanent importance with that sister republic; but her nobility, who still administered her government according to the model assigned them by Andrew Doria, preserved more national spirit, and a more warlike disposition. The neighbourhood of France, and the prevalence of her opinions, had stirred up among the citizens of the middling class a party, taking the name of Morandists, from a club so termed,[292] whose object it was to break down the oligarchy, and revolutionize the government. The nobles were naturally opposed to this, and a large body of the populace much employed by them, and strict Catholics, were, ready to second them in their defence.

The establishment of two Italian democracies upon the Po, made the Genoese revolutionists conceive the time was arrived when their own state ought to pass through a similar ordeal of regeneration. They mustered their strength, and petitioned the doge for the abolition of the government as it existed, and the adoption of a democratic model. The doge condescended so far to their demand, as to name a committee of nine persons, five of them of plebeian birth, to consider and report on the means of infusing a more popular spirit into the constitution.[293]

The three chief Inquisitors of State, or Censors, as the actual rulers of the oligarchy were entitled, opposed the spirit of religious enthusiasm to that of democratic zeal. They employed the pulpit

---

[292] The club held their meetings at the house of an apothecary, named *Morando*. Botta describes him as "un uomo precipitoso, e di estremi pensieri, e che credeva, che ogni cosa fosse licita per arrivare a quella libertà, ch'ei si figurava in mente."—*Storia*, tom. ii., p. 364.
[293] Montholon, tom. iv., p. 152.

and the confessional as the means of warning good Catholics against the change demanded by the Morandists—they exposed the Holy Sacrament, and made processions and public prayers, as if threatened with a descent of the Algerines.

May 22.

Meanwhile, the Morandists took up arms, displayed the French colours, and conceiving their enterprise was on the point of success, seized the gate of the arsenal and that of the harbour. But their triumph was short. Ten thousand armed labourers started as from out of the earth, under the command of their syndics, or municipal officers, with cries of "Viva Maria!" and declared for the aristocracy. The insurgents, totally defeated, were compelled to shut themselves up in their houses, where they were assailed by the stronger party, and finally routed. The French residing in Genoa were maltreated by the prevailing party, their houses pillaged, and they themselves dragged to prison.

The last circumstance gave Buonaparte an ostensible right to interfere, which he would probably have done even had no such violence been committed. He sent his aide-de-camp La Valette to Genoa, with the threat of instantly moving against the city a division of his army, unless the prisoners were set at liberty, the aristocratic party disarmed, and such alterations, or rather such a complete change of government adopted, as should be agreeable to the French commander-in-chief. Against this there was no appeal. The inquisitors were laid under arrest, for having defended, with the assistance of their fellow-citizens, the existing institutions of the state; and the doge, with two other magistrates of the first rank, went to learn at Montebello, the headquarters of Napoleon, what was to be the future fate of the City, proudly called of *Palaces*.[294] They received the outlines of such a democracy as Napoleon conceived suitable for them; and he appears to have been unusually favourable to the state, which, according to the French affectation

---

[294] "On the 6th of June, the deputies from the Senate signed a convention at Montebello, which put an end to Doria's constitution, and established the democratical government of Genoa. The people burned the Golden Book, and broke the statue of Doria to pieces. This outrage on the memory of that great man displeased Napoleon, who required the provisional government to restore it."—Montholon, tom. iv., p. 157.

of doing every thing upon a classical model, now underwent revolutionary baptism, and was called the Ligurian Republic. It was stipulated, that the French who had suffered should be indemnified; but no contributions were exacted for the use of the French army, nor did the collections and cabinets of Genoa pay any tribute to the Parisian Museum.[295]

Nov. 11.

Shortly after, the democratic party having gone so far as to exclude the nobles from the government, and from all offices of trust, called down by doing so a severe admonition from Buonaparte. He *discharged* them to offend the prejudices, or insult the feelings of the more scrupulous Catholics, declaring farther, that to exclude those of noble birth from public functions, is a revolting piece of injustice, and, in fact, as criminal as the worst of the errors of the patricians.[296] Buonaparte says, he felt a partiality for Genoa; and the comparative liberality with which he treated the state on this occasion, furnishes a good proof that he did so.

The King of Sardinia had been prostrated at the feet of France by the armistice of Cherasco, which concluded Napoleon's first campaign; and that sagacious leader had been long desirous that the Directory should raise the royal supplicant (for he could be termed little else) into some semblance of regal dignity, so as to make his power available as an ally. Nay, General Clarke had, 5th April, 1797, subscribed, with the representative of his Sardinian Majesty, a treaty offensive and defensive, by which Napoleon expected to add to the army under his command four thousand Sardinian or Piedmontese infantry, and five hundred cavalry; and he reckoned much on this contingent, in case of the war being renewed with Austria. But the Directory shifted and evaded his solicitations, and declined confirming this treaty, probably because they considered the army under his command as already sufficiently strong, being, as the

---

[295] Montholon, tom. iv., p. 155; Jomini, tom. x., p. 169; Botta, tom. ii., p. 371.
[296] "The Council of Five Hundred at Paris was at this time debating on a motion made by Sièyes, tending to expel all the nobles from France, on giving them the value of their property. This advice, given by Napoleon to the Republic of Genoa, appeared to be addressed, in fact, to the French Republic, which at all events profited by it; for this terrific plan was abandoned."—Montholon, tom. iv., p. 164.

soldiers were, so devoted to their leader. At length, however, the treaty was ratified, but too late to serve Buonaparte's object.

Naples, whose conduct had been vacillating and insincere, as events seemed to promise victory or threaten defeat to the French general, experienced, notwithstanding, when he was in the height of triumph, the benefit of his powerful intercession with the government, and retained the full advantage secured to her by the treaty of Paris of 10th October, 1796.

A most important subject of consideration remained after the pacification of Italy, respecting the mode in which the new republics were to be governed, and the extent of territory which should be assigned to them. On this subject, there had been long discussions; and as there was much animosity and ancient grudge betwixt some of the Italian cities and provinces, it was no very easy matter to convince them, that their true interest lay in as many of them being united under one energetic and active government as should render them a power of some importance, instead of being divided as heretofore into petty states, which could not offer effectual resistance even to invasion on the part of a power of the second class, much more if attacked by France or Austria.

The formation of a compact and independent state in the north of Italy, was what Napoleon had much at heart. But the Cispadane and Transpadane republics were alike averse to a union, and that of Romagna had declined on its part a junction with the Cispadane commonwealth, and set up for a puny and feeble independence, under the title of the Emilian Republic. Buonaparte was enabled to overcome these grudgings and heart-burnings, by pointing out to them the General Republic, which it was now his system to create, as being destined to form the kernel of a state which should be enlarged from time to time as opportunities offered, until it should include all Italy under one single government. This flattering prospect, in assigning to Italy, though at some distant date, the probability of forming one great country, united in itself, and independent of the rest of Europe, instead of being, as now, parcelled out into petty states, naturally overcame all the local dislikes and predilections which might have prevented the union of the Cispadane, Transpadane, and Emilian republics into one, and that important measure was resolved upon accordingly.

CISALPINE REPUBLIC

The Cisalpine republic was the name fixed upon to designate the united commonwealth. The French would more willingly have named it, with respect to Paris, the Transalpine republic; but that would have been innovating upon the ancient title which Rome has to be the central point, with reference to which, all other parts of Italy assume their local description. It would have destroyed all classical propriety, and have confused historical recollections, if, what had hitherto been called the Ultramontane side of the Alps, had, to gratify Parisian vanity, been termed the Hither side of the same chain of mountains.

The constitution assigned to the Cisalpine republic, was the same which the French had last of all adopted, in what they called the year five, having a Directory of executive administrators, and two Councils. They were installed upon the 30th of June, 1797. Four members of the Directory were named by Buonaparte, and the addition of a fifth was promised with all convenient speed. On the 14th of July following, a review was made of thirty thousand national guards. The fortresses of Lombardy, and the other districts, were delivered up to the local authorities, and the French army, retiring from the territories of the new republic, took up cantonments in the Venetian states. Proclamation had already been made, that the states belonging to the Cisalpine republic having been acquired by France by the right of conquest, she had used her privilege to form them into their present free and independent government, which, already recognised by the Emperor and the Directory, could not fail to be acknowledged within a short time by all the other powers of Europe.[297]

---

[297] Thibaudeau, tom. iii., p. 121; Montholon, tom. iv., p. 179; Jomini, tom. x., p. 364.

TREATY OF CAMPO-FORMIO

Buonaparte soon after showed that he was serious in his design of enlarging the Cisalpine republic, as opportunity could be made to serve. There are three valleys, termed the Valteline districts, which run down from the Swiss mountains towards the lake of Como. The natives of the Valteline are about one hundred and sixty thousand souls. They speak Italian, and are chiefly of the Catholic persuasion. These valleys were at this period the subjects of the Swiss Cantons, called the Grisons, not being a part of their league, or enjoying any of their privileges, but standing towards the Swiss community, generally and individually, in the rank of vassals to sovereigns. This situation of thraldom and dependence was hard to endure, and dishonourable in itself; and we cannot be surprised that, when the nations around them were called upon to enjoy liberty and independence, the inhabitants of the Valteline should have driven their Swiss garrisons out of their valleys, adopted the symbol of Italian freedom, and carried their complaints against the oppression of their German and Protestant masters to the feet of Buonaparte.

The inhabitants of the Valteline unquestionably had a right to assert their natural liberty, which is incapable of suffering prescription; but it is not equally clear how the French could, according to the law of nations, claim any title to interfere between them and the Grisons, with whom, as well as with the whole Swiss Union, they were in profound peace. This scruple seems to have struck Buonaparte's own mind.[298] He pretended, however, to assume that the Milanese government had a right to interfere, and his mediation was so far recognised, that the Grisons pleaded before him in answer to their contumacious vassals. Buonaparte gave his opinion, by advising the canton of the Grisons, which consists of three leagues, to admit their Valteline subjects to a share of their franchises, in the character of a fourth association. The moderation of the proposal may be admitted to excuse the irregularity of the interference.

---

[298] Montholon, tom. iv., p. 187.

The representatives of the Grey League, were, notwithstanding, profoundly hurt at a proposal which went to make their vassals their brother-freemen, and to establish the equality of the Italian serf, who drank of the Adda, with the free-born Switzer, who quaffed the waters of the Rhine. As they turned a deaf ear to his proposal, deserted his tribunal, and endeavoured to find support at Bern, Paris, Vienna, and elsewhere, Napoleon resolved to proceed against them in default of appearance; and declaring, that as the Grisons had failed to appear before him, or to comply with his injunctions, by admitting the people of the Valteline to be parties to their league, he therefore adjudged the state, or district, of the Valteline, in time coming, to belong to, and be part of, the Cisalpine republic. The Grisons in vain humbled themselves when it was too late, and protested their readiness to plead before a mediator too powerful to be declined under any ground known in law; and the Valteline territory was adjudged [October 10] inalienably annexed to and united with Lombardy; of which, doubtless, it forms, from manners and contiguity, a natural portion.[299]

The existence of a state having free institutions, however imperfect, seemed to work an almost instant amelioration on the character of the people of the north of Italy. The effeminacy and trifling habits which resigned all the period of youth to intrigue and amusement, began to give place to firmer and more manly virtues—to the desire of honourable minds to distinguish themselves in arts and arms.[300] Buonaparte had himself said, that twenty years would be necessary to work a radical change on the national character of the Italians; but even already those seeds were sown, among a people hitherto frivolous because excluded from public business, and timorous because they were not permitted the use of arms, which afterwards made the Italians of the north equal the French

---

[299] Montholon, tom. iv., p. 185; Botta, tom. ii., p. 461.
[300] "Instead of passing their time at the feet of women, the young Italians now frequented the riding and fencing schools, and fields of exercise. In the comedies and street farces, there had always been an Italian, represented as a very cowardly though witty fellow, and a kind of bullying captain,—sometimes a Frenchman, but more frequently a German—a very powerful, brave, and brutal character, who never failed to conclude with caning the Italian to the great satisfaction of the applauding spectators. But such allusions were now no longer endured by the populace; authors now brought brave Italians on the stage, putting foreigners to flight, and defending their honour and their rights."—Napoleon, *Montholon*, tom. iv., p. 185.

themselves in braving the terrors of war, besides producing several civil characters of eminence.

Amid those subordinate discussions, as they might be termed, in comparison to the negotiations betwixt Austria and France, these two high contracting parties found great difficulty in agreeing as to the pacific superstructure which they should build upon the foundation which had been laid by the preliminaries exchanged at Leoben. Nay, it seemed as if some of the principal stipulations, which had been there agreed upon as the corner stones of their treaty, were even already beginning to be unsettled.

It will be remembered, that, in exchange for the cession of Flanders, and of all the countries on the left side of the Rhine, including the strong city of Mayence, which she was to yield up to France in perpetuity, Austria stipulated an indemnification on some other frontier. The original project bore, that the Lombardic republic, since termed the Cisalpine, should have all the territories extending from Piedmont to the river Oglio. Those to the eastward of that river were to be ceded to Austria as an equivalent for the cession of Belgium, and the left bank of the Rhine. The Oglio, rising in the Alps, descends through the fertile districts of Brescia and Cremasco, and falls into the Po near Borgo-forte, enclosing Mantua on its left bank, which strong fortress, the citadel of Italy, was, by this allocation, to be restored to Austria. There were farther compensations assigned to the Emperor, by the preliminaries of Leoben. Venice was to be deprived of her territories on the mainland, which were to be confiscated to augment the indemnity destined for the empire; and this, although Venice, as far as Buonaparte yet knew, had been faithful to the neutrality she had adopted. To redeem this piece of injustice, another was to be perpetrated. The state of Venice was to receive the legations of Bologna, Ferrara, and Romagna, in lieu of the dominions which she was to cede to Austria; and these legations, it must not be forgotten, were the principal materials of the Cispadane republic, founded by Buonaparte himself. These, however, with their population, which he had led to hope for a free popular government, he was now about to turn over to the dominion of Venice, the most jealous oligarchy in the world, which was not likely to forgive those who had been forward in expressing a desire of freedom. This was the first concoction of the treaty of Leoben, from which it appears that the negotiators of the two great powers regarded the secondary and weaker states, whether ancient or of modern erection, merely as make-weights, to be thrown into either scale, as might be necessary to adjust the balance.

It is true, the infant Cispadane republic escaped the fate to which its patron and founder was about to resign it; for after this arrangement had been provisionally adjusted, news came of the insurrection of Venice, the attack upon the French through her whole territory, and the massacre at Verona. This aggression placed the ancient republic, so far as France was concerned, in the light of a hostile power, and entitled Buonaparte to deal with her as a conquered one, perhaps to divide, or altogether to annihilate her. But, on the other hand, he had received their submission, ratified the establishment of their new popular constitution, and possessed himself of the city, under pretence of assigning it a free government, according to the general hope which he had held out to Italy at large. The right of conquest was limited by the terms on which surrender had been accepted. Austria, on the other hand, was the more deeply bound to have protected the ancient republic, for it was in her cause that Venice so rashly assumed arms; but such is the gratitude of nations, such the faith of politicians, that she appears, from the beginning, to have had no scruple in profiting by the spoils of an ally, who had received a death-wound in her cause.

By the time the negotiators met for finally discussing the preliminaries, the Directory of France, either to thwart Buonaparte, whose superiority became too visible, or because they actually entertained the fears they expressed, were determined that Mantua, which had been taken with such difficulty, should remain the bulwark of the Cisalpine republic, instead of returning to be once more that of the Austrian territories in Italy. The Imperial plenipotentiaries insisted, on the other hand, that Mantua was absolutely necessary to the safety of their Italian possessions, and became more so from the peculiar character of their new neighbour, the Cisalpine republic, whose example was likely to be so perilous to the adjacent dependencies of an ancient monarchy. To get over this difficulty, the French general proposed that the remaining dominions of Venice should be also divided betwixt Austria and France, the latter obtaining possession of the Albanian territories and the Ionian islands belonging to the republic, of which the high contracting powers signed the death-warrant; while Istria, Dalmatia, Venice herself, and all her other dominions, should be appropriated to Austria. The latter power, through her minister, consented to this arrangement with as little scruple, as to the former appropriation of her forlorn ally's possessions on the Terra Firma.

But as fast as obstacles were removed on one side, they appeared to start up on another, and a sort of pause ensued in the deliberations, which neither party seemed to wish to push to a close. In fact, both Napoleon, plenipotentiary for France, and Count Cobentzel,[301] a man of great diplomatic skill and address, who took the principal management on the part of Austria, were sufficiently aware that the French government, long disunited, was in the act of approaching to a crisis. This accordingly took place, under circumstances to be hereafter noticed, on the eighteenth of Fructidor, creating, by a new revolutionary movement, a total change of administration. When this revolution was accomplished, the Directory, who accomplished it, feeling themselves more strong, appeared to lay aside the idea of peace, and showed a strong disposition to push their advantages to the utmost.

Buonaparte was opposed to this. He knew that if war was resumed, the difficulties of the campaign would be thrown on him, and the blame also, if the results were not happy. He was determined, therefore, in virtue of his full powers, to bring the matter to a conclusion, whether the Directory would or not. For this purpose he confronted Cobentzel, who still saw his game in gaining delay, with the sternness of a military envoy. On the 16th October, the conferences were renewed upon the former grounds, and Cobentzel went over the whole subject of the indemnifications—insisting that Mantua, and the line of the Adige, should be granted

---

[301] "Count Cobentzel was a native of Brussels; a very agreeable man in company, and distinguished by studied politeness; but positive and intractable in business. There was a want of propriety and precision in his mode of expressing himself, of which he was sensible; and he endeavoured to compensate for this by talking loud and using imperious gestures."—Napoleon, *Montholon*, tom. iv., p. 239.

to the Emperor; threatening to bring down the Russians in case the war should be renewed; and insinuating that Buonaparte sacrificed the desire of peace to his military fame, and desired a renewal of the war. Napoleon, with stern but restrained indignation, took from a bracket an ornamental piece of china, on which Cobentzel set some value, as being a present from the Empress Catherine. "The truce," he said, "is then ended, and war declared. But beware—before the end of autumn, I will break your empire into as many fragments as this potsherd."[302] He dashed the piece of china against the hearth, and withdrew abruptly. Again we are reminded of the Argantes of Tasso.[303]

The Austrian plenipotentiaries no longer hesitated to submit to all Napoleon's demands, rather than again see him commence his tremendous career of irresistible invasion. The treaty of Campo Formio therefore was signed on the following day; not the less promptly, perhaps, that the affairs at Paris appeared so doubtful as to invite an ambitious and aspiring man like Napoleon to approach the scene where honours and power were distributed, and where jarring factions seemed to await the influence of a character so distinguished and so determined.

The fate of Venice, more from her ancient history than either the value of her institutions, which were execrable, or the importance of her late existence, still dwells somewhat on the memory. The ancient republic fell "as a fool dieth." The aristocrats cursed the selfishness of Austria, by whom they were swallowed up, though they had perilled themselves in her cause. The republicans hastened to escape from Austrian domination, grinding their teeth with rage, and cursing no less the egotistic policy of the French, who, making a convenient pretext of their interest, had pretended to assign them a free constitution, and then resigned them to become the vassals of a despotic government.

---

[302] Montholon, tom. iv., p. 251.
[303] Spiegò quel crudo il seno, e'l manto scosse, Ed a guerra mortal, disse, vi sfido: E'l disse in atto si feroce ed empio Che parve aprir di Giano il chiuso tempio. *La Gerusalemme Liberata, Canto II.*—S.
His lap he open'd and spread forth his cloke, To mortal wars, he saies, I you defie— And this he uttered with fell rage and hate And seem'd of Janus' church t' undoe the gate. Fairfax.

The French secretary of legation, who had played a remarkably active part during the Revolution, hazarded a remonstrance to Buonaparte on the surrender of Venice to Austria, instead of its being formed into a free democracy, or united with the Cisalpine republic.[304] Buonaparte laughed to scorn a man, whose views were still fixed on diffusing and propagating the principles of Jacobinism. "I have received your letter," was the stern and contemptuous reply, "and cannot comprehend it. The Republic of France is not bound by any treaty, to sacrifice its interests and advantages to the Committee of Public Safety in Venice, or to any other class of individuals. France does not make war in behalf and for the benefit of others.[305] I know it costs nothing for a few chattering declaimers, whom I might better describe as madmen, to talk of a universal republic—I wish they would try a winter campaign. The Venetian republic exists no longer. Effeminate, corrupted, treacherous, and hypocritical, the Venetians are unfit for liberty. If she has the spirit to appreciate, or courage to assert it, the time is not unfavourable—let her stand up for it."[306] Thus, with insult added to misery, and great contempt thrown by Napoleon on the friends of liberty all over the world, the fate of Venice was closed. The most remarkable incident of the final transfer to the Austrians was, that the aged Doge Marini dropt down senseless as he was about to take the oath of allegiance to the Imperial commissioner, and died shortly after.

CONGRESS OF RASTADT

Nov. 12.

Napoleon Buonaparte had now finished for the present his career of destiny in Italy, which country first saw his rising talents, and was always a subject of peculiar interest to him. He took an

---

[304] See this remonstrance in Thibaudeau, tom. iii., p. 393.
[305] The language of injustice is alike in similar instances. When Edward I., in the course of over-running Scotland, was reminded of the claims of the candidate for the throne, in whose cause he had pretended to take arms, he answered in the very words of Buonaparte,—"Have we nothing else to do but to conquer kingdoms for other people?"—S.
[306] Daru, tom. vi., p. 60; Thibaudeau, tom. iii., p. 394.

affecting leave of the soldiers,[307] who could scarce hope ever to see him replaced by a general of merits so transcendent, and made a moderate and judicious address to the Cisalpine republic. Finally, he departed, to return through Switzerland to Rastadt, where a congress was sitting for the settlement and pacification of the German empire, and where he was to act as a plenipotentiary on the part of France.[308]

On the journey he was observed to be moody and deeply contemplative. The separation from a hundred thousand men whom he might call his own, and the uncertainty of the future destinies to which he might be summoned, are enough to account for this, without supposing, as some have done, that he already had distinctly formed any of those projects of ambition which Time opened to him. Doubtless, however, his ardent ambition showed him remote and undefined visions of greatness. He could not but be sensible that he returned to the capital of France in a situation which scarce admitted of any mediocrity. He must either be raised to a yet more distinguished height, or altogether broken down, levelled with the mass of subjects, and consigned to comparative obscurity. There was no middle station for the Conqueror and Liberator of Italy.

---

[307] "Soldiers! I set out to-morrow for Rastadt. Separated from the army, I shall sigh for the moment of my rejoining it, and braving fresh dangers. Whatever post government may assign to the soldiers of the army of Italy, they will always be the worthy supporters of liberty, and of the glory of the French name. Soldiers! when you talk of the princes you have conquered, of the nations you have set free, and the battles you have fought in two campaigns, say, 'in the next two campaigns we shall do still more!'"
[308] Montholon, tom. iv., p. 258.

CHAPTER XI

Retrospect—The Directory—they become unpopular—Causes of their unpopularity—Also at enmity among themselves—State of public feeling in France—In point of numbers, favourable to the Bourbons; but the Army and monied Interest against them—Pichegru, head of the Royalists, appointed President of the Council of Five Hundred—Barbé Marbois, another Royalist, President of the Council of Ancients—Directory throw themselves upon the succour of Hoche and Buonaparte—Buonaparte's personal Politics discussed—Pichegru's Correspondence with the Bourbons—known to Buonaparte—He despatches Augereau to Paris—Directory arrest their principal Opponents in the Councils on the 18th Fructidor, and Banish them to Guiana—Narrow and Impolitic Conduct of the Directory to Buonaparte—Projected Invasion of England.

While the conqueror of Italy was pursuing his victories beyond the Alps, the French Directory, in whose name he achieved them, had become, to the conviction of all men, as unlikely to produce the benefits of a settled government, as any of their predecessors vested with the supreme rule.

RETROSPECT

It is with politics as with mechanics, ingenuity is not always combined with utility. Some one observed to the late celebrated Mr. Watt, that it was wonderful for what a number of useless inventions, illustrated by the most ingenious and apparently satisfactory models, patents were yearly issued: he replied, that he had often looked at them with interest, and had found several, the idea of which had occurred to himself in the course of his early studies. "But," said he, with his natural masculine sagacity, "it is one thing to make an ingenious model, and another to contrive an engine which shall work its task. Most of these pretty toys, when they are applied to practical purposes, are found deficient in some point of strength, or correctness of mechanism, which destroys all chance of their ever becoming long or generally useful." Some such imperfection seems to have attended the works of these speculative politicians who framed the various ephemeral constitutions of France. However well they looked upon paper, and however reasonable they sounded to the ear, no one ever thought of them as laws which required veneration and obedience. Did a constitutional rule preclude a favourite measure, to break it down, or leap over it, was the French statesman's unhesitating practice. A rule was always devised applicable to circumstances; and before that, the theory of the constitution was uniformly made to give way.

THE DIRECTORY

The constitution of the year Three was not more permanent than those by which it had been preceded. For some time, the Directory, which contained men of considerable talent, conducted themselves with great prudence. The difficulty and danger of their situation served to prevent their separating, as the weight put above an arch keeps the stones in their places. Their exertions in the attempt to redeem the finances, support the war, and re-establish the tranquillity of the country, were attended at first with success. The national factions also sunk before them for a season. They had defeated the aristocratic citizens of Paris on the 13th Vendemiaire; and when the original revolutionists, or democrats, attempted a conspiracy, under the conduct of Gracchus Babœuf,[309] their endeavours to seduce the troops totally failed, and their lives paid

---

[309] An Italian, by name Buonarotti, and of the same family with the great Michael Angelo, has recently published a full account of the conspiracy of Babœuf,—to this writer the curious reader is referred. "Les fruits sont à tous, la terre à personne," was his favourite text and that of his fellow-levellers, and the burden of their songs, which were to take place of Ça Ira, and La Carmagnole, was "Le Soleil luit pour tout le monde." On being arrested, Babœuf wrote to the Directory—"Whatever may be my fate, my name will be placed with those of Barnevet and Sidney; whether conducted to death or to banishment, I am certain of arriving at immortality!" He was condemned to the guillotine in May, 1797, but stabbed himself in his prison.

the forfeit of their rash attempt to bring back the Reign of Terror. Thus, the Directory, or executive power, under the constitution of the year Three, were for a season triumphant over the internal factions, and, belonging to neither, were in a situation to command both.

But they had few who were really, and on principle, attached to their government, and most endured it only as something better than a new revolutionary movement, and otherwise in no respect eligible. To have rendered their authority permanent, the Directory must have had great unanimity in their own body, and also brilliant success abroad, and they enjoyed neither one nor the other. The very concoction of their body included the principles of disunion. They were a sort of five kings, retiring from office by rotation, inhabiting each his separate class of apartments in the Luxembourg palace, having each his different establishments, classes of clients, circles of courtiers, flatterers, and instruments. The republican simplicity, of late so essential to a patriot, was laid aside entirely. New costumes of the most splendid kind were devised for the different office-bearers of the state. This change took its rise from the weakness and vanity of Barras, who loved show, and used to go a-hunting with all the formal attendance of a prince. But it was an indulgence of luxury, which gave scandal to both the great parties in the state;—the Republicans, who held it altogether in contempt;—and the Royalists, who considered it as an usurpation of the royal dress and appendages.[310]

The finances became continually more and more a subject of uneasiness. In the days of terror, money was easily raised, because it was demanded under pain of death, and assignats were raised to *par* by guillotining those who bought or sold them at less than their full value; but the powerful argument of violence and compulsion being removed, the paper money fell to a ruinous discount, till its depression threatened, unless remedied, altogether to stop the course of public business.[311] It perhaps arose from the difficulty of raising supplies, that the Directory assumed towards other countries

---

[310] Montholon, tom. iv., p. 195.
[311] A decree of the Directory, of the 25th January, 1797, fixed the current value of assignats at twenty sous for a hundred francs.—Montgaillard, tom. v., p. 4.

a greedy, grasping, and rapacious character, which threw disgrace at once upon the individuals who indulged it, and the state whom they represented. They loaded with exactions the trade of the Bavarian republic, whose freedom they had pretended to recognise, and treated with most haughty superiority the ambassadors of independent states. Some of these high officers, and Barras in particular, were supposed accessible to gross corruption, and believed to hold communication with those agents and stockbrokers, who raised money by jobbing in the public funds—a more deservedly unpopular accusation than which can hardly be brought against a minister. It was, indeed, a great error in the constitution, that, though one hundred thousand livres were yearly allowed to each director while in office, yet he had no subsequent provision after he had retired from his fractional share of sovereignty. This penury, on the part of the public, opened a way to temptation, though of a kind to which mean minds only are obnoxious; and such men as Barras[312] were tempted to make provision for futurity, by availing themselves of present opportunity.

Their five majesties (sires) of the Luxembourg, as people called them in ridicule, had also their own individual partialities and favourite objects, which led them in turn to tease the French people with unnecessary legislation. La Reveillere-Lepaux was that inconsistent yet not uncommon character, an intolerant philosopher and an enthusiastic deist. He established a priesthood, and hymns and ceremonies for deism; and, taking up the hopeful project of substituting a deistical worship for the Christian faith, just where Robespierre had laid it down, he harassed the nation with laws to oblige them to observe the *decades* of their new calendar as holidays, and to work at their ordinary trades on the Christian Sabbath.[313] At La Reveillere's theory freethinkers laughed, and religious men shuddered; but all were equally annoyed by the legislative measures adopted on a subject so ridiculous as this new ritual of

---

[312] "When Barras went out of the Directory, he had still a large fortune, and he did not attempt to conceal it. It was not, indeed, large enough to have contributed to the derangement of the finances, but the manner in which it had been acquired, by favouring the contractors, impaired the morality of the nation."—Napoleon, *Montholon*, tom. iv., p. 135.

[313] Montholon, tom. iv., p. 200.

heathenism.[314] Another cause of vexation was the philosophical arrangement of weights and measures upon a new principle, which had, in the meantime, the inconvenience of introducing doubt and uncertainty into all the arrangements of internal commerce, and deranging entirely such as France continued to hold with countries who were only acquainted with the ordinary standard.[315]

It might have been thought that the distinguished success of the French arms under the auspices of the Directory would have dazzled the eyes of the French, attached as they have always been to military glory, and blinded them to other less agreeable measures of their government. But the public were well aware, that the most brilliant share of these laurels had been reaped by Buonaparte on his own account; that he had received but slender reinforcements from France—the magnitude of his achievements considered; and that in regard to the instructions of government, much of his success was owing to his departure from them, and following his own course. It was also whispered, that he was an object of suspicion to the directors, and on his part undervalued their talents, and despised their persons. On the Rhine, again, though nothing could have been more distinguished than the behaviour of the Republican armies, yet their successes had been checkered with many reverses, and, contrasted with the Italian campaigns, lost their impression on the imagination.

While they were thus becoming unpopular in the public opinion, the Directory had the great misfortune to be at enmity among themselves. From the time that Letourneur[316] retired from

---

[314] "La Reveillere-Lepaux was short, and his exterior was as unprepossessing as can well be imagined; in his person he was a true Esop. He wrote tolerably well, but his intelligence was confined, and he had neither habits of business, nor knowledge of mankind. The Jardin des Plantes and the Theophilanthropy, a new sect of which he had the folly to become the founder, occupied all his time. He was an honest man—poor when he became a member of the Directory, and poor when he left it."—Napoleon, *Las Cases*, tom. ii., p. 136.

[315] "The new system of weights and measures will be a source of embarrassment and difficulties for several generations; and it is probable that the first learned commission employed to verify the measure of the meridian, will find it necessary to make some corrections. Thus are nations tormented about trifles!"—Napoleon, *Montholon*, tom. iv., p. 203.

[316] "Letourneur de la Manche was born in Normandy. It is difficult to explain how he came to be appointed to the Directory; it can only be from one of those unaccountable caprices of which large assemblies so often give an example. He was a man of narrow capacity, little

office in terms of the constitution, and Barthelemy was elected in his stead, there was a majority and an opposition in the Directory, the former consisting of Barras, Rewbel,[317] and La Reveillere—the latter, of Carnot and Barthelemy. Of the two last, Carnot (who had been, it may be remembered, a member of the Committee of Public Safety under Robespierre) was a determined Republican, and Barthelemy a Royalist;—so strangely do revolutionary changes, like the eddies and currents of a swollen river, bring together and sweep down side by side in the same direction, objects the most different and opposed. Barthelemy of course dissented from the majority of the Directors, because secretly and warmly he desired the restoration of the Bourbons—an event which must have been fraught with danger to his colleagues, all of whom had voted for the death of Louis XVI. Carnot also differed from the majority, certainly with no such wish or view; but, his temper being as overbearing as his genius was extensive, he was impatient of opposition, especially in such cases where he knew he was acting wisely. He advised strongly, for example, the ratification of the articles of Leoben, instead of placing all which France had acquired, and all which she might lose, on the last fatal cast with an enemy, strong in his very despair, and who might raise large armies, while that of Buonaparte could neither be reinforced nor supported in case of a reverse. Barras's anger on the occasion was so great, that he told Carnot at the council-board, it was to him they owed that infamous treaty of Leoben.

While the Directory were thus disunited among themselves, the nation showed their dissatisfaction openly, and particularly in the two bodies of representatives. The majority indeed of the Council of Elders adhered to the Directory, many of that body belonging to the old republican partisans. But in the more popularly composed Council of Five Hundred, the opposition to the government possessed a great majority, all of whom were decidedly against the Directory, and most of them impressed with the wish of restoring,

---

learning, and of a weak mind. He was, however, a man of strict probity, and left the Directory without any fortune."—Napoleon, *Las Cases*, tom. ii., p. 142.

[317] "Rewbel, born in Alsace, was one of the best lawyers in the town of Colmar. He possessed that kind of intelligence which denotes a man skilled in the practice of the law,—his influence was always felt in deliberations—he was easily inspired with prejudices, and had little faith in the existence of virtue. It is problematical whether he did or did not amass a fortune, during the time he was in the Directory."—Napoleon, *Las Cases*, tom. ii., p. 138.

upon terms previously to be adjusted, the ancient race of legitimate monarchs. This body of persons so thinking, was much increased by the number of emigrants, who obtained, on various grounds, permission to return to their native country after the fall of Robespierre. The forms of civil life began now to be universally renewed; and, as had been the case in France at all times, excepting during the bloody Reign of Terror, women of rank, beauty, talent, and accomplishments, began again to resume their places in society, and their saloons or boudoirs were often the scene of deep political discourse, of a sort which in Britain is generally confined to the cabinet, library, or dining-parlour. The wishes of many, or most of these coteries, were in favour of royalty; the same feelings were entertained by the many thousands who saw no possible chance of settling the nation on any other model; and there is little doubt, that had France been permitted at that moment an uninfluenced choice, the Bourbon family would have been recalled to the throne by the great majority of the French people.

But, for reasons mentioned elsewhere, the military were the decided opponents of the Bourbons, and the purchasers of national domains, through every successive sale which might have taken place, were deeply interested against their restoration. Numbers might be on the side of the Royalists; but physical force, and the influence of wealth and of the monied interest, were decidedly against them.

PICHEGRU

Pichegru might now be regarded as chief of the Royal party. He was an able and successful general, to whom France owed the conquest of Holland. Like La Fayette and Dumouriez, he had been disgusted with the conduct of the Revolution; and like the last of the two generals named, had opened a communication with the Bourbons. He was accused of having suffered his army to be betrayed in a defeat by Clairfait; and the government, in 1796, removed him from the command of the army of the Sambre and Meuse, offering him in exchange the situation of ambassador to Sweden. He declined this species of honourable exile, and, retiring to Franche Compté, continued his correspondence with the Imperial generals.[318] The Royalists expected much from the countenance of a military man of a name so imposing; but we have seen more than once in the course of these memoirs, that a general without an army is like a hilt without the blade which it should wield and direct.

An opportunity, however, offered Pichegru the means of serving his party in a civil capacity, and that a most important one. The elections of May, 1797, made to replace that proportion of the councils which retired by rotation, terminated generally in favour of the Royalists, and served plainly to show on which side the balance of popular feeling now leaned. Pichegru, who had been returned as one of the deputies, was chosen by acclamation President of the Council of Five Hundred, and Barbé Marbois, another Royalist, was elected to the same office by the Council of Ancients, while, as we have already said, Barthelemy likewise friendly to monarchy, was introduced into the Directory.

These elections were evil signs for the Directory, who did not fail soon to be attacked on every side, and upbraided with the continuance of the war and the financial distresses. Various journals were at the disposal of the party opposed to the majority of the directors, and hostilities were commenced between the parties, both in the assemblies, where the Royalists had the advantage, and in the public papers, where they were also favourably listened to. The French are of an impatient temper, and could not be long brought to carry on their warfare within the limits assigned by the constitution. Each party, without much regard to the state of the law, looked about for the means of physical force with which they might arm themselves. The Directory, (that is, the majority of that body,) sensible of their unpopularity, and the predominance of the opposite party, which seemed for a time to have succeeded to the boldness and audacity of the revolutionary class had, in their agony of extremity, recourse to the army, and threw themselves upon the succour of Hoche and of Buonaparte.

---

[318] Montholon, tom. iv., p. 210.

We have elsewhere said, that Buonaparte at this period was esteemed a steady Republican. Pichegru believed him to be such when he dissuaded the Royalists from any attempt to gain over the General of Italy; and as he had known him at school at Brienne, declared him of too stubborn a character to afford the least hope of success. Augereau was of the same opinion, and mistook his man so much, that when Madame de Staël asked whether Buonaparte was not inclined to make himself King of Lombardy, he replied, with great simplicity, "that he was a young man of too elevated a character."[319] Perhaps Buonaparte himself felt the same for a moment, when, in a despatch to the Directory, he requests their leave to withdraw from the active service of the Republic, as one who had acquired more glory than was consistent with happiness. "Calumny," he said, "may torment herself in vain with ascribing to me treacherous designs. My civil, like my military career, shall be conforming to republican principles."[320]

The public papers also, those we mean on the side of the Directory, fell into a sort of rapture on the classical republican feelings by which Buonaparte was actuated, which they said rendered the hope of his return a pleasure pure and unmixed, and precluded the possibility of treachery or engrossing ideas on his side. "The factious of every class," they said, "cannot have an enemy more steady, or the government a friend more faithful, than he who, invested with the military power of which he has made so glorious a use, sighs only to resign a situation so brilliant, prefers happiness to glory, and now that the Republic is graced with triumph and peace, desires for himself only a simple and retired life."[321]

But though such were the ideas then entertained of Buonaparte's truly republican character, framed, doubtless, on the model of Cincinnatus in his classical simplicity, we may be permitted to look a little closer into the ultimate views of him, who was admitted by his enemies and friends, avouched by himself, and

---

[319] "This singular answer was in exact conformity with the ideas of the moment. The sincere Republicans would have regarded it as a degradation for a man, however distinguished he might be, to wish to turn the revolution to his personal advantage."—Mad. de Staël, tom. ii., p. 175.
[320] Moniteur, No. 224, May 3, 1797.—S.
[321] Le Rédacteur, May 1, 1797.

sanctioned by the journals, as a pure and disinterested republican: and we think the following changes may be traced.

Whether Buonaparte was ever at heart a real Jacobin even for the moment, may be greatly doubted, whatever mask his situation obliged him to wear. He himself always repelled the charge as an aspersion. His engagement in the affair of the Sections probably determined his opinions as Republican, or rather Thermidorien, at the time, as became him by whom the Republican army had been led and commanded on that day. Besides, at the head of an army zealously republican, even his power over their minds required to be strengthened, for some time at least, by an apparent correspondence in political sentiments betwixt the troops and the general. But in the practical doctrines of government which he recommended to the Italian Republics, his ideas were studiously moderate, and he expressed the strongest fear of, and aversion to, revolutionary doctrines. He recommended the granting equal rights and equal privileges to the nobles, as well as to the indignant vassals and plebeians who had risen against them. In a word, he advocated a free set of institutions, without the intermediate purgatory of a revolution. He was, therefore, at this period, far from being a Jacobin.

But though Buonaparte's wishes were thus wisely moderated by practical views, he was not the less likely to be sensible that he was the object of fear, of hatred, and of course of satire and misrepresentation, to that side of the opposed parties in France which favoured royalty. Unhappily for himself, he was peculiarly accessible to every wound of this nature, and, anxiously jealous of his fame, suffered as much under the puny attacks of the journalists,[322] as a noble steer or a gallant horse does amid his rich pasture, under the persecutions of insects, which, in comparison to himself, are not only impotent, but nearly invisible. In several letters to the Directory, he exhibits feelings of this nature which would have been more gracefully concealed, and evinces an irritability

---

[322] "All the journals were full of harangues against the General of the Army of Italy: They depreciated his successes, vilified his character, calumniated his administration, threw out suspicions respecting his fidelity to the Republic, and accused him of ambitious designs."—Napoleon, *Montholon*, tom. iv., p. 212.

against the opposition prints, which we think likely to have increased the zeal with which he came forward on the Republican side at this important crisis.[323]

INTRIGUES OF PICHEGRU

Another circumstance, which, without determining Buonaparte's conduct, may have operated in increasing his good-will to the cause which he embraced, was his having obtained the clew of Pichegru's correspondence with the house of Bourbon.[324] To have concealed this, would have been but a second rate merit with the exiled family, whose first thanks must have been due to the partisan whom he protected. This was no part for Buonaparte to play; not that we have a right to say he would have accepted the chief character had it been offered to him, but his ambition could never have stooped to any inferior place in the drama. In all probability, his ideas fluctuated betwixt the example of Cromwell and of Washington—to be the actual liberator, or the absolute governor of his country.

His particular information respecting Pichegru's negotiations, was derived from an incident at the capture of Venice.

When the degenerate Venetians, more under the impulse of vague terror than from any distinct plan, adopted in haste and tumult the measure of totally surrendering their constitution and rights, to be new modelled by the French general after his pleasure, they were guilty of a gross and aggravated breach of hospitality, in seizing the person and papers of the Comte d'Entraigues,[325] agent or

---

[323] See especially his Letter to the Directory, 17th July.—*Correspondence Inédite*, tom. iv., p. 14.
[324] Montholon, tom. iv., pp. 148, 211.
[325] This gentleman was one of the second emigration, who left France during Robespierre's ascendency. He was employed as a political agent by the Court of Russia, after the affair of Venice, which proves that he was not at least convicted of treachery to the Bourbon princes. In July, 1812, he was assassinated at his villa at Hackney, near London, by an Italian domestic, who, having murdered both the Count and Countess, shot himself through the head, leaving no clew to discover the motive of his villany. It was remarked that the villain used Count d'Entraigues' own pistols and dagger, which, apprehensive of danger as a political intriguer, he had always ready prepared in his apartment.—S.

envoy of the exiled Bourbons, who was then residing under their protection. The envoy himself, as Buonaparte alleges, was not peculiarly faithful to his trust; but, besides his information, his portfolio contained many proofs of Pichegru's correspondence with the allied generals, and with the Bourbons, which placed his secret absolutely in the power of the General of Italy, and might help to confirm the line of conduct which he had already meditated to adopt.

Possessed of these documents, and sure that, in addressing a French army of the day, he would swim with the tide if he espoused the side of Republicanism, Buonaparte harangued his troops on the anniversary of the taking the Bastille, in a manner calculated to awake their ancient democratic enthusiasm:—"Soldiers, this is the 14th July! You see before you the names of our companions in arms, dead in the field of honour for the liberty of their country. They have set you an example; you owe your lives to thirty millions of Frenchmen, and to the national name, which has received new splendour from your victories. Soldiers! I am aware you are deeply affected by the dangers which threaten the country. But she can be subjected to none which are real. The same men who made France triumph over united Europe, still live.—Mountains separate us from France, but you would traverse them with the speed of eagles, were it necessary to maintain the constitution, defend liberty, protect the Government and the Republicans. Soldiers, the Government watches over the laws as a sacred deposit committed to them. The Royalists shall only show themselves to perish. Dismiss all inquietude, and let us swear by the manes of those heroes who have died by our sides for liberty—let us swear, too, on our standards—War to the enemies of the Republic, and of the Constitution of the year Three!"[326]

It is needless to remark, that, under the British constitution, or any other existing on fixed principles, the haranguing an armed body of soldiers, with the purpose of inducing them to interfere by force in any constitutional question, would be in one point of view mutiny, in another high treason.

---

[326] Moniteur, No. 305, July 23.

The hint so distinctly given by the general, was immediately adopted by the troops. Deep called to deep, and each division of the army, whatever its denomination, poured forth its menaces of military force and compulsion against the opposition party in the councils, who held opinions different from those of their military chief, but which they had, at least hitherto, only expressed and supported by those means of resistance which the constitution placed in their power. In other words, the soldiers' idea of a republic was, that the sword was to decide the constitutional debates, which give so much trouble to ministers in a mixed or settled government. The Pretorian bands, the Strelitzes, the Janissaries, have all in their turn entertained this primitive and simple idea of reforming abuses in a state, and changing, by the application of military force, an unpopular dynasty, or an obnoxious ministry.

AUGEREAU DESPATCHED TO PARIS

It was not by distant menaces alone that Buonaparte served the Directory at this important crisis. He despatched Augereau to Paris, ostensibly for the purpose of presenting the standards taken at Mantua, but in reality to command the armed force which the majority of the Directory had determined to employ against their dissentient colleagues, and the opponents of their measures in the national councils. Augereau was a blunt, bold, stupid soldier, a devoted Jacobin, whose principles were sufficiently well known to warrant his standing upon no constitutional delicacies.[327] But in case the Directory failed, Buonaparte kept himself in readiness to march instantly to Lyons at the head of fifteen thousand men. There rallying the Republicans, and all who were attached to the Revolution, he would, according to his own well-chosen expression, like Cæsar, have crossed the Rubicon at the head of the popular party—and ended, doubtless, like Cæsar, by himself usurping the

---

[327] "The Directory requested General Buonaparte to send one of his generals of brigade to Paris, to await their orders. He chose General Augereau, a man very decided in action, and not very capable of reasoning—two qualities which rendered him an excellent instrument of despotism, provided the despotism assumed the name of revolution."—Mad. de Staël, tom. ii., p. 180.

supreme command, which he pretended to assert in behalf of the people.[328]

Sept. 4.

But Buonaparte's presence was not so essentially necessary to the support of the Directory as he might have expected, or as he perhaps hoped. They had military aid nearer at hand. Disregarding a fundamental law of the Constitution, which declared that armed troops should not be brought within a certain distance of the Legislative Bodies, they moved towards Paris a part of General Hoche's army. The majority of the Councils becoming alarmed, prepared means of defence by summoning the national guards to arms. But Augereau allowed them no time. He marched to their place of meeting, at the head of a considerable armed force.[329] The guards stationed for their protection, surprised or faithless, offered no resistance; and, proceeding as men possessed of the superior strength, the Directory treated their political opponents as state prisoners, arrested Barthelemey—Carnot having fled to Geneva—and made prisoners, in the hall of the Assembly and elsewhere, Willot, President of the Council of Ancients, Pichegru, President of that of the Five Hundred,[330] and above one hundred and fifty deputies, journalists, and other public characters. As an excuse for these arbitrary and illegal proceedings, the Directory made public the intercepted correspondence of Pichegru; although few of the

---

[328] Montholon, tom. iv., p. 216.

[329] "I spent the night of the 17th in beholding the preparations for the awful scene which was to take place in a few hours. None but soldiers appeared in the streets. The cannon, brought to surround the palace where the Legislative Body assembled, were rolling along the pavements; but, except their noise, all was silence. No hostile assemblage was seen any where; nor was it known against whom all this apparatus was directed. Liberty was the only power vanquished in that fatal struggle. It might have been said, that she was seen to fly, like a wandering spirit, at the approach of the day which was to shine upon her destruction."—Mad. de Staël, tom. ii., p. 182.

[330] "Astonishment was excited by the little respect which the soldiers showed for a general who had so often led them to victory; but he had been successfully represented as a counter-revolutionist—a name which when the public opinion is free, exercises in France a kind of magical power. Besides, Pichegru had no means of producing an effect on the imagination: He was a man of good manners, but without striking expression, either in his features or his words. It has often been said, that he was guided in war by the councils of another. This is, at least, credible; for his look and conversation were so dull, that they suggested no idea of his being fit for becoming the leader of any enterprise."—Mad. de Staël, tom. ii., p. 184.

others involved in the same accusation were in the secret of the Royalist conspiracy. Indeed, though all who desired an absolute repose from the revolutionary altercations which tore the country to pieces, began to look that way, he must have been a violent partisan of royalty indeed, that could have approved of the conduct of a general, who, like Pichegru, commanding an army, had made it his business to sacrifice his troops to the sword of the enemy, by disappointing and deranging those plans which it was his duty to have carried into effect.

Few would at first believe Pichegru's breach of faith; but it was suddenly confirmed by a proclamation of Moreau, who, in the course of the war, had intercepted a baggage waggon belonging to the Austrian general Klinglin, and became possessed of the whole secret correspondence, which, nevertheless, he had never mentioned, until it came out by the seizure of the Comte d'Entraigues' portfolio. Then, indeed, fearing perhaps the consequences of having been so long silent, Moreau published what he knew. Regnier had observed the same suspicious silence; which seems to infer, that if these generals did not precisely favour the royal cause, they were not disposed to be active in detecting the conspiracies formed in its behalf.

THE EIGHTEENTH FRUCTIDOR

The Directory made a tyrannical use of the power which they obtained by their victory of the 18th Fructidor, as this epoch was called. They spilt, indeed, no blood, but otherwise their measures against the defeated party were of the most illegal and oppressive character. A law, passed in the heat of animosity, condemned two directors, fifty deputies, and a hundred and forty-eight individuals of different classes (most of whom were persons of some character and influence,) to be transported to the scorching and unhealthy deserts of Guiana, which, to many, was a sentence of lingering but certain death. They were barbarously treated, both on the passage to that dreadful place, and after they arrived there. It was a singular part of their fate, that they found several of the fiercest of their ancient enemies, the Jacobins, still cursing God and defying man, in the same land of wretchedness and exile.

Besides these severities, various elections were arbitrarily dissolved, and other strong measures of public safety, as they were called, adopted, to render the power of the Directory more indisputable. During this whole revolution, the lower portion of the population, which used to be so much agitated upon like occasions, remained perfectly quiet; the struggle lay exclusively between the middle classes, who inclined to a government on the basis of royalty, and the Directory, who, without having any very tangible class of political principles, had become possessed of the supreme power, desired to retain it, and made their point good by the assistance of the military.

Buonaparte was much disappointed at the result of the 18th Fructidor, chiefly because, if less decisive, it would have added more to his consequence, and have given him an opportunity of crossing, as he termed it, the Rubicon. As it was, the majority of the directors,—three men of no particular talent, undistinguished alike by birth, by services to their country, or even by accidental popularity, and cast as it were by chance, upon supreme power,— remained by the issue of the struggle still the masters of the bold and ambitious conqueror, who probably already felt his own vocation to be for command rather than obedience.

Napoleon appears by his Memoirs to have regretted the violence with which the victorious directors prosecuted their personal revenge, which involved many for whom he had respect. He declares his own idea of punishment would have gone no farther than imprisoning some of the most dangerous conspirators, and placing others under the watchful superintendence of the police. He must have taken some painful interest in the fate of Carnot in particular, whom he seems to have regarded as one of his most effective patrons.[331] Indeed, it is said that he was so much displeased

---

[331] In Carnot's Memoirs, the merit of discovering Buonaparte's talents and taking care of his promotion, is attributed to Carnot, rather than to Barras. However this may be, it is certain that Napoleon acknowledged great obligation to Carnot, and protested to him perpetual gratitude.—See *Moniteur*, No. 140, Feb. 1, 1797.—S.

with the Directory even prior to the 18th Fructidor, that he refused to remit a sum of money with which he had promised to aid them for the purpose of forwarding that event.[332] Barras's secretary was sent to task him with this contumacy: which he did so unceremoniously, that the general, unused to contradiction, was about to order this agent to be shot; but, on consideration, put him off with some insignificant reply.

THE DIRECTORY

It followed, from the doubtful terms on which Buonaparte stood with the Directory, that they must have viewed his return to Paris with some apprehension, when they considered the impression likely to be made on any capital, but especially on that of Paris, by the appearance there of one who seemed to be the chosen favourite of Fortune, and to deserve her favours by the use which he made of them. The mediocrity of such men as Barras never gives them so much embarrassment, as when, being raised to an elevation above their desert, they find themselves placed in comparison with one to whom nature has given the talents which their situation requires in themselves. The higher their condition, their demeanour is the more awkward; for the factious advantages which they possess cannot raise them to the natural dignity of character, unless in the sense in which a dwarf, by the assistance of crutches, may be said to be as tall as a giant. The Directory had already found Buonaparte, on several occasions, a spirit of the sort which would not be commanded. Undoubtedly they would have been well pleased had it been possible to have found him employment at a distance; but as that seemed difficult, they were obliged to look round for the means of employing him at home, or abide the tremendous risk of his finding occupation for himself.

It is surprising that it did not occur to the Directory to make at least the attempt of conciliating Buonaparte, by providing for his future fortune largely and liberally, at the expense of the public. He deserved that attention to his private affairs, for he had himself entirely neglected them. While he drew from the dominions which

---

[332] Las Cases, tom. ii., p. 155.

he conquered or overawed in Italy, immense sums in behalf of the French nation, which he applied in part to the support of the army, and in part remitted to the Directory, he kept no accounts, nor were any demanded of him; but according to his own account, he transmitted sixty millions of francs to Paris, and had not remaining of his own funds, when he returned from Italy, more than three hundred thousand.[333]

It is no doubt true, that, to raise these sums, Buonaparte had pillaged the old states, thus selling to the newly formed commonwealths their liberty and equality at a very handsome rate, and probably leaving them in very little danger of corruption from that wealth which is said to be the bane of republican virtue. But on the other hand, it must be acknowledged, that if the French general plundered the Italians as Cortez did the Mexicans, he did not reserve any considerable share of the spoil for his own use, though the opportunity was often in his power.

The commissary Salicetti, his countryman, recommended a less scrupulous line of conduct. Soon after the first successes in Italy, he acquainted Napoleon that the Chevalier d'Este, the Duke of Modena's brother and envoy, had four millions of francs, in gold, contained in four chests, prepared for his acceptance. "The Directory and the Legislative Bodies will never," he said, "acknowledge your services—your circumstances require the money, and the duke will gain a protector."

"I thank you," said Buonaparte; "but I will not for four millions place myself in the power of the Duke of Modena."

The Venetians, in the last agony of their terrors, offered the French general a present of seven millions, which was refused in the same manner. Austria also had made her proffers; and they were nothing less than a principality in the empire, to be established in Napoleon's favour, consisting of two hundred and fifty thousand inhabitants at least, a provision which would have put him out of danger of suffering by the proverbial ingratitude of a republic. The general transmitted his thanks to the Emperor for this proof of the

---

[333] Montholon, tom. iv., p. 267.

interest which he took in his fortune, but added, he could accept of no wealth or preferment which did not proceed from the French people, and that he should be always satisfied with the amount of revenue which they might be disposed to afford him.[334]

But however free from the wish to obtain wealth by any indirect means, Napoleon appears to have expected, that in return for public services of such an unusual magnitude, some provision ought to have been made for him. An attempt was made to procure a public grant of the domain of Chambord, and a large hotel in Paris, as an acknowledgment of the national gratitude for his brilliant successes; but the Directory thwarted the proposal.

Nov. 5.

The proposition respecting Chambord was not the only one of the kind. Malibran, a member of the Council of Five Hundred, made a motion that Buonaparte should be endowed with a revenue at the public charge, of fifty thousand livres annually, with a reversion to his wife of one half of that sum.[335] It may be supposed that this motion had not been sufficiently considered and preconcerted, since it was very indifferently received, and was evaded by the swaggering declaration of a member,[336] that such glorious deeds could not be rewarded by gold. So that the Assembly adopted the reasonable principle, that because the debt of gratitude was too great to be paid in money, therefore he to whom it was due was to be suffered to remain in comparative indigence—an economical mode of calculation, and not unlike that high-sounding doctrine of the civil law, which states, that a free man being seized on, and forcibly sold for a slave, shall obtain no damages on that account, because the liberty of a citizen is too transcendently valuable to be put to estimation.

---

[334] Montholon, tom. iv., p. 103.
[335] Moniteur, Nov. 8; Thibaudeau, tom. iii., p. 423.
[336] "Un grenadier Français avait fait une action très brillante; son général lui offre trois louis. Plus noble, plus généreux, le grenadier refuse, et lui dit: '*Mon général, on ne fait pas ces choses-là pour de l'argent.*' Irez-vous offrir de l'or à un homme courbé sous le poids des lauriers? Non non, l'ame de Buonaparte est trop grande," &c.—Thibaudeau, tom. iii., p. 423.

Whatever might be the motives of the Directory; whether they hoped that poverty might depress Buonaparte's ambition, render him more dependent on the government, and oblige him to remain in a private condition for want of means to put himself at the head of a party; or whether they acted with the indistinct and confused motives of little minds, who wish to injure those whom they fear, their conduct was alike ungracious and impolitic. They ought to have calculated, that a generous mind would have been attached by benefits, and that a selfish one might have been deterred from more doubtful and ambitious projects, by a prospect of sure and direct advantage; but that marked ill-will and distrust must in every case render him dangerous, who has the power to be so.

Their plan, instead of resting on an attempt to conciliate the ambitious conqueror, and soothe him to the repose of a tranquil indulgence of independence and ease, seems to have been that of devising for him new labours, like the wife of Eurystheus for the juvenile Hercules. If he succeeded, they may have privately counted upon securing the advantages for themselves; if he failed, they were rid of a troublesome rival in the race of power and popularity. It was with these views that they proposed to Napoleon to crown his military glories, by assuming the command of the preparations made for the conquest of England.

Chapter XII

View of the respective Situations of Great Britain and France, at the Period of Napoleon's return from Italy—Negotiations at Lisle—Broken off—Army of England decreed, and Buonaparte named to the Command—He takes up his Residence in Paris—Public Honours—The real Views of the Directory discovered to be the Expedition to Egypt—Armies of Italy and the Rhine, compared and contrasted—Napoleon's Objects and Motives in heading the Egyptian Expedition—those of the Directory regarding it—Its actual Impolicy—Curious Statement by Miot—The Armament sails from Toulon, on 19th May 1798—Napoleon arrives before Malta on 10th June—Proceeds on his course, and, escaping the British Squadron, lands at Alexandria on the 1st July—Description of the various Classes who inhabit Egypt:—1. The Fellahs and Bedouins—2. The Cophts—3. The Mamelukes—Napoleon issues a Proclamation against the Mamelukes—Marches against them on the 7th July—Discontent of the French Troops—Battle of the Pyramids on 21st of July—Cairo surrenders.

It might have been thought, such was the success of the French arms on the land, and of the British upon the sea, that the war must now be near its natural and unavoidable termination, like a fire when there no longer remain any combustibles to be devoured. Wherever water could bear them, the British vessels of war had swept the seas of the enemy. The greater part of the foreign colonies belonging to France and her allies, among whom she now numbered Holland and Spain, were in the possession of the English, nor had France a chance of recovering them. On the contrary, not a musket was seen pointed against France on the continent; so that it seemed as if the great rival nations, fighting with different weapons, and on different elements, must at length give up a contest, in which it was almost impossible to come to a decisive struggle.

NEGOTIATIONS AT LISLE

An attempt accordingly was made, by the negotiation of Lisle, to bring to a period the war, which appeared now to subsist entirely without an object. Lord Malmesbury, on that occasion, gave in, on the part of Britain, an offer to surrender all the conquests she had made from France and her allies; on condition of the cession of Trinidad, on the part of Spain, and of the Cape of Good Hope, Cochin, and Ceylon, on the part of Holland, with some stipulations in favour of the Prince of Orange and his adherents in the Netherlands. The French commissioners, in reply, declared, that their instructions required that the English should make a complete cession of their conquests, without any equivalent whatever; and they insisted, as indispensable preliminaries, that the King of Great Britain should lay aside his titular designation of King of France—that the Toulon fleet should be restored—and that the English should renounce their right to certain mortgages over the Netherlands, for money lent to the Emperor. Lord Malmesbury, of course, rejected a sweeping set of propositions, which decided every question against England even before the negotiation commenced, and solicited the French to offer some modified form of treaty.[337] The 18th Fructidor, however, had in the interim taken place, and the Republican party, being in possession of complete authority, broke off the negotiation, if it could be called such, abruptly, and ordered the English ambassador out of the dominions of the republic with very little ceremony. It was now proclaimed generally, that the existence of the English Carthage in the neighbourhood of the French Rome was altogether inadmissible; that England must be subdued once more, as in the times of William the Conqueror; and the hopes of a complete and final victory over their natural rival and enemy, as the two nations are but overapt to esteem each other, presented so flattering a prospect, that there was scarce a party in France, not even amongst the Royalists, which did not enter on

---

[337] Annual Register, vol. xl., p. 6.

what was expected to prove the decisive contest, with the revival of all those feelings of bitter animosity that had distinguished past ages.

Towards the end of October 1797, the Directory announced, that there should be instantly assembled on the shores of the ocean an army, to be called the Army of England, and that the Citizen-General Buonaparte was named to the command. The intelligence was received in every part of France with all the triumph which attends the anticipation of certain victory. The address of the Directory numbered all the conquests which France had won, and the efforts she had made, and prepared the French nation to expect the fruit of so many victories and sacrifices when they had punished England for her perfidy and maritime tyranny. "It is at London where the misfortunes of all Europe are forged and manufactured—It is in London that they must be terminated." In a solemn meeting held by the Directory, for the purpose of receiving the treaty of peace with Austria, which was presented to them by Berthier and Monge on the part of Buonaparte, the latter, who had been one of the commissioners for pillaging Italy of her pictures and statues, and who looked, doubtless, to a new harvest of rarities in England, accepted, on the part of the army and general, the task imposed by the French rulers. "The Government of England and the French Republic cannot both continue to exist—you have given the word which shall fall—already our victorious troops brandish their arms, and Scipio is at their head."

PARIS—MADAME DE STAËL

Dec. 5.

While this farce, for such it proved, was acting in Paris, the chief of the intended enterprise arrived there, and took up his abode in the same modest house which he had occupied before becoming the conqueror of palaces. The community of Paris, with much elegance, paid their successful general the compliment of changing the name of the street from Rue Chantereine to Rue de la Victoire.

In a metropolis where all is welcome that can vary the tedium of human life, the arrival of any remarkable person is a species of holiday; but such an eminent character as Buonaparte—the conqueror—the sage—the politician—the undaunted braver of every difficulty—the invincible victor in every battle—who had carried the banners of the Republic from Genoa till their approach scared the Pontiff in Rome, and the emperor in Vienna, was no everyday wonder. His youth, too, added to the marvel, and still more the claim of general superiority over the society in which he mingled, though consisting of the most distinguished persons in France; a superiority cloaking itself with a species of reserve, which inferred, "You may look upon me, but you cannot penetrate or see through me."[338] Napoleon's general manner in society, during this part of his life, has been described by an observer of first-rate power; according to whom, he was one for whom the admiration which could not be refused to him, was always mingled with a portion of fear. He was different in his manner from other men, and neither pleased nor angry, kind nor severe, after the common fashion of humanity. He appeared to live for the execution of his own plans, and to consider others only in so far as they were connected with, and could advance or oppose them. He estimated his fellow-mortals no otherwise than as they could be useful to his views; and, with a precision of intelligence which seemed intuitive from its rapidity, he penetrated the sentiments of those whom it was worth his while to study. Buonaparte did not then possess the ordinary tone of light conversation in society; probably his mind was too much burdened or too proud to stoop to adopt that mode of pleasing, and there was a stiffness and reserve of manner which was perhaps adopted for the purpose of keeping people at a distance. His look had the same character. When he thought himself closely observed, he had the power of discharging from his countenance all expression, save that of a vague and indefinite smile, and presenting to the curious investigator the fixed eyes and rigid features of a bust of marble.[339]

When he talked with the purpose of pleasing, Buonaparte often told anecdotes of his life in a very pleasing manner; when

---

[338] Thibaudeau, tom. iii., p. 413; Montholon, tom. iv., p. 266.
[339] Mad. de Staël, Consid. sur la Rév. Franç., tom. ii., p. 199.

silent, he had something disdainful in the expression of his face; when disposed to be quite at ease, he was, in Madame de Staël's opinion, rather vulgar. His natural tone of feeling seemed to be a sense of internal superiority, and of secret contempt for the world in which he lived, the men with whom he acted, and even the very objects which he pursued. His character and manners were upon the whole strongly calculated to attract the attention of the French nation, and to excite a perpetual interest even from the very mystery which attached to him, as well as from the splendour of his triumphs. The supreme power was residing in the Luxembourg ostensibly; but Paris was aware, that the means which had raised, and which must support and extend that power, were to be found in the humble mansion of the newly-christened Rue de la Victoire.

Some of these features are perhaps harshly designed, as being drawn *recentibus odiis*. The disagreement between Buonaparte and Madame de Staël, from whom we have chiefly described them, is well known. It originated about this time, when, as a first-rate woman of talent, she was naturally desirous to attract the notice of the Victor of Victors. They appear to have misunderstood each other; for the lady, who ought certainly to know best has informed us, "that far from feeling her fear of Buonaparte removed by repeated meetings, it seemed to increase, and his best exertions to please could not overcome her invincible aversion for what she found in his character."[340] His ironical contempt of excellence of every kind, operated like the sword in romance, which froze while it wounded. Buonaparte seems never to have suspected the secret and mysterious terror with which he impressed the ingenious author of Corinne; on the contrary, Las Cases tells us, that she combined all her efforts, and all her means, to make an impression on the general.[341] She wrote to him when distant, and, as the Count ungallantly expresses it, tormented him when present. In truth, to use an established French phrase, they stood in a false position with respect to each other. Madame de Staël might be pardoned for thinking that it would be difficult to resist her wit and her talent, when exerted with the purpose of pleasing; but Buonaparte was disposed to repel, rather than encourage the advances of one whose

---

[340] Considerations, tom. ii., p. 197.
[341] Las Cases, tom. iii., p. 191.

views were so shrewd, and her observations so keen, while her sex permitted her to push her inquiries farther than one man might have dared to do in conversing with another. She certainly did desire to look into him "with considerate eyes," and on one occasion put his abilities to the proof, by asking him rather abruptly, in the middle of a brilliant party at Talleyrand's, "whom he esteemed the greatest woman in the world, alive or dead?"—"Her, madam, that has borne the most children," answered Buonaparte, with much appearance of simplicity. Disconcerted by the reply, she observed, that he was reported not to be a great admirer of the fair sex. "I am very fond of my wife, madam," he replied, with one of those brief and yet piquant observations, which adjourned a debate as promptly as one of his characteristic manœuvres would have ended a battle.[342] From this period there was enmity between Buonaparte and Madame de Staël; and at different times he treated her with a harshness which had some appearance of actual personal dislike, though perhaps rather directed against the female politician than the woman of literature. After his fall, Madame de Staël relented in her resentment to him; and we remember her, during the campaign of 1814, presaging in society how the walls of Troyes were to see a second invasion and defeat of the Huns, as had taken place in the days of Attila, while the French Emperor was to enact the second Theodorick.

PARIS—PUBLIC HONOURS

In the meantime, while popular feeling and the approbation of distinguished genius were thus seeking to pay court to the youthful conqueror,[343] the Directory found themselves obliged to render to him that semblance of homage which could not have been withheld without giving much offence to general opinion, and injuring those who omitted to pay it, much more than him who was entitled by the

---

[342] Las Cases, tom. iii., p. 192; Montholon, tom. iv., p. 274; Thibaudeau, tom. iii., p. 429.
[343] "The leaders of all parties called upon him; but he refused to listen to them. The streets and squares through which he was expected to pass were constantly crowded, but Napoleon never showed himself. He had no habitual visitors, except a few men of science, such as Monge, Berthollet, Borda, Laplace, Prony, and Lagrange; several generals, as Berthier, Desaix, Lefebvre, Caffarelli, and Kleber; and a very few deputies."—Montholon, tom. iv., p. 269.

unanimous voice to receive it. On the 10th of December, the Directory received Buonaparte in public, with honours which the Republican government had not yet conferred on any subject, and which must have seemed incongruous to those who had any recollection of the liberty and equality, once so emphatically pronounced to be the talisman of French prosperity. The ceremony took place in the great court of the Luxembourg palace, where the Directory, surrounded by all that was officially important or distinguished by talent, received from Buonaparte's hand the confirmed treaty of Campo Formio.[344] The delivery of this document was accompanied by a speech from Buonaparte, in which he told the Directory, that, in order to establish a constitution founded on reason, it was necessary that eighteen centuries of prejudices should be conquered—"The constitution of the year THREE, and you, have triumphed over all these obstacles."[345] The triumph lasted exactly until the year EIGHT, when the orator himself overthrew the constitution, destroyed the power of the rulers who had overcome the prejudices of eighteen centuries, and reigned in their stead.

Dec. 28.

The French, who had banished religion from their thoughts, and from their system of domestic policy, yet usually preserved some perverted ceremony connected with it, on public solemnities. They had disused the exercises of devotion, and expressly disowned the existence of an object of worship; yet they could not do without altars, and hymns, and rites, upon such occasions as the present. The general, conducted by Barras, the president of the Directory, approached an erection, termed the Altar of the Country, where they went through various appropriate ceremonies, and at length dismissed a numerous assembly, much edified with what they had

---

[344] "Buonaparte arrived, dressed very simply, followed by his aides-de-camp, all taller than himself, but nearly bent by the respect which they displayed to him. M. de Talleyrand, in presenting Buonaparte to the Directory, called him 'the Liberator of Italy, and the Pacificator of the Continent.' He assured them, that 'General Buonaparte detested luxury and splendour, the miserable ambition of vulgar souls, and that he loved the poems of Ossian particularly because they detach us from the earth.'"—Mad. de Staël, tom. ii., p. 203; Montgaillard, tom. v., p. 83.
[345] Thibaudeau, tom. iii., p. 416.

seen. The two Councils, or Representative Bodies, also gave a splendid banquet in honour of Buonaparte. And what he appeared to receive with more particular satisfaction than these marks of distinction, the Institute admitted him a member of its body[346] in the room of his friend Carnot, (who was actually a fugitive, and believed at the time to be dead,) while the poet Chenier promulgated his praises, and foretold his future triumphs, and his approaching conquest of England.[347]

There is nothing less philosophical than to attach ridicule to the customs of other nations, merely because they differ from those of our own; yet it marks the difference between England and her continental neighbour, that the two Houses of Parliament never thought of giving a dinner to Marlborough, nor did the Royal Society choose his successor in the path of victory a member by acclamation; although the British nation in either case acquitted themselves of the debt of gratitude which they owed their illustrious generals, in the humbler and more vulgar mode of conferring on both large and princely domains.

Meantime, the threat of invasion was maintained with unabated earnestness. But it made no impression on the British, or rather it stimulated men of all ranks to bury temporary and party dissensions about politics, and bend themselves, with the whole energy of their national character, to confront and resist the preparations made against them. Their determination was animated by recollections of their own traditional gallantry, which had so often inflicted the deepest wounds upon France, and was not now likely to give up to any thing short of the most dire necessity. The benefits were then seen of a free constitution, which permits the venom of party spirit to evaporate in open debate. Those who had

---

[346] For the class of arts and sciences. Upon the occasion, Buonaparte addressed this note to Camus, the president of the class. "The suffrage of the distinguished men who compose the Institute honours me. I feel sensibly, that before I can become their equal, I must long be their pupil. If there were a manner more expressive of conveying to them my sentiments of respect, that I would employ. The only true conquests, those which awaken no regret, are those we obtain over ignorance. The most honourable, as the most useful pursuit of nations, is that which contributes to the extension of human intellect. The real greatness of the French republic ought henceforth to consist in not permitting the existence of one new idea which has not been added to the national stock."

[347] Thibaudeau, tom. iii., p. 432; Mad. de Staël, tom. ii., p. 204; Montgaillard, tom. v., p. 82.

differed on the question of peace or war, were unanimous in that of national defence, and resistance to the common enemy; and those who appeared in the vulgar eye engaged in unappeasable contention, were the most eager to unite themselves together for these purposes, as men employed in fencing would throw down the foils and draw their united swords, if disturbed by the approach of robbers.

Buonaparte in the meanwhile made a complete survey of the coast of the British channel, pausing at each remarkable point, and making those remarks and calculations which induced him to adopt, at an after period, the renewal of the project for a descent upon England.[348] The result of his observations decided his opinion, that in the present case the undertaking ought to be abandoned. The immense preparations and violent threats of invasion were carried into no more serious effect than the landing of about twelve or fourteen hundred Frenchmen, under a General Tate, at Fishguard, in South Wales. They were without artillery, and behaved rather like men whom a shipwreck had cast on a hostile shore, than like an invading enemy, as they gave themselves up as prisoners without even a show of defence to Lord Cawdor, who had marched against them at the head of a body of the Welsh militia, hastily drawn together on the alarm. The measure was probably only to be considered as experimental, and as such must have been regarded as an entire failure.[349]

The demonstrations of invasion, however, were ostensibly continued, and every thing seemed arranged on either side for a desperate collision betwixt the two most powerful nations in Europe. But the proceedings of politicians resemble those of the Indian traders called Banians, who seem engaged in talking about ordinary and trifling affairs, while, with their hands concealed

---

[348] Buonaparte left Paris on the 8th of February, and returned thither on the 22d. He was accompanied by General Lannes, his aide-de-camp Salkowski, and Bourrienne, his private secretary. "He visited," says the latter, "Etaples, Ambleteuse, Boulogne, Calais, Dunkirk, Furnes, Newport, Ostend, and Walcheren; making at these different ports the necessary surveys, with that patience, presence of mind, knowledge, expertness, and perspicuity, which he possessed in so eminent a degree. He examined till midnight, sailors, pilots, smugglers, fishermen,—making objections, and listening with attention to their replies."
[349] For some curious particulars respecting the Descent of the French in South Wales, see Appendix, No. V.

beneath a shawl that is spread between them, they are secretly debating and adjusting, by signs, bargains of the utmost importance. While all France and England had their eyes fixed on the fleets and armies destined against the latter country, the Directory and their general had no intention of using these preparations, except as a blind to cover their real object, which was the celebrated expedition to Egypt.

While yet in Italy, Buonaparte had suggested to the Directory (13th September, 1797,) the advantage which might be derived from seizing upon Malta, which he represented as an easy prize. The knights, he said, were odious to the Maltese inhabitants, and were almost starving; to augment which state of distress, and increase that incapacity of defence, he had already confiscated their Italian property. He then proceeded to intimate, that being possessed of Corfu and Malta, it was natural to take possession of Egypt. Twenty-five thousand men, with eight or ten ships of the line, would be sufficient for the expedition, which he suggested might depart from the coasts of Italy.[350]

EXPEDITION TO EGYPT

Talleyrand, then minister for foreign affairs, (in his answer of 23d September,) saw the utmost advantage in the design upon Egypt, which, as a colony, would attract the commerce of India to Europe, in preference to the circuitous route by the Cape of Good Hope. This correspondence proves, that even before Buonaparte left Italy he had conceived the idea of the Egyptian expedition, though probably only as one of the vast and vague schemes of ambition which success in so many perilous enterprises had tended to foster. There was something of wild grandeur in the idea, calculated to please an ambitious imagination. He was to be placed far beyond the reach of any command superior to his own, and left at his own discretion to the extending conquests, and perhaps

---

[350] Correspondence Inédite, tom. iv., p. 176. So early as the 10th of August, Buonaparte had written to the Directory,—"Les temps ne sont pas éloignés où nous sentirons que, pour détruire véritablement Angleterre, il faut nous emparer de l'Egypte."—Ibid., tom. iv., p. 77.—See also Jomini, tom. x., p. 512.

founding an empire, in a country long considered as the cradle of knowledge, and celebrated in sacred and profane history, as having been the scene of ancient events and distant revolutions, which, through the remoteness of ages, possess a gloomy and mysterious influence upon the fancy. The first specimens of early art also were to be found among the gigantic ruins of Egypt, and its time-defying monuments of antiquity. This had its effect upon Buonaparte, who affected so particularly the species of fame which attaches to the protector and extender of science, philosophy, and the fine arts. On this subject he had a ready and willing counsellor at hand. Monge, the artist and virtuoso, was Buonaparte's confidant on this occasion, and, there is no doubt, encouraged him to an undertaking which promised a rich harvest to the antiquarian, among the ruins of temples and palaces, hitherto imperfectly examined.

But, although the subject was mentioned betwixt the Directory and their ministers and Buonaparte, yet, before adopting the course which the project opened, the general was probably determined to see the issue of the revolution of the 18th Fructidor; doubting, not unreasonably, whether the conquerors in that struggle could so far avail themselves of the victory which they had obtained over the majority of the national representatives, as to consolidate and establish on a firm foundation their own authority. He knew the Directory themselves were popular with none. The numerous party who were now inclined to a monarchical government, regarded them with horror. The army, though supporting them, rather than coalesce with the Royalists, despised and disliked them; the violent Republicans remembered their active share in Robespierre's downfall, and the condemnations which followed the detected conspiracy of Babœuf, and were in no respect better disposed to their domination. Thus, despised by the army, dreaded by the Royalists, and detested by the Republicans, the Directorial government appeared to remain standing, only because the factions to whom it was unacceptable were afraid of each other's attaining a superiority in the struggle, which must attend its downfall.[351]

This crisis of public affairs was a tempting opportunity for such a character as Buonaparte; whose almost incredible successes,

---

[351] Montholon, tom. iv., p. 281.

unvaried by a single reverse which deserved that name, naturally fixed the eyes of the multitude, and indeed of the nation at large, upon him, as upon one who seemed destined to play the most distinguished part in any of those new changes, which the mutable state of the French Government seemed rapidly preparing.

The people, naturally partial to a victor, followed him every where with acclamations, and his soldiers, in their camp-songs, spoke of pulling the *attorneys* out of the seat of government, and installing their victorious general. Even already, for the first time since the commencement of the Revolution, the French, losing their recent habits of thinking and speaking of the nation as a body, began to interest themselves in Napoleon as an individual; and that exclusive esteem of his person had already taken root in the public mind, which afterwards formed the foundation of his throne.

ARMIES OF ITALY AND THE RHINE

Yet, in spite of these promising appearances, Napoleon, cautious as well as enterprising, saw that the time was not arrived when he could, without great risk, attempt to possess himself of the supreme government in France. The soldiers of Italy were indeed at his devotion, but there was another great and rival army belonging to the Republic, that of the Rhine, which had never been under his command, never had partaken his triumphs, and which naturally looked rather to Moreau than to Buonaparte as their general and hero.

Madame de Staël describes the soldiers from these two armies, as resembling each other in nothing, save the valour which was common to both.[352] The troops of the Rhine, returning from hard-fought fields, which, if followed by victory, had afforded but little plunder, exhibited still the severe simplicity which had been affected under the republican model; whereas the army of Italy had reaped richer spoils than barren laurels alone, and made a display of wealth

---

[352] Considerations sur la Rév. Franç., tom. ii., p. 173.

and enjoyment which showed they had not neglected their own interest while advancing the banners of France.

It was not likely, while such an army as that of the Rhine existed, opposed by rivalry and the jealousy of fame to the troops of Buonaparte, that the latter should have succeeded in placing himself at the head of affairs. Besides, the forces on which he could depend were distant. Fortune had not afforded him the necessary pretext for crossing, as he termed it, the Rubicon, and bringing twenty thousand men to Lyons. Moreau, Jourdan, Kleber, had all high reputations, scarce inferior to his own; and the troops who had served under them were disposed to elevate them, even to an equality with the Conqueror of Italy. Buonaparte also knew that his popularity, though great, was not universal. He was disliked by the middle classes, from recollection of his commanding during the affair of the Sections of Paris; and many of the Republicans exclaimed against him, for his surrendering Venice to the Austrians. In a word, he was too much elbowed and incommoded by others to permit his taking with full vigour the perilous spring necessary to place him in the seat of supreme authority, though there were not wanting those who would fain have persuaded him to venture on a course so daring.[353] To such counsellors he answered, that *"the pear was not ripe,"*—a hint which implied that appetite was not wanting, though prudence forbade the banquet.

Laying aside, therefore, the character of General of the Army of England, and adjourning to a future day the conquest of that hostile island; silencing at the same time the internal wishes and the exterior temptations which urged him to seize the supreme power, which seemed escaping from those who held it, Napoleon turned his eyes and thoughts eastward, and meditated in the distant countries of the rising sun, a scene worthy his talents, his military skill, and his ambition.[354]

---

[353] Montholon, tom. iv., p. 284.
[354] "Napoleon did not think himself popular enough to go alone: he had ideas on the art of governing different from those of the men of the Revolution. He therefore determined to sail for Egypt, resolved, nevertheless, to appear again as soon as circumstances should render his presence necessary, as he already saw they would do. To render him master of France, it was necessary that the Directory should experience disasters in his absence, and

EXPEDITION TO EGYPT

The Directory, on the other hand, eager to rid themselves of his perilous vicinity, hastened to accomplish the means of his expedition to Egypt, upon a scale far more formidable than any which had yet sailed from modern Europe, for the invasion and subjection of distant and peaceful realms.

It was soon whispered abroad, that the invasion of England was to be postponed, until the Conqueror of Italy, having attained a great and national object, by the success of a secret expedition, fitted out on a scale of stupendous magnitude, should be at leisure to resume the conquest of Britain.

But Buonaparte did not limit his views to those of armed conquest; he meant that these should be softened, by mingling with them schemes of a literary and scientific character, as if he had desired, as some one said, that Minerva should march at the head of his expedition, holding in one hand her dreadful lance, and with the other introducing the sciences and the muses. The various treasures of art which had been transferred to the capital by the influence of his arms, gave the general of the Italian army a right to such distinctions as the French men of literature could confer; and he was himself possessed of deep scientific knowledge as a mathematician. He became apparently much attached to learned pursuits, and wore the uniform of the Institute on all occasions, when he was out of military costume. This affectation of uniting the encouragement of letters and science with his military tactics, led to a new and peculiar branch of the intended expedition.

The public observed with astonishment a detachment of no less than one hundred men,[355] who had cultivated the arts and sciences, or, to use the French phrase, *Savans*, selected for the purpose of joining this mysterious expedition, of which the object still remained a secret; while all classes of people asked each other

---

that his return should recall victory to the colours of the nation."—Napoleon, *Montholon*, tom. iv., p. 284.

[355] For a "List of the one hundred and two members of the Commission of the Arts and Sciences attached to the army of the East," see Thibaudeau, tom. iv., p. 424.

what new quarter of the world France had determined to colonize, since she seemed preparing at once to subdue it by her arms, and to enrich it with the treasures of her science and literature. This singular department of the expedition, the first of the kind which ever accompanied an invading army, was liberally supplied with books, philosophical instruments, and all means of prosecuting the several departments of knowledge.[356]

Buonaparte did not, however, trust to the superiority of science to ensure the conquest of Egypt. He was fully provided with more effectual means. The land forces belonging to the expedition were of the most formidable description. Twenty-five thousand men, chiefly veterans selected from his own Italian army, had in their list of generals subordinate to Buonaparte the names of Kleber,[357] Desaix,[358] Berthier, Regnier, Murat, Lannes, Andréossi, Menou,[359] Belliard, and others well known in the revolutionary wars. Four hundred transports were assembled for the conveyance of the troops. Thirteen ships of the line, and four frigates, commanded by Admiral Brueyes, an experienced and gallant officer, formed the escort of the expedition; a finer and more formidable one than which never sailed on so bold an adventure.

We have already touched upon the secret objects of this armament. The Directory were desirous to be rid of Buonaparte, who might become a dangerous competitor in the present unsettled state of the French Government. Buonaparte, on his side, accepted the command, because it opened a scene of conquest worthy of his ambition. A separate and uncontrolled command over so gallant an army seemed to promise him the conquest and the sovereignty, not of Egypt only, but of Syria, Turkey, perhaps Constantinople, the Queen of the East; and he himself afterwards more than hinted, that

---

[356] "The following list of books, for a camp library, I copy from a paper in his own hand. The volumes were in 18mo, and will show what he preferred in science and literature."—Bourrienne, tom. ii., p. 49. See the List in Appendix, No. VI.

[357] "Napoleon offered to leave Desaix and Kleber, whose talents might, he thought, prove serviceable to France. The Directory knew not their value, and refused them. 'The Republic,' said they, 'is not reduced to these two generals.'"—Montholon, tom. iv., p. 282.

[358] "I have beheld, with deep interest, the fleet at Corfu. If ever it sails upon those great enterprises of which you have spoken, in pity do not forget me."—Desaix to Buonaparte.

[359] "Menou, anxious to justify his conduct at Paris on the 13th Vendémiaire, entreated to be allowed to join the army of the East."—Thibaudeau, tom. iv., p. 42.

but for controlling circumstances, he would have bent his whole mind to the establishment of an Oriental dynasty, and left France to her own destinies. When a subaltern officer of artillery, he had nourished the hope of being King of Jerusalem.[360] In his present situation of dignity and strength, the sovereignty of an Emperor of the universal East, or of a Caliph of Egypt at the least, was a more commensurate object of ambition.

The private motives of the government and of the general are therefore easily estimated. But it is not so easy to justify the Egyptian expedition upon any views of sound national policy. On the contrary, the object to be gained by so much risk, and at the same time by an act of aggression upon the Ottoman Porte, the ancient ally of France, to whom Egypt belonged, was of very doubtful utility. The immense fertility of the alluvial provinces irrigated by the Nile, no doubt renders their sovereignty a matter of great consequence to the Turkish empire, which, from the oppressed state of their agriculture every where, and from the rocky and barren character of their Grecian provinces, are not in a condition to supply the capital with grain, did they not draw it from that never-failing land. But France herself, fully supplied from her own resources, had no occasion to send her best general, and hazard her veteran army, for the purpose of seizing a distant province, merely to facilitate her means of feeding her population. To erect that large country into a French colony, would have required a drain of population, of expense, and of supplies of all sorts, which France, just recovering from the convulsion of her Revolution, was by no means fit to encounter. The climate, too, is insalubrious to strangers, and must have been a constant cause of loss, until, in process of time, the colonists had become habituated to its peculiarities. It is farther to be considered, that the most perfect and absolute success in the undertaking must have ended, not in giving a province to the French Republic, but a separate and independent kingdom to her victorious and ambitious general. Buonaparte had paid but slight attention to the commands of the Directory when in Italy. Had he realized his proposed conquests in the East, they would have been sent over the Mediterranean altogether in vain.

---

[360] Las Cases, tom. i.

Lastly, the state of war with England subjected this attempt to add Egypt to the French dominions, to the risk of defeat, either by the naval strength of Britain interposing between France and her new possessions, or by her land forces from India and Europe, making a combined attack upon the French army which occupied Egypt; both which events actually came to pass.

It is true, that, so far from dreading the English forces which were likely to be employed against them, the French regarded as a recommendation to the conquest of Egypt, that it was to be the first step to the destruction of the British power in India; and Napoleon continued to the last to consider the conquest of Egypt as the forerunner of that of universal Asia. His eye, which, like that of the eagle, saw far and wide, overlooking, however, obstacles which distance rendered diminutive, beheld little more necessary than the toilsome marches of a few weeks, to achieve the conquests of Alexander the Great. He had already counted the steps by which he was to ascend to Oriental Monarchy, and has laid before the world a singular reverie on the probabilities of success. "If Saint John d'Acre had yielded to the French arms," said he, "a great revolution would have been accomplished in the East; the general-in-chief would have founded an empire there, and the destinies of France would have undergone different combinations from those to which they were subjected."[361]

In this declaration we recognise one of the peculiarities of Buonaparte's disposition, which refused to allow of any difficulties or dangers save those, of which, having actually happened, the existence could not be disputed. The small British force before Acre was sufficient to destroy his whole plans of conquest; but how many other means of destruction might Providence have employed for the same purpose! The plague—the desert—mutiny among his soldiers—courage and enterprise, inspired by favourable circumstances into the tribes by whom his progress was opposed— the computation of these, and other chances, ought to have taught him to acknowledge, that he had not been discomfited by the only hazard which could have disconcerted his enterprise; but that, had such been the will of God, the sands of Syria might have proved as

---

[361] Las Cases, tom. v., p. 58.

fatal as the snows of Russia, and the scimitars of the Turks as the lances of the Cossacks. In words, a march from Egypt to India is easily described, and still more easily measured off with compasses upon the map of the world. But in practice, and with an army opposed, as the French would probably have been, at every step, if it had been only from motives of religious antipathy, when the French general arrived at the skirts of British India, with forces thus diminished, he would have had in front the whole British army, commanded by officers accustomed to make war upon a scale almost as enlarged as he himself practised, and accustomed to victories not less decisive.[362]

We should fall into the same error which we censure, did we anticipate what might have been the result of such a meeting. Even while we claim the probability of advantage for the army most numerous, and best provided with guns and stores, we allow the strife must have been dreadful and dubious. But, if Napoleon really thought he had only to show himself in India, to ensure the destruction of the British empire there, he had not calculated the opposing strength with the caution to have been expected from so great a general. He has been represented, indeed, as boasting of the additions which he would have made to his army, by the co-operation of natives trained after the French discipline. But can it be supposed that these hasty levies could be brought into such complete order as to face the native troops of British India, so long and so justly distinguished for approaching Europeans in courage and discipline, and excelling them, perhaps, in temperance and subordination?

In a word, the Egyptian expedition, unless considered with reference to the private views of the Directory, and of their General, must have been regarded from the beginning, as promising no

---

[362] "All that Sir Walter Scott says about the expedition to India is not only exaggerated, but wide of the truth. It is not by the mere march of an army across Egypt and Arabia that British India is likely to be conquered, but by establishing and consolidating a French force in Egypt, by opening the ancient communications by Suez, by multiplying the relations between Egypt and India; and, in fine, by so augmenting the French navy in the Mediterranean, that this sea shall become almost inaccessible to the English squadrons."— Louis Buonaparte, p. 31.

results in the slightest degree worthy of the great risk incurred, by draining France of the flower of her army.

Meanwhile, the moment of departure approached. The blockading squadron, commanded by Nelson, was blown off the coast by a gale of wind, and so much damaged that they were obliged to run down to Sardinia. The first and most obvious obstacle to the expedition was thus removed. The various squadrons from Genoa, Civita Vecchia, and Bastia, set sail and united with that which already lay at Toulon.

Yet it is said, though upon slender authority, that even at this latest moment Buonaparte showed, some inclination to abandon the command of so doubtful and almost desperate an expedition, and wished to take the advantage of a recent dispute between France and Austria, to remain in Europe. The misunderstanding arose from the conduct of Bernadotte, ambassador for the republic at Vienna, who incautiously displayed the national colours before his hotel, in consequence of which a popular tumult arose, and the ambassador was insulted. In their first alarm, lest his incident should occasion a renewal of the war, the Directory hastily determined to suspend Buonaparte's departure, and despatch him to Rastadt, where the congress was still sitting, with full powers to adjust the difference. Buonaparte accepted the commission, and while he affected to deplore the delay or miscarriage of "the greatest enterprise which he had ever meditated," wrote in secret to Count Cobentzel, now minister of foreign affairs at Vienna, inviting him to a conference at Rastadt, and hinting at political changes, by which the difficulties attending the execution of the treaty of Campo Formio might be taken away. The tenor of this letter having become known to the Directory, and it appearing to them that Buonaparte designed to make that mission a pretext for interesting Cobentzel in some change of government in France, in which he deemed it advisable to obtain the concurrence of Austria, they instantly resolved, it is said, to compel him to set sail on the expedition to Egypt. Barras, charged with the commission of notifying to the general this second alteration of his destination, had an interview with Buonaparte in private, and at his own house. The mien of the director was clouded, and, contrary to his custom, he scarcely spoke to Madame

Buonaparte. When he retired, Buonaparte shut himself up in his own apartment for a short time, then gave directions for his instant departure from Paris for Toulon. These particulars are given as certain by Miot;[363] but he alleges no authority for this piece of secret history.[364] There seems, however, little doubt, that the command of the Egyptian expedition was bestowed on Buonaparte by the Directory as a species of ostracism, or honourable banishment from France.

At the moment of departure, Buonaparte made one of those singular harangues which evince such a mixture of talent and energy with bad taste and bombast. He promised to introduce those who had warred on the mountains and in the plains, to maritime combat; and to a great part of the expedition he kept his word too truly, as Aboukir could witness. He reminded them that the Romans combated Carthage by sea as well as by land—he proposed to conduct them, in the name of the Goddess of Liberty, to the most distant regions and oceans, and he concluded by promising to each individual of his army seven acres of land.[365] Whether this distribution of property was to take place on the banks of the Nile, of the Bosphorus, or the Ganges, the soldiers had not the most distant guess, and the commander-in-chief himself would have had difficulty in informing them.

---

[363] Mémoires pour servir à l'Histoire des Expéditions en Egypte et en Syrie.—Introduction, p. 20.

[364] "It is an error to state, that the affair at Vienna inspired the idea of abandoning the expedition. The contrary is proved by Buonaparte's letters to Barraguay d'Hilliers, Desaix, and Admiral Brueyes; to whom, on the 20th of April, he wrote: 'Some disturbances, which have just happened at Vienna, require my presence for a few days at Paris. This will in no way affect the expedition. I send an order, by the present courier, for the troops at Marseilles to embark and repair to Toulon. On the evening of the 30th I will send you instructions to get on board, and depart with the squadron for Genoa, where I will join you."—*Correspondence Inédite*, tom. v., p. 3; Thibaudeau, tom. iv., p. 43.

[365] "Je promets à chaque soldat qu'au retour de cette expédition, il aura à sa disposition de quoi acheter six arpens de terre."—*Moniteur*, No. 242, May 21.

SAILS FROM TOULON

May 19.

On the 19th of May, 1798, this magnificent armament set sail from Toulon, illuminated by a splendid sunrise, one of those which were afterwards popularly termed the suns of Napoleon. The line-of-battle ships extended for a league, and the semi-circle formed by the convoy was at least six leagues in extent. They were joined on the 8th June, as they swept along the Mediterranean, by a large fleet of transports, having on board the division of General Desaix.

The 10th June brought the armament before Malta, once the citadel of Christendom, and garrisoned by those intrepid knights, who, half warriors and half priests, opposed the infidels with the enthusiasm at once of religion and of chivalry. But those by whom the order was now maintained were disunited among themselves, lazy and debauched voluptuaries, who consumed the revenues destined to fit out expeditions against the Turks in cruises for pleasure, not war, and giving balls and entertainments in the seaports of Italy. Buonaparte treated these degenerate knights with a want of ceremony, which, however little it accorded with the extreme strength of their island, and with the glorious defence which it had formerly made against the infidels, was perfectly suited to their present condition. Secure of a party among the French knights, with whom he had been tampering, he landed troops, and took possession of these almost impregnable fortresses with so little opposition, that Caffarelli said to Napoleon as they passed through the most formidable defences,—"It is well, general, that there was some one within to open the gates to us. We should have had more trouble in entering, if the place had been altogether empty."[366]

---

[366] "Napoleon said to one of the companions of his exile at St. Helena, 'Malta certainly possessed immense physical, but no moral means of resistance. The knights did nothing disgraceful. They could not hold out against impossibility. No: but they yielded themselves. The successful capture of Malta was assured, before the fleet quitted Toulon.'"—Bourrienne, tom. ii., p. 65.
"The capture of Malta had been secured before Buonaparte left Toulon, by the intrigues and largesses of Poussielque. These have been laid open by the Bailli Teignie, and others, and made the subject of a formal accusation against the Grand-master Hompesch, by the

A sufficient garrison was established in Malta, destined by Buonaparte to be an intermediate station between France and Egypt; and on the 16th, the daring general resumed his expedition.[367] On the coast of Candia, while the *Savans* were gazing on the rocks where Jupiter, it is said, was nurtured, and speculating concerning the existence of some vestiges of the celebrated labyrinth, Buonaparte learned that a new enemy, of a different description from the Knights of Saint John, was in his immediate vicinity. This was the English squadron.

VOYAGE TO EGYPT

Nelson, to the end as unconquerable on his own element as Buonaparte had hitherto shown himself upon shore, was now in full and anxious pursuit of his renowned contemporary. Reinforced by a squadron of ten ships of the line, a meeting with Napoleon was the utmost wish of his heart, and was echoed back by the meanest sailor on board his numerous fleet. The French had been heard of at Malta, but as the British admiral was about to proceed thither, he received news of their departure; and concluding that Egypt must be unquestionably the object of their expedition, he made sail for Egypt. It singularly happened, that although Nelson anticipated the arrival of the French at Alexandria, and accordingly directed his course thither, yet, keeping a more direct path than Brueyes, when he arrived there on the 28th June, he heard nothing of the enemy, who, in the meanwhile, were proceeding to the very same port. The English admiral set sail, therefore, for Rhodes and Syracuse; and thus were the two large and hostile fleets traversing the same narrow sea, without being able to attain any certain tidings of each other's

---

knights who had taken refuge in Germany, Russia," &c.—*Intercepted Correspondence*, part i., preface, p. vi.

"The sum awarded to the grand-master for his baseness was 600,000 francs. On quitting the island which he had not had the courage to defend, he further disgraced himself by kissing the hand of the conqueror who had despoiled him of his dominions."—Thibaudeau, tom. iv., p. 96.

[367] "One of Napoleon's first acts at Malta was to set at liberty the Turkish prisoners, and clear the disgusting galleys. This was a deed of reason and humanity. His time was devoted to providing with equal activity and talent for the administration and defence of the island. His only relaxation was an occasional walk in the beautiful gardens of the grand-master."—Bourrienne, tom. ii., p. 65.

movements. This was in part owing to the English admiral having no frigates with him, which might have been detached to cruise for intelligence; partly to a continuance of thick misty weather, which at once concealed the French fleet from their adversaries, and, obliging them to keep close together, diminished the chance of discovery, which might otherwise have taken place by the occupation of a larger space. On the 26th, according to Denon, Nelson's fleet was actually seen by the French standing to the westward, although the haze prevented the English from observing their enemy, whose squadron held an opposite direction.[368]

Escaped from the risk of an encounter so perilous, Buonaparte's greatest danger seemed to be over on the 1st July, when the French fleet came in sight of Alexandria, and saw before them the city of the Ptolemies and of Cleopatra, with its double harbour, its Pharos, and its ancient and gigantic monuments of grandeur. Yet at this critical moment, and while Buonaparte contemplated his meditated conquest, a signal announced the appearance of a strange sail, which was construed to be an English frigate, the precursor of the British fleet. "What!" said Napoleon, "I ask but six hours—and, Fortune, wilt thou abandon me?"[369] The fickle goddess was then and for many a succeeding year, true to her votary. The vessel proved friendly.[370]

---

[368] "During the whole voyage, Buonaparte passed the greater part of his time below, in his cabin, reclining upon a couch, which, by a ball-and-socket joint at each foot, rendered the ship's pitching less perceptible, and consequently relieved the sickness from which he was scarcely ever free. His remarkable saying to the pupils of a school which he had one day visited, 'Young people, every hour of time lost is a chance of misfortune for future life,' may be considered, in some measure, as forming the rule of his own conduct. Perhaps no man ever better understood the value of time. If the activity of his mind found not wherewithal to exercise itself in reality, he supplied the defect by giving free scope to imagination, or in listening to the conversation of the learned men attached to the expedition. He delighted in discoursing with Monge and Berthollet, when the discussion mostly ran upon chemistry, mathematics, and religion, as also with Caffarelli, whose conversation, rich in facts, was, at the same time, lively, intellectual, and cheerful. At other times, he conversed with the admiral, when the subject always related to naval manœuvres, of which he showed great desire to obtain knowledge; and nothing more astonished Brueyes, than the sagacity of his questions."—Bourrienne, tom. ii., p. 69.
[369] Miot, p. 16.
[370] "On the 30th of June, Buonaparte had the following proclamation printed on board the L'Orient, and issued it to the army:—'Soldiers! You are going to undertake a conquest, the effects of which, upon commerce and civilisation, will be incalculable. You will give the

The disembarkation of the French army took place [July 2] about a league and a half from Alexandria, at an anchorage called Marabout. It was not accomplished without losing boats and men on the surf, though such risks were encountered with great joy by the troops, who had been so long confined on ship-board. As soon as five or six thousand men were landed, Buonaparte marched towards Alexandria, when the Turks, incensed at this hostile invasion on the part of a nation with whom they were at profound peace, shut the gates, and manned the walls against their reception. But the walls were ruinous, and presented breaches in many places, and the chief weapons of resistance were musketry and stones. The conquerors of Italy forced their passage over such obstacles, but not easily or with impunity.[371] Two hundred French were killed. There was severe military execution done upon the garrison, and the town was abandoned to plunder for three hours;[372] which has been justly stigmatized as an act of unnecessary cruelty, perpetrated only to strike terror, and extend the fame of the victorious French general. But it was Napoleon's object to impress the highest idea of his power upon the various classes of natives, who, differing widely

---

English a most sensible blow, which will be followed up by their destruction. We shall have some fatiguing marches—we shall fight several battles—we shall succeed in all our enterprises. The destinies are in our favour. The Mamelouc Beys, who favour the English commerce exclusively, who have injured our merchants, and who tyrannize over the unhappy inhabitants of the banks of the Nile, will no longer exist in a few days after our arrival.

"'The people, among whom you are going to live, are Mahometans. The first article of their faith is "There is no other God but God, and Mahomet is his prophet." Do not contradict them. Act with them as you did with the Jews and with the Italians. Treat their muftis and their imans with respect, as you did the rabbis and the bishops. You must act with the same spirit of toleration towards the ceremonies prescribed by the Koran, that you did to the synagogues and the convents, to the religions of Moses and of Jesus Christ. The Roman legions protected all religions. You will find here customs which differ from those of Europe: you must accustom yourselves to them.

"'The people among whom we are going, treat women differently from us; but in every country, he who violates them is a monster. Pillage enriches but a very few men: it dishonours us, it destroys our resources, and it renders those our enemies whom it is our interest to have for friends. The first city we shall arrive at was built by Alexander, and every step we take we shall meet with objects capable of exciting emulation.'"

[371] "Repulsed on every side, the Turks betake themselves to God and their Prophet, and fill their mosques: Men, women, old, young, children at the breast, all are massacred. At the end of four hours the fury of our troops ceases."—Adjutant-General Boyer to his Parents.—*Intercepted Letters*, part i., p. 150.

[372] Jomini, tom. x., p. 402; Larrey, p. 7.

from each other in manners and condition, inhabit Egypt as their common home.[373]

These classes are, 1st, the Arab race, divided into Fellahs and Bedouins, the most numerous and least esteemed of the population. The Bedouins, retaining the manners of Arabia Proper, rove through the Desert, and subsist by means of their flocks and herds. The Fellahs cultivate the earth, and are the ordinary peasants of the country.

The class next above the Arabs in consideration are the Cophts, supposed to be descended from the pristine Egyptians. They profess Christianity, are timid and unwarlike, but artful and supple. They are employed in the revenue, and in almost all civil offices, and transact the commerce and the business of the country.

MAMELUKES

The third class in elevation were the formidable Mamelukes who held both Cophts and Arabs in profound subjection. These are, or we may say *were*, a corps of professed soldiers, having no trade excepting war. In this they resemble the Janissaries, the Sterlitzes, the Prætorian bands, or similar military bodies, which, constituting a standing army under a despotic government, are alternately the protectors and the terror of the sovereign who is their nominal commander. But the peculiar feature of the constitution of the Mamelukes, was, that their corps was recruited only by the adoption of foreign slaves, particularly Georgians and Circassians. These were purchased when children by the several Beys or Mameluke leaders, who, twenty-four in number, occupied, each, one of the twenty-four departments into which they had divided Egypt. The youthful slave, purchased with a heedful reference to his strength and personal appearance, was carefully trained to arms in the family of his master. When created a Mameluke, he was received into the troop of the Bey, and rendered capable of succeeding to him at his death; for

---

[373] "Alexandria was not given up to pillage, as repeatedly asserted. This would have been a very absurd commencement of the conquest of Egypt, in which there were no fortified places to intimidate by such an example."—Bourrienne, tom. ii., p. 89.

these chiefs despised the ordinary connexions of blood, and their authority was, upon military principles, transferred at their death to him amongst the band who was accounted the best soldier. They fought always on horseback; and in their peculiar mode of warfare, they might be termed, individually considered, the finest cavalry in the world. Completely armed, and unboundedly confident in their own prowess, they were intrepid, skilful, and formidable in battle; but with their military bravery began and ended the catalogue of their virtues. Their vices were, unpitying cruelty, habitual oppression, and the unlimited exercise of the most gross and disgusting sensuality. Such were the actual lords of Egypt.[374]

Yet the right of sovereignty did not rest with the beys, but with the Pacha, or lieutenant,—a great officer despatched from the Porte to represent the Grand Signior in Egypt, where it was his duty to collect the tribute in money and grain, which Constantinople expected from that rich province, with the additional object of squeezing out of the country as much more as he could by any means secure, for the filling of his own coffers. The pacha maintained his authority sometimes by the assistance of Turkish troops, sometimes by exciting the jealousy of one bey against another. Thus this fertile country was subjected to the oppression of twenty-four prætors, who, whether they agreed among themselves, or with the pacha, or declared war against the representative of the Sultan, and against each other, were alike the terror and the scourge of the unhappy Arabs and Cophts, the right of oppressing whom, by every species of exaction, these haughty slaves regarded as their noblest and most undeniable privilege.

---

[374] "The Mameloucs are an invincible race, inhabiting a burning desert, mounted on the fleetest horses in the world, and full of courage. They live with their wives and children in flying camps, which are never pitched two nights together in the same place. They are horrible savages, and yet they have some notion of gold and silver! a small quantity of it serves to excite their admiration. Yes, my dear brother, they love gold; they pass their lives in extorting it from such Europeans as fall into their hands;—and for what purpose?—for continuing the course of life which I have described, and for teaching it to their children. O, Jean Jacques! why was it not thy fate to see these men, whom thou call'st '*the men of nature?*'—thou wouldst sink with shame, thou wouldst startle with horror at the thought of having once admired them! Adieu, my dear brother. This climate kills me; we shall be so altered, that you will discover the change at a league's distance. Remember me to the *legislator* Lucien. He might have sailed with us to advantage; we see more in two days than common travellers in two years."—Louis Buonaparte *to his brother* Joseph, dated Alexandria, July 6th; *Intercepted Correspondence*, part i., p. 8.

From the moment that Buonaparte conceived the idea of invading Egypt, the destruction of the power of the Mamelukes must have been determined upon as his first object; and he had no sooner taken Alexandria than he announced his purpose. He sent forth a proclamation,[375] in which he professed his respect for God, the Prophet, and the Koran; his friendship for the Sublime Porte, of which he affirmed the French to be the faithful allies; and his determination to make war upon the Mamelukes. He commanded that the prayers should be continued in the mosques as usual, with some slight modifications, and that all true Moslems should exclaim, "Glory to the Sultan, and to the French army, his allies!—Accursed be the Mamelukes, and good fortune to the land of Egypt!"[376]

MARCH TO CAIRO

Upon the 7th of July, the army marched from Alexandria against the Mamelukes. Their course was up the Nile, and a small flotilla of gun-boats ascended the river to protect their right flank, while the infantry traversed a desert of burning sands, at a distance from the stream, and without a drop of water to relieve their tormenting thirst. The army of Italy, accustomed to the enjoyments of that delicious country, were astonished at the desolation they saw around them. "Is this," they said, "the country in which we are to receive our farms of seven acres each? The general might have allowed us to take as much as we chose—no one would have abused the privilege." Their officers, too, expressed horror and disgust; and even generals of such celebrity as Murat and Lannes threw their hats on the sand, and trode on their cockades. It required all

---

[375] See it in the Appendix to this volume, No. VII.
[376] "You will laugh outright, you witlings of Paris, at the Mahometan proclamation of the commander-in-chief. He is proof, however, against all your raillery; and the thing itself will certainly produce a most surprising effect. You recollect that produced by the magic cry of 'Guerre aux chateaux, paix aux cabines!'"—Joubert *to* General Bruix; *Intercepted Letters*, part i., p. 31.
"I send you the proclamation to the inhabitants of the country. It has produced an effect altogether astonishing. The Bedouins, enemies of the Mameloucs, and who, properly speaking, are neither more nor less than intrepid robbers, sent us back, as soon as they had read it, thirty of our people whom they had made prisoners, with an offer of their services against the Mameloucs."—Louis Buonaparte; *Intercepted Correspondence*, part i., p. 7.

Buonaparte's authority to maintain order, so much were the French disgusted with the commencement of the expedition.[377]

To add to their embarrassment, the enemy began to appear around them. Mamelukes and Arabs, concealed behind the hillocks of sand, interrupted their march at every opportunity, and woe to the soldier who straggled from the ranks, were it but fifty yards! Some of these horsemen were sure to dash at him, slay him on the spot, and make off before a musket could be discharged at them. At length, however, the audacity of these incursions was checked by a skirmish of some little importance near a place called Chebreis, in which the French asserted their military superiority.[378]

An encounter also took place on the river, between the French flotilla and a number of armed vessels belonging to the Mamelukes. Victory first inclined to the latter, but at length determined in favour of the French, who took, however, only a single galliot.

Meanwhile, the French were obliged to march with the utmost precaution. The whole plain was now covered with Mamelukes, mounted on the finest Arabian horses, and armed with pistols, carabines, and blunderbusses, of the best English workmanship—their plumed turbans waving in the air, and their rich dresses and arms glittering in the sun. Entertaining a high contempt for the French force, as consisting almost entirely of infantry, this splendid barbaric chivalry watched every opportunity for charging them, nor did a single straggler escape the unrelenting edge of their sabres. Their charge was almost as swift as the wind, and as their severe bits enabled them to halt, or wheel their horses at full gallop, their retreat was as rapid as their advance. Even the practised veterans of Italy were at first embarrassed by this new mode of fighting, and lost several men; especially when fatigue caused any one to fall out of the

---

[377] "It would be difficult to describe the disgust, the discontent, the melancholy, the despair of the army, on its first arrival in Egypt: Napoleon himself saw two dragoons throw themselves into the Nile.—One day, losing his temper, he rushed among a group of discontented generals, and addressing himself to the tallest, 'You have held mutinous language,' said he, with vehemence; 'it is not your being six feet high that should save you from being shot in a couple of hours.'"—Las Cases, tom. i., p. 206.
[378] Jomini, tom. x., p. 407.

ranks, in which case his fate became certain. But they were soon reconciled to fighting the Mamelukes, when they discovered that each of these horsemen carried about him his fortune, and that it not uncommonly amounted to considerable sums in gold.

During these alarms, the French love of the ludicrous was not abated by the fatigues or dangers of the journeys. The *Savans* had been supplied with asses, the beasts of burden easiest attained in Egypt, to transport their persons and philosophical apparatus. The general had given orders to attend to their personal safety, which were of course obeyed. But as these civilians had little importance in the eyes of the military, loud shouts of laughter used to burst from the ranks, while forming to receive the Mamelukes, as the general of division called out, with military precision, "Let the asses and the *Savans* enter within the square." The soldiers also amused themselves, by calling the asses *demi-savans*.[379] In times of discontent, these unlucky servants of science had their full share of the soldiers' reproaches, who imagined, that this unpopular expedition had been undertaken to gratify their passion for researches, in which the military took very slender interest.

BATTLE OF THE PYRAMIDS

Under such circumstances, it may be doubted whether even the literati themselves were greatly delighted, when, after fourteen days of such marches as we have described, they arrived, indeed, within six leagues of Cairo, and beheld at a distance the celebrated Pyramids, but learned, at the same time, that Murad Bey, with twenty-two of his brethren, at the head of their Mamelukes, had formed an intrenched camp at a place called Embabeh, with the purpose of covering Cairo, and giving battle to the French. On the 21st of July, as the French continued to advance, they saw their enemy in the field, and in full force. A splendid line of cavalry, under Murad and the other beys, displayed the whole strength of the Mamelukes. Their right rested on the imperfectly intrenched camp, in which lay twenty thousand infantry, defended by forty pieces of cannon. But the infantry were an undisciplined rabble; the guns,

---

[379] Las Cases, tom. i., p. 210.

wanting carriages, were mounted on clumsy wooden frames; and the fortifications of the camp were but commenced, and presented no formidable opposition. Buonaparte made his dispositions. He extended his line to the right, in such a manner as to keep out of gunshot of the intrenched camp, and have only to encounter the line of cavalry.[380]

Murad Bey saw this movement, and, fully aware of its consequence, prepared to charge with his magnificent body of horse, declaring he would cut the French up like gourds. Buonaparte, as he directed the infantry to form squares to receive them, called out to his men, "From yonder Pyramids twenty centuries behold your actions."[381] The Mamelukes advanced with the utmost speed, and corresponding fury, and charged with horrible yells. They disordered one of the French squares of infantry, which would have been sabred in an instant, but that the mass of this fiery militia was a little behind the advanced guard. The French had a moment to restore order, and used it. The combat then in some degree resembled that which, nearly twenty years afterwards, took place at Waterloo; the hostile cavalry furiously charging the squares of infantry, and trying, by the most undaunted efforts of courage, to break in upon them at every practicable point, while a tremendous fire of musketry, grape-shot, and shells, crossing in various directions, repaid their audacity. Nothing in war was ever seen more desperate than the exertions of the Mamelukes. Failing to force their horses through the French squares, individuals were seen to wheel them round, and rein them back on the ranks, that they might disorder them by kicking. As they became frantic with despair, they hurled at the immoveable phalanxes, which they could not break, their pistols, their poniards, and their carabines. Those who fell wounded to the ground, dragged themselves on, to cut at the legs of the French with their crooked sabres. But their efforts were all vain.

The Mamelukes, after the most courageous efforts to accomplish their purpose, were finally beaten off with great

---

[380] Gourgaud, tom. ii., p. 243.
[381] "Pour toute harangue, Buonaparte leur addresse ces mots, qu'on peut regarder comme le sublime de l'éloquence militaire.—'Soldats! vous allez combattre aujourdhui les dominateurs de l'Egypte; songez que du haut de ces Pyramides, quarante siècles vous contemplent!'"—Lacretelle, tom. xiv., p. 267.

slaughter; and as they could not form or act in squadron, their retreat became a confused flight. The greater part attempted to return to their camp, from that sort of instinct, as Napoleon termed it, which leads fugitives to retire in the same direction in which they had advanced. By taking this route they placed themselves betwixt the French and the Nile; and the sustained and insupportable fire of the former soon obliged them to plunge into the river, in hopes to escape by swimming to the opposite bank—a desperate effort, in which few succeeded. Their infantry at the same time evacuated their camp without a show of resistance, precipitated themselves into the boats, and endeavoured to cross the Nile. Very many of these also were destroyed. The French soldiers long afterwards occupied themselves in fishing for the drowned Mamelukes, and failed not to find money and valuables upon all whom they could recover.[382] Murad Bey, with a part of his best Mamelukes, escaped the slaughter by a more regular movement to the left, and retreated by Gizeh into Upper Egypt.[383]

Thus were, in a great measure, destroyed the finest cavalry, considered as individual horsemen, that were ever known to exist. "Could I have united the Mameluke horse to the French infantry," said Buonaparte, "I would have reckoned myself master of the world."[384] The destruction of a body hitherto regarded as invincible, struck terror, not through Egypt only, but far into Africa and Asia, wherever the Moslem religion prevailed.

---

[382] Gourgaud, tom. ii., p. 245; Miot, p. 50; Jomini, tom. x., p. 408; Thibaudeau, tom. iv., p. 184; Larrey, p. 13.

[383] "About nine in the evening, Napoleon entered the country house of Murad Bey at Gizeh. Such habitations bear no resemblance to our *chateaux*. We found it difficult to make it serve for our lodging, and to understand the distribution of the different apartments. But what struck the officers, was a great quantity of cushions and divans covered with the finest damasks and silks of Lyons, and ornamented with gold fringe. The gardens were full of magnificent trees, but without alleys. What most delighted the soldiers (for every one came to see the place,) were great arbours of vines covered with the finest grapes in the world. The vintage was soon over."—Napoleon, *Gourgaud*, tom. ii., p. 249.

[384] Buonaparte made his entry into Cairo on the 26th of July. On the 22d, he issued from Gizeh the following proclamation:—
"People of Cairo! I am satisfied with your conduct. You have done right not to take any part against me: I am come to destroy the race of the Mamelukes, and to protect the trade and the natives of the country. Let all those who are under any fear be composed; and let those who have quitted their houses return to them. Let prayers be offered up to-day, as usual, for I wish that they may be always continued. Entertain no fear for your families, your houses, your property, and, above all, the religion of your Prophet, whom I love."

After this combat, which, to render it more striking to the Parisians, Buonaparte termed the "Battle of the Pyramids," Cairo surrendered without resistance. The shattered remains of the Mamelukes who had swam the Nile and united under Ibrahim Bey, were compelled to retreat into Syria. A party of three hundred French cavalry ventured to attack them at Salahieh, but were severely handled by Ibrahim Bey and his followers, who, having cut many of them to pieces, pursued their retreat without farther interruption. Lower Egypt was completely in the hands of the French, and thus far the expedition of Buonaparte had been perfectly successful. But it was not the will of Heaven, that even the most fortunate of men should escape reverses; and a severe one awaited Napoleon.

CHAPTER XIII

French Fleet—Conflicting Statements of Buonaparte and Admiral Gantheaume—Battle of Aboukir on 1st August, 1798—The French Admiral, Brueyes, killed, and his Ship, L'Orient, blown up—The Victory complete—Effects of this disaster—Means by which Napoleon proposed to establish himself in Egypt—His Administration, in many respects, praiseworthy—in others, his Conduct absurd—He aspires to be regarded an Envoy of the Deity—His endeavours to propitiate the Porte—The Fort of El Arish falls into his hands—Massacre of Jaffa—Admitted by Buonaparte himself—His Arguments in its defence—Replies to them—General Conclusions—Plague in the French Army—Napoleon's Humanity and Courage upon this occasion—Proceeds against Acre to attack Djezzar Pacha—Sir Sidney Smith—His Character—Captures a French Convoy, and throws himself into Acre—French arrive before Acre on 17th March, 1799, and effect a breach on the 28th, but are driven back—Assaulted by an Army of Moslems assembled without the Walls of Acre, whom they defeat and disperse—Personal Misunderstanding and Hostility betwixt Napoleon and Sir Sidney Smith—Explained—Buonaparte is finally compelled to raise the Siege.

FRENCH FLEET

When Buonaparte and his army were safely landed in Egypt, policy seemed to demand that the naval squadron, by which they had been escorted, should have been sent back to France as soon as possible. The French leader accordingly repeatedly asserts, that he had positively commanded Admiral Brueyes, an excellent officer, for whom he himself entertained particular respect,[385] either to carry his squadron of men-of-war into the harbour of Alexandria, or, that being found impossible, instantly to set sail for Corfu. The harbour, by report of the Turkish pilots, was greatly too shallow to admit without danger vessels of such a deep draught of water; and it scarce can be questioned that Admiral Brueyes would have embraced the alternative of setting sail for Corfu, had such been in reality permitted by his orders. But the assertion of Buonaparte is pointedly contradicted by the report of Vice-Admiral Gantheaume, who was himself in the battle of Aboukir, escaped from the slaughter with difficulty, and was intrusted by Buonaparte with drawing up the account of the disaster, which he transmitted to the minister of war. "Perhaps it may be said," so the despatch bears, "that it would have been advisable to have quitted the coast as soon as the disembarkation had taken place. But, *considering the orders of the commander-in-chief,* and the incalculable force afforded to the land-army by the presence of the squadron, the admiral thought it was his duty not to quit these seas."[386]

Looking at the matter more closely—considering the probability of Nelson's return, and the consequent danger of the fleet—considering, too, the especial interest which naval and military officers attach each to their peculiar service, and the relative disregard with which they contemplate the other, we can see several reasons why Buonaparte might have wished, even at some risk, to detain the fleet on the coast of Egypt, but not one which could induce Brueyes to continue there, not only without the consent of the commander-in-chief, but, as Napoleon afterwards alleged, against his express orders. It is one of the cases in which no degree of liberality can enable us to receive the testimony of Buonaparte, contradicted at once by circumstances, and by the positive testimony of Gantheaume.

---

[385] In a letter published in the *Moniteur*, No. 90, December 20, 1797, Buonaparte expresses the highest sense of Admiral Brueyes' firmness and talent, as well as of the high order in which he kept the squadron under his command; and concludes by saying, he had bestowed on him, in the name of the directory, a spy-glass of the best construction which Italy afforded.—S.
[386] Intercepted Letters, part i., p. 219.

We now approach one of the most brilliant actions of the English navy, achieved by the admiral whose exploits so indisputably asserted the right of Britain to the dominion of the ocean. Our limits require that we should state but briefly a tale, at which every heart in our islands will long glow; and we are the more willingly concise that our readers possess it at length in one of the best written popular histories in the English language.[387]

BATTLE OF ABOUKIR

Although unable to enter the harbour of Alexandria, the French admiral believed his squadron safely moored in the celebrated bay of Aboukir. They formed a compact line of battle, of a semicircular form, anchored so close to the shoal-water and surf, that it was thought impossible to get between them and the land; and they concluded, therefore, that they could be brought to action on the starboard side only. On the 1st August, the British fleet appeared; and Nelson had no sooner reconnoitred the French position, than he resolved to force it at every risk. Where the French ships could ride, he argued with instantaneous decision, there must be room for English vessels to anchor between them and the shore. He made signal for the attack accordingly. As the vessels approached the French anchorage, they received a heavy and raking fire, to which they could make no return; but they kept their bows to the enemy, and continued to near their line. The squadrons were nearly of the same numerical strength. The French had thirteen ships of the line, and four frigates. The English, thirteen ships of the line, and one fifty-gun ship. But the French had three eighty-gun ships, and L'Orient, a superb vessel of one hundred and twenty guns. All the British were seventy-fours. The van of the English fleet, six in number, rounded successively the French line, and dropping anchor betwixt them and the shore, opened a tremendous fire. Nelson himself, and his other vessels, ranged along the same French ships on the outer side, and thus placed them betwixt two fires; while the rest of the French line remained for a time unable to

---

[387] Mr. Southey's "Life of Admiral Nelson;" in which one of the most distinguished men of genius and learning whom our age has produced, has recorded the actions of the greatest naval hero that ever existed.—S.

take a share in the combat. The battle commenced with the utmost fury, and lasted till, the sun having set and the night fallen, there was no light by which the combat could be continued, save the flashes of the continuous broadsides. Already, however, some of the French vessels were taken, and the victors, advancing onwards, assailed those which had not yet been engaged.

Meantime, a broad and dreadful light was thrown on the scene of action, by the breaking out of a conflagration on board the French admiral's flag-ship, L'Orient. Brueyes himself had by this time fallen by a cannon-shot.[388] The flames soon mastered the immense vessel, where the carnage was so terrible as to prevent all attempts to extinguish them; and the L'Orient remained blazing like a volcano in the middle of the combat, rendering for a time the dreadful spectacle visible.

At length, and while the battle continued as furious as ever, the burning vessel blew up with so tremendous an explosion, that for a while it silenced the fire on both sides, and made an awful pause in the midst of what had been but lately so horrible a tumult.[389] The cannonade was at first slowly and partially resumed,

---

[388] Buonaparte, on the 19th of August, addressed, from Cairo, the following letter to the widow of the unfortunate admiral:
"Your husband has been killed by a cannon-shot, while fighting on his deck. He died without pain, and by the best death, and that which is thought by soldiers most enviable. I am keenly sensible to your grief. The moment which severs us from the object we love is terrible; it insulates us from all the earth; it inflicts on the body the agonies of death; the faculties of the soul are annihilated, and its relations with the universe subsist only through the medium of a horrible dream, which alters every thing. Mankind appear colder and more selfish than they really are. In this situation we feel that, if nothing obliged us to live, it would be much best to die; but when, after this first thought, we press our children to our hearts, tears and tender feelings revive the sentiments of our nature, and we live for our offspring; yes, madam, see in this very moment, how they open your heart to melancholy: you will weep with them, you will bring them up from infancy—you will talk to them of their father, of your sorrow, of the loss which you and the Republic have sustained. After having once more attached your mind to the world by filial and maternal love, set some value on the friendship and lively regard which I shall always feel for the wife of my friend. Believe that there are a few men who deserve to be the hope of the afflicted, because they understand the poignancy of mental sufferings."
[389] "At ten o'clock a vessel which was burning, blew up with a tremendous noise, which was heard as plainly at Rosetta as the explosion of Grenelle at Paris. This accident was succeeded by a pitchy darkness, and a most profound silence, which continued for about ten minutes."—Poussielque *to his Wife; Intercepted Letters*, part i., p. 208.

but ere midnight it raged with all its original fury. In the morning, the only two French ships who had their colours flying, cut their cables and put to sea, accompanied by two frigates; being all that remained undestroyed and uncaptured, of the gallant navy that so lately escorted Buonaparte and his fortunes in triumph across the Mediterranean.

Such was the Victory of Aboukir, for which he who achieved it felt that word was inadequate. He called it a conquest. The advantages of the day, great as they were, might have been pushed much farther, if Nelson had been possessed of frigates and small craft. The store-ships and transports in the harbour of Alexandria would then have been infallibly destroyed. As it was, the results were of the utmost importance, and the destinies of the French army were altered in proportion. They had no longer any means of communicating with the mother-country, but became the inhabitants of an insulated province, obliged to rely exclusively on the resources which they had brought with them, joined to those which Egypt might afford.

Buonaparte, however surprised by this reverse, exhibited great equanimity. Three thousand French seamen, the remainder of nearly six thousand engaged in that dreadful battle, were sent ashore by cartel, and formed a valuable addition to his forces. Nelson, more grieved almost at being frustrated of his complete purpose, than rejoiced at his victory, left the coast after establishing a blockade on the port of Alexandria.

We are now to trace the means by which Napoleon proposed to establish and consolidate his government in Egypt; and in these we can recognise much that was good and excellent, mixed with such irregularity of imagination, as vindicates the term of Jupiter

---

"L'Orient blew up about eleven in the evening. The whole horizon seemed on fire, the earth shook, and the smoke which proceeded from the vessel ascended heavily in a mass, like an immense black balloon. It then brightened up, and exhibited the objects of all descriptions, which had been precipitated on the scene of conflict. What a terrible moment of fear and desolation for the French, who witnessed this awful catastrophe!"—Louis Buonaparte.

Scapin, by which the Abbé de Pradt distinguished this extraordinary man.[390]

ADMINISTRATION IN EGYPT

His first care was to gather up the reins of government, such as they were, which had dropt from the hands of the defeated beys. With two classes of the Egyptian nation it was easy to establish his authority. The Fellahs, or peasantry, sure to be squeezed to the last penny by one party or other, willingly submitted to the invaders as the strongest, and the most able to protect them. The Cophts, or men of business, were equally ready to serve the party which was in possession of the country. So that the French became the masters of both, as a natural consequence of the power which they had obtained.

But the Turks were to be attached to the conqueror by other means, since their haughty national character, and the intolerance of the Mahometan religion rendered them alike inaccessible to profit, the hope of which swayed the Cophts, and to fear, which was the prevailing argument with the Fellahs. To gratify their vanity, and soothe their prejudices, seemed the only mode by which Napoleon could insinuate himself into the favour of this part of the population. With this view, Buonaparte was far from assuming a title of conquest in Egypt, though he left few of its rights unexercised. On the contrary, he wisely continued to admit the pacha to that ostensible share of authority which was yielded to him by the beys, and spoke with as much seeming respect of the Sublime Porte, as if it had been his intention ever again to permit their having any effective power in Egypt. Their imaums, or priests; their ulemats, or men of law; their cadis, or judges; their sheiks, or chiefs; their Janissaries, or privileged soldiers, were all treated by Napoleon with a certain degree of attention, and the Sultan Kebir, as they

---

[390] "I know not whether the Archbishop of Malines did or did not apply the term *Jupiter Scapin* to Napoleon; but to me it appears incontestable, that the name of Scapin would be much more aptly bestowed on the writer, a bishop and an ambassador, who could be capable of such impertinence towards the sovereign he represented."—Louis Buonaparte, p. 32.

called him, affected to govern, like the Grand Signior, by the intervention of a divan.

This general council consisted of about forty sheiks, or Moslems of distinction by birth or office, who held their regular meetings at Cairo, and from which body emanated the authority of provincial divans, established in the various departments of Egypt. Napoleon affected to consult the superior council, and act in many cases according to their report of the law of the Prophet. On one occasion, he gave them a moral lesson which it would be great injustice to suppress. A tribe of roving Arabs had slain a peasant, and Buonaparte had given directions to search out and punish the murderers. One of his Oriental counsellors laughed at the zeal which the general manifested on so slight a cause.

"What have you to do with the death of this Fellah, Sultan Kebir?" said he, ironically; "was he your kinsman?"

"He was more," said Napoleon; "he was one for whose safety I am accountable to God, who placed him under my government."

"He speaks like an inspired person!" exclaimed the sheiks; who can admire the beauty of a just sentiment, though incapable, from the scope they allow their passions, to act up to the precepts of moral rectitude.

Thus far the conduct of Buonaparte was admirable. He protected the people who were placed under his power, he respected their religious opinions, he administered justice to them according to their own laws, until they should be supplied with a better system of legislation. Unquestionably, his good administration did not amend the radical deficiency of his title; it was still chargeable against him, that he had invaded the dominions of the most ancient ally of France, at a time when there was the most profound peace between the countries. Yet in delivering Egypt from the tyrannical sway of the Mamelukes, and administering the government of the country with wisdom and comparative humanity, the mode in which he used the power which he had acquired, might be admitted in some measure to atone for his usurpation. Not contented with directing his soldiers to hold in respect the religious observances of the country, he showed equal justice and policy in collecting and protecting the scattered remains of the great caravan of the Mecca pilgrimage, which had been plundered by the Mamelukes on their retreat. So satisfactory was his conduct to the Moslem divines, that he contrived to obtain from the clergy of the Mosque an opinion, declaring that it was lawful to pay tribute to the French, though such a doctrine is diametrically inconsistent with the Koran. Thus far Napoleon's measures had proved rational and successful. But with this laudable course of conduct was mixed a species of artifice, which, while we are compelled to term it impious, has in it, at the same time, something ludicrous, and almost childish.

Buonaparte entertained the strange idea of persuading the Moslems that he himself pertained in some sort to their religion, being an envoy of the Deity, sent on earth, not to take away, but to confirm and complete, the doctrines of the Koran, and the mission of Mahomet.[391] He used, in executing this purpose, the inflated language of the East, the more easily that it corresponded, in its allegorical and amplified style, with his own natural tone of composition; and he hesitated not to join in the external ceremonial of the Mahometan religion, that his actions might seem to confirm his words. The French general celebrated the feast of the prophet as it recurred, with some sheik of eminence, and joined in the litanies and worship enjoined by the Koran. He affected, too, the language of an inspired follower of the faith of Mecca, of which the following is a curious example.

On entering the sepulchral chamber in the pyramid of Cheops, "Glory be to Allah," said Buonaparte, "There is no God

---

[391] "It is not true that in Egypt Napoleon showed himself almost persuaded of the truth of the mission of Mahomet. Doubtless, deceit and falsehood should be banished from the language of true policy, since as government ought to be, as much as is in the power of men, the image of God upon earth, its language ought to be that of truth and justice. This, however, does not preclude the right of respecting the religious worship and opinions of a conquered nation, and it was in this sense that the proclamations addressed by my brother to the Mussulmen should be regarded. They would not have been understood by these people, if they had not spoken their language. Whilst I was in Holland, I rejected at first the title of Emperor given to the King of Holland by the Sublime Porte; but upon expressing my astonishment I was assured that the Porte gave this title to the sovereigns of other countries, and that that of king would not be understood."—Louis Buonaparte, p. 34.

but God, and Mahomet is his prophet." A confession of faith which is in itself a declaration of Islamism.

"Thou hast spoken like the most learned of the prophets," said the mufti, who accompanied him.

"I can command a car of fire to descend from heaven," continued the French general, "and I can guide and direct its course upon earth."

"Thou art the great chief to whom Mahomet gives power and victory," said the mufti.

Napoleon closed the conversation with this not very pertinent Oriental proverb, "The bread which the wicked seizes upon by force, shall be turned to dust in his mouth."[392]

Though the mufti played his part in the above scene with becoming gravity, Buonaparte over-estimated his own theatrical powers, and did too little justice to the shrewdness of the Turks, if he supposed them really edified by his pretended proselytism. With them as with us, a renegade from the religious faith in which he was brought up, is like a deserter from the standard of his country; and though the services of either may be accepted and used, they remain objects of disregard and contempt, as well with those to whose service they have deserted, as with the party whom they have abandoned.

---

[392] This conversation appeared officially in the *Moniteur*. Bourrienne, notwithstanding, asserts that Buonaparte never set foot in the pyramid. He acknowledges, indeed, that "with the heads of the Mahometan priesthood he held frequent conversations on these subjects;" but adds, "in all this there was nothing serious; it was rather an amusement. If he ever spoke as a Mussulman, he did so in the capacity of a military and political chief in a Mahometan country. On this depended his success, the safety of the army, and consequently his glory. It is true, he had a Turkish dress made for him, but only as a joke. One morning he desired me to begin breakfast without waiting; a quarter of an hour after, he entered in his new costume. Scarcely was he recognised, when we received him with bursts of laughter. He took his place with a gravity which heightened the effect, but found himself so ill at ease as an Oriental, that he soon went to undress, and never gave a second exhibition of this masquerade."—Bourrienne, tom. ii., p. 164.

INSURRECTION IN CAIRO

The Turks and Arabs of Cairo soon afterwards showed Buonaparte, by a general and unexpected insurrection, [October 22,] in which many Frenchmen were slain, how little they were moved by his pretended attachment to their faith, and how cordially they considered him as their enemy. Yet, when the insurgents had been quelled by force, and the blood of five thousand Moslems had atoned for that of three hundred Frenchmen, Napoleon, in an address to the inhabitants of Cairo, new-modelling the general council or divan, held still the same language as before of himself and his destinies. "Sheriffs," he said, "Ulemats, Orators of the Mosque, teach the people that those who become my enemies shall have no refuge in this world or the next. Is there any one not blind enough to see, that I am the agent of Destiny, or incredulous enough to call in question the power of Destiny over human affairs? Make the people understand, that since the world was a world, it was ordained, that having destroyed the enemies of Islamism, and broken down the Cross,[393] I should come from the West to accomplish the task designed for me—show them, that in more than twenty passages of the Koran my coming is foretold. I could demand a reckoning from each of you for the most secret thoughts of his soul, since to me everything is known; but the day will come when all shall know from whom I have my commission, and that human efforts cannot prevail against me."

It is plain from this strange proclamation, that Buonaparte was willing to be worshipped as a superior being, as soon as altars could be built, and worshippers collected together. But the Turks and Arabs were wiser than the Persians in the case of young Ammon. The Sheik of Alexandria, who affected much devotion to Buonaparte's person, came roundly to the point with him. He remarked the French observed no religious worship. "Why not, therefore," he said, "declare yourself Moslem at once, and remove the only obstacle betwixt you and the throne of the East?" Buonaparte objected the prohibition of wine, and the external rite

---

[393] Alluding to the capture of the island of Malta, and subjection of the Pope, on which he was wont to found as services rendered to the religion of Mahomet.—S.

which Mahomet adopted from the Jewish religion. The officious sheik proposed to call a council of the Moslem sages, and procure for the new proselytes some relaxation of these fundamental laws of the Prophet's faith. According to this hopeful plan, the Moslems must have ceased to be such in two principal articles of their ritual, in order to induce the French to become a kind of imperfect renegades, rejecting, in the prohibition of wine, the only peculiar guard which Mahomet assigned to the moral virtue of his follower's, while they embraced the degrading doctrine of fatality, the licentious practice of polygamy, and the absurd chimeras of the Koran.

Napoleon appears to have believed the sheik serious, which is very doubtful, and to have contemplated with eager ambition the extent of views which his conversion to Islamism appeared to open. His own belief in predestination recommended the creed of Mahomet, and for the Prophet of Mecca himself he had a high respect, as one of those who had wrought a great and enduring change on the face of the world.[394] Perhaps he envied the power which Mahomet possessed, of ruling over men's souls as well as their bodies, and might thence have been led into the idea of playing a part, to which time and circumstances, the character of his army and his own, were alike opposed. No man ever succeeded in imposing himself on the public as a supernatural personage, who was not, to a certain degree, the dupe of his own imposture; and Napoleon's calculating and reflecting mind was totally devoid of the enthusiasm which enables a man to cheat himself into at least a partial belief of the deceit which he would impose on others. The French soldiers, on the other hand, bred in scorn of religion of every description, would have seen nothing but ridicule in the pretensions of their leader to a supernatural mission; and in playing the character which Alexander ventured to personate, Buonaparte would have found in his own army many a Clitus, who would have considered his pretensions as being only ludicrous. He himself, indeed, expressed himself satisfied that his authority over his soldiers was so absolute, that it would have cost but giving it out in the order of the day to have made them all become Mahometans; but, at the same time, he has acquainted us, that the French troops were at times so much discontented with their condition in Egypt,

---

[394] Gourgaud, tom. ii., p. 261.

that they formed schemes of seizing on their standards, and returning to France by force. What reply, it may be reasonably asked, were they likely to make to a proposal, which would have deprived them of their European and French character, and levelled them with Africans and Asiatics, whose persons they despised, and whose country they desired to leave? It is likely, that reflections on the probable consequences prevented his going farther than the vague pretensions which he announced in his proclamations, and in his language to the sheiks. He had gone far enough, however, to show, that the considerations of conscience would have been no hinderance; and that, notwithstanding the strength of his understanding, common sense had less influence than might have been expected, in checking his assertion of claims so ludicrous as well as so profane. Indeed, his disputes with the Ottoman Porte speedily assumed a character, which his taking the turban and professing himself a Moslem in all the forms, could not have altered to his advantage.

OTTOMAN PORTE

It had been promised to Buonaparte, that the abilities of Talleyrand, as minister of foreign affairs, should be employed to reconcile the Grand Signior and his counsellors to the occupation of Egypt.[395] But the efforts of that able negotiator had totally failed in a case so evidently hopeless; and if Talleyrand had even proceeded to Constantinople, as Napoleon alleged the Directory had promised, it could only have been to be confined in the Seven Towers. The Porte had long since declared, that any attack upon Egypt, the road to the holy cities of Mecca and Medina, would be considered as a declaration of war, whatever pretexts might be alleged. They regarded, therefore, Buonaparte's invasion as an injury equally unprovoked and unjustifiable. They declared war against France, called upon every follower of the Prophet to take the part of his vicegerent upon earth, collected forces, and threatened an immediate expedition, for the purpose of expelling the infidels from Egypt. The success of the British at Aboukir increased their confidence. Nelson was loaded with every mark of honour which

---

[395] Gourgaud, tom. ii., p. 363.

the Sultan could bestow, and the most active preparations were made to act against Buonaparte, equally considered as enemy to the Porte, whether he professed himself Christian, infidel, or renegade.

Meantime, that adventurous and active chief was busied in augmenting his means of defence or conquest, and in acquiring the information necessary to protect what he had gained, and to extend his dominions. For the former purpose, corps were raised from among the Egyptians, and some were mounted upon dromedaries, the better to encounter the perils of the desert. For the latter, Buonaparte undertook a journey to the Isthmus of Suez, the well-known interval which connects Asia with Africa. He subscribed the charter, or protection, granted to the Maronite Monks of Sinai, with the greater pleasure, that the signature of Mahomet had already sanctioned that ancient document. He visited the celebrated fountains of Moses, and, misled by a guide, had nearly been drowned in the advancing tides of the Red Sea.[396] This, he observes, would have furnished a splendid text to all the preachers in Europe.[397] But the same Deity, who had rendered the gulf fatal to Pharaoh, had reserved for one, who equally defied and disowned his power, the rocks of an island in the midst of the Atlantic.

Feb. 17.

When Napoleon was engaged in this expedition, or speedily on his return, he learned that two Turkish armies had assembled, one at Rhodes, and the other in Syria, with the purpose of recovering Egypt. The daring genius, which always desired to anticipate the attempts of the enemy, determined him to march with a strong force for the occupation of Syria, and thus at once to alarm the Turks by the progress which he expected to make in that

---

[396] "The night overtook us, the waters began to rise around us, when the horsemen ahead cried out that their horses were swimming. General Buonaparte rescued the whole party by one of those simple expedients which occur to an imperturbable mind. Placing himself in the centre, he bade all the rest form a circle round him, and then ride out each man in a separate direction, and each to halt as soon as he found his horse swimming. The man whose horse continued to march the last, was sure, he said, to be in the right direction; him, accordingly we all followed, and reached Suez, at midnight in safety; though so rapidly had the tide advanced, that the horses were more than breast-high in the water."—*Memoirs of Savary*, vol. i., p. 97.
[397] Las Cases, tom. i., p. 211.

province, and to avoid being attacked in Egypt by two Turkish armies at the same time. His commencement was as successful as his enterprise was daring. A body of Mamelukes was dispersed by a night attack. The fort of El Arish, considered as one of the keys of Egypt, fell easily into his hands. Finally, at the head of about ten thousand men, he traversed the desert, so famous in biblical history, which separates Africa from Asia, and entered Palestine without much loss, but not without experiencing the privations to which the wanderers in those sandy wastes have been uniformly subjected. While the soldiers looked with fear on the howling wilderness which they saw around,[398] there was something in the extent and loneliness of the scene that corresponded with the swelling soul of Napoleon, and accommodated itself to his ideas of immense and boundless space. He was pleased with the flattery, which derived his Christian name from two Greek words, signifying the Lion of the Desert.

MASSACRE OF JAFFA

Upon his entering the Holy Land, Buonaparte again drove before him a body of the Mamelukes, belonging to those who, after the battles of the Pyramids and of Salahieh, had retreated into Syria; and his army occupied without resistance Gaza, anciently a city of the Philistines, in which they found supplies of provisions. Jaffa, a celebrated city during the time of the Crusades, was the next object of attack. It was bravely assaulted, and fiercely defended. But the French valour and discipline prevailed—the place was carried by storm—three thousand Turks were put to the sword, and the town was abandoned to the license of the soldiery, which, by Buonaparte's own admission, never assumed a shape more frightful.[399] Such, it may be said, is the stern rule of war; and if so,

---

[398] "While the army was passing through Syria, there was scarcely a soldier but was heard to repeat these lines from Zaire:—
'Les Français sont las de chercher désormais Des climats que pour eux le destin n'a point faits, Ils n'abandonnent point leur fertile patrie Pour languir aux deserts de l'aride Arabie.'
When the men found themselves in the midst of the Desert, surrounded by the boundless ocean of sand, they began to question the generosity of their general; they thought he had observed singular moderation in having promised each of them only seven acres—'The rogue,' said they, 'might with safety give us as much as he pleases; we should not abuse his good-nature.'"—Las Cases, tom. i., p. 210.
[399] See his despatch to the Directory, on the Syrian campaign.—Gourgaud, tom. ii., p. 374.

most of our readers will acquiesce in the natural exclamation of the Maréchal de Montluc, "Certes, we soldiers stand in more need of the Divine mercy than other men, seeing that our profession compels us to command and to witness deeds of such cruelty." It was not, however, to the ordinary horrors attending the storm of a town, that the charge against Buonaparte is on this occasion limited. He is accused of having been guilty of an action of great injustice, as well as of especial barbarity. Concerning this we shall endeavour to state, stripped of colouring and exaggeration, first the charge, and then the reply, of Napoleon himself.

After the breach had been stormed, a large part of the garrison, estimated by Buonaparte himself at twelve hundred men, which Miot[400] raises to betwixt two and three thousand, and others exaggerate still more, remained on the defensive, and held out in the mosques, and a sort of citadel to which they had retreated, till, at length, despairing of succour, they surrendered their arms, and were in appearance admitted to quarter. Of this body, the Egyptians were carefully separated from the Turks, Maugrabins, and Arnaouts; and while the first were restored to liberty, and sent back to their country, these last were placed under a strong guard. Provisions were distributed to them, and they were permitted to go by detachments in quest of water. According to all appearance they were considered and treated as prisoners of war. This was on the 7th of March. On the 9th, two days afterwards, this body of prisoners were marched out of Jaffa, in the centre of a large square battalion, commanded by General Bon. Miot assures us, that he himself mounted his horse, accompanied the melancholy column, and witnessed the event. The Turks foresaw their fate, but used neither entreaties nor complaints to avert it. They marched on, silent and composed. Some of them, of higher rank, seemed to exhort the others to submit, like servants of the Prophet, to the decree, which, according to their belief, was written on their forehead. They were escorted to the sand-hills to the south east of Jaffa, divided there into small bodies, and put to death by musketry. The execution lasted a considerable time, and the wounded, as in the *fusillades* of the Revolution, were despatched with the bayonet. Their bodies

---

[400] Expédition en Egypte et Syrie, p. 148.

were heaped together, and formed a pyramid which is still visible, consisting now of human bones as originally of bloody corpses.

The cruelty of this execution occasioned the fact itself to be doubted, though coming with strong evidence, and never denied by the French themselves. Napoleon, however, frankly admitted the truth of the statement both to Lord Ebrington and to Dr. O'Meara.[401] Well might the author of this cruelty write to the Directory, that the storming of Jaffa was marked by horrors which he had never elsewhere witnessed. Buonaparte's defence was, that the massacre was justified by the laws of war—that the head of his messenger had been cut off by the governor of Jaffa, when sent to summon him to surrender—that these Turks were a part of the garrison of El Arish, who had engaged not to serve against the French, and were found immediately afterwards defending Jaffa, in breach of the terms of their capitulation. They had incurred the doom of death, therefore, by the rules of war—Wellington, he said, would have, in his place, acted in the same manner.

To this plea the following obvious answers apply. If the Turkish governor had behaved like a barbarian, for which his country, and the religion which Napoleon meditated to embrace, might be some excuse, the French general had avenged himself by the storm and plunder of the town, with which his revenge ought, in all reason, to have been satisfied. If some of these unhappy Turks had broken their faith to Buonaparte, and were found again in the ranks which they had sworn to abandon, it could not, according to the most severe construction of the rules of war, authorise the dreadful retaliation of indiscriminate massacre upon a multitude of prisoners, without inquiring whether they had been all equally guilty. Lastly, and admitting them all to stand in the same degree of criminality, although their breach of faith might have entitled Buonaparte to refuse these men quarter while they had arms in their

---

[401] "I asked him about the massacre of the Turks at Jaffa: he answered, 'C'est vrai; J'en fis fusiller à peu près deux mille.'"—Memorandum of Two Conversations between the Emperor Napoleon and Viscount Ebrington at Porto-Ferraio, p. 12.
"I observed, that Miot asserted that he (Napoleon) had caused between three and four thousand Turks to be shot, some days after the capture of Jaffa. He answered, 'It is not true that there were so many; I ordered about a thousand or twelve hundred to be shot, which was done.'"—O'Meara vol. i., p. 328.

hands, that right was ended when the French general received their submission, and when they had given up the mean of defence, on condition of safety for life at least.[402]

This bloody deed must always remain a deep stain on the character of Napoleon. Yet we do not view it as the indulgence of an innate love of cruelty; for nothing in Buonaparte's history shows the existence of that vice, and there are many things which intimate his disposition to have been naturally humane. But he was ambitious, aimed at immense and gigantic undertakings, and easily learned to overlook the waste of human life, which the execution of his projects necessarily involved. He seems to have argued, not on the character of the action, but solely on the effect which it was to produce upon his own combinations. His army was small; it was his business to strike terror into his numerous enemies, and the measure to be adopted seemed capable of making a deep impression on all who should hear of it. Besides, these men, if dismissed, would immediately rejoin his enemies. He had experienced their courage, and to disarm them would have been almost an unavailing precaution, where their national weapon, the sabre, was so easily attained. To detain them prisoners would have required a stronger force than Napoleon could afford, would have added difficulty and delay to the movement of his troops, and tended to exhaust his supplies. That sort of necessity, therefore, which men fancy to themselves when they are unwilling to forego a favourite object for the sake of obeying a moral precept—that necessity which might be more properly termed a temptation difficult to be resisted—that necessity which has been called the tyrant's plea, was the cause of the massacre at Jaffa, and must remain its sole apology.

It might almost seem that Heaven set its vindictive brand upon this deed of butchery; for about the time it was committed the plague broke out in the army. Buonaparte, with a moral courage deserving as much praise as his late cruelty deserved reprobation, went into the hospitals in person, and while exposing himself, without hesitation, to the infection, diminished the terror of the disease in the opinion of the soldiers generally, and even of the

---

[402] See Jomini, tom. xi., p. 403; Thibaudeau, tom. ii., p. 172; Savary, tom. i., p. 100; Bourrienne, tom. ii., p. 226; Martin, Hist. de l'Expédition d'Egypte, tom. i., p. 289.

patients themselves, who were thus enabled to keep up their spirits, and gained by doing so the fairest chance of recovery.[403]

SAINT JEAN D'ACRE

Meanwhile, determined to prosecute the conquest of Syria, Buonaparte resolved to advance to Saint Jean d'Acre so celebrated in the wars of Palestine. The Turkish Pacha, or governor of Syria, who, like others in his situation, accounted himself almost an independent sovereign, was Achmet; who, by his unrelenting cruelties and executions, had procured the terrible distinction of Djezzar, or the Butcher. Buonaparte addressed this formidable chief in two letters, offering his alliance, and threatening him with his vengeance if it should be rejected.[404] To neither did the pacha return any answer; in the second instance he put to death the messenger. The French general advanced against Acre, vowing revenge. There were, however, obstacles to the success of his enterprise, on which he had not calculated.

The pacha had communicated the approach of Napoleon to Sir Sidney Smith, to whom had been committed the charge of assisting the Turks in their proposed expedition to Egypt, and who, for that purpose, was cruising in the Levant. He hastened to sail for Acre with the Tigre and Theseus, ships of the line; and arriving there two days ere the French made their appearance, contributed greatly to place the town, the fortifications of which were on the old Gothic plan, in a respectable state of defence.

Sir Sidney Smith, who so highly distinguished himself on this occasion, had been long celebrated for the most intrepid courage, and spirit of enterprise. His character was, besides, marked by those traits of enthusiasm at which cold and vulgar minds are apt to sneer, because incapable of understanding them; yet without which great and honourable actions have rarely been achieved. He had also a talent, uncommon among the English, that of acting easily with foreign, and especially with barbarous troops, and understanding

---

[403] O'Meara, vol. ii., p. 128.
[404] See Gourgaud, tom. ii., p. 372.

how to make their efforts availing for the service of the common cause, though exerted in a manner different from those of civilized nations. This brave officer having been frequently intrusted with the charge of alarming the French coast, had been taken on one occasion, and, contrary to the laws of nations, and out of a mean spirit of revenge, was imprisoned in the Temple, from which he was delivered by a daring stratagem, effected by the French Royalist party. He had not been many hours at Acre, when Providence afforded him a distinguished mark of favour. The Theseus, which had been detached to intercept any French vessels that might be attending on Buonaparte's march, detected a small flotilla stealing under Mount Carmel, and had the good fortune to make prize of seven out of nine of them. They were a convoy from Damietta, bound for Acre, having on board heavy cannon, platforms, ammunition, and other necessary articles. These cannon and military stores, destined to form the siege of Acre, became eminently useful in its defence, and the consequence of their capture was eventually decisive of the struggle. General Philippeaux, a French royalist, and officer of engineers, immediately applied himself to place the cannon thus acquired, to the amount of betwixt thirty and forty, upon the walls which they had been intended to destroy. This officer, who had been Buonaparte's school-fellow, and the principal agent in delivering Sir Sidney Smith from prison, possessed rare talents in his profession. Thus strangely met under the walls of Acre, an English officer, late a prisoner in the Temple of Paris, and a French colonel of engineers, with the late general of the army of Italy, the ancient companion of Philippeaux,[405] and about to become almost the personal enemy of Smith.

---

[405] Philippeaux died during the siege, of a fever brought on by fatigue. Buonaparte spoke of him with more respect than he usually showed to those who had been successful in opposing him. One reason might be, that the merit given to Philippeaux was in some degree subtracted from Sir Sidney Smith. The former was a Frenchman, and dead—the latter alive, and an Englishman.—S.—"Sir Sidney Smith behaved very bravely, and was well seconded by Philippeaux, a Frenchman of talent, who had studied with me as an engineer."—Napoleon, *Voice*, &c., vol. i., p. 210.

SIEGE OF ACRE

On the 17th March, the French came in sight of Acre, which is built on a peninsula advancing into the sea, and so conveniently situated that vessels can lie near the shore, and annoy with their fire whatever advances to assault the fortification. Notwithstanding the presence of two British ships of war, and the disappointment concerning his battering cannon, which were now pointed against him from the ramparts, Buonaparte, with a characteristic perseverance, which, on such an occasion, was pushed into obstinacy, refused to abandon his purpose, and proceeded to open trenches, although the guns which he had to place in them were only twelve pounders. The point of attack was a large tower which predominated over the rest of the fortifications. A mine at the same time was run under the extreme defences.

By the 28th March a breach was effected, the mine was sprung, and the French proceeded to the assault upon that day. They advanced at the charging step, under a murderous fire from the walls, but had the mortification to find a deep ditch betwixt them and the tower. They crossed it, nevertheless, by help of the scaling-ladders which they carried with them, and forced their way as far as the tower, from which it is said that the defenders, impressed by the fate of Jaffa, were beginning to fly. They were checked by the example of Djezzar himself, who fired his own pistols at the French, and upbraided the Moslems who were retreating from the walls. The defences were again manned; the French, unable to support the renewed fire, were checked and forced back; and the Turks falling upon them in their retreat with sabre in hand, killed a number of their best men, and Mailly, who commanded the party. Sorties were made from the place to destroy the French works; and although the cries with which the Turks carry on their military manœuvres gave the alarm to the enemy, yet, assisted by a detachment of British seamen, they did the French considerable damage, reconnoitred the mine which they were forming anew, and obtained the knowledge of its direction necessary to prepare a counter-mine.

While the strife was thus fiercely maintained on both sides, with mutual loss and increased animosity, the besiegers were threatened with other dangers. An army of Moslem troops of various nations, but all actuated by the same religious zeal, had formed themselves in the mountains of Samaria, and uniting with them the warlike inhabitants of that country, now called Naplous, formed the plan of attacking the French army lying before Acre on one side, while Djezzar and his allies should assail them upon the other. Kleber, with his division, was despatched by Buonaparte to disperse this assemblage. But though he obtained considerable advantages over detached parties of the Syrian army, their strength was so disproportioned, that at last, while he held a position near Mount Tabor, with two or three thousand men, he was surrounded by about ten times his own number. But his general-in-chief was hastening to his assistance. Buonaparte left two divisions to keep the trenches before Acre, and penetrated into the country in three columns. Murat, at the head of a fourth, occupied the pass called Jacob's Bridge. The attack, made on various points, was every where successful. The camp of the Syrian army was taken; their defeat, almost their dispersion, was accomplished, while their scattered remains fled to Damascus. Buonaparte returned, crowned with laurels, to the siege of Acre.

Here, too, the arrival of thirty heavy pieces of cannon from Jaffa seemed to promise that success, which the French had as yet been unable to attain. It was about this time that, walking on the Mount which still retains the name of Richard Cœur de Lion, Buonaparte expressed himself to Murat in these terms, as he pointed to Saint Jean D'Acre:—"The fate of the East depends upon yonder petty town. Its conquest will ensure the main object of my expedition, and Damascus will be the first fruit of it."[406] Thus it would seem, that, while engaged in the enterprise, Buonaparte held the same language, which he did many years after its failure when at St. Helena.

---

[406] Related by Miot as communicated to him by Murat.—S.—"Le sort de l'Orient est dans cette bicoque; la chute de cette ville est le but de mon expédition; Damas doit en être le fruit."—Miot, p. 184.

Repeated and desperate assaults proved, that the consequence which he attached to taking Acre was as great as his words expressed. The assailants suffered severely on these occasions, for they were exposed to the fire of two ravelins, or external fortifications, which had been constructed under Philippeaux's directions, and at the same time enfiladed by the fire of the British shipping. At length, employing to the uttermost the heavy artillery now in his possession, Buonaparte, in spite of a bloody and obstinate opposition, forced his way to the disputed tower, and made a lodgment on the second story. It afforded, however, no access to the town; and the troops remained there as in a *cul-de-sac*, the lodgment being covered from the English and Turkish fire by a work constructed partly of packs of cotton, partly of the dead bodies of the slain, built up along with them.

At this critical moment, a fleet, bearing reinforcements long hoped for and much needed, appeared in view of the garrison. They contained Turkish troops under the command of Hassan Bey. Yet near as they were, the danger was imminent that Acre might be taken ere they could land. To prevent such a misfortune, Sir Sidney Smith in person proceeded to the disputed tower, at the head of a body of British seamen, armed with pikes. They united themselves to a corps of brave Turks, who defended the breach rather with heavy stones than with other weapons. The heap of ruins which divided the contending parties served as a breast-work to both. The muzzles of the muskets touched each other, and the spear-heads of the standards were locked together. At this moment one of the Turkish regiments of Hassan's army, which had by this time landed, made a sortie upon the French; and though they were driven back, yet the diversion occasioned the besiegers to be forced from their lodgment.

Abandoning the ill-omened tower, which had cost the besiegers so many men, Buonaparte now turned his efforts towards a considerable breach that had been effected in the curtain, and which promised a more easy entrance. It proved, indeed, but too easy; for Djezzar Pacha opposed to the assault on this occasion a new mode of tactics. Confiding in his superior numbers, he suffered the French, who were commanded by the intrepid General Lannes, to surmount the breach without opposition, by which they penetrated into the body of the place. They had no sooner entered, than a numerous body of Turks mingled among them with loud shouts; and ere they had time or room to avail themselves of their discipline, brought them into that state of close fighting, where strength and agility are superior to every other acquirement. The Turks, wielding the sabre in one hand, and the poniard in the other, cut to pieces almost all the French who had entered. General Rambaud lay a headless corpse in the breach—Lannes was with difficulty brought off severely wounded. The Turks gave no quarter; and instantly cutting the heads off of those whom they slew, carried them to the pacha, who sat in public distributing money to those who brought him these bloody trophies, which now lay piled in heaps around him. This was the sixth assault upon these tottering and blood-stained ramparts. "Victory," said Napoleon, "is to the most persevering;"[407] and contrary to the advice of Kleber, he resolved upon another and yet more desperate attack.

On the 21st May the final effort was made. The attack of the morning failed, and Colonel Veneux renewed it at mid-day. "Be assured," said he to Buonaparte, "Acre shall be yours to-night, or Veneux will die on the breach."[408] He kept his word at the cost of his life. Bon was also slain, whose division had been the executioners of the garrison of Jaffa. The French now retreated, dispirited and despairing of success. The contest had been carried on at half a musket shot distance; and the bodies of the dead lying around, putrified under the burning sun, spread disease among the survivors. An attempt was made to establish a suspension of arms for removing this horrible annoyance. Miot says that the pacha returned no answer to the proposal of the French. According to Sir Sidney Smith's official reports, the armistice for this humane purpose was actually agreed on, but broken off by the French firing upon those who were engaged in the melancholy office, and then rushing on to make their last unsuccessful charge and assault upon the breach. This would have been a crime so useless, and would have tended so much to the inconvenience of the French themselves, that we cannot help suspecting some misunderstanding

---

[407] "La victoire est au plus opiniâtre."—Miot, p. 199.
[408] Miot, p. 199.

had occurred, and that the interruption was under a wrong conception of the purpose of the working party.

This is the more probable, as Sir Sidney Smith, who reports the circumstance, was not at this time disposed to put the best construction on any action of Buonaparte's, who, on the other hand, regarded the British seamen with peculiar dislike, and even malignity. The cause of personal quarrel betwixt them was rather singular.

Buonaparte had addressed the subjects of Achmet Djezzar's pachalik, in terms inviting them to revolt, and join the French; yet was much offended when, imitating his own policy, the pacha and Sir Sidney Smith caused letters to be sent into his camp before Acre, urging his soldiers to mutiny and desertion. Sir Sidney also published a proclamation to the Druses, and other inhabitants of the country, calling on them to trust the faith of a Christian knight, rather than that of an unprincipled renegado. Nettled at these insults, Buonaparte declared that the English commodore was mad; and, according to his account, Sir Sidney replied by sending him a challenge. The French general scornfully refused this invitation, unless the challenger would bring Marlborough to meet him, but offered to send one of his grenadiers to indulge the Englishman's desire of single combat. The good taste of the challenge may be doubted, if indeed such was ever sent; but the scorn of the reply ought to have been mitigated, considering it was addressed to one, in consequence of whose dauntless and determined opposition Buonaparte's favourite object had failed, and who was presently to compel him, for the first time, to an inglorious retreat.

Another calumny, circulated by Buonaparte against the English commodore, was, that Sir Sidney Smith had endeavoured to expose his French prisoners to the infection of the plague, by placing them in vessels where that dreadful contagion prevailed. This charge had no other foundation, than in Buonaparte's wish, by spreading such a scandal, to break off all communication between the commodore and the discontented of his own army. After the heat excited by their angry collision had long subsided, it is amusing to find Napoleon, when in the island of Saint Helena, declaring, that his opinion of Sir Sidney Smith was altered for the better, since he had become acquainted with the rest of his countrymen, and that he now considered him as a worthy sort of man—for an Englishman.

THE SIEGE OF ACRE RAISED

The siege of Acre had now continued sixty days since the opening of the trenches. The besiegers had marched no less than eight times to the assault, while eleven desperate sallies were evidence of the obstinacy of the defence. Several of the best French generals were killed; among the rest Caffarelli,[409] for whom Buonaparte had particular esteem; and the army was greatly reduced by the sword and the plague, which raged at once among their devoted bands. Retreat became inevitable. Yet Buonaparte endeavoured to give it such a colouring as might make the measure seem voluntary. Sometimes he announced that his purpose of going to Acre was sufficiently accomplished when he had battered down the palace of the pacha; at other times he affirmed he had left the whole town a heap of ruins; and finally, he informed the Directory that he could easily have taken the place, but the plague being raging within its walls, and it being impossible to prevent the troops from seizing on infected clothes for part of their booty, he had rather declined the capture of Acre, than run the risk of introducing this horrid malady among his soldiers. What his real feelings must have been, while covering his chagrin with such flimsy pretexts, may be conjectured from the following frank avowal to his attendants in Saint Helena. Speaking of the dependence of the most important affairs on the most trivial, he remarks, that the mistake of the captain of a frigate, who bore away, instead of forcing his passage to the place of his destination, had prevented the face of the world from being totally changed. "Acre," he said, "would otherwise have

---

[409] Caffarelli was shot in the elbow, and died of the amputation of the limb. He had before lost a leg, which induced the French soldiers, who disliked him as one of the principal contrivers of the Egyptian expedition, to say, when they saw him hobble past, "He, at least, need care little about the matter—he is sure to have *one* foot in France." He had some days' delirium before he died; but Count Las Cases reports, (vol. i., p. 220,) that whenever Buonaparte was announced, his presence—nay, his name alone—seemed to cure the wanderings of the patient's spirit, and that this phenomenon was renewed so often as the general made him a visit.—S.

been taken—the French army would have flown to Damascus and Aleppo—in a twinkling of an eye they would have been on the Euphrates—the Syrian Christians would have joined us—the Druses, the Armenians would have united with us."—Some one replied, "We might have been reinforced to the number of a hundred thousand men."—"Say six hundred thousand," said the Emperor; "who can calculate the amount? I would have reached Constantinople and the Indies—I would have changed the face of the world."[410]

---

[410] Las Cases, tom. i., partie seconde, p. 384. The extravagance of Napoleon's plan unavoidably reminds us of the vanity of human wishes. The cause to which he ascribes it is the *mistake* of a captain of a frigate, who, instead of forcing his way to Acre, against the opposition of two ships of the line, was unfortunately taken by them. This is a mode of reasoning which Napoleon was very ready to adopt. The miscarriage of his plans was seldom imputed by him to the successful wisdom or valour of an enemy, but to some accidental circumstance, or blunder, which deranged the scheme which must otherwise have been infallible. Some of his best generals were of a different opinion, and considered the rashness of the attack upon Acre, as involving the certainty of failure. Kleber is reported to have said, that the Turks defended themselves with the skill of Christians, and that the French attacked like Turks.—S.

CHAPTER XIV

Discussion concerning the alleged Poisoning of the Sick in the Hospitals at Jaffa—Napoleon acquitted of the charge—French Army re-enter Cairo on the 14th June—Retrospect of what had taken place in Upper and Lower Egypt during Napoleon's Absence—Incursion of Murad Bey—18,000 Turks occupy Aboukir—Attacked and defeated—This Victory terminates Napoleon's Career in Egypt—Admiral Gantheaume receives Orders to make ready for Sea—On the 22d August Napoleon embarks for France—Arrives in Ajaccio on the 30th September—and lands at Frejus on the 9th October.

POISONING OF THE SICK AT JAFFA

The retreat from before Acre was conducted with equal skill and secrecy, though Buonaparte was compelled to leave behind his heavy cannon, which he either buried or threw into the sea. But, by a rumour which long prevailed in the French army, he was alleged to have taken a far more extraordinary measure of preparation for retreat, by destroying with opium the sick in the hospitals, who could not march along with the army.

This transaction is said to have taken place under the following circumstances. The siege of Acre being raised on the 21st of May, 1799, the French army retreated to Jaffa, where their military hospitals had been established during the siege. Upon the 27th, Buonaparte was under the necessity of continuing his retreat, and in the meantime such of the patients as were convalescent were sent forward on the road to Egypt, under the necessary precautions for their safety. There remained an indefinite number, reaching at the greatest computation to betwixt twenty and thirty, but stated by Buonaparte himself to be only seven, whose condition was desperate. Their disease was the plague, and to carry them onward, seemed to threaten the army with infection; while to leave them behind, was abandoning them to the cruelty of the Turks, by whom all stragglers and prisoners were cruelly murdered, often with protracted torture. It was on this occasion that Buonaparte submitted to Desgenettes, chief of the medical staff, the propriety of ending the victims' misery by a dose of opium. The physician answered, with the heroism belonging to his profession, that his art taught him how to cure men, not to kill them.[411]

The proposal was agreeable to Buonaparte's principles, who advocating the legality of suicide, naturally might believe, that if a man has a right to relieve himself of intolerable evils by depriving himself of life, a general or a monarch may deal forth that measure to his soldiers or subjects, which he would think it advisable to act upon in his own case. It was consistent, also, with his character, rather to look at results than at the measures which were to produce them, and to consider in many cases the end as an excuse for the means. "I would have desired such a relief for myself in the same circumstances," he said to Mr. Warden.[412] To O'Meara he affirmed, "that he would have taken such a step even with respect to his own son."[413] The fallacy of this reasoning is demonstrable; but Buonaparte was saved from acting on it by the resistance of Desgenettes. A rear-guard was left to protect these unhappy men; and the English found some of them alive, who, if Desgenettes had been more compliant, would have been poisoned by their physician. If Buonaparte was guilty of entertaining such a purpose, whether entertained from indifference to human life, or from wild and misdirected ideas of humanity, he met an appropriate punishment in the general belief which long subsisted, that the deed had been actually carried into execution, not in the persons of a few expiring wretches only, but upon several hundred men. Miot says the report was current in the French army,—Sir Robert Wilson found it credited among their officers, when they became the English prisoners,—and Count Las Cases admits it was generally believed by the soldiers. But though popular credulity eagerly receives whatever

---

[411] O'Meara, vol. i., p. 331.
[412] Warden's Letters, p. 156.
[413] Voice from St. Helena, vol. ii., p. 333.

stories are marked by the horrible and wonderful, history, on the contrary, demands direct evidence, and the existence of powerful motives,[414] for whatever is beyond the ordinary bounds of credibility. The poisoning of five or six hundred men is neither easily managed nor easily concealed; and why should the French leader have had recourse to it, since, like many a retreating general before him, he had only to leave the patients for whom he had not the means of transportation? To poison the sick and helpless, must have destroyed his interest with the remainder of his soldiers; whereas, to have left them to their fate, was a matter too customary, and too much considered as a point of necessity, to create any discontent[415] among those, whose interest, as well as that of their general, consisted in moving on as fast as possible. Again, had such a horrible expedient been had recourse to, it could not have escaped the knowledge of Sir Sidney Smith, who would not have failed to give the horrid fact publicity, were it only to retaliate upon Buonaparte for the scandalous accusations which he had circulated against the English. But though he mentions various complaints which the prisoners made against their general, and though he states himself to have found seven men alive in the hospitals at Jaffa, (being apparently the very persons whom it had been proposed to despatch by opium,) he says not a word of what he would doubtless have told not unwillingly, had there been ground for believing it. Neither, among the numerous persons to whom the truth must be known, has any one come forward since Buonaparte's fall, who could give the least evidence to authenticate the report otherwise than as a rumour, that had sprung out of the unjustifiable proposal which had indeed been made by Buonaparte to Desgenettes, but never acted upon. The same patient and impartial investigation,

---

[414] History of the British Expedition to Egypt, vol. i., p. 127.
[415] Miot gives a melancholy, but too true a picture, of the indifference with which soldiers, when on a retreat, regard the sufferings of those whose strength does not enable them to keep up with the march. He describes a man, affected by the fear of being left to the cruelties of the Turks, snatching up his knapsack, and staggering after the column to which he belonged, while his glazed eye, uncertain motion, and stumbling pace, excited the fear of some, and the ridicule of others. "His account is made up," said one of his comrades, as he reeled about amongst them like a drunkard. "He will not make a long march of it," said another. And when, after more than one fall, he at length became unable to rise, the observation that "he had taken up his quarters," was all the moan which it was thought necessary to make. It is in these cases, as Miot justly observes, that indifference and selfishness become universal; and he that would be comfortable must manage to rely on his own exertions, and, above all to remain in good health.—S.

therefore, which compels us to record that the massacre of the Turkish prisoners in cold blood is fully proved, induces us to declare, that the poisoning of the sick at Jaffa has been affirmed without sufficient evidence.[416]

Buonaparte continued his retreat from Syria, annoyed by the natives, who harassed his march, and retaliating the injuries which he received, by plundering and burning the villages which lay in the course of his march. He left Jaffa on the 28th May, and upon the 14th June re-entered Cairo, with a reputation not so much increased by the victory at Mount Tabor, as diminished and sullied, for the time, by the retreat from Acre.

Lower Egypt, during the absence of Buonaparte, had remained undisturbed, unless by partial insurrections. In one of these an impostor personated that mysterious individual, the Imaum Mohadi, of whom the Orientals believe that he is not dead, but is destined to return and combat Antichrist, before the consummation of all things takes place. This pretender to supernatural power, as well as others who placed themselves at the head of insurrections without such high pretensions, was completely defeated; and the French showed the greatest severity in punishing their followers, and the country which had furnished them with partisans.[417]

In Upper Egypt there had been more obstinate contention. Murad Bey, already mentioned as the ablest chief of the Mamelukes,

---

[416] See Thibaudeau, tom. ii., p. 272; Martin, tom. i., p. 315; Desgenettes, *Hist. Médicale de l'Armée d'Orient*, p. 97; Larrey, *Relation Chirurgicale de l'Armée d'Orient*, p. 117; Lacretelle, tom. xiv., p. 299. "I feel ashamed," says Savary, "to advert to the atrocious calumny; but the man whose simple assertion was found sufficient to give it currency, has not been able to stifle it by his subsequent disavowal. The necessity to which we were reduced of using roots as a substitute for opium, is a fact known to the whole army. Supposing, however, that opium had been as plentiful as it was scarce, and that General Buonaparte could have contemplated the expedient attributed to him, where could there be found a man sufficiently determined in mind, or so lost to the feelings of human nature, as to force open the jaws of fifty wretched men on the point of death, and thrust a deadly preparation down their throats? The most intrepid soldier turned pale at the sight of an infected person; the warmest heart dared not relieve a friend afflicted with the plague; and is it to be credited that brutal ferocity could execute what the noblest feelings recoiled at? or that there should have been a creature savage or mad enough to sacrifice his own life, in order to enjoy the satisfaction of hastening the death of fifty dying men, wholly unknown to him?"—*Memoirs*, tom. ii., p. 106.
[417] Gourgaud, tom. ii., p. 323.

had maintained himself in that country with a degree of boldness and sagacity, which gave the French much trouble. His fine force of cavalry enabled him to advance or retreat at pleasure, and his perfect acquaintance with the country added much to his advantage.

Desaix, sent against Murad after the battle of the Pyramids, had again defeated the Mameluke chief at Sedinan, where was once more made evident the superiority of European discipline over the valour of the irregular cavalry of the East. Still the destruction of the enterprising bey was far from complete. Reinforced by a body of cavalry, Desaix,[418] in the month of December, 1798, again attacked him, and, after a number of encounters, terminating generally to the advantage of the French, the remaining Mamelukes, with their allies the Arabs, were at length compelled to take shelter in the Desert. Egypt seemed entirely at the command of the French; and Cosseir, a seaport on the Red Sea, had been taken possession of by a flotilla, fitted out to command that gulf.[419]

Three or four weeks after Buonaparte's return from Syria, this flattering state of tranquillity seemed on the point of being disturbed. Murad Bey, re-entering Upper Egypt with his Mamelukes and allies, descended the Nile in two bodies, one occupying each bank of the river. Ibrahim Bey, formerly his partner in the government of Egypt, made a corresponding movement towards the frontiers of Syria, as if to communicate with the right-hand division of Murad's army. La Grange was despatched against the Mamelukes who occupied the right bank, while Murat marched against those who, under the bey himself, were descending the Nile. The French were entertained at the idea of the two Murats, as they termed them, from the similarity of their names, meeting and encountering each other; but the Mameluke Murad retreated before *Le Beau Sabreur*—the handsome swordsman—of the French army.[420]

---

[418] "Brave Desaix! He would have conquered any where. He was skilful, vigilant, daring—little regarding fatigue, and death still less. He would have gone to the end of the world in quest of victory."—Napoleon, *Antommarchi*, vol. i., p. 376.
[419] Jomini, tom. xi., p. 420; Thibaudeau, tom. ii., p. 297; Gourgaud, tom. ii., p. 320.
[420] Gourgaud, tom. iii., p. 328.

THE TURKISH ARMY AT ABOUKIR

Meantime, the cause of this incursion was explained by the appearance of a Turkish fleet off Alexandria, who disembarked eighteen thousand men at Aboukir. This Turkish army possessed themselves of the fort, and proceeded to fortify themselves, expecting the arrival of the Mamelukes, according to the plan which had previously been adjusted for expelling the French from Egypt. This news reached Buonaparte near the Pyramids, to which he had advanced, in order to ensure the destruction of Murad Bey. The arrival of the Turks instantly recalled him to Alexandria, whence he marched to Aboukir to repel the invaders. He joined his army, which had assembled from all points within a short distance of the Turkish camp, and was employed late in the night making preparations for the battle on the next morning. Murat was alone with Buonaparte, when the last suddenly made the oracular declaration, "Go how it will, this battle will decide the fate of the world."

"The fate of this army, at least," replied Murat, who did not comprehend Buonaparte's secret meaning. "But the Turks are without horse, and if ever infantry were charged to the teeth by cavalry, they shall be so charged to-morrow by mine."[421]

Napoleon's meaning, however, referred not to Egypt alone, but to Europe; to which he probably already meditated an unexpected return, which must have been prevented had he not succeeded in obtaining the most complete triumph over the Turks. The leaving his Egyptian army, a dubious step at best, would have been altogether indefensible had there remained an enemy in their front.

Next morning, being the 25th July, Buonaparte commenced an attack on the advanced posts of the enemy, and succeeded in driving them in upon the main body, which was commanded by Seid Mustapha Pacha. In their first attack the French were eminently successful, and pursued the fugitive Turks to their intrenchments,

---

[421] Miot, p. 249.

doing great execution. But when the batteries opened upon them from the trenches, while they were at the same time exposed to the fire from the gun-boats in the bay, their impetuosity was checked, and the Turks, sallying out upon them with their muskets slung at their backs, made such havoc among the French with their sabres, poniards, and pistols, as compelled them to retreat in their turn.[422] The advantage was lost by the eagerness of the barbarians to possess themselves of the heads of their fallen enemies, for which they received a certain reward. They threw themselves confusedly out of the intrenchments to obtain these bloody testimonials, and were in considerable disorder, when the French suddenly rallied, charged them with great fury, drove them back into the works, and scaled the ramparts along with them.

TURKS DEFEATED AT ABOUKIR

Murat had made good his promise of the preceding evening, and had been ever in the front of the battle. When the French had surmounted the intrenchments, he formed a column which reversed the position of the Turks, and pressing them with the bayonet, threw them into utter and inextricable confusion. Fired upon and attacked on every point, they became, instead of an army, a confused rabble, who, in the impetuosity of animal terror, threw themselves by hundreds and by thousands into the sea, which at once seemed covered with turbans.[423] It was no longer a battle, but a massacre; and it was only when wearied with slaughter that quarter was given to about six thousand men; the rest of the Turkish army, originally consisting of eighteen thousand, perished on the field or in the waves. Mustapha Pacha was taken, and carried in triumph before Buonaparte. The haughty Turk had not lost his pride with his fortunes. "I will take care to inform the Sultan," said the victor, meaning to be courteous, "of the courage you displayed in this

---

[422] "Les Turcs maintenaient le combat avec succes; mais Murat, par un mouvement *rapide comme la pensée*, dirigea sa gauche sur les derrières de leur droit," &c.—Buonaparte *to the Directory.*

[423] Gourgaud states, that from three to four thousand Turks were driven into the sea. Berthier calculates the number at ten thousand: "L'ennemi ne croit avoir de ressource que dans la mer; dix mille hommes s'y précipitent; ils y sont fusilés et mitraillés. Jamais spectacle aussi terrible ne s'est presenté."

battle, though it has been your mishap to lose it."—"Thou mayest save thyself the trouble," answered the prisoner haughtily; "my master knows me better than thou canst."

Buonaparte returned in triumph to Cairo on the 9th August; having, however, as he continued to represent himself friendly to the Porte, previously set on foot a negotiation for liberation of the Turkish prisoners.

This splendid and most decisive victory of Aboukir[424] concluded Napoleon's career in the East. It was imperiously necessary, ere he could have ventured to quit the command of his army, with the hope of preserving his credit with the public; and it enabled him to plead that he left Egypt for the time in absolute security. His military views had, indeed, been uniformly successful; and Egypt was under the dominion of France as completely as the sword could subject it. For two years afterwards, like the strong man in the parable, they kept the house which they had won, until in there came a stronger, by whom they were finally and forcibly expelled.

SITUATION AND PROSPECTS

But, though the victory over the Turks afforded the French for the time undisturbed possession of Egypt, the situation of Buonaparte no longer permitted him those brilliant and immense prospects, in which his imagination loved to luxuriate. His troops were considerably weakened, and the miscarriage at Acre dwelt on the recollection of the survivors. The march upon Constantinople was now an impossibility,—that to India an empty dream. To establish a French colony in Egypt, of which Buonaparte sometimes talked, and to restore the Indian traffic to the shores of the Red Sea, thus sapping the sources of British prosperity in India, was a work for the time of peace, when the necessary communication was not impeded by the naval superiority of England. The French general

---

[424] "This is probably the only instance, in the history of warfare, in which an army has been entirely destroyed. It was upon this occasion that Kleber, clasping Buonaparte round the waist, exclaimed, '*General, vous étés grand comme le monde!*'"—Thiers, tom. x., p. 323.

had established, indeed, a chamber of commerce; but what commerce could take place from a closely blockaded harbour? Indeed, even in a more propitious season, the establishment of a pacific colony was no task for the ardent and warlike Napoleon; who, although his active spirit was prompt in striking out commercial schemes, was not possessed of the patience or steadiness necessary to carry them to success. It follows, that if he remained in Egypt, his residence there must have resembled the situation of a governor in a large city, threatened indeed, but as yet in no danger of being besieged, where the only fame which can be acquired is that due to prudent and patient vigilance. This would be a post which no young or ambitious soldier would covet, providing he had the choice of being engaged in more active service. On the other hand, from events which we shall endeavour to trace in the next chapter, there opened a scene of ambition in France, which permitted an almost boundless extent of hopes and wishes. Thus, Napoleon had the choice either of becoming a candidate for one of the greatest prizes which the world afforded—the supreme authority in that fine country—or of remaining the governor of a defensive army in Egypt, waiting the arrival of some new invaders—English, Russians, or Turks, to dispute his conquest with him. Had he chosen this latter line of conduct, he might have soon found himself the vassal of Moreau, or some other military adventurer, (perhaps from his own Italian army,) who, venturing on the course from which he had himself withdrawn, had attained to the government of France, and might soon have been issuing orders from the Luxembourg or the Tuileries to General Buonaparte, in the style of a sovereign to his subject.

There remained to be separated those strong ties, which were formed betwixt Napoleon and the army which he had so often led to victory, and who unquestionably thought he had cast his lot to live or die with them. But, undoubtedly, he might palliate his departure by the consideration, that he left them victorious over their boastful enemy, and without the chance of being speedily summoned to the field; and we can see no reason for supposing, as has been alleged, that any thing like fear had an influence in inducing Napoleon's desertion, as it has been termed, of his army. We cannot, indeed, give him credit for the absolute and pure desire of serving and saving France, which is claimed by his more devoted adherents, as the sole motive of his return to Europe; but we have no doubt that some feelings of this kind—to which, as we are powerful in deceiving ourselves, he himself might afford more weight than they deserved—mingled with his more selfish hopes, and that he took this important step with the desire of serving his country, as well as of advancing his own interest. Nor should it be forgotten, that the welfare even of the Egyptian army, as well as his own ambitious views, required that he should try his fortune at Paris. If he did not personally exert himself there, it seemed highly probable some revolution might take place, in which one of the consequences might be, that the victors of Egypt, deserted by their countrymen, should be compelled to lay down their arms.

The circumstances in which Buonaparte's resolution is said to have originated, as related by himself, were singularly fortuitous. Some intercourse took place with the Turkish fleet, in consequence of his sending the wounded Turks on board, and Sir Sidney Smith,[425] by way of taunting the French general with the successes of the Russians in Italy, sent him a set of newspapers containing an account of Suwarrow's victories, and a deplorable view of the French affairs on the continent.[426] If we may trust other authorities, however, to be quoted in their proper place, he already knew the state of affairs, both in Italy and France, by his own secret correspondence with Paris,[427] informing him, not only of the military reverses which the armies of the latter country had sustained, but of the state of parties, and of the public mind,—intelligence of greater utility and accuracy than could have been communicated by the English newspapers.

However his information was derived, Buonaparte lost no time in acting upon it, with all the secrecy which a matter of such importance required. Admiral Gantheaume, who had been with the army ever since the destruction of the fleet, received the general's

---

[425] "Notwithstanding his unheard-of destiny, Napoleon has often been heard to say, in speaking of Sir Sidney Smith, 'Cet homme m'a fait manquer ma fortune.'"—Thiers, tom. x., p. 314.
[426] See Las Cases, vol. iii., p. 11; Savary's Memoirs, vol. i., p. 112; and Miot, p. 265.
[427] "There existed no secret correspondence, whether private or official. Ten months had already elapsed, and we were still without news from Egypt."—Bourrienne, tom. ii., p. 309.

orders to make ready for sea, with all possible despatch, two frigates then lying in the harbour of Alexandria.

Meantime, determined to preserve his credit with the Institute, and to bring evidence of what he had done for the cause of science, Buonaparte commanded Monge, who is said to have suggested the expedition, and the accomplished Denon, who became its historian, with Berthollet, to prepare to accompany him to Alexandria. Of military chiefs, he selected the Generals Berthier, Murat, Lannes, Marmont, Desaix, Andréossy, and Bessières, the best and most attached of his officers. He left Cairo as soon as he heard the frigates were ready and the sea open, making a visit to the Delta the pretext of his tour. Kleber and Menou, whom he meant to leave first and second in command, were appointed to meet him at Alexandria. But he had an interview with the latter only.

Kleber, an excellent soldier, and a man of considerable parts, was much displeased at the hasty and disordered manner in which the command of an important province and a diminished army were thrust upon him, and remonstrated in a letter to the Directory, upon the several points of the public service, which, by his conduct on this occasion, Buonaparte had neglected or endangered.[428] Napoleon afterwards laboured hard to answer the accusations which these remonstrances implied, and to prove, that, in leaving the Egyptian army, he had no intention of abandoning it; on the contrary, that he intended either to return in person, or to send powerful succours. He blamed Gantheaume, at a later period, for not having made his way from Toulon to Alexandria, with reinforcements and supplies. But Buonaparte, slow to see what contradicted a favourite project, could never be made to believe, unless when in the very act of experiencing it, that the superiority of the British naval power depends upon circumstances totally different from those which can be removed by equal courage, or even equal skill, on the part of the French naval officers; and that, until it be removed, it will be at great

---

[428] Intercepted Letters, part iii., p. 38.

hazard that France shall ever attempt to retain a province so distant as Egypt.[429]

Napoleon left behind him a short proclamation,[430] apprising the army, that news of importance from France had recalled him to Europe, but that they should soon hear tidings of him. He exhorted them, in the meantime, to have confidence in their new commander; who possessed, he said, his good opinion, and that of the government; and in these terms he bade them farewell. Two frigates, La Muiron and La Carére, being ready for sea, the general embarked, from an unfrequented part of the beach, on the 22d August. Menou, who had met him there, came to Denon and others, who had attended the rendezvous without knowing exactly its purpose, as they were gazing in surprise at the unusual sight of two French frigates ready to put to sea, and informed them with agitation, that Buonaparte waited for them. They followed, as in a dream; but Denon had already secured that mass of measurements, drawings, manuscripts, and objects of antiquarian and scientific curiosity, which afterwards enabled him to complete the splendid work, which now contains almost the only permanent or useful fruits of the memorable expedition to Egypt.

Ere the frigates were far from land, they were reconnoitred by an English corvette—a circumstance which seemed of evil augury. Buonaparte assured his companions, by his usual allusions to his own destiny. "We will arrive safe," he said; "Fortune will never abandon us—we will arrive safe in despite of the enemy."

---

[429] General Menou was the last person to whom Napoleon spoke on shore. He said to him, "My dear general, you must take care of yourselves here. If I have the happiness to reach France, the reign of ranting shall be at an end."—Las Cases, tom. iii., p. 13.
[430] "In consequence of the news from Europe, I have determined to return to France. I leave the command of the army to General Kleber. The army will soon hear news of me: I cannot explain more fully. It grieves me to the heart to separate myself from the soldiers, to whom I am so tenderly attached: but the separation shall be but for a moment; and the general whom I leave at your head possesses the confidence of the government, and mine."

AJACCIO

To avoid the English cruizers, the vessels coasted the shores of Africa, and the wind was so contrary, that they made but a hundred leagues in twenty days. During this time, Buonaparte studied alternately the Bible and the Koran;[431] more solicitous, it seemed, about the history of the countries which he had left behind, than the part which he was to play in that to which he was hastening. At length, they ventured to stand northward, and on the 30th September, they entered, by singular chance, the port of Ajaccio in Corsica, and Buonaparte found himself in his native city.[432] On the 7th October, they again put to sea, but, upon approaching the French coast, they found themselves in the neighbourhood of a squadron of English men-of-war. The admiral would have tacked about, to return to Corsica. "To do so," said Buonaparte, "would be to take the road to England—I am seeking that to France." He probably meant that the manœuvre would attract the attention of the English. They kept on their course; but the peril of being captured seemed so imminent, that, though still several leagues from the shore, Gantheaume proposed to man his long-boat, in order that the general might attempt his escape in her. Buonaparte observed, that that measure might be deferred till the case was more desperate.[433]

At length, they passed, unsuspected and unquestioned, through the hostile squadron, and on the 9th October, at ten in the morning, he on whose fate the world so long seemed to depend, landed at St. Rapheau, near Frejus. He had departed at the head of a powerful fleet, and a victorious army, on an expedition designed to alter the destinies of the most ancient nations of the world. The result had been far from commensurate to the means employed. The fleet had perished—the army was blockaded in a distant province, when their arms were most necessary at home. He

---

[431] Las Cases, tom. iii., p. 13.
[432] "Gantheaume informed me, that he saw, at Ajaccio, the house that was occupied by Napoleon's family, the patrimonial abode. The arrival of their celebrated countryman immediately set all the inhabitants of the island in motion. A crowd of cousins came to welcome him, and the streets were thronged with people."—Las Cases, tom. iii., p. 14.
[433] Bourrienne, tom. iii., p. 4; Miot, p. 269.

returned clandestinely, and almost alone; yet Providence designed that, in this apparently deserted condition, he should be the instrument of more extensive and more astonishing changes, than the efforts of the greatest conquerors had ever before been able to effect upon the civilized world.

Chapter XV

Retrospect of Public Events since the Departure of Napoleon for Egypt—Invasion and Conquest of Switzerland—Seizure of Turin—Expulsion of the Pope—The Neapolitans declare War against France—The French enter Naples—Disgraceful Avarice exhibited by the Directory—Particularly in their Negotiations with the United States of America—Russia comes forward in the general Cause—Her Strength and Resources—Reverses of the French in Italy, and on the Rhine—Insurrections in Belgium and Holland against the French—Anglo-Russian Expedition sent to Holland—The Chouans again in the Field—Great and Universal Unpopularity of the Directory—State of Parties in France—Law of Hostages—Abbé Siêyes becomes one of the Directory—His Character and Genius—Description of the Constitution proposed by him for the Year Three—Ducos, Gohier, and Moulins, also introduced into the Directory—Family of Napoleon strive to keep him in the Recollection of the People—Favourable Change in the French Affairs—Holland Evacuated by the Anglo-Russian Army—Korsakow defeated by Massena—and Suwarrow retreats before Lecourbe.

When Napoleon accepted what was to be considered as a doom of honourable banishment, in the command of the Egyptian expedition, he answered to those friends who advised him rather to stay and assert a pre-eminent station in the government at home, "that the fruit was not ripe." The seventeen months, or thereabouts, of his absence, had done much to complete the maturity which was formerly imperfect. The French Government had ceased to be invariably victorious, and at times had suffered internal changes, which, instead of restoring the national confidence, had only induced a general expectation of some farther and decisive revolution, that should for ever overthrow the Directorial system.

When Buonaparte sailed for Egypt, he left France at peace with Austria, and those negotiations proceeding at Rastadt, which no one then doubted would settle on a pacific footing the affairs of Germany. England alone remained hostile to France; but the former being victorious on the sea, and the latter upon the land, it seemed as if the war must languish and die of itself, unless there had been a third element, of which the rivals might have disputed the possession. But though the interests of France, as well as of humanity, peremptorily demanded peace, her rulers, feeling that their own tottering condition would be rendered still more precarious by the disbanding their numerous armies, resolved to continue the war in a new quarter.

Under the most flimsy and injurious pretexts, they attacked the neutral States of Switzerland, so eminent for their moderation; and the French troops, levied in the name of Freedom, were sent to assail that country which had been so long her mountain fortress. The ancient valour of the Switzers was unable to defend them against the new discoveries in the art of war, by which the strongest defiles can be turned, and therefore rendered indefensible. They fought with their ancient courage, particularly the natives of the mountain cantons, and only gave way before numbers and discipline. But these gallant mountaineers sacrificed more than thrice their own amount, ere they fell in their ranks, as became the countrymen of William Tell. The French affected to give the Swiss a constitution on the model of their own, but this was a mere farce. The arsenals, fortresses, and treasures of the cantons, were seized without scruple or apology, and the Swiss were treated in all respects like a conquered nation. The fate of this ancient and unoffending people excited deep and general fear and detestation, and tended more perhaps than any other event to raise the animosity of Europe in general against France, as a country which had now plainly shown, that her ambition could be bounded by no consideration of justice or international law.[434]

---

[434] Lacretelle, tom. xiv., p. 230; Madame de Staël, tom. ii., p. 211.

The King of Sardinia, who had first acknowledged the superiority of Buonaparte, and purchased his existence as a continental sovereign, by surrendering all his fortresses to France, and permitting her troops to march through his country as their own, had surely some claim to forbearance; but now, without even a pretext for such violence, the French seized upon Turin, the capital of this their vassal monarch, and upon all his continental dominions, sending him and his family to the island of Sardinia.[435]

EXPULSION OF THE POPE

Another victim there was of the French grasping ambition, in whose fate the Catholic world was deeply interested. We have seen already that Buonaparte, though he despoiled the Pope of power and treasure, judged it more prudent to permit him to subsist as a petty prince, than by depriving him of all temporal authority, to drive him to desperation, and oblige him to use against the Republic those spiritual weapons, to which the public opinion of Catholic countries still assigned strength. But the Directory were of a different opinion; and though the Pope had submitted passively to every demand which had been made by the French ambassador, however inconsistent with the treaty of Tolentino, the Directory, with the usual policy of their nation, privately encouraged a party in Rome which desired a revolution. These conspirators arose in arms, and, when dispersed by the guards, fled towards the hotel of Joseph Buonaparte, then the ambassador of the French to the Pope. In the scuffle which ensued, the ambassador was insulted, his life endangered, and General Duphot actually killed by his side. This outrage of course sealed the fall of the Pope, which had probably long been determined on. Expelled from his dominions, the aged Pius VI. retired to Sienna, more the object of respect and veneration in his condition of a dethroned exile, than when holding the semblance of authority by permission of France. In place of the Pontiff's government arose the shadow of a mighty name, The Roman Republic. But the Gauls were in possession of the Capitol, nor did the ancient recollections, connected with the title of the new commonwealth, procure for the Romans more independent

---

[435] Lacretelle, tom. xiv., p. 176; Montgaillard, tom. v., p. 126; Jomini, tom. xi., p. 380.

authority than was possessed by any of the other ephemeral republican governments.[436]

In the fall of the Pope, and the occupation of the Roman territories by a French army, the King of Naples saw the nation whom he feared and hated, and by whom he knew he was considered as a desirable subject of plunder, approach his frontiers, and become his neighbours. War he perceived was unavoidable; and he formed the resolution to be the first in declaring it. The victory of Nelson, and the interest which that distinguished hero acquired at what might be called a female court, with the laurels of the Nile fresh upon his brow, confirmed the Neapolitan government in the resolution. Mack, an Austrian general, who had got the reputation of a great tactician, and a gallant soldier, was sent by the emperor to discipline and command the Neapolitan army. Nelson's falcon eye measured the man's worth at once. "General Mack," said he, "cannot move without five carriages—I have formed my opinion—I heartily pray I may be mistaken." He was *not* mistaken. The Neapolitan army marched to Rome, was encountered by the French, fought just long enough to lose about forty men, then fled, abandoning guns, baggage, arms, and every thing besides. "The Neapolitan officers did not lose much honour," said Nelson, "for God knows they had little to lose—but they lost what they had."[437] The prescient eye, which was as accurate by land as by sea, had also foreseen the instant advance of the French to Naples. It took place accordingly, but not unresisted. The naked rabble, called Lazzaroni, showed the most desperate courage. They attacked the French ere they came to the city; and notwithstanding a murderous defeat, they held out Naples for two days with their irregular musketry only, against regular forces amply supplied with artillery. What can we say of a country, where the rabble are courageous and the soldiers cowards? what, unless that the higher classes, from whom the officers are chosen, must be the parties to be censured.[438]

---

[436] Botta, tom. ii., p. 571; Lacretelle, tom. xiv., p. 145; Thiers, tom. x., p. 26; Annual Register, vol. xl., p. 38.
[437] See Southey's Life of Nelson.
[438] Jomini, tom. xiv., p. 316; Lacretelle, tom. xiv., p. 241.

The royal family fled to Sicily; and in Naples a new classical-sounding government was created at the command of the French general—The Parthenopean Republic. The French were now possessed of all Italy, excepting Tuscany, and that was exempted from their authority in name only, and not in effect.

The French people, notwithstanding the success of these several undertakings, were not deceived or flattered by them in a degree equal to what probably their rulers expected. Their vanity was alarmed at the meanness of the motives which the Directory exhibited on almost every occasion. Even the dazzling pride of conquest was sullied by the mercenary views with which war was undertaken. On one occasion the veil was raised, and all Frenchmen who had feelings of decency, not to say of probity or honour, remaining, must have held themselves disgraced by the venal character of their government.

NEGOTIATIONS WITH AMERICA

Some disputes existing between France and the United States of America, commissioners were sent by the latter country to Paris, to endeavour to restore a good understanding. They were not publicly acknowledged by France in the character of ambassadors; but were distinctly given to understand, that they could only be permitted to treat, on condition that the States of America should lend to the Republic the sum of a million sterling; to which was added, the unblushing demand of fifty thousand pounds, as a douceur for the private pocket of the directors. The astonishment of the envoys was extreme at this curious diplomatic proposal, and they could hardly credit their ears when they heard it repeatedly and grossly urged. "The essential part of the treaty," said one of the French agents, "is, *il faut de l'argent—il faut beaucoup d'argent*;" and to render the matter palatable, he told the Americans of other countries which had paid large sums to obtain peace, and reminded them of the irresistible power of France. The Transatlantic Republicans, unmoved by these arguments, stoutly answered, "That it belonged only to petty states to purchase independence by payment of tribute—that America was willing and able to protect herself by arms, and would not purchase with money what she possessed by her powerful means of self-defence." They added, "that they had no power whatever to enter into any engagements concerning a loan."

The agents of France lowered their tone so far as to say, that if the commissioners would pay something in the way of fees, they might be permitted to remain in Paris, whilst one of their number returned to America to obtain instructions from their government; but not even to that modification of bribery would the Americans listen. They would not, according to the expression used in incendiary letters, "put five pounds in a certain place." The treaty became public, to the scandal alike of France and of Europe, which joined in regarding a government that made war on such base principles, as standing, in comparison to those who warred in the spirit of conquest, in the relation of footpads to highwaymen. The only attempt made by Talleyrand towards explanation of this singular transaction, was a shuffling denial of the fact, which he strengthened by an insinuation, that the statement of the American envoys was a weak invention, suggested to them by the English.[439]

Not to multiply instances, the rapacity and domineering insolence with which the Directory conducted themselves towards the new republics, who were at every moment made sensible of their total dependence on the Great Nation—the merciless exactions which they imposed, together with the rapacious peculations of many of their generals and agents, made them lose interest almost as fast as they could acquire territory. Their fair pretexts of extending freedom, and the benefits of a liberal government, to states which had been oppressed by the old feudal institutions, were now valued at no more than their worth; and it was seen, that the only equality which republican France extended to the conquered countries, was to render all classes alike degraded and impoverished. Thus, the successes which we have hastily enumerated rather endangered than strengthened the empire of France, as they rendered her ambition the object of fear and suspicion to all Europe. The Catholic nations beheld the degradation of the supreme Pontiff with abhorrence— every king in Europe feared a similar fate with the sovereigns of

---

[439] Annual Register, vol. xl., p. 244.

Sardinia and Naples—and, after the fate of Switzerland, no people could rely upon a peaceful, unoffending, and strictly neutral character, as ground sufficient to exempt them from French aggression. Thus a general dread and dislike prepared for a new coalition against France, in which Russia, for the first time, was to become an active co-operator.

SUWARROW

The troops of this powerful empire were eminently qualified for encountering with the French; for, added to their hardihood, courage, and discipline, they had a national character—a distinction less known to the Germans, whose subdivision into different states, often at war with each other, has in some degree diminished their natural spirit of patriotism. Accustomed also to warfare on a great scale, and to encounter such an enemy as the Turk, the Russians, while they understood the modern system of tactics, were less servilely bigoted to it than the Austrians. Their ideas more readily went back to the natural and primitive character of war, and they were better prepared either to depart from strict technical rules themselves, or to see them departed from, and calculate the results. These new enemies of France, moreover, were full of confidence in their own character, and unchecked in their military enthusiasm by the frequent recollections of defeat, which clouded the spirit of the Austrians. Above all, the Russians had the advantage of being commanded by Suwarrow, one of the most extraordinary men of his time, who, possessed of the most profound military sagacity, assumed the external appearance of fanatical enthusiasm, as in society he often concealed his perfect knowledge of good-breeding under the show of extravagant buffoonery. These peculiarities, which would not have succeeded with a French or English army, gained for him an unbounded confidence among his countrymen, who considered his eccentric conduct, followed, as it almost always was, by brilliant success, as the result of something which approached to inspiration.[440]

---

[440] "Suwarrow is a most extraordinary man. He dines every morning about nine. He sleeps almost naked: he affects a perfect indifference to heat and cold; and quits his chamber,

The united forces of Austria and Russia, chiefly under the command of this singular character, succeeded, in a long train of bloody battles, to retake and re-occupy those states in the north of Italy, which had been conquered in Buonaparte's first campaigns. It was in vain that Macdonald, whose name stood as high among the Republican generals, as his character for honour and rectitude among French statesmen, marched from Naples, traversing the whole length of Italy, to arrest the victorious progress of the allies. After a train of stubborn fighting, it was only by displaying great military talent that he could extricate the remains of his army. At length the decisive and desperate battle of Novi seemed to exclude the French from the possession of those fair Italian provinces, which had been acquired by such expense of life.[441]

On the Rhine, though her defeats were not of such a decided character, France also lost reputation and territory. Jourdan proved no match for the Archduke Charles, who having no longer Buonaparte to encounter, asserted his former superiority over inferior French generals. His royal highness finally compelled the French to recross the Rhine, while the Austrian generals Bellegarde and Hotze, supported by a Russian division under Korsakow, advanced to the line of the Limmat, near Zurich, and waited the junction of Suwarrow to occupy Switzerland, and even to menace France, who, in a great measure despoiled of her foreign conquests, had now reason to apprehend the invasion of her own territory.

In the Netherlands, the French interest seemed equally insecure. Insurrections had already taken place in what they called Belgium, and it seemed that the natives of these populous districts desired but opportunity and encouragement for a general revolt. Holland, through all its provinces, was equally disaffected; and the reports from that country encouraged England to send to the coast an expedition, consisting of British and Russian forces, to which two

---

which approaches to suffocation, in order to review his troops, in a thin linen jacket, while the thermometer is at ten degrees below freezing. A great deal of his whimsical manner is affected: He finds that it suits his troops, and the people he has to deal with. I dined with him this morning. He cried to me across the table, 'Tweddell, the French have taken Portsmouth. I have just received a courier from England. The king is in the tower, and Sheridan protector!'"—Tweddell's *Remains*, p. 135.
[441] Jomini, tom. xi., p. 275; Thiers, tom. x., p. 279.

divisions of the Dutch fleet delivered up their vessels, hoisting at the same time the colours of the Stadtholder. Here was another risk of an imminent and pressing description, which menaced France and its Directorial government.

It remains to be added to the tale of these foreign calamities, that the Chouans, or Royalists of Bretagne, were again in the field with a number of bands, amounting, it is said, to forty thousand men in all. They had gained several successes, and, though falling short of the chivalrous spirit of the Vendéans, and having no general equal in talents to Charette, were nevertheless sufficiently brave and well commanded, to become extremely formidable, and threaten a renewal of all the evils which had been occasioned by the former civil war.

Amidst these louring appearances, the dislike and disrespect with which the directors were regarded, occasioned their being loaded with every species of accusation by the public. It was not forgotten that it was the jealousy of Barras, Rewbel, and the other directors, which had banished from France the most successful of her generals, at the head of a gallant army, who were now needed to defend the provinces which their valour had gained. The battle of Aboukir, while it annihilated their fleet, had insulated the land forces, who, now cut off from all communication with their mother country, and shut up in an insalubrious province, daily wasted in encounters with the barbarous tribes that valour, and those lives, which, hazarded on the frontiers of France might have restored victory to their standards.

To these upbraiding complaints, and general accusations of incapacity, as well as of peculation, the directors had little to answer. What was a still greater deficiency, they had no party to appeal to, by whom their cause, right or wrong, might have been advocated with the stanch adherence of partisans. They had undergone, as we shall presently show, various changes in their own body, but without any alteration in their principles of administration, which still rested on the principle of *Bascule*, or see-saw,[442] as it is called in English; the

---

[442] The term, it is scarcely necessary to say, is derived from the childish amusement, where two boys swing at the opposite ends of a plank, moving up and down, in what Dr. Johnson

attempt, in short, to govern two contending factions in the state, by balancing the one against the other, without adhering to either. In consequence of this mean and temporizing policy, which is always that of weak minds, the measures of the government were considered, not with reference to the general welfare of the state, but as they should have effect upon one or other of the parties by which it was divided. It followed also, that having no certain path and plan, but regulating their movements upon the wish to maintain an equality between the factions, in order that they might preserve their authority over both, the directors had no personal followers or supporters, save that most sordid class, who regulate their politics on their interest, and who, though faithful adherents of every settled administration, perceive, by instinctive sagacity, the moment that their patrons are about to lose their offices, and desert their cause on such occasions with all convenient speed.

"THE MODÉRÉS"

Yet the directors, had they been men of talent, integrity, and character—above all, had they been united among themselves, and agreed on one steady course of policy, might have governed France with little difficulty. The great body of the nation were exhausted by the previous fury of the revolutionary movements, had supped full with politics, and were much disposed to sit down contented under any government which promised protection for life and property. Even the factions had lost their energy. Those who inclined to a monarchical form, were many of them become indifferent by whom the sceptre was wielded, providing that species of government, supposed by them most suitable to the habits and character of the French, should be again adopted. Many who were of this opinion saw great objection to the restoration of the Bourbons, for fear that, along with their right, might revive all those oppressive feudal claims which the Revolution had swept away, as well as the pretensions of the emigrants to resume their property. Those who entertained such sentiments were called *Modérés*. The ancient blood-red Jacobins could hardly be said to exist. The nation had had a surfeit of blood,

---

calls "a reciprocating motion," while a third urchin, placed in the centre of motion, regulates their movements.—S.

and all parties looked back with disgust on the days of Robespierre. But there existed a kind of white Jacobins; men who were desirous to retain a large proportion of democratical principle in the constitution, either that they might not renounce the classical name of a Republic, or because they confided in their own talents, to "wield at will the fierce democracy;" or because they really believed that a potent infusion of such a spirit in the forms of government was necessary for the preservation of liberty. This party was greatly inferior in numbers to the others; and they had lost their authority over the populace, by means of which they had achieved such changes during the early periods of the Revolution. But they were bold, enterprising, active; and their chiefs, assuming at first the name of the Pantheon, afterwards of the Manège Club, formed a party in the state which, from the character of the leaders, gave great subject of jealousy to the Directory.[443]

The rapacity and insolent bearing of the French Government having, as we have seen, provoked a new war with Austria and Russia, the means to which the directors had recourse for maintaining it were a forced loan imposed on the wealthy, which gave alarm to property, and a conscription of two hundred thousand men, which was alike distressing to poor and rich. Both measures had been submitted to during the Reign of Terror; but then a murmur cost the complainer his head. The Directory had no such summary mode of settling grievances. These two last inflictions greatly inflamed the public discontent. To meet the general tendency to insurrection, they had recourse to a measure equally harsh and unpopular. It was called the Law of Hostages, by which the unoffending relatives of emigrants, or royalists, supposed to be in arms, were thrown into prison, and rendered responsible for the acts of their connexions. This unjust law filled the prisons with women, old men, and children,—victims of a government which, because it was not strong enough to subdue insurrection by direct force, visited the consequences of its own weakness on age, childhood, and helpless females.[444]

---

[443] Gourgaud, tom. i., p. 58.
[444] Thiers, tom. x., p. 269; Lacretelle, tom. xiv., p. 397.

Meantime, the dissensions among the directors themselves, which continued to increase, led to various changes within their own body. When Buonaparte left Europe, the Directory consisted of Barras, Rewbel, Treilhard, Merlin, Reveillière Lepaux. The opposition attacked them with so much fury in the Legislative Assemblies, Boulay de la Meurthe, Lucien Buonaparte, François, and other men of talent leading the way, that at length the directors appear to have become afraid of being made personally responsible, by impeachment, for the peculations of their agents, as well as for the result of the insolences by which they had exasperated the friends and allies of France. Rewbel, he whose character for talent and integrity stood most fair with the public, was removed from office by the lot which announced him as the director who was to retire. It has been said, some art was used to guide fortune on this occasion. His name in the list was succeeded by one celebrated in the Revolution; that of the Abbé Siêyes.

This remarkable statesman had acquired a high reputation, not only by the acuteness of his metaphysical talent, but by a species of mystery in which he involved himself and his opinions. He was certainly possessed of great knowledge and experience in the affairs of France, was an adept in the composition of new constitutions of all kinds, and had got a high character, as possessed of secrets peculiarly his own, for conducting the vessel of the state amidst the storms of revolution. The Abbé, in fact, managed his political reputation as a prudent trader does his stock; and, by shunning to venture on anything which could, in any great degree, peril his credit, he extended it in the public opinion, perhaps much farther than his parts justified. A temper less daring in action than bold in metaphysical speculation, and a considerable regard for his own personal safety, accorded well with his affected air of mystery and reserve. In the National Assembly he had made a great impression, by his pamphlet explaining the nature of the Third Estate;[445] and he had the principal part in procuring the union of the three separate Estates into the National Assembly. A flaming patriot in 1792-3, he voted for the death of the unfortunate Louis; and, as was reported, with brutal levity, using the celebrated expression, "*Mort sans phrase.*" He was no less distinguished for bringing forward the important

---

[445] See *ante*, vol. i.

measure for dividing France into departments, and thus blending together and confounding all the ancient distinctions of provinces.[446] After this period he became passive, and was little heard of during the Reign of Terror; for he followed the maxim of Pythagoras, and worshipped the Echo (only found in secret and solitary places) when he heard the tempest blow hard.

CONSTITUTION FOR THE YEAR THREE

After the revolution of 9th Thermidor, Sièyes came in with the moderate party, and had the merit to propose the recall of the members who had been forcibly expelled by the Jacobin faction on the fall of the Girondists. He was one of the committee of eleven, to whom was given the charge of forming the new constitution, afterwards called that of the year Three. This great metaphysical philosopher and politician showed little desire to share with any colleagues the toil and honour of a task to which he esteemed himself exclusively competent; and he produced, accordingly, a model entirely of his own composition, very ingenious, and evincing a wonderfully intimate acquaintance with political doctrines, together with a multitude of nice balances, capacities, and disqualifications, so constituted as to be checks on each other. As strongly characteristic of the genius of the man, we shall here give an account of his great work.

His plan provided that the constitution, with its powers of judicature and of administration, should emanate from the people; but lest, like that unnatural parent the sow, the people should devour their own nine farrow, the functionaries thus invested with power were to be placed, when created, out of the reach of the parents who had given them birth. The mode in which it was proposed to effect this, was both singular and ingenious. The office-bearers were thus to be selected out of three orders of the state, forming a triple hierarchy. 1. The citizens of each commune were to name one-tenth of their number, to be called the Communal Notables. From these were to be selected the magistrates of the communes, and the justices of peace. 2. The Communal Notables

---

[446] Gourgaud, tom. i., p. 61.

were again to choose a tenth part of their number, who were called the Departmental Notables. The prefects, judges, and provincial administrators, were selected from this second body. 3. The Departmental Notables, in like manner, were to elect a tenth of their number, computed to amount to about six thousand persons; and from this highest class of citizens were to be filled the most dignified and important situations in the state,—the ministers and members of government, the legislature, the senate, or grand jury, the principal judges, ambassadors, and the like. By this system it will be perceived, that instead of equality, three ranks of privileged citizens were to be established, from whose ranks alone certain offices could be filled. But this species of nobility, or, as it was called, Notability, was dependent not on birth, but on the choice of the people, from whom, though more or less directly, all officers without exception received their commissions. The elections were to take place every five years.

To represent the national dignity, power, and glory, there was to be an officer called the Grand Elector, who was to have guards, a revenue, and all the external appendages of royalty; all acts of government, laws, and judicial proceedings, were to run in his name. This species of *Roi-fainéant* was to possess no part of the royal authority, except the right of naming two consuls, one for peace, and the other for war; and the farther right of selecting, from lists of candidates to be supplied by the three ranks of the hierarchy, the individuals who were to fill official situations as they should become vacant. But having exercised this privilege, the grand elector, or proclaimer general, was *functus officio*, and had no active duties to perform, or power to exercise. The two consuls, altogether uncontrolled by him or each other, were to act each in their own exclusive department of peace or war; and the other functionaries were alike independent of the grand proclaimer, or elector, so soon as he had appointed them. He was to resemble no sovereign ever heard of but the queen bee, who has nothing to do but to repose in idleness and luxury, and give being to the active insects by whose industry the business of the hive is carried on.

The government being thus provided for, the Abbé Siêyes's system of legislature was something like that of France in the time of the Parliament. There was to be a Legislative Body of two hundred and fifty deputies; but they were to form rather a tribunal of judges, than a popular and deliberative assembly. Two other bodies, a Council of State on the part of the Government, and a Tribunate of one hundred deputies, on the part of the people, were to propose and discuss measures in presence of this Legislative Council, who then proceeded to adopt or reject them upon scrutiny and by vote, but without any oral delivery of opinions. The Tribunate was invested with the right of guarding the freedom of the subject, and denouncing to the Convocative Senate such misconduct of office-bearers, or ill-chosen measures, or ill-advised laws, as should appear to them worthy of reprobation.

But, above all, Abbé Siêyes piqued himself upon the device of what he determined a Conservative Senate, which, possessing in itself no power of action or legislation of any kind, was to have in charge the preservation of the constitution. To this Senate was given the singular power, of calling in to become a member of their own body, and reducing of course to their own state of incapacity, any individual occupying another situation in the constitution, whose talents, ambition, or popularity, should render him a subject of jealousy. Even the grand elector himself was liable to this fate of *absorption,* as it was called, although he held his crown of Cocaign in the common case for life. Any exertion on his part of what might seem to the Senate an act of arbitrary authority, entitled them to adopt him a member of their own body. He was thus removed from his palace, guards, and income, and made for ever incapable of any other office than that of a senator. This high point of policy was carrying the system of checks and balances as far as it could well go.

The first glance of this curious model must have convinced a practical politician that it was greatly too complicated and technical to be carried into effect. The utility of laws consists in their being of a character which compels the respect and obedience of those to whom they relate. The very delicacy of such an ingenious scheme rendered it incapable of obtaining general regard, since it was too refined to be understood save by profound philosophers. To the rest of the nation it must have been like a watch to a savage, who, being commanded to regulate his time by it, will probably prefer to make the machine correspond with his inclinations, by putting backward and forward the index at pleasure. A man of ordinary talent and honest disposition might have been disqualified for public life by this doctrine of absorption, just as a man ignorant of swimming would perish if flung into a lake. But a stout swimmer would easily gain the shore, and an individual like Buonaparte would set at defiance the new species of ostracism, and decline to be neutralized by the absorption of the Senate. Above all, the plan of the abbé destroyed the true principle of national representation, by introducing a metaphysical election of members of legislation, instead of one immediately derived from the direct vote of the people themselves. In the abbé's alembic, the real and invaluable principle of popular representation was subtilized into smoke.

For these, or other reasons, the commissioners of the year Three did not approve of the plan proposed by Siêyes; and, equally dissatisfied with the constitution which they adopted, he withdrew himself from their deliberations, and accepted the situation of ambassador to Prussia, where he discharged with great ability the task of a diplomatist.

DUCOS—GOHIER—MOULINS

In 1799, Siêyes returned from Berlin to Paris, full of hope to establish his own favourite model on the ruins of the Directorial Constitution, and, as a preliminary, obtained, as we have said, Rewbel's seat in the Directory. Merlin and Lepaux, menaced with impeachments, were induced to send in their resignation. Treilhard had been previously displaced, on pretext of an informality in the choice. Instead of them were introduced into the Directory Roger Ducos, a Modéré, or rather a Royalist, with Gohier and Moulins, men of talents too ordinary to throw any opposition in the path of Siêyes.[447] Barras, by his expenses and his luxurious mode of life, his connexion with stock-jobbers, and encouragement of peculation,

---

[447] "Ducos was a man of narrow mind, and easy disposition. Moulins, a general of division, had never served in war: he was originally in the French guards, and had been advanced in the army of the interior. He was a worthy man, and a warm and upright patriot. Gohier was an advocate of considerable reputation, and exalted patriotism—an eminent lawyer, and a man of great integrity and candour."—Napoleon, *Gourgaud*, tom. i., p. 60.

was too much in danger of impeachment, to permit him to play a manly part. He truckled to circumstances, and allied himself with, or rather subjected himself to, Siêyes, who saw the time approaching when the constitution of the year Three must fall, and hoped to establish his own rejected model in its stead. But the revolution which he meditated could only be executed by force.

The change in the Directory had destroyed the government by bascule, or balance, and that intermediate and trimming influence being removed, the two parties of the Modérés and the Republicans stood full opposed to each other, and ready to try their strength in a severe struggle. Siêyes, though no Royalist, or at least certainly no adherent of the House of Bourbon, stood, nevertheless, at the head of the Modérés, and taxed his sagacity for means of ensuring their victory. The Modérés possessed a majority in the Council of the Ancients; but the Society of the Manège, Republicans if not Jacobins, had obtained, at the last election, a great superiority of numbers in the Council of Five Hundred. They were sure to be in decided opposition to any change of the constitution of the year Three; and such being the case, those who plotted the new revolution, could not attempt it without some external support. To call upon the people was no longer the order of the day. Indeed it may be supposed that the ancient revolutionary columns would rather have risen against Siêyes, and in behalf of the Society of the Manège. The proposers of a new change had access, however, to the army, and to that they determined to appeal. The assistance of some military chief of the first reputation was necessary. Siêyes cast his eyes upon Joubert, an officer of high reputation, and one of the most distinguished among Buonaparte's generals. He was named by the Directors to the command of the department of Paris, but shortly after was sent to Italy with hopes that, acquiring a new fund of glory by checking the progress of Suwarrow, he might be yet more fitted to fill the public eye, and influence the general mind, in the crisis when Siêyes looked for his assistance. Joubert lost his life, however, at the great battle of Novi, fought betwixt him and Suwarrow; and so opportunely did his death make room for the pretensions of Buonaparte, that it has been rumoured, certainly without the least probability, that he did not fall by the fire of the Austrians, but by that of assassins hired by the family of Napoleon, to take out of the way a powerful competitor of their brother. This would have been a gratuitous crime, since they could neither reckon with certainty on the arrival of Buonaparte, nor upon his being adopted by Siêyes in place of Joubert.

Meanwhile, the family of Napoleon omitted no mode of keeping his merits in public remembrance. Reports from time to time appeared in the papers to this purpose, as when, to give him consequence doubtless, they pretended that the Tower guns of London were fired, and public rejoicings made, upon a report that Napoleon had been assassinated. Madame Buonaparte, in the meanwhile, lived at great expense, and with much elegance, collecting around her whoever was remarkable for talent and accomplishment, and many of the women of Paris who were best accustomed to the management of political intrigue. Lucien Buonaparte distinguished himself as an orator in the Council of Five Hundred, and although he had hitherto affected Republican zeal, he now opposed, with much ability, the reviving influence of the democrats. Joseph Buonaparte, also a man of talent, and of an excellent character, though much aspersed afterwards, in consequence of the part in Spain assigned him by his brother, lived hospitably, saw much company, and maintained an ascendance in Parisian society. We cannot doubt that these near relatives of Buonaparte found means of communicating to him the state of affairs in Paris, and the opening which it afforded for the exercise of his distinguished talents.

The communication betwixt Toulon and Alexandria was, indeed, interrupted, but not altogether broken off, and we have no doubt that the struggle of parties in the interior, as well as the great disasters on the frontier, had their full influence in determining Buonaparte to his sudden return. Miot, though in no very positive strain, has named a Greek called Bambuki, as the bearer of a letter from Joseph to his brother, conveying this important intelligence. The private memoirs of Fouché pretend that that minister purchased the secret of Napoleon's return being expected, from Josephine herself, for the sum of a thousand louis, and that the landing at Frejus was no surprise to him. Both these pieces of private history may be safely doubted; but it would be difficult to convince us that Buonaparte took the step of quitting Egypt on the vague intelligence afforded by the journals, and without confidential communication with his own family.

JOURDAN

To return to the state of the French Government. The death of Joubert not only disconcerted the schemes of Siêyes, but exposed him and his party to retaliation. Bernadotte was minister of war, and he, with Jourdan and Augereau, were all warm in the cause of Republicanism. Any of these distinguished generals was capable of leading the military force to compel such an alteration in the constitution as might suit the purpose of their party, and thus reversing the project of Siêyes, who, without Joubert, was like the head without the arm that should execute. Already Jourdan had made in the Council of Five Hundred a speech on the dangers of the country, which, in point of vehemence, might have been pronounced in the ancient hall of the Jacobins. He in plain terms threatened the Modérés with such a general insurrection as had taken place in the year 1792, and proposed to declare the country in danger. He was answered by Lucien Buonaparte, Chenier, and Boulay, who had great difficulty to parry the impetuosity with which the motion was urged forward. Though they succeeded in eluding the danger, it was still far from being over, and the democrats would probably have dared some desperate movement, if any additional reverse had been sustained on the frontier.

But as if the calamities of France, which of late had followed each other in quick succession, had attained their height of tide, the affairs of that country began all of a sudden to assume a more favourable aspect. The success of General Brune in Holland against the Anglo-Russian army, had obliged the invaders of Holland to retreat, and enter into a convention for evacuation of the country on which they had made their descent. A dispute, or misunderstanding, having occurred between the Emperors of Austria and Russia, the Archduke Charles, in order, it was alleged, to repel an incursion of the French into the countries on the Maine, withdrew a great part of his army from the line of the Limmat, which was taken up by the

Russians under Korsakow. Massena took the advantage of this imprudent step, crossed the Limmat, surprised the Russians, and defeated Korsakow, whilst the formidable Suwarrow, who had already advanced to communicate with that general, found his right flank uncovered by his defeat, and had the greatest difficulty in executing a retrograde movement before General Lecourbe.

The news of these successes induced the Republicans to defer their attack upon the moderate party; and on so nice a point do the greatest events hang, that had a longer period intervened between these victories and the arrival of Buonaparte, it is most probable that he would have found the situation of military chief of the approaching revolution, which became vacant on the death of Joubert, filled up by some one of those generals, of whom success had extended the fame. But he landed at the happy crisis, when the presence of a chief of first-rate talents was indispensable, and when no favourite name had yet been found, to fill the public voice with half such loud acclaim as his own.

CHAPTER XVI

General rejoicing on the return of Buonaparte—Advances made to him on all sides—Napoleon coalesces with Siêyes—Revolution of the 18th Brumaire (Nov. 9)—Clashing Views of the Councils of Ancients, and the Five Hundred—Barras and his Colleagues resign—Proceedings of the Councils on the 18th—and 19th—Sittings removed from Paris to St. Cloud—Commotion in the Council of Five Hundred—Napoleon menaced and assaulted, and finally, extricated by his Grenadiers—Lucien Buonaparte, the President, retires from the Hall—Declares the Council dissolved—Provisional Consular Government of Buonaparte, Siêyes, and Ducos.

PARIS

Buonaparte had caused himself to be preceded by an account of his campaigns in Africa and Asia, in which the splendid victory over the Turks at Aboukir enabled him to gloss over his bad success in Syria, the total loss of his fleet, and the danger of Malta, which was closely besieged by the English. Still, however, these despatches could never have led any one to expect the sudden return of a general engaged on a foreign service of the utmost importance, who, without having a better reason to allege, than his own opinion that his talents were more essential to his country in France than in Egypt, left his army to its fate, and came, without either order or permission from his government, to volunteer his services where they were not expected, or perhaps wished for. Another in the same circumstances, or perhaps the same general at another period of the Revolution, would have been received by the public with alienated favour, and by the government with severe inquiry, if not with denunciation.

On the contrary, such was the general reliance on the talents of Buonaparte, that, delighted to see him arrive, no one thought of asking wherefore, or by whose authority he had returned. He was received like a victorious monarch re-entering his dominions at his own time and pleasure. Bells were everywhere rung, illuminations made, a delirium of joy agitated the public mind, and the messenger who carried the news of his disembarkation to Paris, was received as if he had brought news of a battle gained.[448]

The hall of the Council of Five Hundred re-echoed with cries of victory, while the orator, announcing the victories of Brune over the English, and Massena over the Russians, dwelt upon the simple fact of Buonaparte's return, as of interest equal to all these successes. He was heard with shouts of "Long live the Republic!" which, as the event proved, was an exclamation but very indifferently adapted to the occasion.

Josephine, and Joseph Buonaparte, apprised by the government of the arrival of Napoleon, hastened to meet him on the road; and his progress towards Paris was everywhere attended by the same general acclamations which had received him at landing.[449]

The members of Government, it must be supposed, felt alarm and anxiety, which they endeavoured to conceal under the appearance of sharing in the general joy.[450] The arrival of a person so influential by his fame, so decided in his character, engaged with no faction, and pledged to no political system, was likely to give victory to one or the other party who were contending for superiority, as he should himself determine. The eyes of all men were upon Napoleon, while his reserved and retired mode of life prevented any accurate anticipation being formed of the part which he was likely to take in

---

[448] Thiers, tom. x., p. 346; Gourgaud, tom. i., p. 56; Lacretelle, tom. xiv., p. 385.
[449] "It was not like the return of a citizen to his country, or a general at the head of a victorious army, but like the triumph of a sovereign restored to his people."—Gourgaud, tom. i., p. 57.
[450] "The news of his return caused a general delirium. Baudin, the deputy from Ardennes, who was really a worthy man, struck with the idea that Providence had at length sent the man for whom he and his party had so long searched in vain, died the very same night from excess of joy."—Gourgaud, tom. i., p. 59; Fouché, tom. i., p. 107.

the approaching convulsions of the state.[451] While both parties might hope for his participation and succour, neither ventured to call into question his purpose, or the authority by which he had left his army in Egypt, and appeared thus unexpectedly in the capital. On the contrary, they courted him on either hand as the arbiter, whose decision was likely to have most influence on the state of the nation.[452]

Napoleon, meanwhile, seemed to give his exclusive attention to literature, and, having exchanged the usual visits of form with the ministers of the Republic, he was more frequently to be found at the Institute, or discussing with the traveller Volney, and other men of letters, the information which he had acquired in Egypt on science and antiquities, than in the haunts of politicians, or the society of the leaders of either party in the state. Neither was he to be seen at the places of popular resort: he went into no general company, seldom attended the theatres, and, when he did, took his seat in a private box.[453]

A public entertainment was given in honour of the general in the church of St. Sulpice, which was attended by both the Legislative Bodies. Moreau shared the same honour, perhaps on that account not the more agreeable to Buonaparte. Jourdan and Augereau did not appear—a cloud seemed to hang over the festival—Napoleon only presented himself for a very short time, and the whole was over in the course of an hour.[454]

To the military, his conduct seemed equally reserved—he held no levees, and attended no reviews. While all ranks contended in

---

[451] "Having thus arrived in Paris quite unexpectedly, he was in his own house, in the Rue Chantereine, before any one knew of his being in the capital. Two hours afterwards, he presented himself to the Directory, and, being recognised by the soldiers on guard, was announced by shouts of gladness. All the members of the Directory appeared to share in the public joy."—Gourgaud, tom. i., p. 60.
[452] See Mémoires de Gohier, tom. i., pp. 198-212.
[453] Gourgaud, tom. i., p. 65.
[454] "Covers were laid for seven hundred. Napoleon remained at table but a short time: he appeared to be uneasy, and much preoccupied."—Gourgaud, tom. i., p. 63.

offering their tribute of applause, he turned in silence from receiving them.[455]

In all this there was deep policy. No one knew better how much popular applause depends on the gloss of novelty, and how great is the difference in public estimation, betwixt him who appears to hunt and court acclamations, and the wiser and more dignified favourite of the multitude, whose popularity follows after him and seeks him out, instead of being the object of his pursuit and ambition. Yet under this still and apparently indifferent demeanour, Napoleon was in secret employed in collecting all the information necessary concerning the purposes and the powers of the various parties in the state; and as each was eager to obtain his countenance, he had no difficulty in obtaining full explanations on these points.

STATE OF PARTIES

The violent Republicans, who possessed the majority in the Council of Five Hundred, made advances to him; and the generals Jourdan, Augereau, and Bernadotte, offered to place him at the head of that party, provided he would maintain the democratical constitution of the year Three.[456] In uniting with this active and violent party, Buonaparte saw every chance of instant and immediate success; but, by succeeding in the outset, he would probably have marred the farther projects of ambition which he already nourished. Military leaders, such as Jourdan and Bernadotte, at the head of a party so furious as the Republicans, could not have been thrown aside without both danger and difficulty: and it being unquestionably the ultimate intention of Buonaparte to usurp the supreme power, it was most natural for him to seek adherents among those, who, though differing concerning the kind of

---

[455] "Every one of the ministers wished to give him an entertainment, but he only accepted a dinner from the Minister of Justice (Cambacérès.) He requested that the principal lawyers of the Republic might be there. He was very cheerful at this dinner, conversed at large on the criminal code, to the great astonishment of Tronchet, Treilhard, Merlin, and Target, and expressed his desire to see persons and property placed under the guard of a simple code, suitable to an enlightened age."—Gourgaud, tom. i., p. 64.
[456] Gourgaud, tom. i., p. 67.

government which should be finally established, concurred in desiring a change from the republican model.

Barras, too, endeavoured to sound the purposes of the general of the army of Egypt. He hinted to him a plan of placing at the head of the Directory Hedouville,[457] a man of ordinary talent, then general of what was still termed the Army of England, of retiring himself from power, and of conferring on Napoleon the general command of the Republican forces on the frontiers, which he vainly supposed preferment sufficient to gratify his ambition.[458] Buonaparte would not listen to a hint which went to remove him from the capital, and the supreme administration of affairs—he knew also that Barras's character was contemptible, and his resources diminished—that his subsequent conduct had cancelled the merit which he had acquired by the overthrow of Robespierre, and that to unite with him in any degree would be to adopt, in the public opinion, the very worst and most unpopular portion of the Directorial Government. He rejected the alliance of Barras, therefore, even when, abandoning his own plan, the director offered to concur in any which Napoleon might dictate.

A union with Sièyes, and the party whom he influenced, promised greater advantages. Under this speculative politician were united for the time all who, though differing in other points, joined in desiring a final change from a revolutionary to a moderate and efficient government, bearing something of a monarchical character. Their number rendered this party powerful. In the Directory it was espoused by Sièyes and Ducos; it possessed a large majority in the Council of Ancients, and a respectable minority in that of the Five Hundred. The greater part of the middling classes throughout France, embraced with more or less zeal the principles of

---

[457] Hedouville was born at Laon in 1755. In 1801, Buonaparte appointed him ambassador to Petersburgh. On the restoration of the Bourbons he was made a peer of France, and died in 1825.

[458] "On the 8th Brumaire (30th October,) Napoleon dined with Barras: a conversation took place after dinner. 'The Republic is falling,' said the director; 'things cannot go on; a change must take place, and Hedouville must be named president. As to you, general, you intend to rejoin the army; and, for my part, ill as I am, unpopular, and worn out, I am only fit to return to private life. Napoleon looked steadfastly at him without replying a word. Barras cast down his eyes, and remained silent. Thus the conversation ended."—Gourgaud, tom. i., p. 72; Thiers, tom. x., p. 359.

moderation; and agreed, that an executive government of some strength was necessary to save them from the evils of combined revolutionary movements. Though the power of the Moderates was great, yet their subsequent objects, in case of success, were various. Thus Buonaparte saw himself encouraged to hope for victory over the existing government and the Republicans by the united strength of the Moderates of every class, whilst their difference in opinion concerning the ultimate measures to be adopted, afforded him the best opportunity of advancing, during the competition, his own pretensions to the larger share of the spoil.[459]

Napoleon communicated accordingly with Siêyes, upon the understanding that he was to be raised to the principal administration of affairs; that the constitution of the year Three, which he himself had once pronounced "the masterpiece of legislation, which had abolished the errors of eighteen centuries," was entirely to be done away; and that a constitution was to be adopted in its stead, of which he knew nothing more, than that it was ready drawn up, and lay in the portfolio of Siêyes. No doubt, the general mentally reserved the right of altering and adjusting it as it should best suit his own views,—a right which he failed not to exercise to a serious extent. When these great preliminaries had been adjusted, it was agreed that it should be executed between the 15th and 20th Brumaire.

In the interim, several men of influence of both councils were admitted into the secret. Talleyrand, who had been deprived of office by the influence of the Republicans, brought his talents to the aid of Buonaparte.[460] Fouché, according to Napoleon, was not consulted—the Memoirs which bear his name aver the contrary—it is certain, that in his important capacity of minister of police, he acted in Buonaparte's favour during the revolution.[461] Some leading

---

[459] Thiers, tom. x., p. 363.
[460] "Talleyrand availed himself of all the resources of a supple and insinuating address, in order to conciliate a person whose suffrage it was important to him to secure."—Gourgaud, tom. i., p. 66.—"It was he who disclosed to Buonaparte's views all the weak points of the government, and made him acquainted with the state of parties, and the bearings of each character."—Fouché, tom. i., p. 96.
[461] "Napoleon effected the 18th of Brumaire without admitting Fouché into the secret."—Gourgaud, tom. i., p. 66.—"Buonaparte was too cunning to let me into the secret of his means of execution, and to place himself at the mercy of a single man; but he said enough

members of both legislative bodies were cautiously intrusted with what was going forward, and others were generally advised to hold themselves in readiness for a great movement.

A sufficient military force was next to be provided; and this was not difficult, for the reputation of Buonaparte ensured the conspirators unlimited influence among the soldiery. Three regiments of dragoons were enthusiastically petitioning the honour of being reviewed by Napoleon. The adherence of these troops might be counted upon. The officers of the garrison of Paris were desirous to pay their respects to him; so were the forty adjutants of the national guard, whom he himself had appointed when general of the troops in the interior. Many other officers, as well reduced as holding commissions, desired to see the celebrated general, that they might express their devotion to his person, and adherence to his fortunes. All these introductions had been artfully postponed.[462]

Two men of more renowned name, Moreau and Macdonald,[463] had made tenders of service to Buonaparte. These both favoured the moderate party, and had no suspicion of the ultimate design of Napoleon or the final result of his undertaking.

A final resolution on 15th Brumaire determined the 18th (9th November) for the great attempt—an interval was necessary, but the risk of discovery and anticipation made it desirable that it should be as short as possible. The secret was well kept; yet being unavoidably intrusted to many persons, some floating and vague rumours did get abroad, and gave an alarm to the parties concerned.

---

to me to win my confidence, and to persuade me that the destinies of France were in his hands."—Fouché, tom. i., p. 98.

[462] Gourgaud, tom. i., p. 74.

[463] "Moreau, who had been at the dinner of the Legislative Body, and with whom Napoleon had there, for the first time, become acquainted, having learned from public report that a change was in preparation, assured Napoleon that he placed himself at his disposal, that he had no wish to be admitted into any secret, and that he required but one hour's notice to prepare himself. Macdonald, who happened then to be at Paris, had made the same tenders of service."—Gourgaud, tom. i., p. 77.

THE EIGHTEENTH BRUMAIRE

Meanwhile, all the generals and officers whom we have named, were invited to repair to Napoleon's house at six o'clock on the morning of the 18th Brumaire, and the three regiments of cavalry already mentioned were appointed to be ready and mounted in the Champs Elysées, to receive the honour of being reviewed by Buonaparte, according to their petition. As an excuse for assigning so unusual an hour of rendezvous, it is said that the general was obliged to set out upon a journey. Many officers, however, understood or guessed what was to be done, and came armed with pistols as well as with swords. Some were without such information or presentiment. Lefebvre, the commandant of the guard of the Representative Bodies, supposed to be devoted to the Directory, had only received an invitation to attend this military assembly on the preceding midnight. Bernadotte, unacquainted with the project, and attached to the Republican faction, was, however, brought to Buonaparte's house by his brother Joseph.[464]

The surprise of some, and the anxious curiosity of all, may be supposed, when they found a military levee so numerous and so brilliant assembled at a house incapable of containing half of them. Buonaparte was obliged to receive them in the open air. Leaving them thus assembled, and waiting their cue to enter on the stage, let us trace the political manœuvres from which the military were to take the signal for action.

Early as Buonaparte's levee had taken place, the Council of Ancients, secretly and hastily assembled, had met still earlier. The ears of all were filled by a report, generally circulated, that the Republican party had formed a daring plan for giving a new popular impulse to the government. It was said, that the resolution was taken at the Hôtel de Salm, amongst the party who still adopted the principles of the old Jacobins, to connect the two representative bodies into one National Assembly, and invest the powers of

---

[464] Gourgaud, tom. i., p. 78. For some curious historical notes on the 18th Brumaire, furnished to Sir Walter Scott by a distinguished authority, and of which great, although unacknowledged, use has since been made by M. Bourrienne, see Appendix to this volume, No. VIII.

government in a Committee of Public Safety, after the model of what was called the Reign of Terror. Circulated hastily, and with such addition to the tale as rumours speedily acquire, the mind of the Council of Ancients was agitated with much fear and anxiety. Cornudet, Lebrun,[465] and Fargues, made glowing speeches to the Assembly, in which the terror that their language inspired was rendered greater by the mysterious and indefinite manner in which they expressed themselves. They spoke of personal danger—of being overawed in their deliberations—of the fall of liberty, and of the approaching destruction of the Republic. "You have but an instant to save France," said Cornudet; "permit it to pass away, and the country will be a mere carcass, disputed by the vultures, whose prey it must become." Though the charge of conspiracy was not distinctly defined, the measures recommended to defeat it were sufficiently decisive.

By the 102d, 103d, and 104th articles of the Constitution, it was provided, that the Council of Ancients might, if they saw it expedient, alter the place where the legislative bodies met, and convoke them elsewhere; a provision designed, doubtless, to prevent the exercise of that compulsion, which the Parisians had at one time assumed over the National Assembly and Convention. This power the Council of Ancients now exercised. By one edict the sittings of the two councils were removed to St. Cloud; by another, the Council delegated to General Buonaparte full power to see this measure carried into effect, and vested him for that purpose with the military command of the department. A state messenger, the deputy Cornet,[466] was sent to communicate to the general these important measures, and require his presence in the Council of Ancients; and this was the crisis which he had so anxiously expected.[467]

A few words determined the numerous body of officers, by whom the messenger found him surrounded, to concur with him without scruple. Even General Lefebvre, who commanded the

---

[465] Afterwards Third Consul, Arch-Treasurer, and Duke of Placentia.
[466] Buonaparte afterwards made Cornet a member of the Conservative Senate and grand officer of the Legion of Honour. On the restoration of the Bourbons, he became a peer of France.—See his "Notice Historique," published in 1819.
[467] Gourgaud, tom. i., p. 78.

guard of the legislative bodies, declared his adhesion to Buonaparte.[468]

The Directory had not even yet taken the alarm. Two of them, indeed, Siêyes and Ducos, being in the secret of the conspiracy, were already at the Tuileries, to second the movement which was preparing. It is said that Barras had seen them pass in the morning, and as they were both mounted, had been much amused with the awkward horsemanship of Siêyes.[469] He little guessed on what expedition he was bound.

When Buonaparte sallied forth on horseback, and at the head of such a gallant cavalcade of officers, his first movement was to assume the command of the three regiments of cavalry, already drawn up in the Champs Elysées, and to lead them to the Tuileries, where the Council of Ancients expected him. He entered their hall surrounded by his military staff, and by those other generals, whose name carried the memory of so many victories. "You are the wisdom of the nation," he said to the Council: "At this crisis it belongs to you to point out the measures which may save the country. I come, surrounded by the generals of the Republic, to promise you their support. I name Lefebvre my lieutenant. Let us not lose time in looking for precedents. Nothing in history ever resembled the end of the eighteenth century—nothing in the eighteenth century resembled this moment. Your wisdom has devised the necessary measure, our arms shall put it into execution."[470] He announced to the military the will of the Council, and the command with which they had intrusted him; and it was received with loud shouts.

In the meanwhile the three directors, Barras, Gohier, and Moulins, who were not in the secret of the morning, began too late

---

[468] "The messenger found the avenues filled with officers: Napoleon had the folding doors opened; and his house being too small to contain so many persons, he came forward on the steps in front of it, received the compliments of the officers, harangued them, and told them that he relied upon them all for the salvation of France. Enthusiasm was at its height: all the officers drew their swords, and promised their services and fidelity."—Gourgaud, tom. i., p. 80.
[469] Gourgaud, tom. i., p. 85.
[470] Lacretelle, tom. xiv., p. 413; Thiers, tom. x., p. 370; Montgaillard, tom. v., p. 264; Gourgaud, tom. i., p. 82.

to take the alarm. Moulins proposed to send a battalion to surround the house of Buonaparte, and make prisoner the general, and whomsoever else they found there. But they had no longer the least influence over the soldiery, and had the mortification to see their own personal guard, when summoned by an aide-de-camp of Buonaparte, march away to join the forces which he commanded, and leave them defenceless.[471]

Barras sent his secretary, Bottot, to expostulate with Buonaparte. The general received him with great haughtiness, and publicly before a large group of officers and soldiers, upbraided him with the reverses of the country; not in the tone of an ordinary citizen, possessing but his own individual interest in the fate of a great nation, but like a prince, who, returning from a distant expedition, finds that in his absence his deputies have abused their trust, and misruled his dominions. "What have you done," he said, "for that fine France, which I left you in such a brilliant condition? I left you peace, I have found war—I left you the wealth of Italy, I have found taxation and misery. Where are the hundred thousand Frenchmen whom I have known?—all of them my companions in glory?—They are dead."[472] It was plain, that even now, when his enterprise was but commenced, Buonaparte had already assumed that tone, which seemed to account every one answerable to him for deficiencies in the public service, and he himself responsible to no one.

Barras, overwhelmed and stunned, and afraid, perhaps, of impeachment for his alleged peculations, belied the courage which he was once supposed to possess, and submitted, in the most abject terms, to the will of the victor. He sent in his resignation, in which he states, "that the weal of the Republic, and his zeal for liberty alone, could have ever induced him to undertake the burden of a public office; and that, seeing the destinies of the Republic were now in the custody of her youthful and invincible general he gladly resigned his authority."[473] He left Paris for his country seat,

---

[471] Lacretelle, tom. xiv., p. 415.
[472] "Then all at once concluding his harangue, in a calm tone he added, 'This state of things cannot last; it would lead us in three years to despotism.'"—Mad. de Staël, tom. ii., p. 224; Thiers, tom. x., p. 376; Montgaillard, tom. v., p. 265.
[473] Letter to the Directory.—See Gourgaud, tom. i., Appendix, p. 336.

accompanied by a guard of cavalry, which Buonaparte ordered to attend him, as much, perhaps, to watch his motions as to do him honour, though the last was the ostensible reason. His colleagues, Gohier and Moulins, also resigned their office; Siêyes and Ducos had already set the example; and thus, the whole Constitutional Executive Council was dissolved, while the real power was vested in Buonaparte's single person. Cambacérès, minister of justice, Fouché, minister of police,[474] with all the rest of the administration, acknowledged his authority accordingly; and he was thus placed in full possession as well of the civil as of the military power.[475]

The Council of Five Hundred, or rather the Republican majority of that body, showed a more stubborn temper; and if, instead of resigning, Barras, Gohier, and Moulins, had united themselves to its leaders, they might perhaps have given trouble to Buonaparte, successful as he had hitherto been.

This hostile Council only met at ten o'clock on that memorable day, when they received, to their surprise, the message intimating that the Council of Ancients had changed the place of meeting from Paris to St. Cloud; and thus removed their debates from the neighbourhood of the populace, over whom the old Jacobinical principles might have retained influence. The laws as they stood afforded the young Council no means of evading compliance, and they accordingly adjourned to meet the next day at St. Cloud, with unabated resolution to maintain the democratical part of the constitution. They separated amid shouts of "Long live the Republic and the Constitution!" which were echoed by the galleries. The *tricoteuses*,[476] and other more zealous attendants on their debates, resolved to transfer themselves to St. Cloud also, and

---

[474] "Fouché made great professions of attachment and devotion. He had given directions for closing the barriers, and preventing the departure of couriers and coaches. 'Why, good God?' said the general to him, 'wherefore all these precautions? We go with the nation, and by its strength alone: let no citizen be disturbed, and let the triumph of opinion have nothing in common with the transactions of days in which a factious minority prevailed.'"—Gourgaud, tom. i., p. 87.

[475] Gourgaud, tom. i., p. 86.

[476] The women of lower rank who attended the debates of the Council, plying the task of knitting while they listened to politics, were so denominated. They were always zealous democrats, and might claim in one sense Shakspeare's description of
"The *free* maids who weave their thread with bones."—S.

appeared there in considerable numbers on the ensuing day, when it was evident the enterprise of Siêyes and of Buonaparte must be either perfected or abandoned.

The contending parties held counsel all the evening, and deep into the night, to prepare for the final contest on the morrow. Siêyes advised, that forty leaders of the opposition should be arrested;[477] but Buonaparte esteemed himself strong enough to obtain a decisive victory, without resorting to any such obnoxious violence. They adjusted their plan of operations in both Councils, and agreed that the government to be established should be provisionally intrusted to three Consuls, Buonaparte, Siêyes, and Ducos. Proper arrangements were made of the armed force at St. Cloud; and the command was confided to the zeal and fidelity of Murat. Buonaparte used some interest to prevent Bernadotte, Jourdan, and Augereau, from attending at St. Cloud the next day, as he did not expect them to take his part in the approaching crisis. The last of these seemed rather hurt at the want of confidence which this caution implied, and said, "What, general! dare you not trust your own little Augereau?"[478] He went to St. Cloud accordingly.

Some preparations were necessary to put the palace of St. Cloud in order, to receive the two Councils; the Orangerie being assigned to the Council of Five Hundred; the Gallery of Mars to that of the Ancients.

In the Council of Ancients, the Modérés, having the majority, were prepared to carry forward and complete their measures for a change of government and constitution. But the minority, having rallied after the surprise of the preceding day, were neither silent nor passive. The Commission of Inspectors, whose duty it was to convene the Council, were inculpated severely for having omitted to give information to several leading members of the minority, of the extraordinary convocation which took place at such an unwonted hour on the morning preceding. The propriety, nay the legality, of

---

[477] "The recommendation was a wise one; but Napoleon thought himself too strong to need any such precaution. 'I swore in the morning,' said he, 'to protect the national representation; I will not this evening violate my oath.'"—Gourgaud, tom. i., p. 87.
[478] Gourgaud, tom. i., p. 87.

the transference of the legislative bodies to St. Cloud, was also challenged. A sharp debate took place, which was terminated by the appearance of Napoleon, who entered the hall, and harangued the members by permission of the president. "Citizen representatives," said he, "you are placed upon a volcano. Let me tell you the truth with the frankness of a soldier. I was remaining tranquil with my family, when the commands of the Council of Ancients called me to arms. I collected my brave military companions, and brought forward the arms of the country in obedience to you who are the head. We are rewarded with calumny—they compare me to Cæsar—to Cromwell. Had I desired to usurp the supreme authority, I have had opportunities to do so before now. But I swear to you the country has not a more disinterested patriot. We are surrounded by dangers and by civil war. Let us not hazard the loss of those advantages for which we have made such sacrifices—Liberty and Equality."

"And the Constitution!" exclaimed Linglet, a democratic member, interrupting a speech which seemed to be designedly vague and inexplicit.

"The Constitution!" answered Buonaparte, giving way to a more natural expression of his feelings, and avowing his object more clearly than he had yet dared to do—"It was violated on the eighteenth Fructidor—violated on the twenty-second Floreal—violated on the thirtieth Prairial. All parties have invoked it—all have disregarded it in turn. It can be no longer a means of safety to any one, since it obtains the respect of no one. Since we cannot preserve the Constitution, let us at least save Liberty and Equality, the foundations on which it is erected." He went on in the same strain to assure them, that for the safety of the Republic he relied only on the wisdom and power of the Council of Ancients, since in the Council of Five Hundred were found those men who desired to bring back the Convention, with its revolutionary committees, its scaffolds, its popular insurrections. "But I," he said, "will save you from such horrors—I and my brave comrades at arms, whose swords and caps I see at the door of the hall; and if any hired orator shall talk of outlawry, I will appeal to the valour of my comrades, with whom I have fought and conquered for liberty."[479]

The Assembly invited the general to detail the particulars of the conspiracy to which he had alluded, but he confined himself to a reference to the testimony of Siêyes and Ducos; and again reiterating that the Constitution could not save the country, and inviting the Council of Ancients to adopt some course which might enable them to do so, he left them, amid cries of "Vive Buonaparte!" loudly echoed by the military in the courtyard, to try the effect of his eloquence on the more unmanageable Council of Five Hundred.

The deputies of the younger Council having found the place designed for their meeting filled with workmen,[480] were for some time in a situation which seemed to resemble the predicament of the National Assembly at Versailles, when they took refuge in a tennis-court. The recollection was of such a nature as inflamed and animated their resolution, and they entered the Orangerie, when at length admitted, in no good humour with the Council of Ancients, or with Buonaparte. Proposals of accommodation had been circulated among them ineffectually. They would have admitted Buonaparte into the Directory, but refused to consent to any radical change in the constitution of the year Three.

The debate of the day, remarkable as the last in which the Republican party enjoyed the full freedom of speech in France, was opened on nineteenth Brumaire, at two o'clock, Lucien Buonaparte being president. Gaudin, a member of the moderate party, began by moving, that a committee of seven members should be formed, to report upon the state of the Republic; and that measures should be taken for opening a correspondence with the council of Ancients. He was interrupted by exclamations and clamour on the part of the majority.

---

[479] Thibaudeau, tom. i., p. 38; Montgaillard, tom. v., p. 267; Thiers, tom. x., p. 380; Lacretelle, tom. xiv., p. 424; Gourgaud, tom. i., p. 92.

[480] "So late as two o'clock in the afternoon, the place assigned to the Council of Five Hundred was not ready. This delay of a few hours was very unfortunate. The deputies formed themselves into groups in the garden; their minds grew heated; they sounded one another, interchanged declarations of the state of their feelings, and organized their opposition."—Gourgaud, tom. i., p. 89.

"The Constitution! The Constitution or Death!" was echoed and re-echoed on every side. "Bayonets frighten us not," said Delbrel; "we are free men."—"Down with the Dictatorship—no Dictators!" cried other members.

Lucien in vain endeavoured to restore order. Gaudin was dragged from the tribune; the voice of other Moderates was overpowered by clamour—never had the party of democracy shown itself fiercer or more tenacious than when about to receive the death-blow.

"Let us swear to preserve the Constitution of the year Three!" exclaimed Delbrel; and the applause which followed the proposition was so general, that it silenced all resistance. Even the members of the moderate party—nay, Lucien Buonaparte himself—were compelled to take the oath of fidelity to the Constitution, which he and they were leagued to destroy.

"The oath you have just taken," said Bigonnet, "will occupy a place in the annals of history, beside the celebrated vow taken in the tennis-court. The one was the foundation of liberty, the other shall consolidate the structure." In the midst of this fermentation, the letter containing the resignation of Barras was read, and received with marks of contempt, as the act of a soldier deserting his post in the time of danger. The moderate party seemed silenced, overpowered, and on the point of coalescing with the great majority of the Council, when the clash of arms was heard at the entrance of the apartment. All eyes were turned to that quarter. Bayonets, drawn sabres, the plumed hats of general officers and aides-de-camp, and the caps of grenadiers, were visible without, while Napoleon entered the Orangerie, attended by four grenadiers belonging to the constitutional guard of the Councils. The soldiers remained at the bottom of the hall, while he advanced with a measured step and uncovered, about one-third up the room.

He was received with loud murmurs. "What! drawn weapons, armed men, soldiers in the sanctuary of the laws!" exclaimed the members, whose courage seemed to rise against the display of force with which they were menaced. All the deputies arose, some rushed

on Buonaparte, and seized him by the collar; others called out—
"Outlawry—outlawry—let him be proclaimed a traitor?" It is said
that Arena, a native of Corsica like himself, aimed a dagger at his
breast, which was only averted by the interposition of one of the
grenadiers.[481] The fact seems extremely doubtful, though it is certain
that Buonaparte was seized by two or three members, while others
exclaimed, "Was it for this you gained so many victories?" and
loaded him with reproaches. At this crisis a party of grenadiers
rushed into the hall with drawn swords, and extricating Buonaparte
from the deputies, bore him off in their arms breathless with the
scuffle.[482]

It was probably at this crisis that Augereau's faith in his
ancient general's fortune began to totter, and his revolutionary
principles to gain an ascendence over his military devotion. "A fine
situation you have brought yourself into," he said to Buonaparte,
who answered sternly, "Augereau, things were worse at Arcola—
Take my advice—remain quiet, in a short time all this will
change."[483] Augereau, whose active assistance and co-operation
might have been at this critical period of the greatest consequence to
the Council, took the hint, and continued passive.[484] Jourdan and
Bernadotte, who were ready to act on the popular side, had the
soldiers shown the least hesitation in yielding obedience to
Buonaparte, perceived no opening of which to avail themselves.

---

[481] "The Corsican Arena approached the general, and shook him violently by the collar of his coat. It has been supposed, but without reason, that he had a poniard to kill him."—Mad. de Staël, tom. ii., p 239.

[482] "In the confusion, one of them, named Thomé, was slightly wounded by the thrust of a dagger, and the clothes of another were cut through."—Gourgaud, tom. i., p. 95.

[483] Lacretelle, tom. xiv., p. 428; Gourgaud, tom. i., p. 91.

[484] The *Moniteur* is anxious to exculpate Augereau from having taken any part in favour of the routed party on the nineteenth Brumaire. That officer, it says, did not join in the general oath of fidelity to the Constitution of the year Three. The same official paper adds, that on the evening of the nineteenth, being invited by some of the leading persons of the democratic faction, to take the military command of their partisans, he had asked them by way of reply, "Whether they supposed he would tarnish the reputation he had acquired in the army, by taking command of wretches like them?" Augereau, it may be remembered, was the general who was sent by Buonaparte to Paris to act as military chief on the part of the Directory in the revolution of the 18th Fructidor, in which the soldiery had willingly followed him. Buonaparte was probably well pleased to keep a man of his military reputation and resolved character out of the combat if possible.—S.

The Council remained in the highest state of commotion, the general voice accusing Buonaparte of having usurped the supreme authority, calling for a sentence of outlawry, or demanding that he should be brought to the bar. "Can you ask me to put the outlawry of my own brother to the vote?" said Lucien. But this appeal to his personal situation and feelings made no impression upon the Assembly, who continued clamorously to demand the question. At length Lucien flung on the desk his hat, scarf, and other parts of his official dress. "Let me be rather heard," he said, "as the advocate of him whom you falsely and rashly accuse." But his request only added to the tumult. At this moment a small body of grenadiers, sent by Napoleon to his brother's assistance, marched into the hall.

They were at first received with applause; for the Council, accustomed to see the triumph of democratical opinions among the military, did not doubt that they were deserting their general to range themselves on the side of the deputies. Their appearance was but momentary—they instantly left the hall, carrying Lucien in the centre of the detachment.

Matters were now come to extremity on either side. The Council, thrown into the greatest disorder by these repeated military incursions, remained in violent agitation, furious against Buonaparte, but without the calmness necessary to adopt decisive measures.

Meantime, the sight of Napoleon, almost breathless, and bearing marks of personal violence, excited to the highest the indignation of the military. In broken words he told them, that when he wished to show them the road to lead the country to victory and fame, "they had answered him with daggers."

Cries of resentment arose from the soldiery, augmented when the party sent to extricate the president brought him to the ranks as to a sanctuary. Lucien, who seconded his brother admirably, or rather who led the way in this perilous adventure, mounted on horseback instantly, and called out, in a voice naturally deep and sonorous, "General, and you, soldiers! the President of the Council of Five Hundred proclaims to you, that factious men, with drawn daggers, have interrupted the deliberations of the Assembly. He authorises you to employ force against these disturbers—The Assembly of Five Hundred is dissolved!"

Murat, deputed by Buonaparte to execute the commands of Lucien, entered the Orangerie with drums beating, at the head of a detachment with fixed bayonets. He summoned the deputies to disperse on their peril, while an officer of the constitutional guard called out, he could be no longer answerable for their safety. Cries of fear became now mingled with vociferations of rage, execrations of abhorrence, and shouts of *Vive la République*. An officer then mounted the president's seat, and summoned the representatives to retire. "The General," said he, "has given orders."

Some of the deputies and spectators began now to leave the hall; the greater part continued firm, and sustained the shouts by which they reprobated this military intrusion. The drums at length struck up and drowned further remonstrance.

"Forward, grenadiers," said the officer who commanded the party. They levelled their muskets, and advanced as if to the charge. The deputies seem hitherto to have retained a lingering hope that their persons would be regarded as inviolable. They now fled on all sides, most of them jumping from the windows of the Orangerie, and leaving behind them their official caps, scarfs, and gowns. In a very few minutes the apartments were entirely clear; and thus, furnishing, at its conclusion, a striking parallel to the scene which ended the Long Parliament of Charles the First's time, terminated the last democratical assembly of France.[485]

Buonaparte affirms, that one of the general officers in his suite offered to take the command of fifty men, and place them in ambush to fire on the deputies in their flight, which he wisely declined as a useless and gratuitous cruelty.[486]

---

[485] Thibaudeau, tom. i., p. 56; Lacretelle, tom. xv., p. 430; Thiers, tom. x., p. 385; Montgaillard, tom. v., p. 271.
[486] Gourgaud, tom. i., p. 97.

ARENA

The result of these violent and extraordinary measures was intimated to the Council of Ancients; the immediate cause of the expulsion of the Five Hundred being referred to the alleged violence on the person of Buonaparte, which was said by one member to have been committed by Arena, while another exaggerated the charge, by asserting that it was offered in consequence of Buonaparte's having made disclosure of some mal-practices of the Corsican deputy while in Italy. The *Moniteur* soon after improved this story of Arena and his single poniard, into a party consisting of Arena, Marquezzi, and other deputies, armed with pistols and daggers. At other times, Buonaparte was said to have been wounded, which certainly was not the case. The effect of the example of Brutus upon a republican, and an Italian to boot, might render the conduct ascribed to Arena credible enough; but the existence of a party armed with pocket-pistols and daggers, for the purpose of opposing regular troops, is too ridiculous to be believed. Arena published a denial of the attempt;[487] and among the numbers who witnessed the scene no proof was ever appealed to, save the real evidence of a dagger found on the floor, and the torn sleeve of a grenadier's coat, circumstances which might be accounted for many ways. But having served at the time as a popular apology for the strong measures which had been adopted, the rumour was not allowed to fall asleep. Thomé, the grenadier, was declared to have merited well of his country by the Legislative Body, entertained at dinner by the general, and rewarded with a salute and a valuable jewel by Josephine. Other reports were put in circulation concerning the violent purposes of the Jacobins. It was said the ancient revolutionist, Santerre, was setting a popular movement on foot, in the Fauxbourg Saint Antoine, and that Buonaparte, through the ex-Director Moulins, had cautioned him against proceeding in his purpose, declaring, that if he did, he would have him shot by martial law.

---

[487] "I have heard some of Arena's countrymen declare that he was incapable of attempting so rash an act. The contrary opinion was, however, so prevalent, that he was obliged to retire to Leghorn, where he made an appeal to the justice of the first consul; who gave him no reply: but I never heard him say that he had noticed the attitude attributed to Arena."—Savary, tom. i., p. 154.

But the truth is, that although there can be no doubt that the popular party entertained a full purpose of revolutionizing the government anew, and restoring its republican character, yet they were anticipated and surprised by the movement of the 18th and 19th Brumaire, which could not, therefore, in strict language, be justified as a defensive measure. Its excuse must rest on the proposition which seems undoubted, that affairs were come to such extremity that a contest was unavoidable, and that therefore it was necessary for the moderate party to take the advantage of the first blow, though they exposed themselves in doing so to the reproach of being called the aggressors in the contest.[488]

The Council of Ancients had expressed some alarm and anxiety about the employment of military force against the other branch of the constitutional representation. But Lucien Buonaparte, having succeeded in rallying around him about a hundred of the council of the juniors, assumed the character and office of that legislative body, now effectually purged of all the dissidents, and, as President of the Five Hundred, gave to the Council of Ancients such an explanation, as they, nothing loth to be convinced, admitted to be satisfactory. Both councils then adjourned till the 19th February, 1800, after each had devolved their powers upon a committee of twenty-five persons, who were instructed to prepare a civil code against the meeting of the legislative bodies. A provisional consular government was appointed, consisting of Buonaparte, Sièyes,[489] and Roger Ducos.

The victory, therefore, of the eighteenth and nineteenth Brumaire, was, by dint of sword and bayonet, completely secured. It

---

[488] "Metaphysicians have disputed, and will long dispute, whether we did not violate the laws, and whether we were not criminal; but these are mere abstractions, at best fit for books and tribunes, and which ought to disappear before imperious necessity: one might as well blame a sailor for waste and destruction, when he cuts away his masts to avoid being overset. The fact is, that had it not been for us the country must have been lost; and we saved it. The authors and chief agents of that memorable state transaction may, and ought, instead of denials or justifications, to answer their accusers proudly, like the Romans, 'We protest that we have saved our country, come with us and return thanks to the gods.'"—Napoleon, *Las Cases*, tom. iv., p. 331.
[489] "Sièyes, during the most critical moments, had remained in his carriage at the gate of St. Cloud, ready to follow the march of the troops. His conduct during the danger was becoming: he evinced coolness, resolution, and intrepidity."—Gourgaud, tom. i., p. 100.

remained for the conquerors to consider the uses which were to be made of it.

CHAPTER XVII

Clemency of the New Consulate—Beneficial change in the Finances—Law of Hostages repealed—Religious liberty allowed—Improvements in the War Department—Pacification of La Vendée—Ascendancy of Napoleon—Disappointment of Siêyes—Committee formed to consider Siêyes' Plan of a Constitution—Rejected as to essentials—A new one adopted, monarchical in every thing but form—Siêyes retires from public life—General view of the new Government—Despotic Power of the First Consul.

The victory obtained over the Directory and the democrats, upon the 18th and 19th Brumaire, was generally acceptable to the French nation. The feverish desire of liberty, which had been the characteristic of all descriptions of persons in the year 1792, was quenched by the blood shed during the Reign of Terror; and even just and liberal ideas of freedom had so far fallen into disrepute, from their resemblance to those which had been used as a pretext for the disgusting cruelties perpetrated at that terrible period, that they excited from association a kind of loathing as well as dread. The great mass of the nation sought no longer guarantees for metaphysical rights, but, broken down by suffering, desired repose, and were willing to submit to any government which promised to secure to them the ordinary benefits of civilisation.

THE PROVISIONAL GOVERNMENT

Buonaparte and Siêyes—for, though only during a brief space, they may still be regarded as joint authorities—were enabled to profit by this general acquiescence, in many important particulars. It put it in their power to dispense with the necessity of pursuing and crushing their scattered adversaries; and the French saw a revolution effected in their system, and that by military force, in which not a drop of blood was spilt. Yet, as had been the termination of most recent revolutions, lists of proscription were prepared; and without previous trial or legal sentence, fifty-nine of those who had chiefly opposed the new Consulate on the 18th and 19th Brumaire were condemned to deportation by the sole *fiat* of the consuls. Sièyes is said to have suggested this unjust and arbitrary measure, which, bearing a colour of revenge and persecution, was highly unpopular. It was not carried into execution. Exceptions were at first made in favour of such of the condemned persons as showed themselves disposed to be tractable; and at length the sentence was altogether dispensed with, and the more obnoxious partisans of democracy were only placed under the superintendence of the police.[490] This conduct showed at once conscious strength, and a spirit of clemency, than which no attributes can contribute more to the popularity of a new government; since the spirit of the opposition, deprived of hope of success, and yet not urged on by despair of personal safety, gradually becomes disposed to sink into acquiescence. The democrats, or, as they were now termed, the anarchists, became intimidated, or cooled in their zeal; and only a few of the more enthusiastic continued yet to avow those principles, to breathe the least doubt of which had been, within but a few months, a crime worthy of death.

Other and most important decrees were adopted by the consuls, tending to lighten the burdens which their predecessors had imposed on the nation, and which had rendered their government so unpopular. Two of the most oppressive measures of the directors were repealed without delay.

The first referred to the finances, which were found in a state of ruinous exhaustion, and were only maintained by a system of compulsory and progressive loans, according to rates of assessment on the property of the citizens. The new minister of finance, Gaudin,[491] would not even go to bed, or sleep a single night, until he had produced a substitute for this ruinous resource, for which he

---

[490] Gourgaud, tom. i., p 120.
[491] Subsequently Duke of Gaëta, who had long occupied the place of chief clerk of finance. "He was a man of mild manners, and of inflexible probity; proceeding slowly, but surely. He never had to withdraw any of his measures, because his knowledge was practical and the fruit of long experience."—Napoleon, *Gourgaud*, tom. i., p. 109.

levied an additional rise of twenty-five per cent. on all contributions, direct and indirect, which produced a large sum. He carried order and regularity into all the departments of finance, improved the collection and income of the funds of the Republic, and inspired so much confidence by the moderation and success of his measures, that credit began to revive, and several loans were attained on easy terms.

The repeal of the law of hostages was a measure equally popular. This cruel and unreasonable enactment, which rendered the aged and weak, unprotected females, and helpless children of emigrants, or armed royalists, responsible for the actions of their relatives, was immediately mitigated. Couriers were despatched to open the prisons; and this act of justice and humanity was hailed as a pledge of returning moderation and liberality.

Important measures were also taken for tranquillizing the religious discord by which the country had been so long agitated. Buonaparte, who had lately professed himself more than half persuaded of the truth of Mahommed's mission, became now—such was the decree of Providence—the means of restoring to France the free exercise of the Christian faith. The mummery of Reveillière Lepaux's heathenism was by general consent abandoned. The churches were restored to public worship; pensions were allowed to such religious persons as took an oath of fidelity to the government; and more than twenty thousand clergymen, with whom the prisons had been filled, in consequence of intolerant laws, were set at liberty upon taking the same vow. Public and domestic rites of worship in every form were tolerated and protected; and the law of the decades, or Theophilanthropic festivals, was abolished. Even the earthly relics of Pope Pius VI., who had died at Valence, and in exile, were not neglected, but received, singular to relate, the rites of sepulture with the solemnity due to his high office, by command of Buonaparte,[492] who had first shaken the Papal authority; and in

---

[492] "In returning from Egypt, Napoleon had conversed a few minutes at Valence with Spina, the Pope's almoner: he then learnt that no funeral honours had been paid to the Pope, and that his corpse was laid in the sacristy of the cathedral. A decree of the consuls ordered that the customary honours should be rendered to his remains, and that a monument of marble should be raised upon his tomb."—Gourgaud, tom. i., p. 124.

doing so, as he boasted in his Egyptian proclamations, had destroyed the emblem of Christian worship.

The part taken by Cambacérès, the minister of justice, in the revolution of Brumaire, had been agreeable to Buonaparte; and his moderation now aided him in the lenient measures which he had determined to adopt. He was a good lawyer, and a man of sense and information, and under his administration means were taken to relax the oppressive severity of the laws against the emigrants. Nine of them, noblemen of the most ancient families in France, had been thrown on the coast near Calais by shipwreck, and the directors had meditated bringing to trial those whom the winds and waves had spared, as fallen under the class of emigrants returned to France without permission, against whom the laws denounced the penalty of death. Buonaparte more liberally considered their being found within the prohibited territory, as an act, not of violation, but of inevitable necessity, and they were dismissed accordingly.[493]

From the same spirit of politic clemency, La Fayette, Latour Maubourg, and others, who, although revolutionists, had been expelled from France for not carrying their principles of freedom sufficiently high and far, were permitted to return to their native country.

IMPROVEMENT IN WAR DEPARTMENT

It may be easily believed that the military department of the state underwent a complete reform under the authority of Buonaparte. Dubois de Crancé, the minister at war under the directors, was replaced by Berthier; and Napoleon gives a strange picture of the incapacity of the former functionary. He declares he could not furnish a single report of the state of the army—that he had obtained no regular returns of the effective strength of the different regiments—that many corps had been formed in the departments, whose very existence was unknown to the minister at war; and, finally, that when pressed for reports of the pay, of the

---

[493] Gourgaud, tom. i., p. 125.

victualling, and of the clothing of the troops, he had replied, that the war department neither paid, clothed, nor victualled them. This may be exaggerated, for Napoleon disliked Dubois de Crancé[494] as his personal opponent; but the improvident and corrupt character of the directorial government renders the charge very probable. By the exertions of Berthier, accustomed to Buonaparte's mode of arrangements, the war department soon adopted a very different face of activity.[495]

The same department received yet additional vigour when the consuls called to be its head the celebrated Carnot, who had returned from exile, in consequence of the fall of the directors. He remained in office but a short time; for, being a democrat in principle, he disapproved of the personal elevation of Buonaparte; but during the period that he continued in administration, his services in restoring order in the military department and combining the plans of the campaign with Moreau and Buonaparte, were of the highest importance.

Napoleon showed no less talent in closing the wounds of internal war, than in his other arrangements. The Chouans, under various chiefs, had disturbed the western provinces; but the despair of pardon, which drove so many malecontents to their standard, began to subside, and the liberal and accommodating measures adopted by the new Consular government, induced most to make peace with Buonaparte. This they did the more readily, that many of them believed the chief consul intended by degrees, and when the opportunity offered, to accomplish the restoration of the Bourbons. Many of the chiefs of the Chouans submitted to him, and afterwards supported his government. Chatillon, Suzannet, D'Autichamp, nobles and chiefs of the Royalist army, submitted at Montluçon, and their reconciliation with the government, being admitted on liberal terms, was sincerely observed by them. Bernier, rector of St. Lo, who had great influence in La Vendée, also made his peace, and was afterwards made Bishop of Orleans by Buonaparte, and employed in negotiating the Concordat with the Pope.

---

[494] After the 18th Brumaire, Dubois de Crancé withdrew into Champagne. He died in June 1814.
[495] Gourgaud, tom. i., p. 108.

Count Louis de Frotté, an enterprising and high-spirited young nobleman, refused for a long time to enter into terms with Buonaparte; so did another chief of the Chouans, called George Cadoudal, a peasant of the district of Morbihan, raised to the command of his countrymen, because, with great strength and dauntless courage, he combined the qualities of enterprise and sagacity. Frotté was betrayed and made prisoner in the house of Guidal, commandant at Alençon, who had pretended friendship to him, and had promised to negotiate a favourable treaty on his behalf. He and eight or nine of his officers were tried by a military commission, and condemned to be shot. They marched hand in hand to the place of execution, remained to the last in the same attitude, expressive of their partaking the same sentiments of devotion to the cause in which they suffered, and died with the utmost courage. George Cadoudal, left alone, became unable to support the civil war, and laid down his arms for a time. Buonaparte, whose policy it was to unite in the new order of things as many and as various characters as possible, not regarding what parts they had formerly played, provided they now attached themselves to his person, took great pains to gain over a man so resolute as this daring Breton. He had a personal interview with him, which he says George Cadoudal solicited; yet why he should have done so it is hard to guess, unless it were to learn whether Buonaparte had any ultimate purpose of serving the Bourbon interest. He certainly did not request the favour in order to drive any bargain for himself, since Buonaparte frankly admits, that all his promises and arguments failed to make any impression upon him; and that he parted with George, professing still to entertain opinions for which he had fought so often and so desperately.[496]

In another instance which happened at this period, Buonaparte boasts of having vindicated the insulted rights of nations. The Senate of Hamburgh had delivered up to England Napper Tandy, Blackwell, and other Irishmen, concerned in the rebellion which had lately wasted Ireland. Buonaparte took this up in a threatening tone, and expounded to their trembling envoy the

---

[496] Gourgaud, tom. i., p. 137.

rights of a neutral territory, in language, upon which the subsequent tragedy of the Duke d'Enghein formed a singular commentary.[497]

DISAPPOINTMENT OF SIÊYES

While Buonaparte was thus busied in adopting measures for composing internal discord, and renewing the wasted resources of the country, those discussions were at the same time privately carrying forward, which were to determine by whom and in what way it should be governed. There is little doubt, that when Siêyes undertook the revolution of Brumaire, he would have desired for his military assistant a very different character from Buonaparte. Some general would have best suited him who possessed no knowledge beyond that of his profession, and whose ambition would have been contented to accept such share of power as corresponded to his limited views and capacity. The wily priest, however, saw that no other coadjutor save Buonaparte could have availed him, after the return of the latter from Egypt, and was not long of experiencing that Napoleon would not be satisfied with any thing short of the lion's share of the spoil.

Nov. 11.

At the very first meeting of the consuls, the defection of Roger Ducos to the side of Buonaparte convinced Siêyes, that he would be unable to support those pretensions to the first place in the government, to which his friends had expected to see him elevated. He had reckoned on Ducos's vote for giving him the situation of first consul; but Ducos saw better where the force and

---

[497] The Senate of Hamburgh lost no time in addressing a long letter to Napoleon, to testify their repentance. He replied to them thus:—"I have received your letter, gentlemen; it does not justify you. Courage and virtue are the preservers of states; cowardice and crime are their ruin. You have violated the laws of hospitality, a thing which never happened among the most savage hordes of the Desert. Your fellow-citizens will for ever reproach you with it. The two unfortunate men whom you have given up, die with glory; but their blood will bring more evil upon their persecutors than it would be in the power of an army to do." A solemn deputation from the Senate arrived at the Tuileries to make public apologies to Napoleon. He again testified his indignation, and when the envoys urged their weakness, he said to them, "Well! and had you not the resource of weak states? was it not in your power to let them escape?"—Gourgaud, tom. i., p. 128; Thibaudeau, tom. i., p. 169.

talent of the Consulate must be considered as reposed. "General," said he to Napoleon, at the first meeting of the Consular body, "the presidency belongs to you as a matter of right." Buonaparte took the chair accordingly as a thing of course. In the course of the deliberations, Sièyes had hoped to find that the general's opinions and interference would have been limited to military affairs; whereas, on the contrary, he heard him express distinctly, and support firmly, propositions on policy and finance, religion and jurisprudence. He showed, in short, so little occasion for an independent coadjutor, that Sièyes appears from this, the very first interview, to have given up all hopes of establishing a separate interest of his own, and to have seen that the Revolution was from that moment ended. On his return home, he said to those statesmen with whom he had consulted and acted preceding the eighteenth Brumaire, as Talleyrand, Boulay, Rœderer, Cabanis, &c.— "Gentlemen, you have a Master—give yourself no farther concern about the affairs of the state—Buonaparte can and will manage them all at his own pleasure."[498]

This declaration must have announced to those who heard it, that the direct and immediate advantages proposed by the revolution were lost; that the government no longer rested on the popular basis, but that, in a much greater degree than could have been said to have been the case during the reign of the Bourbons, the whole measures of state must in future rest upon the arbitrary pleasure of one man.

It was, in the meantime, necessary that some form of government should be established without delay, were it only to prevent the meeting of the two Councils, who must have resumed their authority, unless superseded by a new constitution previous to the 19th February, 1800, to which day they had been prorogued. As a previous measure, the oath taken by official persons was altered from a direct acknowledgment of the constitution of the year Three, so as to express a more general profession of adherence to the cause of the French nation. How to salve the wounded consciences of those who had previously taken the oath in its primitive form, no

---

[498] Gourgaud, tom. i., p. 107; Fouché, tom. i., p. 128.

care was used, nor does any appear to have been thought necessary.[499]

DISCUSSION ON THE CONSTITUTION

Dec.

The three consuls, and the legislative committees, formed themselves into a General Committee, for the purpose of organizing a constitution;[500] and Siêyes was invited to submit to them that model, on the preparation of which he used to pique himself, and had been accustomed to receive the flattery of his friends. He appears to have obeyed the call slowly, and to have produced his plan partially, and by fragments;[501] probably because he was aware, that the offspring of his talents would never be accepted in its entire form, but must necessarily undergo such mutilations as might fit it for the purposes and to the pleasure of the dictator, whose supremacy he had been compelled to announce to his party.

On being pressed by his colleagues in the committee, the metaphysical politician at length produced his full plan of the hierarchical representation, whose authority was to emanate from the choice of the people and of a Conservative Senate, which was at once to protect the laws of the commonwealth, and *absorb*, as it was termed, all furious and over-ambitious spirits, by calling them, when they distinguished themselves by any irregular exertion of power, to share the comforts and incapacities of their own body, as they say spirits of old were conjured down, and obliged to abide in the Red Sea. He then brought forward his idea of a Legislative Body, which was to vote and decide, but without debate; and his Tribunate,

---

[499] Gourgaud, tom. i., p. 140.
[500] The committee met in Napoleon's apartment, from nine in the evening until three in the morning.—Gourgaud, tom. i., p. 141.
[501] "Siêyes affected silence. I was commissioned to penetrate his mystery. I employed Réal, who, using much address with an appearance of great good-nature, discovered the basis of Siêyes's project, by getting Chenier, one of his confidants, to chatter, upon rising from dinner, at which wines and other intoxicating liquors had not been spared. Upon this information, a secret council was held, at which the conduct to be pursued by Buonaparte in the general conferences was discussed."—Fouché, tom. i., p. 138.

designed to plead for, or to impeach the measures of government. These general outlines were approved, as being judged likely to preserve more stability and permanence than had been found to appertain to the constitutions, which, since 1792, had, in such quick succession, been adopted and abandoned.

But the idea which Siêyes entertained of lodging the executive government in a Grand Elector, who was to be the very model of a King of Lubberland, was the ruin of his plan. It was in vain, that in hopes of luring Buonaparte to accept of this office, he had, while depriving it of all real power, attached to it a large revenue, guards, honours, and rank. The heaping with such distinctions an official person, who had no other duty than to name two consuls, who were to carry on the civil and military business of the state without his concurrence or authority, was introducing into a modern state the evils of a worn-out Asiatic empire, where the Sultan, or Mogul, or whatever he is called, lies in his Haram in obscure luxury, while the state affairs are conducted exclusively by his viziers, or lieutenants.

Buonaparte exclaimed against the whole concoction.—"Who," said he, "would accept an office, of which the only duties were to fatten like a pig upon so many millions yearly?[502]—Or what man of spirit would consent to name ministers, over whom, being named, he was not to exercise the slightest authority?—And your two consuls for war and peace, the one surrounded with judges, churchmen, and civilians,—the other with military men and diplomatists,—on what footing of intercourse can they be said to stand respecting each other?—the one demanding money and recruits, the other refusing the supplies? A government involving such a total separation of offices necessarily connected, would be heterogeneous,—the shadow of a state, but without the efficient authority which should belong to one."

---

[502] "Napoleon now began, he said, to laugh in Siêyes's face, and to cut up all his metaphysical nonsense without mercy. 'You take,' he said, 'the abuse for the principle, the shadow for the body. And how can you imagine, M. Siêyes, that a man of any talent, or the least honour, will resign himself to act the part of a pig fattening on a few millions.' After this sally, which made those who were present laugh immoderately, Siêyes remained overwhelmed."—Napoleon, *Las Cases*, tom, iv., p. 335.

Siêyes did not possess powers of persuasion or promptness of speech in addition to his other talents. He was silenced and intimidated, and saw his favourite Elector-General, with his two Consuls, or rather viziers, rejected, without making much effort in their defence.

Still the system which was actually adopted, bore, in point of form, some faint resemblance to the model of Siêyes. Three Consuls were appointed; the first to hold the sole power of nominating to public offices, and right of determining on public measures; the other two were to be his indispensable counsellors. The first of these offices was designed to bring back the constitution of France to a monarchical system, while the second and third were added merely to conciliate the Republicans, who were not yet prepared for a retrograde movement.

The office of one of these supplementary consuls was offered to Siêyes, but he declined to accept of it, and expressed his wish to retire from public life. His disappointment was probably considerable, at finding himself acting but a second-rate part, after the success of the conspiracy which he had himself schemed; but his pride was not so great as to decline a pecuniary compensation. Buonaparte bestowed on him by far the greater part of the private treasure amassed by the ex-directors. It was said to amount to six hundred thousand francs, which Siêyes called *une poire pour la soif*; in English, a morsel to stay the stomach.[503] He was endowed also with the fine domain and estate of Crosne;[504] and to render the gift more acceptable, and save his delicacy, a decree was issued, compelling him to accept of this manifestation of national gratitude. The office of a senator gave him dignity; and the yearly appointment of twenty-five thousand francs annexed to it, added to the ease of his situation.[505] In short, this celebrated metaphysician disappeared as a

---

[503] Las Cases, tom. iv., p. 333.
[504] "Upon the occasion of this gift, the following sorry rhymes were in every one's mouth:—
"Buonaparte à Siêyes a fait présent de Crôsne, Siêyes à Buonaparte a fait présent du Trône."—Montgaillard, tom. v., p. 318.
[505] "Siêyes was the most unfit man in the world for power, but his perceptions were often luminous, and of the highest importance. He was fond of money; but of strict integrity."—Napoleon, *Gourgaud*, tom. iv., p. 152.

political person, and became, to use his own expression, *absorbed* in the pursuit of epicurean indulgences, which he covered with a veil of mystery. There is no doubt that by thus showing the greedy and mercenary turn of his nature, Siêyes, notwithstanding his abilities, lost in a great measure the esteem and reverence of his countrymen; and this was a consequence not probably unforeseen by Buonaparte, when he loaded him with wealth.

CONSULAR GOVERNMENT

To return to the new constitution. Every species of power and faculty was heaped upon the chief consul, with a liberality which looked as if France, to atone for her long jealousy of those who had been the administrators of her executive power, was now determined to remove at once every obstacle which might stand in the way of Buonaparte to arbitrary power. He possessed the sole right of nominating counsellors of state, ministers, ambassadors, officers, civil and military, and almost all functionaries whatsoever. He was to propose all new laws, and take all measures for internal and external defence of the state. He commanded all the forces, of whatever description, superintended all the national relations at home and abroad, and coined the public money. In these high duties he had the advice of his brother consuls, and also of a Council of State. But he was recognised to be independent of them all. The consuls were to be elected for the space of ten years, and to be re-eligible.

The Abbé Siêyes's plan of dividing the people into three classes, which should each of them declare a certain number of persons eligible to certain gradations of the state, was ostensibly adopted. The lists of these eligible individuals were to be addressed by the various electoral classes to the Conservative Senate, which also was borrowed from the abbé's model. This body, the highest and most august in the state, were to hold their places for life, and had a considerable pension attached to them. Their number was not to exceed eighty, and they were to have the power of supplying vacancies in their own body, by choosing the future senator from a list of three persons; one of them proposed by the chief consul, one by the Legislative Body, and one by the Tribunate. Senators became for ever incapable of any other public duty. Their duty was to receive the national lists of persons eligible for official situations, and to annul such laws or measures as should be denounced to their body, as unconstitutional or impolitic, either by the Government or the Tribunate. The sittings of the Senate were not public.

The new constitution of France also adopted the Legislative Body and the Tribunate proposed by the Abbé Siêyes. The duty of the Legislative Body was to take into consideration such laws as should be approved by the Tribunate, and pass or refuse them by vote, but without any debate, or even an expression of their opinion.

The Tribunate, on the contrary, was a deliberative body, to whom the chief consul, and his Council of State, with whom alone lay the initiative privilege, were to propose such laws as appeared to them desirable. These, when discussed by the Tribunate, and approved of by the silent assent of the Legislative Body, passed into decrees, and became binding upon the community. The Legislative Body heard the report of the Tribunate, as expressed by a deputation from that body; and by their votes alone, but without any debate or delivery of opinion, refused or confirmed the proposal. Some of the more important acts of government, such as the proclamation of peace or war, could only take place on the motion of the chief consul to the Tribunate, upon their recommending the measure to the Legislative Body; and, finally, upon the legislative commissions affirming the proposal. But the power of the chief consul was not much checked by this restriction, for the discussion on such subjects was only to take place on his own requisition, and always in secret committee; so that the greatest hinderance of despotism, the weight of public opinion formed upon public debate, was totally wanting.

A very slight glance at this Consular form of government is sufficient to show, that Buonaparte selected exactly as much of the ingenious constitution of Siêyes as was applicable to his own object of acquiring supreme and despotic authority, while he got rid of all, the Tribunate alone excepted, which contained, directly or indirectly, any check or balance affecting the executive power. The substitution of lists of eligible persons or candidates, to be made up by the people, instead of the popular election of actual representatives, converted into a metaphysical and abstract idea the real safeguard of liberty. It may be true, that the authority of an official person, selected from the national lists, might be said originally to emanate from the people; because, unless his name had received their sanction, he could not have been eligible. But the difference is inexpressibly great, between the power of naming a single direct representative, and that of naming a thousand persons, any of whom may be capable of being created a representative; and the popular interference in the state, which had hitherto comprehended the former privilege, was now restrained to the latter and more insignificant one. This was the main error in Siêyes's system, and the most fatal blow to liberty, whose constitutional safety can hardly exist, excepting in union with a direct and unfettered national representation, chosen by the people themselves.

All the other balances and checks which the Abbé had designed to substitute instead of that which arises from popular election, had been broken and cast away; while the fragments of the scheme that remained were carefully adjusted, so as to form the steps by which Buonaparte was to ascend to an unlimited and despotic throne. Siêyes had proposed that his elector-general should be merely a graceful termination to his edifice, like a gilded vane on the top of a steeple—a sovereign without power—a *roi fainéant*,[506] with two consuls to act as joint *Maires des palais*. Buonaparte, on the contrary, gave the whole executive power in the state, together with the exclusive right of proposing all new laws, to the chief consul, and made the others mere appendages, to be thrown aside at pleasure.

Neither were the other constitutional authorities calculated to offer effectual resistance to the engrossing authority of this all-powerful officer. All these bodies were, in fact, mere pensioners.

---

[506] "The grand elector, if he confine himself entirely to the functions you assign him, will be the shadow, but the mere fleshless shadow, of a *roi fainéant*. Can you point out a man base enough to humble himself to such mockery? Such a government would be a monstrous creation, composed of heterogeneous parts, presenting nothing rational. It is a great mistake to suppose that the shadow of a thing can be of the same use as the thing itself."—Napoleon, *Gourgaud*, tom. i., p. 148.

The Senate, which met in secret, and the Legislative Body, whose lips were padlocked, were alike removed from influencing public opinion, and being influenced by it. The Tribunate, indeed, consisting of a hundred persons, retained in some sort the right of debate, and of being publicly heard. But the members of the Tribunate were selected by the Senate, not by the people, whom except in metaphysical mockery, it could not be said to represent any more than a bottle of distilled liquor can be said to represent the sheaf of grain which it was originally drawn from. What chance was there that, in a hundred men so chosen, there should be courage and independence enough found to oppose that primary power, by which, like a steam-engine, the whole constitution was put in motion? Such tribunes were also in danger of recollecting, that they only held their offices for four years, and that the senators had their offices for life; while a transition from the one state to the other was in general thought desirable, and could only be gained by implicit obedience during the candidate's probation in the Tribunate. Yet, slender as was the power of this tribunate body, Buonaparte showed some jealousy even of this slight appearance of freedom; although, justly considered, the Senate, the Conservative Body, and the Tribunate, were but three different pipes, which, separately or altogether, uttered sound at the pleasure of him who presided at the instrument.

The spirit of France must have been much broken when this arbitrary system was adopted without debate or contradiction; and, when we remember the earlier period of 1789, it is wonderful to consider how, in the space of ten years, the race of men, whose love of liberty carried them to such extravagances, seems to have become exhausted. Personal safety was now a principal object with most. They saw no alternative between absolute submission to a military chief of talent and power, and the return to anarchy and new revolutionary excesses.

During the sitting of Buonaparte's Legislative Committee, Madame de Staël expressed to a representative of the people, her alarms on the subject of liberty. "Oh, madam," he replied, "we are arrived at an extremity in which we must not trouble ourselves about saving the principles of the Revolution, but only the lives of the men by whom the Revolution was effected."[507]

Yet more than one exertion is said to have been made in the committee, to obtain some modification of the supreme power of the chief consul, or at least some remedy in case of its being abused. Several members of the committee which adjusted the new constitution, made, it is said, an effort to persuade Buonaparte, that, in taking possession of the office of supreme magistrate, without any preliminary election, he would evince an ambition which might prejudice him with the people; and, entreating him to be satisfied with the office of generalissimo of the armies, with full right of treating with foreign powers, invited him to set off to the frontier and resume his train of victories. "I will remain at Paris," said Buonaparte, biting his nails to the quick, as was his custom when agitated—"I will remain at Paris—I am chief consul."

Chenier hinted at adopting the doctrine of absorption, but was instantly interrupted—"I will have no such mummery," said Buonaparte; "blood to the knees rather."[508] These expressions may be exaggerated; but it is certain that, whenever there was an attempt to control his wishes, or restrict his power, such a discontented remark as intimated "that he would meddle no more in the business," was sufficient to overpower the opposition. The committee saw no option betwixt submitting to the authority of this inflexible chief, or encountering the horrors of a bloody civil war. Thus were lost at once the fruits of the virtues, the crimes, the blood, the treasure, the mass of human misery, which, flowing from the Revolution, had agitated France for ten years; and thus, having sacrificed almost all that men hold dear, the rights of humanity themselves included, in order to obtain national liberty, her inhabitants, without having enjoyed rational freedom, or the advantages which it ensures, for a single day, returned to be the vassals of a despotic government, administered by a chief whose right was only in his sword. A few reflections on what might or ought to have been Buonaparte's conduct in this crisis, naturally arise out of the subject.

---

[507] Consid. sur la Rév. Française, tom. ii., p. 248.
[508] Mémoires de Fouché, tom. i., p. 104.—S.

We are not to expect, in the course of ordinary life, moral any more than physical miracles. There have lived men of a spirit so noble, that, in serving their country, they had no other object beyond the merit of having done so; but such men belong to a less corrupted age than ours, and have been trained in the principles of disinterested patriotism, which did not belong to France, perhaps not to Europe, in the eighteenth century. We may, therefore, take it for granted, that Buonaparte was desirous, in some shape or other, to find his own interest in the service of his country, that his motives were a mixture of patriotism and the desire of self-advancement; and it remains to consider in what manner both objects were to be best obtained.

The first alternative was the re-establishment of the Republic, upon some better and less perishable model than those which had been successively adopted and abandoned by the French, in the several phases of the Revolution. But Buonaparte had already determined against this plan of government, and seemed unalterably convinced, that the various misfortunes and failures which had been sustained in the attempt to convert France into a republic, afforded irrefragable evidence that her natural and proper constitutional government must be monarchical. This important point settled, it remained, 1st, To select the person in whose hand the kingly power was to be intrusted. 2dly, To consider in what degree the monarchical principle should be mingled with, and qualified by, securities for the freedom of the people, and checks against the encroachments of the prince.

Having broken explicitly with the Republicans, Buonaparte had it in his power, doubtless, to have united with those who desired the restoration of the Bourbons, who at this moment formed a large proportion of the better classes in France. The name of the old dynasty must have brought with it great advantages. Their restoration would have at once given peace to Europe, and in a great measure reconciled the strife of parties in France. There was no doubt of the possibility of the counter-revolution; for what was done in 1814 might have been still more easily done in 1799. Old ideas would have returned with ancient names, and at the same time security might have been given, that the restored monarch should be placed within such legal restraints as were necessary for the protection of the freedom of the subject. The principal powers of Europe, if required, would have gladly guaranteed to the French people any class of institutions which might have been thought adequate to this purpose.

But, besides that such a course cut off Buonaparte from any higher reward of his services, than were connected with the rank of a subject, the same objections to the restoration of the Bourbon family still prevailed, which we have before noticed. The extreme confusion likely to be occasioned by the conflicting claims of the restored emigrants, who had left France with all the feelings and prejudices peculiar to their birth and quality, and those of the numerous soldiers and statesmen who had arisen to eminence during the revolution, and whose pretensions to rank and office would be urged with jealous vehemence against those who had shared the fortunes of the exiled monarch, was a powerful objection to the restoration. The question concerning the national domains remained as embarrassing as before; for, while the sales which had been made of that property could scarce be cancelled without a severe shock to national credit, the restored Bourbons could not, on the other hand, fail to insist upon an indemnification to the spirituality, who had been stripped of their property for their adherence to their religious vows, and to the nobles, whose estates had been forfeited for their adherence to the throne. It might also have been found, that, among the army, a prejudice against the Bourbons had survived their predilection for the Republic, and that although the French soldiers might see with pleasure a crown placed on the brow of their favourite general, they might be unwilling to endure the restoration of the ancient race, against whom they had long borne arms.

THE CONSULATE

All these objections against attempting to recall the ancient dynasty, have weight in themselves, and may readily have appeared insuperable to Buonaparte; especially considering the conclusion to be, that if the Bourbons were found ineligible, the crown of

France—with a more extended empire, and more unlimited powers—was in that case to rest with Buonaparte himself. There is no doubt that, in preferring the title of the Bourbons, founded on right, to his own, which rested on force and opportunity alone, Buonaparte would have acted a much more noble, generous, and disinterested part, than in availing himself of circumstances to establish his own power; nay, that, philosophically speaking, such a choice might have been wiser and happier. But in the ordinary mode of viewing and acting in this world, the temptation was immense; and Buonaparte was, in some measure, unfettered by the circumstances which might have withheld some of his contemporaries from snatching at the crown that seemed to await his grasp. Whatever were the rights of the Bourbons, abstractedly considered, they were not of a kind to force themselves immediately upon the conscience of Buonaparte. He had not entered public life, was indeed a mere boy, when the general voice of France, or that which appeared such, drove the ancient race from the throne; he had acted during all his life hitherto in the service of the French government *de facto*; and it was hard to require of him, now of a sudden, to sacrifice the greatest stake which a man ever played for, to the abstract right of the king *de jure*. Candour will therefore allow, that though some spirits, of an heroic pitch of character, might, in his place, have acted otherwise, yet the conduct of Buonaparte, in availing himself, for his own advantage, of the height which he had attained by his own talents, was too natural a course of action to be loaded with censure by any one, who, if he takes the trouble to consider the extent of the temptation, must acknowledge in his heart the difficulty of resisting it.

But, though we may acknowledge many excuses for the ambition which induced Buonaparte to assume the principal share of the new government, and although we were even to allow to his admirers that he became First Consul purely because his doing so was necessary to the welfare of France, our candour can carry us no farther. We cannot for an instant sanction the monstrous accumulation of authority which engrossed into his own hands all the powers of the State, and deprived the French people, from that period, of the least pretence to liberty, or power of protecting themselves from tyranny. It is in vain to urge, that they had not yet learned to make a proper use of the invaluable privileges of which he deprived them—equally in vain to say, that they consented to resign what it was not in their power to defend. It is a poor apology for theft, that the person plundered knew not the value of the gem taken from him; a worse excuse for robbery, that the party robbed was disarmed and prostrate, and submitted without resistance, where to resist would have been to die. In choosing to be the head of a well-regulated and limited monarchy, Buonaparte would have consulted even his own interest better, than by preferring, as he did, to become the sole animating spirit of a monstrous despotism. The communication of common privileges, while they united discordant factions, would have fixed the attention of all on the head of the government, as their mutual benefactor. The constitutional rights which he had reserved for the Crown would have been respected, when it was remembered that the freedom of the people had been put in a rational form, and its privileges rendered available by his liberality.

Such checks upon his power would have been as beneficial to himself as to his subjects. If, in the course of his reign, he had met constitutional opposition to the then immense projects of conquest, which cost so much blood and devastation, to that opposition he would have been as much indebted, as a person subject to fits of lunacy is to the bonds by which, when under the influence of his malady, he is restrained from doing mischief. Buonaparte's active spirit, withheld from warlike pursuits, would have been exercised by the internal improvement of his kingdom. The mode in which he used his power would have gilded over, as in many other cases, the imperfect nature of his title, and if he was not, in every sense, the legitimate heir of the monarchy, he might have been one of the most meritorious princes that ever ascended the throne. Had he permitted the existence of a power expressive of the national opinion to exist, co-equal with and restrictive of his own, there would have been no occupation of Spain, no war with Russia, no imperial decrees against British commerce. The people who first felt the pressure of these violent and ruinous measures, would have declined to submit to them in the outset. The ultimate consequence—the overthrow, namely, of Napoleon himself, would not have taken place, and he might, for aught we can see, have died on the throne of France, and bequeathed it to his posterity, leaving a reputation which could only be surpassed in lustre by that of an individual who should render similar advantages to his country, yet decline the gratification, in any degree, of his personal ambition.

In short, it must always be written down, as Buonaparte's error as well as guilt, that, misusing the power which the 18th Brumaire threw into his hands, he totally destroyed the liberty of France, or, we would say, more properly, the chance which that country had of attaining a free, and, at the same time, a settled government. He might have been a patriot prince, he chose to be a usurping despot—he might have played the part of Washington, he preferred that of Cromwell.[509]

---

[509] The constitution of the year VIII, so impatiently expected by all ranks of citizens, was published and submitted to the sanction of the people on the 13th of December, and proclaimed on the 24th of the same; the provisional government having lasted forty-three days. The Legislative Body and the Tribunate entered on their functions the 1st day of January, 1800.

Chapter XVIII

Proceedings of Buonaparte in order to consolidate his power—His great success—Causes that led to it—Cambacérès and Le Brun chosen Second and Third Consuls—Talleyrand appointed Minister for Foreign Affairs, and Fouché Minister of Police—Their Characters—Other Ministers nominated—Various Changes made, in order to mark the Commencement of a new Era—Napoleon addresses a Letter personally to the King of England—Answered by Lord Grenville—Negotiation for Peace that followed, speedily broken off—Campaigns in Italy, and on the Rhine—Successes of Moreau—Censured by Napoleon for Over-caution—The Charge considered—The Chief Consul resolves to bring back, in Person, Victory to the French Standards in Italy—His Measures for that purpose.

The structure of government which Buonaparte had selected out of the broken outlines of the plan of Siêyes, being not only monarchical but despotic, it remained that its offices should be filled with persons favourable to the new order of things; and to this the attention of Buonaparte was especially turned. In order to secure the selection of the official individuals to himself, he eluded entirely the principle by which Siêyes had proposed to elaborate his national representatives out of the various signed lists of eligibility, to be made up by the three classes into which his hierarchy divided the French people. Without waiting for these lists of eligible persons, or taking any other rule but his own pleasure, and that of his counsellors, the two new consuls, Buonaparte named sixty senators; the senators named a hundred tribunes, and three hundred legislators; and thus the whole bodies of the State were filled up, by a choice emanating from the executive government, instead of being vested, more or less directly, in the people.

In availing himself of the privileges which he had usurped, the first consul, as we must now call him, showed a moderation as artful as it was conciliatory. His object was to avoid the odium of appearing to hold his rank by his military character only. He desired, on the contrary, to assemble round him a party, in which the predominant character of individuals, whatever it had hitherto been, was to be merged in that of the new system; as the statuary throws into the furnace broken fragments of bronze of every various description, without regarding their immediate appearance or form, his purpose being to unite them by fusion, and bestow upon the mass the new shape which his art destines it to represent.

With these views, Napoleon said to Siêyes, who reprobated the admission of Fouché into office and power, "we are creating a new era. Of the past, we must forget the bad, and only remember the good. Time, habits of business, and experience, have formed many able men, and modified many characters."[510] These words may be regarded as the key-note of his whole system. Buonaparte did not care what men had been formerly, so that they were now disposed to become that which was suitable for his interest, and for which he was willing to reward them liberally. The former conduct of persons of talent, whether in politics or morality, was of no consequence, providing they were willing, now, faithfully to further and adhere to the new order of things. This prospect of immunity for the past, and reward for the future, was singularly well calculated to act upon the public mind, desirous as it was of repose, and upon that of individuals, agitated by so many hopes and fears as the Revolution had set afloat. The consular government seemed a general place of refuge and sanctuary to persons of all various opinions, and in all various predicaments. It was only required of them, in return for the safety which it afforded, that they should pay homage to the presiding deity.

So artfully was the system of Buonaparte contrived, that each of the numerous classes of Frenchmen found something in it congenial to his habits, his feelings, or his circumstances, providing only he was willing to sacrifice to it the essential part of his political principles. To the Royalist, it restored monarchical forms, a court,

---

[510] Gourgaud, tom. i., p. 118.

and a sovereign—but he must acknowledge that sovereign in Buonaparte. To the churchman, it opened the gates of the temples, removed the tyranny of the persecuting philosophers—promised in course of time a national church—but by the altar must be placed the image of Buonaparte. The Jacobin, dyed double red in murder and massacre, was welcome to safety and security from the aristocratic vengeance which he had so lately dreaded. The regicide was guaranteed against the return of the Bourbons—they who had profited by the Revolution as purchasers of national domains, were ensured against their being resumed. But it was under the implied condition, that not a word was to be mentioned by those ci-devant democrats, of liberty or equality: the principles for which forfeitures had been made, and revolutionary tribunals erected, were henceforth never to be named. To all these parties, as to others, Buonaparte held out the same hopes under the same conditions—"All these things will I give you, if you will kneel down and worship me." Shortly afterwards, he was enabled to place before those to whom the choice was submitted, the original temptation in its full extent—a display of the kingdoms of the earth, over which he offered to extend the empire of France, providing always he was himself acknowledged as the object of general obedience, and almost adoration.

The system of Buonaparte, as it combined great art with an apparent generosity and liberality, proved eminently successful among the people of France, when subjected to the semblance of a popular vote. The national spirit was exhausted by the changes and the sufferings, the wars and the crimes, of so many years; and in France, as in all other countries, parties, exhausted by the exertions and vicissitudes of civil war, are in the very situation where military tyranny becomes the next crisis. The rich favoured Buonaparte for the sake of protection,—the poor for that of relief,—the emigrants, in many cases, because they desired to return to France,—the men of the Revolution, because they were afraid of being banished from it;—the sanguine and courageous crowded round his standard in hope of victory,—the timid cowered behind it in the desire of safety. Add to these the vast multitude who follow the opinions of others, and take the road which lies most obvious, and is most trodden, and it is no wonder that the 18th Brumaire, and its consequences, received the general sanction of the people. The constitution of the year Eight, or Consular Government, was approved by the suffrages of nearly four millions of citizens,[511]—a more general approbation than any preceding system had been received with. The vote was doubtless a farce in itself, considering how many constitutions had been adopted and sworn to within so short a space; but still the numbers who expressed assent, more than doubling those votes which were obtained by the constitution of 1792 and of the year Three, indicate the superior popularity of Buonaparte's system.

To the four millions who expressly declared their adherence to the new Consular constitution, must be added the many hundreds of thousands and millions more, who were either totally indifferent upon the form of government, providing they enjoyed peace and protection under it, or who, though abstractedly preferring other rulers, were practically disposed to submit to the party in possession of the power.

Such and so extended being the principles on which Buonaparte selected the members of his government, he manifested, in choosing individuals, that wonderful penetration, by which, more perhaps than any man who ever lived, he was enabled at once to discover the person most capable of serving him, and the means of securing his attachment. Former crimes or errors made no cause of exclusion; and in several cases the alliance between the first consul and his ministers might have been compared to the marriages between the settlers on the Spanish mainland, and the unhappy females, the refuse of great cities, sent out to recruit the colony.—"I ask thee not," said the bucanier to the wife he had selected from the cargo of vice, "what has been thy former conduct; but, henceforth, see thou continue faithful to me, or this," striking his hand on his musket, "shall punish thy want of fidelity."

---

[511] Out of 3,012,569 votes, 1562 rejected the new constitution; 3,011,007 accepted it.—See Thibaudeau, tom. i., p. 117.

CAMBACÉRÈS—LEBRUN—TALLEYRAND

For second and third consuls, Buonaparte chose Cambacérès,[512] a lawyer, and a member of the moderate party, with Lebrun,[513] who had formerly co-operated with the Chancellor Maupeou. The former was employed by the chief consul as his organ of communication with the Revolutionists, while Lebrun rendered him the same service with the Royal party; and although, as Madame de Staël observes, they preached very different sermons on the same texts,[514] yet they were both eminently successful in detaching from their original factions many of either class, and uniting them with this third, or government party, which was thus composed of deserters from both. The last soon became so numerous, that Buonaparte was enabled to dispense with the *bascule*, or trimming system, by which alone his predecessors, the directors, had been enabled to support their power.

In the ministry, Buonaparte acted upon the same principle, selecting and making his own the men whose talents were most distinguished, without reference to their former conduct. Two were particularly distinguished, as men of the most eminent talents, and extensive experience. These were Talleyrand and Fouché. The former, noble by birth, and Bishop of Autun, notwithstanding his high rank in church and state, had been deeply engaged in the Revolution. He had been placed on the list of emigrants, from which his name was erased on the establishment of the Directorial government, under which he became minister of foreign affairs. He resigned that office in the summer preceding 18th Brumaire; and Buonaparte, finding him at variance with the Directory, readily passed over some personal grounds of complaint which he had against him, and enlisted in his service a supple and dexterous

---

[512] "Cambacérès was of an honourable family in Languedoc; he was fifty years old; he had been a member of the Convention, and had conducted himself with moderation: he was generally esteemed, and had a just claim to the reputation which he enjoyed of being one of the ablest lawyers of the republic."—Napoleon, *Gourgaud*, tom. i., p. 153.

[513] "Lebrun was sixty years of age, and came from Normandy. He was one of the best writers in France, a man of inflexible integrity; and he approved of the changes of the Revolution only in consideration of the advantages which resulted from them to the mass of the people, for his own family were all of the class of peasantry."—*Ibid.*, p. 153.

[514] Consid. sur la Rév. Française, tom. ii., p. 255.

politician, and an experienced minister; fond, it is said, of pleasure, not insensible to views of self-interest, nor too closely fettered by principle, but perhaps unequalled in ingenuity. Talleyrand was replaced in the situation of minister for foreign affairs, after a short interval, assigned for the purpose of suffering the public to forget his prominent share in the scandalous treaty with the American commissioners, and continued for a long tract of time one of the closest sharers of Buonaparte's councils.[515]

If the character of Talleyrand bore no strong traces of public virtue or inflexible morality, that of Fouché was marked with still darker shades. He had been dipt in some of the worst transactions of the Reign of Terror, and his name is found among the agents of the dreadful crimes of that unhappy period. In the days of the Directory, he is stated to have profited by the universal peculation which was then practised, and to have amassed large sums by shares in contracts and brokerage in the public funds. To atone for the imperfections of a character stained with perfidy, venality, and indifference to human suffering, Fouché brought to Buonaparte's service a devotion, never like to fail the first consul unless his fortunes should happen to change; and a perfect experience with all the weapons of revolutionary war, and knowledge of those who were best able to wield them. He had managed under Barras's administration the department of police; and, in the course of his agency, had become better acquainted perhaps than any man in France with all the various parties in that distracted country, the points which they were desirous of reaching, the modes by which they hoped to attain them, the character of their individual leaders, and the means to gain them over or to intimidate them. Formidable by his extensive knowledge of the revolutionary springs, and the address with which he could either put them into motion, or prevent them from operating, Fouché, in the latter part of his life, displayed a species of wisdom which came in place of morality and benevolence.

Loving wealth and power, he was neither a man of ardent passions, nor of a vengeful disposition; and though there was no scruple in his nature to withhold him from becoming an agent in the

---

[515] Thibaudeau, tom. i., p. 115; Gourgaud, tom. i., p. 115.

great crimes which state policy, under an arbitrary government, must often require, yet he had a prudential and constitutional aversion to unnecessary evil, and was always wont to characterise his own principle of action, by saying, that he did as little harm as he possibly could. In his mysterious and terrible office of head of the police, he had often means of granting favours, or interposing lenity in behalf of individuals, of which he gained the full credit, while the harsh measures of which he was the agent, were set down to the necessity of his situation. By adhering to these principles of moderation, he established for himself at length a character totally inconsistent with that belonging to a member of the revolutionary committee, and resembling rather that of a timid but well-disposed servant, who, in executing his master's commands, is desirous to mitigate as much as possible their effect on individuals. It is, upon the whole, no wonder, that although Siéyes objected to Fouché, from his want of principle, and Talleyrand was averse to him from jealousy, interference, and personal enmity, Napoleon chose, nevertheless, to retain in the confidential situation of minister of police, the person by whom that formidable office had been first placed on an effectual footing.[516]

Of the other ministers, it is not necessary to speak in detail. Cambacérès retained the situation of minister of justice,[517] for which he was well qualified; and the celebrated mathematician, Laplace, was preferred to that of the Interior, for which he was not, according to Buonaparte's report, qualified at all.[518] Berthier, as we have already seen, filled the war department, and shortly afterwards Carnot; and Gaudin administered the finances with credit to himself.

---

[516] Gourgaud, tom. i., p. 116.
[517] "When Cambacérès afterwards vacated the office, Buonaparte appointed M. d'Abrial, who died in 1828, a peer of France. On remitting the folio to the new minister, the First Consul addressed him thus: 'M. d'Abrial, I know you not, but am informed you are the most upright man in the magistracy; it is on that account I name you minister of justice.'"—Bourrienne, tom. ii., p. 118.
[518] "Laplace, a geometrician of the first rank, soon proved himself below mediocrity as a minister. On his very first essay, the consuls found that they had been mistaken; not a question did Laplace seize in its true point of view: he sought for subtleties in every thing; had none but problematical ideas, and carried the doctrine of infinite littleness into the business of administration."—Napoleon, *Gourgaud*, tom. i., p. 116.

Forfait, a naval architect of eminence,[519] replaced Bourdon in the helpless and hopeless department of the French Admiralty.

A new constitution having been thus formed, and the various branches of duty distributed with much address among those best capable of discharging them, other changes were at the same time made, which were designed to mark that a new era was commenced, in which all former prejudices were to be abandoned and done away.

VARIOUS CHANGES

We have noticed that one of the first acts of the Provisional Government had been to new-modify the national oath, and generalize its terms, so that they should be no longer confined to the constitution of the year Three, but should apply to that which was about to be framed, or to any other which might be produced by the same authority.[520] Two subsequent alterations in the constitution, which passed without much notice, so much was the revolutionary or republican spirit abated, tended to show that farther changes were impending, and that the Consular Republic was speedily to adopt the name, as it already had the essence, of a monarchy. It was scarcely three months since the President of the Directory had said to the people, on the anniversary of the taking of the Bastile,— "Royalty shall never raise its head again. We shall no more behold individuals boasting a title from Heaven, to oppress the earth with more ease and security, and who considered France as their private patrimony, Frenchmen as their subjects, and the laws as the expression of their good-will and pleasure." Yet now, in contradiction to this sounding declamation, the national oath, expressing hatred to royalty, was annulled, under the pretext that the Republic, being universally acknowledged, had no occasion for the guard of such disclamations.

---

[519] "Forfait, a native of Normandy, had the reputation of being a naval architect of first-rate talent, but he was a mere projector, and did not answer the expectations formed of him."— Napoleon, *Gourgaud*, tom. i., p. 115.
[520] *Moniteur*, 31st Dec. 1799.

In like manner, the public observance of the day on which Louis XVI. had suffered decapitation, was formally abolished. Buonaparte, declining to pass a judgment on the action as just, politic, or useful, pronounced that, in any event, it could only be regarded as a national calamity, and was therefore in a moral, as well as a political sense, an unfit epoch for festive celebration. An expression of the first consul to Siêyes was also current at the same time, which, although Buonaparte may not have used it, has been generally supposed to express his sentiments. Siêyes had spoken of Louis under the established phrase of the Tyrant. "He was no tyrant," Buonaparte replied; "had he been such, I should have been a subaltern officer of artillery, and you, Monsieur l'Abbé, would have been still saying mass."[521]

A third sign of approaching change, or rather of the approaching return to the ancient system of government under a different chief, was the removal of the first consul from the apartments in the Luxembourg palace, occupied by the directors, to the royal residence of the Tuileries. Madame de Staël beheld the entrance of this fortunate soldier into the princely residence of the Bourbons. He was already surrounded by a vassal crowd, eager to pay him the homage which the inhabitants of those splendid halls had so long claimed as their due, that it seemed to be consistent with the place, and to become the right of this new inhabitant. The doors were thrown open with a bustle and violence, expressive of the importance of the occasion. But the hero of the scene, in ascending the magnificent staircase, up which a throng of courtiers followed him, seemed totally indifferent to all around, his features bearing only a general expression of indifference to events, and contempt for mankind.[522]

The first measures of Buonaparte's new government, and the expectation attached to his name, had already gone some length in restoring domestic quiet; but he was well aware that much more

---

[521] Las Cases, tom. iv., p. 337.
[522] "The choice of this residence was a stroke of policy. It was there that the King of France was accustomed to be seen; circumstances connected with that monarchy were there presented to every eye; and the very influence of the walls on the minds of spectators was, if we may say so, sufficient for the restoration of regal power."—Mad. de Staël, tom. ii., p. 256.

must be done to render that quiet permanent; that the external relations of France with Europe must be attended to without delay; and that the French expected from him either the conclusion of an honourable peace, or the restoration of victory to their national banners. It was necessary, too, that advances towards peace should in the first place be made, in order, if they were unsuccessful, that a national spirit should be excited, which might reconcile the French to the renewal of the war with fresh energy.

LETTER TO THE KING OF ENGLAND

Hitherto, in diplomacy, it had been usual to sound the way for opening treaties of peace by obscure and almost unaccredited agents, in order that the party willing to make propositions might not subject themselves to a haughty and insulting answer, or have their desire of peace interpreted as a confession of weakness. Buonaparte went into the opposite extreme, and addressed the King of England in a personal epistle. This Letter,[523] like that to the Archduke Charles, during the campaign of 1797, intimates Buonaparte's affectation of superiority to the usual forms of

---

[523] "French Republic—Sovereignty of the People—Liberty—Equality.
"Buonaparte, First Consul of the Republic, to his Majesty the King of Great Britain and Ireland.
"Paris, 5th Nivose, 8th year of the Republic, (25th Dec. 1799.)
"Called by the wishes of the French nation to occupy the first magistracy of the Republic, I think it proper, on entering into office, to make a direct communication of it to your Majesty. The war, which for eight years has ravaged the four quarters of the world, must it be eternal? Are there no means of coming to an understanding? How can the two most enlightened nations of Europe, powerful and strong beyond what their safety and independence require, sacrifice to ideas of vain greatness the benefits of commerce, internal prosperity, and the happiness of families? How is it that they do not feel that peace is the first necessity as well as the first glory? These sentiments cannot be foreign to the heart of your Majesty, who reign over a free nation, and with the sole view of rendering it happy. Your Majesty will only see, in this overture, my sincere desire to contribute efficaciously, for the second time, to a general pacification, by a proceeding prompt, entirely confidential, and disengaged from those forms which, necessary perhaps to disguise the dependence of weak States, prove only in the case of the strong the mutual desire of deceiving each other. France and England, by the abuse of their strength, may still, for a long time, for the misfortune of all nations, retard the period of their being exhausted. But I will venture to say, the fate of all civilized nations is attached to the termination of a war which involves the whole world.
"Buonaparte."

diplomacy, and his pretence to a character determined to emancipate itself from rules only designed for mere ordinary men. But the manner of the address was in bad taste, and ill calculated to obtain credit for his being sincere in the proposal of peace. He was bound to know so much of the constitutional authority of the monarch whom he addressed, as to be aware that George III. would not, and could not, contract any treaty personally, but must act by the advice of those ministers whose responsibility was his guarantee to the nation at large. The terms of the letter set forth, as usual, the blessings of peace, and urged the propriety of its being restored; propositions which could not admit of dispute in the abstract, but which admit much discussion when coupled with unreasonable or inadmissible conditions.

The answer transmitted by Lord Grenville, in the forms of diplomacy, to the Minister for Foreign Affairs, dwelt on the aggressions of France, declared that the restoration of the Bourbons would have been the best security for their sincerity, but disavowed all right to dictate to France in her internal concerns. Some advances were made to a pacific treaty; and it is probable that England might at that period have obtained the same or better terms than she afterwards got by the treaty of Amiens. It may be added, that the moderate principles expressed by the consular government, might, in the infancy of his power, and in a moment of considerable doubt, have induced Buonaparte to make sacrifices, to which, triumphant and established, he would not condescend. But the possession of Egypt, which Buonaparte must have insisted on, were it only for his own reputation, was likely to be an insuperable difficulty. The conjuncture also appeared to the English ministers propitious for carrying on the war. Italy had been recovered, and the Austrian army, to the number of 140,000, were menacing Savoy, and mustering on the Rhine. Buonaparte, in the check received before Acre, had been found not absolutely invincible. The exploits of Suwarrow over the French were recent, and had been decisive. The state of the interior of France was well known; and it was conceived, that though this successful general had climbed into the seat of supreme power which he found unoccupied, yet that two strong parties, of which the Royalists objected to his person, the

Republicans to his form of government, could not fail, the one or other, to deprive him of his influence.

The treaty was finally broken off, on the score that there was great reason to doubt Buonaparte's sincerity; and supposing that were granted, there was at least equal room to doubt the stability of a power so hastily acknowledged, and seeming to contain in itself the principles of decay. There may be a difference of opinion in regard to Buonaparte's sincerity in the negotiation, but there can be none as to the reality of his joy at its being defeated. The voice which summoned him to war was that which sounded sweetest in his ears, since it was always followed by exertion and by victory. He had been personally offended, too, by the allusion to the legitimate rights of the Bourbons, and indulged his resentment by pasquinades in the Moniteur. A supposed letter from the last descendant of the Stuart family appeared there, congratulating the King of Britain on his acceding to the doctrine of legitimacy, and summoning him to make good his principles, by an abdication of his crown in favour of the lineal heir.[524]

EXTERNAL SITUATION OF FRANCE

The external situation of France had, as we before remarked, been considerably improved by the consequences of the battle of Zurich, and the victories of Moreau. But the Republic derived yet greater advantages from the breach between the Emperors of Austria and Russia. Paul, naturally of an uncertain temper, and offended by the management of the last campaign, in which Korsakow had been defeated, and Suwarrow checked, in consequence of their being unsupported by the Austrian army, had withdrawn his troops, so distinguished for their own bravery as well as for the talents of their leader, from the seat of war. But the Austrians, possessing a firmness of character undismayed by defeat, and encouraged by the late success of their arms under the veteran

---

[524] See *Moniteur*, 23 Pluviose, 10th February 1800; and Thibaudeau, tom. i., p. 194.

Melas, had made such gigantic exertions as to counterbalance the loss of their Russian confederates.[525]

Their principal force was in Italy, and it was on the Italian frontier that they meditated a grand effort, by which, supported by the British fleet, they proposed to reduce Genoa, and penetrate across the Var into Provence, where existed a strong body of Royalists ready to take arms, under the command of General Willot, an emigrant officer. It was said the celebrated Pichegru, who, escaped from Guiana, had taken refuge in England, was also with his army, and was proposed as a chief leader of the expected insurrection.

To execute this plan, Melas was placed at the head of an army of 140,000 men. This army was quartered for the winter in the plains of Piedmont, and waited but the approach of spring to commence operations.

Opposed to them, and occupying the country betwixt Genoa and the Var, lay a French army of 40,000 men; the relics of those who had been repeatedly defeated in Italy by Suwarrow. They were quartered in a poor country, and the English squadron, which blockaded the coast, was vigilant in preventing any supplies from being sent to them. Distress was therefore considerable, and the troops were in proportion dispirited and disorganized. Whole corps abandoned their position, contrary to orders; and, with drums beating, and colours flying, returned into France. A proclamation from Napoleon was almost alone sufficient to remedy these disorders. He called on the soldiers, and particularly those corps who had formerly distinguished themselves under his command in his Italian campaigns, to remember the confidence he had once placed in them.[526] The scattered troops returned to their duty, as

---

[525] Thibaudeau, tom. i., p. 182; Jomini, tom. xiii., p. 16, 24.
[526] These disorders gave rise to many general orders from Napoleon; in one of them he said—"The first quality of a soldier is patient endurance of fatigue and privation; valour is but a secondary virtue. Several corps have quitted their positions; they have been deaf to the voice of their officers. Are, then, the heroes of Castiglione, of Rivoli, of Neumark no more? *They* would rather have perished than have deserted their colours. Soldiers, do you complain that your rations have not been regularly distributed? What would you have done, if, like the fourth and twenty second light demi-brigades, you had found yourselves in the midst of the desert, without bread or water, subsisting on horses and camels? *Victory will*

war-horses when dispersed are said to rally and form ranks at the mere sound of the trumpet. Massena, an officer eminent for his acquaintance with the mode of carrying on war in a mountainous country, full of passes and strong positions, was intrusted with the command of the Italian army, which Buonaparte[527] resolved to support in person with the army of reserve.

The French army upon the Rhine possessed as great a superiority over the Austrians, as Melas, on the Italian frontier, enjoyed over Massena. Moreau was placed in the command of a large army, augmented by a strong detachment from that of General Brune, now no longer necessary for the protection of Holland, and by the army of Helvetia, which, after the defeat of Korsakow, was not farther required for the defence of Switzerland. In bestowing this great charge on Moreau, the first consul showed himself superior to the jealousy which might have dissuaded meaner minds from intrusting a rival, whose military skill was often compared with his own, with such an opportunity of distinguishing himself.[528] But Buonaparte, in this and other cases, preferred the employing and profiting by the public service of men of talents, and especially men of military eminence, to any risk which he could run from their rivalry. He had the just confidence in his own powers, never to doubt his supremacy, and trusted to the influence of discipline, and the love of their profession, which induces generals to accept of command even under the administrations of which they disapprove. In this manner he rendered dependant upon himself even those officers, who, averse to the consular form of government, inclined to republican principles. Such were Massena, Brune, Jourdan, Lecourbe, and Championnet. He took care, at the same time, by changing the commands intrusted to them, to break off all combinations or connexions which they might have formed for a new alteration of the government.

---

give us bread, said they; and you—you desert your colours! Soldiers of Italy, a new general commands you; he was always in the foremost ranks, in the moments of your brightest glory; place your confidence in him; he will bring back victory to your colours."—Gourgaud, tom. i., p. 160.

[527] In a proclamation issued to the armies, he said—"Soldiers! it is no longer the frontiers that you are called on to defend, the countries of your enemies are to be invaded. At a fit season I will be in the midst of you, and Europe shall be made to remember that you belong to a valiant race."—Gourgaud, tom. i., p. 162.

[528] Jomini, tom. xiii., p. 35, 43; Thibaudeau, tom. i., p. 182-6: Gourgaud, tom. i., p. 163.

General Moreau was much superior in numbers to Kray, the Austrian who commanded on the Rhine, and received orders to resume the offensive. He was cautious in his tactics, though a most excellent officer, and was startled at the plan sent him by Buonaparte, which directed him to cross the Rhine at Schaffhausen, and, marching on Ulm with his whole force, place himself in the rear of the greater part of the Austrian army. This was one of those schemes, fraught with great victories or great reverses, which Buonaparte delighted to form, and which often requiring much sacrifice of men, occasioned his being called by those who loved him not, a general at the rate of ten thousand men per day. Such enterprises resemble desperate passes in fencing, and must be executed with the same decisive resolution with which they are formed. Few even of Buonaparte's best generals could be trusted with the execution of his master-strokes in tactics, unless under his own immediate superintendence.

Moreau invaded Germany on a more modified plan; and a series of marches, counter-marches, and desperate battles ensued, in which General Kray, admirably supported by the Archduke Ferdinand, made a gallant defence against superior numbers.

SUCCESSES OF MOREAU

In Buonaparte's account of this campaign,[529] he blames Moreau for hesitation and timidity in following up the advantages which he obtained.[530] Yet to a less severe, perhaps to a more impartial judge, Moreau's success might seem satisfactory, since, crossing the Rhine in the end of April, he had his headquarters at Augsburg upon the 15th July, ready either to co-operate with the Italian army, or to march into the heart of the Austrian territory. Nor can it be denied that, during this whole campaign, Moreau kept in view, as a principal object, the protecting the operations of Buonaparte in Italy, and saving that chief, in his dauntless and desperate invasion of the Milanese territory, from the danger which

---

[529] Gourgaud, tom. i., p. 167.
[530] "Moreau did not know the value of *time*; he always passed the day after a battle in total indecision."—Napoleon, *Gourgaud*, tom. i., p. 174.

might have ensued, had Kray found an opportunity of opening a communication with the Austrian army in Italy, and despatching troops to its support.

It may be remarked of these two great generals, that, as enterprise was the characteristic of Buonaparte's movements, prudence was that of Moreau's; and it is not unusual, even when there occur no other motives for rivals undervaluing each other, that the enterprising judge the prudent to be timid, and the prudent account the enterprising rash.

15th July.

It is not ours to decide upon professional questions between men of such superior talents; and, having barely alluded to the topic, we leave Moreau at Augsburg, where he finally concluded an armistice[531] with General Kray, as a consequence of that which Buonaparte had established in Italy after the battle of Marengo. Thus much, therefore, is due in justice to Moreau. His campaign was, on the whole, crowned in its results with distinguished success.[532] And when it is considered, that he was to manœuvre both with reference to the safety of the first consul's operations and his own, it may be doubted whether Buonaparte would, at the time, have thanked him for venturing on more hazardous measures; the result of which might have been either to obtain more brilliant victory for the army of the Rhine, in the event of success, or should they have miscarried, to have ensured the ruin of the army of Italy, as well as of that commanded by Moreau himself. There must have been a wide difference between the part which Moreau ought to act as subsidiary to Buonaparte, (to whom it will presently be seen he despatched a reinforcement of from fifteen to twenty thousand men,) and that which Buonaparte, in obedience to his daring genius, might have himself thought it right to perform. The commander-in-chief may venture much on his own responsibility, which must not be hazarded by a subordinate general, whose motions ought to be regulated upon the general plan of the campaign.

---

[531] For the terms of the armistice, see Gourgaud, tom. i., p. 185.
[532] Jomini, tom. xiii., p. 355, 369; Thibaudeau, tom. i., p. 342.

We return to the operations of Napoleon during one of the most important campaigns of his life, and in which he added—if that were still possible—to the high military reputation he had acquired.

PLAN OF THE CAMPAIGN

In committing the charge of the campaign upon the Rhine to Moreau, the first consul had reserved for himself the task of bringing back victory to the French standards, on the fields in which he won his earliest laurels. His plan of victory again included a passage of the Alps, as boldly and unexpectedly as in 1795, but in a different direction. That earlier period had this resemblance to the present, that, on both occasions, the Austrians menaced Genoa; but in 1800, it was only from the Italian frontier and the Col di Tende, whereas, in 1795, the enemy were in possession of the mountains of Savoy, above Genoa. Switzerland, too, formerly neutral, and allowing no passage for armies, was now as open to the march of French troops as any of their own provinces, and of this Buonaparte determined to avail himself. He was aware of the Austrian plan of taking Genoa and entering Provence; and he formed the daring resolution to put himself at the head of the army of reserve, surmount the line of the Alps, even where they are most difficult of access, and, descending into Italy, place himself in the rear of the Austrian army, interrupt their communications, carry off their magazines, parks, and hospitals, coop them up betwixt his own army and that of Massena, which was in their front, and compel them to battle, in a situation where defeat must be destruction. But to accomplish this daring movement, it was necessary to march a whole army over the highest chain of mountains in Europe, by roads which afford but a dangerous passage to the solitary traveller, and through passes where one man can do more to defend, than ten to force their way. Artillery was to be carried through sheep-paths and over precipices impracticable to wheel-carriages; ammunition and baggage were to be transported at the same disadvantages; and provisions were to be conveyed through a country poor in itself, and inhabited by a nation which had every cause to be hostile to France, and might therefore be expected prompt to avail themselves of any opportunity which should occur of revenging themselves for her late aggressions.[533]

The strictest secrecy was necessary, to procure even the opportunity of attempting this audacious plan of operations; and to ensure this secrecy, Buonaparte had recourse to a singular mode of deceiving the enemy. It was made as public as possible, by orders, decrees, proclamations, and the like, that the first consul was to place himself at the head of the army of reserve, and that it was to assemble at Dijon. Accordingly, a numerous staff was sent, and much apparent bustle took place in assembling there six or seven thousand men with great pomp and fracas. These, as the spies of Austria truly reported to their employers, were either conscripts, or veterans unfit for service; and caricatures were published of the first consul reviewing troops composed of children and disabled soldiers, which was ironically termed his army of reserve.[534] When an army so composed was reviewed by the first consul himself with great ceremony, it impressed a general belief that Buonaparte was only endeavouring, by making a show of force, to divert the Austrians from their design upon Genoa, and thus his real purpose was effectually concealed. Bulletins, too, were privately circulated by the agents of police, as if scattered by the Royalists, in which specious arguments were used to prove that the French army of reserve neither did, nor could exist—and these also were designed to withdraw attention from the various points on which it was at the very moment collecting.[535]

The pacification of the west of France had placed many good troops at Buonaparte's disposal, which had previously been engaged against the Chouans; the quiet state of Paris permitted several regiments to be detached from the capital. New levies were made with the utmost celerity; and the divisions of the army of reserve were organized separately, and at different places of rendezvous, but ready to form a junction when they should receive the signal for commencing operations.

---

[533] Gourgaud, tom. i., p. 261.
[534] "Europe was full of caricatures. One of them represented a boy of twelve years of age, and an invalid with a wooden leg; underneath which was written 'Buonaparte's army of reserve.'"—Napoleon, *Gourgaud*, tom. i., p. 262.
[535] Gourgaud, tom. i., p. 263.

Chapter XIX

The Chief Consul leaves Paris on 6th May, 1800—Has an Interview with Necker at Geneva on 8th—Arrives at Lausanne on the 13th—Various Corps put in motion to cross the Alps—Napoleon, at the head of the Main Army, marches on the 15th, and ascends Mont St. Bernard—On the 16th, the Vanguard takes possession of Aosta—Fortress and Town of Bard threaten to baffle the whole plan—The Town is captured—and Napoleon contrives to send his Artillery through it, under the fire of the Fort, his Infantry and Cavalry passing over the Albaredo—Lannes carries Ivrea—Recapitulation—Operations of the Austrian General Melas—At the commencement of the Campaign, Melas advances towards Genoa—Actions betwixt him and Massena—In March, Lord Keith blockades Genoa—Melas compelled to retreat—Enters Nice—Recalled from thence by the news of Napoleon's having crossed Mont St. Bernard—Genoa surrenders—Buonaparte enters Milan—Battle of Montebello—The Chief Consul is joined by Desaix—Battle of Marengo on the 14th—Death of Desaix—Capitulation on the 15th, by which Genoa, &c., are yielded—Napoleon returns to Paris on the 2d July.

On the 6th of May 1800, seeking to renew the fortunes of France, now united with his own, the chief consul left Paris, and, having reviewed the pretended army of reserve at Dijon on the 7th, arrived on the 8th at Geneva. Here he had an interview with the celebrated financier Necker. There was always doomed to be some misunderstanding between Buonaparte and this accomplished family. Madame de Staël believed that Buonaparte spoke to her father with confidence on his future prospects; while the first consul affirms that Necker seemed to expect to be intrusted with the management of the French finances, and that they parted with mutual indifference, if not dislike.[536] Napoleon had a more interesting conversation with General Marescot, despatched to survey Mont Bernard, and who had, with great difficulty, ascended as far as the convent of the Chartreux. "Is the route practicable?" said Buonaparte.—"It is barely possible to pass," replied the engineer.—"Let us set forward then," said Napoleon, and the extraordinary march was commenced.[537]

On the 13th, arriving at Lausanne, Buonaparte joined the van of his real army of reserve, which consisted of six effective regiments, commanded by the celebrated Lannes. These corps, together with the rest of the troops intended for the expedition, had been assembled from their several positions by forced marches. Carnot, the minister at war, attended the first consul at Lausanne, to report to him that 15,000, or from that to the number of 20,000 men, detached from Moreau's army, were in the act of descending on Italy by St. Gothard, in order to form the left wing of his army.[538] The whole army, in its various divisions, was now united under the command of Berthier nominally, as general-in-chief, though in reality under that of the first consul himself. This was in compliance with a regulation of the Constitution, which rendered it inconsistent for the first consul to command in person.[539] It was a form which Buonaparte at present evaded, and afterwards laid aside; thinking truly, that the name, as well as office of generalissimo, was most fittingly vested in his own person, since, though it might not be the loftiest of his titles, it was that which best expressed his power. The army might amount to 60,000 men, but one-third of the number were conscripts.

---

[536] "The famous Necker solicited the honour of being presented to the first consul. In all he said he suffered it to appear, that he wished and hoped to have the management of the finances. The first consul was but indifferently pleased with him."—Napoleon, *Gourgaud*, tom. i., p. 264. "During this conversation, the first consul made a rather agreeable impression on my father, by the confidential way in which he spoke to him of his future plans."—Mad. De Staël, tom. ii., p. 281.
[537] Thibaudeau, tom. vi., p. 260; Jomini, tom. xiii., p. 176.
[538] Jomini, tom. xiii., p. 177.
[539] Gourgaud, tom. i., p. 260.

PASSAGE OF THE GREAT ST. BERNARD

During the interval between the 15th and 18th of May, all the columns of the French army were put into motion to cross the Alps. Thurreau, at the head of 5000 men, directed his march by Mont Cenis, on Exilles and Susa. A similar division, commanded by Chabran, took the route of the Little St. Bernard. Buonaparte himself, on the 15th, at the head of the main body of his army, consisting of 30,000 men and upwards, marched from Lausanne to the little village called St. Pierre, at which point there ended every thing resembling a practicable road. An immense, and apparently inaccessible mountain, reared its head among general desolation and eternal frost; while precipices, glaciers, ravines, and a boundless extent of faithless snows, which the slightest concussion of the air converts into avalanches capable of burying armies in their descent, appeared to forbid access to all living things but the chamois, and his scarce less wild pursuer. Yet foot by foot, and man by man, did the French soldiers proceed to ascend this formidable barrier, which nature had erected in vain to limit human ambition. The view of the valley, emphatically called "of Desolation," where nothing is to be seen but snow and sky, had no terrors for the first consul and his army. They advanced up paths hitherto only practised by hunters, or here and there a hardy pedestrian, the infantry loaded with their arms, and in full military equipment, the cavalry leading their horses. The musical bands played from time to time at the head of the regiments, and, in places of unusual difficulty, the drums beat a charge, as if to encourage the soldiers to encounter the opposition of Nature herself. The artillery, without which they could not have done service, were deposited in trunks of trees hollowed out for the purpose. Each was dragged by a hundred men, and the troops, making it a point of honour to bring forward their guns, accomplished this severe duty, not with cheerfulness only, but with enthusiasm. The carriages were taken to pieces, and harnessed on the backs of mules, or committed to the soldiers, who relieved each other in the task of bearing them with levers; and the ammunition was transported in the same manner. While one half of the soldiers were thus engaged, the others were obliged to carry the muskets, cartridge-boxes, knapsacks, and provisions of their comrades, as well as their own. Each man, so loaded, was calculated to carry from sixty to seventy pounds weight, up icy precipices, where a man totally without encumbrance could ascend but slowly. Probably no troops save the French could have endured the fatigue of such a march; and no other general than Buonaparte would have ventured to require it at their hand.[540]

He set out a considerable time after the march had begun, alone, excepting his guide. He is described by the Swiss peasant who attended him in that capacity, as wearing his usual simple dress, a grey surtout, and three-cornered hat. He travelled in silence, save a few short and hasty questions about the country, addressed to his guide from time to time. When these were answered, he relapsed into silence. There was a gloom on his brow, corresponding with the weather, which was wet and dismal. His countenance had acquired, during his Eastern campaigns, a swart complexion, which added to his natural severe gravity, and the Swiss peasant who guided him felt fear as he looked on him.[541] Occasionally his route was stopt by some temporary obstacle occasioned by a halt in the artillery or baggage; his commands on such occasions were peremptorily given, and instantly obeyed, his very look seeming enough to silence all objection, and remove every difficulty.

The army now arrived at that singular convent, where, with courage equal to their own, but flowing from a much higher source, the monks of St. Bernard have fixed their dwellings among the everlasting snows, that they may afford succour and hospitality to the forlorn travellers in those dreadful wastes. Hitherto the soldiers had had no refreshment, save when they dipt a morsel of biscuit amongst the snow. The good fathers of the convent, who possess considerable magazines of provisions, distributed bread and cheese,

---

[540] Jomini, tom. xiii., p. 184; Thibaudeau, tom. vi., p. 264; Gourgaud, tom. i., p. 267; Dumas, tom. ii.
[541] Apparently the guide who conducted him from the Grand Chartreux found the Chief Consul in better humour, for Buonaparte says, he conversed freely with him, and expressed some wishes with respect to a little farm, &c. which he was able to gratify. [Gourgaud, tom. i., p. 268.] To his guide from Martigny to St. Pierre, he was also liberal; but the only specimen of his conversation which the latter remembered, was, when shaking the rain water from his hat, he exclaimed, "There! see what I have done in your mountains—spoiled my new hat. Pshaw, I will find another on the other side." For these and other interesting anecdotes, see Mr. Tennant's "Tour through the Netherlands, Holland, Germany, Switzerland," &c.—S.

and a cup of wine, to each soldier as he passed, which was more acceptable in their situation, than, according to one who shared their fatigues,[542] would have been the gold of Mexico.[543]

The descent on the other side of Mont St. Bernard was as difficult to the infantry as the ascent had been, and still more so to the cavalry. It was, however, accomplished without any material loss, and the army took up their quarters for the night, after having marched fourteen French leagues. The next morning, 16th May, the vanguard took possession of Aosta, a village of Piedmont, from which extends the valley of the same name, watered by the river Dorea, a country pleasant in itself, but rendered delightful by its contrast with the horrors which had been left behind.

Thus was achieved the celebrated passage of Mont St. Bernard, on the particulars of which we have dwelt the more willingly, because, although a military operation of importance, they do not involve the unwearied details of human slaughter, to which our narrative must now return.

BARD

Where the opposition of Nature to Napoleon's march appeared to cease, that of man commenced. A body of Austrians at Chatillon were overpowered and defeated by Lannes; but the strong fortress of Bard offered more serious opposition. This little citadel is situated upon an almost perpendicular rock, rising out of the river Dorea, at a place where the valley of Aosta is rendered so very narrow by the approach of two mountains to each other, that the fort and walled town of Bard entirely close up the entrance. This formidable obstacle threatened for the moment to shut up the French in a valley, where their means of subsistence must have been

---

[542] Joseph Petit, Fourrier des grenadiers de la garde, author of "Marengo, ou Campagne d'Italie," 8vo, an. ix.—S.
[543] "Never did greater regularity preside at a distribution. Each one appreciated the foresight of which he had been the object. Not a soldier left the ranks; not a straggler was to be seen. The first consul expressed his gratitude to the Community, and ordered 100,000 francs to be delivered to the monastery, in remembrance of the service it had rendered him."—*Memoirs of Savary*, vol. i., p. 165.

speedily exhausted. General Lannes made a desperate effort to carry the fort by assault; but the advanced guard of the attacking party were destroyed by stones, musketry and hand-grenades, and the attempt was relinquished.

Buonaparte in person went now to reconnoitre, and for that purpose ascended a huge rock called Albaredo, being a precipice on the side of one of the mountains which form the pass, from the summit of which he could look down into the town, and into the fortress. He detected a possibility of taking the town by storm, though he judged the fort was too strong to be obtained by a coup-de-main. The town was accordingly carried by escalade; but the French who obtained possession of it had little cover from the artillery of the fort, which fired furiously on the houses where they endeavoured to shelter themselves, and which the Austrians might have entirely demolished but for respect to the inhabitants. Meanwhile, Buonaparte availed himself of the diversion to convey a great part of his army in single files, horse as well as foot, by a precarious path formed by the pioneers over the tremendous Albaredo, and so down on the other side, in this manner avoiding the cannon of fort Bard.[544]

Still a most important difficulty remained. It was impossible, at least without great loss of time, to carry the French artillery over the Albaredo, while, without artillery, it was impossible to move against the Austrians, and every hope of the campaign must be given up.

In the meantime, the astonished commandant of the fort, to whom the apparition of this large army was like enchantment, despatched messenger after messenger to warn Melas, then opposed to Suchet, on the Var, that a French army of 30,000 men and upwards, descending from the Alps by ways hitherto deemed impracticable for military movements, had occupied the valley of Aosta, and were endeavouring to debouche by a path of steps cut in the Albaredo. But he pledged himself to his commander-in-chief,

---

[544] "The infantry and cavalry passed one by one, up the path of the mountain, which the first consul had climbed, and where no horse had ever stepped; it was a way known to none but goatherds."—Gourgaud, tom. i., p. 271.

that not a single gun or ammunition-waggon should pass through the town; and as it was impossible to drag these along the Albaredo, he concluded, that, being without his artillery, Buonaparte would not venture to descend into the plain.

But, while the commandant of Bard thus argued, he was mistaken in his premises, though right in his inference. The artillery of the French army had already passed through the town of Bard, and under the guns of the citadel, without being discovered to have done so. This important manœuvre was accomplished by previously laying the street with dung and earth, over which the pieces of cannon, concealed under straw and branches of trees, were dragged by men in profound silence. The garrison, though they did not suspect what was going on, fired nevertheless upon some vague suspicion, and killed and wounded artillerymen in sufficient number to show it would have been impossible to pass under a severe and sustained discharge from the ramparts.[545] It seems singular that the commandant had kept up no intelligence with the town. Any signal previously agreed upon—a light shown in a window, for example—would have detected such a stratagem.

A division of conscripts, under General Chabran, was left to reduce fort Bard, which continued to hold out, until, at the expense of great labour, batteries were established on the top of the Albaredo, by which it was commanded, and a heavy gun placed on the steeple of the church, when it was compelled to surrender. It is not fruitless to observe, that the resistance of this small place, which had been overlooked or undervalued in the plan of the campaign, was very near rendering the march over Mont St. Bernard worse than useless, and might have occasioned the destruction of all the chief consul's army.[546] So little are even the most distinguished generals able to calculate with certainty upon all the chances of war.

From this dangerous pass, the vanguard of Buonaparte now advanced down the valley to Ivrea, where Lannes carried the town

---

[545] Gourgaud, tom. i., p. 271; Jomini, tom. xiii., p. 185.
[546] "Supposing it had proved quite impossible to pass the artillery through the town of Bard, would the French army have repassed the Great Saint Bernard? No: it would have debouched as far as Ivrea—a movement which would necessarily have recalled Melas from Nice."—Napoleon, *Gourgaud*, tom. i., p 272.

by storm, and a second time combated and defeated the Austrian division which had defended it, when reinforced and situated on a strong position at Romano. The roads to Turin and Milan were now alike open to Buonaparte—he had only to decide which he chose to take. Meanwhile, he made a halt of four days at Ivrea, to refresh the troops after their fatigues, and to prepare them for future enterprises.[547]

During this space, the other columns of his army were advancing to form a junction with that of the main body, according to the plan of the campaign. Thurreau, who had passed the Alps by the route of Mont Cenis, had taken the forts of Susa and La Brunette. On the other hand, the large corps detached by Carnot from Moreau's army, were advancing by Mont St. Gothard and the Simplon, to support the operations of the first consul, of whose army they were to form the left wing. But ere we prosecute the account of Buonaparte's movements during this momentous campaign, it is necessary to trace the previous operations of Melas, and the situation in which that Austrian general now found himself.

OPERATIONS OF MELAS

It has been already stated, that, at the commencement of this campaign of 1800, the Austrians entertained the highest hopes that their Italian army, having taken Genoa and Nice, might penetrate into Provence by crossing the frontier at the Var, and perhaps make themselves masters of Toulon and Marseilles. To realize these hopes, Melas, having left in Piedmont a sufficient force, as he deemed it, to guard the passes of the Alps, had advanced towards Genoa, which Massena prepared to cover and defend. A number of severe and desperate actions took place between these generals; but being a war of posts, and fought in a very mountainous and difficult country, it was impossible by any skill of combination to ensure on any occasion more than partial success, since co-operation of movements upon a great and extensive scale was prohibited by the character of the ground. There was much hard fighting, however, in

---

[547] Jomini, tom. xiii., p. 188; Gourgaud, tom. i., p. 274.

which, though more of the Austrians were slain, yet the loss was most severely felt by the French, whose numbers were inferior.

In the month of March, the English fleet, under Lord Keith, appeared, as we have already hinted, before Genoa, and commenced a blockade, which strictly prevented access to the port to all vessels loaded with provisions, or other necessaries, for the besieged city.

On the 6th of April, Melas, by a grand movement, took Vado, and intersected the French line. Suchet, who commanded Massena's left wing, was cut off from that general, and thrown back on France. Marches, manœuvres, and bloody combats, followed each other in close detail; but the French, though obtaining advantages in several of the actions, could never succeed in restoring the communication between Suchet and Massena. Finally, while the former retreated towards France, and took up a line on Borghetta, the latter was compelled to convert his army into a garrison, and to shut himself up in Genoa, or at least encamp in a position close under its ramparts. Melas, in the meantime, approached the city more closely, when Massena, in a desperate sally, drove the Austrians from their advanced posts, forced them to retreat, made prisoners twelve hundred men, and carried off some warlike trophies. But the French were exhausted by their very success, and obliged to remain within, or under the walls of the city, where the approach of famine began to be felt. Men were already compelled to have recourse to the flesh of horses, dogs, and other unclean animals, and it was seen that the place must soon be necessarily obliged to surrender.[548]

Satisfied with the approaching fall of Genoa, Melas, in the beginning of May, left the prosecution of the blockade to General Ott, and moved himself against Suchet, whom he drove before him in disorder, and who, overborne by numbers, retreated towards the French frontier. On the 11th of May, Melas entered Nice, and thus commenced the purposed invasion of the French frontier. On the 14th, the Austrians again attacked Suchet, who now had concentrated his forces upon the Var, in hopes to protect the French territory. Finding this a more difficult task than he expected,

---

[548] Gourgaud, tom. i., p. 202; Thibaudeau, tom. vi., p 286.

Melas next prepared to pass the Var higher up, and thus to turn the position occupied by Suchet.

But on the 21st, the Austrian veteran received intelligence which put a stop to all his operations against Suchet, and recalled him to Italy to face a much more formidable antagonist. Tidings arrived that the first consul of France had crossed St. Bernard, had extricated himself from the valley of Aosta, and was threatening to overrun Piedmont and the Milanese territory. These tidings were as unexpected as embarrassing. The artillery, the equipage, the provisions of Melas, together with his communications with Italy, were all at the mercy of this unexpected invader, who, though his force was not accurately known, must have brought with him an army more than adequate to destroy the troops left to guard the frontier; who, besides, were necessarily divided, and exposed to be beaten in detail. Yet, if Melas marched back into Piedmont against Buonaparte, he must abandon the attack upon Suchet, and raise the blockade of Genoa, when that important city was just on the eve of surrender.

Persevering in the belief that the French army of reserve could not exceed twenty thousand men, or thereabouts, in number, and supposing that the principal, if not the sole object of the first consul's daring irruption, was to raise the siege of Genoa, and disconcert the invasion of Provence, Melas resolved on marching himself against Buonaparte with such forces, as, united with those he had left in Italy, might be of power to face the French army, according to his computation of its probable strength. At the same time, he determined to leave before Genoa an army sufficient to ensure its fall, and a corps of observation in front of Suchet, by means of which he might easily resume his plans against that general, so soon as the chief consul should be defeated or driven back.

The corps of observation already mentioned was under the command of General Ellsnitz, strongly posted upon the Roye, and secured by intrenchments. It served at once to watch Suchet, and to cover the siege of Genoa from any attempts to relieve the city, which might be made in the direction of France.[549]

MASSENA SURRENDERS GENOA

Massena, in the meantime, no sooner perceived the besieging army weakened by the departure of Melas, than he conceived the daring plan of a general attack on the forces of Ott, who was left to carry on the siege. The attempt was unfortunate. The French were defeated, and Soult, who had joined Massena, was wounded and made prisoner. Yet Genoa still held out. An officer had found his way into the place, brought intelligence of Buonaparte's descent upon Piedmont, and inspired all with a new spirit of resistance. Still, however, extreme want prevailed in the city, and the hope of delivery seemed distant. The soldiers received little food, the inhabitants less, the Austrian prisoners, of whom they had about 8000 in Genoa, almost none.[550] At length, the situation of things seemed desperate. The numerous population of Genoa rose in the extremity of their despair, and called for a surrender. Buonaparte, they said, was not wont to march so slowly; he would have been before the walls sooner, if he was to appear at all; he must have been defeated or driven back by the superior force of Melas. They demanded the surrender of the place, therefore, which Massena no longer found himself in a condition to oppose.[551]

Yet could that brave general have suspended this measure a few hours longer, he would have been spared the necessity of making it at all. General Ott had just received commands from Melas to raise the blockade with all despatch, and to fall back upon the Po, in order to withstand Buonaparte, who, in unexpected strength, was marching upon Milan. The Austrian staff-officer who

---

[549] Jomini, tom. xiii., p. 198.
[550] Napoleon says, that Massena proposed to General Ott to send in provisions to feed these unhappy men, pledging his honour they should be used to no other purpose, and that General Ott was displeased with Lord Keith for declining to comply with a proposal so utterly unknown in the usages of war.—S. [Gourgaud, tom. i., p. 227.] It is difficult to give credit to this story.
[551] Jomini, tom. xiii., p. 231; Gourgaud, tom. i., p. 228. See also Thiébaut, Journal Historique du Siège de Gênes.

brought the order, had just received his audience of General Ott, when General Andrieux, presenting himself on the part of Massena, announced the French general's desire to surrender the place, if his troops were permitted to march out with their arms. There was no time to debate upon terms; and those granted to Massena by Melas were so unusually favourable, that perhaps they should have made him aware of the precarious state of the besieging army.[552] He was permitted to evacuate Genoa without laying down his arms, and the convention was signed 5th June, 1800. Meantime, at this agitating and interesting period, events of still greater importance than those which concerned the fate of the once princely Genoa, were taking place with frightful rapidity.

Melas, with about one half of his army, had retired from his operations in the Genoese territory, and retreated on Turin by the way of Coni, where he fixed his headquarters, expecting that Buonaparte would either advance to possess himself of the capital of Piedmont, or that he would make an effort to relieve Genoa. In the first instance, Melas deemed himself strong enough to receive the first consul; in the second, to pursue him, and in either, to assemble such numerous forces as might harass and embarrass either his advance or his retreat. But Buonaparte's plan of the campaign was different from what Melas had anticipated. He had formed the resolution to pass the rivers Sesia and Ticino, and thus leaving Turin and Melas behind him, to push straight for Milan, and form a junction with the division of about 20,000 men, detached from the right wing of Moreau's army, which, commanded by Moncey, were on their road to join him, having crossed the mountains by the route of St. Gothard. It was necessary, however, to disguise his purpose from the sagacious veteran.

With this view, ere Buonaparte broke up from Ivrea, Lannes, who had commanded his vanguard with so much gallantry, victorious at Romano, seemed about to improve his advantage. He had marched on Chiavaso, and seizing on a number of boats and small vessels, appeared desirous to construct a bridge over the Po at

---

[552] "Massena ought to have broken off, upon the certainty that within four or five days the blockade would be raised; in fact, it would have been raised twelve hours after."—Napoleon, *Gourgaud*, tom. i., p. 241.

that place. This attracted the attention of Melas. It might be equally a preliminary to an attack on Turin, or a movement towards Genoa. But as the Austrian general was at the same time alarmed by the descent of General Thurreau's division from Mont Cenis, and their capture of Susa and La Brunette, Turin seemed ascertained to be the object of the French; and Melas acted on this idea. He sent a strong force to oppose the establishment of the bridge, and while his attention was thus occupied, Buonaparte was left to take the road to Milan unmolested. Vercelli was occupied by the cavalry under Murat, and the Sesia was crossed without obstacle. The Ticino, a broad and rapid river, offered more serious opposition; but the French found four or five small boats, in which they pushed across an advanced party under General Gerard. The Austrians, who opposed the passage, were in a great measure cavalry, who could not act on account of the woody and impracticable character of the bank of the river. The passage was accomplished; and, upon the 2d of June, Buonaparte entered Milan,[553] where he was received with acclamations by a numerous class of citizens, who looked for the re-establishment of the Cisalpine Republic. The Austrians were totally unprepared for this movement. Pavia fell into the hands of the French; Lodi and Cremona were occupied, and Pizzighitone was invested.[554]

Meanwhile, Buonaparte, fixing his residence in the ducal palace of Milan, employed himself in receiving the deputations of various public bodies, and in re-organizing the Cisalpine government, while he waited impatiently to be joined by Moncey and his division, from Mont Saint Gothard. They arrived at length, but marching more slowly than accorded with the fiery promptitude of the first consul, who was impatient to relieve the blockade of Genoa, which place he concluded still held out. He now issued a proclamation to his troops, in which he described, as the result of

---

[553] Jomini, tom. xiii., p. 210; Gourgaud, tom. i., p. 279.
[554] "One of the first persons who presented themselves to the eyes of the Milanese, whom enthusiasm and curiosity led by all the by-roads to meet the French army, was General Buonaparte. The people of Milan would not believe it: it had been reported that he had died in the Red Sea, and that it was one of his brothers who now commanded the French army."—Napoleon, *Gourgaud*, tom. i., p. 280.

the efforts he expected from them, "Cloudless glory and solid peace."[555] On the 9th of June his armies were again in motion.

SITUATION OF MELAS

Melas, an excellent officer, had at the same time some of the slowness imputed to his countrymen, or of the irresolution incident to the advanced age of eighty years,—for so old was the opponent of Buonaparte, then in the very prime of human life,—or, as others suspect, it may have been orders from Vienna which detained the Austrian general so long at Turin, where he lay in a great measure inactive. It is true, that on receiving notice of Buonaparte's march on Milan, he instantly despatched orders to General Ott, as we have already stated, to raise the siege of Genoa, and join him with all possible speed; but it seemed, that in the meantime, he might have disquieted Buonaparte's lines of communication, by acting upon the river Dorea, attacking Ivrea, in which the French had left much baggage and artillery, and relieving the fort of Bard. Accordingly, he made an attempt of this kind, by detaching 6000 men to Chiavaso, who were successful in delivering some Austrian prisoners at that place; but Ivrea proved strong enough to resist them, and the French retaining possession of that place, the Austrians could not occupy the valley of the Dorea, or relieve the besieged fortress of Bard.[556]

The situation of Melas now became critical. His communications with the left, or north bank of the Po, were entirely cut off, and by a line stretching from Fort Bard to Placentia, the French occupied the best and fairest share of the north of Italy, while he found himself confined to Piedmont. The Austrian army, besides, was divided into two parts,—one under Ott, which was still near Genoa, that had so lately surrendered to them,—one with Melas himself, which was at Turin. Neither were agreeably situated. That of Genoa was observed on its right by Suchet, whose army, reinforced with the garrison which, retaining their arms, evacuated that city under Massena, might soon be expected to renew the

---

[555] Gourgaud, tom. i., p. 282.
[556] Gourgaud, tom. i., p. 283.

offensive. There was, therefore, the greatest risk, that Buonaparte, pushing a strong force across the Po, might attack and destroy either the division of Ott, or that of Melas himself, before they were able to form a junction. To prevent such a catastrophe, Ott received orders to march forward on the Ticino, while Melas, moving towards Alexandria, prepared to resume his communications with his lieutenant-general.

Buonaparte, on his part, was anxious to relieve Genoa; news of the fall of which had not reached him. With this view he resolved to force his passage over the Po, and move against the Austrians, who were found to occupy in strength the villages of Casteggio and Montebello. These troops proved to be the greater part of the very army which he expected to find before Genoa, and which was commanded by Ott, but which had moved westward, in conformity to the orders of Melas.

9th June.

General Lannes, who led the vanguard of the French, as usual, was attacked early in the morning, by a superior force, which he had much difficulty in resisting. The nature of the ground gave advantage to the Austrian cavalry, and the French were barely able to support their charges. At length the division of Victor came up to support Lannes, and the victory became no longer doubtful, though the Austrians fought most obstinately. The fields being covered with tall crops of grain, and especially of rye, the different bodies were frequently hid until they found themselves at the bayonet's point, without having had any previous opportunity to estimate each other's force; a circumstance which led to much close fighting, and necessarily to much slaughter. At length the Austrians retreated, leaving the field of battle covered with their dead, and above 5000 prisoners in the hands of their enemies.[557]

---

[557] Gourgaud, tom. i., p. 287; Thibaudeau, tom. vi., p. 300. At the battle of Montebello, which afterwards gave him his title, General Lannes added to his already high reputation. In describing the desperate conflict—"bones," he said, "crashed in my division; like hailstones against windows."

General Ott rallied the remains of his army under the walls of Tortona. From the prisoners taken at the battle of Montebello, as this action was called, Buonaparte learned, for the first time, the surrender of Genoa, which apprised him that he was too late for the enterprise which he had meditated. He therefore halted his army for three days in the position of Stradella, unwilling to advance into the open plain of Marengo, and trusting that Melas would find himself compelled to give him battle in the position which he had chosen, as most unfavourable for the Austrian cavalry. He despatched messengers to Suchet, commanding him to cross the mountains by the Col di Cadibona, and march on the river Scrivia, which would place him in the rear of the Austrians.

DESAIX—MARENGO

Even during the very battle of Montebello, the chief consul was joined by Desaix, who had just arrived from Egypt. Landed at Frejus, after a hundred interruptions, that seemed as if intended to withhold him from the fate he was about to meet, he had received letters from Buonaparte, inviting him to come to him without delay. The tone of the letters expressed discontent and embarrassment. "He has gained all," said Desaix, who was much attached to Buonaparte, "and yet he is not happy." Immediately afterwards, on reading the account of his march over St. Bernard, he added, "He will leave us nothing to do." He immediately set out post to place himself under the command of his ancient general, and, as it eventually proved, to encounter an early death. They had an interesting conversation on the subject of Egypt, to which Buonaparte continued to cling, as to a matter in which his own fame was intimately and inseparately concerned. Desaix immediately received the command of the division hitherto under that of Boudet.[558]

In the meanwhile, the headquarters of Melas had been removed from Turin, and fixed at Alexandria for the space of two days; yet he did not, as Buonaparte had expected, attempt to move forward on the French position at Stradella, in order to force his

---

[558] Gourgaud, tom. i., p. 289.

way to Mantua; so that the first consul was obliged to advance towards Alexandria, apprehensive lest the Austrians should escape from him, and either, by a march to the left flank, move for the Ticino, cross that river, and, by seizing Milan, open a communication with Austria in that direction; or, by marching to the right, and falling back on Genoa, overwhelm Suchet, and take a position, the right of which might be covered by that city, while the sea was open for supplies and provisions, and their flank protected by the British squadron.

Either of these movements might have been attended with alarming consequences; and Napoleon, impatient lest his enemy should give him the slip, advanced his headquarters on the 12th to Voghera, and on the 13th to St. Juliano, in the midst of the great plain of Marengo. As he still saw nothing of the enemy, the chief consul concluded that Melas had actually retreated from Alexandria, having, notwithstanding the temptation afforded by the level ground around him, preferred withdrawing, most probably to Genoa, to the hazard of a battle. He was still more confirmed in this belief, when, pushing forward as far as the village of Marengo, he found it occupied only by an Austrian rear-guard, which offered no persevering defence against the French, but retreated from the village without much opposition. The chief consul could no longer doubt that Melas had eluded him, by marching off by one of his flanks, and probably by his right. He gave orders to Desaix, whom he had intrusted with the command of the reserve, to march towards Rivolta with a view to observe the communications with Genoa; and in this manner the reserve was removed half a day's march from the rest of the army, which had like to have produced most sinister effects upon the event of the great battle that followed.

MARENGO

Contrary to what Buonaparte had anticipated, the Austrian general, finding the first consul in his front, and knowing that Suchet was in his rear, had adopted, with the consent of a council of war, the resolution of trying the fate of arms in a general battle. It was a bold, but not a rash resolution. The Austrians were more numerous than the French in infantry and artillery; much superior in cavalry, both in point of numbers and of discipline; and it has been already said, that the extensive plain of Marengo was favourable for the use of that description of force. Melas, therefore, on the evening of the 13th, concentrated his forces in front of Alexandria, divided by the river Bormida from the purposed field of fight; and Napoleon, undeceived concerning the intentions of his enemy, made with all haste the necessary preparations to receive battle, and failed not to send orders to Desaix to return as speedily as possible and join the army. That general was so far advanced on his way towards Rivolta before these counter orders reached him, that his utmost haste only brought him back after the battle had lasted several hours.

June 14.

Buonaparte's disposition was as follows:—The village of Marengo was occupied by the divisions of Gardanne and Chambarlhac. Victor, with other two divisions, and commanding the whole, was prepared to support them. He extended his left as far as Castel-Ceriolo, a small village which lies almost parallel with Marengo. Behind this first line was placed a brigade of cavalry, under Kellermann, ready to protect the flanks of the line, or to debouche through the intervals, if opportunity served, and attack the enemy. About a thousand yards in the rear of the first line was stationed the second, under Lannes, supported by Champeaux's brigade of cavalry. At the same distance, in the rear of Lannes, was placed a strong reserve, or third line, consisting of the division of Carra St. Cyr, and the consular guard, at the head of whom was Buonaparte himself. Thus the French were drawn up on this memorable day in three distinct divisions, each composed of a *corps d'armée*, distant about three-quarters of a mile in the rear of each other.

The force which the French had in the field in the commencement of the day, was above twenty thousand men; the reserve, under Desaix, upon its arrival, might make the whole amount to thirty thousand. The Austrians attacked with nearly forty thousand troops. Both armies were in high spirits, determined to fight, and each confident in their general—the Austrians in the bravery and experience of Melas, the French in the genius and talents of Buonaparte. The immediate stake was the possession of Italy, but it was impossible to guess how many yet more important consequences the event of the day might involve. Thus much seemed certain, that the battle must be decisive, and that defeat must prove destruction to the party who should sustain it. Buonaparte, if routed, could hardly have accomplished his retreat upon Milan; and Melas, if defeated, had Suchet in his rear. The fine plain on which the French were drawn up, seemed lists formed by nature for such an encounter, when the fate of kingdoms was at issue.

Early in the morning the Austrians crossed the Bormida, in three columns, by three military bridges, and advanced in the same order. The right and the centre columns, consisting of infantry, were commanded by Generals Haddick and Kaine; the left, composed entirely of light troops and cavalry, made a detour round Castel-Ceriolo, the village mentioned as forming the extreme right of the French position. About seven in the morning, Haddick attacked Marengo with fury, and Gardanne's division, after fighting bravely, proved inadequate to its defence. Victor supported Gardanne, and endeavoured to cover the village by an oblique movement. Melas, who commanded in person the central column of the Austrians, moved to support Haddick; and by their united efforts, the village of Marengo, after having been once or twice lost and won, was finally carried.

The broken divisions of Victor and Gardanne, driven out of Marengo, endeavoured to rally on the second line, commanded by Lannes. This was about nine o'clock. While one Austrian column manœuvred to turn Lannes's flank, in which they could not succeed, another, with better fortune, broke through the centre of Victor's division, in a considerable degree disordered them, and thus uncovering Lannes's left wing, compelled him to retreat. He was able to do so in tolerably good order; but not so the broken troops of Victor on the left, who fled to the rear in great confusion. The column of Austrian cavalry who had come round Castel-Ceriolo, now appeared on the field, and threatened the right of Lannes, which alone remained standing firm. Napoleon detached two battalions of the consular guard from the third line, or reserve, which, forming squares behind the right wing of Lannes, supported its resistance, and withdrew from it in part the attention of the enemy's cavalry. The chief consul himself, whose post was distinguished by the furred caps of a guard of two hundred grenadiers, brought up Monnier's division, which had but now entered the field at the moment of extreme need, being the advance of Desaix's reserve, returned from their half day's march towards Rivolta. These were, with the guards, directed to support Lannes's right wing, and a brigade detached from them was thrown into Castel-Ceriolo, which now became the point of support on Buonaparte's extreme right, and which the Austrians, somewhat unaccountably, had omitted to occupy in force when their left column passed it in the beginning of the engagement. Buonaparte, meantime, by several desperate charges of cavalry, endeavoured in vain to arrest the progress of the enemy. His left wing was put completely to flight; his centre was in great disorder, and it was only his right wing, which, by strong support, had been enabled to stand their ground.

In these circumstances, the day seemed so entirely against him, that, to prevent his right wing from being overwhelmed, he was compelled to retreat in the face of an enemy superior in numbers, and particularly in cavalry and artillery. It was, however, rather a change of position, than an absolute retreat to the rear. The French right, still resting on Castel-Ceriolo, which formed the pivot of the manœuvre, had orders to retreat very slowly, the centre faster, the left at ordinary quick time. In this manner the whole line of battle was changed, and instead of extending diagonally across the plain, as when the fight began, the French now occupied an oblong position, the left being withdrawn as far back as St. Juliano, where it was protected by the advance of Desaix's troops. This division, being the sole remaining reserve, had now at length arrived on the field, and, by Buonaparte's directions, had taken a strong position in front of St. Juliano, on which the French were obliged to retreat, great part of the left wing in the disorder of utter flight, the right wing steadily, and by intervals fronting the enemy, and sustaining with firmness the attacks made upon them.

At this time, and when victory seemed within his grasp, the strength of General Melas, eighty years old, and who had been many hours on horseback, failed entirely; and he was obliged to leave the field, and retire to Alexandria, committing to General Zach the charge of completing a victory which appeared to be already gained.

But the position of Desaix, at St. Juliano, afforded the first consul a rallying point, which he now greatly needed. His army of reserve lay formed in two lines in front of the village, their flanks sustained by battalions *en potence*, formed into close columns of infantry; on the left was a train of artillery; on the right, Kellermann, with a large body of French cavalry, which, routed in the beginning of the day, had rallied in this place. The ground that Desaix occupied was where the high-road forms a sort of defile, having on the one hand a wood, on the other a thick plantation of vines.

The French soldier understands better perhaps than any other in the world the art of rallying, after having been dispersed. The fugitives of Victor's division, though in extreme disorder, threw themselves into the rear of Desaix's position, and, covered by his troops, renewed their ranks and their courage. Yet, when Desaix saw the plain filled with flying soldiers, and beheld Buonaparte himself in full retreat, he thought all must be lost. They met in the middle of the greatest apparent confusion, and Desaix said, "The battle is lost—I suppose I can do no more for you than secure your retreat?"—"By no means," answered the first consul, "the battle is, I trust, gained—the disordered troops whom you see are my centre and left, whom I will rally in your rear—Push forward your column."

14th June.

Desaix, at the head of the ninth light brigade, instantly rushed forward, and charged the Austrians, wearied with fighting the whole day, and disordered by their hasty pursuit. The moment at which he advanced, so critically favourable for Buonaparte, was fatal to himself. He fell, shot through the head.[559] But his soldiers continued

---

[559] The *Moniteur* put in the mouth of the dying general a message to Buonaparte, in which he expressed his regret that he had done so little for history, and in that of the chief consul

to attack with fury, and Kellermann, at the same time charging the Austrian column, penetrated its ranks, and separated from the rest six battalions, which, surprised and panic-struck, threw down their arms; Zach, who, in the absence of Melas, commanded in chief, being at their head, was taken with them. The Austrians were now driven back in their turn. Buonaparte galloped along the French line, calling on the soldiers to advance. "You know," he said, "it is always my practice to sleep on the field of battle."[560]

The Austrians had pursued their success with incautious hurry, and without attending to the due support which one corps ought, in all circumstances, to be prepared to afford to another. Their left flank was also exposed, by their hasty advance, to Buonaparte's right, which had never lost order. They were, therefore, totally unprepared to resist this general, furious, and unexpected attack. They were forced back at all points, and pursued along the plain, suffering immense loss; nor were they again able to make a stand until driven back over the Bormida. Their fine cavalry, instead of being drawn up in squadrons to cover their retreat, fled in disorder, and at full gallop, riding down all that was in their way. The confusion at passing the river was inextricable—large bodies of men were abandoned on the left side, and surrendered to the French in the course of the night, or next morning.[561]

It is evident, in perusing the accounts of this battle, that the victory was wrested out of the hands of the Austrians, after they had become, by the fatigues of the day, too weary to hold it. Had they

---

an answer, lamenting that he had no time to weep for Desaix. But Buonaparte himself assures us, that Desaix was shot dead on the spot. [Gourgaud, tom. i., p. 300.] Nor is it probable that the tide of battle, then just upon the act of turning, left the consul himself time for set phrases, or sentimental ejaculations.—S. Savary, who was aide-de-camp to Desaix, had the body wrapped up in a cloak, and removed to Milan, where, by Napoleon's directions, it was embalmed, and afterwards conveyed to the Hospice of Saint Bernard, where a monument was erected to the memory of the fallen hero. "'Desaix,' said Napoleon, 'loved glory for glory's sake, and France above every thing. Luxury he despised, and even comfort. He preferred sleeping under a gun in the open air to the softest couch. He was of an unsophisticated, active, pleasing character, and possessed extensive information.' The victor of Marengo shed tears for his death."—Montholon, tom. iv., p. 256.
[560] Thibaudeau, tom. vi., p. 312.
[561] Gourgaud, tom. i., p. 296, 303; Jomini, tom. xiii., p. 278, 296; Dumas, tom. ii.; Savary, tom. i., p. 176.

sustained their advance by reserves, their disaster would not have taken place. It seems also certain, that the fate of Buonaparte was determined by the arrival of Desaix at the moment he did,[562] and that in spite of the skilful disposition by which the chief consul was enabled to support the attack so long, he must have been utterly defeated had Desaix put less despatch in his counter-march. Military men have been farther of opinion, that Melas was guilty of a great error, in not occupying Castel-Ceriolo on the advance; and that the appearances of early victory led the Austrians to be by far too unguarded in their advance on Saint Juliano.

In consequence of a loss which seemed in the circumstances altogether irreparable, Melas resolved to save the remains of his army, by entering, upon the 15th June, 1800, into a convention,[563] or rather capitulation, by which he agreed, on receiving permission to retire behind Mantua, to yield up Genoa, and all the fortified places which the Austrians possessed in Piedmont, Lombardy, and the Legations. Buonaparte the more readily granted these terms, that an English army was in the act of arriving on the coast. His wisdom taught him not to drive a powerful enemy to despair, and to be satisfied with the glory of having regained, in the affairs of Montebello and of Marengo, almost all the loss sustained by the French in the disastrous campaign of 1799. Enough had been done to show, that, as the fortunes of France appeared to wane and dwindle after Buonaparte's departure, so they revived with even more than their original brilliancy, as soon as this Child of Destiny had returned to preside over them. An armistice was also agreed upon, which it was supposed might afford time for the conclusion of a victorious peace with Austria; and Buonaparte extended this truce to the armies on the Rhine, as well as those in Italy.

Two days having been spent in the arrangements which the convention with Melas rendered necessary, Buonaparte, on the 17th June, returned to Milan, where he again renewed the Republican constitution, which had been his original gift to the Cisalpine

---

[562] ——"Desaix, who turn'd the scale, Leaving his life-blood in that famous field, (Where the clouds break, we may discern the spot In the blue haze,) sleeps, as thou saw'st at dawn, Just where we enter'd, in the Hospital-church."
Rogers' *Italy*, p. 10.
[563] See Gourgaud, tom. i., p. 303.

state.[564] He executed several other acts of authority. Though displeased with Massena for the surrender of Genoa, he did not the less constitute him commander-in-chief in Italy;[565] and though doubtful of Jourdan's attachment, who, on the 18th Brumaire, seemed ready to espouse the Republican interest, he did not on that account hesitate to name him minister of the French Republic in Piedmont, which was equivalent to giving him the administration of that province.[566] These conciliatory steps had the effect of making men of the most opposite parties see their own interest in supporting the government of the first consul.

PARIS

The presence of Napoleon was now eagerly desired at Paris. He set out from Milan on the 24th June,[567] and in the passage through Lyons paused to lay the foundation-stone for rebuilding the Place Bellecour; a splendid square, which had been destroyed by the frantic vengeance of the Jacobins when Lyons was retaken by them from the insurgent party of Girondins and Royalists. Finally, the chief consul returned to Paris upon the 2d July. He had left it on the 6th of May; yet, in the space of not quite two months, how many hopes had he realized! All that the most sanguine partisans had ventured to anticipate of his success had been exceeded. It seemed that his mere presence in Italy was of itself sufficient at once to

---

[564] "The victory of Marengo had revived the hopes of the Italian people. Each resumed his post; each returned to his functions; and the machinery of government was in full operation in the course of a few days."—Savary, tom. i., p. 186.

[565] "Though Massena was guilty of an error in embarking his troops at Genoa, instead of conducting them by land, he had always displayed much character and energy. In the midst of the fire and confusion of a battle, his demeanour was eminently noble. The din of the cannon cleared his ideas, and gave him penetration, spirit and even gaiety."—Napoleon, *Gourgaud*, tom. i., p. 243.

[566] "General Jourdan felt grateful on finding that the first consul had not only forgotten the past, but was also willing to give him so high a proof of confidence. He devoted all his zeal to the public good."—Napoleon, *Gourgaud*, tom. i., p. 310.

[567] "The first consul's train consisted of two carriages. Duroc and Bourrienne were in the same carriage with him. I followed with General Bassières in the other. There is no exaggeration in saying, that the first consul travelled from Milan to Lyons between two rows of people in the midst of unceasing acclamations. The manifestations of joy were still greater at Dijon. The women of that delightful city were remarkable for the vivacity of an unaffected joy, which threw animation into their eyes, and gave their faces so deep a colour, as if they had trespassed the bounds of decorum."—Savary, tom. i., p. 187.

obliterate the misfortunes of a disastrous campaign, and restore the fruits of his own brilliant victories, which had been lost during his absence. It appeared as if he was the sun of France—when he was hid from her, all was gloom—when he appeared, light and serenity were restored. All the inhabitants, leaving their occupations, thronged to the Tuileries to obtain a glimpse of the wonderful man, who appeared with the laurel of victory in the one hand, and the olive of peace in the other. Shouts of welcome and congratulation resounded from the gardens, the courts, and the quays, by which the palace is surrounded; high and low illuminated their houses; and there were few Frenchmen, perhaps, that were not for the moment partakers of the general joy.[568]

---

[568] "The first consul was partaking also of the prevailing gladness when he learned that a courier from Italy had brought an account of the loss of the battle of Marengo. The courier had been despatched at the moment when Paris every thing seemed desperate, so that the report of a defeat was general in before the first consul's return. Many projects were disturbed by his arrival. On the mere announcement of his defeat, his enemies had returned to their work, and talked of nothing less than overturning the government, and avenging the crimes of the eighteenth Brumaire."—Savary, tom. i., p. 190.

CHAPTER XX

Napoleon offers, and the Austrian Envoy accepts, a new Treaty—The Emperor refuses it, unless England is included—Negotiations with England—fail—Renewal of the War—Armistice—Resumption of Hostilities—Battle of Hohenlinden—Other Battles—The Austrians agree to a separate Peace—Treaty of Luneville—Convention between France and the United States—The Queen of Naples repairs to Petersburgh—Paul receives her with cordiality, and applies in her behalf to Buonaparte—His Envoy received at Paris with the utmost distinction, and the Royal Family of Naples saved for the present—Rome restored to the authority of the Pope—Napoleon demands of the King of Spain to declare War against Portugal—Olivenza and Almeida taken—Malta, after a Blockade of Two Years, obliged to submit to the English.

Napoleon proceeded to manage with great skill and policy the popularity which his success had gained for him. In war it was always his custom, after he had struck some venturous and apparently decisive blow, to offer such conditions as might induce the enemy to submit, and separate his interest from that of his allies. Upon this system of policy he offered the Count de St. Julien, an Austrian envoy, the conditions of a treaty, having for its basis that of Campo Formio, which, after the loss of Italy on the fatal field of Marengo, afforded terms much more favourable than the Emperor of Germany was entitled to have expected from the victors. The Austrian envoy accordingly took upon him to subscribe these preliminaries; but they did not meet the approbation of the Emperor, who placed his honour on observing accurately the engagements which he had formed with England, and who refused to accede to a treaty in which she was not included. It was added, however, that Lord Minto, the British ambassador at Vienna, had intimated Britain's willingness to be included in a treaty for general pacification.[569]

NEGOTIATIONS WITH ENGLAND

Aug. 24.

This proposal occasioned a communication between France and Britain, through Monsieur Otto, commissioner for the care of French prisoners. The French envoy intimated that as a preliminary to Britain's entering on the treaty, she must consent to an armistice by sea, and suspend the advantages which she received from her naval superiority, in the same manner as the first consul of France had dispensed with prosecuting his victories by land. This demand would have withdrawn the blockade of the British vessels from the French seaports, and allowed the sailing of reinforcements to Egypt and Malta, which last important place was on the point of surrendering to the English. The British ministers were also sensible that there was, besides, a great difference between a truce betwixt two land armies, stationed in presence of each other, and a suspension of naval hostilities over the whole world; since in the one case, on breaking off the treaty, hostilities can be almost instantly resumed; on the other, the distance and uncertainty of communication may prevent the war being recommenced for many months; by which chance of delay, the French, as being inferior at sea, were sure to be the gainers. The British statesmen, therefore, proposed some modifications, to prevent the obvious inequality of such armistice. But it was replied on the part of France, that though they would accept of such a modified armistice, if Great Britain

---

[569] "Count St Julien arrived at Paris on the 21st July, 1800, with a letter from the Emperor of Germany to the first consul, containing these expressions: 'You will give credit to what Count Saint Julien will say to you on my behalf, and I will ratify all his acts.' The first consul directed M. de Talleyrand to negotiate with the Austrian plenipotentiary, and the preliminaries were drawn up and signed in a few days."—Gourgaud, tom. ii., p. 2. See also Thibaudeau, tom. vi., p. 384; Jomini, tom. xiv., p. 9.

would enter into a separate treaty, yet the chief consul would not consent to it if Austria was to be participant of the negotiation.[570]

Here, therefore, the overtures of peace betwixt France and England were shipwrecked, and the Austrian Emperor was reduced to the alternative of renewing the war, or entering into a treaty without his allies. He appears to have deemed himself obliged to prefer the more dangerous and more honourable course.

This was a generous resolution on the part of Austria; but by no means politic at the period, when their armies were defeated, their national spirit depressed, and when the French armies had penetrated so far into Germany. Even Pitt himself, upon whose declining health the misfortune made a most unfavourable impression, had considered the defeat of Marengo as a conclusion to the hopes of success against France for a considerable period. "Fold up the map," he said, pointing to that of Europe; "it need not be again opened for these twenty years."

Yet, unwilling to resign the contest, even while a spark of hope remained, it was resolved upon in the British councils to encourage Austria to farther prosecution of the war. Perhaps, in recommending such a measure to her ally, at a period when she had sustained such great losses, and was in the state of dejection to which they gave rise, Great Britain too much resembled an eager and over-zealous second, who urges his principal to continue a combat after his strength is exhausted. Austria, a great and powerful nation, if left to repose, would have in time recruited her strength, and constituted once again a balance against the power of France on the continent; but if urged to farther exertions in the hour of her extremity, she was likely to sustain such additional losses, as might render her comparatively insignificant for a number of years. Such at least is the conclusion which we, who have the advantage of considering the measure with reference to its consequences, are now enabled to form. At the emergency, things were viewed in a different light. The victories of Suwarrow and of the Archduke

---

[570] For copies of the papers relative to the commencement of negotiations for peace with France, through the medium of M. Otto, see Annual Register, vol. xlii., p. 209. See also Jomini, tom. xiv., p. 19; and Gourgaud, tom. ii., p. 4.

Charles were remembered, as well as the recent defeats sustained by France in the year 1799, which had greatly tarnished the fame of her arms. The character of Buonaparte was not yet sufficiently estimated. His failure before Acre had made an impression in England, which was not erased by the victory of Marengo; the extreme prudence which usually tempered his most venturous undertakings was not yet generally known; and the belief and hope were received, that one who ventured on such new and daring manœuvres as Napoleon employed, was likely to behold them miscarry at length, and thus to fall as rapidly as he had risen.

Influenced by such motives, it was determined in the British cabinet to encourage the Emperor, by a loan of two millions, to place himself and his brother, the Archduke John, in command of the principal army, raise the whole national force of his mighty empire, and at the head of the numerous forces which he could summon into the field, either command a more equal peace, or try the fortunes of the most desperate war.

The money was paid, and the Emperor joined the army; but the negotiations for peace were not broken off. On the contrary, they were carried on much on the terms which Saint Julien had subscribed to, with this additional and discreditable circumstance, that the first consul, as a pledge of the Austrian sincerity, required that the three fortified towns of Ingoldstadt, Ulm, and Philipstadt, should be placed temporarily in the hands of the French; a condition to which the Austrians were compelled to submit. But the only advantage purchased by this surrender, which greatly exposed the hereditary dominions of Austria, was an armistice of forty-five days, at the end of which hostilities were again renewed.[571]

In the action of Haag, the Archduke John, whose credit in the army almost rivalled that of his brother Charles, obtained considerable advantages;[572] and, encouraged by them, he ventured

---

[571] Gourgaud, tom. ii.; Thibaudeau, tom. vi., p. 386; Annual Register, vol. xlii., p. 206.

[572] "The manœuvre of the Austrian army was a very fine one, and this first success augured others of great importance; but the archduke did not know how to profit by circumstances, but gave the French army time to rally and recover from its first surprise. He paid dearly for this error, which was the principal cause of the catastrophe of the following day."—Napoleon, *Gourgaud*, tom. xiv., p. 32.

on the 3d of December, 1800, two days afterwards, a great and decisive encounter with Moreau. This was the occasion on which that general gained over the Austrians the bloody and most important victory of Hohenlinden,—an achievement which did much to keep his reputation for military talents abreast with that of the first consul himself. Moreau pursued his victory, and obtained possession of Salzburg. At the same time Augereau, at the head of the Gallo-Batavian army, pressed forward into Bohemia; and Macdonald, passing from the country of the Grisons into the Valteline, forced a division of his army across the Mincio, and communicated with Massena and the French army in Italy. The Austrian affairs seemed utterly desperate. The Archduke Charles was again placed at the head of her forces, but they were so totally discouraged, that a retreat on all points was the only measure which could be executed.

ARMISTICE

Another and a final cessation of arms was now the only resource of the Austrians; and, in order to obtain it, the Emperor was compelled to agree to make a peace separate from his allies. Britain, in consideration of the extremity to which her ally was reduced, voluntarily relieved him from the engagement by which he was restrained from doing so without her participation. An armistice shortly afterwards took place, and the Austrians being now sufficiently humbled, it was speedily followed by a peace. Joseph Buonaparte, for this purpose, met with the Austrian minister, Count Cobentzel, at Luneville, where the negotiations were carried on.

There were two conditions of the treaty, which were peculiarly galling to the Emperor. Buonaparte peremptorily exacted the cession of Tuscany, the hereditary dominions of the brother of Francis, which were to be given up to a prince of the House of Parma, while the archduke was to obtain an indemnity in Germany. The French Consul demanded, with no less pertinacity, that Francis (though not empowered to do so by the Germanic constitution) should confirm the peace, as well in his capacity of Emperor of Germany, as in that of sovereign of his own hereditary dominions.

This demand, from which Buonaparte would on no account depart, involved a point of great difficulty and delicacy. One of the principal clauses of the treaty included the cession of the whole territories on the left bank of the Rhine to the French Republic; thereby depriving not only Austria, but Prussia, and various other princes of the German empire, of their possessions in the districts, which were now made over to France. It was provided that the princes who should suffer such deprivations, were to be remunerated by indemnities, as they were termed, to be allotted to them at the expense of the Germanic body in general. Now, the Emperor had no power to authorise the alienation of these fiefs of the empire, without consent of the Diet, and this was strongly urged by his envoy.

Buonaparte was, however, determined to make peace on no other terms than those of the Emperor's giving away what was not his to bestow. Francis was compelled to submit, and, as the necessity of the case pleaded its apology, the act of the Emperor was afterwards ratified by the Diet. Except in these mortifying claims, the submission to which plainly intimated the want of power to resist compulsion, the treaty of Luneville[573] was not much more advantageous to France than that of Campo Formio; and the moderation of the first consul indicated at once his desire of peace upon the continent, and considerable respect for the bravery and strength of Austria, though enfeebled by such losses as those of Marengo and Hohenlinden.

We have already noticed the disputes betwixt France and America, and the scandalous turn of the negotiations, by which the French Directory attempted to bully or wheedle the United States out of a sum of money, which, in part at least, was to be dedicated to their own private use. Since that time the aggressions committed by the French on the American navy had been so numerous, that the two republics seemed about to go to war, and the United States actually issued letters of marque for making reprisals on the French. New communications and negotiations, however, were opened, which Buonaparte studied to bring to maturity. His brother Joseph acted as negotiator, and on the 30th of September, 1800, a

---

[573] For a copy of the Treaty, see Annual Register, vol. xliii., p. 270.

convention[574] was entered into, to subsist for the space of eight years, agreeing on certain modifications of the right of search, declaring that commerce should be free between the countries, and that the captures on either side, excepting such as were contraband, and destined for an enemy's harbour, should be mutually restored. Thus Buonaparte established peace between France and the United States, and prevented the latter, in all probability, from throwing themselves into a closer union with Britain, to which their common descent, with the similarity of manners, language, and laws, overcoming the recollection of recent hostilities, might have otherwise strongly inclined them.

NAPLES

Still more important results were derived by Napoleon, from the address and political sagacity, with which, in accommodating matters with the court of Naples, he contrived to form what finally became a strong and predominating interest in the councils, and even the affections of a monarch, whose amity was, of all others, the most important to his plans. The prince alluded to was the Emperor of Russia, who had been, during the preceding year, the most formidable and successful enemy encountered by France since her Revolution. A short resumption of facts is necessary, to understand the circumstances in which the negotiation with Naples originated.

When Buonaparte departed for Egypt, all Italy, excepting Tuscany, and the dominions assigned to Austria by the treaty of Campo Formio, was in the hands of the French; while Naples was governed by the ephemeral Parthenopean republic, and the city of the Popes by that which assumed the superb title of Roman. These authorities, however, were only nominal; the French generals exercised the real authority in both countries. Suddenly, and as if by magic, this whole state of affairs was changed by the military talents of Suwarrow. The Austrians and Russians gained great successes in the north of Italy, and General Macdonald found himself obliged to evacuate Naples, and to concentrate the principal resistance of the French in Lombardy and Piedmont. Cardinal Ruffo, a soldier,

---

[574] For a copy of the Convention, see Annual Register, vol. xlii., p. 282.

churchman, and politician, put himself at the head of a numerous body of insurgents, and commenced war against such French troops as had been left in the south, and in the middle of Italy. This movement was actively supported by the British fleet. Lord Nelson recovered Naples; Rome surrendered to Commodore Trowbridge. Thus, the Parthenopean and Roman republics were extinguished for ever.[575] The royal family returned to Naples, and that fine city and country were once more a kingdom. Rome, the capital of the world, was occupied by Neapolitan troops, generally supposed the most indifferent of modern times.

Replaced in his richest territories by the allies, the King of Naples was bound by every tie to assist them in the campaign of 1800. He accordingly sent an army into the March of Ancona, under the command of Count Roger de Damas, who, with the assistance of insurrectionary forces[576] among the inhabitants, and a body of Austrians, was to clear Tuscany of the French. Undeterred by the battle of Marengo, the Count de Damas marched against the French general Miollis, who commanded in Tuscany, and sustained a defeat by him near Sienna. Retreat became now necessary, the more especially as the armistice which was entered into by general Melas deprived the Neapolitans of any assistance from the Austrians, and rendered their whole expedition utterly hopeless. They were not even included by name in the armistice, and were thus left exposed to the whole vengeance of the French. Damas retreated into the territories of the Church, which were still occupied by the Neapolitan forces. The consequence of these events was easily foreseen. The Neapolitan troops, so soon as the French could find leisure to look towards them, must be either destroyed entirely, or driven back upon Naples, and that city must be again forsaken by the royal family, happy if they were once more able to make their escape to Sicily, as on the former occasion.[577]

At this desperate crisis, the Queen of the two Sicilies took a resolution which seemed almost as desperate, and could only have

---

[575] Botta, Storia d'Italia, tom. iii., p. 479.
[576] These were, at this period, easily raised in any part of Italy. The exactions of the French had entirely alienated the affections of the natives, who had long since seen through their pretexts of affording them the benefit of a free government.—S.
[577] Gourgaud, tom. ii., p. 88; Jomini, tom. xiv., p. 215.

been adopted by a woman of a bold and decisive character. She resolved, notwithstanding the severity of the season, to repair in person to the court of the Emperor Paul, and implore his intercession with the first consul, in behalf of her husband and his territories.

We have not hitherto mentioned, except cursorily, the powerful prince whose mediation she implored. The son and successor of the celebrated Catherine, far from possessing the prudence and political sagacity of his mother, seemed rather to display the heady passions and imperfect judgment of his unfortunate father. He was capricious in the choice of his objects, pursuing for the time, with uncommon and irregular zeal and pertinacity, projects which he afterwards discarded and abandoned, swelling trifles of dress or behaviour into matters of importance, and neglecting, on the other hand, what was of real consequence;— governed, in short, rather by imagination than by his reasoning qualities, and sometimes affording room to believe that he actually laboured under a partial aberration of mind. Such characters are often to be met with in private society, the restraints of which keep them within such limits, that they pass through life without attracting much notice, unless when creating a little mirth, or giving rise to some passing wonder. But an absolute prince, possessed of such a disposition, is like a giddy person placed on the verge of a precipice, which would try the soundest head, and must overpower a weak one.

The Emperor had first distinguished himself by an energetic defence of the rights of sovereigns, and a hatred of whatever belonged to or was connected with the French Revolution, from a political maxim to the shape of a coat or a hat. The brother of Louis XVI., and inheritor of his rights, found a refuge in the Russian dominions; and Paul, fond, as most princes are, of military glory, promised himself that of restoring the Bourbon dynasty by force of arms.

SUWARROW

The train of victories acquired by Suwarrow was well calculated to foster these original partialities of the Emperor; and, accordingly, while success continued to wait on his banners, he loaded his general with marks of his regard, elevated him to the rank of a prince, and conferred on him the title of Italiansky, or Italicus.

The very first and only misfortune which befell Suwarrow, seems to have ruined him in the opinion of his capricious master. The defeat of Korsakow by Massena, near Zurich, had involved Suwarrow in great momentary danger as he advanced into Switzerland, reckoning on the support of that general, whose disaster left his right uncovered. Now, although Suwarrow saved his army on this occasion by a retreat, which required equal talent to that which achieved his numerous victories, yet the bare fact of his having received a check was sufficient to ruin him with his haughty sovereign. Paul was yet more offended with the conduct of the Austrians. The Archduke Charles having left Switzerland to descend into Germany, had given occasion and opportunity for Massena to cross the Limmat and surprise Korsakow; and this, notwithstanding every explanation and apology, rankled in the mind of the Czar.[578] He recalled his armies from the frontiers of Germany, and treated his veteran and victorious general with such marks of neglect and displeasure, that the old man's heart sunk under them.

In the meanwhile, Paul gathered up farther subjects of complaint against the Austrian government, and complained of their having neglected to provide for some Russian prisoners,[579] under a

---

[578] "In 1800, Suwarrow returned to Russia with scarcely a fourth of his army. The Emperor Paul complained bitterly of having lost the flower of his troops, who had neither been seconded by the Austrians nor the English. He reproached the Cabinet of Austria with having refused, after the conquest of Piedmont, to replace the King of Sardinia on his throne, and with being destitute of grand and generous ideas, and wholly governed by calculation and interested motives. The first consul did every thing in his power to cherish these seeds of discontent, and to make them productive."—Napoleon, *Gourgaud*, tom. ii., p. 131.

[579] "I had hit upon the bent of Paul's character. I seized time by the forelock; I collected the Russians; I clothed them, and sent them back to him without any expense. From that instant that generous heart was devoted to me."—Napoleon, *Las Cases*, tom. v., p. 174.

capitulation which they made in behalf of their own, at the surrender of Ancona to the French.

The Austrians could not afford to lose so powerful and efficient an ally in the day of their adversity. They endeavoured to explain, that the movement of the Archduke Charles was inevitably necessary, in consequence of an invasion of the Austrian territory—they laid the blame of the omission of the Russians in the capitulation upon the commandant Frœlich, and offered to place him under arrest. The Emperor of Austria even proposed, in despite of the natural pride which is proper to his distinguished house, to place Suwarrow at the head of the Austrian armies,—a proffer, which, if it had been accepted, might have given rise to an extraordinary struggle betwixt the experience, determination, and warlike skill of the veteran Scythian, and the formidable talents of Buonaparte, and which perhaps contained the only chance which Europe possessed at the time, of opposing to the latter a rival worthy of himself; for Suwarrow had never yet been conquered, and possessed an irresistible influence over the minds of his soldiers. These great generals, however, were not destined ever to decide the fate of the world by their meeting.

Suwarrow, a Russian in all his feelings, broke his heart, and died under the unmerited displeasure of his Emperor, whom he had served with so much fidelity.[580] If the memory of his unfortunate sovereign were to be judged of according to ordinary rules, his conduct towards his distinguished subject would have left on it an indelible stigma. As it is, the event must pass as another proof, that the Emperor Paul was not amenable, from the construction of his understanding and temperament, to the ordinary rules of censure.

Meanwhile, the proposals of Austria were in vain. The Czar was not to be brought back to his former sentiments. He was like a spoiled child, who, tired of his favourite toy, seems bent to break

---

[580] Suwarrow died at Petersburgh, in May, 1800, of that accumulated chagrin that proud and sullen resentment which is familiarly called a broken heart; he expired in a small wooden house, under the displeasure of his master, at a distance from his family, and abandoned by his friends.—S.

asunder and destroy what was lately the dearest object of his affection.

When such a character as Paul changes his opinion of his friends, he generally runs into the opposite extreme, and alters also his thoughts of his enemies. Like his father, and others whose imagination is indifferently regulated, the Czar had need of some one of whom to make his idol. The extravagant admiration which the Emperor Peter felt for Frederick of Prussia, could not well be entertained for any one now alive, unless it were the first consul of France; and on him, therefore, Paul was now disposed to turn his eyes with a mixture of wonder, and of a wish to imitate what he wondered at.[581] This extravagance of admiration is a passion natural to some minds, (never strong ones,) and may be compared to that tendency which others have to be in love all their lives, in defiance of advancing age and other obstacles.

When Paul was beginning to entertain this humour, the arrival of the Queen of Sicily at his court gave him a graceful and even dignified opportunity to approach towards a connexion with Napoleon Buonaparte. His pride, too, must have been gratified by seeing the daughter of the renowned Maria Theresa, the sister of the Emperor of Austria, at his court of St. Petersburgh, soliciting from the Czar of Russia the protection which her brother was totally unable to afford her; and a successful interference in her behalf would be a kind of insult to the misfortunes of that brother, against whom, as we have noticed, Paul nourished resentful feelings. He therefore resolved to open a communication with France, in behalf of the royal family of Naples. Lewinshoff, grand huntsman of Russia, was despatched to make the overtures of mediation. He was received with the utmost distinction at Paris, and Buonaparte made an instant and graceful concession to the request of the Emperor

---

[581] "Paul, attacked in so many different directions, gave way to his enthusiastic temper, and attached himself to France with all the ardour of his character. He despatched a letter to Napoleon, in which he said, 'Citizen first consul, I do not write to you to discuss the rights of men or citizens; every country governs itself as it pleases. Wherever I see at the head of a nation a man who knows how to rule and how to fight, my heart is attracted towards him. I write to inform you of my dissatisfaction with the English government, which violates every article of the law of nations, and has no guide but base self-interest. I wish to unite with you to put an end to the unjust proceedings of that government.'"—Gourgaud, tom. ii., p. 133.

Paul. The first consul agreed to suspend his military operations against Naples, and to leave the royal family in possession of their sovereignty; reserving to himself, however, the right of dictating the terms under which he was to grant them such an amnesty.

NAPLES

It was time that some effectual interposition should take place in defence of the King of Naples, who, though he had around him a nation individually brave and enthusiastic, was so ill-served, that his regular army was in the worst and most imperfect state of discipline. Murat, to whom Buonaparte had committed the task of executing his vengeance on Naples, had already crossed the Alps, and placed himself at the head of an army of ten thousand chosen men; a force then judged sufficient not only to drive the Neapolitan general Damas out of the Ecclesiastical States, but to pursue him as far as Naples, and occupy that beautiful capital of a prince, whose regular army consisted of more than thirty thousand soldiers, and whose irregular forces might have been increased to any number by the mountaineers of Calabria, who form excellent light troops, and by the numerous Lazzaroni of Naples, who had displayed their valour against Championet, upon the first invasion of the French. But the zeal of a nation avails little when the spirit of the government bears no proportion to it. The government of Naples dreaded the approach of Murat as that of the Angel of Death; and they received the news that Lewinshoff had joined the French general at Florence, as a condemned criminal might have heard the news of a reprieve. The Russian envoy was received with distinguished honours at Florence. Murat appeared at the theatre with Lewinshoff, where the Italians, who had so lately seen the Russian and French banners placed in bloody opposition to each other, now beheld them formally united in presence of these dignitaries; in sign, it was said, that the two nations were combined for the peace of the world, and general benefit of humanity.[582] Untimely augury! How often after that period did these standards meet in the bloodiest fields history ever recorded; and what a long and desperate struggle was yet in

---

[582] Botta, tom. iv., p. 87; Jomini, tom. xiv., p. 216.

reserve ere the general peace so boldly predicted was at length restored!

The respect paid by the first consul to the wishes of Paul, saved for the present the royal family of Naples; but Murat, nevertheless, made them experience a full portion of the bitter cup which the vanquished are generally doomed to swallow. General Damas[583] was commanded in the haughtiest terms to evacuate the Roman States, and not to presume to claim any benefit from the armistice which had been extended to the Austrians. At the same time, while the Neapolitans were thus compelled hastily to evacuate the Roman territories, general surprise was exhibited, when, instead of marching to Rome, and re-establishing the authority of the Roman republic, Murat, according to the orders which he had received from the first consul, carefully respected the territory of the Church, and re-installed the officers of the Pope in what had been long termed the patrimony of St Peter.[584] This unexpected turn of circumstances originated in high policy on the part of Buonaparte.[585]

We certainly do Napoleon no injustice in supposing, that personally he had little or no influential sense of religion. Some obscure yet rooted doctrines of fatality, seem, so far as we can judge, to have formed the extent of his metaphysical creed. We can scarce term him even a deist; and he was an absolute stranger to every modification of Christian belief and worship. But he saw and valued the use of a national religion as an engine of state policy. In Egypt, he was desirous of being thought an envoy of Heaven; and though uncircumcised, drinking wine and eating pork, still claimed to be accounted a follower of the law of the Prophet. He had pathetically expostulated with the Turks on their hostility towards him. The French, he said, had ceased to be followers of Jesus; and now that they were almost, if not altogether, Moslemah, would the true believers make war on those who had overthrown the cross,

---

[583] Count Roger Damas, on the restoration of the Bourbons, was appointed first gentleman of the King's chamber, and Governor of the 9th military division. He died in 1825.
[584] Jomini, tom. xiv., p. 220.
[585] "This conduct excited the gratitude of the Pontiff, who immediately caused Cardinal Gonsalvi to write to General Murat, on the 31st of January, to express to him 'the lively regard which he felt for the first consul;' on whom, said he, 'depends the tranquillity of religion, as well as the happiness of Europe.'"—Gourgaud, tom. ii., p. 92.

dethroned the Pope, and extirpated the order of Malta, the sworn persecutors of the Moslem faith? On his return to France, all this was to be forgotten, or only remembered as a trick played upon the infidels. He was, as we have said, aware of the necessity of a national faith to support the civil government; and as, while in Egypt, he affected to have destroyed the Catholic religion in honour of that of Mahomed, so, returned to Europe, he was now desirous to become the restorer of the temporal territories of the Pope, in order to obtain such a settlement of church affairs in France, as might procure for his own government the countenance of the Sovereign Pontiff, and for himself an admission into the pale of Christian princes. This restitution was in some measure consistent with his policy in 1798, when he had spared the temporalities of the Holy See. Totally indifferent as Napoleon was to religion in his personal capacity, his whole conduct shows his sense of its importance to the existence of a settled and peaceful state of society.

Besides evacuating the Ecclesiastical States, the Neapolitans were compelled by Murat to restore various paintings, statues, and other objects of art, which they had, in imitation of Buonaparte, taken forcibly from the Romans,—so captivating is the influence of bad example. A French army of about eighteen thousand men was to be quartered in Calabria, less for the purpose of enforcing the conditions of peace, than to save France the expense of supporting the troops, and to have them stationed where they might be embarked for Egypt at the shortest notice. The harbours of the Neapolitan dominions were of course to be closed against the English. A cession of part of the isle of Elba, and the relinquishment of all pretensions upon Tuscany, summed up the sacrifices of the King of Naples, who, considering how often he had braved Napoleon, had great reason to thank the Emperor of Russia for his effectual mediation in his favour.[586]

ROME—PEACE WITH PORTUGAL

These various measures respecting foreign relations, the treaty of Luneville, the acquisition of the good-will of the Emperor Paul,

---

[586] Gourgaud, tom. ii., p. 93.

the restoration of Rome to the Pope's authority, and the mildness of the penalty inflicted on the King of Naples, seemed all to spring from a sound and moderate system, the object of which was rather the consolidation of Napoleon's government, than any wish to extend its influence or its conquests. His plans, in after times, often exhibited a mixture of the greatest good sense and prudence, with rash and splenetic explosions of an over-eager ambition, or a temper irritated by opposition; but it is to be remembered that Buonaparte was not yet so firm in the authority which he had but just acquired, as to encourage any display of the infirmities of his mind and temper.

His behaviour towards Portugal was, however, of a character deviating from the moderation he had in general displayed. Portugal, the ancient and faithful ally of England, was on that account the especial object of the first consul's displeasure. He, therefore, demanded of the King of Spain, who, since the peace between the countries, had been the submissive vassal of France, to declare war on the Prince Regent of Portugal, although the husband of his daughter. War accordingly was declared, in obedience to the mandate of the first consul, and the Spanish armies, together with an auxiliary army of French under Leclerc, entered Portugal, took Olivenza and Almeida, and compelled the prince regent, 6th of June, 1801, to sign a treaty, engaging to shut his ports against the English, and surrendering to Spain, Olivenza, and other places on the frontier of the Guadiana. Buonaparte was highly discontented with this treaty, to which he would not accede; and he refused, at the same time, to withdraw from Spain the army of Leclerc. On the 29th September, he condescended to grant Portugal peace under some additional terms,[587] which were not in themselves of much consequence, although the overbearing and peremptory conduct which he exhibited towards the Peninsular powers, was a sign of the dictatorial spirit which he was prepared to assume in the affairs of Europe.

The same disposition was manifested in the mode by which Buonaparte was pleased to show his sense of the King of Spain's complaisance. He chose for that purpose to create a kingdom and a

---

[587] See the Treaty, Annual Register, vol. xliii., p. 294.

king—a king, too, of the house of Bourbon. An infant of Spain obtained the throne of Tuscany, under the name of Etruria, rent from the house of Austria.[588] Madame de Staël terms this the commencement of the great masquerade of Europe; but it was more properly the second act. The stage, during the first, was occupied by a quadrille of republics, who were now to be replaced by an anti-mask of kings. This display of power pleased the national vanity, and an uproar of applause ensued, while the audience at the theatre applied to Buonaparte the well-known line—

"J'ai fait des rois, madame, et n'ai pas voulu l'être."

While all the continent appeared thus willing to submit to one so ready to avail himself of their subjection, Britain alone remained at war; without allies, without, it might seem, a direct object; yet on the grand and unalterable principle, that no partial distress should induce her to submit to the system of degradation, which seemed preparing for all nations under the yoke of France, and which had placed France herself, with all her affected zeal for liberty, under the government of an arbitrary ruler. On every point the English squadrons annihilated the commerce of France, crippled her revenues, blockaded her ports, and prevented those combinations which would have crowned the total conquest of Europe, could the master, as he might now be called, of the land, have enjoyed, at the same time, the facilities which can only be afforded in communication by sea.

It was in vain that Buonaparte, who, besides his natural hardiness of perseverance, connected a part of his own glory with the preservation of Egypt, endeavoured by various means to send supplies to that distant province. His convoys were driven back into harbour by the English fleets; and he directed against his admirals, who could not achieve impossibilities, the unavailing resentment natural to one who was so little accustomed to disappointment.

The chance of relieving Egypt was rendered yet more precarious by the loss of Malta, which, after a distressing blockade of two years, was obliged to submit to the English arms on the 5th

---

[588] Botta, tom. iv., p. 83; Gourgaud, tom. ii., p. 94; Montgaillard, tom. v., p. 430.

of September, 1800. The English were thus in possession of a strong, and almost impregnable citadel, in the midst of the Mediterranean, with an excellent harbour, and every thing required for a naval station of the first importance; above all, they had obtained the very spot which Buonaparte had fixed upon for maintaining the communication with Egypt, which was now in greater danger than ever.

The capture of Malta was, however, by its consequences, favourable to Napoleon's views in one important respect. The Emperor Paul imagined he had rights upon that island, in consequence of his having declared himself Grand Master of the Order of Saint John; and although, by his deserting the coalition, and abandoning the common cause, he had lost all right to expect that Great Britain should surrender to him an important acquisition made by her own arms, yet, with his usual intemperate indulgence of passion, he conceived himself deeply injured by its being withheld,[589] and nourished from that time an implacable resentment against England and her government, the effects of which are afterwards to be traced.

---

[589] "Paul had been promised Malta, the moment it was taken possession of, and accordingly he was in great haste to get himself nominated Grand-Master. But when Malta had fallen, the English ministers denied that they had promised it to him. It is confidently stated, that Paul felt so indignant, that seizing the despatch, in full council, he ran his sword through it, and ordered it to be sent back in that condition, by way of answer."—Napoleon, *Las Cases*, tom. v., p. 174.

Chapter XXI

Internal Government of France—General Attachment to the Chief Consul—Plot to remove him by Assassination—Defeated—Vain hopes of the Royalists, that Napoleon would restore the Bourbons—Infernal Machine—It fails—Suspicion first falls on the Republicans—The actual Conspirators executed—Use made by Buonaparte of the Conspiracy to consolidate Despotism—System of Police—Fouché—His Skill, Influence, and Power—Apprehension entertained by the Chief Consul of the effects of Literature—Persecution of Madame de Staël—The Concordat—Plan for a general System of Jurisprudence—Amnesty granted to the Emigrants—Plans of Public Education—Hopes of a General Peace.

INTERNAL GOVERNMENT OF FRANCE

We return to the internal government of France under the chief consul.

The events subsequent to the revolution of the 18th Brumaire, seemed to work a miraculous change on the French nation. The superior talents of Napoleon, with the policy exercised by Talleyrand and Fouché, and the other statesmen of ability whom he had called into administration, and who desired at all events to put an end to further revolutionary movements—but, above all, the victory of Marengo, had at once created and attached to the person of the chief consul an immense party, which might be said to comprehend all those, who, being neither decided Royalists nor determined Republicans, were indifferent about the form of the government, so they found ease and protection while living under it.[590]

But, on the other hand, the heads of the two factions continued to exist; and, as the power of the first consul became at once more absolute and more consolidated, it grew doubly hateful and formidable to them. His political existence was a total obstruction to the systems of both parties, and yet one which it was impossible to remove. There was no national council left, in which the authority of the first consul could be disputed, or his measures impeached. The strength of his military power bid defiance alike to popular commotions, if the Democrats had yet possessed the means of exerting them, and to the scattered bands of the Royalist insurgents. What chance remained for ridding themselves of the autocrat, in whom the Republicans saw a dictator, the Royalists an usurper? None, save that, being mortal, Napoleon was subject to be taken off by assassination.

PLOT TO ASSASSINATE THE FIRST CONSUL

The Democrats were naturally the first to meditate an enterprise of this nature. The right of taking off a tyrant was, according to their creed, as proper to any private citizen as to those who opposed him armed in the field. The act of Harmodius and Aristogiton—the noble deed of Brutus and his associates—were consecrated in history, and esteemed so congenial to the nature of a free constitution, that the Convention, on the motion of Jean de Brie,[591] had at one time determined to raise a legion of assassins,

---

[590] "The first consul restored order to all the branches of the administration, and probity in the dealings of private individuals with the government. He caused a strict examination to be made of the accounts of all persons presenting themselves as creditors of the state, and took a detailed cognizance of all the frauds and peculations to which the public purse had been a prey during the administration of the Directory. He had had some misgivings on the subject previously to his coming to power; but he was soon convinced that he had not suspected one half of the disorder which actually existed. Accordingly, from that moment he never could feel either esteem for or confidence in certain individuals, notwithstanding their great wealth. He often said, that he thought better of a highwayman, who at least exposes his life, than he did of those leeches, who carry off every thing without running any risk."—Savary, tom. i., p. 192.
[591] August 26, 1792. See Biographie Moderne, tom. i., p. 338; and Montgaillard, tom. iii., p. 115.

armed with poniards, who should devote themselves to the pious task of exterminating all foreign princes, statesmen, and ministers—in short, all who were accounted the foes of freedom, without pity or distinction. In a party entertaining such principles, there could be no scruple on the score of morality; and where they had been so lately professed by thousands, it seemed natural that, amid the multitude, they must have made a deep impression on some enthusiastic and gloomy disposition, which might be easily provoked to act upon them.

Oct. 10.

It is no wonder, therefore, that some obscure Jacobins should have early nourished the purpose of assassinating Napoleon, as the enemy of his country's freedom, and the destroyer of her liberties; but it is singular, that most of the conspirators against his person were Italians. Arena, brother of the deputy[592] who was said to have aimed a dagger at Buonaparte in the Council of Five Hundred, was at the head of the conspiracy. He was a Corsican.[593] With him, Ceracchi[594] and Diana, two Italian refugees; a painter called Topino-Lebrun;[595] and two or three enthusiasts of low condition, formed a plot for the purpose of assassinating the chief consul at the Opera-house. Their intention was detected by the police; Ceracchi and Diana were arrested in the lobby,[596] armed, it was said, and prepared for the attempt, and Napoleon was congratulated by most of the constituted authorities upon having escaped a great danger.[597]

---

[592] See *ante*.
[593] In 1797, Arena was appointed one of the deputies from Corsica to the Council of Five Hundred.
[594] Giuseppe Ceracchi was born at Rome in 1760. He was a sculptor, had been a pupil of Canova, and had modelled the bust of Napoleon.—"When he entered into the plot, he endeavoured to procure another sitting, under pretence of making an essential improvement on the bust. Fortunately, at that time, the consul had not a single moment's leisure; and thinking that want was the real cause of the urgent solicitations of the sculptor, he sent him six thousand francs."—Napoleon, *Las Cases*, tom. iii., p. 10.
[595] Topino-Lebrun, an historical painter, and pupil of David was born at Marseilles in 1769.
[596] "The first consul's box was in the first tier in front; his access to it was by the public entrance. In this attempt originated the idea of a private entrance."—Savary, tom. i., p. 229.
[597] "An individual named Harel, one of the accomplices, in the hope of large remuneration, made some disclosures to Bourrienne, secretary of the first consul. Harel being brought forward, corroborated his first information, and designated the conspirators."—Fouché,

Crassous, president of the Tribunate, made a singular speech on the occasion, which would almost bear a double interpretation. "There had been so many conspiracies," he said, "at so many different periods, and under so many different pretexts, which had never been followed up either by inquiry or punishment, that a great number of good citizens had become sceptical on the subject of their existence. This incredulity was dangerous," he argued; "it was time it should be ended." With this view, Monsieur Crassous recommended, that the persons guilty on the present occasion should be prosecuted and punished with all the solemnity and rigour of the laws.

Buonaparte replied, with military indifference, that he had been in no real danger. "The contemptible wretches," he said, in something like a renewal of his Egyptian vein, "had no power to commit the crime they meditated. Besides the assistance of the whole audience, I had with me a piquet of my brave guard, from whom the wretches could not have borne a look."[598] So ended this singular discourse; and it is remarkable that neither were the circumstances of the plot made public, nor the conspirators punished, till the more memorable attempt on Napoleon's life by the Royalists.

THE ROYALISTS

The Royalists, as a party, had far more interest with Buonaparte than the Democrats. The former approved of the principles and form of his government,—it was only necessary for their conversion, that they should learn to endure his person; whereas the Jacobins being equally averse to the office to which he aspired, to his power, and to himself, there were no hopes of their being brought to tolerate either the monarch or the man. Of the

---

tom. i., p. 170.—"After dinner, Buonaparte threw a great-coat over his little green uniform, and got into his carriage, accompanied by Duroc and myself. He arrived and entered his box without interruption. In about half an hour he desired me to go into the corridor, and observe what passed. Scarcely had I left the box, when, hearing a great noise, I learned that a number of persons had been arrested. I returned to inform the first consul, and we drove instantly back to the Tuileries."—Bourrienne.
[598] Mémoires de Fouché, tom. i., p. 172.

latter, therefore, Napoleon entertained equal dislike and distrust; while, from obvious causes, his feelings towards the former were in some measure friendly.

The Royalists, too, for some time entertained a good opinion of Buonaparte, and conceived that he intended, in his own time and in his own way, to act in behalf of the exiled royal family. The enthusiastic of the party were at a loss to conceive that the throne of France should be again erected, and that any one but a Bourbon should dare to ascend it. It seemed to them impossible that the monarchy should revive without the restoration of the legitimate monarch, and they could not believe that a Corsican soldier of fortune would meditate an usurpation, or that France would be for a moment tolerant of his pretensions. The word liberty had, indeed, misled the people of France for a time, but, that illusion being dissipated, their natural love to the royal race would return like a reviving spring, and again run in its old channel.

So general was the belief among this class, that Buonaparte meditated the restoration of the Bourbons, that several agents of the family made their way so far as to sound his own mind upon the subject. Louis himself, afterwards XVIII., addressed to the first consul a letter of the following tenor:—"You cannot achieve the happiness of France without my restoration, any more than I can ascend the throne which is my right, without your co-operation. Hasten then to complete the good work, which none but you can accomplish, and name the rewards which you claim for your friends."[599]

Buonaparte answered the letter with cold civility. He esteemed the person, he said, and pitied the misfortunes, of his Royal Highness the Comte de Provence, and should be glad to assist him, did an opportunity permit. But as his royal highness could not be restored to France, save at the expense of an hundred thousand

---

[599] "The letter was forwarded to the Consul Lebrun, through the Abbé de Montesquiou. Lebrun was reprimanded for having received a letter from the king through an underhand channel."—Fouché, tom. i., p. 155.

lives, it was an enterprise in which he, Buonaparte, must decline to aid him.[600]

A less direct, and more artful course, is said to have been attempted, by the mission of the Duchesse de Guiche, one of the most beautiful and pleasing women of the time, who, obtaining permission to come to Paris under pretext of her private affairs, was introduced at the Tuileries, and delighted Josephine with the elegance of her manners.[601] Napoleon did not escape the fascination but the instant she touched on the subject of politics, the interesting duchesse received an order to quit Paris.

As soon as the Royalists discovered, by the failure of these and similar applications, as well as by the gradual tendency of Buonaparte's measures, that the restoration of the Bourbons was the thing farthest from his purpose, their disappointment exasperated them against the audacious individual, whose single person seemed now the only obstacle to that event. Monarchical power was restored, in spirit at least, if not in form; was it to be endured, the more zealous followers of the Bourbons demanded of each other, that it should become the prize of a military usurper? This party, as well as that of the Jacobins, contained doubtless many adherents, whom the enthusiasm of their political principles disposed to serve their cause, even at the expense of great crimes. The sentiments of the princes of the royal family upon such a subject, were becoming their high ranks.[602] They were resolved to combat Buonaparte's

---

[600] Las Cases, tom. i., p. 271; O'Meara's Napoleon in Exile, vol. i., p. 480; Fouché, tom. i., p. 154.
[601] "The duchess breakfasted with Josephine at Malmaison; and the conversation turning on London, the emigrants, and the French princes, Madame de Guiche mentioned, that as she happened, a few days before, to be at the house of the Count d'Artois, she had heard some persons ask the prince what he intended to do for the first consul in the event of his restoring the Bourbons; and that the prince had replied, 'I would immediately make him constable of the kingdom, and every thing else he might choose. But even that would not be enough: we would raise on the Carrousel a lofty and magnificent column, surmounted with a statue of Buonaparte crowning the Bourbons.' As soon as the first consul entered, Josephine eagerly repeated to him the circumstance which the duchess had related. 'And did you not reply,' said her husband, 'that the corpse of the first consul would have made the pedestal of the column?' The duchess received orders that very night to quit Paris."—Las Cases, tom. i., p. 272.
[602] The opinions of the royal family were nobly expressed in a letter written by the Prince of Condé to the Comte d'Artois, at a later period, 24th January, 1802, which will be hereafter quoted at length.—S.

pretensions with open force, such as befitted their pretensions as head of the chivalry of France, but to leave to Jacobins the schemes of private assassination. Still there must have been many, among those characters which are found during the miseries and crimes of civil war, who conceived that the assassination of the chief consul would be received as good service when accomplished, although it might not be authorised beforehand. Nay, there may have been partisans zealous enough to take the crime and punishment on themselves, without looking farther than the advantage which their party would receive by the action.

THE INFERNAL MACHINE

A horrible invention, first hatched, it is said, by the Jacobins,[603] was adopted by certain Royalists of a low description, remarkable as actors in the wars of the Chouans, of whom the leaders were named Carbon and St. Regent. It was a machine consisting of a barrel of gunpowder, placed on a cart to which it was strongly secured, and charged with grape-shot so disposed around the barrel, as to be dispersed in every direction by the explosion. The fire was to be communicated by a slow match. It was the purpose of the conspirators, undeterred by the indiscriminate slaughter which such a discharge must occasion, to place the machine in the street through which the first consul was to go to the opera, having contrived that it should explode, exactly as his carriage should pass the spot; and, strange to say, this stratagem, which seemed as uncertain as it was atrocious, was within a hair's-breadth of success.

On the evening of the 24th December, 1800, Buonaparte has informed us, that though he himself felt a strong desire to remain at

---

[603] It is said in the Memoirs of Fouché, (vol. i., p. 180,) that the infernal machine was the invention originally of a Jacobin named Chevalier, assisted by Veycer, one of the same party; that they even made an experiment of its power, by exploding an engine of the kind behind the Convent de la Saltpétrière; that this circumstance drew on them the attention of the police, and that they were arrested. It does not appear by what means the Royalists became privy to the Jacobin plot, nor is the story in all its parts very probable; yet it would seem it must be partly true, since the attempt by means of the infernal machine was at first charged upon the Jacobins, in consequence of Chevalier's being known to have had some scheme in agitation, to be executed by similar means in the course of the previous year.—S.

home, his wife and one or two intimate friends insisted that he should go to the opera. He was slumbering under a canopy when they awaked him. One brought his hat, another his sword. He was in a manner forced into his carriage, where he again slumbered and was dreaming of the danger which he had escaped in an attempt to pass the river Tagliamento some years before. On a sudden he awaked amidst thunder and flame.[604]

The cart bearing the engine, which was placed in the street St. Nicaise, intercepted the progress of the chief consul's coach, which passed it with some difficulty. St. Regent had fired the match at the appointed instant; but the coachman, who chanced to be somewhat intoxicated, driving unusually fast, the carriage had passed the machine two seconds before the explosion took place; and that almost imperceptible fraction of time was enough to save the life which was aimed at. The explosion was terrible. Two or three houses were greatly damaged—twenty persons killed, and about fifty-three wounded; among the latter was the incendiary St. Regent. The report was heard several leagues from Paris. Buonaparte instantly exclaimed to Lannes and Bessières, who were in the carriage, "We are blown up!" The attendants would have stopped the coach, but with more presence of mind he commanded them to drive on, and arrived in safety at the opera;[605] his coachman during the whole time never discovering what had happened, but conceiving the consul had only received a salute of artillery.[606]

A public officer, escaped from such a peril, became an object of yet deeper interest than formerly to the citizens in general; and the reception of the consul at the opera, and elsewhere, was more enthusiastic than ever. Relief was ostentatiously distributed amongst the wounded, and the relatives of the slain; and every one, shocked with the wild atrocity of such a reckless plot, became, while they execrated the perpetrators, attached in proportion to the object of their cruelty. A disappointed conspiracy always adds strength to the

---

[604] Las Cases, tom. i., p. 374.
[605] "I was in the house when the first consul arrived. On entering his box, as usual, he took the front seat; and as all eyes were fixed upon him, he affected the greatest calm."—Bourrienne.
[606] Las Cases, tom. i., p. 374; Fouché, tom. i., p. 184; Savary, tom. i., p. 227.

government against which it is directed; and Buonaparte did not fail to push this advantage to the uttermost.

Notwithstanding that the infernal machine (for so it was not unappropriately termed) had in fact been managed by the hands of Royalists, the first suspicion fell on the Republicans; and Buonaparte took the opportunity, before the public were undeceived on the subject, of dealing that party a blow, from the effects of which they did not recover during his reign. An arbitrary decree of the Senate was asked and readily obtained for the transportation beyond seas of nearly one hundred and thirty of the chiefs of the broken faction of the Jacobins, among whom were several names which belonged to the celebrated Reign of Terror, and had figured in the rolls of the National Convention. These men were so generally hated, as connected with the atrocious scenes during the reign of Robespierre, that the unpopularity of their characters excused the irregularity of the proceedings against them, and their fate was viewed with complacency by many, and with indifference by all. In the end, the first consul became so persuaded of the political insignificance of these relics of Jacobinism, (who, in fact, were as harmless as the fragments of a bombshell after its explosion,) that the decree of deportation was never enforced against them; and Felix Lepelletier, Chaudieu, Talot, and their companions, were allowed to live obscurely in France, watched closely by the police, and under the condition that they should not venture to approach Paris.[607]

The actual conspirators were proceeded against with severity. Chevalier and Veycer, Jacobins, said to have constructed the original model of the infernal machine, were tried before a military commission, condemned to be shot, and suffered death accordingly.

Arena, Ceracchi, Topino-Lebrun, and Demerville, were tried before the ordinary court of criminal judicature, and condemned by the voice of a jury; although there was little evidence against them, save that of their accomplice Harel, by whom they had been betrayed. They also were executed.

---

[607] Montgaillard, tom. v., p. 414; Fouché, tom. i., p. 191.

At a later period, Carbon and St. Regent, Royalists, the agents in the actual attempt of 24th December, were also tried, condemned, and put to death. Some persons tried for the same offence were acquitted; and justice seems to have been distributed with an impartiality unusual in France since the Revolution.

But Buonaparte did not design that the consequences of these plots should end with the deaths of the wretches engaged in them. It afforded an opportunity not to be neglected to advance his principal object, which was the erection of France into a despotic kingdom, and the possessing himself of uncontrolled power over the lives, properties, thoughts, and opinions, of those who were born his fellow-subjects, and of whom the very meanest but lately boasted himself his equal. He has himself expressed his purpose respecting the Constitution of the year Eight, or Consular Government, in words dictated to General Gourgaud:—

"The ideas of Napoleon were fixed; but the aid of time and events were necessary for their realization. The organization of the Consulate had presented nothing in contradiction to them; it taught unanimity, and that was the first step. This point gained, Napoleon was quite indifferent as to the form and denominations of the several constituted bodies. He was a stranger to the Revolution. It was natural that the will of these men, who had followed it through all its phases, should prevail in questions as difficult as they were abstract. The wisest plan was to go on from day to day—by the polar star by which Napoleon meant to guide the Revolution to the haven he desired."[608]

If there is any thing obscure in this passage, it received but too luminous a commentary from the course of Buonaparte's actions; all of which tend to show that he embraced the Consular government as a mere temporary arrangement, calculated to prepare the minds of the French nation for his ulterior views of ambition, as young colts are ridden with a light bridle until they are taught by degrees to endure the curb and bit, or as water-fowl taken in a decoy are first introduced within a wider circuit of nets, in order to their being gradually brought within that strict enclosure where they are made

---

[608] Gourgaud, tom. i., p. 154.

absolute prisoners. He tells us in plain terms, he let the revolutionary sages take their own way in arranging the constitution; determined, without regarding the rules they laid down on the chart, to steer his course by one fixed point to one desired haven. That polar star was his own selfish interest—that haven was despotic power. What he considered as most for his own interest, he was determined to consider as the government most suited for France also. Perhaps he may have persuaded himself that he was actually serving his country as well as himself; and, indeed, justly considered, he was in both instances equally grievously mistaken.

SPECIAL CRIMINAL TRIBUNAL

With the views which he entertained, the chief consul regarded the conspiracies against his life as affording a pretext for extending his power too favourable to be neglected. These repeated attacks on the Head of the state made it desirable that some mode should be introduced of trying such offences, briefer and more arbitrary than the slow forms required by ordinary jurisprudence. The prompt and speedy justice to be expected from a tribunal freed from the ordinary restraint of formalities and justice, was stated to be more necessary on account of the state of the public roads, infested by bands called Chauffeurs, who stopped the public carriages, intercepted the communications of commerce, and became so formidable, that no public coach was permitted to leave Paris without a military guard of at least four soldiers on the roof. This was used as a strong additional reason for constituting a special court of judicature.

Buonaparte could be at no loss for models of such an institution. As hero of the Revolution, he had succeeded to the whole arsenal of revolutionary weapons forged in the name of Liberty, to oppress the dearest rights of humanity. He had but to select that which best suited him, and to mould it to the temper of the times. The country which had so long endured the Revolutionary Tribunal, was not likely to wince under any less stern judicature.

The court which Government now proposed to establish, was to consist of eight members thus qualified. 1. The president and two judges of the ordinary criminal tribunal. 2. Three military men, bearing at least the rank of a captain. 3. Two citizens, to be suggested by Government, who should be selected from such as were by the constitution qualified to act as judges. Thus five out of eight judges were directly named by the Government for the occasion. The court was to decide without jury, without appeal, and without revision of any kind. As a boon to the accused, the court were to have at least six members present, and there was to be no casting vote; so that the party would have his acquittal, unless six members out of eight, or four members out of six, should unite in finding him guilty; whereas in other courts, a bare majority is sufficient for condemnation.

With this poor boon to public opinion, the special Commission Court was to be the jurisdiction before whom armed insurgents, conspirators, and in general men guilty of crimes against the social compact, were to undergo their trial.

The counsellor of state, Portalis, laid this plan before the Legislative Body, by whom it was, according to constitutional form, referred to the consideration of the Tribunate. It was in this body, the only existing branch of the constitution where was preserved some shadow of popular forms and of free debate, that those who continued to entertain free sentiments could have any opportunity of expressing them. Benjamin Constant, Daunon, Chenier, and others, the gleanings as it were of the liberal party, made an honourable but unavailing defence against this invasion of the constitution, studying at the same time to express their opposition in language and by arguments least likely to give offence to the Government. To the honour of the Tribunate, which was the frail but sole remaining barrier of liberty, the project had nearly made shipwreck, and was only passed by a small majority of forty-nine over forty-one. In the Legislative Body there was also a strong minority.[609] It seemed as if the friends of liberty, however deprived of direct popular representation, and of all the means of influencing

---

[609] Montgaillard, tom. v., p. 422; Fouché, tom. i., p. 196.

public opinion, were yet determined to maintain an opposition to the first consul, somewhat on the plan of that of England.

Another law, passed at this time, must have had a cooling effect on the zeal of some of these patriots. It was announced that there were a set of persons, who were to be regarded rather as public enemies than as criminals, and who ought to be provided against rather by anticipating and defeating their schemes than by punishing their offences. These consisted of Republicans, Royalists, or any others entertaining, or supposed to entertain, opinions inimical to the present state of affairs; and the law now passed entitled the government to treat them as suspected persons, and as such, to banish them from Paris or from France. Thus was the chief consul invested with full power over the personal liberty of every person whom he chose to consider as the enemy of his government.

Buonaparte was enabled to avail himself to the uttermost of the powers which he had thus extracted from the constitutional bodies, by the frightful agency of the police. This institution may, even in its mildest form, be regarded as a necessary evil; for although, while great cities continue to afford obscure retreats for vice and crime of every description, there must be men, whose profession it is to discover and bring criminals to justice, as while there are vermin in the animal world, there must be kites and carrion-crows to diminish their number; yet, as the excellence of these guardians of the public depends in a great measure on their familiarity with the arts, haunts, and practices of culprits, they cannot be expected to feel the same horror for crimes, or criminals, which is common to other men. On the contrary, they have a sympathy with them of the same kind which hunters entertain for the game which is the object of their pursuit. Besides, as much of their business is carried on by the medium of spies, they must be able to personate the manners and opinions of those whom they detect; and are frequently induced, by their own interest, to direct, encourage, nay suggest crimes, that they may obtain the reward due for conviction of the offenders.

Applied to state offences, the agency of such persons, though sometimes unavoidable, is yet more frightfully dangerous. Moral delinquencies can be hardly with any probability attributed to worthy or innocent persons; but there is no character so pure, that he who bears it may not be supposed capable of entertaining false and exaggerated opinions in politics, and, as such, become the victim of treachery and delation. In France, a prey to so many factions, the power of the police had become overwhelming; indeed, the very existence of the government seemed in some measure dependent upon the accuracy of their intelligence; and for this purpose their numbers had been enlarged, and their discipline perfected, under the administration of the sagacious and crafty Fouché. This remarkable person had been an outrageous Jacobin, and dipped deep in the horrors of the revolutionary government[610]—an adherent of Barras, and a partaker in the venality and peculation which characterised that period. He was, therefore, totally without principle; but his nature was not of that last degree of depravity, which delights in evil for its own sake, and his good sense told him, that an unnecessary crime was a political blunder. The lenity with which he exercised his terrible office, when left in any degree to his own discretion, while it never prevented his implicit execution of Buonaparte's commands, made the abominable system over which he presided to a certain extent endurable; and thus even his good qualities, while they relieved individual suffering, were of disservice to his country, by reconciling her to bondage.

THE HAUTE POLICE

The *haute police*, as it is called by the French, meaning that department which applies to politics and state affairs, had been unaccountably neglected by the ministers of Louis XVI., and was much disorganized by the consequences of the Revolution. The demagogues of the Convention had little need of a regular system of the kind. Every affiliated club of Jacobins supplied them with spies, and with instruments of their pleasure. The Directory stood in a different situation. They had no general party of their own, and maintained their authority, by balancing the Moderates and Democrats against each other. They, therefore, were more dependent upon the police than their predecessors, and they

---

[610] See *ante*, and vol. i.

intrusted Fouché with the superintendence. It was then that, destroying, or rather superseding, the separate offices where the agents of the police pretended to a certain independence of acting, he brought the whole system to concentrate within his own cabinet. By combining the reports of his agents, and of the various individuals with whom under various pretexts he maintained correspondence, the minister of police arrived at so accurate a knowledge of the purpose, disposition, adherents, and tools of the different parties in France, that he could anticipate their mode of acting upon all occasions that were likely to occur, knew what measures were likely to be proposed, and by whom they were to be supported; and when any particular accident took place, was able, from his previous general information, to assign it to the real cause, and the true actors.

An unlimited system of espial, and that stretching through society in all its ramifications, was necessary to the perfection of this system, which had not arrived to its utmost height, till Napoleon ascended the throne. Still, before his reign, it existed all through France, controlling the most confidential expressions of opinion on public affairs, and, like some mephitic vapour, stifling the breath though it was invisible to the eye, and, by its mysterious terrors, putting a stop to all discussion of public measures, which was not in the tone of implicit approbation.

The expense of maintaining this establishment was immense; for Fouché comprehended amongst his spies and informers, persons whom no ordinary gratuity would have moved to act such a part. But this expense was provided for by the large sums which the minister of police received for the toleration yielded to brothels, gambling-houses, and other places of profligacy, to whom he granted licenses, in consideration of their observing certain regulations. His system of espial was also extended, by the information which was collected in these haunts of debauchery; and thus the vices of the capital were made to support the means by which it was subjected to a despotic government. His autobiography contains a boast, that the private secretary of the chief consul was his pensioner,[611] and that the lavish profusion of Josephine made even her willing to exchange intelligence concerning the chief consul's views and plans.[612] Thus was Fouché not only a spy upon the people in behalf of Buonaparte, but a spy also on Buonaparte himself.

Indeed, the power of the director of this terrible enginery was so great, as to excite the suspicion of Napoleon, who endeavoured to counterbalance it by dividing the department of police into four distinct offices. There were established, 1st, The military police of the palace, over which Duroc, the grand master of the household, presided. 2d, The police maintained by the inspector of the gendarmes. 3d, That exercised over the city of Paris by the prefect. 4th, The general police, which still remained under the control of Fouché. Thus, the first consul received every day four reports of police, and esteemed himself secure of learning, through some one of them, information which the others might have an interest in concealing.[613]

The agents of these different bodies were frequently unknown to each other; and it often happened, that when, in the exercise of their office, they were about to arrest some individual who had incurred suspicion, they found him protected against them, by his connexion with other bureaus of police. The system was, therefore, as complicated as it was oppressive and unjust; but we shall have such frequent opportunity to refer to the subject, that we need here only repeat, that, with reference to his real interest, it was unfortunate for Buonaparte that he found at his disposal so ready a weapon of despotism as the organized police, wielded by a hand so experienced as that of Fouché.

---

[611] "Bourrienne offered to inform me exactly of all the proceedings of Buonaparte for 25,000 francs per month. The proposal was accepted, and, on my side, I had reason to be satisfied with his dexterity and accuracy. This personage was replete with ability and talent, but his greediness of gain very shortly caused his disgrace."—Fouché, tom. i., p. 163.
[612] "Josephine, in conformity to our conditions, cemented by a thousand francs per day, instructed me in all that passed in the interior of the castle."—Fouché, tom. i., p. 154.
[613] Fouché, tom. i., p. 165.

THE POLICE

It was the duty of the police to watch the progress of public opinion, whether it was expressed in general society, and confidential communication, or by the medium of the press. Buonaparte entertained a feverish apprehension of the effects of literature on the general mind, and in doing so acknowledged the weak points in his government. The public journals were under the daily and constant superintendence of the police, and their editors were summoned before Fouché when any thing was inserted which could be considered as disrespectful to his authority. Threats and promises were liberally employed on such occasions, and such journalists as proved refractory, were soon made to feel that the former were no vain menaces. The suppression of the offensive newspaper was often accompanied by the banishment or imprisonment of the editor. The same measure was dealt to authors, booksellers, and publishers, respecting whom the jealousy of Buonaparte amounted to a species of disease.[614]

No one can be surprised that an absolute government should be disposed to usurp the total management of the daily press, and such other branches of literature as are immediately connected with politics; but the interference of Buonaparte's police went much farther, and frequently required from those authors who wrote only on general topics, some express recognisance of his authority. The ancient Christians would not attend the theatre, because it was necessary that, previous to enjoying the beauties of the scene, they should sacrifice some grains of incense to the false deity, supposed to preside over the place. In like manner, men of generous minds in France were often obliged to suppress works on subjects the most alien to politics, because they could not easily obtain a road to the public unless they consented to recognise the right of the individual who had usurped the supreme authority, and extinguished the

---

[614] "How," exclaims Fouché, "could I possibly reform the state, while the press had too much liberty? I therefore determined upon a decisive blow. At one stroke I suppressed eleven popular journals. I caused their presses to be seized, and arrested their editors, whom I accused of sowing dissension among the citizens, of blasting private character, misrepresenting motives, reanimating factions, and rekindling animosities."—*Mémoires*, tom. i., p. 81.

liberties of his country. The circumstances which subjected Madame de Staël to a long persecution by the police of Buonaparte, may be quoted as originating in this busy desire, of connecting his government with the publications of all persons of genius.

We have been already led to notice, that there existed no cordiality betwixt Buonaparte and the gifted daughter of Necker. Their characters were far from suited to each other. She had manifestly regarded the first consul as a subject of close and curious observation, and Buonaparte loved not that any one should make him the subject of minute scrutiny. Madame de Staël was the centre also of a distinguished circle of society in France, several of whom were engaged to support the cause of liberty; and the resolution of a few members of the Tribunate, to make some efforts to check the advance of Buonaparte to arbitrary power, was supposed to be taken in her saloon, and under her encouragement. For this she was only banished from Paris.[615] But when she was about to publish her excellent and spirited book on German manners and literature, in which, unhappily, there was no mention of the French nation, or its supreme chief, Madame de Staël's work was seized by the police, and she was favoured with a line from Savary, acquainting her that the air of France did not suit her health, and inviting her to leave it with all convenient speed.[616] While in exile from Paris, which she accounted her country, the worthy Prefect of Geneva suggested a mode by which she might regain favour. An ode on the birth of the King of Rome was recommended as the means of conciliation. Madame de Staël answered, she should limit herself to wishing him a good nurse; and became exposed to new rigours, even extending to the friends who ventured to visit her in her exile. So general was the French influence all over Europe, that to shelter herself from the

---

[615] Considerations sur la Révolution Française, tom. ii., p. 301.
[616] "Madame de Staël had not been banished; but she was ordered to a distance from the capital. She has, no doubt, been told, that Napoleon had, of his own accord, ordered her banishment; but this was by no means the case. I know in what manner the circumstance originated, and can safely assert, that when he forced her from her attachment to the world, and ordered her to retire into the country, he only yielded to the repeated entreaties, and the unfavourable reports made to him; for, it must be acknowledged, that he paid far too much deference to her notions of self-consequence, and to her work on Germany. She assumed the right to advise, foresee, and control, in matters in which the Emperor felt himself fully qualified to act upon his own judgment. To get rid of the annoyance, he sent her to distribute her advice at a distance from him."—Savary, tom. iii., p. 4.

persecutions by which she was everywhere followed, she was at length obliged to escape to England, by the remote way of Russia. Chenier, author of the Hymn of the Marseillois, though formerly the panegyrist of General Buonaparte, became, with other literary persons who did not bend low enough to his new dignity, objects of persecution to the first consul. The childish pertinacity with which Napoleon followed up such unreasonable piques, belongs indeed, chiefly, to the history of the Emperor, but it showed its blossoms earlier. The power of indulging such petty passions, goes, in a great measure, to foster and encourage their progress; and in the case of Buonaparte, this power, great in itself, was increased by the dangerous facilities which the police offered, for gratifying the spleen, or the revenge, of the offended sovereign.

THE CONCORDAT

Another support of a very different kind, and grounded on the most opposite principles, was afforded to the rising power of Napoleon, through the re-establishment of religion in France, by his treaty with the Pope, called the Concordat. Two great steps had been taken towards this important point, by the edict opening the churches, and renewing the exercise of the Christian religion, and by the restoration of the Pope to his temporal dominions after the battle of Marengo. The further objects to be attained were the sanction of the first consul's government by the Pontiff on the one hand, and, on the other, the re-establishment of the rights of the Church in France, so far as should be found consistent with the new order of things.

This important treaty was managed by Joseph Buonaparte, who, with three colleagues, held conferences for that purpose with the plenipotentiaries of the Pope. The ratifications were exchanged on the 18th of September 1801; and when they were published, it was singular to behold how submissively the once proud See of Rome lay prostrated before the power of Buonaparte, and how absolutely he must have dictated all the terms of the treaty. Every article innovated on some of those rights and claims, which the

Church of Rome had for ages asserted as the unalienable privileges of her infallible head.

I. It was provided, that the Catholic religion should be freely exercised in France, acknowledged as the national faith, and its service openly practised, subject to such regulations of police as the French Government should judge necessary. II. The Pope, in concert with the French Government, was to make a new division of dioceses, and to require of the existing bishops even the resignation of their sees, should that be found necessary to complete the new arrangement. III. The sees which should become vacant by such resignation, or by deprivation, in case a voluntary abdication was refused, as also all future vacancies, were to be filled up by the Pope, on nominations proceeding from the French Government. IV. The new bishops were to take an oath of fidelity to the Government, and to observe a ritual, in which there were to be especial forms of prayer for the consuls. V. The church-livings were to undergo a new division, and the bishops were to nominate to them, but only such persons as should be approved by the Government. VI. The Government was to make suitable provision for the national clergy, while the Pope expressly renounced all right competent to him and his successors, to challenge or dispute the sales of church property which had been made since the Revolution.[617]

Such was the celebrated compact, by which Pius VII. surrendered to a soldier, whose name was five or six years before unheard of in Europe, those high claims to supremacy in spiritual affairs, which his predecessors had maintained for so many ages against the whole potentates of Europe. A puritan might have said of the power seated on the Seven Hills—"Babylon is fallen,—it is fallen that great city!" The more rigid Catholics were of the same opinion. The Concordat, they alleged, showed rather the abasement of the Roman hierarchy than the re-erection of the Gallic Church.

The proceedings against the existing bishops of France, most of whom were of course emigrants, were also but little edifying. Acting upon the article of the Concordat already noticed, and

---

[617] For a copy of the treaty, see Annual Register, vol. xliii., p. 302.

caused, as the letter[618] itself states, "by the exigencies of the times, which exercises its violence even on us," the Pope required of each of these reverend persons, by an especial mandate, to accede to the compact, by surrendering his see, as therein provided. The order was peremptory in its terms, and an answer was demanded within fifteen days. The purpose of this haste was to prevent consultation or combination, and to place before each bishop, individually, the choice of compliance, thereby gaining a right to be provided for in the new hierarchy; or of refusal, in which case the Pope would be obliged to declare the see vacant, in conformity to his engagement with Buonaparte.

The bishops in general declined compliance with a request, which, on the part of the Pope, was evidently made by compulsion. They offered to lay their resignation at his Holiness's feet, so soon as they should be assured that there was regular canonical provision made for filling up their sees; but they declined, by any voluntary act of theirs, to give countenance to the surrender of the rights of the Church implied in the Concordat, and preferred exile and poverty to any provision which they might obtain, by consenting to compromise the privileges of the hierarchy. These proceedings greatly increased the unpopularity of the Concordat among the more zealous Catholics.

Others of that faith there were, who, though they considered the new system as very imperfect, yet thought it might have the effect of preserving in France some sense of the Christian religion, which, under the total disuse of public worship, stood a chance of being entirely extinguished in the minds of the rising generation. They remembered, that though the Jews in the days of Esdras shed tears of natural sorrow when they beheld the inferiority of the second Temple, yet Providence had sanctioned its erection, under the warrant, and by permission, of an unbelieving task-master. They granted, that the countenance shown by Buonaparte to the religious establishment, was entirely from motives of self-interest; but still they hoped that God, who works his own will by the selfish passions of individuals, was now using those of the first consul to

---

[618] The Pope's Brief to the Archbishops and Bishops of France. See Annual Register, vol. xliii., p. 308.

recall some sense of religion to France; and they anticipated that religion, as the best friend of all that is good and graceful in humanity, was likely, in course of time, to bring back and encourage a sense of rational liberty.

The revolutionary part of France beheld the Concordat with very different eyes. The Christian religion was, as to the Jews and Greeks of old, a stumbling-block to the Jacobins, and foolishness to the philosophers. It was a system which they had attacked with a zeal even as eager as that which they had directed against monarchical institutions; and in the restoration of the altar, they foresaw the re-erection of the throne. Buonaparte defended himself among the philosophers, by comparing his Concordat to a sort of vaccination of religion, which, by introducing a slighter kind into the system of the state, would gradually prepare for its entire extinction.[619]

In the meantime, he proceeded to renew the ancient league betwixt the church and crown, with as much solemnity as possible. Portalis[620] was created minister of religion, a new office, for managing the affairs of the Church. He had deserved this preferment, by a learned and argumentative speech to the Legislative Body, in which he proved to the French statesmen, (what in other countries is seldom considered as matter of doubt,) that the exercise of religion is congenial to human nature, and worthy of being cherished and protected by the state. The Concordat was inaugurated at Notre Dame, [April 1802,] with the utmost magnificence. Buonaparte attended in person, with all the badges and pomp of royalty, and in the style resembling as nearly as possible that of the former Kings of France. The Archbishop of Aix was appointed to preach upon the occasion, being the very individual prelate who had delivered the sermon upon the

---

[619] "One day he assured the prelates, that, in his opinion, there was no religion but the Catholic, which was truly founded on ancient tradition; and on this subject he usually displayed to them some erudition acquired the day before; then, when he was with the philosophers, he said to Cabanis, 'Do you know what this Concordat is which I have just signed? It is the vaccination of religion, and in fifty years there will be none in France.'"— Mad. de Staël, tom. ii., p. 275.

[620] Jean-Etienne-Marie Portalis was born at Beausset in 1746. He died at Paris in 1807. A posthumous treatise, "Sur l'Usage et l'Abus de l'Esprit Philosophique, pendant le 18ᵉ Siècle," was published in 1820, by his son.

coronation of Louis XVI. Some address, it was said, was employed to procure the attendance of the old republican generals. They were invited by Berthier to breakfast, and thence carried to the first consul's levee; after which it became impossible for them to decline attending him to the church of Notre Dame.[621] As he returned from the ceremony, surrounded by these military functionaries, Buonaparte remarked with complacency, that the former order of things was fast returning. One of his generals boldly answered,— "Yes!—all returns—excepting the two millions of Frenchmen, who have died to procure the proscription of the very system now in the act of being restored."[622]

It is said that Buonaparte, when he found the Pope and the clergy less tractable than he desired, regretted having taken the step of re-establishing religion, and termed the Concordat the greatest error of his reign. But such observations could only escape him in a moment of pique or provocation. He well knew the advantage which a government must derive from a national church, which recognises them in its ritual; and at Saint Helena, he himself at once acknowledged the advantage of his compact with the Pope as a measure of state, and his indifference to it in a religious point of view. "I never regretted the Concordat," he said. "I must have had either that or some thing equivalent. Had the Pope never before existed, he should have been made for the occasion."[623]

The first consul took care, accordingly, to make his full advantage of the Concordat, by introducing his own name as much as possible into the catechism of the Church, which, in other respects, was that drawn up by Bossuet. To honour Napoleon, the catechumen was taught, was the same as to honour and serve God

---

[621] Fouché, tom. i., p. 225.
[622] Mad. de Staël, tom. ii., p. 278; Montgaillard, tom. v., p. 443.—"On the way from the Tuileries to Notre Dame, Lannes and Augereau wished to get out of the carriage on finding that they were to be carried to mass; and would have done so, had not an order from Buonaparte prevented them. They went then to Notre Dame; but on the morrow, when the consul asked Augereau how he liked the ceremony, he replied, 'Oh, all was very fine; there only wanted the million of men who devoted themselves to death, in order to destroy what we are now establishing.' Buonaparte was much irritated at this observation."— Bourrienne.
[623] Montholon, tom. i., p. 121.

himself—to oppose his will, was to incur the penalty of eternal damnation.[624]

In civil affairs, Buonaparte equally exerted his talents, in connecting the safety and interests of the nation with his own aggrandisement. He had already laughed at the idea of a free constitution. "The only free constitution necessary," he said, "or useful, was a good civil code;" not considering, or choosing to have it considered, that the best system of laws, when held by no better guarantee than the pleasure of an arbitrary prince and his council of state, is as insecure as the situation of a pearl suspended by a single hair. Let us do justice to Napoleon, however, by acknowledging, that he encountered with manly firmness the gigantic labour of forming a code of institutions, which, supplying the immense variety of provincial laws that existed in the different departments of France, and suppressing the partial and temporary regulations made in the various political crises of the Revolution, were designed to be the basis of a uniform national system. For this purpose, an order of the consuls convoked Messrs. Portalis, Tronchet,[625] Bigot de Préameneu,[626] and Maleville,[627] juris-consults of the highest character, and associated them with the Minister of Justice, Cambacérès, in the task of adjusting and reporting a plan for a general system of jurisprudence. The progress and termination of this great work will be hereafter noticed. The chief consul himself took an active part in the deliberations.

An ordinance, eminently well qualified to heal the civil wounds of France, next manifested the talents of Buonaparte, and, as men hoped, his moderation. This was the general amnesty

---

[624] "The Concordat was necessary to religion, to the Republic, to government: the temples were shut up, the priests were persecuted. The Concordat rebuilt the altars, put an end to disorders, commanded the faithful to pray for the republic, and dissipated all the scruples of the purchasers of national domains."—Napoleon, *Montholon*, tom. i., p. 120.

[625] Tronchet was a lawyer of great celebrity, and was one of Louis Sixteenth's counsel. See *ante*, vol. i. He died in 1806, and was buried in the Pantheon.

[626] Bigot de Préameneu was born in Brittany about the year 1750. In 1808, he succeeded Portalis as minister of public worship, but was removed from office on the restoration of the Bourbons. He died at Paris in 1825.

[627] Jacques de Maleville was born at Domme in 1741. In 1804-5, he published "Analyse raisonnée de la Discussion du Code Civile au Conseil-d'état." He was created a peer by Louis XVIII. in 1814, and died in 1825.

granted to the emigrants. A decree of the Senate, 26th April, 1802, permitted the return of these unfortunate persons to France, providing they did so, and took the oath of fidelity to Government, within a certain period. There were, however, five classes of exceptions, containing such as seemed too deeply and strongly pledged to the house of Bourbon, ever to reconcile themselves to the government of Buonaparte. Such were, 1st, Those who had been chiefs of bodies of armed royalists;—2d, Who had held rank in the armies of the allies; 3d, Who had belonged to the household of the princes of the blood;—4th, Who had been agents or encouragers of foreign or domestic war;—5th, The generals and admirals, together with the representatives of the people, who had been guilty of treason against the Republic, together with the prelates, who declined to resign their sees in terms of the Concordat. It was at the same time declared, that not more than five hundred in all should be excepted from the amnesty. Buonaparte truly judged, that the mass of emigrants, thus winnowed and purified from all who had been leaders, exhausted in fortune and wearied out by exile, would in general be grateful for permission to return to France, and passive, nay, contented and attached subjects of his dominion; and the event in a great measure, if not fully, justified his expectations. Such part of their property as had not been sold, was directed to be restored to them;[628] but they were subjected to the special superintendence of the police for the space of ten years after their return.[629]

PUBLIC EDUCATION

With similar and most laudable attention to the duties of his high office, Buonaparte founded plans of education,[630] and

---

[628] "At one time I intended to form a mass or a *syndicate* of all the unsold property of the emigrants, and on their return, to distribute it in certain proportions among them. But when I came to grant property to individuals, I soon found that I was creating too many wealthy men, and that they repaid my favours with insolence."—Napoleon, *Las Cases*, tom. iii., p. 213.

[629] Fouché, tom. i., p. 226; Montgaillard, tom. v., p. 464.

[630] "One of my grand objects was to render education accessible to every one. I caused every institution to be formed upon a plan which offered instruction to the public, either gratis, or at a rate so moderate, as not to be beyond the means of the peasant. The museums were thrown open to the *canaille*. My *canaille* would have become the best

particularly, with Mongé's assistance, established the Polytechnic school, which has produced so many men of talent. He inquired anxiously into abuses, and was particularly active in correcting those which had crept into the prisons during the Revolution, where great tyranny was exercised by monopoly of provisions, and otherwise.[631] In amending such evils, Buonaparte, though not of kingly birth, showed a mind worthy of the rank to which he had ascended. It is only to be regretted, that in what interfered with his personal wishes or interest, he uniformly failed to manifest the sound and correct views, which on abstract questions he could form so clearly.

Other schemes of a public character were held out as occupying the attention of the chief consul. Like Augustus, whose situation his own in some measure resembled, Napoleon endeavoured, by the magnificence of his projects for the improvement of the state, to withdraw attention from his inroads upon public freedom. The inland navigation of Languedoc was to be completed, and a canal, joining the river Yonne to the Saonne, was to connect the south part of the Republic so completely with the north, as to establish a communication by water between Marseilles and Amsterdam. Bridges were also to be built, roads to be laid out and improved, museums founded in the principal towns of France, and many other public labours undertaken, on a scale which should put to shame even the boasted days of Louis XIV. Buonaparte knew the French nation well, and was aware that he should best reconcile them to his government, by indulging his own genius for bold and magnificent undertakings, whether of a military or a civil character.

But although these splendid proposals filled the public ear, and flattered the national pride of France, commerce continued to languish, under the effects of a constant blockade, provisions became dear, and discontent against the Consulate began to gain ground over the favourable sentiments which had hailed its

---

educated in the world. All my exertions were directed to illuminate the mass of the nation, instead of brutifying them by ignorance and superstition."—Napoleon, *O'Meara*, vol. ii., p. 385.

[631] "At the time of my downfall, the state prisons contained two hundred and fifty individuals, and I found nine thousand in them, when I became consul."—Napoleon, *Las Cases*, tom. v., p. 56.

commencement. The effectual cure for these heart-burnings was only to be found in a general peace; and a variety of circumstances, some of them of a character very unpleasing to the first consul, seemed gradually preparing for this desirable event.

CHAPTER XXII

Return to the external Relations of France—Her universal Ascendency—Napoleon's advances to the Emperor Paul—Plan of destroying the British Power in India—Right of Search at Sea—Death of Paul—Its effects on Buonaparte—Affairs of Egypt—Assassination of Kleber—Menou appointed to succeed him—British Army lands in Egypt—Battle and Victory of Alexandria—Death of Sir Ralph Abercromby—General Hutchinson succeeds him—The French General Belliard capitulates—as does Menou—War in Egypt brought to a victorious Conclusion.

THE EMPEROR PAUL

Having thus given a glance at the internal affairs of France during the commencement of Buonaparte's domination, we return to her external relations, which, since the peace of Luneville, had assumed the appearance of universal ascendency, so much had the current of human affairs been altered by the talents and fortunes of one man. Not only was France in secure possession, by the treaty of Luneville, of territories extending to the banks of the Rhine, but the surrounding nations were, under the plausible names of protection or alliance, as submissive to her government as if they had made integral parts of her dominions. Holland, Switzerland, and Italy, were all in a state of subjection to her will; Spain, like a puppet, moved but at her signal; Austria was brokenspirited and dejected; Prussia still remembered her losses in the first revolutionary war; and Russia, who alone could be considered as unmoved by any fear of France, was yet in a situation to be easily managed, by flattering and cajoling the peculiar temper of the Emperor Paul.

We have already observed, that Buonaparte had artfully availed himself of the misunderstanding between Austria and Russia, to insinuate himself into the good graces of the Czar. The disputes between Russia and England gave him still further advantages over the mind of that incautious monarch.

The refusal of Britain to cede the almost impregnable fortress of Malta, and with it the command of the Mediterranean, to a power who was no longer friendly, was aggravated by her declining to admit Russian prisoners into the cartel of exchange betwixt the French and British. Buonaparte contrived to make his approaches to the Czar in a manner calculated to bear upon both these subjects of grievance. He presented to Paul, who affected to be considered as the Grand Master of the Order of St. John of Jerusalem, the sword given by the Pope to the heroic John de la Valette, who was at the head of the Order during the celebrated defence of Malta against the Turks.[632] With the same view of placing his own conduct in a favourable contrast with that of Great Britain, he new-clothed and armed eight or nine thousand Russian prisoners, and dismissed them freely, in token of his personal esteem for the character of the Emperor.

A more secret and scandalous mode of acquiring interest is said to have been attained, through the attachment of the unfortunate prince to a French actress of talents and beauty, who had been sent from Paris for the express purpose of acquiring his affections. From these concurring reasons, Paul began now openly to manifest himself as the warm friend of France, and the bitter enemy of Britain. In the former capacity, he had the weak and unworthy complaisance to withdraw the hospitality which he had hitherto afforded to the relics of the royal family of Bourbon, who were compelled to remove from Mittau, where they had been hitherto permitted to reside.

To gratify his pique against England, Paul gave hearing at least to a magnificent scheme, by which Buonaparte proposed to accomplish the destruction of the British power in India, which he had in vain hoped to assail by the possession of Egypt. The scheme

---

[632] Gourgaud, tom. ii., p. 131.

was now to be effected by the union of the French and Russian troops, which were to force their way to British India overland, through the kingdom of Persia; and a plan of such a campaign was seriously in agitation. Thirty-five thousand French were to descend the Danube into the Black sea; and then, being wafted across that sea and the sea of Azof, were to march by land to the banks of the Wolga. Here they were again to be embarked, and descend the river to Astracan, and from thence were to cross the Caspian sea to Astrabad, where they were to be joined by a Russian army, equal in force to their own. It was thought that, marching through Persia by Herat, Ferah, and Candahar, the Russo-Gallic army might reach the Indus in forty-five days from Astrabad. This gigantic project would scarce have been formed by any less daring genius than Napoleon; nor could any prince, with a brain less infirm than Paul's, have agreed to become his tool in so extraordinary an undertaking, from which France was to derive all the advantage.[633]

A nearer mode of injuring the interests of England than this overland march to India, was in the power of the Emperor of Russia. A controversy being in dependence betwixt England and the northern courts, afforded the pretext for throwing his weight into the scale against her at this dangerous crisis.

The right of search at sea, that is, the right of stopping a neutral or friendly vessel, and taking out of her the goods belonging to an enemy, is acknowledged in the earliest maritime codes. But England, by her naval superiority, had been enabled to exert this right so generally that it became the subject of much heart-burning to neutral powers. The association of the Northern states in 1780, known by the name of the Armed Neutrality, had for its object to put down this right of search, and establish the maxim that free bottoms made free goods; in other words, that the neutral character of the vessel should protect whatever property she might have on board. This principle was now anxiously reclaimed by France, as the most effective argument for the purpose of irritating the neutral powers against Great Britain, whose right of search, which could not be exercised without vexation and inconvenience to their commerce, must necessarily be unpopular amongst them. Forgetting that the

---

[633] Las Cases, tom. iii., p. 248; O'Meara, vol. i., p. 381.

danger occasioned by the gigantic power of France was infinitely greater than any which could arise from the maritime claims of England, the northern courts became again united on the subject of what they termed the freedom of the seas. Indeed, the Emperor Paul, even before the offence arising out of his disappointment respecting Malta, had proceeded so far as to sequestrate all British property in his dominions, in resentment of her exercising the right of search. But upon the fresh provocation which he conceived himself to have received, the Emperor became outrageous, and took the most violent measures for seizing the persons and property of the English, that ever were practised by an angry and unreasonable despot.

Prussia, more intent on her own immediate aggrandisement, than mindful of the welfare of Europe in general, took advantage of the universal ill-will against England, to seize upon the King's continental dominions of Hanover, with peculiar breach of public faith, as she herself had guaranteed the neutrality of that country.

DEATH OF THE EMPEROR PAUL

The consequences, with regard to the northern powers, are well known. The promptitude of the administration sent a strong fleet to the Baltic; and the well-contested battle of Copenhagen detached Denmark from the Northern Confederacy. Sweden had joined it unwillingly; and Russia altered her course of policy in consequence of the death of Paul. That unhappy prince had surmounted the patience of his subjects, and fell a victim to one of those conspiracies, which in arbitrary monarchies, especially such as partake of the Oriental character, supply all the checks of a moderate and free constitution, where the prerogative of the crown is limited by laws. In these altered circumstances, the cause of dispute was easily removed, by the right of search being subjected to equitable regulations and modifications.

Buonaparte received the news of Paul's death with much more emotion than he was usually apt to testify. It is said, that, for the first time in his life, a passionate exclamation of *"Mon Dieu!"*

escaped him, in a tone of sorrow and surprise. With Paul's immense power, and his disposition to place it at the disposal of France, the first consul doubtless reckoned upon the accomplishment of many important plans which his death disconcerted. It was natural, also, that Napoleon should be moved by the sudden and violent end of a prince, who had manifested so much admiration of his person and his qualities. He is said to have dwelt so long on the strangeness of the incident, that Fouché was obliged to remind him, that it was a mode of changing a chief magistrate, or a course of administration, which was common to the empire in which it took place.[634]

The death of Paul, so much regretted by Buonaparte, was nevertheless the means of accelerating a peace between France and Great Britain, which, if it could have been established on a secure basis, would have afforded him the best chance of maintaining his power, and transmitting it to his posterity. While the Czar continued to be his observant ally, there was little prospect that the first consul would be moderate enough in the terms which he might have proffered, to permit the British Ministry to treat with him.

Another obstacle to peace was at this time removed, in a manner not more acceptable to Buonaparte than was the death of the Emperor Paul. The possession of Egypt by the French was a point which the first consul would have insisted upon from strong personal feeling. The Egyptian expedition was intimately connected with his own personal glory, nor was it likely that he would have sacrificed its results to his desire of peace with Great Britain. On the other hand, there was no probability that England would accede to any arrangement which should sanction the existence of a French colony, settled in Egypt with the express purpose of destroying our Indian commerce. But this obstacle to peace was removed by the fate of arms.

Affairs in Egypt had been on the whole unfavourable to the French, since that army had lost the presence of the commander-in-

---

[634] "Mais enfin, que voulez vous? C'est une mode de destitution propre à ce pais-là!"—S.—"I told him, that whatever might be the mode of deposition practised in Russia, luckily the south of Europe was a stranger to such treacherous habits and attempts; but my arguments could not convince him; he gave vent to his passion in ejaculations, stampings of the foot, and short fits of rage. I never beheld so striking a scene."—Fouché, tom. i., p. 205.

chief. Kleber, on whom the command devolved, was discontented both at the unceremonious and sudden manner in which the duty had been imposed upon him, and with the scarcity of means left to support his defence. Perceiving himself threatened by a large Turkish force, which was collecting for the purpose of avenging the defeat of the vizier at Aboukir, he became desirous of giving up a settlement which he despaired of maintaining. He signed accordingly a convention with the Turkish plenipotentiaries, and Sir Sidney Smith, on the part of the British, by which it was provided that the French should evacuate Egypt, and that Kleber and his army should be transported to France in safety, without being molested by the British fleet. When the British Government received advice of this convention, they refused to ratify it, on the ground that Sir Sidney Smith had exceeded his powers in entering into it. The Earl of Elgin having been sent out as plenipotentiary to the Porte, it was asserted that Sir Sidney's ministerial powers were superseded by his appointment. Such was the alleged informality on which the treaty fell to the ground; but the truth was, that the arrival of Kleber and his army in the south of France, at the very moment when the successes of Suwarrow gave strong hopes of making some impression on her frontier, might have had a most material effect upon the events of the war. Lord Keith, therefore, who commanded in the Mediterranean, received orders not to permit the passage of the French Egyptian army, and the treaty of El Arish was in consequence broken off.

Kleber, disappointed of this mode of extricating himself, had recourse to arms. The Vizier Jouseff Pacha, having crossed the desert, and entered Egypt, received a bloody and decisive defeat from the French general, near the ruins of the ancient city of Heliopolis, on the 20th March, 1800. The measures which Kleber adopted after this victory were well calculated to maintain the possession of the country, and reconcile the inhabitants to the French government. He was as moderate in the imposts as the exigencies of his army permitted, greatly improved the condition of the troops, and made, if not peace, at least an effectual truce, with the restless and enterprising Murad Bey, who still continued to be at the head of a considerable body of Mamelukes. Kleber also raised among the Greeks a legion of fifteen hundred or two thousand men; and with more difficulty succeeded in levying a regiment of Cophts.

ASSASSINATION OF KLEBER

While busied in these measures, he was cut short by the blow of an assassin. A fanatic Turk, called Soliman Haleby, a native of Aleppo, imagined he was inspired by Heaven to slay the enemy of the Prophet and the Grand Seignior. He concealed himself in a cistern, and springing out on Kleber when there was only one man in company with him, stabbed him dead.[635] The assassin was justly condemned to die by a military tribunal; but the sentence was executed with a barbarity which disgraced those who practised it. Being impaled alive, he survived for four hours in the utmost tortures, which he bore with an indifference which his fanaticism perhaps alone could have bestowed.[636]

The Baron Menou, on whom the command now devolved, was an inferior person to Kleber. He had made some figure amongst the nobles who followed the revolutionary cause in the Constituent Assembly, and was the same general whose want of decision at the affair of the Sections had led to the employment of Buonaparte in his room, and to the first rise, consequently, of the fortunes which had since swelled so high. Menou altered for the worse several of the regulations of Kleber, and, carrying into literal execution what Buonaparte had only written and spoken of, he became an actual Mahommedan, married a native Turkish woman, and assumed the name of Abdallah Menou. This change of religion exposed him to

---

[635] The remains of Kleber were interred with great pomp, and a monument was raised to his memory. Buonaparte evinced sincere regret at the loss of this excellent officer, and caused a medal to be struck upon the occasion, with the words "General Kleber, born in 1753, assassinated at Cairo, the 14th of June, 1800;" and on the reverse, "Surnamed, from his stature and intrepidity, the French Hercules; he braved death a thousand times in the field, and fell under the dagger of an assassin." Kleber and Desaix were Napoleon's favourite lieutenants. "Both," he said, "possessed great and rare virtues, though their characters were very dissimilar. Kleber's was the talent of nature: Desaix's was entirely the result of education and assiduity: Kleber was an irreparable loss to France; he was a man of the brightest talents and the greatest bravery."

[636] His body was embalmed and brought by the French savans from Egypt, to be deposited in the museum of natural history at Paris.

the ridicule of the French, while it went in no degree to conciliate the Egyptians.[637]

The succours from France, which Buonaparte had promised in his farewell address to the Egyptian army, arrived slowly, and in small numbers. This was not the fault of the chief consul, who had commanded Gantheaume to put to sea with a squadron, having on board four or five thousand men; but being pursued by the English fleet, that admiral was glad to regain the harbour of Toulon. Other efforts were made with the same indifferent success. The French ports were too closely watched to permit the sailing of any expedition on a large scale, and two frigates, with five or six hundred men, were the only reinforcements that reached Egypt.

Meantime the English Cabinet had adopted the daring and manly resolution of wresting from France this favourite colony by force. They had for a length of time confined their military efforts to partial and detached objects, which, if successful, could not have any effect on the general results of the war, and which, when they miscarried, as was the case before Cadiz, Ferrol, and elsewhere, tended to throw ridicule on the plans of the Ministry, and however undeservedly, even upon the character of the forces employed on the service. It was by such ill-considered and imperfect efforts that the war was maintained on our part, while our watchful and formidable enemy combined his mighty means to effect objects of commensurate importance. We, like puny fencers, offered doubtful and uncertain blows, which could only affect the extremities; he never aimed, save at the heart, nor thrust, but with the determined purpose of plunging his weapon to the hilt.

The consequence of these partial and imperfect measures was, that even while our soldiers were in the act of gradually attaining that perfection of discipline by which they are now distinguished, they ranked—most unjustly—lower in the respect of their countrymen, than at any other period in our history. The pre-eminent excellence of our sailors had been shown in a thousand actions; and it became too usual to place it in contrast with the

---

[637] Montholon, tom. i., p. 78; Memoirs of the Duke of Rovigo, vol. i., p. 243; Las Cases, tom. i., p. 226.

failure of our expeditions on shore. But it was afterwards found that our soldiers could assume the same superiority, whenever the plan of the campaign offered them a fair field for its exercise. Such a field of action was afforded by the Egyptian expedition.

BRITISH EXPEDITION TO EGYPT

This undertaking was the exclusive plan of an ill-requited statesman, the late Lord Melville;[638] who had difficulty in obtaining even Mr. Pitt's concurrence in a scheme, of a character so much more daring than Britain had lately entertained. The expedition was resolved upon by the narrowest possible majority in the Cabinet; and his late majesty interposed his consent in terms inferring a solemn protest against the risk about to be incurred. "It is with the utmost reluctance" (such, or nearly such, were the words of George III.) "that I consent to a measure which sends the flower of my army upon a dangerous expedition against a distant province."[639] The event, however, showed, that in arduous circumstances, the daring game, if previously well considered, is often the most successful.

On the 8th March, 1801, General Sir Ralph Abercrombie, at the head of an army of seventeen thousand men, landed in Egypt, in despite of the most desperate opposition by the enemy. The excellence of the troops was displayed by the extreme gallantry and calmness with which, landing through a heavy surf, they instantly formed and advanced against the enemy. On the 21st of March, a general action took place. The French cavalry attempted to turn the British flank, and made a desperate charge for that purpose, but failed in their attempt, and were driven back with great loss. The French were defeated, and compelled to retreat on Alexandria,

---

[638] Henry Dundas, created in 1802, Baron Duneira and Viscount Melville, died in May, 1811.

[639] At an after period, the good King made the following acknowledgment of his mistake. When Lord Melville was out of power, his majesty did him the honour to visit him at Wimbledon, and partook of some refreshment. On that occasion the King took an opportunity to fill a glass of wine, and having made the company do the same, he gave as his toast, "The health of the courageous minister, who, against the opinion of many of his colleagues, and even the remonstrances of his king, had dared to conceive and carry through the Egyptian expedition."—S.

under the walls of which they hoped to maintain themselves. But the British suffered an irreparable loss in their lamented commander, Sir Ralph Abercrombie, who was mortally wounded in the course of the action. In this gallant veteran his country long regretted one of the best generals, and one of the worthiest and most amiable men, to whom she ever gave birth.

The command descended on General Hutchinson, who was soon joined by the Capitan Pacha, with a Turkish army. The recollections of Aboukir and Heliopolis, joined to the remonstrances and counsels of their English allies, induced the Turks to avoid a general action, and confine themselves to skirmishes, by which system the French were so closely watched, and their communications so effectually destroyed, that General Belliard, shut up in a fortified camp in Cairo, cut off from Alexandria, and threatened with insurrection within the place, was compelled to capitulate, under condition that his troops should safely be transported to France, with their arms and baggage. This was on the 28th of June, and the convention[640] had scarce been signed, when the English army was reinforced in a manner which showed the bold and successful combination of measures under which the expedition had been undertaken.

An army of seven thousand men, of whom two thousand were sepoys, or native Indian troops, were disembarked at Cosseir, on the Red Sea, and, detached from the Indian settlements, now came to support the European part of the English invasion. The Egyptians saw with the extremity of wonder, native troops, many of them Moslemah, who worshipped in the mosques, and observed the ritual enjoined by the Prophet, perfectly accomplished in the European discipline. The lower class were inclined to think, that this singular reinforcement had been sent to them in consequence of Mohammed's direct and miraculous interposition; only their being commanded by English officers did not favour this theory.

In consequence of these reinforcements, and his own confined situation under the walls of Alexandria, Menou saw himself constrained to enter into a convention for surrendering up

---

[640] For a copy of the Convention, see Annual Register, vol. xliii., p. 221.

the province of Egypt. He was admitted to the same terms of composition which had been granted to Belliard; and thus the war in that quarter was, on the part of Great Britain, triumphantly concluded.

The conquest of this disputed kingdom excited a strong sensation both in France and Britain; but the news of the contest being finally closed by Menou's submission, are believed to have reached the former country some time before the English received them. Buonaparte, on learning the tidings, is reported to have said, "Well, there remains now no alternative but to make the descent on Britain." But it seems to have occurred to him presently afterwards, that the loss of this disputed province might, instead of being an argument for carrying the war to extremity, be considered as the removal of an obstacle to a treaty of peace.[641]

---

[641] "Napoleon never ceased to repeat, that Egypt ought to have remained in the possession of the French, which, he said, would infallibly have been the case, had the country been defended by Kleber or Desaix."—Las Cases, tom. i., p. 230.—"However great was the displeasure of the first consul at what had taken place, not an expression of ill-humour escaped him against any one. He showed at all times a marked preference for those who formed a part of the army of Egypt, with the exception of a few officers who had made themselves conspicuous by their bad spirit and ingratitude; and the only revenge he took on these was to forget them altogether."—Duke of Rovigo, vol. i., p. 251.

Chapter XXIII

Preparations for the Invasion of Britain—Nelson put in command of the Sea—Attack of the Boulogne Flotilla—Pitt leaves the Ministry—succeeded by Mr. Addington—Negotiations for Peace—Just punishment of England, in regard to the conquered Settlements of the enemy—Forced to restore them all, save Ceylon and Trinidad—Malta is placed under the guarantee of a Neutral Power—Preliminaries of Peace signed—Joy of the English Populace, and doubts of the better classes—Treaty of Amiens signed—The ambitious projects of Napoleon, nevertheless, proceed without interruption—Extension of his power in Italy—He is appointed Consul for life, with the power of naming his Successor—His Situation at this period.

As the words of the first consul appeared to intimate, preparations were resumed on the French coast for the invasion of Great Britain. Boulogne, and every harbour along the coast, was crowded with flat-bottomed boats, and the shores covered with camps of the men designed apparently to fill them. We need not at present dwell on the preparations for attack, or those which the English adopted in defence, as we shall have occasion to notice both, when Buonaparte, for the last time, threatened England with the same measure. It is enough to say, that, on the present occasion, the menaces of France had their usual effect in awakening the spirit of Britain.

The most extensive arrangements were made for the reception of the invaders should they chance to land, and in the meanwhile, our natural barrier was not neglected. The naval preparations were very great, and what gave yet more confidence than the number of vessels and guns, Nelson was put into command of the sea, from Orfordness to Beachyhead. Under his management, it soon became the question, not whether the French flotilla was to invade the

British shores, but whether it was to remain in safety in the French harbours. Boulogne was bombarded, and some of the small craft and gun-boats destroyed—the English admiral generously sparing the town; and not satisfied with this partial success, Nelson prepared to attack them with the boats of the squadron. The French resorted to the most unusual and formidable preparations for defence. Their flotilla was moored close to the shore in the mouth of Boulogne harbour, the vessels secured to each other by chains, and filled with soldiers. The British attack in some degree failed, owing to the several divisions of boats missing each other in the dark; some French vessels were taken, but they could not be brought off; and the French chose to consider this result as a victory, on their part, of consequence enough to balance the loss at Aboukir;—though it amounted at best to ascertaining, that although their vessels could not keep the sea, they might, in some comparative degree of safety, lie under close cover of their own batteries. Meantime, the changes which had taken place in the British administration, were preparing public expectation for that peace which all the world now longed for.

PITT LEAVES THE MINISTRY

Mr. Pitt, as is well known, left the Ministry, [Feb. 1801,] and was succeeded in the office of first Minister of State by Mr. Addington, now Lord Sidmouth. The change was justly considered as friendly to pacific measures; for, in France especially, the gold of Pitt had been by habit associated with all that was prejudicial to their country. The very massacres of Paris, nay, the return of Buonaparte from Egypt, were imputed to the intrigues of the English minister; he was the scape-goat on whom were charged as the ultimate cause, all the follies, crimes, and misfortunes of the Revolution.

A great part of his own countrymen, as well as of the French, entertained a doubt of the possibility of concluding a peace under Mr. Pitt's auspices; while those who were most anti-Gallican in their opinions, had little wish to see his lofty spirit stoop to the task of arranging conditions of treaty on terms so different from what his hopes had once dictated. The worth, temper, and talents of his successor, seemed to qualify him to enter into a negotiation to which the greater part of the nation was now inclined, were it but for the sake of experiment.

TREATY OF AMIENS

Buonaparte himself was at this time disposed to peace. It was necessary to France, and no less necessary to him, since he otherwise must remain pledged to undertake the hazardous alternative of invasion, in which chances stood incalculably against his success; while a failure might have, in its consequences, inferred the total ruin of his power. All parties were, therefore, in a great degree inclined to treat with sincerity; and Buonaparte was with little difficulty brought to consent to the evacuation of Egypt, there being every reason to believe that he was already possessed of the news of the convention with Menou. At any rate, the French cause in Egypt had been almost desperate ever since the battle of Alexandria, and the first consul was conscious that in this sacrifice he only resigned that which there was little chance of his being able to keep. It was also stipulated, that the French should evacuate Rome and Naples; a condition of little consequence, as they were always able to reoccupy these countries when their interest required it. The Dutch colony of the Cape of Good Hope was to be restored to the Batavian republic, and declared a free port.

In respect of the settlements which the British arms had conquered, England underwent a punishment not unmerited. The conquest of the enemy's colonies had been greatly too much an object of the English Ministry; and thus the national force had been frittered away upon acquisitions of comparatively petty importance, which, from the insalubrity of the climate, cost us more men to maintain them than would have been swept off by many a bloody battle. All the conquests made on this peddling plan of warfare, were now to be returned without any equivalent. Had the gallant soldiers, who perished miserably for the sake of these sugar-islands, been united in one well-concerted expedition, to the support of Charette, or La Rochejacquelein, such a force might have enabled these chiefs to march to Paris; or, if sent to Holland, might have replaced the Stadtholder in his dominions. And now, these very sugar-islands, the pitiful compensation which Britain had received for the blood of her brave children, were to be restored to those from whom they had been wrested. The important possessions of Ceylon in the East, and Trinidad in the West Indies, were the only part of her conquests which England retained. The integrity of her ancient ally, Portugal, was, however, recognised, and the independence of the Ionian islands was stipulated for and guaranteed. Britain restored porto Ferrajo, and what other places she had occupied in the isle of Elba, or on the Italian coast; but the occupation of Malta for some time threatened to prove an obstacle to the treaty. The English considered it as of the last consequence that this strong island should remain in their possession, and intimated that they regarded the pertinacious resistance which the first consul testified to this proposal, as implying a private and unavowed desire of renewing, at some future opportunity, his designs on Egypt, to which Malta might be considered as in some measure a key. After much discussion, it was at length agreed that the independence of the island should be secured by its being garrisoned by a neutral power, and placed under its guarantee and protection.

The preliminaries of peace were signed 10th October, 1801. General Law de Lauriston,[642] the school companion and first aide-de-camp of Buonaparte, brought them over from Paris to London, where they were received with the most extravagant joy by the populace, to whom novelty is a sufficient recommendation of almost any thing. But amidst the better classes, the sensation was much divided. There was a small but energetic party, led by the celebrated Windham, who, adopting the principles of Burke to their utmost extent, considered the act of treating with a regicide government as indelible meanness, and as a dereliction, on the part of Great Britain, of those principles of legitimacy, upon which the social compact ought to rest. More moderate anti-Gallicans, while they regretted that our efforts in favour of the Bourbons had been totally unavailing, contended with reason, that we were not so closely leagued to their cause as to be bound to sacrifice our own country, in a vain attempt to restore the exiled family to the throne

---

[642] General Law of Lauriston was born at Pondicherry in 1768. He died at Paris in 1828.

of France. This was the opinion entertained by Pitt himself, and the most judicious among his followers. Lastly, there was the professed Opposition, who, while rejoicing that we had been able to obtain peace on any terms, might now exult in the fulfilment of their predictions of the bad success of the war. Sheridan summed up what was perhaps the most general feeling in the country, with the observation, that "it was a peace which all men were glad of, and no man could be proud of."

Amiens was appointed for the meeting of commissioners, who were finally to adjust the treaty of pacification, which was not ended till five months after the preliminaries had been agreed on. After this long negotiation, the treaty was at length signed, 25th March, 1802. The isle of Malta, according to this agreement, was to be occupied by a garrison of Neapolitan troops, while, besides Britain and France, Austria, Spain, Russia, and Prussia, were to guarantee its neutrality. The Knights of St. John were to be the sovereigns, but neither French nor English were in future to be members of that order. The harbours were to be free to the commerce of all nations, and the order was to be neutral towards all nations save the Algerines and other piratical states.

Napoleon, had he chosen to examine into the feelings of the English, must have seen plainly that this treaty, unwillingly acceded to by them, and only by way of experiment, was to have a duration long or short, in proportion to their confidence in, or doubt of, his own good faith. His ambition, and the little scruple which he showed in gratifying it, was, he must have been sensible, the terror of Europe; and until the fears he had excited were disarmed by a tract of peaceful and moderate conduct on his part, the suspicions of England must have been constantly awake, and the peace between the nations must have been considered as precarious as an armed truce. Yet these considerations could not induce him to lay aside, or even postpone, a train of measures, tending directly to his own personal aggrandisement, and confirming the jealousies which his character already inspired. These measures were partly of a nature adapted to consolidate and prolong his own power in France; partly to extend the predominating influence of that country over her continental neighbours.

By the treaty of Luneville, and by that of Tolentino, the independent existence of the Cisalpine and Helvetian republics had been expressly stipulated; but this independence, according to Buonaparte's explanation of the word, did not exclude their being reduced to mere satellites, who depended on, and whose motions were to be regulated by France, and, by himself, the chief governor of France and all her dependencies. When, therefore, the Directory was overthrown in France, it was not his purpose that a directorial form of government should continue to subsist in Italy. Measures were on this account to be taken, to establish in that country something resembling the new consular model adopted in Paris.

For this purpose, in the beginning of January, 1802, a convention of 450 deputies from the Cisalpine states arrived at Lyons, (for they were not trusted to deliberate within the limits of their own country,) to contrive for themselves a new political system. In that period, when the modelling of constitutions was so common, there was no difficulty in drawing up one; which consisted of a president, a deputy-president, a legislative council, and three electoral colleges, composed, first, of proprietors; second, of persons of learning; and, third, of commercial persons. If the Italians had been awkward upon the occasion, they had the assistance of Talleyrand; and soon after, the arrival of Buonaparte himself at Lyons gave countenance to their operations. His presence was necessary for the exhibition of a most singular farce.

A committee of thirty of the Italian convention, to whom had been intrusted the principal duty of suggesting the new model of government, gave in a report, in which it was stated, that, from the want of any man of sufficient influence amongst themselves to fill the office of president, upon whom devolved all the executive duties of the state, the new system could not be considered as secure, unless Buonaparte should be prevailed upon to fill that situation, not, as it was carefully explained, in his character of head of the French government, but in his individual capacity. Napoleon graciously inclined to their suit. He informed them, that he concurred in the modest opinion they had formed, that their republic did not at present possess an individual sufficiently gifted with talents and impartiality to take charge of their affairs, which he should, therefore, retain under his own chief management, while circumstances required him to do so.

PROJECTS OF AMBITION—CONSUL FOR LIFE

Having thus established his power in Italy as firmly as in France, Buonaparte proceeded to take measures for extending his dominions in the former country and elsewhere. By a treaty with Spain, now made public, it appeared that the duchy of Parma was to devolve on France, together with the island of Elba, upon the death of the present duke—an event at no distant date to be expected. The Spanish part of the province of Louisiana, in North America, was to be ceded to France by the same treaty. Portugal, too, though the integrity of her dominions had been guaranteed by the preliminaries of the peace with England, had been induced, by a treaty kept studiously private from the British court, to cede her province of Guiana to France. These stipulations served to show that there was no quarter of the world in which France and her present ruler did not entertain views of aggrandisement, and that questions of national faith would not be considered too curiously when they interfered with their purpose.

While Europe was stunned and astonished at the spirit of conquest and accumulation manifested by this insatiable conqueror, France was made aware that he was equally desirous to consolidate and to prolong his power, as to extend it over near and distant regions. He was all, and more than all, that sovereign had ever been; but he still wanted the title and the permanence which royalty requires. To attain these was no difficult matter, when the first consul was the prime mover of each act, whether in the Senate or Tribunate; nor was he long of discovering proper agents eager to gratify his wishes.

Chabot de L'Allier took the lead in the race of adulation.— Arising in the Tribunate, he pronounced a long eulogium on Buonaparte, enhancing the gratitude due to the hero by whom France had been preserved and restored to victory. He therefore proposed that the Tribunate should transmit to the Conservative

Senate a resolution, requesting the Senate to consider the manner of bestowing on Napoleon Buonaparte a splendid mark of the national gratitude.

There was no misunderstanding this hint. The motion was unanimously adopted, and transmitted to the Convention, to the Senate, to the Legislative Body, and to the Consuls.

The Senate conceived they should best meet the demand now made upon them, by electing Napoleon first consul for a second space of ten years, to commence when the date of the original period, for which he was named by the Constitution, should expire.

The proposition of the Senate being reduced into the form of a decree, was intimated to Buonaparte, but fell short of his wishes; as it assigned to him, however distant it was, a period at which he must be removed from authority. It is true, that the space of seventeen years, to which the edict of the Senate proposed to extend his power, seemed to guarantee a very ample duration; and in point of fact, before the term of its expiry arrived, he was prisoner at Saint Helena. But still there was a termination, and that was enough to mortify his ambition.

CONSUL FOR LIFE

He thanked the Senate, therefore, for this fresh mark of their confidence, but eluded accepting it in express terms, by referring to the pleasure of the people. Their suffrages, he said, had invested him with power, and he could not think it right to accept of the prolongation of that power but by their consent. It might have been thought that there was now nothing left but to present the decree of the Senate to the people. But the second and third consuls, Buonaparte's colleagues at a humble distance, took it upon them, though the constitution gave them no warrant for such a manœuvre, to alter the question of the Senate, and to propose to the people one more acceptable to Buonaparte's ambition, requesting their judgment, whether the chief consul should retain his office, not for ten years longer, but for the term of his life. By thus juggling, the proposal of the Senate was set aside, and that assembly soon found it wisest to adopt the more liberal views suggested by the consuls, to whom they returned thanks, for having taught them (we suppose) how to appreciate a hint.

The question was sent down to the departments. The registers were opened with great form, as if the people had really some constitutional right to exercise. As the subscriptions were received at the offices of the various functionaries of government, it is no wonder, considering the nature of the question, that the ministers with whom the registers were finally deposited, were enabled to report a majority of three millions of citizens who gave votes in the affirmative. It was much more surprising, that there should have been an actual minority of a few hundred determined Republicans, with Carnot at their head, who answered the question in the negative. This statesman observed, as he signed his vote, that he was subscribing his sentence of deportation; from which we may conjecture his opinion concerning the fairness of this mode of consulting the people. He was mistaken notwithstanding. Buonaparte found himself so strong, that he could afford to be merciful, and to assume a show of impartiality, by suffering those to go unpunished who had declined to vote for the increase of his power.[643]

He did not, however, venture to propose to the people another innovation, which extended beyond his death the power which their liberal gift had continued during his life. A simple decree of the Senate assigned to Buonaparte the right of nominating his successor, by a testamentary deed. So that Napoleon might call his children or relatives to the succession of the empire of France, as to a private inheritance; or, like Alexander, he might leave it to the most favoured of his lieutenant-generals. To such a pass had the

---

[643] Montgaillard, tom. v., pp. 470, 476; Jomini, tom. xv., p. 17. "For six weeks," says Fouché, "the ministry was busily engaged in collecting and transcribing the registers in which the suffrages for the consulship for life were inscribed. Got up by a special committee, the report presented 3,568,185 votes in the affirmative, and only 9074 in the negative. On the 2d August, a *senatus consultum*, called organic, conferred the perpetual power on the First Consul Buonaparte; and on the 15th, the anniversary of his birth, solemn prayers were offered up to God for having, in his ineffable bounty, granted to France a man who had deigned to consent to bear the burden of supreme power for his whole life."—Tom. i., p. 236.

domination of a military chief, for the space of betwixt two and three years, reduced the fierce democracy and stubborn loyalty of the two factions, which seemed before that period to combat for the possession of France. Napoleon had stooped on them both, like the hawk in the fable.

The period at which we close this chapter was a most important one in Napoleon's life, and seemed a crisis on which his fate, and that of France, depended. Britain, his most inveterate and most successful enemy, had seen herself compelled by circumstances to resort to the experiment of a doubtful peace, rather than continue a war which seemed to be waged without an object. The severe checks to national prosperity, which arose from the ruined commerce and blockaded ports of France, might now, under the countenance of the first consul, be exchanged for the wealth that waits upon trade and manufactures. Her navy, of which few vestiges were left save the Brest fleet, might now be recruited, and resume by degrees that acquaintance with the ocean from which they had long been debarred. The restored colonies of France might have added to the sources of her national wealth, and she might have possessed—what Buonaparte on a remarkable occasion declared to be the principal objects he desired for her—ships, colonies, and commerce.

In his personal capacity, the first consul possessed all the power which he desired, and a great deal more than, whether his own or the country's welfare was regarded, he ought to have wished for. His victories over the foes of France had, by their mere fame, enabled him to make himself master of her freedom. It remained to show—not whether Napoleon was a patriot, for to that honourable name he had forfeited all title when he first usurped unlimited power—but whether he was to use the power which he had wrongfully acquired, like Trajan or like Domitian. His strangely-mingled character showed traits of both these historical portraits, strongly opposed as they are to each other. Or rather, he might seem to be like Socrates in the allegory, alternately influenced by a good and a malevolent demon; the former marking his course with actions of splendour and dignity; while the latter, mastering human frailty by means of its prevailing foible, the love of self, debased the history of a hero, by actions and sentiments worthy only of a vulgar tyrant.

Chapter XXIV

Different Views entertained by the English Ministers and the Chief Consul of the effects of the Treaty of Amiens—Napoleon, misled by the Shouts of a London Mob, misunderstands the Feelings of the People of Great Britain—His continued encroachments on the Independence of Europe—His conduct to Switzerland—Interferes in their Politics, and sets himself up, uninvited, as Mediator in their concerns—Ney enters Switzerland at the head of 40,000 men—The patriot, Reding, disbands his Forces, and is imprisoned—Switzerland is compelled to furnish France with a Subsidiary Army of 16,000 Troops—The Chief Consul adopts the title of Grand Mediator of the Helvetic Republic.

The eyes of Europe were now fixed on Buonaparte, as master of the destinies of the civilized world, which his will could either maintain in a state of general peace, or replunge into all the miseries of renewed and more inveterate war. Many hopes were entertained, from his eminent personal qualities, that the course in which he would direct them might prove as honourable to himself as happy for the nations over whom he now possessed such unbounded influence. The shades of his character were either lost amid the lustre of his victories, or excused from the necessity of his situation. The massacre of Jaffa was little known, was acted afar off, and might present itself to memory as an act of military severity, which circumstances might palliate, if not excuse.

Napoleon, supposing him fully satiated with martial glory, in which he had never been surpassed, was expected to apply himself to the arts of peace, by which he might derive fame of a more calm, yet not less honourable character. Peace was all around him, and to preserve it, he had only to will that it should continue; and the season seemed eminently propitious for taking the advice of Cineas to the King of Epirus, and reposing himself after his labours. But he was now beginning to show, that, from the times of Pyrrhus to his own, ambition has taken more pleasure in the hazards and exertions of the chase than in its successful issue. All the power which Buonaparte already possessed seemed only valuable in his eyes, as it afforded him the means of getting as much more; and, like a sanguine and eager gamester, he went on doubling his stakes at every throw, till the tide of fortune, which had so long run in his favour, at length turned against him, and his ruin was total. His ruling and predominating vice was ambition—we would have called it his only one, did not ambition, when of a character intensely selfish, include so many others.

It seems the most natural course, in continuing our history, first to trace those events which disappointed the general expectations of Europe, and after a jealous and feverish armistice of little more than a year, again renewed the horrors of war. We shall then resume the internal history of France and her ruler.

TREATY OF AMIENS

Although the two contracting powers had been able to agree upon the special articles of the peace of Amiens, they possessed extremely different ideas concerning the nature of a state of pacification in general, and the relations which it establishes between two independent states. The English minister, a man of the highest personal worth and probity, entertained no doubt that peace was to have its usual effect, of restoring all the ordinary amicable intercourse betwixt France and England; and that, in matters concerning their mutual allies, and the state of the European republic in general, the latter country, on sheathing the sword, had retained the right of friendly counsel and remonstrance. Mr. Addington could not hope to restore the balance of Europe, for which so much blood had been spilled in the eighteenth century. The scales and beams of that balance were broken into fragments, and lay under the feet of Buonaparte. But Britain did not lie prostrate. She still grasped in her hand the trident of the ocean, and had by no event, in the late contest, been reduced to surrender the right of remonstrating against violence and injustice, and of protecting the feeble, as far as circumstances would still permit.

But Buonaparte's idea of the effects of the treaty of Amiens was very different. It was, according to his estimation, a treaty, containing every thing that Britain was entitled to expect on the part of herself and her allies, and the accepting of which excluded her from all farther right of interference in the affairs of Europe. It was like a bounding charter, which restricts the right of the person to whom it is granted to the precise limits therein described, and precludes the possibility of his making either claim or acquisition beyond them. All Europe, then, was to be at the disposal of France, and states created, dissolved, changed and rechanged at her pleasure, unless England could lay her finger on the line in the treaty of Amiens, which prohibited the proposed measure. "England," said the *Moniteur*, in an official tone, "shall have the treaty of Amiens, the whole treaty of Amiens, and nothing but the treaty of Amiens!" In this manner the treaty was, so far as England was concerned, understood to decide, and that in favour of France, all questions which could possibly arise in the course of future time between the two countries; while, in ordinary candour, and in common sense, it could be only considered as settling the causes of animosity between the parties, as they existed at the date of the pacification.

The insular situation of England was absurdly alleged as a reason why she should not interfere in continental politics; as if the relations of states to each other were not the same, whether divided by an ocean or a line of mountains. The very circumstance had been founded upon eloquently and justly by one of her own poets, for claiming for Britain the office of an umpire,[644] because less liable to be agitated by the near vicinity of continental war, and more likely to decide with impartiality concerning contending claims, in which she herself could have little interest. It was used by France in the sense of another poet, and made a reason for thrusting England out of the

---

[644] "Thrice happy Britain, from the kingdoms rent, To sit the Guardian of the Continent." Addison.—S.

European world, and allowing her no vote in its most important concerns.[645]

To such humiliation it was impossible for Britain to submit. It rendered the treaty of Amiens, thus interpreted, the counterpart of the terms which the Cyclops granted to Ulysses, that he should be the last devoured. If Britain were compelled to remain, with fettered hands and padlocked lips, a helpless and inactive witness, while France completed the subjection of the Continent, what other doom could she expect than to be finally subdued? It will be seen afterwards that disputes arose concerning the execution of the treaty. These, it is possible, might have been accommodated, had not the general interpretation, placed by the first consul on the whole transaction, been inconsistent with the honour, safety, and independence of Great Britain.

It seems more than probable, that the extreme rejoicing of the rabble of London at signing the preliminaries, their dragging about the carriage of Lauriston, and shouting "Buonaparte for ever!" had misled the ruler of France into an opinion that peace was indispensably necessary to England: for, like other foreigners, misapprehending the nature of our popular government, he may easily enough have mistaken the cries of a London mob for the voice of the British people. The ministers also seemed to keep their ground in Parliament on condition of their making and maintaining peace; and as they showed a spirit of frankness and concession, it might be misconstrued by Buonaparte into a sense of weakness. Had he not laboured under some such impression, he would probably have postponed, till the final pacification of Amiens, the gigantic steps towards farther aggrandisement, which he hesitated not to take after signing the preliminaries, and during the progress of the Congress.

We have already specified Napoleon's acceptance of the presidency of the Cisalpine Republic, on which he now bestowed the name of Italian, as if it was designed at a future time to comprehend the whole peninsula of Italy. By a secret treaty with

---

[645] ——"penitus toto divisos orbe Britannos." Virgil.—S.

Portugal, he had acquired the province of Guiana, so far as it belonged to that power. By another with Spain, he had engrossed the Spanish part of Louisiana, and, what was still more ominous, the reversion of the duchy of Parma, and of the island of Elba,[646] important as an excellent naval station.

In the German Diet for settling the indemnities, to be granted to the various princes of the empire who had sustained loss of territory in consequence of late events, and particularly of the treaty of Luneville, the influence of France predominated in a manner which threatened entire destruction to that ancient confederation. It may be in general observed, that towns, districts, and provinces were dealt from hand to hand like cards at a gaming-table; and the powers of Europe once more, after the partition of Poland, saw with scandal the government of freemen transferred from hand to hand, without regard to their wishes, aptitudes, and habits, any more than those of cattle. This evil imitation of an evil precedent was fraught with mischief, as breaking every tie of affection betwixt the governor and governed, and loosening all attachments which bind subjects to their rulers, excepting those springing from force on the one side, and necessity on the other.

In this transfer of territories and jurisdictions, the King of Prussia obtained a valuable compensation for the Duchy of Cleves, and other provinces transferred to France, as lying on the left bank of the Rhine.[647] The neutrality of that monarch had been of the last service to France during her late bloody campaigns, and was now to be compensated. The smaller princes of the empire, especially those on the right bank of the Rhine, who had virtually placed themselves under the patronage of France, were also gratified with large allotments of territory; whilst Austria, whose pertinacious opposition was well remembered, was considered as yet retaining too high pretensions to power and independence, and her indemnities were as much limited as those of the friends of France were extended.

---

[646] See Annual Register, vol. xliv., p. 608.
[647] Jomini, tom. xv., p. 25; Annual Register, vol. xliv., p. 640.

The various advantages and accessions of power and influence which we have hitherto alluded to, as attained by France, were chiefly gained by address in treating, and diplomatic skill. But shortly after the treaty of Amiens had been signed, Buonaparte manifested to the world, that where intrigue was unsuccessful, his sword was as ready as ever to support and extend his aggressions.

SWITZERLAND

The attack of the Directory on the Swiss Cantons had been always considered as a coarse and gross violation of the law of nations, and was regarded as such by Buonaparte himself. But he failed not to maintain the military possession of Switzerland by the French troops; nor, however indignant under the downfall of her ancient fame and present liberties, was it possible for that country to offer any resistance, without the certainty of total destruction.

The eleventh article of the treaty of Luneville seemed to afford the Swiss a prospect of escaping from this thraldom, but it was in words only. That treaty was declared to extend to the Batavian, Helvetic, Cisalpine, and Ligurian Republics. "The contracting parties guarantee the *independence* of the said republics," continues the treaty, "and the right of the people who inhabit them to adopt what form of government they please."[648] We have seen how far the Cisalpine republic profited by this declaration of independence; the proceedings respecting Switzerland were much more glaring.

There was a political difference of opinion in the Swiss Cantons, concerning the form of government to be adopted by them; and the question was solemnly agitated in a diet held at Berne. The majority inclined for a constitution framed on the principle of their ancient government by a federative league, and the plan of such a constitution was accordingly drawn up and approved of. Aloys Reding, renowned for wisdom, courage, and patriotism, was placed at the head of this system. He saw the necessity of obtaining

---

[648] Annual Register, vol. xliii., p. 273.

the countenance of France, in order to the free enjoyment of the constitution which his countrymen had chosen, and betook himself to Paris to solicit Buonaparte's consent to it. This consent was given, upon the Swiss government agreeing to admit to their deliberations six persons of the opposite party, who, supported by the French interest, desired that the constitution should be one and indivisible, in imitation of that of the French Republic.

This coalition, formed at the first consul's request, terminated in an act of treachery, which Buonaparte had probably foreseen. Availing themselves of an adjournal of the Diet for the Easter holidays, the French party summoned a meeting, from which the other members were absent, and adopted a form of constitution which totally subverted the principles of that under which the Swiss had so long lived in freedom, happiness, and honour. Buonaparte congratulated them on the wisdom of their choice. It was, indeed, sure to meet his approbation, for it was completely subversive of all the old laws and forms, and so might receive any modification which his policy should dictate, and it was to be administered of course by men, who, having risen under his influence, must necessarily be pliant to his will. Having made his compliments on their being possessed of a free and independent constitution, he signified his willingness to withdraw the troops of France, and did so accordingly. For this equitable measure much gratitude was expressed by the Swiss, which might have been saved, if they had known that Buonaparte's policy rather than his generosity dictated his proceedings. It was, in the first place, his business to assume the appearance of leaving the Swiss in possession of their freedom; secondly, he was sure that events would presently happen, when they should be left to themselves, which would afford a plausible pretext to justify his armed interference.

July 19.

The aristocratic cantons of the ancient Swiss League were satisfied with the constitution finally adopted by the French party of their country; but not so the democratic, or small cantons, who, rather than submit to it, declared their resolution to withdraw from the general league, as new-modelled by the French, and to form under their own ancient laws a separate confederacy.[649] This was to consist of the cantons of Schweitz, Uri, and Underwalden, forest and mountain regions, in which the Swiss have least degenerated from the simple and hardy manners of their ancestors. A civil war immediately broke out, in the course of which it was seen, that in popularity, as well as patriotism, the usurping Helvetic government, established by French interest, was totally inferior to the gallant foresters. These last were guided chiefly by the patriotic Reding, who strove, with undaunted though ultimately with vain resolution, to emancipate his unfortunate country. The intrusive government were driven from Berne, their troops every where routed, and the federative party were generally received with the utmost demonstrations of joy by their countrymen, few adhering to the usurpers, excepting those who were attached to them by views of emolument.

But while Reding and the Swiss patriots were triumphing in the prospect of restoring their ancient constitution, with all its privileges and immunities, the strong grasp of superior power was extended to crush their patriotic exertions.

Sept. 30.

The fatal tidings of the proposed forcible interference of France, were made known by the sudden arrival of Rapp, adjutant-general of Buonaparte, with a letter addressed to the eighteen Swiss cantons.[650] This manifesto was of a most extraordinary nature. Buonaparte upbraided the Swiss with their civil discords of three years standing, forgetting that these discords would not have existed

---

[649] "In the conviction, that for a forced and unfortunate marriage, divorce is the only reasonable remedy, and that Helvetia and ourselves cannot recover repose and content, except by the rupture of this forced tie, we are firmly resolved to labour at that separation with all possible activity."

[650] "The first consul instructed Ney to enter Switzerland with a corps of troops, and caused Reding, the instigator of the disturbances, to be arrested; and he despatched Rapp, in all haste, who providentially arrived at the moment when the parties were coming to blows. Rapp, with a rare presence of mind, alighted from his carriage, placed himself between the two armies, loudly declaring, in the German language, that he was authorised to denounce, as an enemy of the French nation, whichever of the two parties should commence firing, and that he was ordered to introduce a fresh body of French troops into the Swiss territory. His firmness produced the greater effect, as both parties had the same consequences to apprehend, from a second invasion."—Savary, tom. i., p. 301.

but for the invasion of the French. He told them that, when he, as a boon granted, had been pleased to withdraw his troops from their country, they had immediately turned their arms against each other. These are singular propositions enough to be found in a proclamation addressed by one independent nation to another. But what follows is still more extraordinary. "You have disputed three years, without understanding one another; if left any longer to yourselves, you will kill each other for three years more, without coming to any better result. Your history shows that your intestine wars cannot be terminated without the efficacious intervention of France. It is true, I had resolved not to intermeddle with your affairs, having always found that your various governments have applied to me for advice which they never meant to follow, and have sometimes made a bad use of my name to favour their own private interests and passions. But I neither can, nor ought to remain insensible to the distress of which I see you the prey. I recall my resolution of neutrality. I consent to be the mediator of your differences; but my mediation shall be effectual, such as becomes the great nation in whose name I address you."[651]

This insulting tone, with which, uninvited, and as if granting a favour, the chief consul took upon him, as a matter of course, to exercise the most arbitrary power over a free and independent people, is equally remarkable at the close of the manifesto. The proclamation commands, that a deputation be sent to Paris, to consult with the chief consul; and concludes with an assertion of Buonaparte's "right to expect that no city, community, or public body, should presume to contradict the measures which it might please him to adopt." To support the reasoning of a manifesto which every schoolboy might have confuted, Ney, with an army of forty thousand men, entered Switzerland at different points.

As the presence of such an overpowering force rendered resistance vain, Aloys Reding, and his gallant companions, were compelled to dismiss their forces after a touching address to them. The Diet of Schweitz also dissolved itself in consequence of the interference, as they stated,[652] of an armed force of foreigners,

---

[651] Annual Register, vol. xliv., p. 671.
[652] Annual Register, vol. xliv., p. 678.

whom it was impossible, in the exhausted state of the country, to oppose.

Switzerland was thus, once more, occupied by French soldiers. The patriots, who had distinguished themselves in asserting her rights, were sought after and imprisoned. Aloys Reding was urged to conceal himself, but he declined to do so; and when upbraided by the French officer who came to arrest him, as being the head of the insurrection, he answered nobly, "I have obeyed the call of conscience and my country—do you execute the commands of your master." He was imprisoned in the castle of Aarsbourg.[653]

The resistance of these worthy patriots, their calm, dignified, and manly conduct, their simple and affecting pleas against overmastering violence, though they failed to procure the advantages which they hoped for their country, were not lost to the world, or to the cause of freedom. Their pathetic complaints, when perused in many a remote valley, excited detestation of French usurpation, in bosoms which had hitherto contented themselves with regarding the victories of the Republic with wonder, if not with admiration. For other aggressions, the hurry of revolution, the extremity of war, the strong compulsion of necessity might be pleaded; but that upon Switzerland was as gratuitous and unprovoked as it was nefariously unjust. The name of the cantons, connected with so many recollections of ancient faith and bravery, hardy simplicity, and manly freedom, gave additional interest to the sufferings of such a country; and no one act of his public life did Buonaparte so much injury throughout Europe, as his conduct towards Switzerland.[654]

---

[653] Aloys Reding was born in 1755. After being confined several months in the castle of Aarsbourg, he was liberated, and being in 1803 elected landemann of the canton of Schweitz, he assisted, in that capacity, at the diet of Fribourg, in 1809. He died at Schweitz in 1819.

[654] "Never did Buonaparte less abuse his vast preponderance; and Switzerland is, without contradiction, of all states, near or distant, over which he has exerted his influence, that which he has spared the most, during the fifteen years of his ascendency and glory. In order to pay a proper tribute to truth, I will add, that the act of mediation was impregnated, as much as possible, with the conciliatory and characteristically moderate spirit of Barthélemi."—Fouché, tom. i., p. 254.

The dignified resistance of the Swiss, their renown for courage, and the policy of not thwarting them too far, had some effect on the chief consul himself; and in the final act of mediation, by which he saved them the farther trouble of taking thought about their own constitution, he permitted federalism to remain as an integral principle. By a subsequent defensive treaty, the cantons agreed to refuse all passage through the country to the enemies of France, and engaged to maintain an army of a few thousand men to guarantee this engagement. Switzerland also furnished France with a subsidiary army of sixteen thousand men, to be maintained at the expense of the French Government. But the firmness which these mountaineers showed in the course of discussing this treaty was such, that it saved them from having the conscription imposed on them, as in other countries under the dominion of France.[655]

HELVETIC REPUBLIC

Notwithstanding these qualifications, however, it was evident that the voluntary and self-elected-Mediator[656] of Switzerland was in fact sovereign of that country, as well as of France and the north of Italy; but there was no voice to interdict this formidable accumulation of power. England alone interfered, by sending an envoy (Mr. Moore) to the diet of Schweitz, to inquire by what means she could give assistance to their claims of independence; but ere his arrival, the operations of Ney had rendered all farther resistance impossible. A remonstrance was also made by England to the French Government upon this unprovoked aggression on the liberties of an independent people.[657] But it remained unanswered and unnoticed, unless in the pages of the *Moniteur*, where the pretensions of Britain to interfere with the affairs of the Continent,

---

[655] Montgaillard, tom. vi., p. 5; Jomini, Vie Politique et Militaire de Napoléon, tom. i., p. 532; Savary, vol. i., p. 302.

[656] "The deputies, pleased with the result of their mission, requested the first consul to retain the title of Mediator which had been conferred upon him. The country was restored to its wonted tranquillity without the effusion of blood; and the celebrated M. de la Harpe (formerly tutor to the Emperor Alexander,) who had governed it under the title of Director, came to fix his residence in Paris."—Savary, tom. i., p. 302.

[657] For Lord Hawkesbury's note-verbal to M. Otto, Oct. 10, 1802, together with his lordship's directions to Mr. Moore, and Mr. Moore's reply, see Annual Register, vol. xliv., pp. 674-678.

were held up to ridicule and contempt. After this period, Buonaparte adopted, and continued to bear, the title of Grand Mediator of the Helvetian Republic, in token, doubtless, of the right which he had assumed, and effectually exercised, of interfering in their affairs whenever it suited him to do so.[658]

---

[658] "That which Sir Walter Scott here advances concerning the blameable policy of Napoleon with respect to the Swiss, when he gave them this act of mediation, is not correct, and I will prove it to be so. I was in Switzerland in 1814, after the invasion of the allies, and certainly this was the period of the greatest enmity towards my brother; it was the epoch of the calumniators and libellers; nay, there existed those who carried their effrontery so far, as to declare that the name of Napoleon was not his own, and that he was called Nicholas. Nevertheless, even at this period, some of the deputies of the Diet, and the landemanns of the different cantons, and the principal Swiss, who frequented the baths of Baden, near Zurich, where I then was, did not refrain from openly declaring, that they could not complain of the Emperor Napoleon, that he had put an end to their difficulties, and that they could feel nothing but gratitude towards him."—Louis Buonaparte, p. 38.

Appendix

No. I

Buonaparte's Letter to General Paoli

General,

I was born when our country was perishing. Thirty thousand Frenchmen, vomited on our coasts, drowning the throne of liberty in streams of blood—such was the odious spectacle which first presented itself to my sight.

The cries of the dying, the groans of the oppressed, the tears of despair, were the companions of my infancy.

You quitted our island, and with you disappeared the hope of happiness. Slavery was the reward of our submission; weighed down under the triple chain of the soldier, the legislator, and the collector of imposts, our countrymen live despised—despised by those who have the forces of the administration in their hands. Is not this the severest of suffering for those who have the slightest elevation of sentiment? Can the wretched Peruvian, groaning under the tortures of the rapacious Spaniard, experience a vexation more galling?

The traitors to our country—the wretches whom the thirst of sordid gain has corrupted—to justify themselves, have circulated calumnies against the national government, and against you in particular. Writers, adopting them as truths, transmit them to posterity.

While reading them, my blood has boiled with indignation; and at length I have resolved to disperse these delusions, the offspring of ignorance. An early study of the French language, long observation, and documents drawn from the portfolios of the patriots, have led me to promise myself some success.

I wish to compare your government of our country with the present one. I wish to brand with infamy the men who have betrayed the common cause. I wish to summon before the tribunal of public opinion the men now in power—to set forth their vexatious proceedings, expose their secret intrigues, and if possible, interest the present minister[659] in the deplorable situation we are now in.

If my fortune had permitted me to live in the capital, I should doubtless have found out other means of making known the wrongs of my country: but, obliged to serve in the army, I find myself compelled to resort to this, the only means of publicity; for, as to private memorials, they would either not reach those for whom they were intended, or, stifled by the clamour of interested individuals, they would only occasion the ruin of the author.

Still young, my undertaking may be a rash one; but a love of truth, my native land, and fellow-countrymen—that enthusiasm, with which the prospect of an amelioration in our state always inspires me, will be my support. If you, general, condescend to approve of a labour, of which your deeds will form so large a portion—if you condescend to encourage the efforts of a young man, whom you have known from the hour of his birth, and whose parents were always attached to the good cause, I shall dare to augur favourably of my success.

I at one time indulged a hope, that I should have been able to go to London, to express to you in person the sentiments you have given birth to in my bosom, and to converse together on the misfortunes of our country; but the distance is an obstacle. The day, perhaps, will arrive, when I shall be able to overcome it.

Whatever may be the success of my work, I am sensible that it will raise against me the whole host of French employés, who misgovern our island, and against whom my attack is directed. But

---

[659] M. Necker.

what imports their enmity, when the interest of our country is at stake! I shall be loaded with their abuse; and, when the bolt falls, I shall descend into my own bosom, call to memory the legitimacy of my motives, and from that moment defy it.

Permit me, general, to offer you the homage of my family. And, ah! why should I not say, of my countrymen? They sigh at the recollection of a time when they had hoped for liberty. My mother, Madame Letitia, charges me especially to recall to your memory the years long since past at Corté

I am, with respect,
General,
Your very humble, and very obedient Servant,
Napoleon Buonaparte,
Officer in the Regiment of La Fère.

Auxonne-en-Bourgoyne, }
12th June, 1789. }

No. II
Letter of Napoleon Buonaparte to M. Matteo Buttafuoco, Deputy from Corsica to the National Assembly

Sir,

From Bonifacio to Cape Corso, from Ajaccio to Bastia, there is one chorus of imprecations against you. Your friends keep out of sight, your relations disown you, and even the man of reflection, who does not allow himself to be swayed by popular opinion, is, for once, led away by the general effervescence.

But what have you done? What are the crimes to justify such universal indignation, such complete desertion? This, sir, is what I wish to inquire into, in the course of a little discussion with you.

The history of your life, since the time at least when you appeared on the stage of public affairs, is well known. Its principal features are drawn in letters of blood. Still, however, there are details comparatively unknown. In these I may be mistaken; but I reckon upon your indulgence, and hope for information from you.

After having entered the service of France, you returned to see your relations: you found the tyrants vanquished, the national government established, and the Corsicans, entirely governed by noble sentiments, vying with each other in daily sacrifices for the prosperity of the state. You did not allow yourself to be seduced by the general enthusiasm; far from that, you looked with nothing but pity on the nonsensical stuff about country, liberty, independence, and constitution, which had got into the heads of our meanest peasants. Deep reflection had taught you to set a proper value on those artificial sentiments, the maintenance of which is a general evil. In fact, the peasant must be taught to mind his work, and not play the hero, if it is wished that he should not starve, that he should bring up his family, and pay respect to authority. As to those who are called, by their rank and fortune, to occupy stations of power, they cannot long remain such dupes as to sacrifice their comforts and consideration in society for a mere chimera, or stoop to pay court to a cobbler, that they may at last play the part of Brutus. Still, as it was necessary for your designs that you should gain the favour of Paoli, you had to dissemble;—M. Paoli being the centre of all the movements of the political body. We shall admit that he had talent—even a certain degree of genius; he had, in a short time, placed the affairs of the island on a good footing; he had founded a university, in which, for the first time, perhaps, since the creation, the sciences which are useful for the developement of reason were taught among our mountains. He had established a foundery for cannon, powder-mills, and fortifications, which increased the means of defence; he had formed harbours, which, while they encouraged commerce, improved agriculture; he had created a navy, which protected our communication with other countries, while it injured our enemies. All these establishments, in their infancy, were a mere presage of what he one day might have done. Union, peace, and liberty, seemed the precursors of national prosperity, had not a government, ill-organized, and placed on an unsound basis, afforded still surer indications of the misfortunes which were to happen, and of the total ruin into which every thing was to fall.

M. Paoli had dreamed of being a Solon, but had been unsuccessful in his imitation. He had placed every thing in the hands of the people or their representatives, so that it was impossible even to exist without pleasing them. A strange error which places under the control of a brutal and mercenary plebeian, the man who alone, by his education, his illustrious birth, and his fortune, is formed for governing. In the long run, so palpable a dereliction of reason cannot fail to bring on the ruin and dissolution of the body-politic, after having exposed it to every species of suffering.

You succeeded to your wish. M. Paoli, constantly surrounded by enthusiastic and hot-headed persons, never imagined that there could be any other passion than the devotion to liberty and independence. Finding that you had some knowledge of France, he did not trouble himself to do more than take your own word for your moral principles. He got you appointed to treat at Versailles respecting the accommodation which was negotiating under the mediation of the cabinet. M. de Choiseul saw you, and knew you; minds of a certain stamp are speedily appreciated. In a short time, in place of being the representative of a free people, you transformed yourself into the clerk of a minister; you communicated to him the instructions, the plans, the secrets of the Cabinet of Corsica.

This conduct, which is considered here as base and atrocious, appears to me quite natural; but this is because, in all sorts of affairs, we should understand one another, and reason with coolness.

The prude censures the coquette, and is laughed at by her in return; this, in a few words, is your history. The man of principle judges you harshly, but you do not believe that there is a man of principle. The common people, who are always led away by virtuous demagogues, cannot be appreciated by you, who do not believe in virtue. You cannot be condemned but by your own principles, like a criminal by the laws; but those who know the refinement of your principles, find nothing in your conduct but what is very simple. This brings us back, then, to what we have already said, that, in all sorts of affairs, the first thing requisite is to understand one another, and then argue coolly. You are also protected by a sort of sub-defence, not less effectual, for you do not aspire to the reputation of a Cato or a Catinat. It is sufficient for you to resemble a certain class; and, among this certain class, it is agreed that he who may get money, and does not profit by the opportunity, is a ninny; for money procures all the pleasures of sense, and the pleasures of sense are the only pleasures. Now, M. de Choiseul, who was very liberal, made it impossible for you to resist him—particularly as your ridiculous country paid you for your services, according to her laughable custom, by the honour of serving her.

The treaty of Compiégne being concluded, M. de Chauvelin and twenty-four battalions landed on our shores. M. de Choiseul, to whom the celerity of the expedition was most important, had uneasiness on the subject, which, in his confidential communications, he could not disguise from you. You suggested that he should send you there with a few millions. As Philip took cities with his Mule, you promised to make every thing yield to him without opposition. No sooner said than done—and there you are, recrossing the sea, throwing off the mask, and, with money and your commission in your hand, opening negotiations with those whom you thought would be most easily gained over.

Never imagining that a Corsican could prefer himself to his country, the Cabinet of Corsica had intrusted you with her interests. Never dreaming, for your part, that any man would not prefer money and himself to his country, you sold yourself and hoped to buy every body. Profound moralist as you were, you knew how much the enthusiasm of each individual was worth; some pounds of gold, more or less, formed, in your eyes, all the shades which diversify character.

You are mistaken, however:—the weak-minded were certainly shaken, but they were terrified by the horrible idea of mangling the bosom of their country. They thought they saw their fathers, their brothers, their friends, who perished in defending her, raise their heads from the tomb to load them with curses. These ridiculous prejudices were strong enough to stop you in your career; you lamented having to do with a people so childish in its notions. But, sir, this refinement of sentiment is not bestowed on the multitude; and, therefore, they live in poverty and wretchedness; while a man who has got proper notions, if circumstances favour him ever so little, knows the way to rise very speedily. This is pretty exactly the moral of your story.

When you made your report of the obstacles which prevented you from realizing your promises, you proposed that the Royal Corsican regiment should be bought. You hoped that its example would enlighten our too simple and honest peasants, and accustom them to things to which they felt so much repugnance. But what happened? Did not Rossi, Marengo, and some other madmen, inflame the minds of the regiment to such a pitch, that the officers in a body protested, by an authentic writing, that they would throw up their commissions, sooner than violate their oaths, or their duties, which were still more sacred?

You thus found yourself reduced to stand alone as an example to others. Without being disconcerted, at the head of a few friends and a French detachment, you threw yourself into Vescovato; but the terrible Clement[660] unkennelled you from thence. You retired upon Bastia with your companions in adventure. This little affair was not much to your credit; your house, and those of your associates, were burnt. But, in a place of safety, you laughed at these impotent efforts.

People here charge you with having endeavoured to arm the Royal Corsicans against their brethren. They also wish to impeach your courage, from the small resistance you made at Vescovato. There is little foundation for these accusations; for the first was an immediate consequence of your projects, indeed one of your means of executing them; and, as we have already proved that your conduct was perfectly simple and natural, this incidental charge goes for nothing. As to your want of courage, I do not see how this is settled by the action of Vescovato: You did not go there with the serious purpose of fighting, but for the sake of encouraging, by your example, those who were wavering in the opposite party. And after all, what right has any one to require that you should have run the risk of losing the fruits of two years' good conduct, by being shot like a common soldier? But you must have felt a good deal, say some folk, on seeing your own house, and those of your friends, become a prey to the flames. Good God! when will narrow-minded people give over trying to judge of every thing? Your letting your house be burnt, put M. de Choiseul under the necessity of indemnifying you. Experience proved the accuracy of your calculations; you received much more than the value of what you lost. To be sure you are accused of having kept all to yourself, and of having given nothing but a trifle to the poor creatures whom you had seduced. In order to justify your having acted in this way, it is

---

[660] Clement Paoli, elder brother of the general, a good soldier, an excellent citizen, a real philosopher. At the beginning of an action he could not bring himself to engage in personal combat; he gave his orders with the *sang froid* which characterises the good officer. But he no sooner saw his men begin to fall, than he seized his arms with a convulsive movement of indignation, and made use of them, exclaiming—"Unjust men! why break down the barriers of nature? why must you be enemies of your country?" Austere in his manners, simple in his habits, he has always lived retired. It was only in great emergencies that he came forward to give his opinion, which was very seldom departed from.—S.

only necessary to inquire if you could do it with perfect safety. Now, the poor people who were so dependent on your protection, were neither in a condition to demand restitution, nor even to understand very clearly the injustice which was done them. They could not become malecontents, and rebel against your authority; being held in detestation by their countrymen, their return to their former sentiments could no longer be held as sincere. It was then very natural that, when a few thousand crowns thus came in your way, you should not let them out of your hands;—to have done so, would have been cheating yourself.

The French, beaten in spite of their gold, their commissions, the discipline of their numerous battalions, the activity of their squadrons, the skill of their artillerymen,—defeated at La Penta, Vescovato, Loretto, San Nicolai, Borgo Barbaggio, Oletta,—intrenched themselves, excessively disheartened. Winter, the time of their repose, was for you, sir, a period of the greatest labour; and if you could not triumph over the obstinacy of prejudices so deeply rooted in the minds of the people, you found means to seduce some of their chiefs, whom you succeeded, though with some difficulty, in bringing to a right way of thinking. This, along with the thirty battalions whom M. de Vaux brought with him the following spring, forced Corsica to yield to the yoke, and drove Paoli and the greatest fanatics into banishment.

One portion of the patriots had died in the defence of their independence, another had fled from a land of proscription, and which, from that time, was a hideous den of tyrants. But a great number could neither die nor take flight; they became the objects of persecution. Minds, whom it had been found impossible to corrupt, were of such a stamp, that the empire of the French could only be established on their total destruction. Alas! this plan was but too punctually executed. Some perished, victims of crimes unjustly imputed to them; others, betrayed by their own hospitality, and by their own confidence, expiated on the scaffold the sighs and tears into which they had been surprised by dissimulation. A great number, crowded by Narbonne-Fridzelar into the town of Toulon, poisoned by unwholesome food, tortured by their chains, and sinking under the most barbarous treatment, lived a short time in their misery, merely to see death slowly approaching. O God, witness of their innocence, why didst thou not become their avenger?

In the midst of this general calamity, in the midst of the groans and lamentations of this unfortunate people, you, however, began to enjoy the fruit of your labours—honours, dignities, pensions, all were showered upon you. Your prosperity would have advanced still more rapidly, had not Du Barri overthrown M. de Choiseul, and deprived you of a protector, who duly appreciated your services. This blow did not discourage you: you turned your attention to the *bureaux*; you merely felt the necessity of greater assiduity. This flattered the persons in office, your services were so notorious. All your wishes were granted. Not content with the lake of Biguglia, you demanded a part of the lands of many communities. Why, it is said, did you wish to deprive them of these lands? I ask, in my turn, what regard ought you to have for a nation by whom you knew yourself to be detested?

Your favourite project was, to divide the island among ten Barons. How! not satisfied with having assisted in forging the chains with which your country was bound, you wished still further to subject her to the absurd feudal government! But I commend you for having done as much harm to the Corsicans as you possibly could. You were at war with them; and, in war, to do evil for one's own advantage, is a first principle.

But let us pass over all these paltry matters—let us come to the present moment, and conclude a letter, which, from its frightful length, cannot fail to fatigue you.

The state of affairs in France prognosticated extraordinary events. You became alarmed for the effect of them in Corsica. The same madness with which we were possessed before the war, began, to your great scandal, to infect that amiable people. You comprehended the consequences; for, if noble sentiments were to gain an ascendency in public opinion, you would become no better than a traitor, instead of being a man of prudence and good sense. What was still worse, if ever noble sentiments were again to stir the blood of our ardent countrymen, and if ever a national government were to be the result of such sentiments, what would become of you? Your own conscience then began to terrify you. Restless, however, and unhappy as you were, you did not yield to your conscience. You resolved to risk every thing for every thing—but you played your game skilfully. You married, to strengthen your interest. A respectable man, who, relying on your word, had given his sister to your nephew, found himself abused. Your nephew, whose patrimony you had swallowed up in order to increase an inheritance which was to have been his own, was reduced to poverty, with a numerous family.

Having arranged your domestic affairs, you cast your eyes over the country. You saw it smoking with the blood of its martyrs, heaped with numerous victims, and, at every step, inspiring only ideas of vengeance. But you saw the ruffian soldier, the insolent pettifogger, the greedy tax-gatherer, lord it without contradiction; and the Corsican, groaning under the weight of triple chains, neither daring to think of what he was, nor to reflect on what he still might be. You said to yourself, in the joy of your heart, "Things go on well, and the only thing is to keep them so." And straightway you leagued yourself with the soldier, the pettifogger, and the tax-gatherer. The only point now to be attended to was, to procure deputies who should be animated by congenial sentiments; for, as to yourself, you could never suppose that a nation which was your enemy would choose you for her representative. But you necessarily changed your opinion, when the letters of convocation, by an absurdity which was perhaps the result of design, determined that the deputy from the nobility should be appointed by an assembly composed of only twenty-two persons. All that was necessary was to obtain twelve votes. Your associates in the higher council laboured with activity. Threats, promises, caresses, money, all were put in action. You succeeded. Your friends were not so successful among the Commons. The first president failed; and two men of exalted ideas—the one the son, the brother, the nephew, of the most zealous defenders of the common cause—the other a person who had seen Sionville and Narbonne, and whose mind was full of the horrid actions he had seen, while he lamented his own want of power to oppose them;—these two men were proclaimed deputies, and their appointment satisfied the wishes of the nation. The secret chagrin, the suppressed rage, which were every where caused by your appointment, form the best eulogy on the skill of your manœuvres, and the influence of your league.

When you arrived at Versailles, you were a zealous Royalist. When you now arrived at Paris, you must have seen with much concern, that the government, which it was wished to organize upon so many ruins, was the same with that which, in our country, had been drowned in so much blood.

The efforts of the unprincipled were powerless; the new constitution being admired by all Europe, and having become an object of interest to every thinking being, there remained for you but one resource. This was, to make it be believed that this constitution was not adapted to our island; although it was exactly the same with that which had produced such good effects, and which it cost so much blood to deprive us of.

All the delegates of the former administration, who naturally entered into your cabal, served you with the zeal arising from personal interest. Memorials were written, the object of which was to prove how advantageous for us was the existing government, and to demonstrate that any change would be contrary to the wish of the nation. At this time the city of Ajaccio obtained some knowledge of what was going on. This city roused herself, formed her national guard, organized her committee. This unexpected incident alarmed you—the fermentation spread in all directions. You persuaded the ministers, over whom you had gained some ascendency in relation to the affairs of Corsica, that it was of importance to send thither your father-in-law, M. Gaffory, with a command; and immediately we saw M. Gaffory, a worthy precursor of M. Narbonne, endeavouring, at the head of his troops, to maintain by force that tyranny which his late father, of glorious memory, had resisted and confounded by his genius. Innumerable blunders left no room for concealing your father-in-law's mediocrity of talent; he possessed no other art but that of making himself enemies. The people rallied against him on every side. In this imminent danger you lifted up your eyes, and saw Narbonne! Narbonne, profiting by a moment of favour, had laid the plan of establishing firmly, in an island which he had wasted with unheard-of cruelty, the despotism which oppressed it. You laid your heads together; the plan was determined on; five thousand men received orders; commissions for increasing by a battalion the provincial regiment were prepared. Narbonne set out. This poor nation, unarmed and disheartened, without hope and without resource, is delivered into the hands of her executioner.

O unhappy countrymen! Of what odious treachery were you to be the victims! You would not perceive it till it was too late. How were you, without arms, to resist ten thousand men? You would yourself have signed the act of your degradation; hope would have been extinguished; and days of uninterrupted misfortune would have succeeded. Emancipated France would have looked upon you with contempt; afflicted Italy with indignation; and Europe, astonished at this unexampled degree of degradation, would have effaced from her annals the traits which do honour to your character. But your deputies from the Commons penetrated the design, and informed you of it in time. A king, whose only wish was the happiness of his people, being well informed on the subject by M. La Fayette, that steady friend of liberty, dissipated the intrigues of a perfidious minister, who was certainly impelled by the desire of vengeance to do you injury. Ajaccio showed resolution in her address, in which was described with such energy the miserable state to which you were reduced by the most oppressive of governments. Bastia, till then stupified as it were, awoke at the sound of danger, and took up arms with that resolution for which she has been always distinguished. Arena came from Paris to Boulogne, full of those sentiments which lead men to the boldest enterprises. With arms in one hand, and the decrees of the National Assembly in the other, he made the public enemies tremble. Achilles Meurate, the conqueror of Caprana, who had carried desolation as far as Genoa, and who, to be a Turenne, wanted nothing but opportunity and a more extensive field, reminded his companions in glory, that this was the time to acquire additional fame,—that their country in danger had need, not of intrigues, which he knew nothing about, but of fire and sword. At the sound of so general an explosion, Gaffory returned to the insignificance from which he had been brought, so *mal-à-propos*, by intrigues;—he trembled in the fortress of Certe. Narbonne fled from

Lyons, to hide in Rome his shame, and his infernal projects. A few days afterwards Corsica is united to France, Paoli recalled; and in an instant the prospect changes, and opens to your view a course of events which you could not have dared to hope for.

I beg your pardon, sir; I took up my pen to defend you; but my heart revolts against so uniform a system of treason and atrocity. What! did you, a son of the same country, never feel any thing for her? What! did your heart experience no emotion at the sight of the rocks, the trees, the houses, the spots which were the scenes of your infant amusements? When you came into the world, your country nourished you with her fruits; when you came to the years of reason, she placed her hopes in you; she honoured you with her confidence; she said to you, "My son, you see the wretched state to which I am reduced by the injustice of men;—through my native vigour, I am recovering a degree of strength which promises me a speedy and infallible recovery; but I am again threatened! Fly, my son, hasten to Versailles; inform the great king of every thing, dissipate his suspicions, request his friendship."

Well! a little gold made you betray her confidence; and forthwith, for a little gold, you were seen, like a parricide, tearing open her bosom. Ah, sir, I am far from wishing you ill; but there is an avenging conscience! Your countrymen, to whom you are an object of horror, will enlighten France as to your character. The wealth, the pensions, the fruits of your treasons, will be taken from you. In the decrepitude of old age and poverty, in the frightful solitude of wickedness, you will live long enough to become a prey to the torments of conscience. The father will point you out to his son, the master to his pupil, saying, "Young people, learn to respect your country, virtue, fidelity, and humanity."

And you, respectable and unhappy woman, whose youth, beauty, and innocence were vilely prostituted, does your pure and chaste heart beat under a hand so criminal? In those moments in which nature gives the alarm to love, when, withdrawn from the chimeras of life, unmingled pleasures succeed each other with rapidity, when the mind, expanded by the fire of sentiment, enjoys only the pleasure of causing enjoyment, and feels only the pleasure of exciting feeling,—in those moments you press to your heart, you become identified with that cold and selfish man, who has never deviated from his character, and who, in the course of sixty years, has never known any thing but the care of his own interest, an instinctive love of destruction, the most infamous avarice, the base pleasures of sense! By and by, the glare of honours, the trappings of riches, will disappear; you will be loaded with general contempt. Will you seek, in the bosom of him who is the author of your woes, a consolation indispensable to your gentle and affectionate mind? Will you endeavour to find in his eyes tears to mingle with yours? Will your failing hand, placed on his bosom, seek to find an agitation like that in your own? Alas, if you surprise him in tears, they will be those of remorse; if his bosom heave, it will be with the convulsions of the wretch who dies abhorring nature, himself, and the hand that guides him.

O Lameth! O Robespierre! O Pétion! O Volney! O Mirabeau! O Barnave! O Bailly! O La Fayette! this is the man who dares to seat himself by your side! Dropping with the blood of his brethren, stained by every sort of vice, he presents himself with confidence in the dress of a general, the reward of his crimes! He dares to call himself the representative of the nation—he who sold her—and you suffer it! He dares to raise his eyes, and listen to your discourse, and you suffer it! Is it the voice of the people that sent him? He never had more than the voice of twelve nobles. Ajaccio, Bastia, and most of the districts, have done that to his effigy which they would have been very glad to do to his person.

But you, who are induced, by the error of the moment, or perhaps temporary abuses, to oppose any fresh changes, will you tolerate a traitor? a man who, under the cool exterior of a man of sense, conceals the avidity of a lacquey? I cannot imagine it. You will be the first to drive him away with ignominy, as soon as you are aware of the string of atrocities of which he has been the author.

I have the honour, &c.
Buonaparte.
From my closet at Milleli,

23d January, 1790

No. III

THE SUPPER OF BEAUCAIRE

JULY 29, 1793

I happened to be at Beaucaire on the last day of the fair, and by chance had for my companions at supper two merchants from Marseilles, a citizen of Nimes, and a manufacturer from Montpelier.

After the first few minutes of mutual survey, they discovered that I came from Avignon, and was in the army. The attention of my companions, which, all the week, had been fixed on the details of that traffic which is the parent of wealth, was at this moment turned to the issue of those passing events, upon which the security of all wealth so much depends. They endeavoured to come at my opinion, in order that, by comparing it with their own, they might be enabled to form probable conjectures respecting that future, which affected us so differently. The two citizens of Marseilles, in particular, appeared to be perplexed in spirit. The evacuation of Avignon had taught them to doubt of every thing. They manifested but one great solicitude as to their future fate. Confidence soon made us talkative, and our conversation ran in nearly the following terms:—

Nimois.—Is Cartaux's army strong? It is said to have lost a great many men in the attack; but if it be true that it has been repulsed, why have the Marseillese evacuated Avignon?

Militaire.—The army was four thousand strong when it assaulted Avignon; it now amounts to six thousand, and within four days will reach ten thousand men. It lost five men killed and eleven wounded. It has never been repulsed, since it never made a formal attack; the troops only manœuvred about the place, in order to ascertain where an attempt to force the gates, by means of petards, might be made to the best advantage; a few cannon were fired, to try the courage of the garrison, and it was then necessary to draw back to the camp, to combine the attack for the following night. The

Marseillese were three thousand six hundred men; they had a heavier and more numerous artillery, and yet they have been obliged to recross the Durance. This surprises you; but it is only veteran troops who can endure the uncertain events of a siege. We were masters of the Rhone, of Villeneuve, and of the open country; we had intercepted all their communications. They were under the necessity of evacuating the town, were pursued by our cavalry, and lost many prisoners, with two guns.

Marseillese.—This is a very different story from what we have been told. I do not dispute what you say, since you were present; but you must confess, that, after all this, they can do you no good. Our army is at Aix. Three good generals are come in place of the former ones: at Marseilles they are raising fresh battalions; we have a new train of artillery, several twenty-four pounders; in a few days, we shall be in a position to retake Avignon, or at worst we shall remain masters of the Durance.

Militaire.—Such is the story you have been told, to entice you to the brink of the abyss, which is deepening every moment, and which perhaps will engulf the finest town of France—the one which has deserved most of the patriots. But you were also told, that you should traverse France—that you should give the *ton* to the Republic—and yet your very first steps have been checks. You were told that Avignon could resist for a long time a force of twenty thousand men—and yet a single column, without a battering train, gained possession of it in four-and-twenty hours. You were told that the south had risen—and you found yourselves *alone*! You were told that the Nimes cavalry were about to crush the Allobroges—and yet the Allobroges were already at Saint-Esprit, and at Villeneuve. You were told that four thousand Lyonese were marching to your assistance—and yet the Lyonese were negotiating an accommodation for themselves. Acknowledge, then, that you have been deceived—open your eyes to the want of skill among your leaders, and put no faith in their calculations. Of all counsellors, self-love is the most dangerous. You are naturally impetuous: they are leading you to your destruction, by the self-same means which have ruined so many nations—by inflaming your vanity. You possess considerable wealth, and a large population—these they exaggerate.

You have rendered signal services to the cause of liberty—of these they remind you, without, at the same time, pointing out to you, that the genius of the republic was at that time with you, that it has now abandoned you.

Your army, you say, is at Aix with a large train of artillery, and skilful generals; well, do what it may, I tell you it will be beaten. You had three thousand six hundred men—a full half is dispersed. Marseilles, and a few refugees from the department, may offer you four thousand: that is the utmost. You will then have between five and six thousand troops, without unity, without order, without discipline.

You have, you say, good generals. I do not know them, and shall not, therefore, dispute their abilities; but they will be absorbed in details, they will not be seconded by the subalterns, they will be unable to do any thing to maintain the reputation they may possess; for it would require at least two months to get their army into tolerable discipline; and in four days Cartaux will have passed the Durance—and with what soldiers? Why, with the excellent light troop of the Allobroges, the old regiment of Burgundy, and the brave battalion of the Cote d'Or (which has been a hundred times victorious in battle,) and six or seven other corps, all disciplined soldiers, encouraged by their successes on the frontiers, and *against your army*! You have some twenty-four pounders, and eighteen pounders, and you fancy yourselves impregnable. In this you but follow the vulgar opinion; but military men will tell you, and fatal experience is about to convince you, that good four-pounders and eight-pounders are preferable on many accounts to pieces of heavy calibre! You have cannoneers of the new levy—your adversaries have gunners from regiments of the line, the best masters of their art in all Europe!

What will your army do if it concentrates itself at Aix? It is lost. It is an axiom in the military art, that the army which remains in its intrenchments is beaten: experience and theory agree upon this point; and the walls of Aix are not equal to the worst field-intrenchment, especially if you bear in mind their extent, and the houses which skirt them on the exterior within pistol-shot. Be you well assured then that this course, which to you appears the best, is the very worst. Besides, what means will you possess of supplying the town, in so short a time, with every kind of provisions? Will your army offer battle? Why, it is the weaker in numbers—it has no cavalry—its artillery is less adapted for the field—it would be broken, and from that moment defeated without resource, for the cavalry would prevent it from rallying.

Expect, then, to see the war carried into the Marseilles territory. There a tolerably powerful party is for the Republic; this will be the moment for the struggle; the junction will be made; and your city, the centre of the commerce of the Levant, the *entrepôt* of the south of Europe, is lost! Recollect the recent example of Lisle,[661] and the barbarous laws of war.

What infatuation has all at once possessed your townsmen? What fatal blindness is leading them to their ruin? How can they fancy themselves powerful enough to oppose the whole Republic? Even should they compel this army to fall back upon Avignon, can they doubt that, in a few days, fresh troops would come to supply the place of the former? The Republic, which gives the law to Europe, will she receive it from Marseilles?

United with Bourdeaux, Lyons, Montpellier, Nimes, Grenoble, the Jura, the Eure, the Calvados, you undertook a revolution. You had a probability of success: those who spurred you on might be ill-intentioned men; but you were an imposing mass of strength. On the contrary, now that Lyons, Nimes, Montpellier, Bourdeaux, the Jura, the Eure, Grenoble, Caen, have accepted the constitution;—now that Avignon, Tarascon, Arles, have submitted, acknowledge that in obstinacy there is folly. The fact is, that you are under the influence of individuals who, *having no property of their own to look after*, are involving you in their ruin.

Your army will be composed of the best-conditioned, the richest portion of your city; for the Sans-Culottes could but be too easily turned against you. You are about, then, to risk the *élite* of

---

[661] A small town in the department of Vaucluse, four leagues east of Avignon, having resisted Cartaux's army, was carried by assault, 26th July, 1793.—S.

your youthful population, young men accustomed to hold the commercial balance of the Mediterranean, and enrich you by their economy and their speculations, against veteran soldiers a hundred times stained with the blood of the desperate aristocrat or the ferocious Prussian.

Let poor countries fight to the last extremity. The inhabitant of the Vivarais, of the Cevennes, of Corsica, exposes himself without fear to the issue of a battle; if he gains it, he has obtained his object; if he is beaten, he finds himself as before, in the condition to make peace, and in the same position. But you!—lose but a battle, and the fruits of a thousand years of industry, of economy, of prosperity, become the prey of the soldier.

Marseillese.—You get on a great rate, and you alarm me. I agree with you that our situation is critical. It is perhaps true, that we do not sufficiently consider the position in which we now stand; but you cannot but acknowledge that we have still immense resources to oppose you. You have persuaded me that we could not resist at Aix: your observation as to the want of subsistence is perhaps unanswerable, as applied to a siege of long duration; but do you imagine that all Provence can, for a long period, witness with indifference the blockade of Aix? It will rise spontaneously; and your army, hemmed in on all sides, will be but too happy to repass the Durance.

Militaire.—Ah! how little you know of the spirit of men, and of the times, to talk thus! Everywhere there are two parties. The moment you are besieged, the Sectionary party will be put down in all the country places. The example of Tarascon, Saint-Remy, Organ, Arles, should convince you of this; a score of dragoons have sufficed to restore the old authorities, and put the new ones to flight.

Henceforward, in your department, any powerful movement in your favour is impossible. It might have taken place when the army was on the other side the Durance, and you were unbroken. At Toulon, the active spirits are much divided; and there the Sectionaries have not the same superiority as at Marseilles; they must therefore remain in the city to keep down their adversary. As for the department of the Lower Alps, nearly the whole of it, as you know, has accepted the constitution.

Marseillese.—We shall attack Cartaux in our mountains, where his cavalry will be of no service to him.

Militaire.—As if an army engaged in protecting a town could choose the point of attack. Besides, it is a fallacy to suppose there are any mountains near Marseilles sufficiently inaccessible to render cavalry ineffective: your hills are just steep enough to render the use of artillery more difficult, and to give a great advantage to your enemy; for it is in a country intersected by rivers that the skilful artilleryman, by the rapidity of his movements, the exactness in serving his pieces, and the accuracy of his elevations, is the most sure of having the superiority.

Marseillese.—You fancy us, then, to be without resources: Is it then possible, that it can be the destiny of a town who resisted the Romans, and preserved a portion of its laws under the despots who succeeded them, to become the prey of a handful of brigands? What! the Allobroge, laden with the spoils of Lisle, shall he give law to Marseilles? What! Dubois du Crancé, and Albitte, shall they rule over us uncontrolled? Those men, steeped in blood, whom the miseries of the times have placed at the head of affairs, shall they be our absolute masters? Sad, indeed, is the prospect you set before us! Our property, under different pretences, would be invaded; at every instant we should be the victims of a soldiery, whom plunder unites under the same banner: our best citizens would be imprisoned, and perish by violence. The Club would again rear its monstrous head to execute its infernal projects! Nothing can be worse than this; better to expose ourselves to the chance of warfare, than become victims without alternative!

Militaire.—Such is civil war! men revile one another—detest one another—kill one another, without knowing one another! The Allobroges! what do you suppose them to be? Africans? inhabitants of Siberia? Oh, not at all! They are your countrymen,—the men of Provence, of Dauphiny, of Savoy. Some people fancy them to be barbarians, because the name they have taken sounds oddly. If your own troops were to be called the Phocœan phalanx, every species of fable would be accredited respecting them.

You have reminded me of one fact, the assault of Lisle. I do not justify it, but will explain to you how it happened. The inhabitants killed the trumpeter who was sent to them; they resisted without the slightest chance of success; the town was taken by assault; the soldiers entered it amidst fire and slaughter: it was impossible to restrain them, and fury did the rest.

Those soldiers whom you call brigands, are our best troops, and most disciplined battalions: their reputation is above calumny.

Dubois-Crancé and Albitte, constant friends of the people, have never deviated from the right line. Certainly they are "wicked men" in the eyes of the bad: but Condorcet, Brissot, Barbaroux, were also "wicked men," so long as they remained uncontaminated. It will ever be the fate of the good to be ill-spoken of by the worthless. You imagine they show you no mercy; on the contrary, they are treating you like wayward children. Do you think, if they had been otherwise disposed, that the merchants of Marseilles would have been suffered to withdraw the goods which they had at Beaucaire? They could have sequestered them till the war was over. They were unwilling to do so; and, thanks to them, you can now return quietly to your homes.

You call Cartaux an assassin. Well! let me tell you, that that general takes the greatest pains to preserve order and discipline; witness his conduct at St. Esprit and at Avignon. He ordered a sergeant to prison because he had violated the asylum of a citizen who concealed one of your soldiers. In the eyes of the general, this sergeant was culpable for having entered, without direct orders, a private dwelling. Some people of Avignon were punished for pointing out a house as belonging to an aristocrat. A prosecution is now going on against a soldier, on a charge of theft. On the contrary, your army killed, assassinated more than thirty persons, violated the asylums of families, and filled the prisons with citizens, on the vague pretence that they were brigands.

Do not be in alarm about the army. It esteems Marseilles, because it knows that no town has made so many sacrifices for the public good. You have eighteen thousand men on the frontier; and you have not spared yourselves under any circumstances. Shake off, then, the yoke of the few aristocrats who govern you; return to sounder principles, and you will have no truer friend than the army.

Marseillese.—Ah! your army! It has greatly degenerated from the army of 1789. That army would not take up arms against the nation. Yours should imitate so worthy an example, and not turn their arms against their fellow-citizens.

Militaire.—With such principles, La Vendée would now have planted the white flag on the again reared walls of the Bastile, and the Camp of Jalès been dominant at Marseilles.

Marseillese.—La Vendée is anxious for a king—a counter-revolution: the war of La Vendée, of the camp of Jalès, is that of fanaticism, of despotism. Ours, on the contrary, is that of true Republicans, friends of the laws, of order; enemies of anarchy and of bad men. Is not ours the tri-coloured flag? and what interest could we have in wishing for slavery?

Militaire.—I well know that the people of Marseilles differ widely from those of La Vendée as to the subject of counter-revolution. The people of La Vendée are robust and healthy: the people of Marseilles weak and sickly. They stand in need of honey, to induce them to swallow the pill: to establish among them the new doctrine, they must be deceived. But after four years of revolution, after so many plots, and counterplots, and conspiracies, all the perversity of human nature has been developed under all its different aspects, and bad men have perfected their subtlety. You have, you say, the tri-coloured flag? Paoli also hoisted it in Corsica to have time to deceive the people, to crush the true friends of liberty, to entice his countrymen to join him in his ambitious and criminal projects; he hoisted the tri-coloured flag, and he nevertheless fired upon the vessels of the Republic, and drove our troops from the fortresses; he disarmed all the detachments he could surprise; he collected forces to drive the garrison from the island; he plundered the magazines, selling at a low price every thing found within them, to secure money to carry on his revolt; he confiscated the property of the wealthiest families, because they were attached to the unity of the Republic; he got himself appointed generalissimo, and he declared all those who should continue in our armies enemies of their country. Before this, he had caused the failure of the expedition to Sardinia; and yet he had the shamelessness to call himself the friend of France and a good Republican; and he deceived the Convention still, after all. He acted, in short, in such a way, that when at length he was unmasked by his own letters found at Calvi,—it was too late,—the fleets of our enemies intercepted all intercourse with the island.

It is no longer to words that we must trust. We must analyse deeds; and in appreciating yours, it is easy, you must acknowledge, to show you to be counter-revolutionary. Take my advice, people of Marseilles: shake off the yoke of the handful of wretches who are leading you to a counter-revolution; restore your constituted authorities; accept the constitution; liberate the representatives; let them go to Paris and intercede for you: you have been misled—it is no new thing for the people to be so—by a few conspirators and intriguers. In all ages, the flexibility and ignorance of the multitude have been the causes of most civil wars.

Marseillese.—Ah! sir, who is to bring the good about? Can it be the refugees who arrive on all sides from the department? They are interested in acting with desperation. Can it be those who at this moment govern us? Are not they in the same situation? Can it be the people? One portion of them knows nothing of its real position; it is blinded and *fanaticized*; the other portion is disarmed, suspected, humbled. I see, therefore, with deep affliction, miseries without remedy.

Militaire.—At last you are brought to reason. Why should not a like change be effected in the minds of a large portion of your fellow-citizens, who are deluded and sincere? In that case, Albitte, who can have no other wish than to spare French blood, will send you some honest and able man; matters will be arranged; and without a moment's delay, the army will march under the walls of

Perpignan, to make the Spaniard dance the Carmagnole; and Marseilles will continue to be the centre of gravity to liberty. The only thing necessary will be to tear a few leaves out of its history.

This happy prognostic put us all in excellent humour. The citizens of Marseilles, with great readiness, treated us to some bottles of champagne, which dispelled all our doubts and anxieties. We retired to rest at two in the morning, having agreed to meet again at breakfast; where my new acquaintance had still many doubts to suggest, and I many interesting truths to impart.

July 29, 1793.

No. IV

LETTERS OF NAPOLEON TO JOSEPHINE

[In the first Edition of this Work, Sir Walter Scott introduced, by way of foot notes, a few translations from the Letters of Napoleon and Josephine during the campaign of 1796, published in 1824 by Mr. Tennant. But the larger collection of those letters, edited by Josephine's daughter, the Duchess of St. Leu, had not then appeared. We now reprint the *versions* which Sir Walter thought fit to give; and append to them some specimens of the native style and orthography of the correspondence.]

(1.)

NAPOLEON TO JOSEPHINE

(*Translation.*)

"*Port Maurice, the 14th Germinal, (April 4,) 1796.*

"I have received all thy letters: but not one of them has affected me so much as thy last. Dost thou think, my adorable love, of writing to me in such terms? Dost thou imagine, then, that my position is not already cruel enough, without an increase of my sorrows, and an overthrow of my soul? What a style! what sentiments dost thou describe. They are of fire—they burn my poor heart. My only Josephine!—far from thee there is no joy;—far from thee the world is a desert, where I remain an isolated being, without enjoying the sweets of confidence. Thou hast deprived me of more than my soul; thou art the only thought of my life. If I am tired of the troubles of business—if I dread the result—if mankind disgust me—if I am ready to curse this life—I place my hand upon my heart—there thy portrait beats—I look at it, and love becomes to me absolute happiness; all is smiling, save the time when I am separated from my beloved.

"By what is it that thou hast been able to captivate all my faculties, and to concentrate in thyself my moral existence? It is a magic, my sweet love, which will finish only with my life. To live for Josephine—there is the history of my life. I am trying to reach thee—I am dying to be near thee. Fool that I am, I do not perceive that I increase the distance between us. What lands, what countries separate us! What a time before you read these weak expressions of a troubled soul in which you reign! Ah! my adorable wife! I know not what fate awaits me, but if it keep me much longer from thee, it will be insupportable—my courage will not go so far. There was a time when I was proud of my courage; and sometimes, when contemplating on the ills that man could do me, on the fate which destiny could reserve for me, I fixed my eyes steadfastly on the most unheard-of misfortunes without a frown, without alarm. But now, the idea that my Josephine may be unwell, the idea that she may be ill, and, above all, the cruel, the fatal thought, that she may love me less, withers my soul, stops my blood, renders me sad, cast down, and leaves me not even the courage of fury and despair. Formerly I used often to say to myself, men cannot hurt him who can die without regret; but now, to die without being loved by thee, to die without that certainty, is the torment of hell; it is the lively and striking image of absolute annihilation—I feel as if I were stifled. My incomparable companion, thou whom fate has destined to make along with me the painful journey of life, the day on which I shall cease to possess thy heart will be the day on which parched nature will be to me without warmth or vegetation.

"I stop, my sweet love, my soul is sad—my body is fatigued—my head is giddy—men disgust me—I ought to hate them—they separate me from my beloved.

"I am at Port Maurice, near Oneille; to-morrow I shall be at Albenga; the two armies are in motion—We are endeavouring to deceive each other—Victory to the most skilful! I am pretty well satisfied with Beaulieu—If he alarm me much, he is a better man than his predecessor. I shall beat him I hope in good style. Do not be uneasy—love me as your eyes—but that is not enough—as yourself, more than yourself, than your thought, your mind, your sight, your all. Sweet love, forgive me—I am sinking. Nature is weak for him who feels strongly, for him whom you love!!"

(2.)

"Albenga, 16th Germinal, (April 6.)

"[It is one hour after midnight. They have just brought me a letter. It is sad—my soul is affected by it: It is the death of Chauvet. He was commissary-in-chief of the army. You have seen him sometimes with Barras. My love, I feel the want of consolation that is to be obtained by writing to thee—to thee alone!—Chauvet is dead! He was attached to me. He has rendered essential services to his country. His last words were, that he was setting off to join me. Soul of my existence! write to me by every courier, otherwise I cannot live. I am here very much occupied; Beaulieu moves his army. We are in sight. I am a little fatigued; I am every day on horseback. Adieu, adieu, adieu. I am going to sleep. Sleep consoles me—it places me at thy side. But alas! on waking, I find myself three hundred leagues from thee!"

(3.)

"Albenga, 18 Germinal, (April 8.)

"My brother [Joseph] is here. He has heard of my marriage with pleasure. He is most anxious to know thee. I am trying to decide him to go to Paris. His wife has been brought to bed of a girl. He sends you a present of a box of Genoese sugar-plums. You will receive some oranges, perfumes, and orange-flower water, which I send you. Junot and Murat present you their respects."]

(4.)

"Headquarters, Carru, April 24.

"To my Sweet Love,

"My brother [Joseph] will give you this letter. I have the warmest regard for him. I hope he will obtain yours. He merits it. Nature has endowed him with a character, gentle, equal, and unchangeably good. He is made up of good qualities. I have written to Barras, that he may be appointed consul in some part of Italy. He wishes to live with his little wife, far away from the great whirlwind, and from great affairs. I recommend him to thee.

"Junot carries to Paris twenty-two standards. You must return with him. Should he come without thee—misfortune without remedy, grief without consolation, endless sufferings!—My adorable love, he will see thee—he will breathe in thy temple—perhaps even thou wilt accord him the rare and invaluable favour of a kiss on thy cheek. And I—I shall be alone, and far, very far away. But thou art coming, art thou not? Take wings!—come! come! but travel gently—the road is long, bad, fatiguing. If you were to be overturned, or to be taken ill! If the fatigue * * *. Go gently, my adorable love: but be often and rapidly with me in your thoughts.

"I have received a letter from Hortense. She is altogether lovely. I am going to write to her. I love her dearly, and I will soon send her the perfumes she wishes to have.

"I do not know whether you want money, for you have never spoken to me of these matters. If you do, speak to my brother, who has 200 Louis of mine.—N. B."

(5.)

tortone midi le 27 prarial.

A Josephine

Ma vie est un cochemar perpetuel un presentiment funeste m empeche de respirer. je ne vis plus j'ai perdu plus que la vie plus que le bonheur plus que le repos je suis presque sans espoir. je t expedie un courrier. il ne restera que 4 heure a paris et puis m aportera ta reponse—ecris moi 10 pages cela seul peut me consoler un peu—tu es malade, tu m aime, je t ai affligé, tu es grosse et je te ne vois pas! cett idée me confond. j'ai tant de tord avec toi que je ne sais comment les expier je t accuse de rester a paris et tu y etois malade—pardonne moi ma bonne amie l amour que tu m a inspiré m a ote la raison je ne la retrouverai jamais l'on ne guerit pas de ce mal la. mes presentimens sont si funestes que je me bornerois a te voir te presser 2 heures contre mon cœur et mourir ensemble! qu est ce qui a soin de toi. j'imagine que tu a fait appeller hortense j aime mille fois plus cet aimable enfant depuis que je pense qu'elle peut te consoler un peu quand a moi point de consolation point de repos, point d espoir jusqu 'a ce que j' ai reçu le courrier que je t expedie et que par une longue lettre tu m explique ce que c est que maladie et jusqu' a quel point elle doit etre serieuse—si elle est dangereuse, je t en previens je pars de suite pour paris. mon arrivé vaudra ta maladie. J'ai ete toujours heureux. jamais mon sort n a resiste a ma volonte et aujourdhui je suis frappe dans ce qui me touche uniquement. Josephine comment peut tu rester tant de tems sans m ecrire—ta derniere lettre laconique est du 3 du mois encore est elle affligante pour moi je l ai cependant toujours dans ma poche—ton portrait et tes lettres sont sans cesse devant mes yeux.

je ne suis rien sans toi je concois a peine comment j ai existe sans te connoitre ah! Josephine si tu eusse connu mon cœur serois tu rester depuis le 29 au 16 pour partir? aurois tu prete l oreil a des amis perfides qui vouloient peutetre te tenir eloignée de moi? je l avoue* tout le monde, j en veux a tout ce qui t entourre je te calculois partie depuis le 5 et le 15 arrivé a Milan.

josephine si tu m 'aime si tu crois que tout depend de ta conservation, ménage toi, je n ose pas te dire de ne pas entreprendre un voyage si long et dans les chaleurs a moins si tu es dans le cas de fair la route va a petites journées ecris moi a toutes les couchés et expedie moi d avance tes lettres.

toutes mes pensées sont concentrées dans ton alcove dans ton lit sur ton cœur ta maladie voyla ce qui m occupe la nuit et le jour— sans apetit, sans someil, sans interet pour l amitie, pour la gloire, pour la patrie, toi, toi et le reste du monde n existe pas plus pour moi que s il etoit anneanti je tiens a l honneur puisque tu y tiens, a la victoire puisque cela te fait plaisir sans quoi j aurois tout quitte pour me rendre a tes pieds.

quelquefois je me dis je m allarme sans raison deja elle est guerie elle part elle est partie, elle est peutetre deja a lion—vaine imagination—tu es dans ton lit souffrante, plus belle, plus interessante plus adorable tu es palle et tes yeux sont plus languissans mais quand sera tu guerie? si un de nous deux devoit etre malade ne doit il pas etre moi, plus robuste et plus courageux jeusse suporte la maladie plus facilement la destinée est cruelle elle me frappe dans toi.

ce qui me console quelque fois c est de penser qu il depend du sort de te rende malade mais qu il ne depend de personne de m obliger a te survivre.

dans ta lettre ma bonne amie aie soin de me dire que tu est convaincue que je t aime au dela de ce qu il est possible d imaginer, que tu es persuade que tous mes instans te sont consacrés que jamais il ne se passe une heure sans penser à toi, que jamais il ne m est venu dans l idée de penser a une autre femme qu elles sont toutes a mes yeux sans grace sans beauté et sans esprit que toi toi toute entière telle que je te vois telle que tu est pouvoit me plaire et absorber toutes les facultes de mon ame que tu en a touché toute l etendue que mon cœur n a point de replis que tu ne voye, point de pensées qui ne te sont subordonnes, que mes forces mes bras mon esprit sont tout a toi, que mon ame est dans ton corps, et que le jour ou tu aurois change ou ou tu cesserois de vivre seroit celui de ma mort, que la nature, la terre n est belle a mes yeux que parceque tu l habite—si tu ne crois pas tout cela si ton ame n'en est pas convaincue penetree, tu m afflige, tu ne m aime pas—il est un fluide magnetique entre les personnes qui s aiment———tu sais bien que jamais je ne pourrois te voir un amant encore moins t en offrir un, lui dechirois le cœur et le voir seroit pour moi la meme chose et puis si je † porter la main sur ta personne sacrée—non je ne l'oserai jamais mais je sorterois d une vie ou ce qui existe de plus vertueuse m auroit trompé.

Mais je suis sur et fier de ton amour—les malheurs sont des epreuves qui nous decellent mutuelment toute la force de notre passion un enfant adorable comme la maman va voir le jour et pourroit passer plusieurs ans dans tes bras—infortuné! je me contenterais d une journèe—Mille baise sur tes yeux, sur tes levres sur ta langue sur ton cœur—adorable femme quelle est ton ascendant je suis bien malade de ta maladie,j ai encore une fiévre brulante! ne garde pas plus de 6 heure le Simple* et qu il retourne de suite me porter la lettre cherie de ma Souveraine.

te souviens tu de ce reve ou j etois tes souliers tes chiffons et je te faisois entrer toute entière dans mon cœur—pourquoi la nature n a-t-elle pas arrange cela comme cela—il y a bien des choses a faire.

N. B.

A la Citoyenne Bonaparte,
Rue Chautreine, No. 6
Paris.

(6.)

de Pistoa en toscane le 8 messidor.

A Josephine,

Depuis un mois je n'ai reçu de ma bonne amie que 2 billets de trois lignes chacun—a-t-elle des affaires? celle d'écrire a son bon ami n'est donc pas un besoin pour elle des lors celle d'y penser—vivre sans penser a josephine ce seroit pour ton mari etre mort et ne pas exister—ton image embelit ma pensée et egaye le tableau sinistre et noire de la melancolie et de la douleur———un jour peuttere viendra ou je te verai, car je ne doute pas que tu ne sois encore a paris et bien ce jour la je te montrerai mes poches pleines de lettres que je ne t'ai pas envoyé par qu'elles etoient trop bete, bien c'est le mot. bon dieu dis mois toi qui sais si bien faire aimer les autres sans aimer sauras tu me guerir de l'amour??? je pairai ce remede bien chère tu devois partir le 5 prairal—bon que j'etois je tendois le 13 comme si une jolie femme pouvoit abandoner ses habitudes, ses amis, et Me. tallien et un diné chez baras, et une representation d'une piece nouvelle et fontane* oui fontane* tu aime tout plus que ton mari tu n'a pour lui qu'un peu d'estime et une portion de cette bienveillance dont ton cœur abonde tous les jours †† recapituler tes tord, tes fautes je me bat le flanc pour ne te plus aimer bah n' est* ce* pas que je taime davantage enfin mon incomparable petite mere je vais te dire mon secret. Mocque toi de moi reste a Paris, aie des amans, que tout le monde le sache, n ecris jamais eh! bien je t en aimerai 10 fois davantage—et ce n est pas folie fiévre delire!! et je ne guerirai pas de cela—oh si par dieu j'en guerirai—mais ne vas pas me dire que tu es malade—n entrepend pas de te justifie bon dieu tu es pardonnée je t aime a la folie et jamais mon pauvre cœur ne cessera de donner tout* a* l'*amour* si tu ne m aimois pas mon sort seroit bien byzare. tu ne m'a pas ecrit—tu etois malade—tu n es pas venue. †† n'a pas voulu et puis ta maladie et puis ce petit enfant qui se remuoit si fort qu il te faisoit mal? mais tu as passe lion tu seras le 10 a turin le 12 a milan ou tu m atendira. tu seras en italie et je serois encore loin de toi—adieu, ma bien aimé, un baisé sur ta bouche—un autre sur ton cœur—et un autre sur ton petit enfants.

Nous avons fait la paix avec Rome qui nous donne de l'argent—nous serons demain a livourne et le plutot que je pourrois dans tes bras, a tes pieds, sur ton sein.

A la Citoyenne
Bonaparte,
Rue chautreinne No. 6
Paris.

No. V
Descent of the French in South Wales, under General Tate

We have found some curious particulars respecting Tate's descent in the Memoirs of Theobald Wolfe Tone, one of the unfortunate and misguided Irish gentlemen who were engaged in the Rebellion 1796, and who, being taken on his return to Ireland with a French expedition, was condemned and executed there. The author, for whom we entertain much compassion, seems to have been a gallant light-hearted Irishman, his head full of scraps of plays, and his heart in a high fever on account of the supposed wrongs which his country had sustained at the hands of Great Britain. His hatred, indeed, had arisen to a pitch which seems to have surprised himself, as appears from the conclusion of the following extracts, which prove that nothing less than the total destruction of Bristol was expected from Tate and his merry-men, who had been industriously picked out as the greatest reprobates of the French army.

We have that sort of opinion of Citizen Wolfe Tone, which leads us to think he would have wept heartily had he been to witness the havoc of which he seems ambitious to be an instrument. The violence of his expressions only shows how civil war and political fury can deform and warp the moral feelings. But we should have liked to have seen Pat's countenance when he learned that the Bande Noire had laid down their arms to a handful of Welsh militia, backed by the appearance of a body of market women, with red cloaks, (such was the fact,) whom they took for the head of a supporting column. Even these attempts at pillage, in which they were supposed so dexterous, were foiled by the exertions of the sons of Owen Glendower. The only blood spilt was that of a French straggler, surprised by a Welsh farmer in the act of storming his hen-roost. The bold Briton knocked the assailant on the head with his flail, and, not knowing whom he had slain, buried him in the dunghill, until he learned by the report of the country that he had slain a French invader, when he was much astonished and delighted with his own valour. Such was the event of the invasion; Mr. Tone will tell us what was expected.

Nov. 1st and 2d, 1796, (Brest.)

Colonel Shee tells me that General Quantin has been dispatched from Flushing with 2000 of the greatest reprobates in the French army, to land in England, and do as much mischief as possible, and that we have 3000 of the same stamp, whom we are also to disgorge on the English coast....

Nov. 24th and 25th.

Colonel Tate, an American officer, has offered his services, and the general has given him the rank of chef-de-brigade, and 1050 men of the Legion Noire, in order to go on a bucaneering party into England. Excepting some little errors in the locality, which, after all, may seem errors to me from my own ignorance, the instructions are incomparably well drawn; they are done, or at least corrected, by the general himself; and if Tate be a dashing fellow, with military talents, he may play the devil in England before he is caught. His object is Liverpool; and I have some reason to think the scheme has resulted from a conversation I had a few days since with Colonel Shee, wherein I told him that, if we were once settled in Ireland, I thought we might make a piratical visit in that quarter; and, in fact, I wish it was we that should have the credit and profit of it. I should like, for example, to pay a visit to Liverpool myself, with some of the gentlemen from Ormond Quay, though I must say the citizens of the Legion Noire are very little behind my countrymen either in appearance or morality, which last has been prodigiously cultivated by three or four campaigns in Bretagne and La Vendée. A thousand of these desperadoes, in their black jackets, will edify John Bull exceedingly, if they get safe into Lancashire.

Nov. 26th.

To-day, by the general's orders, I have made a fair copy of Colonel Tate's instructions, with some alterations from the rough draught of yesterday, particularly with regard to his first destination, which is now fixed to be Bristol. If he arrives safe, it will be very possible to carry it by a *coup-de-main*, in which case he is to burn it to the ground. I cannot but observe here that I transcribed, with the greatest *sang froid*, the orders to reduce to ashes the third city of the British dominions, in which there is, perhaps, property to the amount of L.5,000,000.

No. VI

Buonaparte's Camp Library

BIBLIOTHEQUE DU CAMP.

VOL.

Sciences et Arts.

Mondes de Fontenelle,	1
Lettres à une Princess d'Allemagne,	2
Le Cours de l'Ecole—Normande,	6
Aide nécessaire pour l'Artillerie,	1
Traité des Fortifications,	3
Traité des Feux—d'Artifice,	1

Géographie et Voyages.

Géographie de Barclay,	12
Voyages de Cook,	3
Voyages Française de la Harpe,	24

Histoire.

Plutarque,	12
Turenne,	2
Condé,	4
Villars,	4
Luxembourg,	2
Duguesclin,	2
Saxe,	3
Mémoires des Maréchaux de France,	20
President Henault,	4
Chronologie,	2
Marlborough,	4
Prince Eugene,	6

Histoire Philosophique des Indes,	12
D'Allemagne,	2
Charles XII.,	1
Essai sur les Mœurs des Nations,	6
Pierre-le-Grand,	1
Polybe,	6
Justin,	2
Arrien,	3
Tacite,	2
Tite-Live,	
Thucydide,	2
Vertot,	4
Denina,	8
Frédéric II.,	8

Poésie.

Ossian,	1
Tasse,	6
Arioste,	6
Homère,	6
Virgile,	4
Henriade,	1
Télémaque,	2
Les Jardins,	1
Les Chefs-d'Œuvre du Théâtre-Français,	20
Poésies Légères (choisies,)	10
Fontaine,	

Romans.

Voltaire,	4
Héloïse,	4
Werther,	1
Marmontel,	4
Romans Anglais,	40
Le Sage,	10

Prevost, 10
Politique et Morale.
Le Vieux Testament.
Le Nouveau.
Le Coran.
Le Vedam.
Mythologie.
Montesquieu—L'Esprit des Lois.

(In all, about 320 vols.)

No. VII

BUONAPARTE, MEMBER OF THE NATIONAL INSTITUTE, COMMANDER-IN-CHIEF, TO THE PEOPLE OF EGYPT

Alexandria, July the _____, 6th Year of the Republic, One and Indivisible, the _____ of the Month of Muharrem, the Year of the Hegira 1213.

For a long time the Beys, who govern Egypt, have insulted the French nation, and covered her merchants with injuries: the hour of their chastisement is come.

For too long a time this rabble of slaves, purchased in Caucasus and in Georgia, has tyrannized over the fairest part of the world; but God, on whom every thing depends, has decreed that their empire shall be no more.

People of Egypt! you will be told that I am come to destroy your religion; do not believe it. Reply, that I am come to restore your rights, to punish usurpators; and that I reverence more than the Mameloucs themselves, God, his prophet Mahomet, and the Koran!

Tell them that all men are equal before God. Wisdom, talents, and virtue, are the only things which make a difference between them.

Now, what wisdom, what talents, what virtues, have the Mameloucs, that they should boast the exclusive possession of every thing that can render life agreeable?

If Egypt is their farm, let them show the lease which God has given them of it! But God is just and merciful to the people.

All the Egyptians shall be appointed to all the public situations. The most wise, the most intelligent, and the most virtuous, shall govern; and the people shall be happy.

There were formerly among you great cities, great canals, and a great commerce. What has destroyed them all? What! but the avarice, the injustice, and the tyranny of the Mameloucs.

Cadis, Cheiks, Imans, Tchorbadgis! tell the people that we are the friends of the true Mussulmans. Is it not we, who have destroyed the Pope; who said that it was necessary to make war on Mussulmans? Is it not we, who have destroyed the Knights of Malta, because these madmen believed that it was the good pleasure of God, that they should make war on Mussulmans? Is it not we, who have been in all ages the friends of the Grand Signior, (on whose desires be the blessings of God!) and the enemy of his enemies? And, on the contrary, have not the Mameloucs always revolted against the authority of the Grand Signior, which they refuse to recognize at this moment?

Thrice happy those who shall be with us! they shall prosper in their fortune and their rank. Happy those who shall be neutral! they shall have time to know us thoroughly, and they will range themselves on our side.

But woe, woe, woe, to those who shall take up arms in favour of the Mameloucs, and combat against us! There shall be no hope for them: they shall all perish.

(Signed) Buonaparte.
A true copy.
(Signed) Berthier.

No. VIII

HISTORICAL NOTES ON THE EIGHTEENTH BRUMAIRE.[662]

The following facts, which have never been made public, but with which we have been favoured from an authentic channel, throw particular light on the troubled period during which Napoleon assumed the supreme power—the risks which he ran of being anticipated in his aim, or of altogether missing it.

In the end of July, 1799, when all those discontents were fermenting, which afterwards led to the Revolution of the 18th Brumaire.

General Augereau, with one of the most celebrated veterans of the Republican army, attended by a deputation of six persons, amongst whom were Salicetti and other members of Convention, came on a mission to General Bernadotte, their minister at war, at an early hour in the morning.

Their object was to call the minister's attention to a general report, which announced that there was to be a speedy alteration of the constitution and existing order of things. They accused Barras, Siêyes, and Fouché, as being the authors of these intrigues. It was generally believed, they said, that one of the directors (Barras) was for restoring the Bourbons; another (Siêyes is probably meant) was for electing the Duke of Brunswick. The deputation made Bernadotte acquainted with their purpose of fulminating a decree of arrest against the two official persons. Having first inquired what proofs they could produce in support of their allegations, and being informed that they had no positive proof to offer, the minister

---

[662] "Les notes historiques, qui sont inserees comme appendice à la fin du dernier volume de la Vie de Napoleon, sont attribées au General Bernadotte, actuellement Roi de Suède, mais qu'il faut plutôt regarder comme l'ouvrage d'un ami indiscret. C'est pourtant dans ces notes que, sans les citer jamais, Bourrienne a évidemment puisé à pleines mains."—*Observations sur le 18 Brumaire de M. de Bourrienne*, par M. Boulay de la Meurthe, *Ancien Ministre d'Etat*.

informed them that he would not participate in the proposed act of illegal violence. "I require your word of honour," he said, "that you will desist from this project. It is the only mode to ensure my silence on the subject." One of the deputation, whom the minister had reason to regard as a man of the most exemplary loyalty, and with whom he had had connexions in military service, replied to him, "Our intention was to have placed you in possession of great power, being well persuaded that you would not abuse it. Since you do not see the matter as we do, the affair is at an end. We give up our scheme. Let the affair be buried in complete oblivion." In less than two months afterwards, Buonaparte's arrival gave a new turn to the state of affairs.

He landed, as is well known, at Frejus, after having abandoned his army, and broke the quarantine laws. When this intelligence reached Bernadotte, he intimated to the Directory, that there was not an instant to lose in having him brought before a council of war. General Debel was instructed to make this communication to a member of the Directory, who was one of his friends. Colonel St. Martin, of the artillery, spoke to this director to the same purpose. His answer was, "We are not strong enough." On its being said that Bernadotte was of opinion that Buonaparte should be proceeded against according to the principles of military discipline, and that the opportunity which occurred should be laid hold of, the director replied, "Let us wait."

Buonaparte arrived at Paris. All the generals went to visit him. A public dinner to him was proposed, and a list for that purpose handed about. When it was presented to Bernadotte by two members of the Council of Five Hundred, he said to them, "I would advise you to put off this dinner till he account satisfactorily for having abandoned his army."[663]

---

[663] When Bernadotte came into the ministry, it became a question whether Buonaparte should not be sent for from Egypt.—"It is the army you mean," said the minister,—"for as to the general, you know he has an eye to the dictatorship; and sending vessels to bring him to France, would just be giving it to him."
A French fleet was at that time cruizing in the Mediterranean,—the minister insisted that it should be ordered to Toulon.

More than twelve days had elapsed before Bernadotte saw Buonaparte. At the request of Joseph, his brother-in-law, and of Madame Leclerc, Buonaparte's sister, Bernadotte at length went to visit him. The conversation turned upon Egypt. Buonaparte having begun to talk of public affairs, Bernadotte allowed him to enlarge on the necessity of a change in the government; and at last, perceiving that Buonaparte, aware of the awkwardness of his situation, was exaggerating the unfavourable circumstances in the situation of France,—"But, general," said Bernadotte, "the Russians are beaten in Switzerland, and have retired into Bohemia; a line of defence is maintained between the Alps and the Ligurian Apennines; we are in possession of Genoa; Holland is saved—the Russian army that was there is destroyed, and the English army has retired to England:— 15,000 insurgents have just been dispersed in the department of the Upper Garonne, and constrained to take refuge in Spain:—at this moment we are busied in raising two hundred auxiliary battalions of 1000 men each, and 40,000 cavalry; and in three months at most, we shall not know what to do with this multitude of torrents. Indeed, if you had been able to bring the army of Egypt with you, the veterans who compose it would have been very useful in forming our new corps. Though we should look upon this army as lost, unless it return by virtue of a treaty, I do not despair of the safety of the Republic, and I am convinced she will withstand her enemies both at home and abroad." While pronouncing the words *enemies at home*, Bernadotte unintentionally looked in the face of Buonaparte, whose confusion was evident. Madame Buonaparte changed the conversation, and Bernadotte soon after took leave.

Some days afterwards, M. R——, formerly chief secretary to the minister of war, begged General Bernadotte to introduce him to Buonaparte. The general carried him along with him. After the usual compliments, they began to talk of the situation of France. Buonaparte spoke much of the great excitement of feeling among the republicans, and particularly in the *"club du manège."* Bernadotte said in answer, "When an impulse is once given, it is not easily stopped. This you have often experienced. After having impressed on the army of Italy a movement of patriotic enthusiasm, you could not repress this feeling when you judged it proper to do so. The same thing happens now. A number of individuals, and your own brothers principally, have formed the club you speak of. I have never belonged to it. I was too busy, and had too many duties to perform as minister, to be able to attend it. You have alleged that I have favoured these meetings. This is not correct. I have indeed supported many respectable persons who belonged to this club, because their views were honest, and they hoped to give prevalence to a spirit of moderation and prudence, which is generally thrown aside by ambitious men. Salicetti, a particular friend and secret confidant of your brothers, was one of the directors of that meeting. It has been believed by observers, and is believed still, that the state of excitement which you complain of, has originated in the instructions received by Salicetti."

Here Buonaparte lost temper, and declared that he would rather live in the woods, than continue to exist in the midst of a society which gave him no security.

"What security do you want?" answered General Bernadotte. Madame Buonaparte, fearing that the conversation would become too warm, changed the subject, addressing herself to M. R——, who was known to her. General Bernadotte did not persist in his questions, and, after some general conversation, he withdrew.

A few days afterwards, Joseph had a large party at Morfontaine. Buonaparte, meeting General Bernadotte coming out of the *Théâtre Française*, inquired if he was to be of the party on the following day. Being answered in the affirmative—"Will you," said he, "give me my coffee to-morrow morning? I have occasion to pass near your house, and shall be very glad to stop with you for a few moments." Next morning, Buonaparte and his wife arrived; Louis followed them a moment afterwards. Buonaparte made himself very agreeable.[664] In the evening there was some conversation between Regnault de St. Jean d'Angely, Joseph, and Lucien. Buonaparte conversed with Bernadotte, who saw, from his embarrassed air, and frequent fits of absence, that his mind was deeply occupied. He had

---

[664] It was by no means from friendship that Buonaparte went to Bernadotte's on this occasion; but really to render the Directory and the friends of the Republic suspicious as to that general's intentions.

no longer any doubt that it was Buonaparte's determined purpose to save himself, by the overthrow of the constitution, from the danger with which he was threatened in consequence of his leaving Egypt, abandoning his army, and violating the quarantine laws. He resolved to oppose it by every means in his power. On his return to Paris, he happened, accidentally, to be in a house belonging to a fellow-countryman and friend of Moreau's. That general having inquired if he had been at the party at Morfontaine, and if he had spoken with Buonaparte, and Bernadotte having told him he had, Moreau said, "That is the man who has done the greatest harm to the Republic."—"And," added Bernadotte, "who is preparing the greatest."—"We shall prevent him," replied Moreau. The two generals shook hands, and promised to stand by each other in resisting the deserter from Egypt. So they called him in presence of a number of persons, among whom was the ex-minister, Petiet.

The Directory, it is true, did not enjoy the public esteem. Sièyes stood first in reputation among the five members, but he was looked upon as being timid and vindictive. He was believed to be disposed to call the Duke of Brunswick to the throne of France. Barras was suspected by some persons of being in treaty with the Comte Lille. Gohier, Moulines, and Roger Ducos, were very respectable men, but considered to be unfit for the government of a great nation. Gohier, however, was known to be one of the first lawyers of that period, to be of incorruptible integrity, and an ardent lover of his country.

When Sièyes obtained a place in the Directory, he had desired to have General Bernadotte for war-minister. Some confidential relations between them, and a certain degree of deference which Bernadotte paid to Sièyes, in consequence of his great celebrity, had flattered his self-love. Buonaparte's two brothers, Joseph and Lucien, thinking they should find in Bernadotte a ready instrument for the execution of the plans of their brother, whom they believed to be on the point of landing in France, agreed with Sièyes in bringing Bernadotte into the ministry. Gohier, Moulines, and Roger Ducos joined the Buonapartes and Sièyes; Barras alone inclined towards Dubois-Crancé; but he yielded with a good grace to the opinion of his colleagues.

The proposal was made to Bernadotte at a dinner at Joseph's, in the *rue du Rocher*. Joubert, one of the party, who had recently formed an intimacy with the candidate for the place of minister, was chosen by the Buonapartes to propose it to him. The proposal was refused, and the remonstrances of Joubert had no effect on the resolution of Bernadotte, which at that time appeared immovable. The Buonapartes, who were the prime movers of all the changes which took place, and enjoyed the distribution of all the great posts, were astonished when they heard General Joubert's report. They got several members of the council to endeavour to induce Bernadotte to accept. Their attempts were vain. Every solicitation was followed by a most obstinate refusal. But what could not be done by Bernadotte's friends and partisans, duped by the apparent friendship of the Buonapartes for him, was accomplished by his wife and sister-in-law. After many days spent in entreaties, Bernadotte yielded, and received the *porte-feuille* from the hands of General Millet-Moreau, who then had the charge of that department. The Buonapartes were not slow in showing a desire to exercise a direct influence in the war department. Many of their creatures were raised, by the new minister, to higher situations; but the number of fresh applications continually made to him, convinced him that they considered him as holding his place merely to serve their purposes, and prepare the way for their elevation.

The minister, who went regularly at five o'clock in the morning to the office of the war-department, where he had to repair heavy disasters, recruit the army, put a stop to dilapidations, organise two hundred battalions of a thousand men each, bring back to their corps 80,000 men, who had, in the course of a few years, absented themselves without permission, and accomplish an extraordinary levy of 40,000 horse, did not return to his house, in the *rue Cisalpine*, till between five and six in the evening. Joseph and his wife were almost always there. Joseph sometimes turned the conversation on the incapacity of the Directory, the difficulty of things remaining as they were, and the necessity of new-modelling the administration.

Bernadotte, on the contrary, thought that if the five directors were reduced to three, one of whom should go out of office every three years, the constitution would go on very well. He found in that form of government the creation of a patrician order exclusively charged with the government of the state. The Roman republic was his model, and he saw in the constitution of the year four a great analogy to the consular privileges and the rights of senators. By the 135th article of that constitution, no one could aspire to become a Director, without having been first a member of one of the two councils, a minister of state, &c. As that condition was already fulfilled in his case, it was natural that he should incline towards the preservation of a form of government which placed him on an equality with kings, and gave him the hopes of seeing many kings tributary to, or at least protected by, the Republic. These discussions sometimes became rather unreserved, and it was at such a time that Joseph intimated to Bernadotte, in a sort of half-confidence, the possibility of his brother's speedy return. The minister had sufficient presence of mind to conceal his indignation; but his surprise was so visible that Joseph was alarmed by it. He endeavoured to diminish the impression which his communication had produced. He said, "That what he had advanced was merely a simple conjecture on his part, which might become a probability—perhaps, even (added he) a reality; for he has conquered Egypt—his business is at an end—he has nothing more to do in that quarter."—"Conquered!" replied Bernadotte—"Say rather, *invaded*. This conquest, if you will call it so, is far from being secure. It has given new life to the coalition, which was extinct; it has given us all Europe for our enemies; and rendered the very existence of the Republic doubtful. Besides, your brother has no authority to quit the army. He knows the military laws, and I do not think that he would be inclined, or would dare, to render himself liable to punishment under them. Such a desertion would be too serious a matter; and he is too well aware of its consequences." Joseph went away a few moments afterwards; and this conversation having proved to him that Bernadotte did not concur in his opinions, it became an object to produce a breach between him (Bernadotte) and Siêyes.

Bernadotte retired from the ministry, and Buonaparte arrived about three weeks afterwards. Not being able to doubt that the Directors themselves were either dupes of Buonaparte's ambition, or his accomplices, and that they were meditating with him the overthrow of the established order of things, General Bernadotte persevered in offering his counsels and services to those members of the government, or of the Legislative Body, who might have opposed those designs. But the factions and the intriguing went on at a more rapid pace; and every day Buonaparte increased his party by the accession of some distinguished personage.

On the 16th Brumaire, at five o'clock, Bernadotte went to General Buonaparte's where he was invited to dinner. General Jourdan was of the party. He arrived after they had sat down to table. The conversation was entirely on military subjects; and Bernadotte undertook to refute the maxims which Buonaparte was laying down relative to the system of war by invasion. Bernadotte concluded nearly in these words:—"There is more trouble in preserving than in invading;" alluding to the conquest of Egypt. The company rose and went to the drawing-room. Immediately afterwards there arrived several very distinguished members of the council, and a good many men of letters; Volney and Talleyrand were of the number. The conversation was general, and turned on the affairs of the west of France. Buonaparte, raising his voice a little, and addressing somebody near him, said—"Ah! you see a Chouan in General Bernadotte." The general, in answering him, could not refrain from smiling. "Don't contradict yourself," said he; "it was but the other day that you complained of my favouring the inconvenient enthusiasm of the friends of the Republic, and now you tell me that I protect the Chouans. This is very inconsistent." The company continued to increase every minute; and, the apartments not being very spacious, Bernadotte went away.

Many persons have thought that the answers given by Bernadotte to Buonaparte on this occasion, had retarded for twenty-four hours the movement which had been prepared. Others, on the contrary, have alleged that, the 17th being a Friday, Buonaparte, naturally superstitious, had deferred the execution of the project till the 18th.

On the 17th Brumaire, between eleven and twelve at night, Joseph Buonaparte, returning to his house in the *rue du Rocher* by the way of the *rue Cisalpine*, called at the house of Bernadotte. He, being in bed, sent to request Joseph to return next day. He did so before seven o'clock in the morning of the 18th. He told Bernadotte that his brother desired to speak with him; that the measures to be taken had been discussed the evening before, and that they wished to inform him of them. They both went immediately to Buonaparte's house in the *rue de la Victoire*. The court, the vestibule, and the apartments, were filled with generals and officers of rank. Many of the officers had the air of persons in a state of excitation from wine. Bernadotte was shown into a small room; Joseph did not go in. Buonaparte was sitting at breakfast with one of his aides-de-camp, who, as far as can be remembered, was Lemmarois. General Lefebvre, afterwards Duke of Dantzic, then commanding the 17th military division, of which Paris was the headquarters, was standing. Bernadotte, seeing him in that attitude, did not doubt that he was detained a prisoner. He immediately took a chair, sat down, and made a sign to Lefebvre to do the same. Lefebvre hesitated, but a glance from Buonaparte reassured him. He sat down respectfully, looking at Buonaparte. The latter, addressing himself to Bernadotte, said, with embarrassment,—"Why, you are not in uniform!" On Bernadotte answering—"I am not on duty," Buonaparte replied—"You shall be immediately."—"I do not think so," said Bernadotte. Buonaparte rose, took Bernadotte by the hand, and carried him into an adjoining room. "This Directory governs ill," said he; "it would destroy the Republic if we did not take care. The Council of Ancients has named me commandant of Paris, of the national guard, and of all the troops in the division. Go and put on your uniform, and join me at the Tuileries, where I am now going."

Bernadotte having declined doing this, Buonaparte said—"I see you think you can count upon Moreau, Bournonville, and other generals. You will see them all come to me—Moreau himself;" and, speaking very fast, he named about thirty members of the Council of Ancients, whom Bernadotte had believed to be the greatest friends of the constitution of the year IV. "You don't know mankind," added he; "they promise much, and perform little."

Bernadotte having declared that he did not choose to be involved in a rebellion of this kind, nor to overturn a constitution which had cost the lives of a million of men,—"Well," said

Buonaparte, "you will stay till I receive the decree of the Council of Ancients; for till then I am nothing." Bernadotte, raising his voice, said—"I am a man whom you may put to death, but whom you shall not detain against his will."—"Well, then!" said Buonaparte, softening his voice, "give me your word that you will do nothing against me."—"Yes, as a citizen; but if I am called upon by the Directory, or if the Legislative Body gives me the command of its guard, I shall oppose you, and you shall not have the upper hand."—"What do you mean by *as a citizen*?"—"I will not go to the barracks, nor places of public resort, to inflame the minds of the soldiers and the people."

"I am quite easy," answered Buonaparte; "I have taken my measures; you will receive no appointment; they are more afraid of your ambition than of mine. I wish merely to save the Republic; I want nothing for myself; I shall retire to Malmaison, after having brought about me a circle of friends. If you wish to be of the number, you shall be made very welcome." Bernadotte said in reply, as he was going away—"As to your being a good friend, that may be; but I am convinced that you will always be the worst of masters."

Bernadotte left the room; Buonaparte followed him into the lobby, and said to Joseph with an agitated voice—"Follow him." Bernadotte passed through a crowd of generals, officers of rank, and soldiers, who filled the court of the house, and a part of the street, making some impression upon them by his looks, which expressed his disapprobation of their conduct. Joseph followed Bernadotte, and came up to him in the court of the house. He asked him to go to his house, in the *rue du Rocher*, where he had assembled several members of the Legislative Body. When he arrived at Joseph's, he found a dozen of persons, among whom were several deputies devoted to Buonaparte, and particularly Salicetti. Breakfast was served. During the few moments they remained at table, they spoke of the resolutions which would be taken, and Joseph repeated that his brother wished for nothing but the consolidation of freedom, that he might then have it in his power to live like a philosopher at Malmaison.

Bernadotte went to the garden of the Tuileries, and passed along the front of the 79th demi-brigade. The officers having recognised him, though not in uniform, came up to him, and asked him for information as to what was going to happen. Bernadotte answered in general terms, expressing his wish that the public tranquillity might not be endangered by the movement about to take place. The soldiers, having in their turn recognised the general who had commanded them at the siege and taking of Maestricht, loudly expressed their astonishment at his not being along with the generals, who, said they, were then deciding, in the palace, the fate of France.

Bernadotte having observed what he might expect, in case of need, from this corps, and from some detachments before whom he had presented himself on the *Boulevard* and on the *Pont de la Révolution*, went to General Jourdan's, presuming that the Directory would send for him to take care of the safety of the government. He found at Jourdan's a good many members of the Council of Five Hundred, among others Augereau, afterwards Duke of Castiglione. He had scarcely arrived, when a great number of the members came to announce the communication of the decree of the Council of Ancients, which, in virtue of the 102d article of the Constitution, transferred the sitting of the Legislative Body to St. Cloud.

Bernadotte, on his return home, learned from his wife that the Adjutant-General Rapatel, attached to General Moreau's staff, had just been there, and that he had been sent by Buonaparte and Moreau, to persuade him to join them at the Tuileries. Buonaparte had said to him—"You have served under General Bernadotte. I know that he has confidence in you. Tell him that all his friends are assembled at the Tuileries, and that they are desirous of seeing him among them; add that they love their country as much as he, and that they strongly wish to see him appear among the number of those to whom she this day owes her safety."

Siêyes and Roger Ducos had already joined Buonaparte at the Tuileries. The three Directors, Gohier the President, Moulins and Barras, remained at the Luxembourg. The secretary-general, Lagarde, was still faithful to the majority of the Directory. As

General Bernadotte had foreseen, that majority cast their eyes on him for the ministry of war, and the general command of the troops, and of the national guards of the 17th division. The resignation of Barras, and the defection of the secretary-general, put a stop to this nomination. Buonaparte, having no longer any thing to fear, made a new division of the different commands, and assigned to Moreau, with an hundred horse, that of the Luxembourg, where Gohier and Moulins were detained.

Moreau, dissatisfied with the indifference with which he had been treated by Buonaparte, and acquainted with his intentions and projects, was already thinking of forsaking his cause, which he regarded as unjust and traitorous to the nation. He again desired Rapatel to go, towards evening, to Bernadotte's, to invite him, on the part of Moreau, to go to the Luxembourg, that they might consult together as to the measures to be taken for preventing Buonaparte from seizing the Dictatorship. Bernadotte's answer to these overtures was, that he was bound by the word of honour which he had given, not to undertake any thing as a citizen; but that he was free to act if called on or summoned to do so by a public man; that if Moreau would march out of the Luxembourg, at the head of the detachment which he commanded, present himself at his door, and summon him, in the name of the public good, to make common cause with him in the defence of liberty and of the constitution which had been sworn to, he, Bernadotte, would mount his horse with his aides-de-camp, put himself under Moreau's command, address the troops, and cause Buonaparte to be immediately arrested and tried as a deserter from the army of Egypt, and as having violated the constitution, by accepting a command given him by a mere fraction of the Legislative Body. Moreau, bound down by the duty of military discipline, according to which he was under the orders of General Buonaparte, did not agree to Bernadotte's proposal; and the latter, therefore, did not think himself at liberty to go to the Luxembourg.

Bernadotte, from seven o'clock till ten, had conferences with Salicetti, Augereau, Jourdan, Gareau, and a dozen of the most influential members of the Council of Five Hundred. It was decided, that, next morning, Bernadotte should be named commandant of the guard of the Legislative Body, and of all the troops in the capital, and they separated. Salicetti ran to the Tuileries to tell Buonaparte what had happened, and he, who dreaded so courageous an adversary as Bernadotte, charged Salicetti to be present next morning at five o'clock, at the preparatory meeting which was to take place before going to St. Cloud, and to tell every one of the deputies, that he, Buonaparte, had made the greatest efforts to prevent a decree of deportation being issued against the deputies who had formed the design of giving to Bernadotte the command of the armed force.

On the 19th, at seven o'clock in the morning, Generals Jourdan and Augereau, followed by eight or ten deputies of the Council of Five Hundred, (among whom were Gareau and Talot,) went to General Bernadotte's in the *rue Cisalpine*. They informed him that Salicetti had made them aware, on the part of Buonaparte, that Sièyes had proposed to arrest a number of the deputies of the two Councils, in order to prevent their appearing at St. Cloud. They asked Bernadotte what he thought of the events of the day. He saw nothing in the communication of Salicetti, but the desire of rendering these deputies favourable to Buonaparte. Some of these legislators seemed to feel grateful for the service which Buonaparte had done them the evening before. Bernadotte did not appreciate this act of generosity as they did; but he agreed in their opinion as to the conciliatory measures which they seemed to wish to adopt, and, entering into their views, he explained himself in these terms:—"Let one of you mount the tribune; let him describe succinctly the internal situation of France, and her successes abroad; let him say, that the departure of an army for Egypt, while it has involved us in war, has deprived us of an army of more than 30,000 veterans, and a great many experienced generals; that, nevertheless, the Republic is triumphant; that the coalition is broken up, since Suwarrow is returned to Russia; that the English, with a prince of the blood at their head, have left the Batavian republic and retired to England; that the line of defence is maintained between the Alps and the Ligurian Appenines; that 200,000 conscripts are hastening to arrange themselves into battalions to reinforce the armies, and 40,000 cavalry are raising; that the insurrection of the west is reduced to a few scattered bands, and that a royalist army in the Upper Garonne has been destroyed or dispersed; that, to obtain a peace quite as honourable as that of Campo Formio, it is only necessary for France to maintain this formidable attitude; that, in order to maintain it, union and mutual confidence are indispensable; that, although the Council of Ancients have violated the constitution, in naming Buonaparte general-in-chief of the 17th division, and in giving him the command of the national guard and the guard of the Directory, the Council of Five Hundred is not now engaged in deliberating on this violation of the constitution, but rather on the means of giving security to the French people, the two Councils, and the Government of the State; that, for this purpose, the Council of Five Hundred names General Bernadotte colleague to General Buonaparte; that these two generals shall understand each other in regard to the employment of the armed force, and the distribution of commands, in case of this force being employed; but that the tranquillity which prevails in Paris and the vicinity, renders it certain that there will be no occasion for this force being put in motion. Send me this decree; in twenty minutes after receiving it, I shall be in the midst of you with my aides-de-camp; I shall take the command of the corps that I shall find on my way, and we shall see what is to be done. If it is necessary to declare Buonaparte an outlaw, you will always have on your side a general, and a great proportion at least of the troops."

The deputies immediately set off for St. Cloud. The unhappy custom of delivering set speeches from the tribune, produced the loss of precious time. The debate became warm: and the taking individually the oath to the constitution caused a useless loss of more than an hour and a half. No other resolution was taken. Buonaparte made his appearance, and the events which then happened at St. Cloud are well known.

After having been repulsed from the Council of Five Hundred, Buonaparte, stammering with agitation, addressed the soldiers. "Are you for me?"—"We are for the Republic," said they—(It was at this time that Lucien, President of the Council, harangued the troops.) What would have become of him had Bernadotte been there? Buonaparte felt this himself; for he said, at this period—"I am not afraid of Bernadotte's consenting to my being assassinated; but he will harangue the troops, and that is what I have to fear."

Buonaparte was made aware, the same evening, of the language which Bernadotte had used to the deputies at his house in the *rue Cisalpine*. The expressions he had really made use of, though they must have been disagreeable enough to Buonaparte, particularly in so far as related to his escape from Egypt, and his ulterior designs against the liberty of France, were exaggerated, and represented to Buonaparte so as to indicate personal hatred.

Buonaparte, though he never found an opportunity of taking open revenge against Bernadotte, let slip no opportunity of injuring him, by placing him, as a general, in difficult situations, and leaving him, in the most perilous and delicate circumstances, without instructions or orders. The following occurrence, which took place soon afterwards, will give a correct idea of this conduct on the part of Buonaparte.

The measures for restoring tranquillity in the west of France, in the month of January 1800, had never been entirely completed; for, at the same moment that they were taken, several departments were put out of the pale of the constitution. The Chouans of these departments were organised as militia, and as guerillas, who plundered the diligences, and murdered the persons who became proprietors of the national domains. They were regularly paid, and had communications with the enemies of the Republic, by means of the English fleets which threatened the coasts. At this critical moment, Bernadotte was invested with the civil and military command of these departments. By his firm and prudent conduct, he repressed the seditious movements, and re-established good order and obedience to the laws. Many free corps, numbers of individuals belonging to which, for want of being properly employed, were in the pay of the Chouan chiefs, were organised as regular troops; and by this measure he furnished government with the means of drawing from these departments troops for the army of Italy. But when these troops were to begin their march to Dijon, a serious insurrection broke out at Vannes, on the 28th Fructidor, year VIII., (4th September 1800.) The 52d demi-brigade refused to march till they should receive their arrears of pay. The commandant and officers who wished to restore order among them were maltreated. Bernadotte being informed of this transaction, hastened to Vannes to quell the insurrection; but the corps had left the place. He gave orders to General Liebert, commanding the 22d military division, to assemble the 52d demi-brigade on its way to Tours; to come before it, followed by his staff and the council of war; to make the military penal code be read; to order the colonels to point out one or two men in each company who had made themselves most remarkable in the revolt of the 28th; to deliver these men to the council of war, and to have them tried on the spot, &c. &c.

Bernadotte's orders were executed on the 4th Vendemaire, (25th September,) when the 52d demi-brigade was drawn up on the parade at Tours, and the ringleaders of the revolt arrested in presence of a great number of spectators, without the smallest disturbance taking place.

Bernadotte made a report of this event to the First Consul, and to Carnot, the minister of war; but as the result of the measures he had taken was not yet known, the Consul put on the margin of the report:—"General Bernadotte has not done well in taking such severe measures against the 52d demi-brigade, not having sufficient means to bring them to order in the heart of a town where the garrison is not strong enough to repress mutiny."

The result was different. The soldiers returned to their duty, and themselves denounced the authors of the insurrection. The demi-brigade continued its route to Italy; and, two days afterwards, the Consul was profuse in his encomiums on the prudence, foresight, and firmness of the general whose conduct he had been so hasty in disapproving.—The letter which he wrote to Bernadotte on this subject, was in these terms:—

"Paris, 10th Vendemaire, year IX.

"I have read with interest, Citizen-general, the account of what you have done to restore order in the 52d, and also the report of General Liebert, of the 5th Vendemaire. Give this officer the assurance of the satisfaction of Government with his conduct. Your promotion of the colonel of brigade to the rank of general of brigade is confirmed. I desire that this brave officer may come to Paris. He has given an example of firmness and energy most honourable to a military man.

"I salute you,

"Buonaparte."

All men, doubtless, are liable to err; but the eagerness of the Consul to attach blame to the conduct of a military and political commander, charged with the maintenance of discipline and obedience to the laws, appears evidently to have proceeded more from private hatred than from any duty which the government had to perform; for there was no occasion to give his judgment so precipitately, and he might have waited the final result of the measures he censured, more especially as the scene had taken place in a district agitated by faction and civil war. Bernadotte's friends, who were still in the ministry of war, and even frequented the saloons of the Consul, were anxious to make him acquainted with Buonaparte's evil intentions towards him. Every despatch which he received informed him that the police were forming secret intrigues and conspiracies; that agents were scattered among the Army of the West and the Army of the Rhine, to endeavour to make the staffs of those armies commit themselves, in order to have a pretext for disgracing the generals who commanded them. Reports were circulated among the members of these staffs; one day the Consul was dying; next day the population of Paris had risen, and the constitution of the year IV. was re-established, with the necessary modifications. The persons employed in raising these reports, watched the looks of the generals, and reported their slightest expressions. These snares roused the indignation of General Bernadotte, and the army he commanded; and it is not going too far to say, that it was in the Army of the West and the Army of the Rhine that plans for the preservation and security of constitutional freedom originated. Men who were obliged by profession and duty to yield to the force of military discipline, and who neither had, nor wished to have any thing to do with the intricacies of civil policy, were all at once inspired with a new spirit, and tacitly formed an association guided by their opinions; so much so, that, during the course of the year 1801, the Consul perceived, from the reserve and behaviour of many of the generals towards him, that a change had taken place in the confidence entertained as to his intentions on the subject of public liberty and individual security.

This reserve, the cause of which he penetrated, determined him to make a set of new creatures, and bring around him men from whom he was sure, as he said, to meet with no contradiction. His having laid down this principle of action, and his well-known system of degrading every thing, were the cause of the entry of foreign armies into France, and the fall of his dynasty.

END OF VOLUME SECOND

www.ingramcontent.com/pod-product-compliance
Lightning Source LLC
Chambersburg PA
CBHW060258230426
43663CB00009B/1508